At the 2006 Monde Selection World Quality Awards, everything wer
Cobra was awarded an incredible 12 Gold Medals.
That's more than any other beer in the world.

Unusual thing, excellence

2008 COBRA GOOD CURRY GUIDE

PAT CHAPMAN

THE 2008 COBRA GOOD CURRY GUIDE

Joint Editor and Database Management:
Dominique Chapman (DBAC)

Design: PCP Graphics developed from Peter Ward

Text Editor: Helen Bendel

Statistics: Taylor Nelson, Sub Continent Publishing

Researchers: Sarika Azad, Jonelle Bester, Zubin Bhedwar, Aftab Bhatti, Shahnoor Chowdhury, Roopa Gulati, Khurram Nelson, Horshang Noria, Ajay Patel, Biren Parikh, Buela Samuel, Samson Sohail and Puja Vedi.

Good Curry Guide Frequent and Prolific Reporters:
Dave Bridges, The Wirral; N.K.Campbell, Edinburgh; Hilary Chapchal, Surrey; Bill Parkes-Davis, Kent; Rod Eglin, Cumbria; Ray & Ruby Elliot, Worcs; Tony Emmerson, Lancs; Prof Bob Giddings, Poole; Justin Harper, Hemel; Tony and Monika Hetherington, Yorks; Andy Glazier, London; Tim & Katherine Morgan, Scotland; Paul Motley, e-mail; Steve Osborne, Bucks; Grahame and Melida Payne, Coventry; Prof Dirk Pilat, e-mail; Nigel Thomas, Lincoln; Ralph Warrington, Hyde; Cheshire (GM); Jeanette Wickes, Kent,; Malcolm Wilkins, Gravesend, Kent; Mick Wright, Beds.
plus many hundreds of others, without whom this Guide would not exist, and whose names appear at the end of this book..

This ninth edition first published in Great Britain in 2007
by The Curry Club, PO Box 7, Haslemere, Surrey, UK. GU27 1EP,
in association with John Blake Publishers, W14 9BP

Previous Editions of this Guide:
First edition 1984, Second: 1987, Third 1991,
Fourth: 1995, Fifth: 1998, Sixth: 1999, Seventh 2001, Eighth 2004

ISBN 9781844543113

Printed and bound in Great Britain by Blackmore Ltd, Shaftesbury, Dorset.
A CIP catalogue recommendation for this book is available from the British Library

CONTENTS

THE ENTRIES

Café Spice Namaste Café Spice Namaste Café Spice Namaste

Nominated
Cobra Good Curry
Guide
Best in London
2007/8

CURRY CLUB

CAFE SPICE NAMASTE

County Index

See page 469 for Town Index

London

England

The Isles and Islands

Ireland

Scotland

Wales

Author's Notes

Sponsorship The continuing sponsorship by Cobra Beer as the *Guide*'s sole sponsor, enables the author to finance the considerable costs of operating and producing this *Guide*, which include: maintaining the restaurant database on computer; subscribing to a press-cutting service and other information suppliers; printing a detailed questionnaire and mailing it to all 9,000 restaurants twice a year; mail-shotting the 1,500-plus restaurants that are selected to appear in the *Guide*; telephoning many for verification of information; producing, supplying and mailing the selected restaurants (free of charge) their wall certificates and window stickers; printing and mailing restaurant report forms for interested parties; collating and recording the info received (some 5,000 reports per annum) and operating the Awards Ceremony *(see page 32)*.

Accuracy The contents of this *Guide* are as up-to-date and accurate as possible, but we cannot be held responsible for any changes regarding quality, price, menu details, decor, ownership, health offences or even closure, following our processing of the reports.

Connections Pat Chapman, the publishers of this *Guide* and the proprietors of The Curry Club wish to make it quite clear that they have absolutely no financial or ownership connections with any restaurants, including those mentioned in this *Guide*.

False Representation Restaurant reports are welcomed from any bona-fide source. We do not pay for reports – they are sent in spontaneously and voluntarily. Our own research and restaurant testing is normally done anonymously, the bill is paid, and often no disclosure is made as to our presence. On some occasions, such as openings, we accept invitations to visit restaurants as 'guests of the house'. Under no circumstances do we tout for free hospitality, and anyone doing so in the name of The Curry Club is an impostor. We have heard of cases where people claiming to be members of The Curry Club, or *Good Curry Guide* 'inspectors', request payment and/or free meals in return for entry into this *Guide*. In such cases, we would recommend that restaurants threaten to call the police. We would also like to be informed of any such incidents and we will not hesitate to take action against people acting illegally in our name.

Discounts We used to invite all restaurants selected to appear in this *Guide* to participate in a discount scheme for members of The Curry Club. We have now discontinued this scheme, but we urge all readers of this Guide to request a discount from any restaurant in this Guide, and if necessary to show the restaurant their entry in the Guide.

Certificates & Window Stickers
We send all restaurants appearing in this *Guide* a 2007 certificate, hand-signed by Pat Chapman, and a 2007 window sticker. These items are supplied free of charge. Some choose not to display them, others display them proudly and prominently. You may observe that our certificate is not displayed alone. There may well be a host of others, some bigger and flashier than ours, including the Dome Grading certificates issued by Peter and Colleen Groves, which are genuine, as are certificates issued by London's *Time Out*, Ronay, local council health departments and certain others. Unfortunately, some certificates are a pure sham. They are issued to any restaurant who cares to pay for them, in some cases with a promise of entry into a *Guide* which does not even exist. We reported last time on a scam by *Good Food Guide*, yet again, but this is not The *Good Food Guide*. There is no *Guide* and this is the same outfit that were sued by the Consumers' Association some time ago and have now re-emerged at a

Sailing ahead on an award-winning course

BRITANNIA Spice's combination of stylish yacht-inspired interior and exotic cuisine, together with immaculate service means it has amassed an array of awards since it opened in Edinburgh in 1999.

The culmination of these honours came when the restaurant was named Best Curry House in Scotland at the British Curry Awards 2005, having just months before picked up a Top 30 award at the Best in Britain Awards (the BIBAs).

Britannia Spice specialises in exotic food from four countries: Bangladesh, Thailand, Nepal and India. Using only the finest produce and freshest of ingredients, the chefs, under the guidance of Britannia Spice's Executive Chef Abu Zaman, prepare mouth-watering dishes. It means a voyage of discovery, exploring the highlights of south-east Asian cuisine. Always popular is Gaeng Kiew Waan, a green

curry from Thailand. Its coconut cream, galanga. lemon grass, kaffir lime leaves and basil perfectly compliment the tender chicken.

One of the signature dishes is Bangladeshi Special Chicken where prawns in a rich, mild sauce add an unexpected twist to the meat. Another favourite is Harrey Masaley Ka Gosht, a Bangladeshi dish which teams lamb with green masala of coriander, mint, green chilli, curry leaves and spices.

Britannia Spice won't be resting on its laurels its chief executive, Dr Wali Uddin, assures us. "My customers know we will be striving to do even better in the future. And I look forward to welcoming everyone to enjoy the Britannia Spice experience."

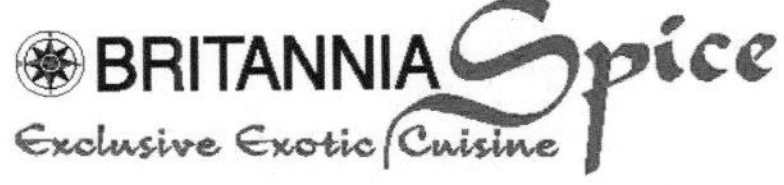

150 Commercial Street, Leith, EH6 6LB.
Telephone 0131 555 2255
Open 7 days: 12 noon -2:15pm (except Sundays) and 5pm-11:45pm

different address. Masterchef returned after being exposed by BBC 'Food and Drink' in June. Certificates are on offer for £67.50 (£10 for extra copies) and £5 for window stickers. The *Asian Food Guide* was caught out on Radio 4. There are others on the bandwagon. Like Peter Groves, we would like to see this scam stopped. But how do you know that the *Good Curry Guide* certificate you see is genuine?

For those of you who like to follow events, we reported last time about a scam-operator called Ian Cowan of Inc Software, Paisley, Scotland. He was attempting to charge for *Good Curry Guide* certificates for a cost of £30. Remember, we give our certificates free of charge. -It seems that, as we predicted, he has sunk without trace. And so too has the mania to operate copy-cat websites. Infact we have become relaxed about it. If you want to read this ***Guide's*** words on some 'unauthorised' website, so be it. And if you are contemplating rewriting all the words on this Guide, I point out that there are 250,000 words to copy. Enjoy!

About this Guide

The Good Curry Guide broke new ground when it was first published in 1984, by being the first restaurant guide to specialise only in the British curry. This, its eighth edition.. As usual, there there have been demotions and promotions since last time. We want continuity in each edition of the *Guide*, and because we do expect changes, we feel it is important that each restaurant completes our questionnaire. For one thing, it means the restaurant actually wants to be in the *Guide*. It also verifies its current name, address, telephone number, and above all, prices. Despite our earnest endeavours, not all restaurants reply, even if they did so last time. So if we have not received a reply from a restaurant that was in the previous edition, after it has been sent a form three times, should it be delisted? I believe it should if it cannot be bothered, for whatever reason, to talk to us. But curry restaurants are a peculiar trade; communications aren't always easy and normal rules don't apply.

A completed form from a restaurant does not guarantee entry to the Guide. We rely on various other sources of information. We can only visit a handful of restaurants each year, and do not have a team of paid inspectors. Most important to us are the opinions of the customers – you, the diners. We do not pay for such reports, though from time to time The Curry Club gives prizes for your efforts. The report itself can be a simple short note, though we have a special form (see final page) for all who want one. A report may deal with a single restaurant or several. Some reporters write to us only once, others write repeatedly. For this Guide, we received about 5,000 reports, yielding information on up to 50,000 restaurant visits. We read and record every report, although it is becoming increasingly difficult to reply to all of them. I would like, therefore, to thank all those who have taken the time to tell us where they have found the best, good, mediocre and even bad curries.

Of course reporting standards vary, and the The Wind of India, Puddlecome-on-the-Marsh may well be reported as the best in the world by an ardent, novice, local fan (and I want such opinions), but may not rate highly if compared with London's best. Nevertheless, it will be a competent curry house in that area, serving standard formula curry. Numerous entries in this *Guide* come into this category, and they are here because someone, maybe more than one person, has taken the trouble to write in and praise the place, and to exclude it would be wrong. We want to know what you know.

Answering the question 'Name your

favourite curry restaurant(s) may not always be as easy as it sounds. It is worth again quoting Sutton Coldfield's John Brockingham, a retired college lecturer: 'My favourite restaurants,' he wrote, 'range from opulent establishments like Rajdoot, Birmingham, where I might take the family on special occasions, to cheap and cheerful places like Erdington's Balti Express, where a meal costs £11 a head. I have a favourite posh curry restaurant, when I can afford it, and a favourite posh Balti. But I have a favourite plonk version of both, and a favourite takeaway, and then there's a favourite lucky dip. Some of my favourites are good enough to tempt me in whenever I'm in the district, but could not be nominated for the highest accolade.'

Of course we do not receive reports on every single establishment. On occasion a restaurant we normally receive good reports about gets damned. If this is the exception, we will probably still carry that restaurant. Some will have closed, and others should perhaps have been omitted. But none get into this *Guide* unless we have had at least one recent good report on it, preferably several. To get into the TOP 100 we need several detailed excellent reports, including at least one by one of our elite 60 or so regular reporters. As editors we visit a TOP 100 restaurant anonymously whenever we can, but it's impossible to go to them all within one year. We do our best to filter out 'good' reports on bad restaurants, particularly those written by their hopeful owners. This time we requested that restaurants selected for entry get their customers to write to us, and many did. This way, we have almost weeded out the few restaurants who previously sent us phoney reports, purportedly from adoring customers. However, even after twenty five years in the editor's chair, it is possible that I've been conned and a 'bad' restaurant has slipped in. Equally, I'll guarantee that we've missed someone's favourite, and that there are a few *faux pas* too. Please let us know about these. No doubt, we'll continue to get irate letters from people who won't have bothered to read this section, telling us that, because this or that restaurant was awful when they visited, 'it casts doubt on the credibility of the entire *Guide*'. We certainly do not enter restaurants just because they ask us to. After twenty five years of bona-fide operations, you would imagine that curryhouse owners would clamour to be in the *Guide*. Indeed some do. As I have said in previous *Guides*, more than one restaurant has made veiled references to the benefits that would be made available to the editors if that restaurant were declared the UK's number one. The very idea is abhorrent. Besides, if one did accede to such bribery, word would soon get round risking the credibility of both author and publication. The book is paid for through book sales, ads and sponsorship, not through bribes.

So what's new in this edition? Regular readers will know that we go alphabetically by county, then within that, by town and then restaurant. We are continuing with this system, since it is easier to see at a glance what alternative choices are nearby. We have also continue with the town index at the end of the book. At the start of each county's entry, we have also improved our thumbnail county maps, which help pinpoint the location of that particular county, along with the feature, which lists adjacent counties. It should make this *Guide* more informative and finding your way around it easier. And that, after all, is what this *Guide* is all about finding good curries easily, and nothing else.

Well almost: this time we have introduced a fun quiz *(see page 468)*. The whole idea is to make the avid curryholic read every page, and then tell us so by giving us the correct answers. We give the winner(s) a super prize, but the winning is in reading the Guide.

So please, get going!!!

Welcome to the Ninth Edition

When you only appear every three years or so, there is a lot to tell. Good news is a healthy clutch of new openings, some of which are stunning. Standards are becoming increasingly high across the nation, so much so that Birmingham now has the Top UK restaurant. Regional food is also catching on nationwide albeit slowly. Trends seem to be for café bars with 'Indian" canapés and street-food, pioneered by Masala Zone and remarkably elegant presentation at the high end, pioneered again by the same operators at Chutney Mary. Modern furnishing has arrived to stay, although the industry dinosaurs will never get it, nor will they let CTM die the death. Food colouring has correctly come in for a hammering, but it too lingers on and on. Open-ended credit card slips are giving way to electronics, but still request at tip.

We are delighted to have introduced a number of innovations this time. Firstly the *Guide* is in full colour throughout. Secondly, we have introduced a completely new category called our **A-LIST** – the 60 Best UK restaurants, which we list from p33. Find out which is Britain's' oldest curry house on p98. and the whereabouts of the world's best Tandoori Restaurant on p460. This truly is the Guide as chosen by you. We list you on page462 and hear your views on p52. The Curry Magazine's ***Gastronome*** makes his *Guide* debut here with some Hot Gossip and for fun, try our new-to-the-*Guide* quiz on p467. Finally, if you don't tell us your views, we can't print them. Use the form on page 465 or better still e-mail me on <pat@patchapman.co.uk>

The Currynation

The Curry Magazine's Gastronome takes a light-hearted look at the nation's curranigans.

The Fish War

If you thought that the fish-war was something which takes place between Europe and Britain in Atlantic waters, think closer to home. ***Good Houskeeping's*** annual survey finds that *'apple crumble is the nation's favourite pudding whilst curry replaces fish and chips as the nation's most popular fast food'.* Replaces? What IS all this about? Once a year we get treated to the ***National Federation of Fish Friers' (NFFF)*** survey which tells us the fish and chips as the nation's most popular fast food. But wait! another annual survey finds differently: ***WindSetlers*** (aka ***BiSodol***) indigestion cures asks people what gives them indigestion. Its wealth of data informs us that 43% bought Chinese takeaways; 24% Indian while just 14% bought fish and chips. So that's that then! Ignore the Chinese bit ... curry is way ahead of fish and chips. And just to nail it, let *Gastronome* prove it once and for all using NFFF's own naff, fishy evidence versus our hot statistics.

- They say the first fish and chip shop opened in Cleveland Street, London E1 in 1860*. We say the first curry shop opened in 1809. (see p xxx).
- There are now around UK 8,500 fish and chip shops* employing approximately 27,000 people. There are now over 9,000 UK curry restaurant and takeaways employing approximately 80,000.
- The British consumed nearly 300 million servings of fish and chips*, totalling some £1.2bn. They spent over £3.2 billion a year at the curry restaurant.
- As noted the ***WindSetlers*** survey tells us 24% of takeaway purchases were Indian takeaways compared with just 14% fish and chips.
- Fewer fish and chip products are sold as ready-meals or ingredients at the supermarket and delis. Curry accounts for £800m per year in this sector. ***Sharwoods*** tell us the chilled sauces category alone is worth £50 million and growing 7% pa.
- The fish and chip market has remained static (apart from inflated fish prices) whilst the curry market continues to show a 10% true annual growth.
- Only 5% of the dishes ordered at the curry restaurant are fish (most of which are prawns).

**Source: The National Federation of Fish Friers*

You are What You Eat

That same ***WindSetlers*** survey of 3,000 adults reveals that Brits scoff over 2 billion takeaway meals each year! 40% of us have a takeaway at least once a week whilst 14% order two or more every seven days. 38% admit feeling guilty after eating a takeaway, with women twice as likely to feel guilty as men, but 78% of British adults are happy to feed a takeaway to their children. 58% admit that they have no idea of the fat and calorie content of their favourite takeaways – the average takeaway meal contains over 1,000 calories. 68% say the main reason they order a take-away is because they are too tired or busy to cook whilst 39% say it was simply because they love the taste. 23% say they have a takeaway number stored on their mobile phone. 43% admit that they order the same takeaway dishes each time whilst a staggering 21% admit their local take-away restaurant knows their name and order by memory! The north east orders the most takeaways and the south east the least. Of the Indian takeaways, Tikka Masala is, as ever the first choice and Korma second. Getting to the point ***WindSetlers*** reveal that 33% regularly suffer from indigestion following eating a takeaway. Nutritionist spoil-sport Dr Chris Fenn says: *'Take-away food should be regarded as a rare treat but they are becoming increasingly popular for a variety of reasons including people's hectic lifestyles. Consistent consumption can also lead to obesity in the long-term. In Britain two-thirds of the adult population is currently overweight.'* Bet he's good fun on a girl's night out. Not!

Dr A weighs In

Guess who suffers most in the weight department? A survey by Dr Amelia Lake of Newcastle Uni finds that women put on more weight after setting up home with their male partner, while men loose weight. (Not in my household, Dr A!). Women it seems use food as a comfort-zone when dealing with the emotional stress of a relationship. Men get used to previously untried food such as fresh fruit and vegetables. One of Dr Lakes' couples, area manager Jo Tough, 33 and her cop husband Gary agreed. Jo said *'I weighed 9 stone when we married. After meeting Gary he introduced me to curry and before long I went up to size 18.'* PS: She went on a diet lost it all again.

Researching the Night Away

Good for you Jo, besides curry is good for you. The usual parade of professors have been dipping into the academic pot in the interest of curry. The latest research from Dr Tze-Pin-Ng of Singapore University reveals that turmeric inhibits the build-up of amyloid plaques, protein deposits found in the brains of Alzheimer's disease sufferers. 1000 Asians aged 60 to 93 who did not have the disease were given mental agility tests. Their results were all above average and all ate curry. The Scottish Executive has found that cumin, turmeric and paprika are particularly rich sources of salicylic acids, the active ingredient in aspirin and could help treat migraine and prevent colon cancer. Texas medical researchers concurred, stating that turmeric helps ward off cancer; Columbia Uni New York has pronounced that it has an anti-inflammatory effect on people with the bowel disease Crohn's disease; and Mr Ah-Ng Tony Kong, pharmaceutics professor, Rutgers Uni, New Jersey was inspired to investigate diets when he noted that prostrate cancer is rare in India yet common in the US. He proscribes cauliflower, broccoli, sprouts, watercress and turnips (all having curcurmin – aka turmeric) and indeed curry to retard the growth of cancerous tumours. So we can all curry on taking the yellow spice for the green light to health, or is that the red one? ... The New Scientist reported that researcher Andrew Davies of Tasmania Uni spent eight weeks surveying the sleep patterns of 25 volunteers. For half the time they ate bland food, then they had 30g of chilli added to their daily diet. Result: they needed 20 minutes less sleep a night and had up to 30% more energy during the day. Capsaicin, the chilli heat-giving chemical, is reckoned to act on sensors in our brain which control our sleep cycles. Co-researcher Dominic Geraghty found that even small amounts of chilli has a beneficial effect on cardio-vascular activity.

Mr Naga Napalms the US

Talking of chilli, according to Tesco consultant John Hale, 42, a sensory analysts *'curry, Chinese and Thai meals are now a weekly staple and have made such a culinary impact that our tastebuds have begun to adapt.'* Retail analysts TNS say that in 2006 demand for Vindaloo ready meal curries grew by 50% and Vindaloo cooking sauces by 33%; Red Thai curry ready meals jumped by 27%; Hot pepper sauces by 19% and hot fresh chillies by 16%. To meet demand Tesco has launched Britain's hottest 'triple X rated' pizza with extra chillies, also a hotter range of traditional curry dishes which have already become popular sellers. Until recently, the hottest known to New Mexico State Uni's Dr. Paul Bosland, the world's premier chilli breeder were Mexican Habeneros and Caribbean Scotch Bonnets. Using the Schoville heat-measuring scale (SHU) these each register some 350,000 units. Put into perspective, Tabasco registers about 140,000 units and those fat chillies at the supermarket, c40,000 units. Then the ***International Herald Tribune*** featured story about a chilli variety grown in the Indian Assam and Bengali hills called the *'Naga Jolokia'* or *'Tezpur chilli.'* Although well known for years to Bengalis and Bangladeshis including those resident in the UK, it was unknown to the American chill fraternity. Bosland tested the Naga and astonishingly the tests revealed that its high heat level was a whopping 1,001,304 SHU. *'It's like Napalm'*, he spluttered. *'It's a heat level previously seen only with ultra-hot sauces using pepper extract oleoresin.'* Naga dishes are increasingly available at the UK curryhouse, and have a totally different characteristic to Phal. Ask at the Asian stores for the new Bangladeshi pickle called Mr Naga.

Balderdash and Piffle

So popular is British curry that the BBC TV's first series of *Balderdash and Piffle* chose 'balti' as a word to examine with the intention of updating the Oxford English Dictionary, the definitive record of the English language ,flatteringly observed: *'The winter 1984 issue of the Curry Club's Curry Magazine contains the first printed evidence the OED has for 'balti'. But where the term comes from (India, Pakistan — perhaps Baltistan) remains something of a mystery at present. The Curry Club say it first appeared in the Birmingham area in the early 80s. But is there any printed evidence for the term earlier, and can the origin be confirmed?'* The programme asked viewers: *'Are you one of Britain's original curry kings or queens? If so, did you cook or serve Britain or the world's first balti — or do you know who did? Knocking around at the back of the kitchen drawer do you have an old takeaway menu with a balti on it from before 1984?'* Following transmission, only one piece of written evidence predated our own: an advert from a local paper, as the revised for the OED indicates: This ad has come to light from July 8th 1982. *'Heathan (Balsall Heath, Birmingham) Specialists in kebab, tikah, balti meats, tandoori chicken and all kinds of curry.'* Re our own evidence, the OED have retained it. Here it is in full:Curry Mag. Winter 1984, Edition 11, Restaurant Roundup page 29 col 1: *'Can anyone tell me what Balti is? As you peer through the two large windows, full of happy diners and catch the delicious smell exuding from the interior, you'll find it impossible to pass the place.Some unusual dishes on the menu are Curried Quail, Balti chicken or meat. We found the food wholesome and satisfying'.* from Mr.G.Loughlin, Formby. We were as surprised as the OED that no printed evidence came from the 1970s. But all is not lost; maybe you, our curryholic readers can produce evidence. If you can please reply to us in Haslemere, address p4. Our first Guide balti reference was in the second (1986) when we mentioned the baltis at Adils (still in this Guide). Meanwhile here is the new OED definition:

balti, n.2 Cookery. Also with capital initial. Origin uncertain and disputed.

The word was first used in connection with restaurants chiefly in the area of Birmingham, England, in the early 1980s. One source claims that that first Balti house opened in 1977, but no printed evidence for this has been found. It is unclear whether there is any antecedent in languages of northern India, Pakistan, or Kashmir; it is not recorded among the many borrowings from these languages in R. J. Baumgartner Eng. Lang. Pakistan (1993). It is widely suggested that the word is derived from the Hindi for pail or bucket referring to the small, two-handled pan used in balti houses (Urdu – karahi), or Punjabi, Hindi, Bengali – deep brass dish but as there is no evidence that the Hindi word was used for vessels of this kind, this is probably a folk etymology. It has also been suggested that the word has some connection with Baltistan. The cuisine is found throughout Pakistan and north-western India, but

with the notable exception of Baltistan, which has a subsistence economy (although sharing of food from a communal pot, or bucket is a feature of Balti culture). The first balti houses may have been so named because of their simple, bring-and-share style, or because an early proprietor of such a restaurant was a Balti from Pakistani Kashmir. The predominant British pronunciation with back vowel is perh. after BALTIC a. and n.]
© Oxford University Press 2006
www.oed.com/bbcwords/balti-new2.html
If you have some evidence on any of the words listed in this appeal, please email wordhunt@bbc.co.uk.

Curry gets the V-sign

Some 60 'official National Icons of England' have been voted for by the public. They include: the Tube Map, Stonehenge, Punch and Judy, Holbein's Henry VIII, the FA Cup, Alice in Wonderland, the Routemaster bus, King James Bible, the Angel of the North, the Spitfire, Jerusalem, the St George Flag and The V-sign. In addition, there are now 900 nominations which have not joined the ranks of official Icons, including Concorde, and the RAF, but not the QE2. Food Icons include Roast Beef and Yorkshire Pudding, a cup of tea, Cheddar Cheese, Mrs Beeton's Book Of Household Management, a Pint of Beer and Fish and Chips, of which the website says: 'Gourmets may sneer, but love 'em or hate 'em, Fish and Chips is indisputably a national dish and it's here to stay. The iconic status of England's favourite take-away supper is confirmed.' Funny that ... I thought we've proved above that curry is our number one takeaway supper!!! Yet Curry does not yet feature even as a nominee, although Vindaloo , the Curry Mile, Rusholme Belgrave Road Leicester, Chicken Tikka Masala and South Asian Food are nominated. However Brick Lane, rather unexpectedly does, as a full Icon. The website <www.ICONS.org.uk> says of it: *'Brick Lane, a vibrant London thoroughfare, otherwise known as Banglatown, is the epicentre of the capital's Bangladeshi community. In earlier times, the street was a place of refuge for French Protestants, before playing host to the Jewish community, though they have dwindled away. Fortunately you can still buy bagels at one Brick Lane shop. Now its iconic fame comes some of London's best Asian cooking. The area is also a hotbed of fashion, music and the visual arts.'* Here are more Brick Lane facts: The Sheraz at no 13 was formerly the notorious Frying Pan pub, where Jack The Ripper's victim Mary Nichols was seen leaving shortly before her body was discovered in Bucks Row. You can go on free tours of the former Truman Brewery, near Hanbury Street. Chicksand Street is reputed to be where Dracula author Bram Stoker stayed on his return from Transylvania. In 1999 David Copeland exploded a nail-bomb in Brick Lane, fortunately causing no deaths or serious injuries Habitat's head office is in nearby Princelet Street. Brick Lane's Banglatown International Curry Festival runs over two weeks each September, attracting 60,000 visitors and hosts its annual Curry Chef of the Year Competition.

Hot Gossip by Gastronome

• So Tesco, along with M&S, Next and ASDA on on the lookout for sites in India and Bangladesh?. Tesco are well established in Thailand, but have they pipped the others to the post in Sylhet. New stores open every day in the rickshaw-jammed city, fuelled, as we know by the wealth created by the Great British curry. But who owns it? If you have information, every little helps.

• *'It is getting harder to find servants in India these days'*, says Bangalore's Mrs Balasubramanium, wife of the former Cobra beer brewery owner. *'They are getting properly educated these days and don't want to do domestic work. We are a good case in point'*, she says. *'We paid for our servants' children to go to the same schools as our own. Some do even better than ours at exam time Now their parents are retiring, and we have no one to cook and clean; their kids are all lawyers and doctors'.* Never mind Raji, there's plenty of cheap labour in Romania, meanwhile read on ...

• The burgeoning Indian female middle class is getting busier in the work place, something unheard of by their mothers. (It has risen from 1% to 15% of India's white-collar labour force in the last decade). With an average monthly income of 18,000 rupees (about £225), And with more and more shopping malls opening up in them, are India's newest discovery, self-service supermarkets. And on offer in them come ready-meals. Ravi Naware CEO of ITC foods *(see page 389)* have jumped onto the bandwagon. *'We already have sales of £10m, up from £3m three years ago'*, he says *'We intend to treble it in the next three years.'* Mostly ITC are selling boil-in-the-bag items with such unoriginal, but new to India slogans as *'curry-in-a-hurry'*. Says Delhi's Mrs Kanchan Chawla, 29. *'At 45p per bag, I can afford it, and work instead. Besides who needs to spend hours chopping food, when it's all done for you.'* So that's that then. We welcome India to the 21st century and can look forward to the decline of her real home cooking in favour of supermarket crud. It happened here, it happened there, it happened everywhere.

• Talking of crud, Tushar Gandhi, great-grandson of Mahatma is outraged by the choice of name of an Australian curry firm. Under the brand name ***Handi Ghandi,*** it sells a range of meat and vegetarian curries. *'For one thing,'* decries Tushar, *'they are selling beef products. No self-respecting Hindu eats beef, and Mahatma Gandhi was a vegan. And secondly, they have misspelled our family name. It is Gandhi not Ghandi, and a handi is a pot!'* Gandhi's name and image are well-protected in India against such use, but not in other countries. And ***Handi Ghandi's*** reaction? ... *'We're recipe-testing right now, and haven't got the time to beef'.*

• Besides who needs home cooking. Asll you need is cash! An American art dealer spent £45,000 on a meal at Mayfair's Tamarind restaurant. Did he leave a tip, one wonders. Tamarind is used to such bonanzas. It recently catered for a polo tournament in Geneva, and regularly jets takeaways to the Sultan of Brunei in his private jet, price of these two, unknown.

- Anyone who has served in the forces know that compo rations are a day's pack of food, all capable of being stored for years before being eaten. In Gastronome's service days in the 1960s, some of the canned compo rations dated from the war! But times are a-changing. New rations include burger and beans, bacon, tuna, toffees, and Yorkie bars. But star meals with all troops are chicken balti, chicken and lamb curries. Cpl Saunders of No 2 Sqn RAF Regiment tried the new packs out while on the Thetford firing range and ruefully observed *'the French get wine, and the US get self-heating ready-meals, and we get spotted dick and custard.'* His oppo, Cpl Lovejoy said of the curries *'what do you expect for boil-in-the-bag.'*
- Perhaps the ever-hungry troops fare better. during the annual autumn National Curry Week. Honey Top Foods hold the record for the World's Biggest Naan which was over 7 feet long and needed four strapping members of the Army Catering Corps to display it ... they did not tell us how many pongoes it took to eat it. At one Curry Weeks event, the Army set the record for the number of Indian meals cooked and served from scratch, with a feast for 652 hungry racegoers at Kempton Park. Not to be outdone, Chef Abdul Salam from Lichfield claimed the World's Biggest Curry record in 2000 with a bubbling 3 tonnes of it. He beat this in 2005 by having a special stainless steel vat built and brewed up a whopping ten tonnes of curry to set a new record.

A Hairy End Piece

Lijjat the Chennai poppadum manufacturer exports 700 million to the UK annually. ***Menu Magazine's*** Mrs Grove worked out that if placed end to end, they would cover the circumference of the Earth 2.8 times. (she does these things!) She put it another way: if they were stacked on top of each other they would make a tower 156 times the height of Mount Everest. They are undoubtedly the world's finest poppadums, each one being made by hand by local women. But beware: inspect carefully! It is not uncommon to find a black hair imbedded in the disk.

The Hall of Fame ~ once a Winner, always a Winner

The UK's first ever restaurant awards ceremony was ours, celebrating curry.
It was held at the overall winner,'s venue Chutney Mary's SW10 on 9th October 1991.

Left to right: Abdul Latif Rupali Newcastle, Sanjay Anand Madhus, the late Latif Tarafder Khyber Plymouth, Wali Udin Scotland, Namita Panjabi Chutney Mary, Hansa of Hansa's Leeds, Cyrus, Rashmi Jashan N8, Des Sarda Rajdoot Group (now retired) , and far right John Loosemore, the Guide's most Prolific Reporter. Most are still around at the top of their professions.

Our Ultimate Achievers

BOMBAY BRASSERIE, SW 7

Lifetime Best Restaurant award – 1982 to 2008

CHUTNEY MARY, SW10

Best in UK 1991-1994 – *Third Edition of this Guide*

Best in UK 1999-2000 – *Sixth Edition*

BOMBAY BRASSERIE, SW 7

Best in UK 1995-7 – *Fourth Edition*

LA PORTE DES INDES, LONDON, W1

Best Indian and Best in UK 1998-1999 – *Fifth Edition*

THE QUILON, SW1

Best in UK 2001-2003 – *Seventh Edition*

MADHU'S, SOUTHALL, MIDDLESEX

Best in UK 2004-2006 – *Eighth Edition*

ITHIHAAS, BIRMINGHAM

Best in UK 2007-2008 – *This Edition*

Welcome to the seventh

2007 Good Curry Awards Ceremony and Luncheon

The ceremony which brings the very best representatives of the British Asian restaurant industry to the stage to receive the most prestigious awards in the business before some of our most illustrious industry personalities.

Presented by Sky-TV's Lisa Aziz and Guide founder Pat Chapman.

Televised world-wide by Sony Entertainment TV Asia.

19th December 2006
London's Park Lane Hilton

Treasure of India

Whisky dream comes true

A DREAM is coming true in Britain for a young man from Bangalore. His vision - of an Indian Single Malt Whisky on sale across the UK - has turned into reality as curry houses and specialist whisky shops see sales soar.

In Bangalore, Rackshit Jagdale, the son of a family of Indian distillers, had dreamed of exporting a Single Malt Whisky that could stand up with pride on the world stage.

The family company, Amrut Distilleries Ltd, had been making malt whisky since the 1980s to mix with neutral alcohol and create whisky brands to sell locally. So, when Rackshit was studying for an MBA at the University of Newcastle upon Tyne, he investigated the idea of marketing Amrut Single Malt Whisky in Indian restaurants in Britain for his thesis.

As the student test-marketed Amrut Single Malt Whisky he received very favourable responses. It's not surprising, the single malt whisky received such a good reception: it has been lovingly created.

The barley, which is the pick of the crop from the fertile north-western frontier states of the Punjab and Rajasthan, is malted to Amrut's exacting standards in Jaipur and Delhi.

Amrut Single Malt Whisky's unique flavour – notes of fruit and chocolate laced with spices – appears as it is distilled and matured in Bangalore. There the high altitude and tropical climate combine to increase evaporation, giving the whisky a flavour beyond its years.

Taking the lessons learned in Rackshit's MBA thesis, Amrut Distilleries have adopted his marketing plan and now Amrut Single Malt Whisky is available here in the UK at specialist whisky shops and curry restaurants.

And it's receiving rave reviews. Jim Murray, the whisky writer, described the "sweet richness" of the malt on the palate as a "joy, with boundless energy that pulses through to the prickly, oaky finish" in his Whisky Bible 2006 (Carlton Books, 2005). He also recommends it after a curry: "Solid, honest whisky (with a non-scotch flourish at the finish) that would, after a black coffee, follow the finest Chicken Korma."

For more information contact:
Amrut Distilleries Ltd
53 Bothwell Street
Glasgow, G2 6TS
Tel: + 44 141 221 4297
amrutmaltwhisky@yahoo.co.uk
www.amrutwhisky.co.uk

DOUBLE FILTERED
EXTRA SMOOTH
COBRA®
कोबरा
0.0%
ALCOHOL FREE
PREMIUM LAGER BEER

The Elite ~ The A-LIST and TOP 100

Only one in every twelve of the nation's curry restaurants has achieved entry into this *Guide*, so they are all top restaurants and a cut above the norm.

But, naturally, we are always asked to identify the best of the best, so to speak. And it is true that there is an élite number of really excellent restaurants including, by definition, those establishments about which we receive many consistently good reports. Since our 1992 edition we have listed them as our **TOP 100** restaurants. As usual, this year there has been quite a lot of change. There is the usual demotion from the list because of a decline in performance or closure. Fortunately, from the many you have brought to our attention, we have promoted 68 'new' entrants (indicated •). Some are indeed new, although some are long-established. Once again we do not have an exact 100. This time the total is some 150. As ever, if there are yet others you feel we have missed, please report to us. For a restaurant to remain in our **TOP 100** list, we also need your views. There is a further, even more élite list, the cream of the cream, winners of our **AWARDS** all of whom attend the Guide's prestigious ceremony in London to receive their awards. The 2007 Nominees and Winners are listed below. For the record, our previous award winners are indicated from page 38, since they all remain at the top of our **TOP 100.** Indeed we have now described all these as our **A-LIST** (A for Awards + Nominees). At the request of the worldwide media, we commenced our **BEST IN THE UK AWARDS** in 1992, in our third edition of this *Guide.* To date there have only been six such winners. Although our judgements at the time were nearly always received with some surprise, we are proud they have all stood the test of time. Each of these restaurants continue to thrive and deliver outstanding food and service. Last year we moved a little outside London for the first time. Once again we hope to surprise you again by going to the Midlands for our **BEST.** Once again we are proud to awarding two unique and special **LIFETIME ACHIEVEMENT AWARDS.**

Here are the élite of the élite:

Award Winners and Nominees, 2007 ` The A-LIST

British Regions

Best in the North Best Indian

Indian Ocean, 83 Stamford Street E, Ashton 0161 343 3343, Winner
Last Days of the Raj, 168 Kells La, Low Fell 0191 482 6494
Magna, 39 Bridge Street, Berwick 01289 302736
Sachins, Forth Banks, Quayside, Newcastle 0191 261 9035
The Valley, The Old Station House, Corbridge 01434 633434

Best in Midlands

Itihaas, 18 Fleet St Birmingham B3 0121 212 3383, Winner
Bolaka Spice, 41 Stockwell Street, Leek 01538 373734
Café Lazeez, The Mail Box, 116 Wharfside Street B1, 0121 643 7979
Ek Maya, 28 Dysart Way, Leicester, LE1 2JY 0116 262 1118
Lasan, 3 Dakota Bldgs, James St, St Paul's B3, 0121 212 3664
Rajnagar, 256 Lyndon Rd, Olton, Solihull, B92 0121 742 8140
Sweet Chillies Cuisine, 836 Yardleywood Rd, Moseley, B13 0121 443 2737

Best in Scotland

Ashoka at the Mill, 10 Clydeholm Road, Glasgow, G14 0141 576 5123, Winner
Balaka Bangladeshi, 3 Alexander Place, Market St, St Andrews 01334 474825
Café India, 171 North St, Charing Cross, Central Glasgow 0141 248 4074
Verandah, 17 Dalry Rd, Edinburgh 0131 337 5828

Best in the South and West

Tamasha, 131 Widmore Rd Bromley, Kent (Gtr London) 020 8460 3240, Winner
Eastern Eye, 8a Quiet Street, Bath, Somerset 01225 422323
Jalori, 23 High Street, Woburn, MK, 01908 2812393.
Malik's, Royal Exchange, High St, Cookham, Surrey 01628 520085
Mumtaj, 115 London Road, St Albans 01727 858399
Origin Asia, 100 Kew Road, Richmond, Surrey (Gtr London) 020 8948 0509

Best in London

Mint Leaf, Suffolk Place SW1 020 7839 6673, Winner
Babur Brasserie, 119 Brockley Rise, SE23 020 8291 2400
Cinamon Club, Old Westminster Library, Great Smith Street, SW1 020 7222 2555
Kasturi, 57 Aldgate High Street, EC3 020 7480 7402
Mala, St Katherine's Dock, E1 020 7480 6356
Nayab, 309 New Kings Rd, SW6 020 7731 6993

Best in Wales

Misbah, 9 Priory Street, Monmouth NP25 3BR 01600 714940 Winner
Bengal Dynasty, 106 Chester Road East, Shotton, Deeside, Flintshire 01492 875928
Balti Empire, 157-159 Albany Rd Roath Cardiff, 029 2048 5757
Juboraj, 10 Mill La, Hayes, Cardiff, 029 2037 7668

National Cuisines

Best Bangladeshi

Kuti's, 37 Oxford Street, Southampton, 023 8022 1585 Winner
Aziz, 228 Cowley Road, Oxford 01865 794945
Kafé La, 15 Perry Vale, Forest Hill, SE23 020 8699 2028
Café Naz, 46 Brick Lane, E, 020 7247 0234
Hason Raja, Southampton Row, WC2, 020 7242 33773.
Shampan, 79 Brick Lane, E1 020 7375 0475
Spicery, Denton Bank, Denton Rd, Newcastle 0191 274 9464

Best Indian

Imli, 167 Wardour Street, W1 020 7287 4243 Winner
Popadom Express, 48 Oxford Street, Southampto, 023 8063 2444
Rasa, 55 Church Street, N16 020 7249 0344
Kovalam, 12 Willesden Lane NW6 7SR 020 7625 4761
Club Baylis, Baylis House, Stoke Poges Lane, Slough 01753 555555

nint leaf

t Leaf, hailed as one of London's most stylish and contemporary aurants, brings a touch of class to Indian dining. Winner of numer- awards and accolades, the restaurant has become a hotspot for and international celebrities; London's trendy residents; and bar usiasts.

d Chef K.K Anand's innovative Indian cuisine has hit all the right spots Mint Leaf fans. Delicate flavours, light textures and stunning entations are Mint Leaf's hallmark for sophisticated dining. With the ch of a new a la carte menu, the restaurant continuously strives to ver the best for its discerning clientele.

ous for its high profile parties, the website features a stunning vie' highlighting some of its headline grabbing events.

Leaf also holds a licence to host civil wedding ceremonies.

nt Leaf does for Indian opulence what Hakkasan does for Chinese." er Peyton for GQ

remarkable for its flamboyant, post modern Indian design as for its y, evolved cooking." Tatler

avernous restaurant that blends dark wood, leather and stone with er touches in the flowers and flickering candles… great food!" am Norton for Evening Standard.

n 7 days, except Saturday and Sunday lunch.

folk Place, Haymarket, SW1
7930 9020
: 020 7930 6205
w.mintleafrestaurant.com
ervations@mintleafrestaurant.com
Piccadilly/Leicester Square

Awarded Cobra Good Curry Guide Best in London 2007/8

Best Nepalese

Monty's, 224 South Ealing Road, W5 020 8560 2619 Winner
Gurkha Kitchen, 111 Station Rd, East Oxted, Surrey 01883 722621
Gurkha Palace Nepalese, 97 Enbrook Valley, Folkestone. Kent 01303 257700
Gurkha Square, 327 Fleet Road, Fleet, Hampshire 01252 810286
Rara, 528 Victoria Road S.Ruislip, Middlesex 020 8845 7094

Best Pakistani

Kinara at Pitt's Cottage, High Street, Limpsfield Road, Westerham, Kent 01959 562125 Winner
Aagrah, BBC Building St Peter's Square, Quarry Hill, Leeds, W.Yorkshire 0113 245 5667
Adils, 148 Stoney Lane, Sparkbrook, B11, 0121 449 0335
Moj Masti, 37 Featherstone Rd, Southall, Middlesex 020 8893 6502
Royal Naim, 417 Stratford Road, Sparkhill, Birmingham, B11 0121 766 7849
Lahore Kebab House, 2 Umberton Street, E1 020 7488 2551

Best Sri Lankan

Elephant Walk, 98 West End Lane, NW6 020 7328 3308 Winner
Jaffna House, 90 High Street, SW1, 020 8672 7786
Palm Palace, 80 South Road, Southall, Middlesex 020 8574 9209

Miscellaneous

Best Vegetarian

Chai Pani 64 Seymour Street, W1 020 7258 2000 Winner
Hansa's, 72 North Street, Leeds, W.Yorkshire 0113 244 4408
Sagar, 157 King Street, W6 020 8741 8563
Shahee Bhel Poori Vegan, 1547 London Road, SW16 020 8679 6275

Chef of the Year

Stephen Gomes Café Naz group, E1, Cambridge and Cardif

Manager of the Year

Bhim Singh, Kosturi, 18 Station Approach, Bromley 020 8462 8594

Most welcome Newcomer (since last edition of the Guide)

Amaya, Halkin Arcade Knightsbridge SW , 020 7823 1166
Hara The Circle Bar, Queen Elizabeth St, SE1 08452 269 411
Moti Mahal, 45 Great Queen Street, WC2 020 7240 9329 Joint Winner
Victoria's India,, The Manse, Church St, Longridge, Lancs 01727 785111 Joint Winner

Best Oriental Asian UK restaurant

Orchid Lounge Thai at Jaipur, 1st Floor, 599 Grafton Gate E, Milton Keynes, Bucks 01908 669 811
Awana Malaysian, 85 Sloane Avenue, SW3 020 7584 8880
Blue Elephant Thai, 4 Fulham Broadway, SW6, 020 7385 6595
Georgetown Malaysian, Colwick Hall Hotel, Racecourse Rd Nottingham 0115 9500 566
Mandalay Burmese, 444 Edgware Rd, W2 020 7258 3696
Nipon Kan Japanese, Old Thorns Hotel, Griggs Green, Liphook, Hampshire 01428 724555

Best European Restaurant

Tandoor Palace, Charanjit Singh., ul. Marszalkowska 21, Warsaw 00-825+48228252375
Indian Taj, Jernbanegade 3-5 ,DK 1608 , Copenhagen, +33 131 010
Rasas, Bayernallee 42, 14052, BERLIN, 030 33 77 29 41
Sagar Royal, Zahid Ali Khan, Stationsstraat 7-11,1182. JM Amsterdam , 020 641 84 45

Special Awards

UK Lifetime Achievement Award.

Kewal Anand, Brilliant Restaurant,72 Western Road, Southall 020 8574 1928

International Lifetime Achievement Award

Satish Arora, Chef Culinaire, Taj Hotels Group, Chef Director, Chef Director of Food Production,

Best UK Restaurant

Itihaas, 18 Fleet St Birmingham B3, 0121 212 3383

A-LIST AND TOP 100

KEY:
A-LIST (see pagesabove)
• = NEW TO OUR TOP 100
† = One of a group of restaurants

London

E1	•† **CAFE NAZ** A-LIST, **AWARD WINNER BEST BANGLADESHI AND BEST CHEF, 2007-8**
	Café Spice Namaste A-LIST, **(Best chef 1992-5 / 1996-8 / Culinary excellence 2001-3)**
	Lahore Kebab House A-LIST, **NOMINATED BEST PAKISTANI RESTAURANT**
	• Mala
	Shampan **(Best Bangladeshi 2001-3)**
	Tiffin Indian
E14	• Dockmasters
EC1	† **The Coconut Lagoon** A-LIST, **(Best Restaurant group 2004-5)**
EC3	**KASTURI** A-LIST **NOMINATED BEST IN LONDON, 2007-8**
N1	• Afghan Kitchen
	MASALA ZONE A-LIST, **(Best New Concept Award 2004-5)**
N3	Rani Vegetarian **(Best Vegetarian 2001-3)**
N16	† Rasa A-LIST
	Rasa Travancore A-LIST
N19	Parsee A-LIST
NW1	Diwana Bhel Poori House
	Great Nepalese **(Best Nepalese 2001-3)**
NW3	• Eriki
NW4	Prince of Ceylon **(Best Sri Lankan 2001-3)**
NW5	• Chetna
NW6	• **ELEPHANT WALK** A-LIST, **BEST SRI LANKAN 2007-8**
	Geeta South Indian
	Vijay
SE1	Bengal Clipper
	Georgetown **(Best Restaurant group 2004-5)** *See Kenilworth Warks.*
	• **HARA THE CIRCLE BAR** A-LIST, **NOMINATED BEST NEWCOMER 2007-8**
SE13	Spice of Life
SE23	**BABUR BRASSERIE** A-LIST, **NOMINATED BEST IN LONDON, 2007-8**

THE AWARD WINNING RESTAURANT

Unique & Luxurious Environment
warm and Friendly service

café Naz

Nominated
Cobra Good
Curry Guide
Best Bangladeshi
2007/8

Cafe Naz
46-48 Brick Lane
London E1 6RF

Awarded
Cobra Good
Curry Guide
Best
Chef
2007/8

020 7247 0234
www.cafenaz.co.uk

• Celebrate your birthday & have a cake on us •

•Winner of food hygiene award
•Featured in BBC
•"Best Indian Restaurant"- *'Independent'*

Resolutely modern from its shiny black facade and chilli-patterned glass 'n' chrome bar, 'this is Banglatown's flagship buzzing brasserie'
Charles Champion.

'Cafe Naz is sleek and elegant, lunchtime buffet is superb, as is dinner'
Time Out.

'Best contemporart Indian restaurant'
ITV Dinner Date.

† Three Monkeys
SW1 • **AMAYA** A-LIST, **NOMINATED BEST NEWCOMER, 2007-8**
Cinnamon Club A-LIST
• **MINT LEAF** A-LIST, **BEST IN LONDON, 2007-8**
THE QUILON A-LIST, **(BEST IN UK 2001-3 and OUTSTANDING RESTAURANT AWARD 2004-5 & 2007-8)**
Saloos
† Woodlands
SW3 **Haandi** A-LIST, **PREVIOUS AWARD WINNER**
• Rasoi Vineet Bhatia A-LIST
SW5 • Masala Zone A-LIST
Nizam
Star of India
SW6 **BLUE ELEPHANT THAI** A-LIST, **PREVIOUS AWARD WINNER**
• Darbar
NAYAAB A-LIST, **NOMINATED BEST IN LONDON, 2007-8**
SW7 **BOMBAY BRASSERIE** A-LIST, **(BEST IN UK 1995-7 / LIFETIME BEST RESTAURANT AWARD – 1982 TO 2004-5 & 2007-8)**
Café Lazeez A-LIST,
Shezan Indian
SW10 **CHUTNEY MARY** A-LIST, **(BEST IN UK 1991-4 AND 1999-2000) OUTSTANDING RESTAURANT AWARD 2004-5)**
PAINTED HERON A-LIST, **BEST CHEF AWARD**
Vama The Indian Room A-LIST
SW12 **TABAQ** A-LIST, **(BEST PAKISTANI 1998-99, 1999-2000 , 2001-3 & 2004-5)**
SW15 Ma Goa
SW16 • Mirch Masala
• Shahee Bhel Poori Vegan
SW17 **JAFFNA HOUSE** A-LIST **(BEST SRI LANKAN 2004-5) & NOMINATED 2007-8**
Radha Krishna Bhavan
Sree Krishna
SW18 **SARKHEL'S** A-LIST, **(BEST NEWCOMER 1999-2000 / BEST INDIAN 2001-3 OUTSTANDING RESTAURANT AWARD 2004-5 & 2007-8)**
SW19 Dalchini
W1 Anwars
• Benares
† Café Lazeez
• **CHAI PANI RAJASTHANI** A-LIST, **BEST VEGETARIAN 2007-8**
Chor Bizarre **(BEST NORTH INDIAN 2001)**
Chowki
Gaylord
• **IMLI** A-LIST, **AWARD WINNER BEST INDIAN 2007-8**
† **MASALA ZONE** A-LIST, **(BEST NEW CONCEPT AWARD 2004-5)**
LA PORTE DES INDES A-LIST, **(BEST INDIAN AND BEST IN UK 1998-9 / OUTSTANDING RESTAURANT AWARD 2004-5 & 2007-8)**
Ragam South Indian
† Rasa A-LIST
† Rasa Samudra A-LIST
• Red Fort A-LIST
•† Soho Spice
Tamarind A-LIST, **(BEST NEWCOMER 1995-97 / BEST INDIAN 1998-9 / BEST CHEF 1999-2000)**
VEERASWAMY A-LIST, (BEST NEWCOMER 1998-9 & **OUTSTANDING RESTAURANT AWARD 2007-8)**
† Woodlands
W2 Bombay Palace
• Durbar
Ginger **(BEST BANGLADESHI 2004-5)**
Khans
Mandalay Burmese A-LIST

W4	† Woodlands, South Indian Vegetarian
W5	• **MONTY'S NEPALESE CUISINE** A-LIST **BEST UK NEPALESE, 2007-8**
W6	• Agni
	• Green Chilli
	• Indian Zing
	SAGAR A-LIST, **NOMINATED BEST VEGETARIAN, 2007-8**
	Tandoori Nights
W8	Malabar
W8	Zaika A-LIST
W13	• Laguna
WC1	• Hason Raja A-LIST**, NOMINATED BEST BANGLADESHI**
	Malabar Junction (Best South Indian 1999-2000)
WC2	**India Club** A-LIST, **(Special Award Winner 1995-97)**
	Mela
	• **MOTI MAHAL** A-LIST, **MOST PROMISING NEWCOMER AWARD**
	Punjab A-LIST, **(Best North Indian 1999-2000)**

England

BERKSHIRE

Cookham	Malik's
Slough	• **BAYLIS HOUSE** A-LIST, **NOMINATED BEST INDIAN, 2007-8**
Sunningdale	Tiger's Pad
Theale	**Café Blue Cobra (Best in the West 1995-7)**
Twyford	• Hawelli
Windsor	Spice Route
Wokingham	Sultan Balti Palace

BUCKINGHAMSHIRE

Milton Keynes	**JAIPUR** A-LIST, **(BEST RESTAURANT OUTSIDE LONDON 1995-97, 1998-99, 1999-2000 , 2001-3 & 2004-5)**
	• Jaloril
	• **ORCHID LOUNGE AT JAIPUR** A-LIST, **BEST UK ORIENTAL ASIAN RESTAURANT, 2007-8**
Newport Pagnell	Mysore
Stony Stratford	Moghul Palace

CAMBRIDGESHIRE

Cambridge	• **CAFE NAZ** A-LIST, **AWARD WINNER BEST BANGLADESHI AND BEST CHEF, 2007-8**

CHESHIRE

Ellesmere Port	**The Taj of Agra Fort (Best in the North 1998-9)**
Northwich	† Bengal Dynasty A-LIST

DEVON

Ilfracombe	Rajah

ESSEX

Gants Hill	Kanchans
Ilford	Curry Special
	Jalalabad

HAMPSHIRE

Fleet	**GURKHA SQUARE** A-LIST **(BEST NEPALESE 1998-9) & NOMINATED BEST NEPALESE, 2007-8**
Liss	Madhuban
Southampton	• Café Mumbai
	• **KUTI'S BRASSERIE** A-LIST **BEST BANGLADESHI, 2007-8**
	• Popadom Express
Southsea	• Bombay Bay
	Golden Curry

HERTFORDSHIRE

Abbots Langley	Viceroy of India
St Albans	**MUMTAJ** A-LIST, **NOMINATED BEST IN THE SOUTH, 2007-8**

KENT

Ashford	• Zarin
Bromley	• Kosturi
	TAMASHA A-LIST, **BEST IN THE SOUTH, 2007-8 (BEST IN THE SOUTH 1998-9)**
Folkestone	**• GURKHA PALACE** A-LIST **NOMINATED BEST NEPALESE, 2007-8**
	India
Welling	Tagore A-LIST
Westerham	**• KINARA AT PITT'S COTTAGE** A-LIST , **NOMINATED BEST PAKSITANI, 2007-8**
	Tulsi

LANCASHIRE

Adlington	Sharju
Longridge	**• VICTORIA'S INDIA, MOST WELCOME NEWCOMER, 2007-8**

LEICESTERSHIRE

Leicester	**CURRY FEVER** A-LIST, **(BEST IN THE MIDLANDS 2001-3)**
	• EK MAYA A-LIST, **NOMINATED BEST IN THE MIDLANDS, 2007-8**
	Friends Tandoori

LINCOLNSHIRE

Boston	Star of India
Lincoln	• Malabar Junction at Barbican hotel

MANCHESTER (GREATER)

Altrincham	Barindar
	• Dilli
Ashton-u-Lyne	**INDIAN OCEAN** A-LIST, **BEST IN THE NORTH, 2007-8**
Manchester	Gaylord
Rochdale	La Tandoor

MERSEYSIDE

Liverpool	**GULSHAN (BEST IN THE NORTH 1999-2000 AND 2001-3)**
	• Maharaja South Indian

MIDDLESEX

Brentford	Pappadums
Edgware	• Haandi
Southall	**BRILLIANT** A-LIST, **(BEST PUNJABI RESTAURANT 1998-9, 2004/6 2007/8)**
	MADHU'S BRILLIANT A-LIST, **(SPECIAL AWARDS 1991-2000 BEST RESTAURANT IN UK AWARD 2004-5, OUTSTANDING , 2007-8)**
	• Moj Masti
	New Asian Tandoori Centre
	Omi's
	• PALM PALACE NOMINATED BEST SRI LANKAN, 2007-8
Wembley	Chetna's Bhel Puri
	Clay Oven
	Curry Craze
	† Woodlands

NORTHUMBERLAND

Berwick	**MAGNA** A-LIST, **BEST IN THE NORTH EAST, 2007-8**
Corbridge	**THE VALLEY** A-LIST, **(BEST IN THE NORTH 1995-7)**

NOTTINGHAMSHIRE

Nottingham	• 4500 miles from Delhi
	Saagar

OXFORDSHIRE

Oxford	**AZIZ** A-LIST, **NOMINATED BEST BANGLADESHI, 2007-8**
	(ALSO BRANCHES: AZIZ BURFORD AND AZIZ WITNEY)

SOMERSET

Bath	**EASTERN EYE** A-LIST, **NOMINATED BEST IN THE WEST, 2007-8**

STAFFORDSHIRE

Kingsley Holt — Thornbury Hall Rasoi
Leek — Bolaka Spice
Lichfield — Eastern Eye

SUFFOLK

Woodbridge — Royal Bengall

SURREY

Croydon — Planet Spice A-LIST
Epsom — Le Raj
Oxted — GURKHA KITCHEN A-LIST, NOMINATED , 2007-8 (BEST NEPALESE 1999-2000)
Richmond — • Origin Asia
Woking — Jaipur

SUSSEX

Crawley — • Blue India
Haywards Heath — • Blue India
Nutbourne — • Tamarind and Moonlight Express
Worthing — • Indian Ocean Takeaway

TYNE & WEAR

Gateshead — THE LAST DAYS OF THE RAJ A-LIST, NOMINATED BEST IN THE NORTH, 2007-8
Newcastle — SACHINS A-LIST, NOMINATED BEST IN THE NORTH, 2007-8
VALLEY JUNCTION 397 A-LIST (MOST ORIGINAL 1999-2000), NOMINATED BEST IN THE NORTH, 2007-8
VUJON (BEST IN THE NORTH EAST 2004-5)

WARWICKSHIRE

Kenilworth — † THE COCONUT LAGOON A-LIST (BEST IN THE MIDLANDS 2002-3 AND BEST RESTAURANT GROUP AWARD 2004-5)
† RAFFLES, MALAYSIAN A-LIST, (BEST RESTAURANT GROUP AWARD 2004-5)
Stratford on Avon — †THE COCONUT LAGOON A-LIST, (BEST RESTAURANT GROUP 2004-5)
† GEORGETOWN, MALAYSIAN A-LIST, (BEST RESTAURANT GROUP AWARD 2004-5)

WEST MIDLANDS

Birmingham — ADIL (BEST BALTI HOUSE 1999-2000)
†THE COCONUT LAGOON A-LIST, (BEST RESTAURANT GROUP 2004-5)
• ITIHAAS A-LIST, BEST IN THE MIDLANDS , 2007-8 AND BEST IN UK AWARDS, 2007-8
• LASAN NOMINATED BEST IN MIDLANDS , 2007-8
MAHARAJAH (BEST IN THE MIDLANDS 1998-99 &1999-2000)
• PRÂNA A-LIST, NOMINATED BEST IN MIDLANDS , 2007-8
ROYAL NAIM (BEST BALTI HOUSE1995-98)
• SWEET CHILLIES CUISINE NOMINATED BEST IN MIDLANDS, 2007-8
Coventry — Monsoon
Solihull — • Mango Tree
Rajnagar International A-LIST, NOMINATED BEST IN THE MIDLANDS, 2007-8

WILTSHIRE

Marlborough — • The Palm
Salisbury — • Anokaa
Swindon — Rafu's Tandoori

WORCESTERSHIRE

Worcester — Monsoon
Spice Cuisine

NORTH YORKSHIRE

Skipton — † AAGRAH A-LIST, (BEST RESTAURANT GROUP, 1998-2000) & NOMINATED BEST PAKISTANI, 2007-8 ALSO AAGRAH, Tadcaster and York
York — † Jinnah

SOUTH YORKSHIRE

Doncaster — † AAGRAH A-LIST, (BEST RESTAURANT GROUP, 1998-99 &1999-2000)
Sheffield — Ashoka A-LIST
• Saffron Club

WEST YORKSHIRE

Bradford	• Sweet Centre
Garforth	† **AAGRAH** A-LIST, **(BEST RESTAURANT GROUP, 1998-2000) & NOMINATED BEST PAKISTANI, 2007-8,** also **AAGRAH,** Huddersfield, Pudsey, Shipley and Wakefield
	• Akbars and Akbar's The Grand
	Darbar
	Polash

Eire

Dublin	• Jaipur
	• Shalimar

Scotland

FIFE

ST ANDREWS	**BALAKA** A-LIST, **NOMINATED BEST IN SCOTLAND, 2007-8 (BEST IN SCOTLAND 1995-7 & BEST BANGLADESHI 1999-2000)**

LOTHIAN

Edinburgh	Far Pavillion
	Lancers Brasserie
	SHAMIANA (BEST CHEF 1998-99)
	Verandah
Leith	**BRITANNIA SPICE** A-LIST, **NOMINATED BEST IN SCOTLAND, 2007-8 (BEST IN SCOTLAND 2001-3)**
	GULNAR'S PASSAGE TO INDIA (BEST IN SCOTLAND 1999-2000)

STRATHCLYDE

Glasgow	† **ASHOKA AT THE MILL** A-LIST, **BEST IN SCOTLAND, 2007-8**
	• Café India
	Koh-i-noor
	Mister Singh's India
	• Mother India
	† Murphy's Pakora Bar

TAYSIDE

Dundee	**DIL SEE** A-LIST, **(BEST IN SCOTLAND 2004-5)**

Wales

CLWYD

Colwyn Bay	† **BENGAL DYNASTY** A-LIST, **(BEST IN WALES 2004-5 – FOURTH TIME)**

GLAMORGAN

Cardiff	• **CAFE NAZ** A-LIST, **AWARD WINNER BEST BANGLADESHI AND BEST CHEF, 2007-8**
	† **JUBRAJ** A-LIST, **(BEST IN WALES 1999/2000)**
Swansea	Bonophul
	Moghul Brasserie

GWENT

Monmouth	**MISBAH TANDOORI** A-LIST, **BEST IN WALES, 2007-8**

GWYNEDD

Llandudno	† **BENGAL DYNASTY** A-LIST, **(BEST IN WALES 2004-5 – FOURTH TIME)**

U- Raitabout ~ a few letters from the postbag

Hi Pat, Looking forward to your new *Guide.* We take our copy where ever we go. Tried at least 35 restaurants from it. Our favourite is Jaipur in Milton Keynes. We stay in the Hilton for the week-end and always visit the Jaipur Saturday night. A place to dress up for. **Regards Dot (Dorothy Vaughan-Williams, e-mail)**

Hi Pat, My mum's name is Pat Chapman and on a visit to the Knowle Indian Brasserie near Solihull, my parents were seated at a table with the Curry Club certificate just above as they had booked a table as Chapman. Even though they did not know my mum's Christian name, she was quite embarrassed!
Rod Chapman, e-mail.

Pat: Please enclosed an attachment containing reviews of the 150 restaurants that I reported on over the last 12 months – there have been a lot of changes recently. After due deliberation my restaurants of the year are as follows: 1: Coconut Lagoon, Kenilworth; 2; Eastern Eye, Bath; 3: Spice Avenue, B13.
Graham & Melinda Paine, Coventry

Re: GOOD CURRY GUIDE (NOT): I very disappointed by some of the restaurants you have recommended. I think your advisers should check them with local environmental health officers first. The best way to judge any restaurant is to see how much regular custom there is and if there is evidence of food poisoning! **Mansoor.**
From: Pat: I would very much appreciate it if you will tell me which restaurants you are referring to.
From: Mansoor: I will just give you one recent example: Radcliffe Charcoal Tandoori, Blackburn Street Radcliffe Manchester. They boast that they are in the **TOP 100** Indian Restaurants in *The Real Curry Guide.* This is what was delivered: Poppadoms stale with very watered down mango chutney and stale tomato onions. Seekh Kebabs probably reheated in microwave and tasteless. Lamb Karai really mutton with a lot of tomato/onions and very mild spices fairly tasteless for any pallet. Vegetable Karai could not eat as it was clearly off. We were told that they had cooked the vegetables the previous night and kept it refrigerated. They do not even use fresh vegetables (frozen). Tandoori Nans not cooked in a tandoor clay oven but under a normal grill. The restaurant itself is shabby with dirty carpets I would hate to see the kitchen. And you give this restaurant a high recommendation to your readers! Do I need to say more! Now see if you will share this with your readers. I have no axe to grind but I think people should not be hoodwinked. I tried this restaurant because of your guide!
From: Pat: Now we are getting somewhere. Firstly the *Cobra Good Curry Guide* is not the *Real Curry Guide* and they had a **TOP 30** (not TOP 100). It used to be published by a 'rival' and has been defunct for years. Radcliffe Charcoal Tandoori are are entered into our 2004 edition but they are not and have never been in our **TOP 100**. They are entered largely but not entirely because of the recommendation of MB (Mike Bates) who lives nearby and who reliably reports about restaurants up and down the UK. Finally, and the most important point of all. If you believed the food was off at any restaurant it is your duty to report it to the EHO at once, not to leave it until later to report it to me in a critical side-swipe. Now please let me know the other restaurants where you claim to have a bad experience. Tell you what ... let's find out what the public think of your remarks about the advice in my *Guide.* I have nothing to hide. I will publish your e-mail in full with its address and let's see what response we / you get. Thanks for giving me the opportunity.
From: Mansoor <asimzain@nildram.co.uk>: I am in the process of reporting this restaurant to Bury Council's EHO. The e-mail I sent you was sparked off because this was just last Sunday and this restaurant has a flyer which states that it received the Top 100 Indian Restaurant Award from the *Real Curry Guide.* I never mentioned the *Cobra Good Curry Guide.* **(could have fooled me, Ed)** I am not in the catering business but we do eat out a lot. My comments are not made out of anger but of genuine concern. I do hope you will be a little more cautious on how some restaurants may exploit your guide. I do not wish to go into anymore dialogue. **And he didn't. So now your views, dear readers please.**

Hello Mr Chapman, I was just wondering why are there not many Indian and Bangladeshi restaurants in the north east of England with AA ratings. **Samsul Hoque, e-mail**
Couldn't tell you Samsul. We are not the *AA Guide.* We are the *Cobra Good Curry Guide,* and there are numerous Bangladeshi restaurants with high ratings in our *Guide.*

Dear Pat, I was really sad recently to learn that Edinburgh's Raj failed to meet health standards and had to close for four days to bring it up to standard. I just thought it was a sad day for Bangladeshi restaurateurs. Just that you can confirm what I said, it's the Scotsman newspaper which published the article.
S.R.Miah e-mail.

Sir: I had a takeaway last week from a local restaurant. It stated on the front of their menu *"Recommended by Curry Club. The best food critic in the UK."* and that was the reason my husband and I tried it. It was the worst meal I have ever had in my life. The chicken tikka, lamb bhuna and curry all tasted the same, absolutely horrible. We then found a black hair in the chicken tikka. I rang to complain and they offered us another chicken tikka. The entire meal went in the bin. I presume the Curry Club they mentioned was yours and would appreciate your feedback on the matter. I have checked the restaurant time in Curry Club list and it does not appear anywhere. The restaurant is the Taj Mahal 4 Willow Tree Lane, Yeading, Hayes, Middlesex, UB4 9BB. I await your comments.
Jacinta Mussett Cintgrant@aol.com

Hi Jacinta: You are quite correct to say that this restaurant is not in the *Cobra Good Curry Guide,* nor on any of our 'recommended' listings. It is one of the pitfalls we suffer, presuming they are claiming it is our Curry Club, and worse still using our logo. Incidentally both the logo and the name are trade marks and are

copyright. Just how to prevent such usage is another matter. We will publish your e-mail in a the next *Guide* (done here), but short of getting our lawyers involved, (expensive) we can do little else.

Sir: The Akash Tandoori, Leicester displays a Cobra recommendation. It was for this reason that a friend and I ate there recently. The meal was one of the worst we have had in 40 years of visiting Indian restaurants. The meat was of poor quality, the rice cold, the vegetables victims of much reheating and the spices overwhelmingly pepper and chilli. I complained in a manner not likely to be soon forgotten. We weren't looking for the best Indian meal in Leicester but for a reasonable one among the many restaurants close to the railway station. I do not know whether the Akash features in your current *Guide.* If it does, then the guide is seriously misleading; if it doesn't, you have an equally serious problem.
Roger; Not sure what the latter comment means, but yes it is in my *Guide* because of satisfied reports received. I do get occasional complaints that the *Guide* is misleading when diners have a bad experience, and they look for someone to blame. Of course one puncture does not mean you buy a new car. As I put in the *Guide's* long intro, restaurants change in quality, and we cannot be held responsible for this. This is the first complaint received re Akash. But I will publish you remarks in full and see what comments we get from our members, if any. Of course if you had read the *Guide* you would know that the best in Leicester is the Curry Fever on Belgrave Road.

Dear Pat, I picked up a copy of your *Guide* recently when eating at Curry Fever in Leicester and I must confess, have hardly put it down. It is currently sitting in what is euphemistically called the smallest room, so is read at least a couple of times daily! (**only a couple, John?**). In my job, as a sports correspondent for the BBC and the Guardian, I spend inordinate amounts of money eating out. It is, in my opinion, one of life's finest extravagances although, a little sadly, it is sometimes necessary to wade through the mediocre in order to appreciate the exceptional. But curries, or more precisely Indian food are my gastronomic passion. So, bearing that preamble in mind, I have to say I am astonished that the restaurant I regard as the best in Leicestershire, the Khyber, does not merit an entry in your publication.. Best Wishes, **John Rawling, e-mail.**

Pat: I saw you piece on tipping in Tandoori Magazine. Very good point: my husband and I went to Leicester' Tiffin the other night. We sent the meal back as didn't even resemble a curry (Curry Fever still the best in Leicester) and we got charged the full price and a 12.5% service charge to add insult to serious hunger!
Chloe Malik"
<chloe.malik@hotmarketing.co.uk>
And I sincerely hope you did not pay the service charge, indeed you had every right to pay nothing.

Pat: Thanks for the *Guide* . It is, as always, an absorbing read. One point of issue is the removal of Bengal Mangrove, Halstead Kent and the Tulsi Westerham Kent from the **TOP 100** because of their ploy of leaving the credit card slip open after charging a service charge. If this is your policy why not delist all the others who do it? I feel as strongly as you, but it will not stop them from doing it because they know they will loose any business at all, so strong is their loyal following. Nor will it stop me going to these restaurants as they are so good. **Chris Osler, Biggin Hill.**
OK, you win, they go back in as **TOP 100**s, but you loose if you pay.

This weird reply to our restaurant questionnaire arrived with postage unpaid (it cost £1.21 to retrieve it). *'Your Guide is written by intelligent crooks who have never worked and never will. Money doesn't grow on the tree making people full* (sic). *Waste of time.'* The anonymous respondent was fool enough to put his address on the rear of the envelope as follows: Kajal, 53 Liskeard Rd, Walsall, WS5.

I found a copy of the *Guide* at a local bookshop. It is in my opinion quite astonishing how the detail in your book is so varied, and how the book collates years of experience from from your Club and the public. This is an ideal way of playing a little part in gastronomy and reviewing meals, and I hope you find my comments useful, if not written by an expert.
Duncan Weaver, Bury St Edmunds
Hello Duncan, I do not get many fluent letters from 17 year-olds, in fact none that I can recall. And even those from people two, three or even five times your age are rarely so articulate. Mind you I am only too pleased to get any correspondence on restaurants even if it is a one-liner. Your powers of observation and literacy are extremely good and I enjoyed your general remarks, and your reviews.

I have belatedly been reading the current (2004) *Cobra Good Curry Guide* (appropriate since I now live in Bury St Edmunds home of the excellent Abbot Ale) and I was most interested to learn of the dodgy Scot Ian Cowan. Did the story get picked up at the time – is he still at it? **Richard Goss, Anglia Press Agency.**
See page 13, Richard.

Dear Mr Chapman. I work for the London Correspondents Unit of the Foreign and Commonwealth Office (FCO) and you're probably wondering why I've contacted you. Foreign journalists are the major source of opinion about the UK overseas and we are the FCO's specialist link with the foreign press. We encourage accurate, balanced and in-depth reporting of all aspects of the UK . We have close links with many of the London-based correspondents from South Asia where, I know, they are fascinated by the UK's obsession with curry. I know they enjoy reading your *Guide.*
David Dearnley

Out for a takeaway tonight from Patching near Brighton, cannot remember when I last had 3 curries in one week, life is on the up. However we need to stoke up; we're signing off for a "round-the-world-in-74-days" trip, and will be suffering from curry deprivation on our return I fear. **Chris and Maureen Coleman**

Last word to Malcolm ...
Hello Pat,
Another Saturday curry excursion and another disappointment!
I sometimes question why I bother to put my stomach at the disposal of research rather than enjoy my curry at somewhere I know is good!
Malcolm Wilkins, Kent

Pat Chapman's New Curry Bible

published by

John Blake Publishing

This best-selling definitive, gorgeously illustrated book is a 'must-have' for all curryholics. It brings together a wealth of information on how to prepare a perfect Indian meal. In an innovative presentation for a cookery book, all your favourite curryhouse dishes are arranged in menu order, with descriptions, recipes and pictures of every one. Some are compared with their authentic classic counterparts. The book begins with a colour-picture study of ingredients and utensils, then continues with step-by-step colour sequences of important techniques. The 150 recipes are subdivided into chapters including Starters, Kebabs, Tandoori/Tikka, 32 Top Curries plus the most popular Specials, Vegetable, Dhal and Rice Dishes and Breads and Desserts. The book concludes with thumbnail essays on the cuisine of the Curry World, Menu Suggestions. a Store Cupboard list. and an extensive Glossary. Running throughout the recipe section is an exciting A to Z of 40 spices. Each spice is illustrated full size in colour and has a fascinating description. All the recipes are easy to cook and give superb results. *Please note this book was first entitled Pat Chapman's Curry Bible.*

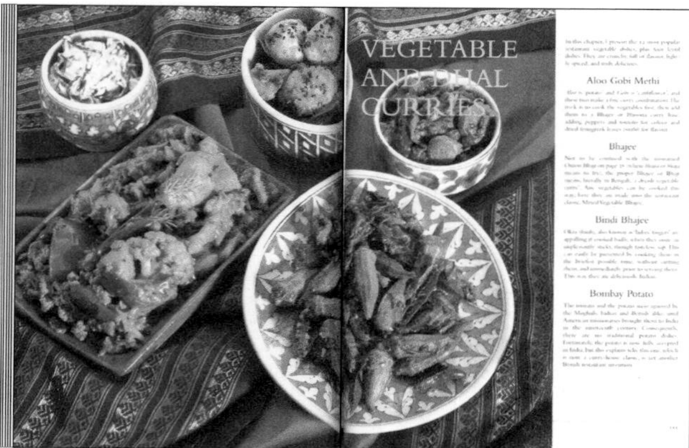

"A truly authoritative book. Pat Chapman is to curry what God is to the Old Testament."
Max Davidson,
Daily Telegraph.

208 pages: 280 x 230mm.
150 full colour photographs

Available in bookshops now. Or order your signed copy directly from The Curry Club. Add £4.01 to the prices below for p&p.

Hardback ISBN: 9781843580874 £19.99. *Paperback ISBN: 9781843581598 £12.99.*

LIFETIME ACHIEVEMENT AWARD

Kewal Krishan Anand

BRILLIANT RESTAURANT
72 Western Road, Southall, Middlesex
020 8574 1928

The Anand family are typical Kenyan Asians who came to Britain in the 1970s; they are energetic, prolific, ambitious, hard-working chefs and restaurateurs. Their elder statesman is Kewal Krishan Anand. His nephews, Sanjay and Sanjeev run Madhu's Southall. Leicester's Curry Fever is owned by cousins Anil and Sunil Anand. Brother in-law Sartaj Luther and his son Paul has a restaurant in Newbury Park's Curry Special. Kewal and his brother Gulu began it all in the UK with Southall's irreplaceable Brilliant. All are award winning Punjabi-style restaurants.

Kewal was born in Nairobi in 1936. His father Bishen Das Anand, opened in Nagara's Kashmir Paradise, the family's first restaurant and before long became known as the King of Chefs. At sixteen Kewal was helping out. In 1963 he obtained a remarkable contract for Kenya's Independence celebrations when the restaurant provided breakfast, lunch and dinner for 60,000, continually for two weeks, an achievement repeated in the next year. After that the restaurant moved and changed name to Brilliant Nightclub and Hotel. A bigger venture was opened on Desai Road, Nairobi – The Brilliant Restaurant. Over-looking the much-used Gymkhana Cricket Club, it was built in the shape of a ship the inside of which featured a grand bar and open-plan seating for 500, whose cosmopolitan regulars included Punjabis, Gujaratis, Europeans and local Africans.

Following the loss of his father Kewal brought the family to the UK in 1972 where he started a small Asian wedding catering business operating from home. Wishing to restart the Brilliant, in 1975 Kewal and Gulu bought a fish monger's shop on Western Road and it became a 36 seater restaurant, with the family living in the tiny flat above. Although their father had taught Kewal and Gulu to cook, they concentrated on front of house while Kewal's wife Avinash was head cook. Since those heady days the brothers have extended the restaurant no less than six times. Even with its current 250 seats, the restaurant gets so busy it has a wait-list. Customers have been known to say *'we wouldn't mind sitting on the floor as long as we get the Brilliant food'.*

Neither Kewal nor Gulu foresaw that success. The Brilliant appeared in the first (1984) edition of this Guide, and we said of it then: *'Probably the best restaurant in Southall, and that's an accolade. When in Southall we never go anywhere else. Prince Charles visited ... and declared the food excellent.'* It has appeared in every edition since, and has continuously achieved both TOP 100 status and the highly prestigious Best Punjabi Restaurant Award, which it achieves once again in 2007/8.

The family accords this reputation to Kewal. Family, friends and customers know him as a very hard working, genuine father-figure whose restaurant is his life. He is easing off a little now but still involves himself with the accounts. The future is bright; Kewal has inspired Gulu's young daughter and son, Dipna and Shanker into running the business, ensuring that the name Brilliant carries on for years to come.

Largest ever Asian Lifestyle Show

An overview of the first Asian Lifestyle Show at the Grand Hall Olympia

London's thriving Indian community gathered in full force at the Grand Hall Olympia, from 9 to 11 July, for the first Asian Lifestyle Show.

The event was organized to showcase the wide diversity of contemporary Asian culture and society, and to celebrate the best in British Asian life.

Over 40,000 visitors participated in the event that encompassed all aspects of the Asian community's vibrant lifestyle, featuring fashion shows, entertainment, health, technology and communications, food and drink, beauty, jewellery, sports and a wide variety of exhibitors.

The exhibitors had something to cater to the needs of each and every guest, from live demonstrations, astrology readings and beauty makeovers to a cookery theatre and also a recruitment village.

The presence of three leading Bollywood stars – Sonali Bendre, Bipasha Basu and John Abraham – provided a touch of glamour. Chart toppers like Raghav, Rishi Rich, Jay Sean, Juggy D, Stereo Nation, and DCS also performed at the festival, along with the likes of Sonu Nigam who had flown in from India.

Earls Court and Olympia Group chief executive Anthony Lyons praised the event as one of the most successful launch shows ever to be staged at the venue. "The opening day of Asian Lifestyle saw one of the highest attendances for a launch show at Olympia, which I believe is a tribute to the event's unique combination of imaginative content and the organisers' ability to tap into public interest and enthusiasm for Asian culture. It is a pleasure to welcome such a bold, creative and successful show to our venue and I look forward to watching the show go from strength to strength," he said.

Asian Lifestyle 2004 is the largest exhibition of Asian culture in Europe and the first Asian show ever to be staged at Olympia. The event was sponsored by Sunrise Radio and supported by Sony Entertainment TV (SET) Asia, the Mayor of London, the GLA and British Airways supported the festival.

Piece courtesy India Digest, Govt of India

Baylis House chef with guest demonstrator Pat Chapman, right, author of the 'Indian Curry Guide' and founding patron of The Curry Club, cooking up some culinary delights in the demonstration theatre at the Asian Lifestyle Show.

India DIGEST

INTERNATIONAL LIFETIME ACHIEVEMENT AWARD

Satish Arora

Director of Food Production, Chef Culinaire Taj Group of Hotels.

Satish Arora was born into a Delhi Punjabi family in 1947. Despite the efforts of his civil servant father, OM Prakash Arora to apply strict discipline to his daughter Kusum sons Chander and Satish, the latter tells us he was a very naughty boy, not helped by the fact that he skipped school many times; on one occasion he was caught playing marbles in the street with his friends.

In 1963 it was time to choose his career. Not surprisingly his low-percentage exam marks gave his long-suffering family considerable difficulty in selecting a suitable professional course for their wayward son. Luckily for the world, at just the right moment one of his friends brought him a prospectus from the fledgling New Delhi Catering Institute. Satish was delighted to find they taught subjects like cookery, bakery, food and beverage; subjects dear to his heart and tummy. Much against his fathers wish Satish was admitted to that college. It was a turning point in his life Coming top of the class each year, he was the college's first student to get a distinction for his Hotel Management & Catering Diploma. It enabled him to join the elite kitchen brigade at Mumbai's Taj Mahal Hotel as trainee. After ten months he was sent to Germany for a further year's practical training. On his return he was promoted to the highly prestigious position of Sous Chef at Mumbai's Taj Mahal Hotel, India's top hotel under Executive Chef Mascarenhas who had been a remarkable 55 years in Taj service. Less than four years later, Chef Mascarenhas retired and Satish was given the position of Executive Chef. At just 26 years of age and with only 6 years in the hotel, Satish became the youngest Exec Chef in the world at a 5 star deluxe hotel.

The going was tough, but Satish gave it everything. He was always first to work at 0630 am and last to leave at 1 am after locking all cold rooms and closing all gas valves. He married Sushma in 1972, herself a home-science student from Delhi and a very good cook at home. And with her full support Satish enjoyed a expanded his career. As luck would have at this stage Taj also started expanding from one hotel to today's 55 Indian hotels and 15 overseas. It was Satish who established the in-house chef training systems that such expansion required.

His individual achievements are too long to list here, but one highlight was in 1983 when he was in charge of all cuisine for a summit meeting of 48 Commonwealth Heads of Government in Goa for which Margaret Thatcher and Indira Gandhi personally thanked him. Since then he has cooked all over the world for Queens Elizabeth and

Beatrix, numerous Princes, Prime Ministers and Presidents (including Clinton, Gorbachov and Mitterand) and an A-LIST, of celebrities. 1985 he was appointed Chef Culinaire Taj Group and in 1990 he was promoted to Taj Director of Food Production, where his talents include reinventing Taj's in-flight catering at Mumbai airport.

Satish's son Puneet Arora works in London for Bombay Halwa as Production Manager and Executive Chef and his daughter Kanika is a Mumbai fashion designer.

90% of the chefs in now working in the Taj the chain, and a good many more in London, the US and Australia were trained by him personally. The are the world's top chefs, and it is therefore true to say that no one has done more to bring Indian food to public awareness, yet there is no one more modest or more dedicated than Chef Satish Arora.

Chef Satish has exclusively carried out cookery demonstrations for our Gourmet Tours to India. Here we see him at work at Taj Mumbai for our second tour in 1984. Story and pictures are from The Curry Magazine, Winter 1984.

BOMBAY

Satish Arora

Satish Arora is Chef Culinaire in one of the most prestigious hotels in the world – the Taj Mahal Intercontinental, Bombay. He is responsible for the cuisine of the hotels many restaurants and banqueting suites. Whether it is Indian, Chinese, Nouveau, Western or a room service English breakfast, Satish and his kitchen brigade of 150 can prepare it to perfection. It is nothing for the hotel to prepare 5,000 meals in the course of one day. Satish is responsible for all the Taj Groups hotels in Southern India and Sri Lanka including Fort Aguada in Goa and the Caromandel in Madras. A role he greatly enjoys is chef training, which is done at Bombay. At any one time 40 apprentice chefs are learning their trade under Satish for up to three years each.

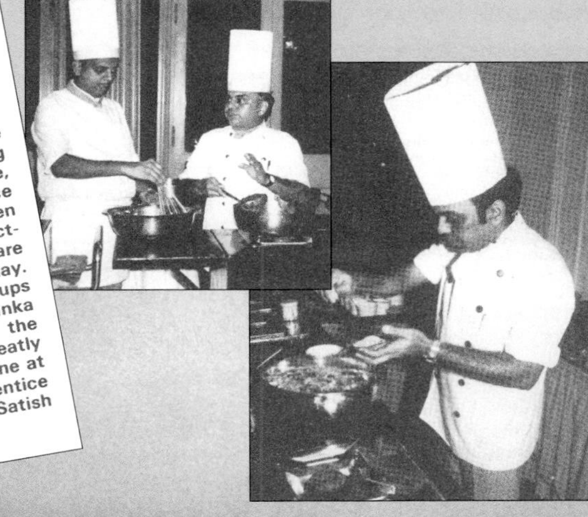

The Curry Club's Next Gourmet Tour

Oct / Nov 2007

Total 18 days inc 2 long-haul flights:

BA 257 direct flight **Heathrow to Delhi** and Indian Airlines to **Kajuraho,** *stay Taj Chandella Hotel, 1 night.*

Varanassi, *stay Taj Ganges Hotel, 2 nights.*

Kanpur/Lucknow *stay Taj Residency, 2 nights.*

Fly to **Delhi**, *stay Taj Mahal Hotel, 2 nights.* Cooking Demo: by Chef Director Arvind Saraswat and Chef Irshad Ahmed Qureshi by the dinner they have cooked.

Darjeeling via Bagdogra *stay Fortune, 3 nights.*

Calcutta (Kolkata) *stay Taj Bengal, 2 nights.*

Hyderabad, *stay Taj Krishna, 2 nights.*

Bangalore, *stay Taj West End, 2 nights.* Visit Grover winery. Demo south Indian food.

BA 118 direct flight **Bangalore to Heathrow, arr 1235.**

6 day Extension to Bangladesh:

This is Bangladesh's first such tour.

Fly from Bangalore via Calcutta to **Chitagong,** *stay Hotel Agrabad, 1 night.* Bangladeshi Cooking Demonstration on hotel rooftop followed by dinner.

Coach to **Cox's Bazaar,** *stay Seagull Hotel, 1 night.*

Fly to **Sylhet,** *stay Parjatan Hotel, 2 nights.* coach to **Mouli Bazaar & Srimongal.**

Fly to **Dhaka,** *stay Pan-Pacific Sonargaon Hotel, 2 nights.* Cooking Demonstration at hotel by Bangladesh's foremost chef Albert Gomes.

BA 114 direct flight **Dhaka to Heathrow, arr 1405.**

Hotels: We stay at the best in each destination. Sightseeing: full guided tours at each destination. Gourmet: The Groups' daily meals are specially selected to show off the best regional food. Plus exclusive chef demos. The tour is operated by TransIndus (see below). Dominique and Pat Chapman host the tour, assisted by a tour leader.

BOOKINGS ARE BEING TAKEN NOW.

Full details <www.patchapman.co.uk> Tours to the Spicy Lands ~ Gourmet Tours

To book your holiday of a lifetime call us now on 020 8566 2729

TransIndus are one of the UK's leading specialists in high quality tours and tailor-made holidays to India, China, Japan and other countries in the Indian subcontinent and South East Asia.
We offer: Tailor-made journeys, bespoke private tours, designed just for you – our speciality!
Guest lecturer tours: small groups led by eminent experts
Escorted group tours: small and intimate (10 - 12 persons), with experienced, friendly tour escorts
Independent tours: a selection of carefully devised itineraries for private travel.

www. transindus.co.uk
enquiries@transindus.com

75 St Mary's Road, Old Fire Station, Ealing, W5 5RH

+44 (0) 20 8566 2729

Britain's best known Indian chef,
Cyrus Todiwalla, OBE.
Even before he came to London in 1991 the Cobra Good Curry Guide made him Best Indian chef.
Ten year earlier, Cyrus gave his first cooking demonstration for Pat Chapman's Gourmet Tour Group who were enjoying the food of Goa at Taj Fort Aguada.

Fishy business!

We were out in the balmy Goan night air, captivated by the demo. On Cyrus' right is Stephen Morgan, who is coming with us in Oct 2007. It is his fourth Gourmet Tour with us. Want to join him? See alongside.

Pictures from Curry Club Magazine Spring 1983

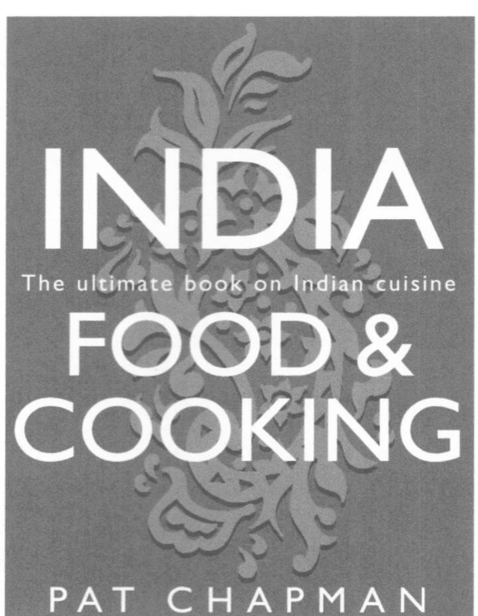

Pat Chapman's new book

published by

New Holland

September 2007

Readers in the 'developed' world all know and love our local curry houses, but this is not a curry book, if by curry we mean the pastiche which is served at many curryhouses outside India herself.

This is a collection of recipes from real India and Pat Chapman has spent over three years travelling the length and breadth of India's 26 federal states collecting thousands of culinary secrets from home cooks, chefs, and foodies. The 200 recipes represent the tip of the iceberg from a country whose a landmass exceeds that of Europe, has several main culinary styles; with numerous minor variations.

The recipes give the reader the widest range of ingredients, tastes and methods, with all the principal signature dishes of each region included. They are in short, the dishes the reader is most likely to encounter whilst travelling in that enigmatic and contradictory land called India. They are cooked in the manner which Indian householders would be proud to offer to their friends and family. Each recipe includes a short introduction with regional or other relevant information.

Indian food began its development thousands of years ago. At a time when Britain was covered in ice and populated with individuals in bearskins and wode, whose main activities included picking berries and clubbing to death anything alive, including each other, India was already cooking refined spicy food.

To understand how India and her food evolved, the book goes on an exciting journey over the last nine millennia. The book comes right up to date by examining modern Indian food trends. Then it explains in detail the utensils and cooking methods, spices, herbs, and ingredients we need to cook Indian food.

The book is a good read, and every recipe is enjoyable and easy to cook.

256 pages   265 x 195 mm   ISBN 9781845376192   over 80 full-colour photographs   hardback

The Subcontinent

The subcontinent includes Pakistan, India, Nepal, Bhutan, Bangladesh, Myanmar (Burma) and Sri Lanka. Until 1947 this was one country ruled by the British. Now as independent states, each has its own unique culinary style. India has ten major regional cuisines and several minor ones, colour-grouped in the map. The main cuisines of the subcontinent are outlined in the following pages.

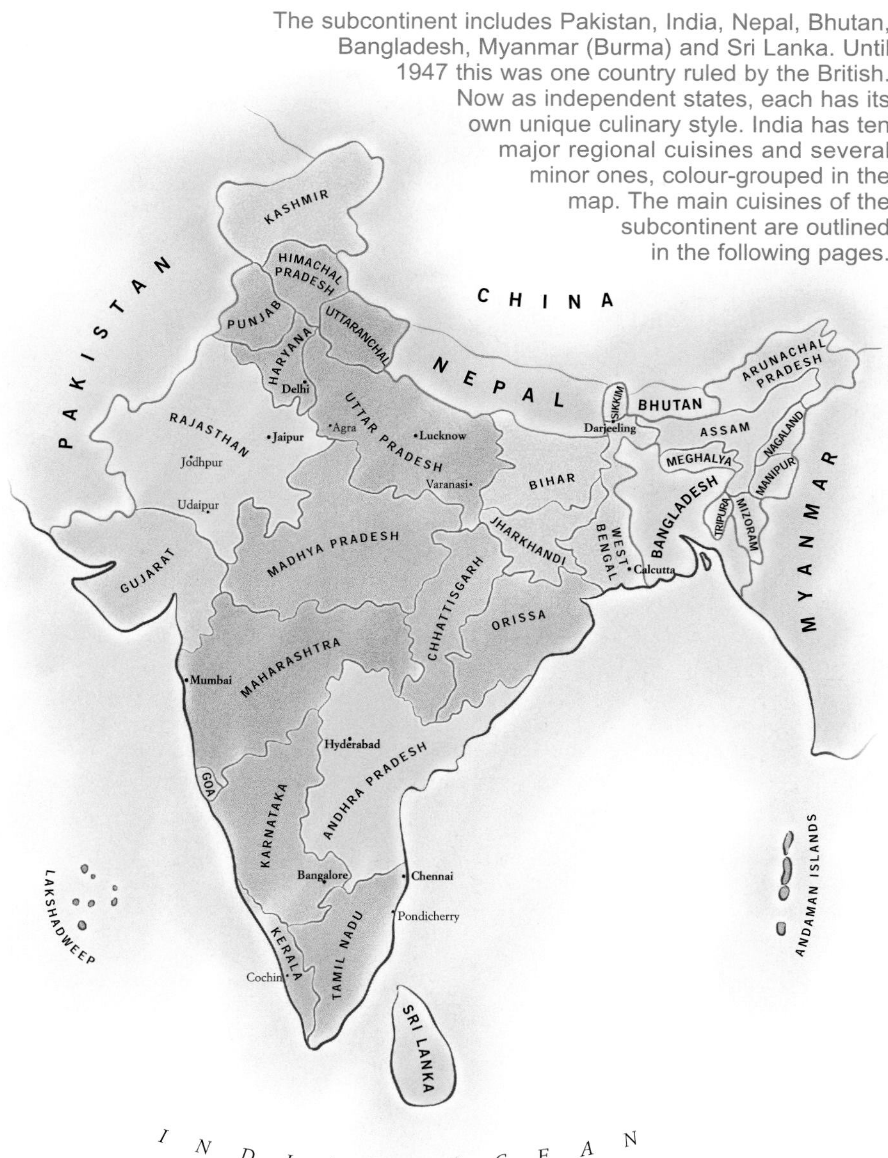

The Cuisine of the Subcontinent

It is a pleasant duty to enlarge this section for the second time in two editions. As we said before, the average overseas tourist expects to find a gastronomic desert when they visit the UK, although many it seems, are intensely relieved to find to that they can populate the proliferation Macdonalds and its clones just as they do back home. Gourmets know better and head for culinary delights the like of which many can only dream of in their home countries. Despite our enduring reputation for boring, tasteless food, it is now several years since London has held the crown as the world's food capital. London boasts the unique and remarkable fact that every nation on the planet is represented with at least one restaurant serving its national food, and most of our bigger cities offer thirty or forty national cuisines. Their streets abound with serious cooks and restaurateurs whose mission is to produce good food and serve it well. Certainly that is the case in the 'Indian 'sector., whether it is haute cuisine in highly-starred restaurants or simple home cooking in cosy, tiny venues. And the good news is that all over Great Britain standards are rising and authentic food is becoming more readily .

For years the majority of curry restaurants have been Bangladeshi-owned, profiting on a food style which is so alien to them they they won't eat it. In the last two decades, some have begun to 'come out' and declare their nationality, in some cases with a full menu of Bangladeshi dishes. There are rather less Pakistani, Sri Lankan, Nepalese and Indian restaurants. However most of these have always been true to their culinary roots, which is why we highlight as many of them as we can in this Guide.

In London you can dine in restaurants who specialise in the Indian region of their owners cooked to the highest, most authentic quality. Bengal, Goa, Gujarat, Hyderabad, Indian Kosher, Kashmir, Lucknow and Nawabi Dum Pukht, Maharashtra and Mumbai, Parsee, Punjab, Rajahsthan and South India which itself has restaurants specialising in the cuisines of Kerela, Chetinad, Coorg, the Nairs, the Syrian Christians, Tamil Nadu and Udipi. They are all in London; their restaurants are all in this Guide and their cuisines and those of the subcontinent are outlined below (between here and page 75). Not even India you can get such an array of good regional Indian cuisine in any one city. **The A to Z of the Curry Menu** (from page 85) details every one of the items at these and all our British Asian restaurants, Outside London, such restaurants are beginning to open up and down the country. It is up to you the diners to become their regular diners.

Afghani Afghanistan's location had always held the strategic key to India until this century, for it was through the solitary mountain passes that the invaders came and possessed India from as early as 3000 BC. Located between Iran (formerly Persia) and Pakistan (formerly NW India), it brought the cuisine of the Middle East to India – and that of India to the Middle East. Afghan food features Kebabs and Birianis, and skewered spiced lamb over charcoal. The only UK Afghan restaurant is Afghan Kitchen, London N1. (*See Pashtoon*).

Balti The Philistines continue to denigrate Balti cooking with references to *'it doesn't exist'* and *'Balti means a bucket'*. Usually these comments come from Indians or the media. The fact is that Balti is a Pakistani phenomenon and so it does not exist in India and with Pakistan and India in a permanent state of war, communications between them are limited and bitter. The reality is that in north Pakistan's high mountains is the ancient state of Baltistan, sharing its border with China and India's Kashmir, and once on the Spice Route to China. Little may have been known about Balti food outside its indigenous area, had it not been for a small group of Pakistani Kashmiris, many from Mirpur, who settled in east Birmingham in the 1960s. There, they opened small cafés in the back streets, serving curries made aromatic with Kashmiri Garam Masala, and herbs, with plentiful coriander, in two-handled pots called the 'karahi' in India, but known here as the 'Balti pan'. Eating with no cutlery, using fingers and bread to scoop up the food, is the norm to the community, but a revelation to Birmingham's white population, who made Balti their

Mayor of Monmouth

Cancer Research UK

Awarded Cobra Good Curry Guide Best in Wales 2007/8

Refurbished to highest standard.

Welcome to Misbah Tandoori

Awarded top 100 restaurant in the UK. It is the only recommendation in SE Wales and one of only a handful of restaurants throughout Wales.

Misbah Tandoori is a family run restaurant, offering authentic Bangladeshi cuisine.

It is located in a grade II listed building in the heart of Monmouth, within the picturesque Wye valley. The restaurant offer a function room, taking the capacity of the premises 80 diners.

We use only the best quality ingredients and all dishes are freshly cooked to order.

We have introduced some dishes including Goan with new flavours, which are unique to 'Misbah'.

Mission Statement:

We place the Customers at the centre of our business.

Many celebrities patronise at the Misbah such as:-

Alan Cox. KB, CBE : *"A wonderfully deserved place in the Top 100, Monmouth should be very proud"!*

Eileen Goodrich (Mayor of Monmouth) *'Food always fabulous and company superb ..Nowhere better in Wales ! Thank you Miah'*

Elinor Jones (BBC) "Around Wales with Elinor" *What a wonderful evening!*

David Bellamy : *"Great food, Great welcome".*

Shirley-Ann Field : // Dave Edmunds :

Anoushka Shankar : *'The food was lovely' !*

ASH: *'Fantastic Thank you xx '(Charlotte hatherley)*

REM: *"Stupendously good curry".*

Oasis // Bob Geldof // The Charlatans // Julian Lennon:

Mark Owen: *(Take That) "Thank you very much, nice Music".*

Judas Priest : *'Will be back".*

Nick Faldo : *"Excellent".*

Sir David Steel : *"Great Lamb Passanda".*

Malcom Bruce : *(House of Commons) "Very Pleasant".*

Peter Snape MP : *Again! "Steel Excellent".*

Arthur Scargill : *'Thanks for a first class meal & Excellent service"*

Also Huw Edwards MP & David Davies AM are regular patrons.

(And many more; too many to mention)

Misbah Tandoori

Fully Air Condition

9 PRIORY STREET

MONMOUTH, NP25 3BR

TEL: 01600 714940/772346

www.misbahtandoori.co.uk

Sarkhel's

Sarkhel's Indian Cuisine is the award winning restaurant of Udit Sarkhel, former executive chef at London's Bombay Brasserie and author of the Bombay Brasserie Cookbook.

The restaurant features Sarkhel's unique Indian Cuisine with recipes drawn from his years of cooking throughout the subcontinent as head chef for the Taj Hotel Group.

At Sarkhel's, the emphasis is on authentic, classical and fresh quality Indian cooking, the kind of food served in Indian homes. Each dish is explained in detail, but if you want to know more, the staff would love to help you order a well balanced, delicious meal to remember.

Sarkhel's

INDIAN CUISINE

199 Replingham Road, Southfields, London, SW18 5LY

Telephone 020 8870 1483 - email info@sarkhels.com

Outside Catering and Party Service - why not give us a call and ask for a quote

Home delivery service now available for £2 - call 020 8871 0808

Magic Wok Cuisine

199, Richmond Road West, London, SW14 8QT
Reservations: 020 8876 6220

Addictively robust wok cooking of the colonial Chinese of Calcutta in India. The food executed by Chef Madan Khapangi who has worked shoulder to shoulder with Udit at his previous venture in Wimbledon Park.

own. Bear in mind that Balti served in the average curry house bears no resemblance to the real thing. *See* West Midlands, Birmingham Balti Zone for information.

Bangladeshi Most of the standard curry houses in the UK are owned by Bangladeshis and nearly all of those serve standard formula curries (from mild to very hot). Bangladesh, formerly East Pakistan, is located at the mouth of the River Ganges. Before Partition, the area either side of the Ganges was Bengal. Today Bengal is the Indian state that shares its border with Bangladesh. Bangladesh is Muslim, so pork is forbidden. Unlike Hindu India, beef is eaten. The area enjoys prolific fresh and seawater fish – pomfret, boal, ruhi, hilsa and ayre, and tiger prawns – and specialises in vegetable dishes such as Shartkora and Niramish, some quite bitter, such as Shuktoni; Shatkora, a kind of grapefruit is an ingredient in meat/poultry dishes. Until recently, true Bangladeshi cuisine was nigh on impossible to find in the UK. Now more of our Bangladeshi restaurants are serving the delights of their own country. Of these good examples are found at Aziz, Oxford, Café Naz E1, Hason Raja, London wc1, Kuti's Southampton, Kafé La SE23, Shampan, E1, and Spicery , Newcastle

Bengali Bengal is one of India's major culinary areas with Bengali cuisine India's second oldest-established. Mustard oil and seeds and the aromatic nigella seeds have been around in Bengali cuisine for thousands of years, as has the spice mixture unique to Bengal, Panch Phoran. Over time two states, East and West Bengal developed, their main difference being religion. In 1947 East Bengal was partitioned to Muslim Pakistan. In 1972 it became Bangladesh *(see above)*. West Bengalis are mainly Hindu, and this proscribes no beef. Many dishes are common to both Bengals, for example, their adoration of sour tastes as seen in Dal Doyi Jhol – a runny lentil and yoghurt Soup, other dishes they have in common include Chachchori Morog – stir-fried mild chicken curry, Rezala Morgh – rich-tasting hot chicken, creamier curry than Korma in which green chillies are mandatory., Kalia – a thin red sauce. Aubergine (eggplant) were indigenous with Begun Shorshe, fried aubergines in yogurt and mustard sauce. while Baigan Burtha is the smoky puréed version. Niramish is another remarkable Vegan Curry. Potoler Dolma is a small wax gourd stuffed with a spicy filling. The 16th century Portuguese taught the Bengalis to make cheese (Paneer). Bengalis have a sweet tooth and they adore their sweet chutneys. J A Sharwood, a Victorian Raj merchant exported sweet Bengali mango chutney into Britain in the 1800s, and it is now a major feature at the curryhouse. It is not eaten in this form in India, but its basis was the Bengali Choti Mature sweet Mango Pickle. Calcutta is India's city of culture and in the 19th century it became famous for those wonderful, sticky sweets, such Gulab Jamun, Jalebi, Ras Malai and Ros Gulla *(see glossary)*. The UK's one and only truly authentic Bengali restaurant is Sarkhel's, London, SW18.

Chetinad A style of cooking from the southern Indian state of Tamil Nadu. A meat-eating community called Chetiyars, have been resident in the Madras area since the earliest times. Under the British, they became merchants and money lenders, owning large amounts of Burmese farmland. Fish Kozambhu – sour sauce tamarind & chillies. Chetinad dishes appear on menus all over the place but Coconut Lagoon restaurants *(see Kenilworth, Warks)* are owned by Chetiyars so are one of the few places to do them correctly.

Dum Pukht A cooking term meaning 'containing the steam'. The technique originated in ancient Persia deriving from the Persian word 'dampukht' or baked. A pot was filled with meat and spices. A tightly-fitting lid was sealed with chupatti dough. A hole was dug in the desert sands. and hot coals were placed in its bottom. Next the sealed pot was surrounded with hot coals, buried in the sand and left undisturbed to cook for a few hours. The magical moment comes when the lid is opened in front of the diners, releasing all those captured fragrances. This was the perfect vehicle for cooking Biriani. The contemporary exponent is Delhi master chef Imtiaz Qureshi. His modern versions use pastry as the lid, and of course the modern oven. Qureshi has not ventured to London, but we have the next best chef, Mohammed Rais. He also hails from Lucknow and he too claims ancestry back to the Nawab court and Qureshi is his uncle. Rais worked at the Red Fort (W1) from 1997, but moved to Darbar, SW6. *See also Kasturi,* EC3 *and Naresh Matta (Rias' former assistant at the Red Fort) now at Eriki.* NW3.

Goan The tiny state of Goa had always depended on spices, fish and coconut.In 1492 it was taken the Portuguese who occupied it until 1962. Christianity prevails and there are no objections to eating pork or beef. Modern Goan curries are based on all these ingredients, often combined with palm todi (feni) vinegar to create a gently unique sour taste. Goans are mostly non-vegetarian. Meat is usually confined to Sundays. Fish is mandatory at least once a day in the Goan diet. Bread-making was introduced by the Portuguese and though rice is important to Goa, bread takes precedence and is eaten with most meals. Portuguese dishes, some unspiced, are to be found on the Goan menu. Many have evolved to be unique to Goa, with the addition of spices and coconut, yet have Portuguese names such as Cafreal, Xacutti and their most famous dish, Vindaloo. But it is not the dish from the standard curry house; the real thing is derived from the Portuguese dish Vino d'Alhos, traditionally pork marinated (the longer the better) in wine vinegar and garlic, then simmered until tender. To this the Goans added hot red chillies, creating a rich red curry gravy. But nothing is simple in Goa. Many dishes can appear with two different names in Portuguese or Goan (Konkani). And even same-named dishes can be cooked in different ways by the three different Goan communities. The majority of the population is Christian (Catholic) who eat everything including pork and beef and use plentiful chillies, todi-vinegar and sugar for piquancy, sweet and sour tastes. There is also a significant Goan Hindu population. Hindu Goans use less heat, tamarind or kokum for souring and jaggery for sweetening. The use asafoetida, chick peas, curry leaves, fenugreek, mustard and urid dhal. They don't eat beef, of course, and generally abstain from pork. Goa was occupied by Moslems for centuries before the Portuguese and there is still a significant Goan Moslem population. They do not eat pork or beef, mutton (goat) being their preferred meat, and the rather more complex dishes from Kashmir and the Moghals (Roghan Josh Gosht, kormas and birianis) are to be found in the Goan Muslim home. There is only one true Goan restaurant in the UK, Ma Goa in London sw15, although Goan dishes do appear at the better Indian restaurants such as Bombay Brasserie, sw7.

Gujarati Gujarat is a major culinary region, with a unique and abundant indigenous cuisine. It is home to more vegetarians (about 70%) than anywhere else in India, and their food is also India's least spicy. The Parsees, who lived in Gujarat for 500 years (*see below*), influenced the food, with subtleties of sour and sweet. Prime ingredients in savoury dishes are yoghurt and gram flour, with a little sugar being added, the penchant for sweet tastes. Khadi is just one dish showing Gujarati adoration of these ingredients. This soup-like dish, often served with with gram flour dumplings, is called Kari or Khadi, whose yellow gravy is made with turmeric, lentils, spices, sugar and yoghurt. The first British diplomat docked at the port of Surat in 1608, and Kadhi may have been the very dish which gave curry its name. Surat was used as a British trading post, until Bombay was built in 1674. Despite her long Arabian Sea coastline, fish does not prevail. No other Indian state makes a greater variety of pickles than Gujarat. The famous Pakora / Bhaji also originated in Gujarat, as did the lesser known Dahi Vada, a gram flour dumpling in a tangy yoghurt sauce. Two further recipes worth highlighting are Ravaiya, stuffed baby aubergine (eggplant) and Sevian Tamatar, wheat vermicelli noodles, a rare Indian ingredient. Bombay Mix, the general name for crunchy spicy snack nibbles are made from a deep-fried spicy gram flour dough and originated in Gujarat, where they are known are known as Murukus. Sev is the very fine vermicelli-sized version. Gujarati vegetarian restaurants are prevalent in Leicester and Wembley, Middlesex, and they pop up elsewhere, too. Not all Gujaratis are Hindus or vegetarians. As a result of ancient Moslem occupations, there remains a small group of Gujarati meat-eating Moslems, called the Bohris Community. One of their dishes is the outstanding Gosht Tikkea Malai ke Bohris, Baked marinated Beef. In this dish cubes of best beef are marinated in cream, garlic and ginger. They are coated with breadcrumbs and baked.

Hyderabadi (Andhra Pradesh) Andhra Pradesh (AP) formerly called Hyderabad, after its major city is the fifth largest state in India, both in area and population. In the 1930s, Hyderabad's royal ruler, the Nizzam was alleged to be the richest man in the world. The state is strategically situated in the south central India and forms a major link between north and south of India. It has a widely diversified agricultural base with a variety of cash crops. It is the granary of the south and produces a surplus of food grain. Hyderabad has been south India's strongest Moslem enclave since the 14th century. Today it is 40% Moslem. Hyderabad also has a Parsee population. Consequently, it is a meat-eating cuisine, but its cuisine is also one of India's hottest, as indicated by Mirchi Ka Salan, Chilli Curry. Mirchi means chilli, 'ka' means 'of' and Salan is a type of Urdu spicing speciality of Hyderabad and we encounter it twice more in Macchi ka Salan (Fish) and Baigan ka Salan (aubergine / eggplant. Biriani is a Hyderabadi speciality and we represent it with Tahiri a Vegetable Biriani speciality. Koftas and Kebabs are popular and the Parsee Khara Soti Boti Kebab, Omelette-enrobed Meat chunks Two dishes represent yoghurt's popularity, Chowgra a Yoghurt-based Vegetable curry and Churri a Herbal Yoghurt dip. Thoran lightly spiced Coconut and shredded Cabbage, is called Thoora in Andhra Pradesh.

Kashmiri Kashmir is India's most northerly state, located in the Himalayas thousands of feet above sea level. At partition in 1947 Kashmir was split between India and Pakistan, leading to conflict. On both sides of the border most Kashmiris are meat-eaters (even Hindu Kashmiris) whose rich sauces and ghee help to combat the cold. Lotus, apples, saffron and rice but not wheat are specifically Kashmiri. The Moghuls built a summer retreat in the 16th century and brought with them aromatic spices, such as cardamom, cinnamon, clove, and aniseed. Nothing shows this off better than Kashmir's most celebrated dish, Korma. The Kashmiri Moslem wedding feast, the Wazwan at which the number of guests expected to attend always exceeds 500, is unique. Traditionally, the feast must contain exactly 36 different dishes, including chutneys and accompaniments. At least

seven mutton dishes must be served. A 15kg male sheep considered ideal. All parts are used. Leg for dhaphol, ribs for tabak maz, neck for roghan josh, entrails for methi maz, quorma soured with apricots, jakhni soured with curds. Gushtaba giant meatball, with curd gravy, is traditionally the final dish, though a semolina might follow. *See Chor Bizare, London,* W1.

Maharashtran and Bombay food Maharashtra is located in central India's Deccan plains. Maharashtran, or Marathi food has developed over the centuries as a minor cuisine. It is mild and delicately spiced and uses tamarind and fresh coconut. The climate is perfect for viticulture and supports two grape crops a year. One brand of method-champagne is widely exported under the name Omar Khyam. Bombay (Mumbai) is the vibrant, buoyant, commercial centre of India, with some of the highest property prices in the world, Bollywood, expensive restaurants, and home-delivery Pizza, contrasting with the apalling poverty of shanti-towns, and street-begging. Bombay was the creation of the British and as such it has never developed a large cuisine. A favourite UK curryhouse dish, Bombay Potato (*see A-Z glossary*) is not found in Bombay, but it is typical of Bombay tastes. Gujarat's Murukus was re-invented as 'Bombay Mix' in Southall in the 1970s. Sev *(qv)* is one ingredient of Bhel Puri, Bombay's favourite street food. It is served cold and is delicious. Restaurants such as London's Masala Zones, Bhel Puri Houses in Drummond Street, Wembley, SW16 and other places around London specialise in it. The original fishing tribes, the Kholis, however, had a couple of delicacies up their sleeve; Bombay Duck and Bangda (fish head) curry. The largest Parsee community *(see below)* are Bombay residents.

Moghul Almost surrounded by Haryana is Delhi, the small state containing India's capital city. Delhi has no cuisine in its own right; it was during the 16th century that Indian food was taken to its supreme culinary heights in the Moghul capital city of Delhi, as well as Agrah, Lahore and Kashmir (see below). East of Delhi is the largely Muslim state of Uttar Pradesh, with Moghul Agra and its Taj Mahal in the west and the river Ganges flowing through its length. No one was richer than the Moghuls, and it was during their time, four centuries ago, that Indian food was perfected. Authentically, this style of food should be subtly spiced. The French may believe they invented 'haute cuisine', but they were pipped to the post by Moghul chefs, who did to Indian food what the French chef Varenne did to French cooking a century later; they perfected sauces using garlic, butter and cream with the addition of something uniquely Indian; a marriages of spices. They created supremely aromatics curries with sensual sauces like Classic Korma, Pasanda, Rhogan Josh Gosht and Raan, roast lamb. The standard curry-house has based some of its formula on mild, rich, creamy dishes such as these, albeit lacking the subtlety of the real thing. Rather more authentic interpretations can be found in an increasing number of 'haute cuisine' restaurants around the country, spelt variously Moghul, mogul, moglai, muglai mugal, mugul, etc.

Nawabi Of culinary importance, is Lucknow, now an Indian army city, and one which is of immense historical importance especially during the time of the wealthy Nawabs, who came to royal prominence as the Moghuls declined. One inheritance is Nawabi cuisine. Lucknow, being Moslem, enjoys meat, but its cooking is unique. Flavours are spicy aromatic and subtle and the food is luxurious. One process is called Dum or Dum Pukht. It means slow-cooking by steaming the curry or rice dish, in a handi or round pot, whose lid is sealed into place with a ring of chapatti dough. The resulting dish is opened in front of the diners, releasing all those captured fragrances.

Nepalese Beautiful Himalayan mountains, the world's only Hindu kingdom, home of Gurkas, sherpas, yak and yeti, Kumari the living virgin goddess-princess, Everest, and unique food. Some similarities to north Indian, with curry (tarkari), rice (bhat), and wheat breads (roti haru). Kukhura (chicken), Khasi (lamb), Dumba (mutton), Bhutwa (pork), Hach Ko (duck), Jhinge (prawn) and Maccha (fish) are cooked in the clay oven (chula) or curried. Specialities include Aloo Achar, potatoes in pickle sauce, Momo/Momocha, keema-filled dumplings, and Tama Bodi, bamboo shoots and black-eye beans, a dish showing Tibetan/Chinese roots. More examples will be found in the entries for Great Nepalese, NW1, Gurkha Kitchen, Oxted, Surrey and Gurkha Square, Fleet, Hants.

Pakistani Until independence in 1947, Pakistan formed the north-western group of Indian states. Located between Afghanistan and India, it contains the famous Khyber Pass. The people are predominantly meat-eaters, favouring lamb and chicken (being Muslim, they avoid pork). Charcoal cooking is the norm, and this area is the original home of the tandoor. Breads such as Chupatti, Nan and Paratha are the staple. Balti cooking originated in the northernmost part of Pakistan (*see earlier*). In general, Pakistani food is robustly spiced and savoury. The area called the Punjab was split by the formation of Pakistan, and it is the Punjabi tastes that formed the basis of the British curry house menu (*see Punjab, London* WC2). Bradford, Glasgow and Southall have sizeable Pakistani populations.

Parsee/Persian This is not a regional cuisine; it is the cuisine of a religious sect, and their unique cuisine has evolved over the last 800 years from when the Parsees migrated from Persia. There are now only around 100,000 Parsees. Most live in Bombay, but there are other groups in Hyderabad and Gujarat. It is quite common to see Persian dishes listed on the standard curry house menu. Dishes such as Biriani and Pullao did indeed originate in Persia (Iran) while Dhansak and Patia. are Parsee dishes. However they are a pastiche of the real thing. Parsees have no religious proscriptions on eating, so they eat pork, beef as well as lamb and shellfish and they love egg dishes. Meat mixed with vegetables and fruit is typical of Persian and Parsee food, though the latter has now incorporated the Indian spice palette and sweet and sour combinations, typified in their Patia. The most celebrated and popular of all Parsee dishes is Dhansak, where in the real thing meat on-the-bone is incorporated with four types of lentil (polished moong, masoor, chana and toovar). Slow cooking in a heavy lidded pot amalgamates the flavours. During the cooking, a kind of ratatouille of aubergine, tomato, spinach and fresh chillies is added. Sweet and sour comes from jaggery (palm sugar) and a slight overtone of sour from fresh tamarind juice. Jardaloo Boti is lamb cooked with dried apricots and the coriander coated fish dish, Patrani Maachli is a Parsee speciality. Their roasted vegetable dish, Oonbhariu is one of the best vegetable dishes in India. True Persian food is hard to find in the UK, although it is served at the Old Delhi, London W1. There is one Parsee restaurant in the UK (Parsee N19) but south-west London's Bombay Brasserie and Chutney Mary both have Parsee chefs who cook authentic Parsee dishes.

Pashtoon It refers to tribal people and their language from the rugged mountain passes of Afghanistan (q.v.) and Pakistan (q.v.) in the former North-West Frontier Province, whose name for themselves is Pathan, Pashtun, Phuktana or Pukhtun. Afghan food is pretty basic, especially at tribal level, involving hunting wild life then grilling it or slow-cooking it in pots. Grills, Kebabs, Koftas and Birianis are popular, spiced with the unique Afghan spice mix, Char Masala (four aromatic spices) and cooked mostly in their own juices. Visit Tagore, Welling Kent and Kasturi EC1.

Punjabi For the purposes of this Guide we link together India's north-central states Haryana, Himachal Pradesh ,Uttaranchal and Punjab. The former have little culinary interest, though the very best Basmati rice comes from Himachal Pradesh, which as its name suggests is in the foothills of the Himalayas: Dehradun Basmati is to rice what Krug or Dom Perignon is to champagne. The Punjab, like Kashmir was another state split into two after partition, with western Punjab and the Moghul city of Lahore in Pakistan. Food knows no boundaries, and Punjabi food is a major culinary style which is identical in both the Punjabs and in Haryana (meaning 'green land') Punjabi cuisine began to evolve from early in the first millennium AD. It is perhaps the best known Indian food because the original curry restaurants in the developed world based their menus on Punjabi cuisine. Dairy farming is a major Punjabi industry and its prolific wheat and grain crops, earn it the title 'the granary of India', and Parathas and Puris are staples. Oilseeds, spices, peas and beans and much else. grows prolifically in the area. The food is very savoury and fenugreek leaf (methi) and mustard leaf (rai) are virtually staples. Robust curries like Punjabi Keema, Methi Gosht, Aloo Ghobi Methi and Sag Paneer ,Mattar Valor – pea and bean curry are typical. Best Punjabi exponents are found in Southall, but look out for other Punjabi references throughout the Guide.

South Indian South India consists of three sub-tropical and very fertile states, Karnataka, Kerela and Tamil Nadu and also includes the Konkan Coast or Karavali (800 miles of rugged and beautiful Indian coastline stretching from Mumbai to Mangalore). The area was first occupied in about 1000BC by the Dravidians, who are still the largest racial group. South India's cuisine has remained virtually unmodified since that time, making it India's longest-established cuisine. When the Dravidians first arrived and cultivated the area, they encountered South India's main indigenous ingredients: ginger, coconut, curry leaves, peppercorns, turmeric and curry leaf. The food is rice-based, with no wheat. Yoghurt and tamarind provide two quite differing sour tastes. Many dishes use all these ingredients, and many dishes are common to all three south Indian states, albeit under different names, and with subtle differences in flavourings. Common to all states is Dosa, huge, thin, crisp rice-lentil-flour pancakes, with a curry filling (Masala) and Idlis – steamed rice or lentil-flour dumplings accompanied by Sambar, a lentil-based curry, Rasam, a hot and spicy consommé and coconut chutney. Other rice-based items include Upuma and Uthappam (*see* poo). Because of the intense heat and frequent high humidity, thin curries are preferred because they are more easily digested than the thick-sauced versions of the north. Day to day, much of the area's population is fish-eating or vegetarian, but most will eat meat or poultry on special occasions. Many exotic vegetables include, drumstick, mooli, snake gourd, doodi, bottle gourd, bittergourd (karela). tindoora, and long beans. Vegetable curries using them include Avial, Thoran and many others. Some specialist groups, such as Coorgs, Malabaris, Nairs, Mophlas, Syrian Christians and Jews (see below) eat meat and chicken dishes on a regular basis. Specialist restaurants have long been found been in

and around London (especially Tooting SW17). The specialist food of Udipi (a small town north of Mangalore) is to be found at Sagar, W6. The good news is that they are becoming established in Britain's other cities and should be visited. The first restaurant to bring south Indian meat, chicken and sea food dishes to the UK was Chutney Mary. But other restaurants have developed the theme as specialisations. The best are Kerela, N1, Rasa Travanvore, N19 and Coconut Lagoon restaurants *(see Kenilworth, Warks)*. One conservation-minded, zero-cost serving method dating from 1000BC and still in daily use is the banana leaf. This fleshy, pliable, ribbed, inedible leaf serves as your plate and on which is placed the traditional meal (the Sadya), all courses together, but with each item in an invariable position on the leaf. No cutlery is needed and once you have eaten, the plate leaf is wrapped up and disposed of to bio-degrade. When will the Sadya appear in a UK restaurant as a trendy (and no doubt costly) dining experience, one wonders?

Tandoori The ancient Egyptians created the side-entry clay-oven in which to bake their bread. Later they were used in ancient Persia where they are still called the' tonir', and their bread 'nane lavash'. A small variant seems to have been invented in India at the same time. Instead of having a side-entry, this egg-shaped vessel's entry hole was at the top, which was narrower than its centre point. It was the ancestor of today's tandoori oven. Its base had a small air-hole, below which was placed an even earlier invention, charcoal. Easily transported, this oven was probably invented to enable travelling traders to cook at their camp-sites. Corroborative evidence exists in the form of oven remains found all along ancient trade routes. By 300BC Sanskrit writings on cooking techniques describes meat spread with a honey-coloured spicy paste and cooked in the clay-oven, the 'kavan kunndu' (fire-container). Could kunndu be the derivation of the Hindi word 'tandoor'? The paste 'kunndu pachitam' (fire-paste) 'spread on meat' sounds remarkably like a marinade, the contents of which are unclear, but to achieve the colour as described, it could well contain yoghurt to assist in tenderising the flesh, plus spices, garlic, salt and indeed honey itself. For the first time we know that spiced meat, and probably poultry too was cooked in the tandoor.. The ancient Iranians also have a claim to the derivation of the word tandoor. It could have derived from their words 'tata', meaning 'hot', and 'andar', meaning 'inside'. Either way the tandoor remained on the Afghan/Pakistan border until modern times. The world's first tandoori restaurant, the Moti Mahal was established there in 1922. Partition forced its Hindu owner to move to Delhi in 1947. It remained as India's only tandoori restaurant until recent times. Even now, outside the five-star hotels, tandoori food is rarely found in India. Conversely tandoori food is ubiquitous in the UK and is some of the most popular dishes. Recently a Moti Mahal branch opened in London WC2

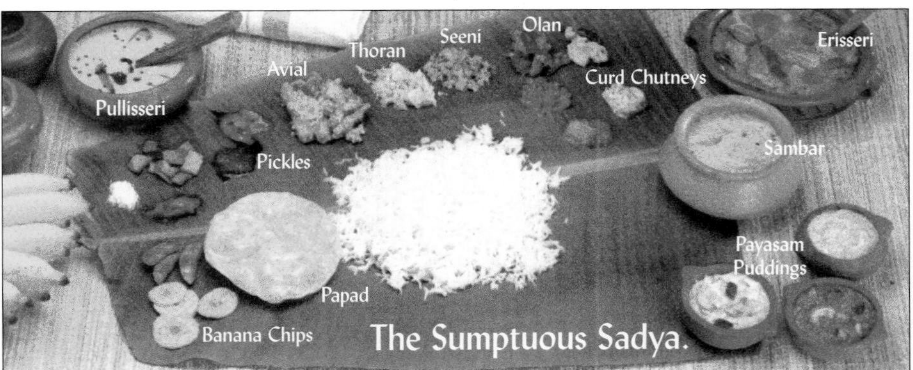

The Sumptuous Sadya.

Sri Lanakan Sri Lanka is the small, pearl-shaped island, formerly Ceylon, at the southern tip of India. Its cuisine is distinctive and generally chilli hot. They eat similar fare to that eaten in south India, i.e. vegetarian dishes, but they also enjoy very pungent meat, squid, chicken and duck curries. Look out for black curries and white ones, and deviled doshes. Hoppers are pancakes made of fermented rice, mixed with highly alcoholic palm toddy) and a little sugar, and are available in both sweet and savoury versions, String hoppers are rice-flour noodle nests. A festive dish introduced by a Dutch burger centuries ago is called Lampries (Longkirist). here a full meal of meat curry, kofta, rice and sambols is wrapped inside a banana leaf parcel and cooked. Samols made of coconut and onion accompany all meals. Good Sri Lankan restaurants include Palm Paradise, Southall, Middlesex, Prince of Ceylon, London n4, a .Elephant Walk NW6, and Jaffna House sw17

The Cuisine of South East Asia

Indo China

South East Asia, called 'farther India' is the peninsula between India and China containing Burma, Thailand, Malaysia, Singapore, and Indonesia. Britain is blessed with an ever-increasing number of restaurants serving these spicy cuisines. Here we examine their cuisines:

Burmese Burma, now renamed Myanmar, shares its boundaries with Bangladesh, India, China, Laos and Thailand. Its food is a combination of these styles. Rice is the staple and noodles are popular too. The curries are very hot and there are no religious objections to eating pork, beef or other meats. Duck and seafood are commonly eaten. The only UK Burmese restaurant is the Mandalay, London W2.

Malaysian Malysia's only border is a narrow strip at her north where the peninsula joins that of Thailand, and it shares many tastes in food. Such similarities include the love of lemon grass, shrimp paste (belacan pronounced blachan) sweet lime (kaffir) and, above all chillies (the taste for really hot food diminishes in popularity as one goes southwards, away from Thailand). Differences include the use of tamarind (asam) to achieve a tart taste, turmeric for yellow colour and peanut to thicken. Instead of galangal, Malaysians use aromatic pink ginger buds with their flowers and or zedoary (cekur), both hard to obtain (ginger or galangal can substitute). Noodles are more ubiquitous in Malayasia than in Thailand, and curry with noodles is as common there as curry with rice. Curries prevail, showing their Indian, Chinese and Thai influences. Thinner fragrant gravies, often based on coconut milk, also contain chillies, ginger, and lemon grass. Satay, meat coated in a lightly spiced peanut sauce, is well known, and a curry version is Inche Kabin, where curry paste is added to the sauce, which is coated onto a whole chicken, then grilled. Wet curries are flavoured with lemon grass and shrimp paste, along with the robust spices of India. Soto Ayam and Redang are two of Malaysia's better known curries. Malaysia's population is composed of Chinese, Indians, and Malayans, and this results in a distinctive cuisine also known as Nonya. Best UK restaurants: Georgetown Malaysian, Nottingham, Stratford, Leeds and Kenilworth

Thai Thailand shares her borders with Burma, Laos, Kampuchea and Malaysia, yet her cuisine is little influenced by them. It is the combination of tastes which makes Thai cuisine unique. Key items are fragrance from lime leaves (markrut), lemon grass stalks (takrai) and holy basil leaves; heat from explosive tiny chillies and to a lesser extent from galangal, a peppery type of ginger. Savoury tastes come from shrimp paste (kapi), sweet from palm sugar and seasoning from thin clear fish sauce (nam-pla) which never dominates, but enhances the other ingredients. Thailand grows dozens of vegetables which have no translation in the west. Appearance matters greatly in Thai cooking, and no where else on earth makes prettier carved garnishes than the Thai. Roses from radishes, carnations from carrots and coronets from cucumbers are examples. Chicken, pork, duck, beef, fish, shellfish are regularly in the diet. Wheat, dairy products, potato, tomato and potato are largely absent from the diet. Glutinous rice, tamarind, soy sauce, noodles and chops sticks are common to the far north. The south prefers fragrant non-sticky rice, coconut milk which gives Thai curries a creamy sauce. Indian spiced mutton is eaten in the Moslem far south, as one approaches Malaysia. The best UK Thai restaurants UK is Orchid Lounge at Jaipur, Milton Keynes, Bucks with Blue Elephant, London, SW6 and Rumwong Guildford close behind.

Singaporean Singapore is a small island country in Southeast Asia. It lies near the southern tip of the Malay Peninsula about where the South China Sea and the Indian Ocean meet. The sea is an arm of the Pacific Ocean. Singapore consists of a large island and more than 50 smaller islands. founded in 1819 by Sir Stamford Raffles, and was used by the British as their major trading post in the area, the legacy of which is today's major business centre. Singapore's population is the most cosmopolitan of the area, with Indian, Chinese, Malay, Indonesian and European influences. The Chinese or Hokkien predominate, and little wonder, so do noodles. Because Singapore, like Hong Kong were created from nothing, and then populated by such a mixture of races, there has been insufficient time for few, if any true Singaporean dishes to evolve. Fish Head Curry and Hokkien stir-fry Noodles are two.

Indonesian Adjacent to Malaysia is Indonesia, the former Dutch East Indies. It consists of in excess of 13,600 islands, some of which are uninhabited. The world's fourth largest population lives on the remaining islands, which include Sumatra, Borneo, Java, New Guinea, Bali. Indonesia likes its spicy dishes and it contains the celebrated Molucans, the spice islands, the original home of clove, mace and nutmeg, its cuisine never uses these spices. Spices, ironically earn relatively little income for Indonesia. The Chinese introduced Nasi Goreng (fried rice with vegetables), Bhami Goreng (noodles). The Indians brought their curries and spices, the Portuguese brought chilli, peanuts and tomatoes while the Dutch brought sweets and cakes, and of course Rijstaffel (a selection of up to 40 dishes of meat, vegetables and rice served in individual bowls).

LUNCH 12 NOON – 2.30PM
DINNER 6PM – 11PM

OPEN MONDAY TO FRIDAY
AND SATURDAY DINNER ONLY

From India's beautiful south,
The BB's sister restaurant,
The Quilon features sublime
cuisine from Kerala.

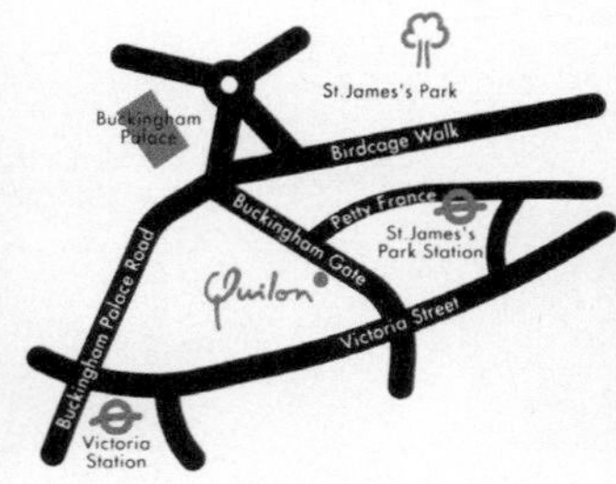

41 Buckingham Gate London SW1E 6AF
Tel 020 7821 1899 Fax 020 7828 5802
www.thequilonrestaurant.com

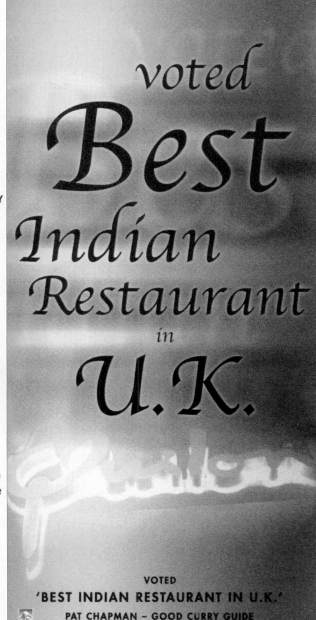

voted Best Indian Restaurant in U.K.

VOTED
'BEST INDIAN RESTAURANT IN U.K.'
PAT CHAPMAN – GOOD CURRY GUIDE

CURRY CLUB

The A to Z of the Curry Menu

To the first-timer, the Indian restaurant menu is a long and complex document. This glossary explains many of the standard, and some of the specialised, dishes and items that you are likely to encounter. See also **The Cuisine of the Subcontinent** (*page* 65). Spellings of vowel sounds will vary from restaurant to restaurant, reflecting the 15 languages and hundreds of dialects of the subcontinent. (See *Masala, Moglai, Papadam and Rhogan Josh Gosht for some examples.*) Our spelling here is as near as possible to the standard accepted way of spelling, when translating phonetically from the main languages to English.

AAM or AM Mango.

ACHAR or ACHAAR Pickle, such as lime, mango, aubergine, etc. *Achar Gohst* is meat curry, curried in a pickle base, *Achar Murgh* is the chicken version.

AFGHANI CURRY Nuts and fruit are added for the standard curry house interpretation.

ALOO Potato.

BAIGAN or BEGUN *see* Brinjal.

BALTI Balti originated centuries ago in north Pakistan's Mirpur, Kashmir and Skardu (Baltistan). It found its way to east Birmingham in the 1970s, where any combination of ingredients was curried in a two-handled pot known as the *karahi* (q.v.) elsewhere, but the Balti there. Served to the table still cooking, the art is to eat the food – which should be spicy, herby and aromatic – Indian-style, with the bread as the scoop in the right hand. In the 1990s, Balti spread rapidly all over the UK and beyond. The Balti found at the standard Bangladeshi curry house, however, owes its flavours more to Patak's acidic Balti paste than to Mirpur, and unless it is cooked in its pan and served cutlery-free, it will (correctly) never convince the Brummy purist that it is anything other than hype.

BARFI or BURFI Indian fudge-like sweet made from reduced condensed milk (*koya* or *khoa*), in various flavours.

BASMATI The best long-grained rice.

BATERA Football-sized puri (q.v.) becoming increasingly popular.

BATTAR Quail.

BENGAL CURRY A chicken or meat curry with chilli, sugar, potato cubes and halves of tomato.

BHAJI or BHAJEE Dryish, pan-fried mild vegetable curry.

BHAJIA Deep-fried fritter, usually with sliced onion, mixed with spiced gram flour batter, then deep-fried. Bhajia is the correct term, meaning fried. Bhaji or Bhajee is the anglicisation. For the real thing, visit Maru's Bhajia House, Wembley, Middlesex. *See also* Pakora.

BHEL PURI This is the delicious street food snack from Bombay. It is a cold combination of those crunchy squiggles you find in Bombay Mix (q.v.), the smallest of which is called *Sev*. To this is added small-diced cooked potato, puffed rice (*mamra*), coriander leaf, onion and chilli. It is laced with brown sweet and sour tamarind (*imli*) sauce, green coriander chutney (*dhania*) and red chilli/garlic sauce, and topped with crispy puri biscuit

chippings. The result is an exquisite combination of crisp, chewy and soft textures with sweet, hot, savoury and sour tastes. Variations include differing amounts of ingredients, under various similar names, such as *Sev Batata Puri, Dahi* (yoghurt) *Batata Puri, Chat Aloo Papri* and *Batata Pava. Bhel* can be accompanied by Gol Goppas (q.v.). This delicious food is generally beyond the abilities of the average curry house, so is rarely found. Try it when you can (*see* London NW1's Drummond Street NW1, Shahee Bhel SW16 and Masala Zone W1).

BHOONA or BHUNA Cooking process involving slowly frying out all the water content to produce a dry, usually mild curry.

continued on page 85

Passing the test of time

When did your love of Indian cooking begin? Chances are, if you're over 40, it's probably only over the last 15-20 years you've noticed that certain Indian restaurants have become more sophisticated, more adventurous, more stylish and, perhaps, more interested in you as a customer. There is a reason for this; The Bombay Brasserie has influenced many of the Indian restaurants that have opened over the last 25 years.

In the eighties the Indian restaurant business recognised that the British love of Indian cuisine was not receiving the respect it deserved. The wake-up call came from India herself, from one of its most successful companies, the Taj Group.

The Bombay Brasserie opened in late 1982 and was an immediate sensation. As Fay Maschler, doyen of restaurant critics noted: *'The Bombay Brasserie, known by its aficionados as the BB, changed the perception that Indian cooking was little more than meat and veg combination with an all-purpose sauce. Indian cuisine, which had developed over hundreds of years, influenced by so many external influences (not least the British Raj) was now of a new age.'*

Expansion followed quickly. The BB doubled the size of its celebrated conservatory a few

The celebrated Bombay Brasserie Cobra Coffee.
Ingredients are strongly brewed black coffee, sugar, orange liqueur, orange peel and cream.
Top left:, the sugar, is melted to a thick syrup.
Middle: As sugar-work, it is enrobed snake-like around a glass. Dangerous stuff if it touches your hand.
Next: the coffee is heated.
Top right: In goes the liqueur.
Next: The orange peel now resembles a cobra, and it decorates the glass.
Finally, thick cream is dolloped on top.

years ago. Today, **The Bombay Brasserie** is a world class, international brand. Its premium chilled dishes

are sold exclusively by Sainsbury's, and its home-made Chutneys by Harrods. Yet the restaurant has always resisted the temptation of creating a chain of Bombay Brasserie restaurants, set in the belief that there can only ever be one restaurant by that name. Even when it decided to open a sister restaurant four years ago, again the logic was to be innovative and unique. The Quilon forged its own identity and has been acclaimed at a level that is entirely in keeping with Bombay Brasserie standards. Fay Maschler noted that it is *"confidently producing the most interesting and delicious southern Indian food in London."*

In 2001, The Cobra Good Curry Guide went further by voting The Quilon the best Indian restaurant in the whole of the UK, having already given the BB that accolade in 1995. The father of all that excellence among Indian restaurateurs, as a shining example of how imaginative, yet authentic Indian cuisine can be is **The Bombay Brasserie**

And it just gets better. The Cobra Good Curry Guide has just announced that **The Bombay Brasserie** has again been awarded the industry's unique and only **LIFETIME ACHIEVEMENT AWARD**, recognising the completion of its first 25 years, an achievemnt it shares with the Guide itself.

Congratulations BB.
Here's to the next 25 years.

Bindi A pulpy, rather sappy vegetable also known as okra or ladies fingers. Correct cooking of this dish is a good test of a chef's ability.

Biriani Traditionally, rice baked between layers of meat or vegetable filling, enhanced with saffron and aromatic spices, served topped with edible silver leaf (*vark*). The restaurant interpretation is a cooked rice, artificially coloured, with filling stir-fried in. It is usually heavily garnished and served with a vegetable curry sauce (*see* Pullao).

Bombay Duck A smallish fish native to the Bombay docks, known locally as *bommaloe macchi*. This was too hard for the British Raj to pronounce, so it became Bombay Duck. It is dried and appears on the table as a crispy deep-fried starter or accompaniment to a curry.

Bombay Mix An age-old traditional Indian snack nibble, called *muruku*, made from a savoury, gram-flour, spiced batter called *ompadi*, which is forced through a press straight into the deep-frier, to give different shapes and thicknesses of squiggly nibbles. Nuts, pulses, seeds and other ingredients are added. It should always be really crunchy and fresh. Re-invented by GK Noon, owner of Royal Sweets in Southall, under the catchy name Bombay Mix, it will keep you going at the bar.

Bombay Potato A popular invention of the curry house. Potatoes in curry sauce with onions and tomato.

Boti Kebab Marinated cubes of lamb cooked in a tandoor oven (*see* Tandoori).

Brinjal Aubergine, also called *baigan* or *began*. In *Baigan Burtha*, aubergine is smoked, spiced and mashed, in *Baigan Bhaji* it is chopped and curried by pan-frying.

C

CTM Chicken Tikka Masala. Invented by a British curry house chef (identity unknown) *c.* 1980, as a way to exploit his already popular Chicken Tikka by adding a creamy, pink, mild sauce made tasty by skilful blending of curry sauce, tomato purée, tandoori paste, cream, coconut, mango chutney, ground almonds and a surfeit of red food colouring. It is a dish not found in India (because they do not have red food colouring nor Tandoori dishes – see page 75). In any case India already had a dish from the 16th century Moghuls (*See* Murgh Makhani). CTM is now ordered by 65% of all diners. Not only that, it appears in supermarket sandwiches, flavours crisps, is a pizza topping and even spices mayonnaise. If only that chef had copyrighted it, he'd be earning millions in royalties a year. *See* Tikka.

Ceylon Curry At the curry house, this is usually cooked with coconut, lemon and chilli.

Chana A yellow lentil resembling, but not identical to, the split pea, used in Dhal (q.v.) and to make gram flour. *Kabli chana* is the chickpea. Both can be curried or dried and deep-fried as in Bombay Mix (q.v.). *See also* Paneer.

Chasni, Chicken A central Scotland Pakistani restaurant name for CTM (q.v.).

Chat or Chaat Literally means 'snack', though often it can be a salad.

Chilli Fleshy members of the capsicum family, ranging in heat from zero (the bell pepper) to incendiary. All chillies start green and, if left long enough, eventually turn red, the one being no hotter than the other. The chilli normally used in Indian cooking is the narrow 7.5cm (3in) cayenne. The hottest in the world are Mexican habañeros, Caribbean Scotch bonnets and Bangladeshi nagas. People build up a tolerance to chillies, but they should never be inflicted upon the novice, not even in fun.

Chupatti A 15cm (6in) flat disc of unleavened bread, cooked dry on the tava (q.v.). It should always be served hot and pan-fresh. The spelling can vary – Chupati, Chapatti, etc.

Chutney The common ones are onion chutney, mango chutney and tandoori chutney. There are dozens of others that rarely appear on the standard menu. *See* Sambals.

CURRY The only word in this glossary to have no direct translation into any of the subcontinent's 15 or so languages. The word was coined centuries ago by the British in India. Possible contenders for the origin of the word are: *Karahi* or *Karai* (Hindi) – the wok-like frying pan used all over India to prepare *masala* (spice mixtures); *Karhi* or *Khadi* – a soup-like dish made with spices, gram-flour dumplings and buttermilk; *Kari* – a spicy Tamil sauce; *Turkuri* – a seasoned sauce or stew; and *Kari Phulia* – Neem leaves, which are small and rather like bay leaves, used for flavouring. The Dutch, who were in India in the 17th century have their own derivation. They say it was used in Malaya for their Malay curries, and that it derived from the word *Lekker* meaning delicious, or in colloquial Dutch, *Lekkerie*.
CURRY HOUSE *See* Formula Curries.

DABBA or DHAABA The subcontinent's version of the transport café, it's a ubiquitous roadside eatery usually made of tin sheets and thatch or tarpaulin. Millions exist. If packed with truckers (their lorries parked all around) it's good. A limited menu offers dhals, spicy omelettes, mutton and vegetable curries, tea (chai) and soft drinks at truly low prices. Seating usually a charpoy or rope-strung cot in the open air in front of the eatery. Primitive kitchen fully visible. Vertical neon tubes are its night time symbol. Dabba dishes are appearing on some London chi-chi menus, at rather more expensive prices.
DAHI or DOHI Yoghurt, used as a chutney (*see* Raita) and in the cooking of some curries. Most curry houses make their own, and it is delicious as an accompaniment to curry, being less sharp than the shop-bought equivalent. Incidentally, Dahi, not water, is the best antidote if you eat something that's too hot for you.
DAHI VADA South Indian savoury gram-flour doughnut, deep-fried, cooled and dunked into cold, spicy yoghurt (*see* Vada).
DAL or DHAL LENTILS There are over sixty types of lentil in the subcontinent, all packed full of nutrients. The common restaurant types are *massor* (red, which cooks yellow), *moong* (green), *chana* (also used to make gram flour) and *urid* (black).
DEGCHI or DEKHCHII Brass or metal saucepan without handles.
DHANIA Coriander leaf or spice.
DHANSAK Traditional Parsee meat dish cooked in a purée of lentils, aubergine, tomato and spinach. Restaurants use dal and methi, and sometimes chilli and pineapple.
DOPIAZA Traditional meat dish. *Do* means two, *piaza* means onions. Onions appear twice in the cooking, first fried and second raw. They give the dish a sweetish taste.

DOSA South Indian pancake made from rice and *urid* (lentil) flour, which, when made into a batter, soon ferments to give a superb sour taste. The batter is ladeled onto a hot plate and spread thinly to achieve a pancake shape. *Masala Dosa* is a Dosa filled with mashed potato curry spiced with onion, chilli, turmeric and mustard seed.
DUM Cooking by steaming in a sealed pot, invented by the Royal Nawabs (*see* The Cuisine of the Subcontinent), e.g. *Aloo Dum*, steamed potatoes. Also called Dum Pukt or Pukht (pronounced 'pucked').

ELAICHI Cardamom. Can major in curries – for example, *Elaichi Murgh* is chicken curried with a predominance of green cardamom.

FOOGATH Lightly cooked vegetable dish found in the Malabar area of South India. Any vegetable such as gourds or plantain can be used.
FORMULA CURRIES Many of our 'Indian' (q.v.) restaurants operate to a formula which was pioneered in the late 1940s. In those days, a way had to be found to deliver a variety of curries, without an unreasonable delay, from order to table. Since all authentic Indian recipes require hours of cooking in individual pots, there was no guarantee that they would even be ordered. So cubed meat, chicken or potatoes, dal and some vegetables were lightly curried and chilled, and a large pot of thick curry gravy, a kind of master stock, was brewed to medium-heat strength. To this day, portion by portion, on demand, these ingredients are reheated by pan-frying them with further spices and flavourings. At its simplest, a Medium Chicken Curry, that benchmark of middle ground, is still on many menus, though sometimes

disguised as Masala, and requires no more than a reheat of some gravy with some chicken. For instance, take a typical mixed order for two. Chicken Korma (fry a little turmeric, coriander and cumin, add six pieces of chicken, add a ladleful of curry gravy, plenty of creamed coconut, almonds maybe and a little cream – result, a mild dish, creamy-golden in colour), with Vegetable Dhansak (fry some cumin seeds, dry methi leaves (q.v.), chopped onions, a little sugar, tomato, red and green capsicum with the gravy, add dhal and some cooked veg – result, colourful, and still medium-strength). Meat Korma (as for the chicken, using meat), and Prawn Vindaloo (fry spices and chilli powder, add the gravy which at once goes red and piquant, then cooked peeled prawns, fresh tomato and potato, simmer and serve). Maybe also a Sag Paneer (fry cummin, some thawed creamed spinach and pre-made crumbled paneer together, add fresh coriander – done). One cook can knock all these up, simultaneously, in five pans, within minutes. Rice is pre-cooked, breads and tandoori items made to order by a different specialist. And, hey presto, your order for two! The menu can be very long, with a huge variety of dishes, sometimes numbered, sometimes heat-graded, mild, medium and hot, hotter, hottest, and any dish is available in meat, poultry, prawn, king prawn, and most vegetables, too. That's the formula of the standard curry house. Just because this is not authentic does not make it bad. It can be, and variously is, done well. This *Guide* is full of many such restaurants, about which we say 'a standard curry house, doing the formula well'.

G

Garam Masala Literally meaning hot mixture, there are as many recipes for Garam Masala as there are cooks. A combination of whole aromatic spices including pepper, are weighed the lightly roasted then ground.It originated in Kashmir and is added towards the end of cooking in certain north Indian curries. *See also* Masala.

Ghee Clarified butter or vegetable oil used in high-quality north Indian cooking.

Gobi Cauliflower.

Gol Goppas or Pani Puri are mouth-sized puffed-up crispy biscuits, served with *Jeera Pani* (water spiced predominantly with chilli, black salt and cumin water) and *Aloo Chaat* (potato curry) at Bhel Puri (q.v.) houses. To eat the correct way, gently puncture the top of the biscuit, pour in some *Jeera Pani,* and pop into the mouth in one. Chew and then add some *Aloo Chaat.*

Gosht Meat, usually refering to lamb or mutton.

Gulab Jaman An Indian dessert of cake-like texture. Balls of curd cheese paneer, or flour and milk-powder, are deep-fried to golden and served in light syrup.

Gurda Kidney. *Gurda Kebab* is marinated kidney, skewered and cooked in the tandoor.

H

Haleem A Muslim speciality found in Pakistan and Hyderabad (central India) where it is regarded as a delicacy to them but an acquired taste to everyone else. Pounded mutton is cooked with wheat, chillies, ginger, garam masala and onion tarkaI to become a sort of gruel. A bread called Girda is traditionally eaten with

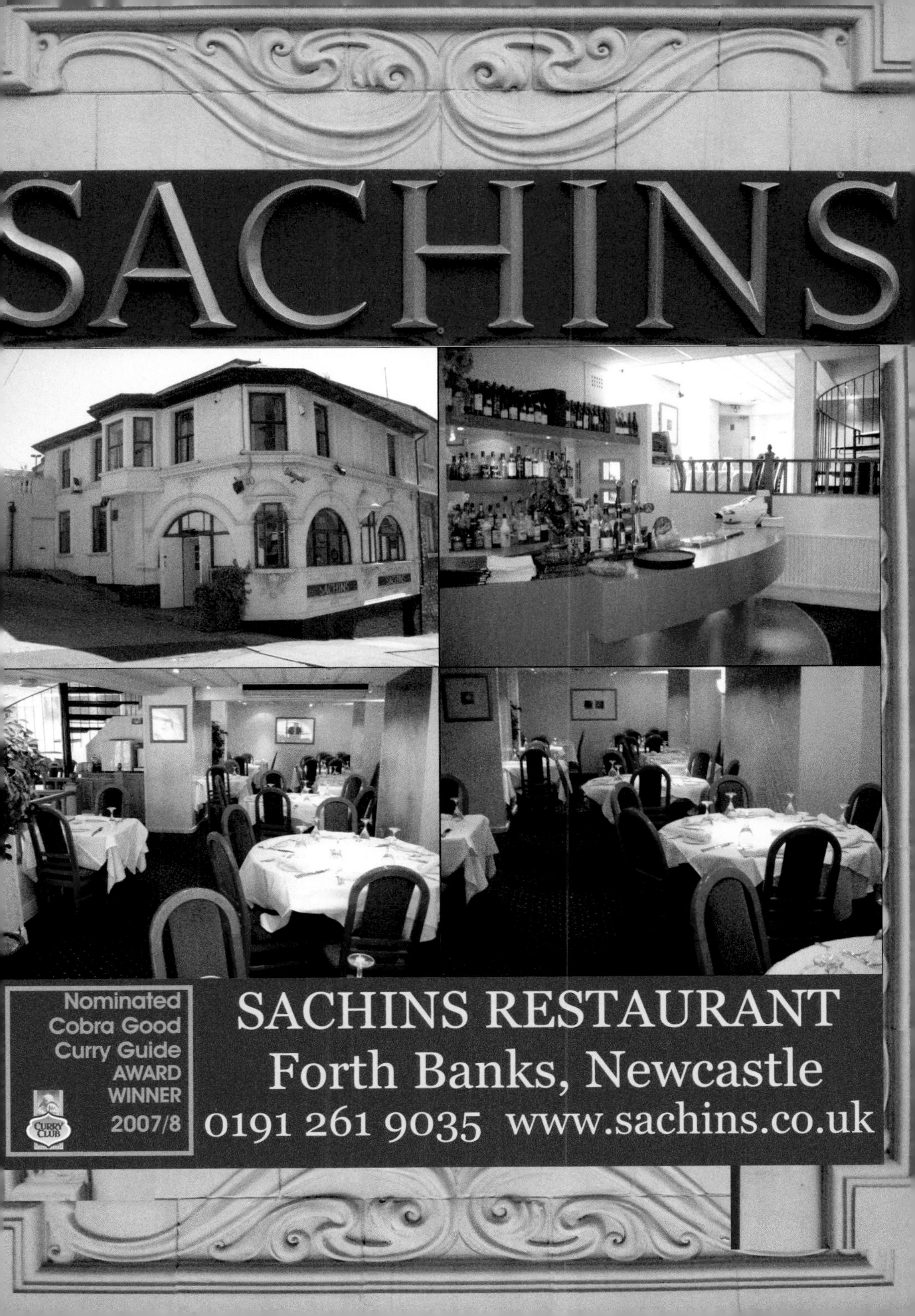
SACHINS
SACHINS
SACHINS
Nominated
Cobra Good
Curry Guide
AWARD
WINNER
2007/8
CURRY CLUB
SACHINS RESTAURANT
Forth Banks, Newcastle
0191 261 9035 www.sachins.co.uk

Haleem. Found at Salloos SW1 and Lahori Kebab E1.

HALVA Sweets made from syrup and vegetables or fruit. Served cold in small squares, it is translucent and comes in bright colours depending on the ingredients used. Orange – carrot; green – pistachio; red – mango, etc. Has a texture thicker than Turkish Delight. Sometimes garnished with edible silver leaf.

HANDI OR HAANDI Is a traditional round-bellied, sometimes earthenware, sometimes metal, narrow-necked cooking pot used in many parts of India, and especially Gujarat. Pottery shards have dated it from 2500BC.

HASINA KEBAB Pieces of chicken breast, lamb or beef marinated in a yoghurt and spice (often tandoori) mixture, then skewered and barbecued/baked, interspersed with onions, capsicum and tomato. Turkish in origin. *See* Shaslik.

I

IDLI Rice- and lentil-flour steamed cake, about the size and shape of a hockey puck, served with a light but fiery curry sauce. South Indian in origin.

IMLI Tamarind. A very sour, date-like fruit used in cooking or chutney which is of purée consistency, sweetened with sugar.

INDIAN In 1947, the subcontinent of India was partitioned. To cut a long story short, in Britain and the West we still generally erroneously refer to our curry restaurants as 'Indian'. In fact, over 85% are Bangladeshi, with only around 8% run by Indians and 8% run by Pakistanis. There is a smattering of Nepalese and Sri Lankan restaurants, and only a single Afghan and a single Burmese restaurant in Britain. *See* Formula Curries.

J

JALEBI An Indian dessert. Flour, milk-powder and yoghurt batter are squeezed through a narrow funnel into a deep-frier to produce golden, curly, crisp rings. Served in syrup. (*see* bottom of picture, right).

JAL FREZI Sautéed or stir-fried meat or chicken dish, often with lightly cooked onion, garlic, ginger, green pepper and chilli.

JEERA Cumin or cummin seed or powder, hence *Jeera Chicken,* the signature dish at Madhu's Southall.

JINGRI OR CHINGRI Prawns of any size.

K

KALIA Traditional Bengali/Bangladeshi meat, poultry or fish dish in which red-coloured ingredients are mandatory, especially red chillies and tomatoes. *See* Rezala.

KARAHI A two-handled Indian kitchen dish. Some restaurants reheat curries in small karahis and serve them straight to the table with the food sizzling inside. *See also* Curry and Balti.

KASHMIR CHICKEN Whole chicken stuffed with minced meat. *See* Kurzi.

KASHMIR CURRY Often a medium curry to which is added cream and coconut and/or lychees, pineapple or banana.

KEBAB Kebab means 'cooked meat' in ancient Turkish, traditionally cooked over charcoal, in a process over 4,000 years old. It was imported to India by the Muslims centuries ago. Shish, incidentally, means 'skewer'. *See* Boti, Hasina, Nargis, Shami and Sheek Kebab.

KEEMA Minced meat, e.g. as used in curry. *See also* Mattar.

KOFTA Balls made from ground meat, poultry or fish/shellfish or vegetables, then deep-fried and simmered in a curry sauce.

KORMA Probably derived from the Persian *Koresh,* a mild stew. The Moghuls made it very rich, using cream, yoghurt and ground almonds, fragranced with saffron and aromatic spices. But, traditionally, Kormas need not be mild. In Kashmir a popular dish is the *Mirchwangan Korma,* red in colour because it is full of Kashmiri chillies. To the curry house, Korma is terminology for the mildest curry, sometimes made sickly by the overuse of creamed coconut block, cream and nuts.

KULCHA Small leavened bread. Can be plain or stuffed, e.g. *Onion Kulcha*.

KULFI Indian ice cream. Traditionally made in cone-shaped moulds in vanilla, pistachio or mango flavours.

KURZI Leg of lamb or whole chicken given a long marination, then a spicy stuffing, e.g. rice and/or Keema (q.v.), then slowly baked until tender. This is served with 'all the trimmings'. It is many a curry house's Special, requiring 24 hours' notice (because of the long preparation) and a deposit to make sure you turn up to eat it). Often for two or four, it is good value. Also called Khurzi, Kasi, Kozi, Kushi, etc. *See also Murgh Masala.*

LASSI A refreshing drink made from yoghurt and crushed ice. The savoury version is *Lassi Namkeen* and the sweet version is *Lassi Meethi.*

M

MACCI or MACHLI Fish. Today, fresh exotic fish from India and Bangladesh are readily available and, when a restaurant offers them, you have the chance of getting a truly authentic dish.

MADRAS You will not find a Madras Curry in Madras. It does not exist. But the people of the south eat hot curries, firing them up with as many as three different types of chilli – dry, powdered and fresh – added to the cooking at different stages. As the Brits got used to their early formula curries, they began to demand them hotter. With no time to add chillies in the traditional way, one of the pioneer curry house chefs simply added one teaspoon of extra-hot chilli powder to his standard sauce, along with tomato and ground almonds, and ingeniously called it 'Madras'. The name stuck. *See also* Chilli, Phal and Vindaloo.

MAKHANI Butter. *See* Murgh Makhani

MALAI Cream. So *Malai Sabzi Kofta*, for example, means vegetable balls in a creamy curry gravy. *See* Rasmalai.

MALAYA The curries of Malaya are traditionally cooked with coconut, chilli and ginger. In the Indian restaurant, however, they are usually based on the Korma (q.v.), to which is added pineapple and/or other fruit.

MASALA A mixture of spices which are cooked with a particular dish, e.g. *Garam Masala* (q.v.). It can be spelt a remarkable number of ways – Massala, Massalla, Masalam, Mosola, Moshola, Musala, etc.

MASALA DOSA *See* Dosa.

MATTAR Green peas. So *Mattar Paneer* is peas with Indian cheese, *Keema Mattar* is mince meat curry with peas,etc.

MEDIUM CURRY *See* Formula Curries.

METHI Fenugreek, pronounced 'maytee'. Savoury spice. The seed is important in masalas. The leaves, fresh or dried, are used particularly in Punjabi dishes. At the curry house, the flavour of these leaves predominates in their *Dhansak*.

MOGLAI Cooking in the style of the Moghul emperors, whose chefs took Indian cookery to the heights of gourmet cuisine centuries ago. Few restaurateurs who offer Moglai dishes come anywhere near this excellence. Authentic Moglai dishes are expensive and time-consuming to prepare. Can also be variously spelt Muglai, Mhogulai, Moghlai, etc.

MULLIGATAWNY A Tamil vegetable consommée (*molegoo* pepper, *tunny* water), adapted by the Raj to create the thick, meat-based British soup.

MURGH Chicken.

MURGH MASALA or MURGH MASSALAM Whole chicken, marinated in yoghurt and spices for hours, then stuffed and roasted. *See* Kurzi.

Murgh MAKHANI A 16th century Moghal dish. Chicken is cooked in butter ghee, in a creamy, lightly spiced red sauce, nowadays using tomato. This was the derivation of CTM (q.v.).

NAGA The world's hottest chilli. Native to Assam and Bangladseh.

NAN or NAAN Pronounced 'narn', it is flat, leavened bread, usually made from plain white flour (*maida*) dough, but sometimes from wholemeal flour (*atta*). After the dough rises, it is rolled out and baked in the tandoor (q.v.). It is teardrop-shaped and about 20-25cm (8-10 inches) long. It must be served fresh and hot. As well as *Plain Nan,* there are many variations involving the addition of other ingredient(s). *Keema Nan* is stuffed with a thin layer of minced, spiced kebab meat. *Peshwari Nan* is stuffed with almonds and/or cashew nuts and/or raisins. Garlic, onion, pineapple, tomato, indeed anything, can be added. Double- or treble-sized *Karak,* Elephant or Family Nans are offered at Balti houses to share to scoop your food up with.

NARGIS KEBAB Indian scotch egg – spiced, minced meat around a hard-boiled egg.

NIRAMISH A Bangladeshi mixed vegetable, often cooked without garlic, and spiced only with *Panch Phoran* – Indian Five Spice mixture.

OOONBARIOU (or Umberio/ Oberu) Parsee vegetable dish which evolved from Undhui, Gujarat baked vegetables. Like Undhui (sic) it uses root vegetables slow-baked for several hoursin a charcoal-lined pit..

OOTHAPPAM *See* Uthappam.

Arabi
india
ashoka
Sheffield

P

PAAN Betel leaf folded, samosa-fashion, around a stuffing of aniseed, betel nut, sunflower seeds, lime paste, etc. and eaten in one mouthful, as a digestive after a meal. The leaf is bitter, the mouth-feel coarse and the taste acquired; but more acceptable (to Westerners) small spices and seeds (*supari*), sometimes sugar-coated in lurid colours, are often offered by the curry house after the meal.

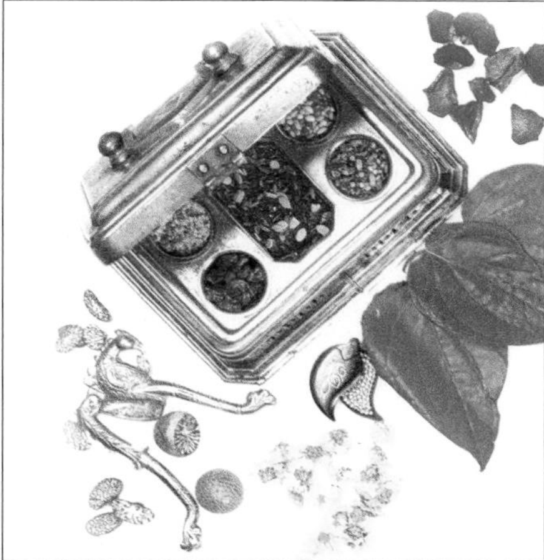

PAKORA The true pakora is a whole piece of vegetable, lightly coated in gram-flour batter and deep-fried, although at the curry house it is to all intents and purposes the same as the Bhajia (q.v.).
PALAK *See* Sag
PANEER Cheese made from milk by separating the whey (liquid) from the curds (solids) which, when compressed, can be crumbled, chopped, fried, tandoori-baked and/or curried (*see* Mattar). In Bengali, Paneer is called *Chhana*, not to be confused with the lentil, Chana (q.v.).
PAPADAM or PAPAD Thin lentil-flour wafers. When cooked (deep-fried or baked) they expand to about 20cm (8 ins). They must be crackling crisp and warm when served. If not, send them back and deduct points from that restaurant. They come either plain or spiced, with lentils, pepper, garlic or chilli. There are many ways to spell papadam, using any combination of the vowels 'a', 'o' and 'u', and double 'p' and double 'd'. But, despite many people calling it so, it should never be referred to as a pampadom.
PARATHA Dough combined with ghee (q.v) thinly rolled out and folded over itself to create a layered disc, like puff pastry. Pan-fried to create a soft bread.
PASANDA Meat, usually lamb, which traditionally is thinly beaten, then cooked in a creamy curry gravy to which some chefs add red wine. The dish and wine were both true treats of Moghul emperor Jehangir who, though Muslim, blessed the wine to make it 'holy water' thus circumventing the rules of Islam. Then he and his court proceeded to drink themselves legless while enjoying this dish.
PATIA Restaurant curry with a thick, dark, red sweet and sour sauce. Based on a Parsee prawn or fish dish.
PATRA A Gujarati speciality, in which colcasia (*patra*) leaves are rolled in gram-flour paste, like a Swiss roll, then steamed, sliced and deep-fried.
PESHAWARI NAN *See* Nan.
PHAL The hottest curry, also known as a Bangalore Phal, invented by the British curry house restaurateurs.
PICKLE Pungent, hot, pickled vegetables essential to an Indian meal. The most common are lime, mango, brinjal and chilli. Though rarely seen at the restaurant, meat and game are made into traditional and very delicious Rajasthani pickles.
PODINA Mint. A fresh chutney, puréed from fresh mint, chilli and onion. Can also be spelt Pudina.
PRAWN BUTTERFLY Usually a large or giant king prawn, cut so that it opens out and flattens, butterfly-shaped, marinated in spices and immersed in gram-flour batter, then deep-fried. A curry house invention, whose name could also have derived from 'batter-fry'.
PRAWN PURI Prawns in a hot sauce served on a Puri (q.v.) bread. Although sometimes described as Prawn Puree it is not a purée.
PULLAO Ancient Persia invented *Pollou,* with rice and meat and/or vegetables, cooked together in a pan until tender. Following Muslim invasions it evolved into Turkey's *Pilav,* Greece's *Pilafi,* Spain's *Paella* and, of course, India's *Pullao.* In many curry houses, the ingredients are mixed after cooking, to save time. (*See* Biriani.) There are many other ways to spell it: *Pillau, Puloa, Pillar, Pilaw, Polaw,* etc.
PULLAO RICE The restaurant name for rice fried with aromatic spices, usually with rice grains coloured yellow and/or red and/or green.
PURI Unleavened wholemeal bread: rolled out flat to about 10cm (4 ins) in diameter, it puffs up when deep-fried, and should be served at once.

Q

QUAS CHAWAL or KESAR CHAVAL Rice fried in ghee (q.v.), flavoured and coloured with saffron (*kesar*).

R

RAITA A cooling chutney of yoghurt on its own (*see also* Dhai) or vegetable, e.g. cucumber or mint (sometimes called Tandoori Sauce) to accompany papadoms, the starter or the main course.

RASGULLA Walnut-sized balls or ovals of paneer (q.v.), or semolina and cream cheese, cooked in syrup (literally meaning 'juicy balls'). They are white or pale gold in colour and served cold or warm. *See* Rasmalai.

RASHMI KEBAB Kebab of minced meat inside an egg net or omelette.

RASMALAI Rasgullas cooked in cream, served cold. Very rich, very sweet. They are the white spheres in the picture To their right is Gulab Jaman, below is Rasgulla.. Above are Indian sweetmeats, Burfi and Halva, In the bowl is Shrikand, the Bombay yoghurt sweet syllabub..

REZALA Bengali/Bangladeshi speciality. Lamb cooked in

evaporated milk, rich and subtly spiced, it would be milder than Korma except that green chillies are mandatory. Traditionally no red- or orange-coloured ingredients should be used. *See* Kalia.

RHOGAN JOSH GOSHT Literally meaning 'lamb in red gravy'. Traditionally, in Kashmir, lamb is marinated in yoghurt, then cooked with ghee, aromatic spices and natural red colorants. It should be creamy but not hot. The curry house version omits the marinade and the aromatics, and uses tomato and red pepper to create a red appearance. There are many ways of spelling it – Rogon, Roghan, Rugon, Rugin, Rowgan, Ragan, etc, Just, Joosh, Juice, Jash, etc, Goosht, Goose, Gost, etc.

ROTI Indian bread of any type, rolled out into thin flat discs.

S

SABZI Vegetable.

SAG or SAAG Spinach, also called *Shak* in Bengali, *Palak* in the Punjab and *Rai*, although these are mustard leaves. *Lalshak* is delicious red spinach.

SAMBAL/SAMBOL A Malaysian and Sri Lankan term describing the chutneys accompanying a meal. Sometimes referred to on the Indian menu. Malaysians also refer to Sambal as a dish of various ingredients cooked in a hot sauce, e.g. prawn sambal.

SAMBAR A hot and spicy, runny, almost consommé-like south Indian vegetable curry made from lentils and exotic vegetables, such as the drumstick. In the Manchester/Merseyside area, the curry houses have a dish called *Samber*. It bears no resemblance to Sambar, except that lentils and a lot of chilli powder are added to meat, chicken or prawn curry.

SAMOSA Celebrated triangular, deep-fried meat or vegetable patties, supreme as starters or snacks.

SHAMI KEBAB Round minced meat rissoles.

SHASHLIK KEBAB Shashlik in Armenia means 'to grill'. Cubes of skewered lamb or chicken are marinated (in an oil, garlic and chilli mixture) then grilled. *See* Hasina.

SHATKORA A Bangladeshi citrus fruit, the size of a grapefruit but sharper in flavour. Can be eaten fresh or used in cooking.

SHEEK KEBAB or SEEKH Literally means (from Turkish *shish*) a skewer. Spiced minced meat, usually coloured lurid red at the curry house (from proprietary tandoori/kebab paste), is moulded onto the skewer, then baked in the tandoori and grilled.

SINGARA Bengali for Samosa (q.v.).

STANDARD CURRY *See* Formula Curries.

T

TANDOORI An ancient style of cooking, which originated in the rugged north-west frontier of India (now Pakistan). It gets its name from the cylindrical clay oven, the tandoor, with its opening at the top, fired with charcoal in its base. Originally the ingredients were chicken and lamb, marinated for many hours in a spiced yoghurt-based sauce, traditionally slightly reddened with red chilli, then skewered and baked in the tandoor. Now the curry house product also includes fish, prawns, paneer (q.v.) and vegetables. But its lurid red or orange colour is created by the unnecessary use of tartrazine food colouring in proprietary ready-to-use pastes. *See* Boti Kebab, Tikka, Nan Bread and Raita.

TARKA DHAL A tasty, spicy lentil dish, the Dhal being *massoor* (red) lentils, cooked to a purée, to which the Tarka (crispy, fried caramelized onion and/or garlic) is

kinara

Pakistani, Indian and Eastern Cuisine

www.pittscottage.co.uk

Kinara at Pitt's Cottage
High Street,
Limpsfield Road, Westerham,
Kent

01959 562125

Lunch: Friday, Saturday and Sunday 12.30pm - 3pm
Dinner: Seven nights a week from 6pm - 11.30pm

Awarded
Cobra Good Curry Guide
Best Pakistani Restaurant
2007/8

est for the cook. It should taste very slightly burnt (from the Tarka), and be subtly, yet decisively, spiced, neither too thick nor too thin.

TAVA A heavy steel, rimless, flattish frying pan, used to cook items such as Parathas.

THALI or TALI A round tray (*thali*) with a low rim, averaging about 34cm (12in) in diameter. It is a plate on which an entire meal is served. Dry items (rice, bread and even dry curries) are placed directly on the thali. Wet portions (curries, dhals, soups and sweets, etc) are placed in matching serving bowls (*tapelis*), and they too reside on the thali. They were made of gold for the Moghul emperors, silver for the Maharajas, and stainless steel for the rest of us. To be found at certain restaurants serving 'special' meals.

TIKKA Literally, a small piece. For example, *Chicken Tikka* is a filetted chunk of chicken, marinated (*see* Tandoori), skewered and baked in the tandoor. Traditionally, the marinade is identical to Tandoori marinade, and cooks a naturally russet brown colour. Proprietary Tikka paste, as used in the curry house, is lurid orange or yellow because of the tartrazine it contains.

TINDALOO *see* Vindaloo.

UNDHUI A baked vegetable dish from Gujarat.

UPPUMA South Indian dish. Lightly fried semolina with onion and spices.

UTHAPPAM Uthappam or Oothappam South India

pancakes made of rice and urid dhal which is soaked and ground, then allowed to ferment. The rice should be sambar (south Indian) rice, a small oval-grained variety, available at the Asian store. Traditionally the batter contains dried red chilli, ginger and onion. Recent developments include Pizza-style toppings of garlic, tomato, onion and green chilli

URID A type of lentil, its husk is black, and it comes whole, split or polished. Available as a dhal dish in some restaurants, e.g. *Maharani Dhal.*

VADA or VADAI Lentil-flour spicy doughnut, enjoyed in Gujarat and south India. *See* Dahi Vada.

VARK Edible silver or gold leaf, made today in Hyderabad, but a Moghul speciality, said to be an aphrodisiac.

VINDALOO A fiery dish from Goa. (*See page* 50). It now means the second hottest dish (two spoonfuls of chilli powder), usually with a chunk of potato (Aloo). Also sometimes called *Bindaloo* or *Tindaloo* (even hotter). *See also* Chilli, Madras and Phal.

YAKNI Literally mutton, or a spicy meat-based stock.

ZAFFRON Saffron, also known as *Kesar* or *zafron.* The stigma (stamen) of the crocus flower. Though never as expensive as gold it is world's most expensive spice, because picking is is laboriuos and expensive..

ZEERA Alternatively called Jeera, which is cumin. *Zeera Gosht* is lamb cooked with cumin.

Kings' Man was First Curry King

Holborn's short-lived Kaiser-e-Hind has long been credited as being the UK's first Indian restaurant to open (in 1911), possibly predated by a few undocumented café-venues in the London Docks. In fact the Hindoostanee Coffee House, opened at 34, George Street near London's Marble Arch a century earlier in 1809. As with other contemporary coffee houses, it was opened in the hope that it would attract businessmen to its doors. Its owner, Bengali Dean Mahomet was targeting a small but specific market at a time when the East India Company was in the ascendancy. Billed as *'being for the entertainment of gentlemen where they may enjoy the Hoakha, with real Chilm tobacco and Indian dishes, in the highest perfection, and allowed by the greatest epicures to be unequalled to any curries ever made in England with choice wines and every accommodation'* Mahomet was aiming at those who traded in Indian and Far Eastern goods. Furnished with ornate bamboo chairs and tables, and decorated with Chinese and Japanese tableware and artwork, the Hindoostanee was, it seems a curiosity which though evidently enjoyed by its members, never received enough such patronage to survive.

CITY OF WESTMINSTER
SITE OF
HINDOOSTANE
COFFEE HOUSE
1810
LONDON'S FIRST
INDIAN RESTAURANT
OWNED BY
SAKE DEAN MAHOMED
1759-1851
THE PORTMAN ESTATE

Mahomet was born in Patna, in 1759, at exactly the time that Clive of India and his like were defeating the Moghuls and curtailing French and Dutch power in India, indeed his father

was subadar in the Company's Bengal Army. Dean followed suit as trainee surgeon/barber in the unit of one Captain Godfrey Baker, a minor Irish aristocrat. Upon leaving the army Mahomet emigrated to Ireland and with Baker's patronage built his position in society, fell in love with, eloped and married an Irish woman, Jane Daly. He then moved to London and persuaded the Honourable Basil Cockrane in Portman Square to finance the development of a 'vapour bath' which introduced 'shampooing' – therapeutic massage, now known as aromatherapy. But Mahomet had other ambitions and went it alone with his Hindoostanee coffee shop venture. By 1812, it filed for bankruptcy the Mahomets moved to Brighton where they opened Mahomed's (sic) Bath House, on the site now occupied by the Queen's Hotel. Described in the local paper as *'The Indian Medicated Vapour Bath (type of Turkish bath); a cure to many diseases and giving full relief when every thing fails; particularly Rheumatic and paralytic, gout, stiff joints, old sprains, lame less, aches and pains in the joints'*. Mahomet became known as *'Dr Brighton'*. Hospitals referred patients to him and he was appointed as shampooing surgeon to both Kings George IV and William IV.

Mahomet died in 1851 aged 92. As is often the way with a pioneer, he led a colourful life. His Indian restaurant was simply was way ahead of its time. Had he been around today, would he have resented the vast 21st century curry industry? Unlikely, because he would have been leading from the front. Fortunately he is not forgotten, and it is fitting that he gets the recognition he deserves. In September 2005 the City of Westminster unveiled a Green Plaque at 34 George Street, commemorating the opening of the Hindoostanee Coffee House.

As for no 34 itself, it is now the site of the Japanese restaurant *Defune.*

2008 COBRA GOOD CURRY GUIDE

THE ENTRIES

The Entries
An explanation of our method

There is no perfect system for laying out a nationwide restaurant Guide. Many Guides simply list their entries in town alphabetical order. The problem here is that there is no geographical relationship between each town.

The method we have adopted in our Guides is to record the entries by county. We believe that most people understand the ancient British counties. We list them alphabetically. Unlike some Guides, we do not group the counties in National Regions (such as 'The Midlands' or the 'West Country', etc), since this too lacks logic. Counties are not without confusion. In some cases, their once sacrosanct borders have been altered by frequent local government tinkering. Greater Manchester is one example. When it was established as a 'Unitary Region' in 1965, it nibbled away parts of Cheshire and Lancashire. Many residents prefer to stick to these counties in their addresses, though we have adopted 'Greater Manchester' as a 'county' in this *Guide.* Other bodies, such as the Post Office, add to the confusion of recent years. Their postcodes are far from logical and do not follow county borders. BT also have their own system of geographical reference. It is because few people understand postcode logic, and even fewer understand phone codes, that we use the counties.

Following London, we cover the English counties. With the demise of Avon (which was in any case, not a county, but a Unitary Region), we now start with Bedfordshire. Within each county, we record the relevant towns alphabetically, and within each town, we record each restaurant alphabetically. In Bedfordshire, for example, the first town we record is Arlesey, and its first restaurant is Raj Villa, and so on. Following England, we then look at the Isles and Islands, Northern Irelaand, and after some years of absence, Eire returns to this Guide. Then it's Scotland and finally Wales.

We start with London, as is explained alongside. Before we are accused of London bias, it is worth giving our usual caveat: Of the 9,000 British curry restaurants on our nationwide database, nearly 20% of them are in London. Naturally, with such competition, many of the country's best are in the capital. Our coverage reflects this, with a strong London section.

CENTRAL LONDON

Area: British capital
Postcodes: E, EC, N, NW, SE, SW, W & WC
Population: 5,735,000

For the purpose of this Guide we define Central London as its 1870 postal districts, now known as postcodes. We run them alphabetically as follows: E, EC, N, NW, SE, SW, W *and* WC. *Within each individual postcode, we run numerically, starting with* E1 *and ending with* WC2. *As with all postcode logic, this is not in any geographical order. For example,* W5 *Ealing, shares its borders with* W13, *West Ealing and* W3, *Acton. For 95 years these postcodes comprised all of London. In 1965 Greater London, (GL) was established. It includes these postcodes and expanded its borders, absorbing Middlesex and parts of Essex, Hertfordshire, Kent and Surrey (shown in lilac in the drawing below). For GL (Greater London) towns/boroughs in these areas, please see the relevant county (Essex, Herts, Kent, Middlesex and Surrey) –* *see list on page 9.*

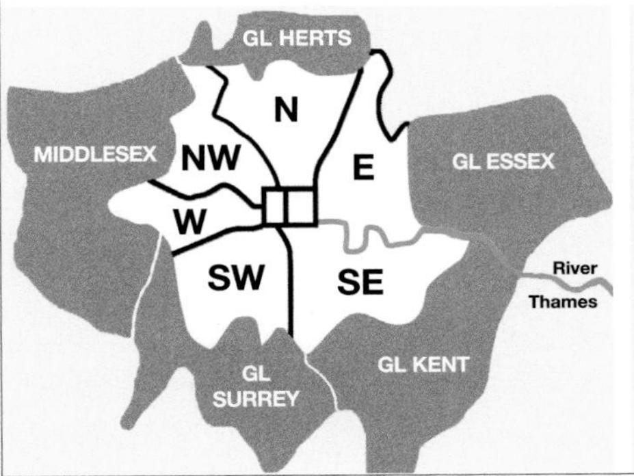

Greater London covers 1579 km^2 (609 sq. mi) and had in 2006, an estimated population of 7,500,000. The highest point is Westerham Heights, in the North Downs on the Kent / SE London border, at 245 metres. The River Thames flows west to east through central London, and forms the natural boundary between E and SE London and Essex and Kent

London E

Area: East London
Postcodes: E1 to E18
Population: 1.050,000

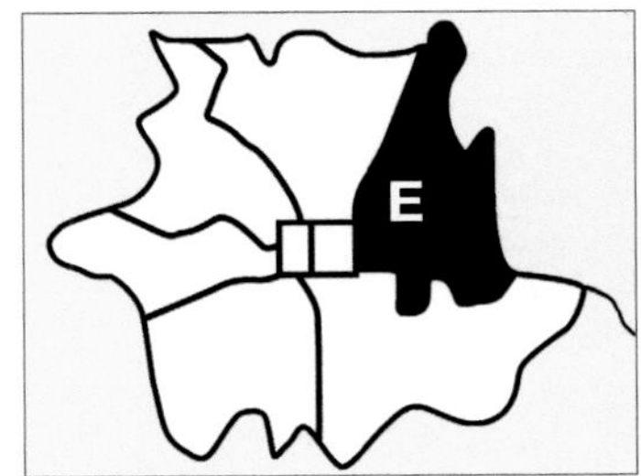

London E1

Brick Lane – Banglatown

Once predominantly Jewish, and bustling with tailors, salt-of-the-earth street markets and cab drivers, (to emphasise its roots you'll still find a 24 hr fresh-baked bagel shop at 159 where cabbies queue for sustenance) the long and narrow Brick Lane, has, since 1971, become home to the country's largest Bangladeshi community. Running north between Shoreditch and Aldgate East tube stations, it is now called Banglatown, indicating its proliferation of cheap and cheerful curry cafés, snack bars, restaurants and provisions shops, run by the thriving community. Some of these establishments have remained fairly spartan, and unlicensed (you can BYO). Others have redecorated and become licensed. We're not convinced that a Balti house is PC on the street, but there is one. But the curry-hungry can get breakfast from 8am here (Sweet & Spice, no 40). The late arrivals can get into Shampan until 2.30am. Many other on the Lane are open all day. Here are your favourites:

BENGAL CUISINE

12 Brick Lane, E1 0120 7377 8405

'Rashid has finished refurbishment from plate windows, new fittings, new staff dress.' says BF. *'Continues to provide best food on Brick Lane. Buy his privilege card and you get a 10% discount on all meals, and notes of functions, special evenings etc.'*BF. Those special evenings sound good, Bernard, let's hear more details about them. Bernard ate Jha, which he says is really hot. Delivery: 3-mile radius. Hours: 12 to 12 non stop, daily. Branch: Taja, E1.

CAFE NAZ BEST BANGLADESHI

46-48 Brick Lane, E1 020 7247 0234

'Resolutely modern from its shiny black facade and chilli-patterned glass'n'chrome bar, Cafe Naz is sufficiently confident to allow itself the odd splash of kitsch such as the splendid, smoking fountain by the door. After all, this is Banglatown's buzzing Bangladeshi brasserie', says Caf'Naz about Caf'Naz *'.Presentation is very European, and just as well, as the large deep plates are necessary for coping with monster main courses such as Hyderabadi achar Gost - chunks of lamb slow cooked on the bone in a dark rich sauce flavored with pickling spices and limes.'* It enjoys a very busy and lively buffet lunchtime trade. Above the main restaurant there is a large room, which can be used for private meetings and functions. The food very good indeed, including some authentic dishes. All round very happy reports with some saying best in Brick Lane, though as these pages show, opinions about everything vary. *'Why have I never discovered Brick Lane before? What a colourful, vibrant and lively cobbled street this is, with every second building being a thriving Indian restaurant (including two in the Top 100). Café Naz is an excellent restaurant, very deserving of it is Top 100 listing. Ambience is lively and the decor is bright and airy. The staff were welcoming, professional and efficient, coping with a large group of us from a local graduate art show, all of whom had to leave at different times. Dishes that really stood out were their Tandoori/Tikka Fish which was succulent, perfectly cooked and nicely balanced. The Lamb Korai was also very nicely balanced and the meat was truly melt in the mouth texture. Chicken Madras and Chicken Korma were also much enjoyed by my teenage daughters. Overall Opinion – excellent and would definitely return (although there are at least a dozen other establishments deserving of attention in this great street).'*SO. *'Add perfect pilou rice and a nice fluffy garlic naan - if you're planning to sleep alone.'* Takeaway Service. Free Delivery over £12 and within 2 miles Hours: Mon to Weds: 12- 12; Thurs & Friday: to 1am Saturday: 6 - 1, and 12 - 3 /6 -12 on Sunday: Branches Cambridge, Chelmsford Essex and Cardiff. New branch: Café Naz at Corvino, 7 Middlesex Street, Aldgate, E1 *See page 40.*

LE TAJ

134 Brick Lane, E1 020 7247 4210

Opened in 1995, seats 40 diners. Authentic Bengali food on the stylish purple and cream menu. Biran Mass – a slice of boal fish marinated in a mixture of freshly ground herbs, then fried with onions. Singara – golden triangle of pastry filled with cottage cheese and spiced chicken, served with a chunky pineapple chutney. Shorisha Raja Chingri – grilled gholda king prawns in a chilli and fresh mustard marinade served sizzling. Lal Gootha – pumpkin and King Prawn dish, extremely popular in the fishing districts of Bangladesh. Beguner Borta – smoked aubergine pulp, muddled with green chillies, ginger and fresh lime. Pepe Bhajia – green papaya diced and tossed with light chillies and aromatic spices. Tomato Bhorta charcoal grilled tomatoes, puréed with a hint of spices, mustard oil and chillies. Set lunch: £7.50. Set dinner: from £15 to £22.

SHAFIQUES BENGAL BLUES CAFE BRASSERIE

94 Brick Lane, E1 020 7377 9123

Popular venue seating 80. Chicken and Lamb Haryali is the most popular dish. Snack menu available, including Chicken Tikka, Prawn Puri, Salmon Dhaka , Shobji Golati Kebab. Set lunch: £7.95, set dinner: £10.95. Hours: 12 to 12 non stop, daily.

SHAMPAN

PREVIOUS AWARD WINNER & TOP 100

79 Brick Lane, E1 020 7375 0475

'If you want something unusual, THIS is the place to go,' says NP. *'Came one lunch time, on strength of Guide, very good indeed. I unimaginatively began with a meat spring roll, very nice. Can't remember the main course except that it was a Bangladeshi Chicken recipe involving a whole/half spring chicken – delicious. Impressed with food, although wasn't cheap.'* NP. Mr Haque, the owner runs the annual September Bangaltown Festival. Here's the fully licensed place for the night owls. Hours: 12AM to 2.30AM non stop, daily. Branch Clifton, E1 and Docklands.

SHEBA

36 Brick Lane, E1 020 7247 7824

It just serves standard curries, without any claim to Bangladesh, but good and reliable. *'Still the best place in*

Brick Lane for formula curries,' says NP. *'I've tried others – Nazrul and Nazrul II and while I can't remember much about them, I remember thinking they weren't nearly as good as Sheba. If you want cheap, enjoyable curry, Sheba is definitely the place to go. Prawn Puri and Chicken Bhuna – both very good, never been disappointed. Egg and Mushroom Curry is ideal to soak up the Friday night alcohol! Extremely reasonable prices. Place often packed with city workers, atmosphere often merry and smokey, service almost always polite and well-timed.'* NP. Lunch and dinner daily.

SWEET AND SPICY

40 Brick Lane, E1 020 7247 1081

One of the Lane's oldest (1968). It's the cuisine you go for and it's Pakistani. Seats 40 diners in simple clean cafeteria style. Prices here are very good indeed, choose from the counter established favourites such as Seikh Kebab or Aloo Bora for 80p each. Chicken Karahi or Vindaloo or Korma for £3.95. Karahi Gosht or Madras Chuppatis, Puris and Popadoms are all 30p each. A favourite is the Kebab Roll from 90p to £2. Specials: Halwa Puri and Chana. Set lunch, set dinner, delivered to your table. Sunday Buffet: £4.50. One of the few places where you can get curry breakfast in London. Hours: 8am to 10pm non stop, daily.

Elsewhere in E1

CAFE SPICE NAMASTE
A-LIST PREVIOUS AWARD WINNER

16 Prescot Street, E1 020 7488 9242

When he opened in 1995 Cyrus and his front of house wife Pervin Todiwala did busier lunch trades than evening and did not even bother to open on Saturdays! Lunch – weekdays remains frantic and the crew have learned to turn around a full house within the hour!. The former magistrates' office had been wrecked by the DHSS, who seem to achieve immunity from Grade I listings, and it cost a packet to get it suitable for restaurant business. The secret weapons were Cyrus and Parveen friends of mine since 1982, he as Exec Chef and she as Maitre D at Taj Fort Aguada properties in Goa. I knew then that Cyrus can really cook, specialising in Parsee and Goan cuisine. The former because he is Parsee, Goan because he was in Goa where he learned to cook wonderful Portuguese-influenced curries. Cyrus is a great talker and dooer too, and we gave him his first Award in 1992, barely a month after he opened his first UK restaurant. 'Well presented and tasty food from a varied menu , in an attractive décor, with prompt lunchtime service'. SH. 'Usual good food at this place. £3 for a small cobra is a bit steep. Pickle selection well above average. Nice touch on current menu is naming dishes after regulars. Interesting to conjecture how often folk have to go to get so honoured. "Jacobs" aloo chat at £4.50 was a cold dish, but very spicy."Jenny's" chicken was a hearty full breast portion at £12.75 with piquant sauce. "Danglers?" scallops made for a different ingredient at £14.95. The pork in "Carvalho's(? CFC centre half) vindaloo could have been fat trimmed. Most disappointing dish was "Dhanki's" palakh, a very bland veg. curry for £4.75. Service very good, full by 8.30 on a Tuesday evening. 10% CC discount without quibble. Cost net £135 with 12.5 % service. Can see why it gets awards.' C & MC. The small alfresco patio out back, with Indian snacks and cold beer, opens in summer. Cyrus is a bundle of energy, and he achieved one of his dreams to open an Asian cookery school. which it got him the MBE. See Zen Satori London n15. Main courses £10 - £17. Set meals £25 - £40 (min 2), Service charge: 12.5% Takeaway service; delivery service (within 2-mile radius). Hours: 12-3 / 6.15-10.30 Mon-Fri; Closed on Sundays. Branch Café T WI <www.cafespice.co.uk> . *See page 8.*

CLIFTON — NEW ENTRANT

1 Whitechapel Road, E1 — 020 7377 5533

The iconic Clifton closed in 1997 when its owner passed away. Though unable to build on the original site, current owner Shiraj Haque of

Shampan fame, wanted to resurrect the name and recreate the fine cuisine and great reputation that Clifton once had, and he found a site virtually at the entrance to Brick Lane. It opened in 2005. With its beautiful Indian and Bangladeshi art in a variety of mediums adorning the walls on both the ground and lower ground floors, the eatery has a simple but modern feel and seats 200 covers. Chef Musavir Ahmed and his kitchen team have designed an extensive menu. The open-plan kitchen on the ground floor entices passers by and customers can see and understand how the dishes are prepared. *Puja Vedi, Tandoori Magazine.*

EMPRESS TANDOORI

141 Leman Street, E1 — 020 7265 0745

Owned by Mr Islam since 1992. Good Bangladeshi choices here, including the restaurant's most popular dishes: Skiandari Lamb – marinated and roasted. Cox's Bazar Crab – soft crabs cooked with ginger, garlic, coconut and fresh herbs, garnished with cucumber and lemon. Annan's Haash – succulent roasted breast of duck, cooked in aromatic spices, served with pineapple and cherry tomatoes, fairly hot. Takeaway: 10% discount. Minimum charge: £12. Delivery. Lunch to 3pm weekdays. Dinner to 11.30pm.

HALAL

2-6 St Mark Street, E1 — 020 7481 1700

Established way back in 1939, making it the second oldest in London.*'I went to the Halal Mark Lane E1). Better than the trendy places in Brick Lane with their freebie inducements. Cost £51 with a tip for 3 people. Still about the only place where I have meat vindaloo(£4.30).Have been going there for twenty years but still regarded as a newcomer-plenty of city retirees of older vintage still go for old times' sake.Good value for money, quiet in the evening, but 8 "city gents", obviously regulars came in.'* CC. Fully licensed. Hours: 12-12, Sat /Sun 12 - 10.30.

EASTERN SPICE

2a Artillery Passage, Bishopsgate, E1 — 020 7247 0772

A full range of Tandooris, Baltis, Kebabs, Samosa. Bhajis and Curries are available at this well-established City curry house. 'We often drop in here for lunch, and very good it is too' HEG. Hours: 12-3/6-11.30. Closed Sat/Sun.

LAHORE KEBAB HOUSE A-LIST
NOMINATED BEST PAKISTANI RESTAURANT

2 Umberton Street, E1 020 7488 2551

For anyone who has not been to either Pakistan or to Sparkbrook, the LKH is what it's all about. Despite Brum's claim to be the inventor of the currinary world, this gaff has been doing Balti, under what some say is its true name, Karahi – or Karrai (sic.) – since it opened in the seventies – serving darned good food, geared to Asian tastes, without compromising it for Westerners. At least that's what it used to be. But its relatively new-found glory as a lunchtime dive for the money boys and girls from the City has permeated into the evenings, and it's had an effect on management. The redec has now become old hat, and tatty even, much to the delight of LKH's aficionados and its Asian patrons, who were wary of such inventory as arty line drawings. Cutlery is still for wimps (though you no longer have to ask for it). But when in Rome, eat the correct way, please, using a piece of Roti to scoop up your curry, in your right hand only – too bad if you're left-handed. And expect limitations if you're a veggie. Halal mutton, chicken and quail are it, in the karahi, from the tandoor as tikkas or kebabs, or as steam roast (Choosa), with robust lentils and fragrant rice. Real veterans show their spurs by enjoying the celebrated, and very filling and satisfying, Paya (lamb's trotters), laced with the Hot Chilli Raita, followed by their gorgeous Kheer rice pudding. Service is swift and accurate, but don't expect pampering, and don't expect to pay more than a tenner, including tip, in cash, please – nothing fancy like credit cards. It has a different atmosphere at different times of the day, different again at the weekend, depending on who's eating when. *'The eight downstairs tables are communal, each seating 6 – 12. There are eight more tables upstairs. One wall is covered with mirrors. The restaurant is worn but clean. The main dishes are on display in a glass-fronted heater. I sat next to two businessmen and ordered Saffron Rice and Chicken Karahi. Almost but not quite – too hot. My Spinach and Potato offers a pleasant counter note, flavoured with nutmeg'* LB, Dallas. *'Service very good: they're used to large crowds with diners in and out very quickly. This place is my Mecca, my Garden of Eden, my Golden Temple. It's the best food anywhere.'* RCE. *'Please. please delist this restaurant from your Guide. It's already too busy, and we don't need you piling in more people.'* ANON. Hours: 12-12 non stop, daily.

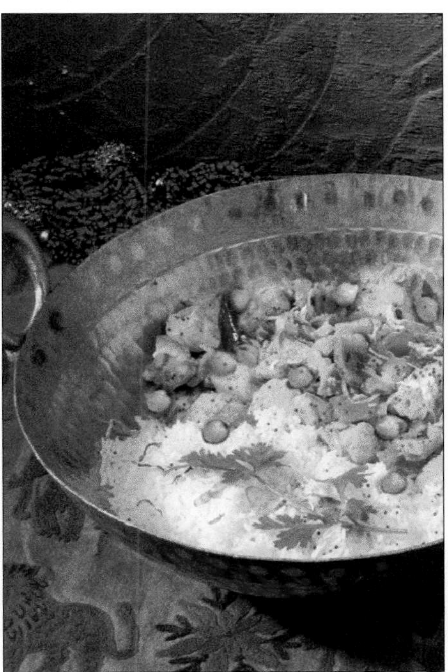

MALA NEW ENTRANT

St Katherine's Dock, E1 020 7480 6356

Mala restaurant was established in 1987 by clothing and property tycoon brothers, Charanjit and Malkit Roy Sandhu intitally as a place to entertain their clients. Located in the unique and beautiful St Katherine's Dock Marina, it started off as an 80-seater. The restaurant became an instant success with the public, and was often fully booked weeks in advance. In 1996 they took over the next-door premises, enabling the seating to be expanded to 200, as well as creating a generous-size seated bar area. Marble, exquisite murals, paintings and antiques, imported from all over Asia complement the extension, giving Mala a traditional and unique atmosphere, almost like a museum within a restaurant. This is coupled with spectacular views from anywhere in the restaurant. It is now run by Charanjit's son, Vinnie Sandhu, whose corporate and tourism businesses connections bring Mala clients from all over the world. This perfect cultural melting pot is matched by the international floor staff from from Ecuador to China to Poland to India, who are all trained in Indian cuisine.

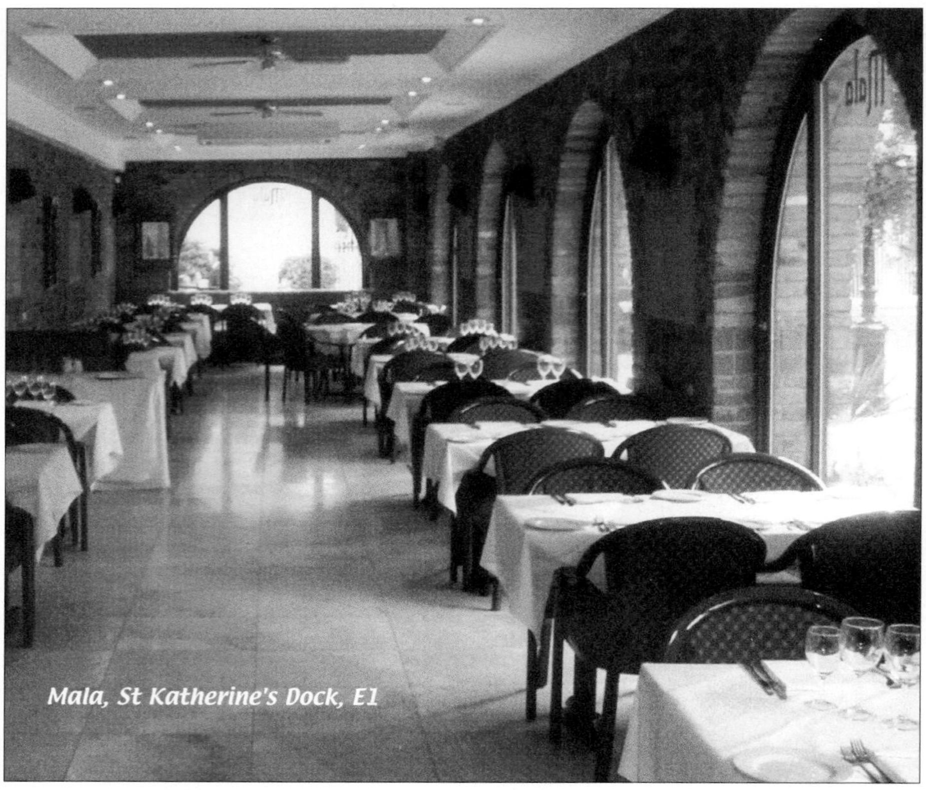

Mala, St Katherine's Dock, E1

The menu contains dishes from all over India such as Malabari sea food and fish dishes from the south, to Chingiri Jhol from the east, to Dal Makhani from Punjab. There is also a range of curries and tandoori dishes, all under the professional expertise of head chef Madhur Sheel, whose wide knowledge and experience of running kitchens all over India has taken Mala to the next successful level. Says Vinnie 'This multicultural environment meets all our customers needs, be it a private meeting, a wedding or a fantastic night out with your friends and family.

PRIDE OF ASIA

207 Mile End Rd, E1 020 7780 9321

A bog-standard, 65-seater owned and managed by Abdul Habiz. Chef Amir Uddin continues to provide all the favourites at prices made all the better with the Curry Club Discount. Delivery: £10 min, 3 mile radius.12-2.30pm. Dinner to 12, daily.

SCARLET DOT NEW ENTRANT

4 Crispin Sq, Crispin Place, E1 0207 375 0880

Referring to the traditional Indian symbol for a married woman, the bindi, Scarlet Dot is the first Indian haute cuisine restaurant to open its doors in London's famous Spitalfields. Part of a modern complex of restaurants and posh shops behind the famous indoor market, it does much to challenge your idea of what an Indian restaurant should look like. For starters, it's as much drinking-den as restaurant. The Scarlet Spice Bar is 30 feet of tropical wood, dark blinds and marble floors and walls, providing a seriously cool place to meet for lunch or after-work drinks. Neon floor-lights lead up to the bar where chill-out music plays by day and the tempo picks up by night. The adjoining 120-cover restaurant also attracts a diverse group of people from lawyers and bankers, to designers and artists, who pour in for delicious meals and a traditional Indian breakfast that is not to be missed. Five-star Indian chefs who are adept at whipping up contemporary dishes support the adjoining restaurant For the summer months, there is an outdoor eating area under an impressive glass and steel canopy. Scarlet Dot's restaurant has 120 covers (200 standing) reservable for a variety of private and corporate functions and parties. You can also hire 'zones' in the chic bar for groups of up to 25 – complete with a DJ if you want one. A further 125 can sit outside on the modern terrace. Full range of party menus on offer, from a la carte to drinks-only. *Puja Vedi, Ed, Tandoori Magazine.* <www.scarletdot.co.uk>

TAJA

199a Whitechapel Road, E1 020 7247 3866

Taja, they tell us, translates as *'fresh'* which applies to the food. Specials: Mushroom Kebab, Mango and Coconut Curry and Goan Prawn Sag. This 80 seater can get busy at times. Ask about their loyalty club for instant savings, which will ensure you get your fill for under a tenner. Hours: 11AM to midnight, non stop, daily. Branch: 1 Brick Lane. E1

TIFFIN INDIAN TOP 100

165 Cannon Street Road, E1 020 7702 3832

Abul Kalam's Tiffin continue to thrive according to its fans. It starts with the menu. *'Very dramatic and stylish glossy purple menu for the food, wine and other drinks are listed in an equally good looking orange and green menu.'* RL. Start with Tiffin Special, an absolute feast, including Murghi Tikka – chicken marinated in yogurt and spices cooked in a clay oven. Keema Chops – seasoned mince coated in finely mashed potato and breadcrumbs lightly fried. Sheek Kebab – finely minced meat mixed with onion, coriander and an assortment of rich exotic spices, skewered and cooked in a clay oven, all served with salad. The vegetarian alternative is also equally tempting, lightly spiced aubergine slices in batter; vegetables in a spicy sauce wrapped in filo pastry and fried. But do leave room for your main course, for example Tandoori Batak – duck breast marinated in curd and coriander or the Murgh Ur Saag – chicken cooked in a dry sauce with spinach, onion and spices. And many more such delights. Minimum charge: £8, set lunch: £5.95. Lunch and dinner daily.

London E2

Bethnal Green

AL AMIN

483 Cambridge Heath Road, E2 020 7739 9619

Abdul Noor's two-room 39-seater is a popular standard curry house, with all the trimmings, including Balti. It pleases everyone. Reasonable prices. Delivery: £10 minimum, 2-mile radius. Lunch to 2.30pm. Dinner to midnight, daily.

Al fresco fun in and around Brick Lane for the Banglatown Curry Festival, held annually each September.

London E4

Chingford, Highams Park

PURBANI

34 The Avenue, E4 020 8531 8804

Established 1983. Owner Tony Turu Miah's air conditioned 54-seater is a regular in the Guide, and has built up a good loyal following. Chicken Tikka, Chicken and Prawn Bhoona with green salad and Special Pullao Rice for nigh on a tenner. Bamboo Shoot Bhajia is something different. Lunch to 2.30 and dinner to 11.30 daily.

London E6

Upton Park

LAZZAT KAHAR NEW ENTRANT

18 Plashet Grove, E6 020 8552 3413

Busy, cheerful, basic, friendly, buzzing, friendly ... these are your words, and above all cheap! We add to that Punjabi so expect meats, savoury flavours , no holds barred on the chilli front, al dente-perfect rice and super breads. And let's add another word: superb. You watch them cook, and you know it's fresh. The lettuce, onion, tomato, and chilli salad is free.. With main courses £3.95-£4.95 and starters much less, it's hard to spend a tenner here, so cash is best here. Alcohol not permitted.. Takeaway service. Hours: 11am-midnight daily.

London E7

Forest Gate

MOBEEN NEW ENTRANT

224 Green Street, E7 020 8470 2419

An all-day caff which takes credit cards. Hm ... Bliss! Furthermore it has escaped gentrification. Because of it or despite it, it is busy, busy with Asian families high on the attendance list. The mainly Punjabi food is churned out by a battery of cooks, in view and female servers. Meat and veg dishes alike are competent, maybe not brilliant but ample and tasty. One veggie tried the Vegetable mince curry and rejected it because it tasted like meat! Entertainment too!. (it is made with granulated soya). And the balance of opinion favours the veggie dishes over the meat (just), so take your choice. Besides, it's hard to spend a tenner here, so what the heck! A 20-seat party room is billed, but it always seems to be a party here. Main courses£2-£5.50. No smoking. Takeaway service. 11-10 daily. Branch Ilford, Essex.

VIJAY'S CHAWALLA NEW ENTRANT

268 Green Street, E7 020 8470 3535

And just down the road is another all-day caff which takes credit cards. More bliss! Again, it's a non-nonsense value-for-money caff, but with a different food-style from Mobeen. It is Gujarati, which means considering its apt address, that vegetarian is king, and there is an abundance of gram flour, albeit used in rissole form, sauces, curries et al.Yoghurt also prevails in the cooking, as does the typically Gujarati sweetness in savoury dishes. Sev Khaman, is gram-flour dumplings with topped gram flour squiggles (sev) with yoghurt and sweet and sour imli (tamarind chutney). Ragada patties, balls of mashed potato stuffed with curried chickpea are deep-fried and served in a tangy sauce. *'I started with that delightful Bombay street snack Bhel Poori'* (see glossary) *'and it was sublime. Then I went on to a fab thali'.* HEG.. They dosh up good Indian desserts here, and someone, not sure if is VJ himself, makes Indian tea as it should be made (bring milk to the simmer with green cardamoms. Add too much sugar and serve in a large cup. Well that's what Chawalla means – tea maker! If you've not had it before, this is the place to indulge. (especially if you didn't BYO). Main courses £4 - £7. Thalis £7. Unlicensed. BYO allowed. Corkage no charge. Hours: 11 - 9 daily.

London E11

Leytonstone

CHANDNI NEW ENTRANT

715 High Rd, E11 020 8539 1700

Vegetarian food here including South Indian in this licensed café.. *'I thought hang it, money is no object today ignoring the £5 thali, I splashed out on the top-priced version (£6.50). I enjoyed a platter of mixed vegetable pakoras (very fresh, very tasty) while I pondered whether I would regret this impulsive act. The rather bumbling but amiable waiter eventually ambled up with my thali, and placed it in front of me with a flourish I never suspected he had in him. Now I've had salvadors all over India, and I have to say this one was worth every penny the extra investment. I'll be back!'* HEG. House wine: £8. Credit cards OK. Hours: 11 -11 daily.

London E14

Docklands, Dogs, Limehouse, Poplar

MEMSAHEB ON THAMES

65 Amsterdam Road, E14 020 7538 3008

Mridul Kanti Das, managing partner of Memsaheb, puts on regular food festivals, specialising in regional food with delights such as Machli Amritsar – boneless pieces of white Indian fish in a spicy batter which is deep-fried. Murghi Lababdar – minced chicken cooked in a thick spicy tomato sauce, garnished with fresh coriander. Punjabi Roghan – on the bone lamb cooked with medium hot spices with fresh tomatoes and fresh coriander. A popular place with several reporters in the area, who speak reverentially of the views (of the Dome across the and the staff curry, oh yes and *'the adorable staff!'*' They spin that you can see the Dome from this restaurant. We couldn't care less if we saw it or not, but if you are drawn there by the spin, caveat emptor, on the day we went, unless it had moved, we could see only the tip of its top. But parking was easy, we could sort of see the Thames, the food curryhouse but competent., and the service amiable.'DBAC. Lunch to 2.30 weekdays and dinner to 11.30 daily.

DOCKMASTERS

NEW TO OUR TOP 100

Dockmaster's House, West India Dock Gate, Hertsmere Road, E14 020 7345 0345

The huge house was built in 1807 by Thomas Morris, to house the all-powerful Dockmaster. A century later it became the Jamaica Tavern, but reverted the post-war dock manager's office, fIt was restored by the Docklands development Corporation and was used by its marketing department. So successful were they that today the charms of this once prominent Georgian building, are utterly dwarfed by Canary Wharf's sky-tech towers, the snaking overhead tracks of the Docklands railway and the surrounding drab, gloomy overparked streets. The movie *Batteries Not Included* spring to mind, but such is progress. It is work a visit, however. There are three elements. A 100-seat a/c restaurant with a satisfying range of Indian regional dishes. Down in the extensive cellars, is now a 200-seat bar offering a range of spicy pub grub. Outside there is a garden large enough to accommodate 100 seats which serves summer barbecues of Indian kebabs, grills and tandooris on platters alongside pitchers of beer. Chef Trepan Singh Rawat produces competent Indian food. His Murgh Makhni Paneer and Biriani was above average, with a medium price tag. (Avg pp: £22.5). House Wine: £12 Hours: Weekdays: 11:30 - 15:00 / 18:00 - 23:00 Weekends: 18:00 - 22:45 <dockmastersindianrestaurant.co.uk>

SPICE MERCHANTS **NEW ENTRANT**

38 Salter Street, E14 020 7987 8779

'A recently opened restaurant, managed by Mr Uddin, previously of the Tale of India across the West India Dock Road. A very pleasant environment, with most tables on the first floor for a slightly better view, and an interesting variety of dishes, including a good value (£8.95) fixed price 2 course lunch menu, and in the last couple of months a seasonal (£14.95) lunch menu with some dishes not presented on their à-la-carte. Recommended.' SH.*'Although it was a busy Friday night the friendly helpful waiters moved things around to accommodate us. Nothing was to much for them. The contemporary decor was non the less warm and inviting. The food was equally inspiring. The popadoms were fresh, thin and crisp. Starters of Salmon Tikka (£4.95) , Chingri puree a sort of prawn puree (£3.45) and Mish Mash a mixed kebab dish(£4.95), all excellent. Main dishes of e Xacuti chicken, Karaki Lamb, King Prawn dhansak, and Goan lamb shank all excellent and around £8.00 p e r dish. The popadoms and rice were to cooked to perfection as were the side vegetables. A very pleasant experience'* IC. <www.thespicemerchants.com>

TALE OF INDIA

53 West India Dock Rd, E14 020 7987 3418

Seats forty diners in air-conditioned comfort. Check out the interesting starters which include: Cauliflower Pakora, Iribeesi Baja – runner beans fried with onions and Fish Bora – salmon, mixed with fresh coriander and onions, lightly spiced and deep-fried with egg and breadcrumbs. Main courses are just as exciting: Shathkora Bhuna – chicken spiced and flavoured with shathkora, a sour citrus fruit, Rezalla – tikka cooked in sauce of yoghurt and green chilli and Dal Samber – vegetables and lentils lavishly flavoured with garlic and butter. Delivery: 3 miles, £10 minimum. Lunch to 2.30 weekdays and dinner to 11.30.

London E15

Stratford

SPICE INN

22 Romford Road, E15 020 8519 1399

'Dark interior, tasteful Indian drawings on walls. Swift and polite service, but lacks interpersonal skills. Mixed Kebab – sheik kebab, chicken and lamb tikka, reshmi kebab, all very well spiced and delicious, but lukewarm. Methi Gosht – best I've had since the untimely demise of the Shish Mahal in Dumbarton, but again warm. Nevertheless very, very good. £17 for food plus 2 pints Cobra.' DP.

London E18

Redbridge, S. Woodford, Woodford

MEGHNA GRILL

219 Woodford High Rd, E18 020 8504 0923

Siddiqur Rahman's long-established (1971), competent Bangladeshi curry house. It's one of those places which is always busy. Says it all really. For those who don't eat curry (they won't be reading this then) let them eat chips, as Marie Antoinette didn't say. But the Meghna serve them and Roast Chicken. But I'd plump for the Tikka Duck or Bangladeshi Fish-on-the-bone, myself. Half price Mondays if you book. Home delivery and takeaway.

THE ROSE

65 Woodford High Rd, E18 020 8989 8726

The Rose has been operated for 25 years by Messrs Miah and Hoque, who offer all the favourite tandooris and curries at sensible prices. The media often ask the editors for flock-wallpapered venues, presumably so that they can make disparaging remarks about curry. Well the flock went and the food got better. *'Food delicious, service exemplary, as ever'* says SSTC. *'Chef's Rallwa – chicken or lamb tikka with prawns, keema and spring onions in ginger sauce, very tasty. Generous portions and rice served in little china dishes (Villeroy and Bosch) with matching lids.'* SSTC. Be more adventurous and try the Garlic Mussels on Puri – mussels cooked in a garlic, red onion and white wine sauce, served on a puri. 20% discount on collected takeaways. Lunch to 2.30pm. Dinner to 11.30pm.

London EC

Area: The City of London
Postcodes: EC1 to EC4
Population: 145,000

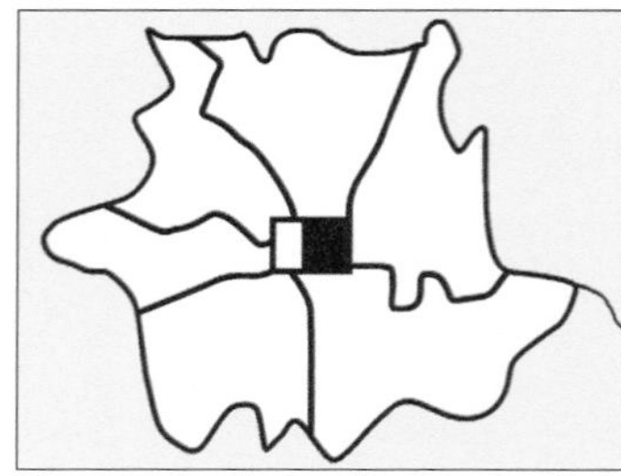

See page 109 for key to this map.

London EC1

Angel, Barbican, Clerkenwell, Farringdon, Old Street, Smithfield

ANAKANA

Olivers Yard, City Rd, EC1 0845 262 5262

'Street-food' is the new thing on new trendy venue's menus, whatever street-food means. I take it to mean Indian items you purchase from kerbside vendors, and since you can purchase just about anything in this manner, I am still not able to define it in terms of the UK . Chef Simon Koo's definition is 'small-eats' and I guess that is OK. Except aren't starters small-eats? And in any case India does not have a concept of 'starters".such as Bhel Puri (qv). The other new thing on the block is the bar aimed at the pre-married, pre-mortgaged young workers in employment and affluence. The bar here is pink and alluring to such wallets who think nothing of paying heartily for cocktails and 'small-eats' such as mini tandoori quail and mini utthapam (south Indian pancakes). Those with a heartier appetite go to the rear and share table with other happy diners, happy because we have received such reports from the. They like Mr Koo's cooking. Menu Snapshot: A version of Patrani Maachli (seabass wrapped in banana leaves) a green vegetable biriyani, and char-grilled cuttlefish / black ink pilau are original. Char-grilled red pepper stuffed with vegetables. Pre CocaCola India's major fizzy drink brand was the cutely misspelled Thums Up, and it's here. Not cheap if you go for the works (about £90 for two for a starter cocktail and small-eat followed by a meal with beer and tip. Hours: Mon-Sat 11.30 - 11 / Sun -10.30. Bar Sun-Wed -12/Thur-Sat -2.

CAFE GULSHAN

33 Charterhouse Square, Barbican, EC1
020 7600 7277

'A large restaurant, a very pleasant building in an excellent location. We had been there twice before, not long after it opened. We were always happy enough with the food but something was missing. This time it was different from the moment we stepped through the door. We were welcomed immediately, shown to an upstairs table, (before we had always been ushered downstairs even though upstairs was not full), promptly handed menus and wine list and generally given the impression that the whole place was much more professional. Apparently the owner is the same but the whole staff has changed, with a 'proper chef', keen waiters and an ambitious manager who has already made changes and has plans for more. The menu has a few less common items, unfortunately no fish except the usual prawns and a crab dish. The food was very good, portions generous and prices very fair for central London. Very good to find an Indian restaurant with a better wine list and offering espresso coffee. Coffee is usually a dreadful let down in Indian restaurants. Unfortunately there wasn't a single Indian dessert. Perhaps they will offer these in the future if the improvements continue as planned.' HC.

CARDAMOM ROOMS

NEW ENTRANT

33 Charterhouse Sq, EC1 020 7600 7277

Launched by brothers, Jay and Sal Abedin , India meets Thailand in this new (2005) 140-cover restaurant. It is airy and spacious, combining dark wood floors and black marble with shades of cream, crimson and chocolate. Large round tables encourage a social dining experience. Chef Himmat Singh (ex Cinnamon Club) offer the Indian menu with signature dishes including Muglai Rost Gosht, slow-cooked lamb shank with whole spices and onion in a tomato and cashew based sauce. Chef Saowanee Franklin delivers the Thai menu, with dishes such as Plah Neung Si-ew, steamed whole sea bass with soya sauce, chilli, ginger and spring onions. *Puja Vedi, Ed, Tandoori Magazine.*

A warm welcome at the Cardamom Rooms

COCONUT LAGOON

A-LIST

7 – 21 Goswell Road, EC1 020 7253 4546

This new 160 seat branch from the owners of the original Coconut Lagoon restaurants in Kenilworth and Stratford upon Avon, is located in alongside a decent hotel, so check in, fill up and flop out in bed. The restaurant is decorated in the company style, displaying the bright colours so redolent of South India. For those who need a restaurant that can serve a decent dinner before curtain up at the Barbican theatre, this place is for you. *'I was walking around the Barbican and couldn't believe my luck. Very large, decor is almost over the top, very colourful, masses of silk flowers, some arrangements with mock parrots in them, cane furniture, all very eye catching. The menu is Southern Indian, which made a very pleasant change and all the food comes plated on colourful plates. The main courses are good value as all come complete with the rice and vegetable the chef thinks appropriate. The food was very good and very attractively presented. There is a pretheatre menu for £12.95, particularly good value with a reasonable choice. We saw from the menu that its sister restaurant is one of the* **TOP 100,** *this one certainly deserves to be and will no doubt become so. Service was excellent, all the waiters in Nehru style suits, all very friendly, helpful and professional. It is an upmarket Indian restaurant and the whole meal was a wonderful experience. Stuffed Roti for starter – served with a silver paper, frilled holder, like one end of a cracker, very attractive and practical. Wonderful Stuffed Pomfret with Prawns. One of the best Parathas I have ever had. Large piece of Halwa dessert, very good served with pretty slices of kiwi and cream.'* HC. For discerning diners who enjoy excellence, albeit at a price, you'll be pleased to hear that we've awarded this and the owners' other restaurants our Award for the Best Group of Restaurants. See Coconut Lagoon, Kenilworth, Warwickshire for full menu details. Lunch-2.30. Dinner 5-11, daily. *See pages 78 and 80..*

CURRY LEAF

NEW ENTRANT

20 City Road, EC1 020 7374 4842

Curry Leaf opened in 2004 and is owned by S. Rehman, T. Ali, P. Chowdhery, and S. Sohail who between them for the past 30 years own twelve other top-end restaurants across London. This 120-cover restaurant is pretty and modern, with an intimate 15-seat bar/lounge area, a 25-seat balcony and the main dining area (70 seats) on the ground level. There is also a basement, with a private 35-seat room. The walls are noticeably bare and the only obvious embellishment is the arched Burma teak beams, which coordinate with the curved-back chairs and give the restaurant a bit of flair. The illuminated glass panel at the back of the restaurant enhances the chic simplicity and the generous space between tables again emphasises the minimalism of the eatery, while allowing the diners a bit of privacy during their meal to a backdrop of Indian classical music. The bar area also projects a contemporary vibe, with comfortable bar stools for a small group of people and dim lighting to create a cool atmosphere for diners. The man behind the food, Executive Chef, Ramu Sharma trained in Dehradun's School of Food and Arts and worked for Moti Mahal group of restaurants in Delhi (see London W1) before moving to London. He has emphasised the cuisine on north India, with regional dishes from across India peppered into the menu. Ones to try include Sikandari Raan, which is a leg of spring lamb soaked overnight in run marinade and oven-cooked, Allepey Seafood Curry, which is a mixture of seafood stewed in coconut milk with shredded ginger soured with raw mangoes and Lamb Hyderabadi Biryani. *Puja Vedi, Ed, Tandoori Magazine.* . <www.curryleaf.co.uk>

INDIA — NEW ENTRANT

182 St John Street — 020 7490 8295

After a wealth of family restaurant experience stretching back to the Shangri La in London's East End in 1967, Harun Khan, who owns four restaurants in the Chingford area and one in Upminster. has opened this 80 seater restaurant, India in Clerkenwell. The downstairs Saffron Bar is run by Mark Powers, former Saudi Royal family butler then beverage manager at the St James Club. The chef came from Chutney Mary and this reflects in the menu. Reports please.

SEMA INDIAN BALTI — U BYO

141 White Cross Street, EC1 — 020 7253 2927

Proprietor, Abdul Khalique Choudhury says he'll provide the glasses, you just BYO at his friendly 25 seater. He tells us Chicken Jalfrezi Balti £5.75 including a Nan bread is his most popular dish,probably because all Balti dishes come with a free Nan bread. Interesting starters : Liver Hazri £2, I can hear screeches of 'yuk' but liver curries very well. Semi Balti Soup £1.75. Main courses: Ginger Chicken, Chicken Tikka Pepper Balti and Nan around a fiver. Set lunch: £5.50, set dinner: £6.40. Delivery: 1 mile, £10 minimum Takeaway: 10% discount. Lunch to 2.30pm. Dinner to 11.30pm.

SMITHFIELD'S TANDOORI

4 Lindsey Street, EC1 — 020 7606 3868

"The decor has had a complete facelift. The menu is fairly standard and the prices are on the low side for central London, but the portions are average and the cooking well above average. Had Tandoori King Prawns, a meal I haven't had for years. The prawns were gorgeous, well spiced, moist, small areas of burned tandoori patches, lots of sizzling onions. Full marks – they had several Indian sweets – I had Gulab Jamun, served warm, lovely. Danny made to feel welcome even though he wasn't eating. An unplanned and unexpected Indian meal turned out to be a real pleasure. Service really good, particularly one waiter who really added to the evening. HC.

SONIA BALTI HOUSE

1 Lever Street, EC1 — 020 7253 3398

Brisk takeaway trade. Service is very homely and friendly. Very tender and tasty Sheek Kebab £1.95, with a cool crisp salad and very yellow and garlicky yoghurt sauce. Lamb Taba Gosht £5.95 – rather tough lamb in well spiced and appetising, but thin gravy. Very doughy Garlic Nan £1.40.' RW. No credit cards. Takeaway: 10% discount. Delivery: £10 minimum. Hours: 5.30 to 12.

London EC2

Barbican, City, Liverpool Street, Moorgate

MEHEK

45 London Wall, EC2 — 020 7588 5043

A pretty Indian girl, who takes coats etc, shares space with a comfortable leather sofa (for the takeaway customer) and a clutch of tables. An extremely long bar leads to more tables at the back. Throughout our visit, suited men, men and more men arrived. Some perched themselves on high stools, drank pints of beer and talked loudly while crunching on woven metal baskets piled high with Popadoms. We were swiftly seated and passed menus. However, all chutneys and no pickle, cachumber or raitha does make quite dull eating. From the short menu, we chose a starter of Bhalla Papria Chaat – light, fluffy buns of fermented and steamed rice flour, smothered in natural yoghurt and imli which were quite plain. I decided on a firm vegetarian favourite, Aloo Tikki. Three nicely shaped patties of spiced potato and green peas were delivered with salad and yoghurt dip. The main course Achari Gosht £12.50 – tender lamb, mildly spiced, was too sweet for us both. Madri Murgh £12, a new twist on CTM, this dish contained Vodka (and that's why I ordered it!). Side dishes of Jaipuri Bhindi £5, diagonal slices of okra, deep-fried in a very light batter of besan and sprinkled, too sparingly, in my opinion, with mango powder and kala namak. Though still a good dish. Our benchmark Dal Makhni was £5. I try this one everywhere I go. It was well cooked, creamy, not over salted, wonderful. While we ate, our waitress 'stalked' our table. I strongly object to this habit. She could have chatted to the coats girl, who wasn't doing anything, except for, of course, flirting with the floor manager. He took delight in showing off like a peacock in front of her reception desk. While, she in turn, giggled and fluttered her long, well mascared eye lashes at him in appreciation. In between his performances, he stood on the pavement outside, glancing left and right as if about to cross the road. In fact, he went no where, he just stood and smoked. The Sommelier was also at a loose end. He constantly returned to our table to fill our drinking receptacles, very annoying and quite rude. You should not overfill a glass, wine needs to breath. After a short rest and totally unlike our normal eating habits, we decided to indulge in a pudding. HC will be over the moon – real Indian sweets on offer. We shared Dudhi (marrow) Halwa. Service charge at 12.5% was added to our bill and the credit card slip was returned, closed – congrats! Food OK. Staff need training. Lunch and dinner.

London EC3

Aldgate, Fenchurch Street, Tower of London

KASTURI — **BEST IN LONDON**

57 Aldgate High St, EC3 — 020 7480 7402

Nur Monie's Tanjore, Welling, Kent has been in our **TOP 100** for ages. In late 2002 he teamed up

with Bashir Ahmed (owner of five popular Kohinoor restaurants in Holland) to open their 80-seater Kasturi. It has the current look of blonde wood floor, bright lights, colourful walls and pot plants. Management tell us, Kasturi means *'the strong scented secretion found in rare musk deer, used in expensive perfumes'.* Phew! I don't know about that, but the scent of the tandoor is more likely to be encountered. Kasturi has an ace up its sleeve – Chef Rajandra Balmiki, head chef at The Tangore. He trained at the Delhi's Mauyra Sheraton Hotel, under chef Imtiaz Qureshi of Dum Pukht fame and former training chef, the highly respected C.P Rahman. Maurya has the best Tandoori restaurant in the world. What a background for Balmiki. Kasturi claims to specialise in Pakhtoon cuisine. It's a far cry from Delhi and Welling. It refers to the tribal people of Afghanistan from the rugged mountain passes in the former North-West Frontier Province, whose name for themselves is Pathan, Pashtun, Phuktana or Pukhtun. Afghan food is pretty basic (*see pages* 66 & 73), especially at tribal level, involving kebab-skewer cooking and slow-cooking in pots. Grills, Kebabs, Koftas and Birianis are popular, spiced with the unique Afghan spice mix, Char Masala (four aromatic spices) and cooked mostly in their own juices. Try the Kebab Ke Karishma, a selection of kebabs. It includes Chicken, Lamb and Minced meat kebabs. Served as a starter for two persons with special bread: £10.95. Kadak kebab Samarkand – minced lamb roll stuffed with cheese and grilled.. Then there's Mahi-e-Ghazni – whole pomfret fish marinated in fresh coriander and mint and roasted in the Tandoor £9.95, or Grilled Seabass – marinated in a sauce of yoghurt and olive oil with black and white pepper £10.95. Any of the Biryanis will 'blow you away'. HEG. Our benchmark Dal-Dera Ismail Khan – 'A harmonious combination of black dal and herbs, simmering on slow charcoal fire' (aka Dal Makhani) is just £3.50. Kasturi has attracted rave reviews from our reporters But such a menu and such a skilled Indian chef will of course bring adverse comments from what Monie calls *'those with their brains closed'.* He's prepared for it, and he offers them formula curries. [How sad.] We're prepared for it too, and have no hesitation in saying if it's formula that you want go to nearby Brick Lane and enjoy it. Takeaway and Delivery. Hours: 11-11 weekdays. 5.30 -11.30 Saturdays. Closed Sundays. <www.kasturi-restaurant.co.uk>

MATAB'S

76 Aldgate High Street, EC3 020 7481 4010

Owned by the personable Matab Choudhury, one of the prime movers and Chief Treasurer of the Bangladeshi Caterers Association, this restaurant in some way acts as a flagship and example to the 12,000 other restaurants which the BCA quotes as its membership. One is struck by the vibrant wall paintings and ceilings, with contrasting crisp white tablecloths, King's cutlery and wooden floor. The deft service provides all the old favourites that one has come to expect of the Bangladeshi formula curry venue. And it is a favourite haunt of many a city regular, of which VW-P and LD-W are two.

PLANTERS INN

25 Great Tower Street, EC3 020 7621 1214

The original owners named this venue after Bangladesh's major industry, tea planting. Of the 138 tea estates in Bangladesh, 128 are in Sylhet. Now under new management with partners Vernon Menezes, a personable Goan, formerly of Zaika and Chor Bizarre Chef Joydeep Chatterjee, from Calcutta and formerly chef of Ophim and Pitts Cottage. The 64-seater, opposite the Tower of London, is uncluttered, with white walls, mirrors, polished wood, tiled floor and potted glossy palm trees which divide the tables. The restaurant gets busy at lunchtime with suited City folk grabbing a served-within-the-hour quick lunch before resuming their afternoon business. *'Different atmosphere in the evening. I like both, and I like the food. It's not your typical curry house.'* RCF.

RAJASTHAN

49 Monument Street, EC3 020 7626 1920

'Closest to my work, occasionally go at lunchtimes. Packed with city workers, so specialise in getting you in and out quickly. Good fast service, nice decor and food varies from OK to pretty good. Duck Pineapple, very nice, enjoyably unusual. Obviously priced to reflect that it's in the city, although not bad.' NP. Bhuna £9, silver pomfret, marinated, medium sauce. Air conditioned. Menu extracts: Tangri Kebab £3.50, marinated chicken drumstick, tandooried. Lamb Rezala £8 – lamb tikka, hot, tangy sauce, fresh green chillies, coconut and tomatoes. Roop Chanda – a Bangladeshi fish dish. Lunch to-3pm. Dinner to-11pm., daily.

London N

Area: North London
Postcodes: N1 to N22
Population: 1,250,000

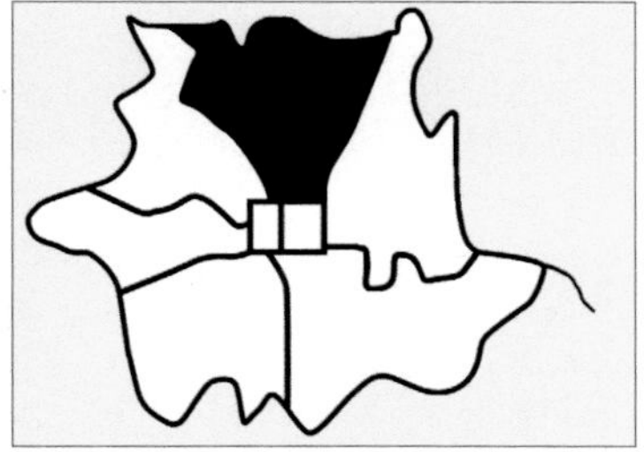

See page 109 for key to this map.

London N1

Islington, King's Cross, Shoreditch

AFGHAN KITCHEN

NEW TO OUR TOP 100

35 Islington Green, N1 020 7359 8019

Then there was one (UK Afghan restaurant) with the demise of Caravan Serai since our last edition. Or so we thought, then lo there are two, nay, three, and with our new-found relationship with that country they may be more to come. (*see also page* 49). Afghani food is Muslim, big on Halal goat (here they use lamb) and goat's milk. Yoghurt always accompanies a meal. Try Dogh – Savoury Yoghurt with mint, and the Tourshis or chutneys. The food is less spicy than Indian, but the names are similar. Bread isn't Naan, it is Nane Lawash – thinner, glazed and basket-shaped. Qurma is Korma, etc, etc. *'Not knowing anything about Afghan food, four of us were delighted to find that it bore a close resemblance to Indian with the Murgh Kofta – chicken meat balls in sauce, Gosht Qurma, a type of meat Korma, Suzhi Gosht – meat with spinach spiced with Char Masasa (a four-spice version of India's Garam Masala), each £4.50 with the bread as the staple, chilli pickle to liven up the delicate spicing, house wine to wash to it all down.'* GR. Small menu. No credit cards. Average spend £9. Hours: 12pm-12am Tues.-Sat.

INDIAN VEG BHEL POORI HOUSE

92 Chapel Market, N1 020 7837 4607

'Although I have sung the praises of the excellent value eighteen buffet dishes e-a-m-a-y-l £2.95, I feel I must praise it again. I now lunch there once a week and the quality is always consistent. Occasionally there is a superb mashed potato and onion curry. Always a friendly welcome and my half lager is now brought automatically.' TN. *'All the dishes are superb, and I'm no veggie. The Bhel Puri is still my favourite though.'* ME. Hours: 12-11.30.

MASALA ZONE

A-LIST

80 Upper Street, N1 020 7359 3399

This is the second of five Masala Zones. They are a clever idea from a clever family. Briefly it is basic food, but cooked as if it is at the Indian food. You can't reserve, and it is inexpensive. Hard in fact to exceed £15 per head (more with wine). You won't find better real Indian food at such prices. Mon-Fri 12 -3, 5.30-11.30; Sat, Sun 12-11. *See page* 28, SW5 & W1..

PARVEEN

6 Theberton Street, N1 020 7226 0504

Established 1977 and seating 60 diners on two floors. It's now an air-conditioned, contemporary restaurant, decorated in bright colours – turquoise, red, royal blue, canary yellow. Polished blonde wooden floor, spot lights and marbled bar. You'll find the curry formula done well here. Here are the views of some of Parveen's many friends: *'Great decor and food that tastes authentic!'* HN. *'Faruk and staff are so amazing, makes everyone feel special. Food lovely and decor fantastic.'* JO B. *'Great food and service.'* HM. *'By far the best Indian in Islington, highly recommended.'* CR. Rupchandra £8.95 and Lamb Pasanda £7.95 are regular favourites. Set dinner £33.95 for two. Hours: 12-3 and 6-12.

RAJ MONI

279 Upper Street, N1 020 7354 1270

Small, about fifty covers, pleasantly decorated. *'Prompt service. Standard menu – Silsila Masala Chicken and Afgani Chicken new to me. Started with Rajmoni Special which was basically Chicken Chat – good portion, nicely spiced with tender chicken, OK, but nothing special. Main course – Chicken Tikka, good portion, 10 pieces, served on sizzler; Madras Curry Sauce – nice and hot; Plain Rice – generous portion, light and fluffy. Standard formula curry house.'* DB. Lunch and dinner daily. Delivery evenings only.

ZEN SATORI RESTAURANT AT THE ASIAN AND ORIENTAL SCHOOL OF CATERING

40 Hoxton Street, N1. 020 7613 9590

Named after the Buddhist term for enlightenment, Zen Satori is designed to do just that. Opened by

Zen Zatori, N1

The Asian and Oriental School of Cookery in September 2002, the restaurant offers a selection in Chinese, Indian and Thai cuisine prepared, cooked and served by its students. Located just off fashionable Hoxton Square, the school was set up in 1998 as a response to a catering industry report that revealed a skills gap in the ethnic food industry and an urgent need to address the issue. The school provides training in all aspects of the restaurant trade. Students are taught practical cooking techniques in a fully equipped kitchen that features the best in ethnic catering equipment, most of which was donated by companies in the industry that were keen to help the school. The courses have been designed by the industry experts, and provide students with real skills by using a combination of expert knowledge, demonstration and hands-on practice. The board of the school involves well-known restaurateurs like Holland Kwok of the Good Earth Group, Antique Choudhury of Yum Yum and Cyrus Todiwala MBE of Cafe Spice Namaste.

'The trendy ground floor restaurant offers a unique Asian eating experience. Diners enter into a light and relaxed area where they can enjoy the bar. The drinks menu features an international selection of wines with recommendations on food and wine pairing. It also features a wide selection of both alcoholic and non-alcoholic drinks. The long, open restaurant offers three types of seating: traditional fine dining, contemporary refectory seating or an area where diners can enjoy the activity in the open kitchen. The menu is fun, exotic and diverse. It is great value for money, as the prices are very low for the quality of food and service. The reason being is that it is a training ground for the students where they can learn to cook quality food for paying customers. And it is worth every penny! Starters like Tom Yum with lemon grass and coriander, Mysore Bonda (deep-fried potato cake served with coconut chutney) and spicy Oriental spring rolls is like having three different cuisines under one roof! Main course and dessert are equally good, with food from across Asia. But if eating here is not enough for you then you can even learn how to cook the food on the menu by joining one of their evening classes at the school.' Puja Vedi, Ed, Tandoori Magazine. The School has already successfully placed several hundred people in employment and handles up to 800 students a year on a range of courses with a time-span of anything from an afternoon to three years. Zen Satori restaurant is split into a 'fine-dining' area

Zen Zatori, N1

and casual section situated close to the bar area. The open kitchen enables diners to watch the fledgling chefs working tandoori ovens, flaming woks and hot grills. Manager Leon Zhang has an ever-changing team of young, enthusiastic floor staff, the school's students, who have reached a certain standard before beginning a spell in Zen Satori. Hoxton Street gained notoriety when a certain Jamie opened his own restaurant at no 15. Why go there when you can enjoy the output of youthful students, keen to impress their first real customers, at far more reasonable prices. Lunch Mon to Friday. Dinner, Tuesdays to Saturdays. Closed Sundays Hours differ, so ring to check.

London N2

East Finchley

COCHIN — NEW ENTRANT

111 High Rd, N2 — 020 8444 5666

This South Indian & vegetarian restaurant serves all the dishes you'd expect for such a menu. Thali set meal from £8.95. A-la-carte meal for two with wine and service: around £60. Hours: 12-2.30/6-11.30.

MAJJOS

1 Fortis Green, N2 — 020 8883 4357

Established in 1993 by Mrs Ashraf. Manager S Mogul. A shop with a seating area for just 10 diners, so you can enjoy some spicy dishes while shopping for your Indian groceries. Kashmiri, Pakistani and Indian food. Great prices: Meat curries £5.50 or £4. Veg curries £3.50 or £2.30 Hours: 10.30am-10.30pm (10pm on Sun.).

London N3

Finchley, Fortis Green

RANI VEGETARIAN

PREVIOUS AWARD WINNER — TOP 100

7 Long Lane, N3 — 020 8349 4386

Jyoti Patni is front of house in this venue tastefully decorated in shades of turmeric and red, with Georgian chairs and glass-topped tables. Rani means Queen, and the term could as well refer to the cooks, Jyoti's wife and his mother, because their Gujarati vegetarian food cannot be bettered anywhere. The menu features mainly Gujarati items which are tasty enough to please all but the most obdurate non-veggie. India's most western state, Gujarat, is the home of mild, slightly sweet dishes, with a love of yoghurt and gram flour. The soup-like curry Khadi is one dish showing Gujarati adoration of both. The famous bhajia also originated in Gujarat, as did the lesser known Dahi Vada, a gram flour dumpling in a tangy yoghurt sauce. Kachoris – Spicy mashed potato and peas spicy ball, coated in batter and deep-fried. Bhel Puri are all there along with Gujarati curries e.g. Undui – five vegetable stew, and a Gujarati national dish. Traditionally the five vegetables are beans, aubergine, red pumpkin, sweet potato and a further vegetable. These are cooked in a sauce made from gram flour, asafoetida and yoghurt. It is often served with besan kofta balls in it. Another superb dish is Lasan Bateta, literally garlic potato, but it's not that simple, it is baby new potatoes, and the stuffing includes spices and red chilli.the whole is dipped in gram-flour batter, deep-fried and served in imli (sweet tamarind chutney). Wow!!! Innovations to prevent diner boredom make this restaurant different. How about pizzas (which are after all just Naan bread cooked in the oven) with Indo-Italian toppings, such as banana (plantain) methi with green chilli and mozzarella. Great stuff. And they are innovations retaining the ethos of Indian, rather than fusion food which does not. *'The menu has some cold starters which are "to die for". Rashia Vall, great. Rice and breads as good as usual.'* CT. Says the highly critical RL: *'Menu includes unusual and tasty dishes. Recommended to me by so many people. Aloo Shai Poori (crispy pooris, potatoes, onions with yoghurt) and Vall Papri (spicy beans and onions on pooris with tamarind and yoghurt), both a taste of heaven. This restaurant is pure quality. It's world class.'* RL. Sunday lunch 12.15-2.30. Dinner 6-10.30 daily.

London N4

Stroud Green

JAI KRISHNA

161 Stroud Green Road, N4 — 7272 1680

Vegetarian food and the quality is good. *'The set-menu feast* (£6.75 for 2 courses) *s home-style, plentiful and wonderful.'* RL. An added advantage is that it is **BYO**. Cash only and the WC is accessed from outside the venue. Hours: 12-2/ 5.30-11 Mon-Sat

London N7

Tufnell Park

BENGAL BALTI HOUSE

6 Brecknock Road, N7 020 7609 7075

A popular haunt in the area owned by Ashik Ali since 1994. This air-conditioned restaurant seats 86 in two rooms, serves all the favourites, *'with friendly panache'*. HEG. Hours: 12-2.30pm/6pm-12am (Sat. to 12.30am). Branch: Hillmarton Tandoori, Hillmarton Terrace, N7.

London N8

Crouch End, Hornsey, Turnpike Lane

MASALA DELI BAR

59 Park Road, N8 020 8442 9222

Gujarati food, predominately vegetarian, e.g.: Kachori 60p – minced peas / split mung beans in pastry balls. Patra 50p, spiced gram flour wrapped in arvi leaves. Pani Puri £2.50, six small puffed puris filled with sprouted mung beans and potato, served with tamarind and date dressing (yum yum!). Roti Wraps £1.50, bread filled with a choice of sweet corn; potato and nut; shredded cabbage with carrot and lime. Light lunches include: Tuna Thali £6, plain rice served with spicy tuna, a vegetable dish or your choice, a roti and a juice drink. Falafel Meal £3, spicy lentil fritters served with salad and dressing in pitta bread. <www.masala-uk.com> Hours: 11-9.30.

London N10

Muswell Hill

TASTE OF NAWAB

93 Colney Hatch Lane, N10 020 8883 6429

Established in 1996 the comfortable air-conditioned Nawab has all the old favourites plus exciting dishes. Owner Abdul says it all. *'If you as customers are happy, then I'm happy. If I'm happy the waiters and the cooks are happy'*. And it seems Abdul's customers really are happy. Won the local area Curry Chef Award, *'All dishes are large, reasonably priced and tasty.Service great!'* SM. Delivery: £10 minimum, 3 miles. Hours: 12-2.30/6-12am. Sunday buffet 12-5.30, eat all you can.

London N11

Friern Barnet, New Southgate

BEJOY

72 Bounds Green Road, N11 020 8888 1 2 6 8

Established 1995, Abdul Sukur's restaurant seats 54, party room 16. Bangladeshi standards cooked by chef M Rahman. Price check: Papadam 65p, CTM £6.75, Pullao Rice £1.80, Peshwari Nan £1.85. Delivery: £8 minimum, 2-mile radius. Hours: 12-2.30pm (Sat.-Thurs.)/6-12am. Sunday buffet £5.95 per person, 12-11pm. Branch: Sunderban, N4.

London N12

North Finchley, Woodside Park

FINCHLEY PAN CENTRE

15 Woodhouse Road, N12 020 8446 5497

A tiny, unlicensed Indian snack bar, frequented by Indians. Kebabs, samosas, veg rissoles, etc., very inexpensive. Friendly service. Cash please. Oh, and as for Pan or Paan, it's not a cooking vessel, it is a collection of edible ingredients, ranging from very bitter to very sweet wrapped in the paan or bright dark green paan or betel leaf. Paan is an acquired taste, used as an aid to digestion. The observant visitor to India will have noticed very busy street kiosks dispensing paan all hours. We only know of a few other Paan houses (in Asian communities such as Southall). *See page 95 for more about Paan.* Hours: 12-10pm (Fri., 3.30-10); closed Tues.

London N13

Broomfield Park, Palmers Green

DIPALI INDIAN

82 Aldermans Hill, N13 020 8886 2221

This popular restaurant has appeared in all our *Guides*. Specials: Murghi Shassle, chicken marinated in mint sauce, cooked with selected spices and topped with salad. Murghi Tamatar, chicken cooked in fresh green chilli and coriander ginger, very spicy hot. Achar Murghi, cooked with pickle, slightly hot. Sunday buffet 12-3.30. Hours: 12-2.30/6-12.

London N14

Oakwood, Southgate

BEKASH

6-8 Hampden Square, N14 020 8368 3206

Owned by Nazrul Miah (manager) and Harun Ali (chef), decorated in yellow, seats 55. Delivery. House wine £7.80. Price check: Papadam 50p, CTM £6.25, Pullao Rice £1.60. Hours: 5.30-11.30pm (Sat. to 12am).

London N15

Stoke Newington

ABI RUCHI NEW ENTRANT

42 Church Street, N15 020 7923 4564

Kerala meat, fish and shellfish, as well as vegetable dishes. *'Had Veg Pakodas (bhajias) crunch and fresh and for mains Bekal Meen Kootan, fish curry with smoked tamarind and Koonthal Masala, spiced baby squid, stuffed with tomato, pepper, coconut, and chilli. Friendly helpful service.'* BD. 2 courses et lunch £5.95, vegetarian), £7.50, non-veg. House wine £9. Hours; 12-3/6-11 Mon-Thur; to 11.45 Fri/Sat; 1-10.15 on Sun.

London N16

Stoke Newington

RASA A-LIST

55 Church Street, N16 020 7249 0344

Shiva Das Sreedharan's and his wife Alison's first restaurant. He worked at a Delhi hotel before coming to England to manage a small restaurant. Believing he could do things better, he set up this restaurant in 1994 in this then unfashionable street serving then unfashionable south Indian vegetarian food. Thanks to enthusiasts like Das, we know that there is so much more to Keralan food than Masala Dosas. Rasa chefs are expert vegetarian cooks. Cooking uses coconut, mustard, curry leaves, curds, chillies, lentils and rice. Exotic vegetables include plantains, drumsticks, gourds, sour mango, and beans. The differences between the cooking of the five Kerelan groups is intensely subtle, including the names of the similar dishes. But differences there are, so try it out. Ask managers Usha or Bhaskar or the staff for advice. Favourites include Nair Dosa – a Keralan speciality, usually eaten during festivals and celebrations. A rice and black gram flour pancake filled with a mixture of

Paan

potatoes, beetroot, carrot, onions and ginger, served with sambar and fresh coconut chutney, c£6. Chef Narayanan's signature dish is the Rasa Kayi, a mixed vegetable speciality from the Southern State of Karnataka. A spicy curry made of beans, carrots, cauliflower, potatoes and simmered in a sauce of garlic, ginger and fennel, c£4. Cheera Curry is Paneer and spinach cooked with garlic, peppers and tomato in a creamy sauce, c£3. For pudding, if you have room, try Banana Dosa, the Palakkad Iyer (Brahmin) speciality with a difference. These tiny pancakes are made from bananas, plain flour and cardamom. Lots of reports. Most love the food and are happy with the service. An added extension has not really helped its being crowded. Like adding a lane to the M25, it simply fills up again. It's the problem of being popular. Sun to Thurs: 6–10.45. Fri, Sat to 11.30. Saturday/Sunday Lunch: 12– 3. Service: 12.5%. <www.rasarestaurants.com>

RASA TRAVANCORE — A-LIST

56 Church Street, N16 — 020 7249 1340

This recent Rasa is nearly opposite the original at 55 (*see above*). You can't miss it. The colour is the key. Das just loves pink – the hue that is blackcurrant yoghurt. It's the colour of his venue frontages, decor, menu and his web site. So why this new venue? We normally think of Kerala as a vegetarian state. In fact there have been passionate non-vegetarians – Muslims, Jews and Christians – living there side by side for centuries, each with a distinctive cooking style. As for the latter, St Thomas the Apostle landed in Kerala in AD50 and made many converts to Christianity. His language was Syriac Armenaic, his converts known as Syrian Christians. To this day they eat offal, chicken, duck, fish, shellfish, beef, and wild boar. Dishes with very unfamiliar names crowd the menu. A great introduction is the Travancore Feast, where you get a good selection of dishes for £20. Chicken Puffs, spicy chicken masala stuffed in puff pastry are frankly Anglo Indian Raj stuff, but they're great stuff, £3.50, and eat them with Meen Achar – Chicken pickle. More traditional Syrian Christian specialities include Kerala Fish fry, £3.95, kingfish marinated in a spicy paste made of ginger, green chillies and coriander, then shallow fried in the traditional fashion. Chicken Stew, £5.25, chicken cooked in fresh coconut milk, with finely chopped ginger, green chillies and flavoured with cinnamon, cardamom, cashewnut and raisins. Erachi Olathiathu, £6.95, cubes of lamb and dry cooked in turmeric water, then stir-fried in an open kadai with an abundance of black pepper, curry leaves, and finely sliced fresh coconut slivers. Tharavu roast, £6.95, duck cooked in a thick sauce with ginger, garlic, onion and coriander. Rasa in Sanskrit means amongst other things, taste, flavour, liking, pleasure, delight and essence. There is so much more. The venue is managed by Jinu and Mustafa. Let them and the staff guide you. Hours: as Rasa alongside. Branches: previous entry, and London NW1, and W1.

London N19

Archway, Tufnell Park, Upper Holloway

PARSEE — A-LIST

34 Highgate Hill, N19 — 020 7272 9091

The Parsee is the his brain child of one of our longest correspondents, Dr CF. It was set up in a failing curry house with Cyrus Todiwalla, himself a Parsee.(*see page 8*). This is the only authentic Parsee restaurant outside Mumbai, (where Cyrus and the largest Parsee population come from). Even there it's hard to find. I know of only six where Parsi food appears amongst other cuisines (such as Italian), though probably the best is the improbably named Strand Coffee House on Colaba. Authentic delights here in N19 include Akoori on Toast, scrambled eggs on toast spiced with chilli and garlic. Papeta Na Pattis, mashed potato cakes filled with green peas, grated coconut, chopped nuts and spices, rolled in breadcrumbs and fried, served with green coconut chutney. Keema Pao, minced lamb flavoured with garam masala, served with a warm chilli roll. Laal Masala, chops marinated in red masala of red chillies, garlic, ginger, cumin and spices, chargrilled and served with Dhaan (rice) and Daar (lentils). Haran Na Kabab, venison minced with fresh ginger, garlic, coriander and chillies, flavoured with mint and garam masala, formed over skewers and chargrilled. Patra Ni Machci, Pomfret, filetted and filled with green coconut chutney, wrapped in a banana leaf and steam baked. Sali Boti, lamb with chopped shallots, whole spices and pitted Hunza apricots, garnished with sali (straw potatoes). Khattu Mitthu Istew, green peas, carrots, cauliflower, whole baby shallots, baby potatoes, yam and sweet potato make this a delightful stew, served with Jeera Pullao if ordered as a main course. Hours: 12 to 3, Sunday only and 6 to 10.45, Sunday to 10.

London N22

Wood Green

AKBAR TAKEAWAY NEW ENTRANT

13 Salisbury Rd, N22 020 8881 7902

Chef Proprietor - Mostakin Miah (Mintu) has been running this takeaway since 1988 and his Chicken Korma and Chicken Tikka Masala literally runs out of the door, he says they are just so popular. His set dinner for £7 a person is also a favourite and consists of a Popadom, Onion Bhajia, a Chicken Curry, a Vegetable Curry, Pullao Rice and Onion Salad - good value I know we will all agree! Delivery: 2.5 miles, £7 minimum. Price Check: Popadom 25p, CTM £4.50, Pullao Rice £1.00. Is this the cheapest popadom in the Guide? Hours: 5.30 - 11.30.

London NW

Area: North West London,
Postcodes: NW1 to NW11
Population: 680,000

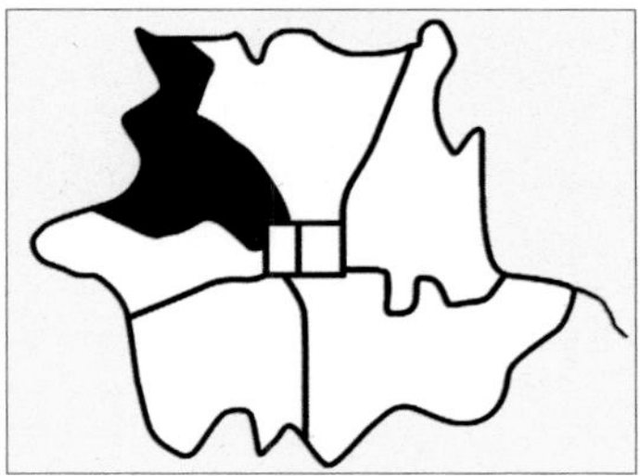

See page 109 for key to this map.

London NW1

Drummond Street, Euston

I am often asked where the best restaurants are. It's the reason for producing this Guide. Drummond Street is one such area. West of Euston Station, it will not win any beauty awards, and it lacks the ethnic glamour of Southall and Wembley, or the intensity of purpose of Brick Lane. Its assets are a concentrated selection of extremely good, mainly inexpensive Indian food vendors. There are greengrocers, a Halal butcher and ingredient stores, such as Viranis, where Pataks began trading in the 60s. It is open all hours for all things Indian including Cobra (useful for the nearby BYOs), a dozen or so takeaways and restaurants. Here in alphabetical order are your Drummond Street favourites:

AMBALA SWEET CENTRE

112 Drummond Street, NW1 020 7387 3521

Ambala started trading in 1965. It specialises in takeaway-only savoury snacks (Pakoras and Samosa, etc.), Indian sweets (Halva, Jalebi, Gulab Jamun, Barfi, etc.) and a few vegetarian curries such as chickpea. Established initially for Asians, it now has branches in Birmingham, Bradford, Derby, East Ham, Finchley, Glasgow, Leicester, Leyton, Luton, Manchester, Slough, Southall, Tooting and Wembley. All branches serve identical items at identical prices. The quality is first-class and the prices are always reasonable. Be prepared to queue, and pay cash. Open daily 10am-11pm.

CHUTNEYS

134 Drummond Street, NW1 020 7387 6077

Good vegetarian food at good prices. Lunch and dinner daily.

DIWANA BHEL POORI HOUSE
TOP 100

121 Drummond Street, NW1 020 7387 5556

It's a café-style, unlicensed, open all day, still very cheap, highly successful. 100-seat restaurant, divided into two ground-floor sections plus a further floor. The food is all vegetarian, with much vegan, and above all, it's all fabulous, and it's most certainly all authentic. Diwana pioneered Bombay pavement kiosk snack food in the UK and is undoubtedly still the best of its kind. The ownership change could have dethroned Diwana, but it has remained one of London's iconic eating-holes. *'Not to be visited for the decor, nor for a long and relaxing meal – sitting on the floor would be more comfortable than sitting on the bolted-down benches, so opt for chairs if you can. I have the same thing every time I visit, Papadam with Coconut Chutney, Rasam, a soup, whose chillies without fail give me attention-drawing hiccups, then a Dosa £3 to £4.60 depending on type, with more Coconut Chutney, with its mustard seed and chilli and Sambar. If Pat and I share, I try to get all the drumsticks before him. And of course I never miss out on one of their adorable Bhel Puris, their masthead and their most ordered dish.'* DBAC. Bhel Puri, or Poori, is defined on *page* 81. Diwana offers several types – Batata Puri, Dahi Batata Puri, Chat Aloo Papri and Batata Pava, all £2.10. Bhel can be accompanied by Gol Goppas (*see page* 88). A super alternative starter is Dahi Vada (*see page* 87). By now you've spent £5 or £6, and you're probably full. But try to leave a little space for the Diwana's desserts. Their legendary Kulfi, perhaps, or *'the highlight of our meal, the Falooda – an Indian knickerbocker glory – probably the best in London. The quality of the food outweighs the numbness in your backside!'* DB. *'All first class. Reasonably priced.'* MW. *'Consistently good quality and low prices. Never changes.'* JR. *"On one of the hottest days in July, I needed lunch in Drummond Street. I chose Diwana because of the jug of water that is automatically provided. It was too hot for alcohol and lassis is too filling when there is serious eating to be done.'* BS. *'Will certainly go back, but not for buffet.'* NP. *'The back of the bill has a questionnaire. I was pleased to tick excellent for everything.'* HC. Booking is hit and miss, and they won't even try on Fri. to Sun. so expect a queue (especially at peak hours). Great value and don't forget to **BYO** (no corkage charge). Off-license with chilled Cobra available at Viranis up the street. Thali from £4.00 to £6.00. E-a-m-a-y-l lunch to 2.30pm, £4.50. Hard to exceed £12 for a good veggie blow-out! It remains very high in our **TOP 100.** Hours: 12-11.

GUPTA CONFECTIONERS

100 Drummond Street, NW1 020 7380 1590

Overshadowed, perhaps by the nearby Ambala, Gupta is nonetheless a very good, long-established, less flashy vegetarian snack and sweet takeaway. Samosas and Pakoras, plus their unique, delightful, and often still-hot Pea Kebab, a Gujarati speciality, are freshly cooked in the kitchens behind. Their sweets achieve a lightness of touch, and seem to avoid the taste of tinned evaporated milk that sometimes spoils those made by others. Cash or cheque. Branch: Watford Way, Hendon, NW4.

RAVI KEBAB HALAL

125 Drummond Street, NW1 020 7388 1780

Not the first on the street., but one of the longest stayers (opened 1978). As the name says this is a Pakistani meat venue. 'Kebab' tells you it's very much a meat place, Halal that there's no pandering to Western tastes, as one can tell by its local mostly Muslim patronage (so no alcohol permitted). Grilled and curried meats are all there at bargain prices. There are some vegetable and dhal dishes but this is no place for the veggie. *'One of my favourites. Cheap and cheerful. Food superb. Sheek Kebabs amongst the best anywhere.'* RE.

RAVI SHANKAR

133 Drummond Street, NW1 020 7388 6458

Vegetarian restaurant similar to the Diwana which it followed into Drummond Street. Prices are still very reasonable and it is usually busy at peak hours. Recommended are the two Thali set dishes, the Mysore and the Shankar, and the Shrikand dessert. *'Every dish was excellent – flavoursome, spicy and delicious. Prices are extremely reasonable.'* MW Daily specials at under £4. Hours: 12pm-11pm. Branches: Chutneys, and Haandi, both on Drummond Street.

Elsewhere in NW1

Camden Town, Chalk Farm, Marylebone, Regent's Park

CAFE INDIYA

71 Regents Park Road, NW1 020 7722 5225

Seats 28 in two rooms. We hear of Goan Fish Curry with coconut milk, £7.95, and Chicken

Xacutti £7.25, fairly hot. Sabziyon Ki Shaslick £5.95, fresh vegetables, marinated in a special tandoori sauce and grilled in the clay oven. Paneer Simla Mirch £3.25, medium spiced stir-fry of homemade cottage cheese, green peppers and fresh tomatoes. Service: 10%. Hours: 12-2.30 (Saturday only) and 5.30 Saturday 6.00) to 11.30. Sunday 12-11.30.

GREAT NEPALESE
BEST NEPALESE AWARD & TOP 100

48 Eversholt Street, NW1 020 7388 6737

Started by Gopal P Manandhar in 1982, this Nepalese restaurant has stood the test of time, Chef is son Jeetendra, whose charming wife Mandira also adds her culinary expertise, especially with Nawari (an Nepalese ethnic group) food, for example the starter, Momo, or Momocha – steam-cooked meat-filled pastries, £4. Other Nepalese specialities include Masco Bara, black lentil pancakes with curry sauce £4, Kalezo Ra Chyow (chicken liver). Main courses include Dumba (mutton), Pork Bhutwa (the Nepalese have no proscriptions of either pork or alcohol) and Hach Ko (duck) curries. There is also a range of eleven Nepalese vegetable dishes. Add those to sixteen 'standard' curry house vegetable dishes and the vegetarian will be spoilt for choice. In addition, the Great does all the standard curries and tandooris, from Phal, 'very very hot', to Shahi Korma, 'very very mild', though why you'd go there for these is beyond me. Go for Nepalese food, and if virgin to it, ask the staff to explain. Ask Ghopla for a shot of Coronation rum. Brewed in 1975 in Katmandu, its bottle is kukri-shaped, its contents lethal. Set Nepalese meal £14. Service 10%. Average spend: £15. Takeaway: 10% discount. Delivery: £12 minimum 5-miles. Hours: 5.30 - 11.30. Sat. to 12.

RASA EXPRESS

327 Euston Road, NW1 020 7387 8974

Rasa Express is a simple, inexpensive, no fuss brand, and clearly the pilot (along with the wI Rasa Express) for a franchise operation nationwide. It's fast food with just seven items on the menu at prices ranging from £1.50 to £2.95. In the latter category are Mysore Bonda – Potato balls laced with ginger, curry leaves, coriander cashew nuts and mustard seeds, dipped in besan batter and crisply fried. Fish Cutlet, spiced cassava and tuna breadcrumbed and Veg Samosa, all served with coconut chutney. Top of the bill is the Rasa Lunch Box, two curries, a stir-fried vegetable dish, bread, rice and sweet of the day. Monday to Friday: 12.3 . Credit cards: over £15. Branches: *Rasa London N16, W1 and Rasa Express, 5 Rathbone Street, W1T*

London NW3

Belsize Park, Hampstead, Finchley Road, Swiss Cottage

BOMBAY BICYCLE CLUB
NEW ENTRANT

3a Downshire Hill, Hampstead 0207 435 3544

Located on one of Hampstead's most beautiful roads, joining the High Street to the Common, is The BBC's second restaurant. Seating seventy people in is on former site of Keats restaurant. The philosophy of the restaurant is to create simple, yet fresh and inventive Indian food, using raw ingredients of the highest quality. Head Chef Kul Acharya specialises in North Indian cooking with signature dish like the Barra Channa Shahi. Their menu is designed to suit the European palate; spicy and aromatic but not searing hot, and the restaurant has become very popular. The restaurant is open every evening and all day Sunday. *Puja Vedi, Ed, Tandoori Magazine.*

CUMIN
NEW ENTRANT

02 Centre, 255 Finchley Road, Swiss Cottage 020 7794 5616

Opened in 2005 by Pam and Sirneet Kalwan who like to think of it in Wagamama terms. It certainly has uncomfortable Wagamama-style bench seating and a technicolour interior. The menu is quite extensive. King Prawn Peri Peri, chilli- fried in the Goan style sit comfortably with many old favourites. *'But some seem to work and others don't. We wondered whether the menu might work better if it were shorter.'* RL. Certainly it is not a place for a long romantic night out, but then neither is Wagamama. For a bright quick turn-around, the this is for you.

ERIKI
NEW TO OUR TOP 100

4 Northways Parade, Finchley Road, NW3 020 7722 0606

Entrepreneur Sat Lally opened here in 2002 in a former Italian restaurant. Pictured below it's a 75-seater with a modern Indian look with orange and

Ekori, NW3

Ekori, NW3

magenta walls, Indian cushions, carvings and chairs and a huge bar. Sat requests that you don't nick the trendy cutlery imported from Rajasthan; it's for sale if you fall for it! The place has a homely yet upmarket feeling. It is a place which could well become your local. The welcome is certainly one for regulars and newcomers alike: friendly, swift and sure-footed. Lally has recruited serious talent here: Naresh Matta was for many years one of Amin Ali's Indian chefs at Jamdani then the Red Fort, W1, working under Mohammed Rias, a Dum Pukht practitioner *(see pages 69 & 87)* and more latterly at Soho Spice. Matta learned Goan cuisine from former head chef Jude Pinto (ex Goan specialist at Veeraswami and Chutney Mary). This gave Matta a very wide Indian palette to work from. He says *"The menu offers a tour of India, with dishes starting from the northern regions of Hyderabad, Punjab, midway through Delhi and Bombay (Mumbai), moving south to the coastline of Goa"* Such a background also ensures good presentation. Main courses c£8 to £12. 1 course Set lunch £7. Service charge: 12.5%. Hours: 12-3 Mon-Fri & Sun. and 6-11 daily. <www.eriki.co.uk>

Ekori, NW3

FLEET TANDOORI

104 Fleet Road, NW3 020 7485 6402

'A good restaurant for those seeking a dependable, quiet and inexpensive meal. The Sunday buffet is a must for those who wish a cheap alternative to meat and two veg. An additional attraction is the Special on the menu – Pomfret Fish, which comes either tandoori or, for those with a rich palate, bathed in a curry sauce flavoured with a multitude of spices' AD . Good prices enhanced by a 10% discount if you show them this *Guide* !

WOODLANDS NEW ENTRANT ~ TOP 100

37 Panton Street, SW1 020 7930 8200

New branch of the much -loved vegetarian chain. *See SW1 for details.* Hours: 6-11, M - Th; 12-11 F - Sun.

London NW4

Hendon

KAVANNA NEW ENTRANT

60 Vivian Ave, Hendon, NW4
020 7722 0606

There are, it seems, 1,000 Indian-born Jews in the Hendon/Golders Green area. One of these is Nathan Moses who was born in India, lived in Israel and came to Hendon in 1978, where he runs a kosher and Indian bakery in Vivian Avenue, Hendon. Moses felt sure there was a demand for a kosher Indian restaurant, and Kavanna is it. We have not heard directly from this restaurant, but soon after it opened in 2005, it came to the notice of our scribes, thrilled to tell us of yet another first in London's Indian cuisine: Kosher Indian. There are kosher Chinese restaurants in Philadelphia and

New York, and Moses claims there is a kosher Indian in Paris. Kosher is a protocol for orthodox Jews. Any food style can be kosher if it is prepared and supervised in accordance with certain laws. Kosher and Halal rules have in common meat slaughtering rules and a proscription on pork. Kosher goes further with stating no shellfish and that meat cannot be cooked or eaten with dairy and according to some views, fish with meat. Mosses employs Indian chefs, who adapt traditional Indian recipes to be kosher. Most Indian dishes need no adaptation. Meat and chicken cannot be marinated in yoghurt, cooked in ghee, nor mixed with cream; soy or coconut milk substitutes. At the Kavanna, non-Jews are welcome, and will hardly notice any difference. Apart from the absence of prawns, the menu reads much like the standard curry house, at prices normal prices. Hours: 5.30 - 11, Sun - Thur.

LAHORE ORIGINAL KEBAB HOUSE

150 Brent Street NW4 020 8203 6904

Lahore Kebab House E1 was, of course, the original the food being pure super Pakistani / Punjabi food, geared to Asian tastes, without compromising it for Westerners. Meat is the main player; Halal meat is a given, with dark, thick-gravied, pungent, savoury curries served in the karahi, or with items from the tandoor in the form of succulent tikkas or kebabs. But the observant tell of a seed change here. The menu has a Kenyan Asian twist with an emphasis on vegetable dishes such as Paneer or Chilli mogo, cassava stir-fried with garam masala and a heap of fresh coriander and chillies, then combined with tamarind sauce. The lentil dishes, a great test of the cook's skills. are to die for. Try the Mung Makhani (a green lentil version of black urid makhni dhal, makhni being butter). Prices remain excellent, eg: Main courses £5-£6.50. Takes some credit cards. Party room seats 35. Takeaway service. 11-11.30 daily.

PRINCE OF CEYLON FORMER BEST SRI LANKAN AWARD AND TOP 100

39 Watford Way, NW4 020 8202 5967

Abdul Satter has been here since 1979, during which time it has grown to 150 seats split over five rooms. Manager Nelson presides over a kind of bamboo/coir jungle with yellow-ochre and brown linen, olive green leather seats, and a lot of natural dark wood – tables given privacy by carved wood screens. The Prince's standard menu of tandooris, kebabs, curries and all the business, all perfectly competently cooked, are not what you go there for. It is the Sri Lankan specials. And if these items are unfamiliar, ask the waiter's advice, but be patient if explanations are unclear at first. It is a rice (Buth) cuisine. Jaffna Thossai, soft pancake made of soaked and ground urid dal, served with coconut chutney. Devilled curries are there, including Squid curry. Fried Cabbage with onion £3. Coconut Chutney £2. Hoppers or Appas are rice and coconut-flour pancakes; String Hoppers, like string made of wheat or rice flour dough, but resembling vermicelli nests (10 for £3.50); or Pittu – ditto dumpling. These or straight rice are accompanied by pungent watery curries, in which coconut, turmeric, tamarind, curry leaves and chillies feature. But they can be mild, too. Look out for aromatic black curries and fragrant white ones. Fish dishes, such as Ambul Thial (a Sri Lankan national dish – a sour, spicy tuna fish dish) and the Ceylon Squid (Dhallo) curry are popular. And there are substantial curries such as Lumpri (chicken, meat and egg). Sambols, or relishes, include dried fish and chilli. Contented reports, for example, Average spend £15. Sunday buffet, noon-5pm, £8.50. Hours: 12-3/6-12, weekdays. 12-12, Saturday and Sunday.

London NW5

Kentish Town

CHETNA

56 Chetwynd Road, NW5 020 7482 2803

Established as the Indian Lancer in 1990, then Indian Brasserie in 1999 this 42-seater's owner Edward Graham has decorated in a minimalist style with very pale pink walls, redwood furniture with pinky red cushions, modern spot lighting and red carpets. His chef, Ramdas, was Gujarati region chef of the year 1993 and has held post as executive chef at the Sayji group of hotels in northern India. Ramdas' signature dishes include: Dover Sole Kaliwala, fresh dover sole, cooked with red chillies, yoghurt and curry leaves, spicy!, Chicken 65, dry-fried Hyderbadi style in a light batter, topped with fried green chillies and curry leaves, Phaldari Kofte Paneh Phoran and Chicken Malwari. The most popular dish ordered is Dum Pukht Gosht – a royal favourite. Set lunch: c£3.50 to £5.50. Hours: 12-2.30 (Sun 4) and 6-12 (Sun -1 0). Closed Monday.

London NW6

Kilburn, South and West Hampstead

BENGAL SPICE

245 West End Lane, NW6 020 7794 5370

Established 1957. Fully licensed and air-conditioned. *'When your daughter graduates as a lawyer, leaves home and moves to London with her partner a dad experiences many emotional feelings – will she be safe in London, will she succeed, will she live near a good quality Indian restaurant? I am relieved to say that their new flat is near to the Bengal Spice. External and internal decor is in 'modern brasserie' style. On entering we were shown to our table, drinks served swiftly, fresh Popadoms, good selection of pickles. Shish Kebab, Onion Bhajia £1.95 and Meat Samosa £1.95 – proved to be excellent starters. CTM, CT Bhuna and C Jalfrezi £5.95 were served with Pullao Rice, Peshwari Nan £1.75 and chunky chips (sorry Pat but they were great) all generous portions and beautifully spiced. Highly satisfactory at £15 per person.'* AIE. Hours: 6-12, Friday and Saturday -12.30.

ELEPHANT WALK BEST SRI LANKAN

98 West End Lane, NW6 020 7328 3308

Specialising in Sri Lankan and South Indian food, it opened in 2005, fronted by Kannan Rajapakse, with his Head Chef wife, Deepthe. With her background is in accountancy, she ran a successful catering business before being encouraged to open up her own restaurant by enthusiastic customers. The couple make no secret of the fact that the decor was largely from IKEA installed by friends and family. If true this puts Llewllyn Bowen Whatsit Carol Oversmiley and the TV make-over bore-shows to shame ... it's gorgeous. The floors are hardwood, the furniture is ebony black solid wood. The chairs match the hardwood floor. The highlights are the traditional Batik paintings by renowned Sri Lankan artist, Manawadu from his art studio Bravo Batiks. Located a stone's throw from fashionable St. John's Wood and Lord's Cricket Ground, Elephant Walk seats 42 people in the main dining area, with an additional function room on the lower level that can hold up to 30 people. The front patio opens its French folding doors every summer for outdoor dining, while the outdoor patio at the back offers a more zen-style atmosphere and is complete with a canopy. Mrs R has put together a typical south Indian and Sri Lankan menu. The charm is the fact that the dishes Deepthe serves to diners are ones that her own mother prepared for her in their family home. So Deepthe guarantees authentic dishes prepared in a traditional method. Typical Sri Lankan treats include String Hoppers, steamed noodle made of

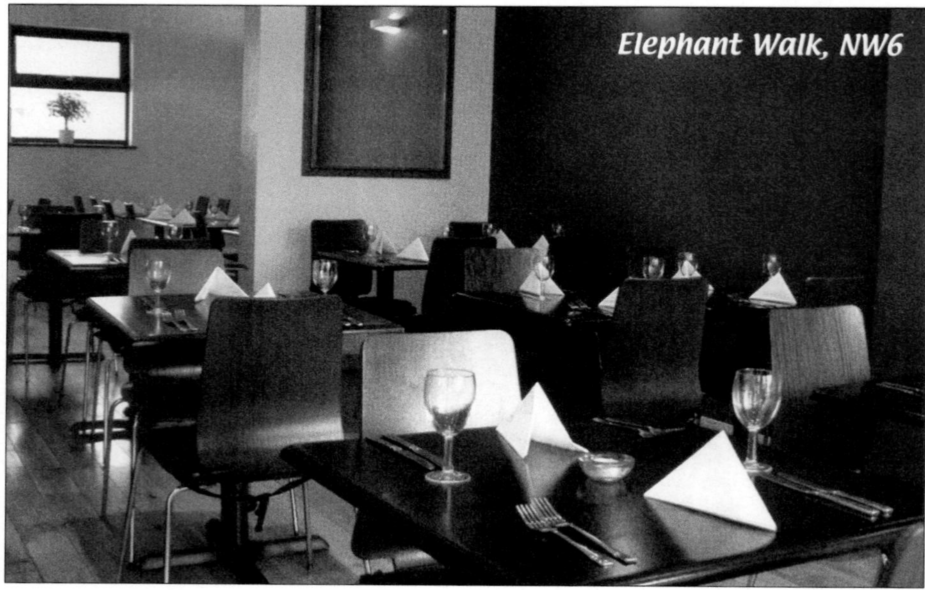
Elephant Walk, NW6

rice flour and Kotthu Rotis, a flatbread that is shredded and chopped in a wok with vegetables and other ingredients and served with sauce on the side. Devil Dishes, mainly served the clubs in colonial times – dry dish served on a hot plate, wp. Planters introduced some European vegetables to Ceylon, as it was then known. Try curries like Beetroot & Potato Kari, Green Cabbage stir fried with coconut, Green Beans kari, Swede kari, Leaks stirfried with coconut, Turnip kari. There are some unusual exotic karies like Breadfruit kari, Manioc kari, Drumsticks & Potato kari, Bitter Gourd kari, Pumpkin kari, Snake Gourd kari, Aubergine kari and Green Banana kari. Thali's and masala dosa's are other specialties coming out of the kitchen.

Puja Vedi, Ed, Tandoori Magazine. Sunday buffet – min12 items, 12-5. Weekdays 12-3/5 - 10:45; Weekends 12-10.45 <www.elephantwalk.biz>

GEETA SOUTH INDIAN TOP 100

57 Willesden Lane, NW6 020 7624 1713

The recent refurb still leaves the requisite homely feel and certainly hasn't detracted from the mainly south Indian vegetarian food at which Geeta excels, and has done since the 70s, with never a decline in standard.. Geeta and son work front of house and a safe-hands, elderly male chef commands the kitchens. Try his Dosa, Idli, Sambar, Upamas Karela (bitter gourds), drumsticks (long pithy marrow which you suck to extract the tender flesh), Ravaiya – baby aubergine and plantains stuffed with a coconut spicy filling Rasam – and more. And with most of these around the £2 mark, and providing you keep off the carnivorous items, you'll fill up for less than a tenner, with drink. You can get standard meat (inc beef) and chicken curries, et al, and from the reports I get, the thoroughly devoted following adore it. It's all fine stuff, served in less than glamourous, but typically Indian surroundings, to a thoroughly devoted following. *'This and Vijay (below) are different and should not be missed.'* DMW. Hours: 12-2.30pm/6-10.30pm, Fri & Sat. to 11.30.

KOVALAM

12 Willesden Lane, NW6 020 7625 4761

Kovalam restaurant opened in 2001 in a former curry house. Kovalam is a rather good government-run (Ashoka Group) beach hotel at the town of Trivandrum, just 30 miles north of India's southern most tip. Actually it's probably the best hotel in that chain. Coconut palms, temple elephants, white dotis, sea, sun and sand. Ah me!.Their restaurant is called Sea Shells and it serves a range of south Indian dishes, protein as well as vegetable. I digress; Trivandrum is a far cry from Willesden, but you'll get the picture from the pictures on the wall. And as at Sea Shells, the food is spot on. It offers south Indian dishes such as dosas, Idli, Sambar, Upamas and Vaadia (*see glossary page* 73). Pazham pori plantain pakora make an unusual starter. It also does Keralan seafood and meat dishes. Try the traditional Lamb Fry where the meat is dry-fried with pepper, coconut and curry leaves. Though we cannot imagine why the do it, the south Indian chefs offer curry-house dishes. Takeaway service; delivery (3-mile radius on over £15). 12-2.30 daily/ 6-11 Sun-Thur, 6-12 Fri & Sat. <www.kovalamrestaurant.co.uk>

SURYA

59 Fortune Green Road, NW6 020 7435 7486

Mr (front of house) and Mrs Tiwari (chef) really pack 'em in at this tiny, 34-seat vegetarian, licensed restaurant – there's no room to move, almost literally – it's always full. The dish of the day (it changes daily) excites several of our regulars. We hear well of Gujarati dishes such as Patra and Kaddu Kari and inexpensive prices. Hours: 6-10.30pm, and Sun. lunch. Branch: Shree Ganesha, 4 The Promenade, Edgwarebury Lane, Edgware, Middx.

VIJAY TOP 100

49 Willesden Lane, NW6 020 7328 1087

Vijay was founded in 1966, and predated nearby Geeta (*see above*) by several years, so it can take the crown for being the earliest to provide south Indian food for NW6, and its menu contains all the vegetarian items listed in Geeta's entry, at much the same prices. Indeed my remarks are the same, since Vijay like Geeta does carnivorous dishes too. Vijay has its own clan of loyal regulars who know they'll get 'very nice tasty food.' B&WW. Prices are much the same, perhaps just a tad higher here, but again, even with the ridiculous 10% service charge (please get rid of it) you'll only spend a tenner if you stick to the scrumptious vegetarian delights. *'This and Geeta (above) are different and should not be missed.'* DMW. Hours: 12-2.45/6-10.45 (Fri & Sat to 11.45pm).

London NW7

Mill Hill

DAYS OF THE RAJ

123 The Broadway, NW7 020 8906 3477

Established in 1989 by S Miah, who tells us that he changes the wallpaper every six months to 'maintain standards'. M Miah manages the 100-seater, whose extensive menu appears to be formula stuff from Kurma to Phal, etc. But a closer look provides a number of 'unique' dishes. What are Noorane, Sherajee, Kushboo, Dilkush and Bakhara curries, for example? Each available in chicken, lamb, beef, prawn, king prawn and vegetables (the menu explains their attributes), they are clearly house inventions. So is the dish Days of the Raj, gently cooked with pineapple, lychees and sultanas in a thick creamy sauce sprinkled with nuts. It sounds like a fruit salad but is, we're assured, *'really quite delicious, the chicken quite succulent, and mild enough for my boss who is a curry novice.'* GC. It is more than a 'safe-bet' curry house. It is very smart indeed and is a place to go for an enjoyable meal out. Service 10%. E-a-m-a-y-l lunch buffet daily £7. Delivery: £12 minimum, 3-mile radius. Hours: 12-2pm/5-11.30.

London NW9

Kingsbury, Neasden

LAHORE KEBAB HOUSE

248 Kingsbury Road, NW9 020 8424 8422

This branch of the celebrated London E1 original, never achieved the glory. So it was sold to H. Hameed as far back as 1994. No longer connected, it was permitted to keep the name and menu, and it has now built its own following. It's licensed, and the kebabs are good and the curries. For the menu see the e1 Lahore Kebab House review. No credit cards. 1pm to midnight, daily.

TANDOOR NEW ENTRANT

232 Kingsbury Road,NW9 020 8205 1450

Although new to this Guide, Tandoor is an old hand and very popular with the local Punjabi population. The fact it's in a pub is an added attraction. It's on two levels, and has a party room for 60. As for the food, it is spot on. Savoury, meat dishes, super veg dishes, breads. 12 - 3.30/6 - 11.30.

London NW10

Harlesden, Kensal Green, Willesden

ANN MARIE AT THE TASTE OF THE TAJ

43 Chamberlayne Rd, NW10 020 8991 5366

'Hello Pat. My restaurant has relocated and.we want to continue to use your curry club logo, please confirm this is OK and that we are enlisted in the next Guide. Love, Ann Marie.' For those who like to know these things, I do love Ann Marie. She is a one-off. She is the undisputed of Queen of Quormas, the Majesty of Masalas. She is epitome of the perfect front-of-house host. I first met her at the Ealing Taj Mahal where she made her debut in that role in 1965. She opened her own restaurant in 1989, and sold up in 2003. Although strictly speaking retired, she does make the occasional appearance. So if you see the great lady, get her autograph and enjoy a welcoming taste experience. Delivery: £12 minimum. Hours: lunch weekdays only/6-12am.

GALLE CAFÉ NEW ENTRANT

91 Dudden Hill Lane NW10 020 8459 7921

A Sri Lankan in the area is a precious gem. Named after the town (pron Gaul) in south Sri Lanka, it's an unpretentious café with unpretentious prices, very popular with local Asians. And look at the hours. Fancy breakfast? There is the typical British greasy spoon stuff: eggs, bacon, beans et al, but why not try String Hopper (steamed noodle) with a thin curry or Egg Hopper (ditto with an egg)? See page 75 for more explanations. The dishes of the day are on the board. Main stream curries may include, Cashew, or tuna fish, or beetroot. Meat might be beef or it might be lamb. Sambols (chutneys) add to the fun. Cash only (and not much of that either. You can exit with filled tummy for a fiver! Hours 8 - 8, Mon-Sat.

SARAVANAS NEW ENTRANT

77 Dudden Hill La, NW10 020 8459 4900

As if Sri Lankan on the street (see previous entry0 the lucky locals have a South Indian too, and it too is popular with the Asian population. It is vegetarian, and inexpensive.(even so it does take credit cards): There are two dining areas, the formica tabled café and the cane-seating 'smarter' room with bar. South Indian food is described on

page 85 and in the A-Z glossary. The Rasam soup and Sambar are competent, as are the curries, and the Thalis (£6 to 8) are a splendidly filling, economical meal. Hours: 12 - 10.30, Tue-Sun

RAJ — NEW ENTRANT

43 Chamberlayne Rd, NW10 0208 960 7090

Misbah's smart and popular Bangladeshi curryhouse is there for those who enjoy the fix cooked and served well. The menu contains all your favourites, and you can dine in, have it delivered free. (minimum order £10.00) or get a 10% discount on collection for orders over £15.00. Hours 12 - 2/6- 11.30. <rajlondon.com>

London SE

Area: South East London
Postcodes SE1 to SE28
Population: 910,000

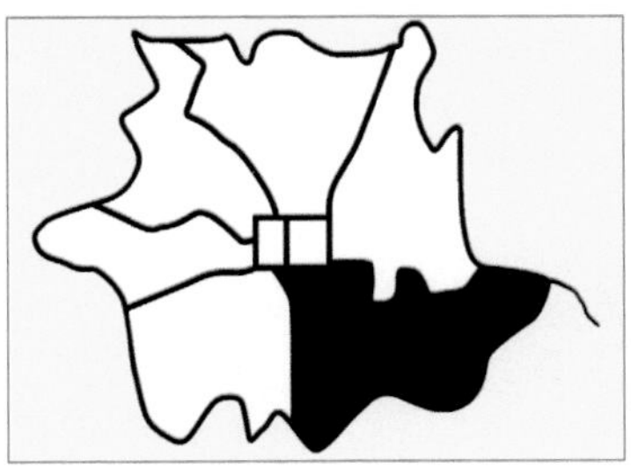

See page 109 for key to this map.

London SE1

Borough, Elephant & Castle, London Bridge, Old Kent Road, Southwark and Waterloo

BENGAL CLIPPER — TOP 100

Cardamom Building,
31 Shad Thames, SE1 020 7357 9001

Finding it is the problem. It's a fair walk from the tube! Taxis will find it (it's behind Conran's). If you're driving, and you've squeezed through the narrow one-way streets, you'll then have to find a parking space (min. £4). Once inside, you'll find Kenneth Lynn's sophisticated and expensive interior. Chef Ram Das turns out excellent curry house food, and the Bangladeshi dishes are the best bet. *'Another good value lunch, with fairly quick service, whilst the food, as ever, is tasty and quite hot as they go.' sh.* Average £30. Lunch and dinner daily. Branches: Bengal Trader, E1, Bengal Mangrove, Halstead, Kent, and the original Bengal Lancer, Chislehurst, Kent. *<www.bengalclipper.co.uk>*

CASTLE TANDOORI

200 Elephant & Castle Shopping Centre, SE1
020 7703 9130

Mr Uddin's Castle is a spirited place, and a regular entrant in our *Guide*. He once told us, and will tell you, if you care to be entertained by him, that he's outlived twenty-two Hoovers, two recessions, and several prime ministers, and served enough nan bread to stretch from Waterloo to Paris. Still no update on this yet; but I expect he's calculating anew. The menu is pretty much formula (135 items) but includes duck, lamb chops and trout in various guises. Reports tell of the value for money. We know of no longer hours in London (let us know if you know better). So, if you're an insomniac curryholic, or just a late-night reveller, note this place well. Hours: Lunch Mon.-Fri./6-1am daily (Fri. & Sat. to 2.30am).

HARA THE CIRCLE BAR

NOMINATED BEST NEWCOMER

Queen Elizabeth St, SE1 0845 226 9411

Opened in 2005 and designed by Shelley Singh, Hara is set on two floors, with the 80 seat restaurant on the mezzanine level overlooking the stylish Circle Bar. Located in Butler's Wharf 200 guests be accommodated for pre or post-dinner drinks before you dine in the Hara restaurant. Designed by Europe's famous Zoran Zafaria, he bar front is fitted with a translucent marble pieces sourced from Rajasthan and finished in Italy. Modern European furniture and a mixture of dark brown leather seating and elegant stools are scattered round the bar. With impressive credentials (Conran's Bluebird, and a TGI's Master Bar Tender),Tony Rozario is head barman. In the restaurant, Chef Bhuwan presents modern Indian food but still uses traditional methods of preparation by generations of chefs from the villages from Punjab and Nepal of North India. There is also an Ayurvedic menu known as 'Jeyarani Food'. Ayurveda promises youth, long life and vitality that you can attract to you in a perfectly natural way with lifestyle counselling and enjoyable food. Amongst its features, Hara is also one of the few restaurants to provide lead-free drinking glasses. While the glass is environmentally friendly, it was also recently discovered that lead in glasses

presents an unacceptable exposure to hazardous toxins. Puja Vedi, Ed, Tandoori Magazine. Hours: 12 - 3 / 6 - 12. <www.hararara.co.uk>

SILKA

6 Southwark Street, SE1 020 7378 6161

With the pedigree of cheffing at Tamarind, Chutney Mary, Three Monkeys and the Red Fort, Abdul Mushahid turned proprietor and opened his 80-seat Silka in 2003 in the basement of a Grade II listed building. Managed by A. Hannan, it is between London Bridge and Tate Modern. The design has inspired the idea of a horizontal and layered landscape with clouds hovering above. Depth is created through the back-lit wall cladding made from different exotic timbers such as indian rosewood, ebony and makore. Lighting and decor lead the eye to Mushahid's window kitchen from where emanates cooking with Ayurvedic (low-fat, health-conscious) principles leading to an original menu. *'Our starters included Baked Lemon Sole wrapped in a banana leaf, Stir-fried Baby Squid, and Mixed Sprout Lentil Soup – a modern take on a traditional Indian staple. Interesting salads such as a lotus leaves coated with white sesame seeds and spiced gram flour batter is refreshingly innovative and served with a typically tangy tamarind chutney. Other gems include Wild Duck braised with delicate spices, Roasted Cauliflower marinated with cheese, yoghurt and cashew nuts and fiery Peri Peri Prawns. Try the tasting Ayurvedic platters. Potatoes cooked in a creamy sauce, and spiced vegetable and rice, served with tiger prawns is one example of the choice on offer. Side dishes include pan-fried fresh mustard leaves and the steadfast Indian favourite of simmered black lentils.'* RG. Lunch platter at £7.95. Dinner average £25. Take Out. Free Delivery. Valet Parking. Hours 12 - 3/6 - 11.

THAMES TANDOORI

79 Waterloo Road, SE1 020 7928 3856

Kalkur Rahman established this one in 1985. Managed by Amirul Islam this air-conditioned 52-seater is still there under the railway bridge, and, yes, its neighbour, the fab-named Fishcotheque [it's a fish & chip shop for those new to this *Guide*] is still there. *'Fell out of Waterloo Station into this restaurant'* [I can think of worse places to fall into, Bernard.] *'Confirm all your comments about the food and service. Only one small complaint – food a touch cool, in cooking sense. King Prawn Jalfrezi absolutely excellent.'* BF. *'Keeps a consistently high standard. Staff welcoming, food above average, very modest prices. Definitely in a higher league.'* HLC. *'On another occasion, had such a good meal, an unassuming restaurant, staff are pleasant and food is so good – deserves to be praised.'* HLC. Delivery: 2 miles, £20 minimum. Hours: 12-2.15 / 5.30-11.45.

TOWER TANDOORI

74 Tower Bridge Road, SE1 020 7237 2247

8 minutes walking distance from Tower Bridge. Tower Tandoori Specialities include: Shatay Chicken £6.45, three quarters of breast chicken marinated in special sauce then cooked in tender clay oven, served with separate mossala sauce and with green salad. Me Gori £6.75, a special biriani consisting of meat, prawn, king prawn and pullao rice, green salad on top, served with mixed vegetable curry. *'It was a delicious meal – especially the King Prawn Dopiaza £6.50. All prices were very favourable.'* NB.

London SE3

Blackheath Village

TASTE OF RAJ

9 Royal Parade, SE3 020 8344 2823

'Continues to be v g indeed. Shared a wonderful Afgan Puri followed by a chilli-hot Sag Chana Dhansak, also v go with plenty of sag and chickpeas. Garlic Nan was light and fluffy and Tarka Dall full of mustard seed and garlic – good food and good value all round.' AG.

London SE8

Deptford

TANDOORI XPRESS — NEW ENTRANT

111B Deptford High St, SE8 020 8320 2555

The one to find for good cheap comfort food. It's a takeaway with a couple of tables. *'I use the street market (it's near the office) and I use this takeaway too. It;s in Douglas Way (off the main drag) Every time I've been in the tables are taken.'* JGS. It's home cooking, Punjabi-style. Cooking is done in view and it's no frill, no toilet and no credit cards. But, hey, who cares, it's so inexpensive: expect to pay around a fiver for a good fill. Hours: 11.30-11 Mon-Sat; 12-3/6-10.30 Sun.

London SE9

Eltham, Falconwood

CROWN TANDOORI TAKEAWAY

7, Lingfield Crescent, SE9 020 8294 1313

Owned and managed by Saiful Abedin, since January 1997. Set meal excellent value from c£4for Chicken Tikka and Nan to c£8 for Onion Bhajia, Chicken Bhuna, Bombay Aloo, Pullao Rice and Nan. Complimentary Popadoms, Mint Sauce and Onion salad with all orders. Delivery: 3-mile radius. Hours: 5-11.30.

CURRY GARDEN

144 Westmount Road, SE9 020 8850 2250

Opened in 1992, taken over in 1999 by A Miah (manager), F Haque, S Miah and K Miah. Interesting menu additions: Koleze Puree £2 – chicken liver delicately prepared and served with pancake, Bahari Nan £1.75 – with green chilli and coriander. Delivery: 5-mile radius, £15 minimum, no delivery to high rise buildings. Hours: 5-10.30. .

RUCHITA TAKEAWAY

31 Avery Hill Road, SE9 020 8850 1202

Unusually for a takeaway-only, Miss Salma, Mohammed Yousuf's and Chef A Mukid's Ruchita is licensed. It's been going since 1975, so they know what they're doing. Their Chicken Tikka is still easily their most popular dish (surprise, surprise). Delivery: £10, 3-mile radius. Hours: 5.30-12.

London SE13

Hither Green, Lee, Lewisham, New Cross, Deptford, Lewisham & Catford

ARRU SUVAI NEW ENTRANT

19 Lee High Rd Lewisham 020 8297 6452

This Sri Lankan gaff is almost a club too its aficionados. The telly blares out Bollywood, the the fruit machine spews out cash (now and again), the decor is, well Sri Lankan and the atmosphere great. The menu includes such Sri Lankan delights as devilled dishes, Koththu Roi, Pittu, Tuna Curry, vadas, and wonderfully light, huge Masala Dosa. *(see page 75)*. Cash only, but it is another of those gems where you fill for a fiver. Hours: 10-11 daily.

BABU SAHEEB

406-408 High Street, SE13 020 8690 7667

Decorated with white ceiling, spot lights, light blue walls with chandeliers, blue carpet. Fully licensed: £2.95 pint lager, £6.95 bottle house wine. Service: 10% Buffet Dinner Nights: Sunday to Thursday £8.50 adult and £4.50 child under 12. Delivery: 3 miles, £2 charge. Hours: lunch by appointment and 6 to 12.30. Branch: Ladywell Tandoori, 81, Ladywell Road, Lewisham, SE13.

BENGAL BRASSERIE

79 Springbank Road, SE13 020 8461 5240

This 60-seater restaurant, prettily decorated in pale shades of pink, is owned and managed by Syed Ahmed. CT describes chef M Chowdhury's efforts as *'a nice little menu, now containing a few originals'. 'The spinach in Lobster Saghee makes this a fine dish.'* ES. And others enjoy the Sea Thali – clever name. Most popular dish Sali Ana Roshi, chicken or meat with pineapple and honey, lightly spiced. Minimum charge £15. Parties of 20 diners, eat and drink as much as you like for £25 per diner! Service 10%. Cover charge £1. Delivery: 3-mile radius. Hours: 5.30-11.30 (12am Sat.).

GREEN CABIN SRI LANKAN

244 High Street, SE13 020 8852 6666

40 seater opened in 1996 by SE Jebarajan and serving Sri Lankan and South Indian food asa well as the safe-bet Korma-through-Vindaloo range. Forget all that and go for the real stuff – you won't be disappointed. Meat Roll (diced lamb, onions, chillies and potato wrapped in a pancake, bread crumbed and deep-fried, served with spicy sauce), Potato Kulambu (deep-fried cubes of potato cooked in coconut milk with dry roasted chilli), Cabbage Mallung (shredded cabbage stir-fried with mustard seed, turmeric and spices), Koththu Roti, soft and thin as a silk cloth sliced into pieces and mixed with shredded chicken on a hot griddle and blended together). Delivery: 2-mile radius, £15 minimum, dinner only. Takeaway: 10% discount, £15 minimum. Hours: 12-3 /6-11; closed Mon.

EVEREST CURRY KING NEW ENTRANT

24 Loampit Hill, Lewisham 020 8691 2233

Don't be fooled by the name. It's yet another Sri Lankan in SE13. Everest is 1500 miles to the north of Sri Lanka, but it's the food which counts. *(see page 75)*. It's a typical caff with no menu, just items on display in the cabinet. Fill up, pay up (and not much of that and by card if you wish) and have a superbly tasty, authentic experience. Hours: 11-11.30 daily

SPICE OF LIFE TOP 100

260 Lee High Road, SE13 020 8244 4770

Owner, Mahmud (Moody) Miah, head chef, has a multi-talented crew – Jilad Miah, head waiter and menumaster, Moshaid Miah, barman, music master and tandoori chef, Harris (Harry) Miah-head barman and decor coordinator. Their fully licensed, air-conditioned venue seats 58. *'Small, cosy restaurant which is hard to fault. Its special gourmet nights and daily blackboard specials lift it well above average.'* say C &GM. Blackboard specials showing dish(es) of the day are still rare in the curry business. *'Food is simply out of this world. It is quite small and does not do a delivery service, helps keep the quality high. Special vegetarian dishes – Garlic Chilli Vegetables – are outstanding, King Prawn Chilli Vegetables – absolutely superb. Nans fluffy and hot. Long may this restaurant continue to prosper!'* AG. *' Thursday evenings are Fish Specials, what ever is fresh at the market Moody's wife cooks – super dishes.'* G&CM Takeaway: 10% discount. Lunch and dinner daily.

London SE15

Peckham

GANAPATI NEW ENTRANT

38 Holly Grove, Peckham 020 7277 2928

Its a simple café, on a corner site which is easy to

spot., especially in the summer with its 4 outside tables (4 more in the 'garden'). Ganapati (aka Ganesh) by the way, is the the elephant-headed god and the bringer of good luck. So lucky Peckham, enjoy the South Indian delights on offer. The thali is great stuff with Rasam soup, bean curries, shredded veg curry (Thoran), lentils (Sambar) gourds and the like. at lunch from £4.50 to £5.50 and Main courses £8 to £11. Service charge: 10%. Credit cards: accepted. Hours 12-10.45 Tue-Sun. Closed Mondays.

London SE22

East Dulwich

AL AMIN TANDOORI

104b Forest Hill Road, SE22 020 8299 3962

Established in 1994 by Kabir Khan. It has all the curryhouse standards and we hear that it's all done well. *'I love their Dhansak — creamy lentils, slightly sweet, yet a chill bite and succulent chicken'* DBAC. Try Chicken Roll – spicy boneless chicken roll in thin pancake. Chuza Mossala – baby chicken with thick gravy. Set meal for one: £7.95 includes: CTM, Pullao Rice, Nan and 2 Pops. Delivery: 3 miles, min £15. Hours: 5.30-12.

THE CORIANDER NEW ENTRANT

120 Lordship Lane, SE22 020 8613 1500

It is a new sister to the Coriander in Buckhurst Hill, Essex. The high quality of the food, service, decor and comfort has been replicated here under the supervision of the owner J Islam. *'A visit to either of these branches is a MUST. The food is of a consistently high quality and is always freshly cooked. All the portions are generous in size. The menu is comprehensive and many of the dishes have an individual style. I visited with my husband and to start we had: Hara kebab - spinach and potatoes stuffed with cottage cheese and roasted cashew nuts - superb - £2.95 and Coriander special - a mixture of starters - chicken tikka, lamb tikka, onion bhaji and hara kebab - great value - £3.50. We followed with the Chef's specials of Mahi masala - salmon cooked with the Chef's special masala sauce - the salmon is succulent and tasty - £7.95 and Adha diya - lamb or chicken cooked with garlic, ginger, coconut and cream - is absolutely delicious - £6.95. The main dishes were accompanied by brinjal bhaji and sag bhaji - first class - £2.50 each and mushroom rice - great - £2.25. The staff are helpful, efficient, polite and friendly and you receive a warm welcome on every visit. The waiters are knowledgeable about the ingredients of each dish and the way it's cooked. The restaurant is spotlessly clean (as are the toilets). It is tastefully decorated and has comfortable seating. They have a Sunday Buffet at East Dulwich that is served all day (which we haven't tried) but if it's as good as the one served at the Buckhurst Hill branch it is truly value for money. Both establishments are WELL WORTH A VISIT.'* MF.

PISTACHIO CLUB NEW ENTRANT

44 Lordship Lane, SE22 020 8693 7584

Better than average curryhouse with some special specials. We hear of their aptly named Pista Murgh pistachio chicken whose sensuous sauce is made from cream, yoghurt, garlic, ginger, chilli and turmeric, punctuated with succulent fresh pistachio nuts. Their Raan, roast lamb Lucknow-style is marinated with cardamom, kewra water (screwpine) and saffron and served with a thick aromatic sauce. Bangladeshi fish such as ayer, rui and boal are available. Reasonable prices. Hours: 12 - 2.30/6 - 11

SURMA CURRY HOUSE

42 Lordship Lane, SE22 020 8693 1779

Surma Curry House is what is says. It's one of those venues which delivers the goods exactly as enjoyed by a wide range of regular customers. It's been around for years. *'We just love going here. We go with our parents and with our kids. What more could you ask for?'* AAR. Lunch and dinner, daily. Sunday 12-11.

London SE23

Forest Hill, Honor Oak

BABUR BRASSERIE

NOMINATED BEST IN LONDON

119 Brockley Rise, SE23 020 8291 2400

Babur established the Moghul Empire in 1483 through his courage and daring in capturing Delhi. This restaurant captured Forest Hill in 1985, though its ownership by the dynamic Rahman brothers did not occur until 1992. Quite simply, it's in our AWARD-WINNING category because everything the Rahmans do, they do well. Enam Rahman's cooking is bright and fresh, while front of house is equally so, under the careful supervision of co-owner manager Emdad Rahman. Regulars get frequent mail-shots telling of festivals and al-fresco dining. Talking about outside, the front is really attractive, with white Mogul arches, each one enhanced by hanging baskets and floor tubs. The white decor continues inside, offset by 56 air-force-blue chairs. Dining is intimate in a screened area or in the conservatory. The menu is interesting with no formula stuff done here. The restaurant seats 56 and serves unusual delights such as Patra £2.25, avari leaves layered with a spicy chick pea paste, steamed, sliced and then deep-fried. Harrey Tikka £5.95, diced chicken marinated in green sauce of pureed coriander and mint, cooked in the tandoor. Shah Jahani £5.95, smoked river fish, marinated, cooked in tandoor. Shugati Masala £5.50, chicken in masala sauce of coconut and white poppy seeds. Dum Tori £2.50, courgettes with turmeric and mango. Aloo Makhani £2.50, tiny whole round potatoes with rich masala sauce. Fully licensed. Sunday lunch: buffet £8.95 adult, children up to 7 years, free. Delivery: 6-12, closed Tuesday. Hours: 12-2.30 (not Friday) and 6-11.30 daily. Branch: Planet Spice, 88, Selsdon Park Road, Croydon, Surrey.

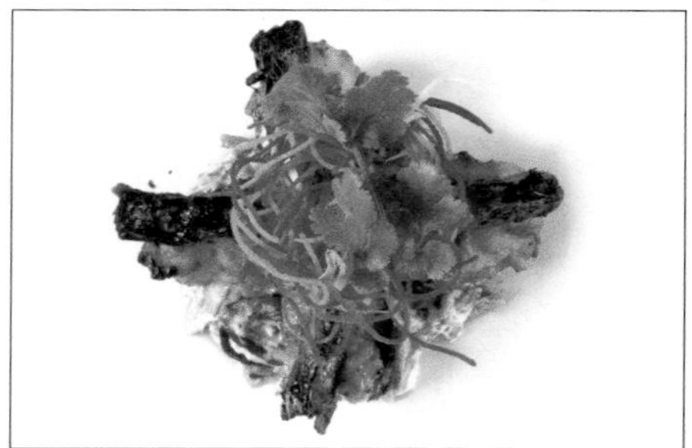

Babur, SE23

Babur, SE23

KAFÉ LA
15 Perry Vale,
SE23
020 8699 2028
Authentic
Bangladeshi food

KAFÉ LA **NEW ENTRANT**

15 Perry Vale, SE23 020 8699 2028

Opened in 2005 as joint venture between Iqbal Ahmed, Ruhel Hasan, Jewel Zaman and Anwar Haq, it's trendy name perhaps does not reveal four partners' main mission – to delve back to their roots and serve home-style Bangladeshi cuisine in an upmarket environment. Divided on two floors, Kafé La seats 52 people and exudes elegance and simplicity with a touch of ethnicity. Open space and natural light to pour in, via skylights to create fresh, uncluttered surroundings, with ethnic lounge music to help busy Londoners relax. In the evenings, the skylights themselves turn into lights and change colour depending on the mood – for instance over the Valentines period the management turn it red. The cream walls are decked out with paintings specially imported from Dubai, depicting an abstract fusion of Arabic and Far Eastern cultures. Comfortable dark brown leather chairs and white linen contrast the scene with classy appeal. The Bangladeshi food is in the hands Nazrul Hussin. At 29 he is probably one of the youngest Head Chefs in the industry, but the British-Bangladeshi was selected for his innovative approach in the kitchen and his readiness to recreate traditional favourites. Dishes with meat on the bone are commonly eaten in Bangladesh, especially lamb shanks, which was the inspiration for a house favourite, Lamb Lau ('Lau' means pumpkin in Bengali), which is lamb shanks served with green pumpkin and lentil curry (dal). Their Chicken Korma is a perfect example of home-style. Most korma sauces are very creamy and nutty, but Hussin has kept true to his roots and prepares a more mild, onion-based korma sauce. Bangladeshis are also fond of beef, an ingredient hard to find in most South Asian restaurants, but is available at Kafé La cooked in several traditional ways. *Puja Vedi, Tandoori Magazine.*

London SE24

Herne Hill

THREE MONKEYS **TOP 100**

136 Herne Hill, SE24 020 7738 5500

The 110 seater Three Monkeys opened in a former bank building in 1998. Its modern lines are graced by a remarkable entry bridge, which looks down onto the bar below. In the centre of the main dining area you can watch chefs in the open kitchen. Both floors give an airy spacious feel. In late 2004 the restaurant changed ownership. to chef-proprietor Kuldeep Singh, of Chowki / Mela fame. The cooking is highly accomplished and there are regular menu changes. Prices are very fair. Two course set lunch from £7.95 / dinner £12.95 Sun to Thur 2 course. Sunday buffet £6.95. Service charge: 12.5.% Hours: 12-2.30/5.30-10.30 Mon-Sat; 12-10.30 Sun.

London SW

Area: South West London,
Postcodes: SW1 to SW20
Population: 705,000

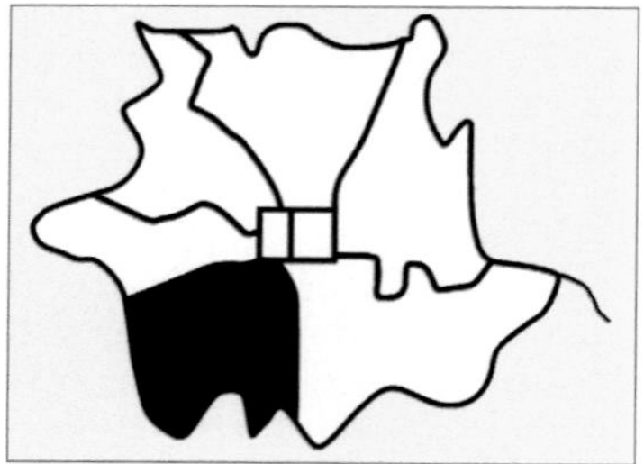

See page 109 for key to this map.

London SW1

Belgravia, Knightsbridge. Pimlico, St James's, Sloane Square, Victoria, Westminster

AMAYA — A-LIST

Halkin Arcade, Knightsbridge SW1
020 7823 1166

Without doubt the cleverest restaurateurs not just in London, but anywhere,are the owners of this restaurant. They already have five Masala Zones, Chutney Mary and Veeraswami. Those alone make a formidable portfolio. Masala Zone for the quick in-and-out dining experience. The other two for Indian regional fine-dining. So why Amaya? It's address, Knightsbridge, home to Harrods and London's highest house prices, gives us a clue. A further clue came from the fact that the Panjabis have long bemoaned the fact that their rent, rates, ingredients and wages and supplies cost every bit as

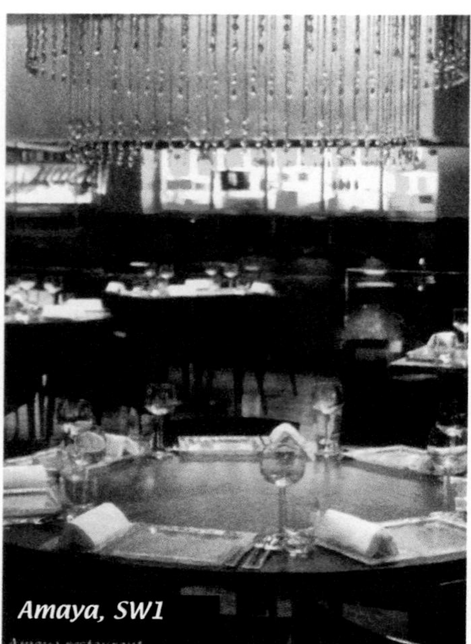

Amaya, SW1

much as any other restaurant, yet because it is Indian they are obliged ton charge less. Well not any more. This restaurant has broken all grounds, not only price-wise, but food-wise. The average meal costs over £60 and you can add drink and service to that. And the clients flock in.. And this is what they find. The decor is stunning. First there is a most attractive bar, encased in rosewood and vibrant red panels, which opens at 6pm. There is also a private dining room seats 14. Day time provides a totally different atmosphere to night where the moody chandeliers, spotlights and candles do the work. I don't know which I prefer. Statues, dark wood fittings, Indian sandstone and rosewood panelling, .tasteful use of colour, subtle table settings, separate areas, yet a view of them all. And above all, a view of the kitchen running full-length at the end. The owners call it the India Grill. But this is no ordinary grill. There on view are a wide range of cooking implements used in India for thousands of years such as Sigrhi (open fire grill), Tawa (griddle), Mahi Tawa (walled griddle), Kadhai (wok), Lagan (steam pot) Shilajit Stone (special stones from Hyderabad, with aphrodisiac properties) and of course the Tandoor. Expertly positioned spotlights illuminate the equipment and the food, but not the chefs, discretely dressed in black. A big range of kebabs are produced in full view in a theatrical show kitchen - creating a culinary spectacle. Other dishes are seasoned with subtle marinades. These sit alongside fragrant light soups and exotic salads. The food is designed to be shared and is served as it is prepared. There are no conventional first courses or main courses. This, of course has led to a fair bit of flack for those who like to get things in the order they believe they should be served. And usually the criticism lands unfair but square on the waiting staff. *'The waitress couldn't answer a single question about what was in offer. Was she newly over from Poland?'* RL. Indeed on our own visit, the waitress was condescending to such an extent that DBAC called her *'snotty nosed'* Others complain of a noisy ambience. Shrill noise is what you get with so many hard surfaces – it's the price you pay for the current trendy decor. Others complain that this is not 'curry' as they know it. The Panjabis explain this very tactfully. *'Our restaurants are very different from the inexpensive neighbourhood curry restaurants started in Britain by enterprising non-Indian entrepreneurs who developed their own brand of curry totally different from the tastes of real Indian food.'* Put it another way, curryhouse they are not. And of course we hear about it being pricey with small portions to boot. However is not only one of the most highly rated restaurant s in this Guide, it won the Tio Pepe ITV 2005 Best Restaurant and Best Newcomer (and this was for all restaurant categories, not just Indian.) It is also a Michelin Star holder. Main courses £8.50 to£25 Dinner with wine costs about £55 per head. Express lunch is £14.50. Many desserts are light, and some are sugar free. A favourite is plum compote with chilli custard and rose sorbet. Three-course lunch of less than 400 calories Hour:. 12.30-2.15 Mon-Fri; 12.30-2.30pm Sat; 12.45-2.45Sun./ 6.30-11.15 Mon-Sat; 6.30-10.15 Sun. <www.realindianfood.com>

CINNAMON CLUB A-LIST

The Old Westminster Library,
Great Smith Street, SW1 020 7222 2555

The conversion of the former Westminster library is well documented. It was a labour of love by its founder who has now moved onto other ventures. The location is genius. To put it in catchment terms, it is one of the nearest restaurants to the House of Commons, the Lords, vast numbers of media types, numerous parliamentary offices, an expensive convention centre and a million tourists.

Chef Vivek Singh and a shot of The Cinnamom Club, displaying its former library heritage..

Excluding the latter, the average wage of the indigenous workforce is in six figures. And there are thousands of them; ministers, shadow ministers, MPs, peers, civil servants and diplomats. And they love the Cinnamon Club. It's a great name too; because there is a membership-only bar and lounge at £1000 pa for the privilege. And so you are more than likely to see some of these high-flyers along with a sprinkling of celebs from all walks of life. Indeed when the House is 'sitting' the venue now echoes to the sound of the Division bell. This also happens at the previous curry king of the castle, the Kundan, Horseferry Road, and I ran a much copied gag about when the bell goes and the suits evacuate, its not the fire alarm it's the division bell!. So location, location, locations is perfect. The other maxim at the forefront of a venue owner's mind is utilisation. If your venue is only open for lunch and dinner, or worse just dinner, then its fixed costs are higher per hour than if it operates 24 hours. Unlike New York, London is not a 24 hour city, but this venue operates the longest hours of any restaurant in this Guide. It opens at 07.30 and diners often leave after midnight. Its current success is largely down to its chef. Chef Vivek Singh ex Jaipur Raj Vilas Hotel is used to cooking for dignitaries. He once cooked for President Bill Clinton. Vivek also has a brigade of 20 chefs. And he needs them. For breakfast try Bombay spiced vegetables with cumin pao. Spicy scrambled eggs (Parsee Ekori) on layered bread. Uttapam - rice pancake with choice of toppings: onion, green chilli, tomato or peppers served with coconut chutney and lentil broth. Or there's Anglo Indian Kedgeree If you must, there's a Full English or Continental breakfast. Average price £25. The lunch and dinner menu literally changes daily, so this review gives you a flavour. On the lunch and dinner menu, there are ten starters from c £7 to £9.

The lunch and dinner menu literally changes daily, so this snapshot gives you an idea of the things on offer. Starters: Seafood Selection – Scallop, Salmon and King Prawn Kebab; Mussels with pickled Carrot and Beetroot; Green Moong Lentil and Basmati Kedgeree; Sandalwood flavoured Tandoori Chicken Breast;. Potatoes stuffed with cottage cheese in a sweet and sour sauce £9. Hyderbadi-style aubergine steaks with coconut rice The mains go in the same unusual direction: Fillet mullet with a Bengali style shrimp and vegetable broth;. Mustard-flavoured tandoori king prawns with saffron kedgeree; Goan-spiced duck with curry leaf flavoured semolina; Calves liver with masala-mashed potatoes and stir-fried okra; Rack of lamb with a mint and onion sauce, peas pullao £17. Rajasthani spiced rack of 'Oisin' red deer with pickling sauce, pilau rice. The caveat remains. A lot of diners have found Cinnamon Club not to their liking, as is to be expected. It is far removed form the curryhouse formula as can be. No pickles and pops, and a futuristic/fusion slant on the food. But we agree with others that Vivek has moved the frontiers forward. But it is an experience all true devotees of Indian food should try. *'on our first visit, we sat in the buzzing bar, I drank Gimlets – really good, 2nd best I've tasted – (best in Goa's Fort Aguada, by the pool). After a relaxing chat, we moved to the dining room, where a cleanly laid table, situated in the corner awaited us. We dined on fab food – I liked my duck curry, and the venison better! (I also ate half his Pat and I don't really eat puddings in Indian restaurants, (too full) but we were seduced by chef's delectable selection and finished with fruit stuffed Samosas, home made sorbets and ice creams – delicious.'* DBAC. Main courses £12-£26. 2 course set lunch £19; 3 course £22. 5 course set dinner £60. A-la-carte average £80 + drinks. Party rooms, seating 30 and 50. Service charge: 12.5%. Hours: Breakfast: 7.30-9.30AM, lunch: 12-2.30, Mon-Fri, dinner 6-10.45 Mon-Sat. Closed Sundays. <www.cinnamonclub.com>

MINT LEAF — BEST IN LONDON

Suffolk Place, Haymarket, SW1 020 7930 9020

After an uncertain start, Dinu Bhattessa's venture has reached maturity in the three years since it opened. It highly justifies this *Guide's* **BEST IN LONDON AWARD.** This 4,000 sq f basement 140-seater is simply gorgeous. The decor is breathtaking. It is intensly dark, but its spotlighting creates the most sexy environment. You down the stairs enter into the bar. And you must enjoy it. Have a drink or three and watch the cocktails being 'thrown and juggled', and have some bar-snacks. When you do move into the main dining area, it is in fact several areas, expertly divided, yet all in vision. There are private areas and public areas.The food is from ex Cinnamon Club chef KK Anand Starters range from Yellow Lentil Soup with Garlic Kulcha, £6; through Rabbit Keema Roll with Cardamom, or Guinea fowl breast marinated in Archar Pickle, both £9.50; to Tandoor-grilled King Scallops spiced with chilli, £11. Mains include Jumbo Prawn, Salmon, Bream,Tilapia Rack of Lamb, Chicken Thigh, from c£18 to £20. Vegetarian Platter is £30, while Meat is £45 and Seafood, £48. There is a wide selection of side dishes and desserts. *'We were invited to the 40th wedding anniversary of the original Cobra brewery owner from Bangalore. We were in a private room, about 20 of us, and it was a truly great occasion. The food lived up to everyone's expectations (and it isn't always easy to please south Indians). The service was discrete yet perfect. It is a venue highly suitable for private dos.'* DBAC. We were asked to recommend a venue for a pre-Christmas office party for 6 senior execs of a multi-national US company. They wanted a venue where they could arrive at lunch time and relax until evening. We suggested Mint Leaf. *'We enjoyed the pre-lunch drinks and lunch, then we returned to the bar sofas and enjoyed our drinks. Next I knew it was midnight and they were closing. Our bill? £1200 + Tip. Worth every dime!'* GR Hours: 12-3, Mon-Fri, dinner 5.30-11 daily. Bar 12-12, Mon-Weds; to 1am Thurs & Fridays; to 5-1am 12, Saturdays; and to 12am Sunday. *<mintleafrestaurant.com>*

Mint Leaf, SW1

THE QUILON — A-LIST & PREVIOUS BEST IN UK AWARD

St James Court Hotel, 45 Buckingham Gate, SW1 020 7821 1899

Taj Hotels Group have owned London's unique Bombay Brasserie (SW7) and the elegant St James's Court Hotel for many years. But it took until 1999 to open an Indian restaurant here. Though within the complex, the restaurant is only accessible from the street. It is modern, with clean lines and sparkly mosaics running discreetly around the room and a splendid monkey mural on one wall. It's a modern, light and airy restaurant, seating 92 diners in two areas. The restaurant's name comes from Quilon,

an unremarkable town on the coast road in the south of Kerala, not far from India's southernmost tip. This is the clue that the food is from the various states of south India. Indeed, the restaurant reflects what has been happening in Taj Hotels across India, where regional food of a high order is on their menus. In fact, Taj piloted this restaurant in Bangalore in 1988. Called Karavali, (meaning coastal food) it has become one of the city's favourites. Karavali owes its success to its original chef, Chef Aylur V Sriram. He originally trained with his father at the Hotel Sriram, and went on to work in some of India's top hotel restaurants. While at Karavali, the New Statesman described him as 'One of the top five chefs in India.' In 1999 he opened Quilon; his mission to recreate Karavali in London. Chef Sriram is a master; his spicing lyrical; his balance of flavour dreamlike; his menu a super choice of meat, fish and vegetable dishes. Unlike others in town, Sriram proves that there is no need for flamboyance, spin or new wave, *'Do not take a traditional dish and mess around with it,;* he says. In typical understated Taj style, he simply and quietly goes about his business of producing perfect Indian cooking. His reward is that he is now Quilon's General Manager as well as Chef. His small but perfectly balanced menu awaits you. It's an education. Here are some of the wonderful delights that you could sample. Starters: Partridge Masala, cooked in red chilli, ginger, garlic, fried onion flakes, tomatoes, lime juice and freshly ground roast masala of cardamom, cinnamon, aniseed and cloves – one of Pat's favourites, it's the red chilli that does it. Crab Cakes, crab meat sauteed with curry leaves, ginger, green chillies and cooked on a skillet until golden brown. Coorg Chicken, tangy preparation of sautéed chicken with roasted and ground coriander, peppercorns, mustard seeds, cinnamon, cumin seeds, laced with Coorg vinegar – I've eaten this dish many times and find it a must for those particular Coorg flavours. Masala Vada, crispy dumplings of yellow lentil, green chilli, fennel and curry leaves. Delicious main courses: Masala Fried Stuffed Squid (Quilon's most ordered dish) – squid, crispy fried and stuffed with spiced spinach, potatoes and drizzled with lemon and curry oil dressing. Mangalorean Chicken Curry (Kori Gassi), succulent pieces of chicken cooked in finely ground fresh coconut and roasted red chilli, peppercorns, cumin seeds, coriander seeds, tempered with chopped onion, fenugreek seeds and cumin seeds. Eat with a delicious Appam, soft-centred, lace-edged rice-pancake, (cooked on view in the restaurant) perfect for dipping into the rich masala sauce – I know its traditionally eaten with Istew, lamb or vegetable cooked Keralan-style, but hey! – let's break a few rules. Malabar Lamb Biryani, lamb marinated in traditional Malabar spices and cooked with basmati rice in a sealed pot, served with Pachadi (whole wheat layered bread cooked on skillet with pure ghee) and a lamb sauce. This dish is particularly delicious and outshines any other Biryani that you might have tried. Finish off with cooling and refreshing ice creams with traditional desserts of Bibinca or Dodal, unconventional to the western palate perhaps, but you will be converted – fabulous! In conclusion, a restaurant with management of this calibre means its quality remains rock-solid. It won our **BEST UK RESTAURANT** award last time, which means what it says. Though this award goes elsewhere this time, nothing will change our opinion. Main courses £8.50-£23. 2 course set lunch £12.95, 3 course £15.95 Service charge: 12.5%. Hours: 12-2.30 Mon-Fri and 6-11. Mon-Sat.

St James Court Hotel, SW1

The Quilon, SW1

SALOOS A-LIST

62 Kinnerton Street, SW1 020 7235 4444

M Salahuddin's Saloos is a Pakistani institution. It's been around for decades and at the beginning it set a new standard of service, decor and, yes, expense. Even 18 years ago, it was easy to spend £100 for two there. The elegant Farizeh Salahuddin (daughter of the house – she can be heard out of hours on the answer machine) handles bookings with considerable aplomb. It's still much hallowed by my Pakistani and Indian friends, well-educated wealthy citizens, who ignore politics when it comes to conviviality. But I am beginning to wonder if it has become overtaken by so many really excellent newer venues. Being Pakistani, meat, meat and more meat predominates (*'A vegetarian-free heaven'* says RA who, like Bernard Shaw, despises vegetables). The faithful still adore it. *'Succulent, natural-coloured, divinely-flavoured offerings like Chicken Shashlik, Lamb chop and Shami Kebab are insurmountable'* HEG. Hard-to-find, acquired taste Haleem, (see glossary) is one speciality. But we get somewhat reserved reports about Salloos from occasional or first-time visitors these days. The place is an institution and is worth at least one visit. The last time we were there seemed to be family day. There were kids all over the place (well behaved ones, Asian and white), thoroughly enjoying themselves as were their parents, the staff and us. An unmissable treat for the aficionado. High in our **A-LIST.** Set lunches at £13 and £17, (2 & 3 courses). Main courses c£11 to £16. Cover charge £1.50. Service 12.5%. Hours; 12-2.15/7-11, .Mon.-Sat.

SEKARA NEW ENTRANT

3 Lower Grosvenor Place, SW1 020 7834 0722

A combination of Indian and Sinhalese Sri Lankan cuisine. Go for the latter, and if you like it hot, ask the helpful personnel for it done as it would be back home. Menu snapshot: Sri Lankan Starters, mutton Rolls or Fish Rolls £3.50 two deep-fried crispy pancake rolls stuffed with a mixture of lightly spiced savoury lamb or fish and potato; Vadai £2.00, two deep-fried crunchy, spicy lentil cakes. Some mains: Mutton Lamprais £12.95, deep-fried pieces of mutton mixed with basmati rice flavoured with saffron and spices and served with mutton curry, aubergine and seeni sambola (fried onions). Lamprais or Lampries (singular from the Dutch word, 'Longkirist') was a festive dish introduced to Sri Lanka by a Dutch burger centuries ago: a full meal of meat curry, kofta, rice, and sambols is wrapped inside a banana leaf parcel and served like a hot picnic. This is the only venue we know of where you will find this dish. Chicken Koththu Roti £8.95, soft home made roti bread chopped up and stir-fried with chicken, fresh leeks, tomatoes and carrots to a historic recipe. Tandoori Mixed Grill, £14.95, pricey but contains all you need: King prawns, lamb tikka, chicken tikka, tandoori chicken and sheek kebab served with salad and naan bread; String Hoppers £10.95, steamed Sri Lankan noodles served with seer fish curry and pol sambola (coconut); Devilled chicken, pork or squid £5.95, with sweet green and red capsicums, onions and fresh green chillies in a rich, sweet, spicy-hot sauce. Dessert: Wattalapam £4.95, coconut milk, sweet jaggery, cashew nuts and pure kithul treacle and spiced with cinnamon and nutmeg. A postscript. We were going to nominate this restaurant for best Sri Lankan *(see page 37)* but the manager / owner told our researchers that they weren't interested in the *Guide,* nor in receiving an Award. So we dropped it. Inexplicable behaviour but we do get 'em from time to time. Normally we drop those-that-think-they-don't-need-help from the *Guide* altogether, but we do believe this restaurant has plenty going for it, not least the Lamprais, though this is no further helped by open credit card slips with the 10% service charge already added. To stay in the *Guide,* it needs your opinions. Hours: 12-3/6-10. <www.sekara.co.uk>

SPICY WORLD

76 Wilton Road, Pimlico, SW1 020 7630 9951

Mohammed Uddin carefully runs this venue. Whilst it doesn't have red flock (I wish I got a tenner every time I am asked where one is!) it has ruby red walls, crisp white table linen, kings' design cutlery, bouncy carpeting, Indian background music and the tacky laminated menu. Despite its expensive postcode, prices are normal, and the food lives up to its name, being deliciously spicy. All your favourites are on the menu. Baltis, curries, specials, nothing is missing (RCF loves the Nargis Kebabs – kebab mince around an egg). Get your weekday 3 course fill for £15. Sunday e-a-m-a-y-l lunch at £5.95 is really good value. Hours: 12 -12, daily.

WOODLANDS TOP 100

37 Panton Street, SW1 020 7930 8200

Long-established (1985) licensed, vegetarian, south

Indian 55-seat restaurant, just off Haymarket. It is the tiniest of UK Woodlands. The big news is that they've opened a new fifth London branch in Chiswick, NW3 (there some 30 are branches in India, Singapore and LA, each serving an identical menu. Bhel, Dosa, Idli, Vada, Samosa, Pakoda, Uthappams (*see page 75*). *'I particularly like southern Indian food, and find the menu so appealing, it makes choice difficult. We chose one exceptionally good-value set meal, Thali, £6.50, which was quite generous, with good variety, and the Paper Dosa, £3.95. Upma, £2.95, Lhassi, £1.25, and Channa, £3.75 are as good as ever. Also glad to have a choice of Indian desserts. Good value.'* HC. *'Gulab Jamun, slightly chewy cardamom-scented fried milk balls in a sticky syrup, Kulfi, Indian ice-cream in a variety of flavours and Carrot Halva, a dense pudding that has the consistency of fudge, are enough to satisfy any sweet tooth. And, if you missed out on a Dosa for your main course or want to continue the pancake theme, you could always end the meal with a butter dosa with sugar'.* TY. *'Enjoyed my lunchtime visit, indulging in the vegetarian buffet. Plenty of flavoursome dishes.'* RL Lunch,c £8; Dinner c £20. Service 12.5%. Hours: 11-2.45/5.30-10.45. Branches: London NW3, W1, W4 & Wembley, Mddx.

London SW3

Chelsea, King's Road, Sloane Square, Knightsbridge

HAANDI

PREVIOUS AWARD WINNER A-LIST

136 Brompton Rd, Knightsbridge, SW3
020 7823 7373

A restaurant with bar and two entrances. One at the rear on Cheval Place is at street level, while the one on Brompton Road is down a generous staircase, leading to a bright, clean and tidy reception and the bar, which serves snacks, and on the left is the restaurant. The lemony-yellow decor, with inviting tables and chairs, give a cheerful sunshine welcome. *'We propped up the bar on high stools, and sipped glasses of red wine, which Ray (proprietor) had chosen for us – very good. We chatted about India, its food and his Kenyan connections (Ray has a highly regarded restaurant there). We enjoyed Kebabs and Tikkas – a chef speciality; you can see them cooking through a plate glass window, followed by Chicken Tikka Butter Masala , fantastic, not overly tomatoey, creamy, smoky, with a little chilli kick, Gosht-Ki-Haandi , one of Pat's favourites with Dal Dera Ismail Khan , creamy black lentils, rice and Pudina Nan £2.10, quite thin, not doughy, sprinkled with finely chopped mint – lovely (Pat liked it and he's not a bread fan!). All dishes cooked properly, presented carefully, served professionally and in generous portions.* DBAC. Other diners think the same. *'Excellent menu, food and presentation with a warm welcome. A wonderful restaurant.'* RB *'Chakula Mzuri Sana is Kenyan for Good Food!'* NH. *'Absolutely gorgeous, good food, wine and service.'* JH. *'A great experience, not only the place was relaxing, the atmosphere and the staff really helpful. We had one of the best Indian meals we have ever come cross. We'll definitely go back.'* NM. *'I have become a regular. Absolutely amazing food, a great ambassador of Indian cuisine.'* AB. *'Absolutely love Haandi. Food so flavourful, spicy and delicious. Courteous staff are welcoming.'* CM. Menu Extracts: Khajy Til Rolls, vegetable roll with cashew nuts and mint. Bindya Prawns £12.20, crispy queen prawns. Diwani Haandi, mix of peas, corn, carrots and beans. Gosht Kabuli, lamb with chickpeas, lentils and fresh mint. Lunch Menus: from £9. Bar Hours: drinks served between 12-10.30, light meals and snacks available all day. Lunch -3. Dinner: 6-1130.

RASOI VINEET BHATIA

NEW ENTRANT A-LIST

10 Lincoln Street, Sloane Square SW3
020 7225 1881

This restaurant is chef led, but Vineet Bhatia in no ordinary chef. He is one of the most determined hard-workers I know. He worked his way up via the Star of India to Zaika, Chelsea then South Ken, where he gained his Star, Michelin, that is. But he also wanted total freedom, and he settled for a tiny venue (38 seats) where he could cook as he calls it *'properly rather than for a 300 cover factory with a more hands-on approach'.* Rasoi appropriately meaning 'kitchen' is housed in a 100 year old property which was

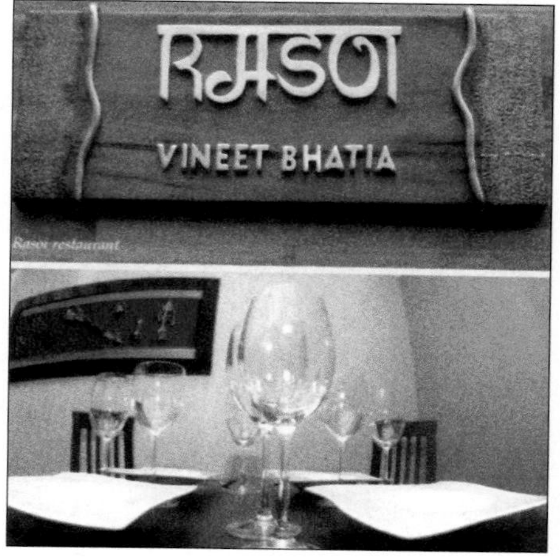

previously home to Richard Corrigan's English Garden restaurant. Vineet, with his wife Rashima, has revamped the Chelsea property into a mini-Indian palace. It is divided into two floors; the lower is the main dining area and bar and the upper level is split into two private function rooms and named after Rajasthan's twin cities – Udaipur and Jaipur, seating 8 and 15. . A myriad of rich eastern treasures creates a regal air. Rajasthani jharokas, –beautifully crafted wood frames, wedding saris draping the walls, a stunning Kashmiri rug, vibrant Benaris saris framing the windows and antiquated Indian chests placed throughout the restaurant. All embody the rustic charms and colourful culture of India. Being perfectionists, Vineet and Rashima have not overlooked their staff. Together with Rashima, Bobby Gudka who has designed clothes for some of India's biggest fashion houses, including Satya Paul has exclusively designed the staff uniforms using a theme of chocolate brown and turquoise. Vineet and Rashima have globe-trotted to source many of their furnishings and crockery. Chic chocolate brown dining tables are imported from Turkey, plates (there are over fifty types) have been brought in from countries like Spain and America, the silverware is from France and the Rosenthal glassware is German. A glass covered wall adds depth to the modest space and overlooks the teak wood surface of the bar. Frequently reported is the *'delicately explosive individual spicing'* RCF countered with *'rather bland. but enhanced with some green chillies'* JGS. As you would expect Vineet varies his menu and he experiments with non-Indian ingredients. Samosa fillings the like of spinach and sultana, chopped asparagus tips mixed with south Indian coconut chilli and curry leaf chutney, and shiitake mushroom with chopped roasted peanut are not liked by all. But the Tandoori platter gets universal acclaim for the different marinades and subtlety. There is an array of chicken, lamb, king prawn, fish, lobster and Indian vegetable main dishes. And you will find ingredients we do not normally associate with Indian food; items like broccoli, chestnuts, beetroot, pine nuts, Stilton (in the Naan) and honey. Vineet's Dum Pukht Biriani *(see page 69)* has always been fabulous. Vineet consults world-wide. Travellers to Mauritius must visit Safran, at Le Touessrok Hotel. Opened in 2002, following a £39m hotel refurbishment, Vineet's menu, and especially the caught-that-day sea food dishes have got the venue 'The Best Resort Food in The World' by Tatler Awards, 2004. General Manager, Thomas Heimann, also the sommelier has carefully selected an extensive range of wines, in addition to the range of spirits and cocktails. *'Exceptionally good food , much fresher and more creative than average. Good wines too.'* Jancis Robinson. Slightly understated Jancis; the list is as fabulous as the food. Not cheap though, the wines, nor the food. Main courses £15 to £36. Set meal £60 to £70. Service charge: 12.5%. Hours: 12-2.30 Mon-Fri. 6-10.30 Mon-Sat <www.vineetbhatia.com>

SHAHEEN OF KNIGHTSBRIDGE

225 Brompton Road, SW3 020 7581 5329

With Shaheen 150 yards from Harrods, if you are feeling a bit battered and worn, elbowing your way past the tourists, why not drop in at Shaheen to revive yourself and rest your feet! It's a long-standing restaurant, which understands its regulars and tourists equally well. *'very happy with the meal. Decor plain and menu short. Prices very fair, considering location. All food very good and all chose something different, so had a good range. Full marks for having a dessert menu that wasn't the usual fancy ice-creams. Very pleasant Gajar Halva'* HJC Lunch to-3pm. Dinner to-11.30, weekdays. Saturday and Sunday 12-11.30.

London SW4

Clapham

CLAPHAM TANDOORI

10 Clapham Common S, SW4 020 7622 4470

Clapham's second oldest (1971), owned by Abdur Rhaman Choudhury. His restaurant seats 72 diners, and head chef Shiraze Ahamed serves well-liked curries and side dishes and has some Indo-French specials up his sleeve, £7-7. Sunday lunch e-a-m-a-i-l £6.50, children (under 12) £3.50. Delivery: 3-mile radius, £10 min. Hours: 12-2.30/6-12.

MAHARANI

117 Clapham High Street, SW4 020 7622 2530

The 104-seat Maharani was established in 1958, at which time there were under 200 curry houses in the whole of the UK. It was not only Clapham's first curry house, opened long before Cla'am became trendy ma'am, it was one of the first to open in a London suburb. It has always earned its keep by providing good, bog-standard, formula curries; indeed, owner SU Khan was one of the pioneers of the formula.

Under the same ownership for all these years, Khan has kept up with the trends, though, and everything is as it should be. Hours: 12-2.30/6-12; Sun. 12-12.

London SW5

Earls Court

MASALA ZONE A-LIST NEW ENTRANT

147 Earl's Court Road, SW5 020 7373 0220

London's most exciting chain is expanding. Its distinctive decor and food make it stand out. From a simple selection of street food dishes to a thali – a complete meal on a plate, noodle bowls, curry & rice plates, tandoors & grills and Masala burgers. Most meals served within five minutes of ordering. *'Quality Very good Quantity Adequate Decor Minimalist Service Prompt and pleasant Comfort Adequate and very clever Comments Starters: Chicken Vada £3.95 dry and subtly spiced. Slightly too salty; Aloo Tikka Chat £3.50 lovely flavours, well spiced. Main Courses: Clove Smoked Lamb Korma £7.45 intense flavours and subtly spiced. Chicken Mangalore £6.55 very rich sauce, extremely tasty. Accompaniment: Vegetable side £1 delicious. Drinks: Stella £2.75; Cobra £3.15. Bill: £31.19. Mark: 8/10'* G&MP. Delivery telephone: 08700 841 330. Delivery lunch offer – 25% off. Hours 12.30 – 2.30, 5.30 – 10. Sit-in hours: Mon-Fri 12 -3, 5.30-11.30; Sat, Sun 12-11. *See page* 28, Branches:N1 & W1, WC2.

NIZAM TOP 100

152 Old Brompton Road, SW5 020 7373 0024

The Nizam was the former ruler of Hyderabad. Until partition he was the richest man in the world, and his dining table seated 101 guests, yes, at one table! On it was a silver model railway which chugged around the table dispensing whisky et al to the guests. M Mian's 1989 vintage Nizam is rather smaller, seating 65 on several tables in two rooms. *'Attractive appearance and warm reception. The food was varied and excellent with a number of dishes new to me and my guests. Chicken and prawn main courses with excellent vegetables, especially the smoked aubergine. Service was superb throughout.'* RH. Service is exemplary, with smartly waistcoated waiters, exuding expertise. NW Frontier and Moghul cuisine is carefully executed by chef M Riaz. Specialities include smoky Baingan Bharta, (charcoal-grilled aubergine, its flesh then mashed to a purée), Prawn Piri Piri, (coconut milk and chilli). Cover charge £1. Takeaway 10% discount. Delivery: £12 min. Hours: 12-2.30/6-11.45.

STAR OF INDIA TOP 100

154 Old Brompton Road, SW5 020 7373 2901

Reza and Azam Mahammad run this startling restaurant. I say startling for two reasons. One is because Vineet was once chef here. (see Rasoi Vineet Bhatia, SW3, earlier). Vineet is a larger-than-life character, but he fades to insignificance alongside Reza. Get him talking to you and you'll see what I mean. It is startling too because the decor is a dead-ringer of Michael Angelo's Sistine Chapel. Starters include: Galouti Kebab, smooth mince lamb patties, served with onion and cumin relish. Samundri Ratan, Saffron infused chargrilled scallops served in a creamy sauce. Chenna Samosa crispy parcels filled with a trio of goat, buffalo and cow's cheese, mixed with leeks, ginger and green peppercorns, served with a spiced tomato and chive chutney. Main courses: Murghabi Tawe Wale, escallops of mallard marinated with garlic, nutmeg, lemon and chilli oil, pan fried on an iron griddle. Raan Mussallam (serves two), roasted leg of baby lamb marinated in a mixture of spices then cooked over a gentle flame in a rich onion and tomato gravy, flavoured with nutmeg and flambéed with rum. If you can spare room for a pudding, try either the Dum Malai Chikki, steamed milk pudding scented with nutmeg and cardamom, topped with caramelised jaggery and carom seeds, served chilled, or the Phalon Ka Muzaffar, home made seasonal fruit compote, served with cardamom ice cream, or have both! Lunch and dinner daily. Some say the Star has passed its zenith. Tell that to its regulars! Hours 12.30 - 2.30, 6 - 10.30.

London SW6

Fulham, Parson's Green, West Brompton

BLUE ELEPHANT THAI

AWARD WINNER

4 Fulham Broadway, SW6 020 7385 6595

The benchmark for best Thai restaurant anywhere, this group, headed by Belgian Karl Steppe, and his Thai wife has branches worldwide, recently including a cookery school in Bangkok. London's Blue Elephant has always been the group's flagship. The stunning Blue Bar, based on the Royal Thai Barge, enhances the whole experience. The bar menu includes a salad of young sour mango, palm sugar and roast coconut. On entering this enchanted kingdom, allow yourself to be taken on a wonderful journey, tasting some of the finest Thai cuisine in the country. Cross the delightful bridge stretching over a picturesque lily pond and enter the heart of lush jungle, exotic blooms and thatched Thai dining 'Houses'. Bundles of redolent orchids, freshly imported from Bangkok's famous floating market fill the light and airy interior. Specialist chefs prepare the finest in Royal Thai cuisine, ensuring each dish possesses the stamp of authenticity. Friendly and efficient staff are at hand to recommend and advise from the extensive menu that boasts a fabulous array of vegetarian dishes. The spectacular Sunday Brunch includes entertainment for children and unlimited servings for only £16.75! All this is why we have frequently rated it the best Thai restaurant in the country. Lunch and dinner daily.

DARBAR NEW TO OUR TOP 100

92 Waterford Road, SW6 020 7348 7373

Pravin Chauhan's family run and very successful London's Diwan-e-Am, But Pravin wanted his own venue and Darbar, (meaning royal court) is the outcome. His choice of chef shows the astrologers were smiling on Pravin. To establish things he got Mohammed Rais from the Red Fort London w1, having been there since 1997. His final ace is his advisor. Kris Patel owned the fabulous Diwana Bhel Poori House, Drummond Street, NW1, in fact he pioneered this type of food into Britain.. He sold up a few years ago, but the restaurant bug didn't leave him and he is now a sleeping partner, advising Pravin on the running of the restaurant. This combination ensures the restaurant is promoted into our **TOP 100.** Although Rias has now returned to the Red Fort, his Dum Pukht *(see page 69)*. legacy remains Starters include Galauti Kebab – the smoothest patties of minced lamb and spices. These are often cooked at your table to add to the drama. Teetar gilafi kebab – spiced roasted minced partridge. Monkfish tikka – chunks of monkfish smoked with ginger. For main course, the wallets love Dum ka lobster – lobster steamed in a delicate sauce of mace, cumin and saffron, £28. But the Dum Pukht cogniscenti go for any of Rais' Birianis cooked in a sealed pot: Avadhi gosht biryani – Rais' 300 year old family recipe of lamb and rice. Samudari biryani – scallops, squid, prawns and rice. Subz biryani – moist basmati rice, vegetables and spices. Desserts include Strawberry Shirkhand – yoghurt flavoured with

Blue Elephant, SW 6

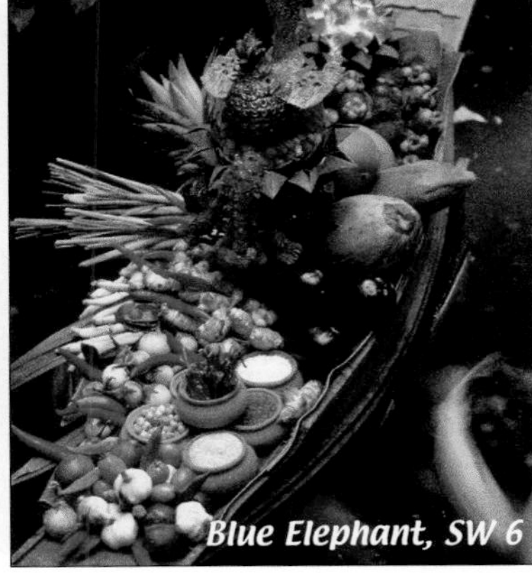

Blue Elephant, SW 6

fresh raspberry couli, £6. Not cheap, but this is Chelsea. Min spend £25 lunch and £45 dinner.

LILY TANDOORI NEW ENTRANT

86c Lillie Road, West Brompton SW6
020 7385 1922

'Everything very good – the food, service, the price! The original Bengali cuisine, the one I was brought up with, the old fashioned taste. The Vindaloo was fantastic and the people so friendly. We were working at the Ideal Home Exhibition, erecting stands for a week prior to the opening of the show, and again, a month later to dismantle the stands. I'm in my 50's now and was pleased to get that authentic taste. We need more old fashioned restaurants as they used to be, not the fancy types which we are getting now.' PC. Peter, you are not alone with this comment.

MEMSAAB NEW ENTRANT

7 The Boulevard, Imperial Wharf, SW6:
020 7736 0077

The 96-cover Memsaab is Bilal Ali and Abdul Jalil's third restaurant. This flagship branch veers away from their popular Sussex Memories of India located in Brighton Marina, and Chichester for several years. Sited in Chelsea's swanky Imperial Wharf, the Memsaab offers diners a variety of regional Indian dishes that amalgamate traditional recipes with modern food trends developing in India today. Memsaab's interior decor reflects the modern and stylish surroundings of Imperial Wharf. Don't expect a river view though: it overlooks the railway. For pre-dinner drinks there is a special 16-seater lounge area where brown leather furnishings and American walnut hardwood flooring invite guests to enjoy custom cocktails like the Attitude Adjuster and Bombay Swinger, before heading off for some food. Cool toffee-coloured leather chairs and banquettes, cherry hardwood floors, traditional carved wooden screens and special Cold Cathode lighting are just some of the interesting features in the main dining area. Blown up pictures of various spices in Indian markets deck the walls and offer an ethnic flavour, but the focal point is a specially preserved palm tree that adds a touch of the tropics to west London contrasting with smart tableware and place-settings. South Indian Head Chef Muraalindharan, formerly at Chutney Mary, has created an a la carte menu that encompasses some of the best Indian cuisine from across the country. Menu Snapshot: Punjabi starter of Chana chickpeas and Aloo Chop, fried potato cake with a whisp of chilli; Chettinad Quails; Madras pot-roasted quails with shallots, star anise and toasted garlic; Palak Tikka Masala, roasted pepper with spinach patties served with tomato cumin sauce; and Quilon Seabass, seabass fillet marinated in red Keralan style masala pan fried in banana leaves. Special desserts include Kheer Brulee and fresh fruit skewers with honey yoghurt. Puja Vedi, Ed, Tandoori Magazine. Lunch £6.95, meat curry, boiled rice, paneer, and yogurt. Dinner for two with wine and service: around £80. Mon-Sat 12-11.30 / Sun 11 <www.memsaabrestaurant.co.uk>

Memsahib, SW 6

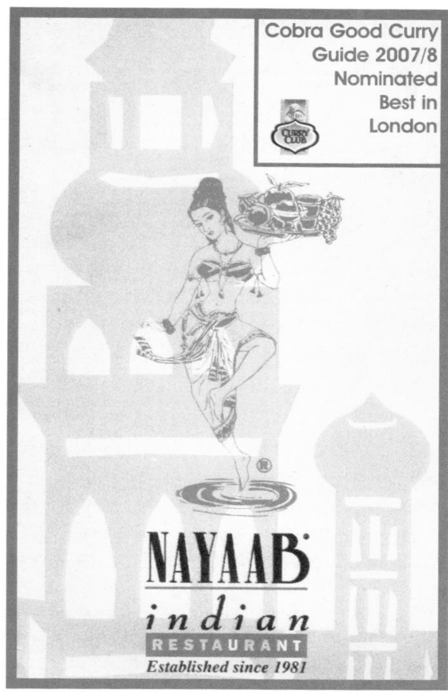

Cobra Good Curry Guide 2007/8 Nominated Best in London
NAYAAB
indian
RESTAURANT
Established since 1981

NAYAAB **NOMINATED BEST IN LONDON**

309 New Kings Rd (jnct'n Munster Rd), SW6
020 7731 6993

Praveen Rai has been around for a long time (est 1981) and this ensures that he runs a very good upmarket restaurant and superior Indian cooking will greet you. There are a lot of lovely dishes to choose from, so take your time and enjoy! Praveen's menu is full of *'some dishes you won't recognise and some that you will'.* The former are Indian and Pakistani specials cooked by head chef Akeel Ghani. Menu Snapshot: Lamb's Liver £4.95 - medium spiced, sautéed with onions and plum tomatoes; Baingan Pakoras £3.95 - gram flour coated aubergine roundels filled with cheese and herbs, crispy fried; Dhingree Chicken £5.95 - supreme breast of chicken stuffed with delicately spiced garlic mushrooms, rolled in gram-flour batter and deep-fried; Nihari £7.95 - lamb shank, slow cooked, pot roasted, sautéed, sealed, spicy sauce, slow cooked; Chuza Anardana £7.95 - whole poussin rubbed with home-made chutney (mint, pomegranate, spices) grilled in tandoor, hot and tangy; Monk Caldini £12.95 - spicy fish curry, cooked with 'kokum' (butternut berries), coconut, palm vinegar, garlic, curry leaves; Red Pumpkin £3.95 - lightly spiced, sautéed with onions, mustard and garlic; Mooli Ka Paratha £3.50 - multi-layer bread stuffed with spiced grated white radish. This is all dedicated stuff, and well spoken of by the regulars. For the if-you-must-brigade, Mr Rai offers 'old curry-house favourites' which include everything except Phal (he'll explain how it came to be 'invented by chefs as a revenge against the lager lout – and he'd never serve it or them!'). So if you are chilli-addicted, as Praveen himself is, then choose the hotter specials. Praveen is from the old-school of owner-management. He is gracious, articulate, witty and thoroughly good company. We cannot recommend it highly enough. And the added advantage is the discount:: Show Praveen your copy of this *Guide* and receive a massive 25% discount on food bill. Price Check: Popadom 60p, CTM £6.95, Pullao Rice £2.50. Set menus for two at £13 and £16 pp. Delivery: 3 miles, £10 minimum. Hours: 6-11.45 (11.30 on Sun.) <www.nayaab.com>

London SW7

Kensington

BOMBAY BRASSERIE **A-LIST**
LIFETIME BEST RESTAURANT AWARD

14 Courtfield Close, Courtfield Road, SW7
020 7370 4040

The Bombay Brasserie (BB to its friends) pioneered Indian regional cooking in this country, in fact the world when it opened in 1982. It hadn't even been done in India It is now the 50-strong Taj Hotel Group's flagship venue, earning millions of profit each year. It is an icon. And its management by Adi and Harun is exemplary. Staff turn-round is minimal. Locals and regulars, of which there are very many greet the same staff faces year after year. Of our many thousands of reports received each year, we typically get around 100 about the BB. It way out does any other venue. Despite seating a considerable 265, you are advised to book. Some nights they serve 400 guests, split between a stylish restaurant and conservatory. It's nothing to see Madonna on one table, Hugh Grant on another, and the odd politician or Peer on a third. None of this phases the waiters. The chefs are all Taj-trained regional specialists And this is some of their work: Samosa Chaat, vegetable samosas, served with chick peas, sweet yoghurt and a medley of chutneys. Aloo Tuk, crispy fried baby potatoes in jacket, topped with sweet yoghurt and imli (tamarind chutney). Sev Batata Puri , small biscuits like puris topped with cubed boiled potatoes, gramflour straws, sprouted lentil, coriander leaves and covered with a mix of mint, tamarind and chilli chutneys. And for mains: Chicken Tikka Makhani, chicken tikka immersed in a spiced butter sauce – fantastic CTM done the proper way. Lamb Chops with ginger and green herbs, French cut, English lamb cooked Indian style. Margi Ni Sali , chicken curry topped with straw potatoes. *'Pat and I enjoyed a candle-lit dinner for two, sitting in the conservatory. After finishing a bottle of well chilled champagne in the bar, we sampled an abundance of delicious starters and main dishes and enjoyed everything immensely, but we always do at the BB! We finished off in the bar with their unique Cobra coffee - if you haven't had it, you don't know what you are missing!! It's absolutely fabulous as is the whole BB experience.'* DBAC. *(see page 82). 'A friend booked six of us after our annual 'Messiah from Scratch' at the Royal Albert Hall. The BB is the sort of restaurant in which to spend a whole evening, and our concert made us late, but it was still such a treat. Surroundings are lovely, menu different, wonderfully tempting, food fantastic. Usual grumble – service. Professional when it came but had to attract attention to order drinks, ditto food. But atmosphere made up for everything. First class restaurant whatever its cuisine. Not cheap but top quality never is. Haven't been since 1984, so pleased it has kept up high standard. Had an out-of-this-world lobster dish. All superb, generous, and individual. Most impressed, we all were. £72 per couple.'* HC. *'Attended the London International Trade Fair at Olympia and stayed in a hotel near the BB. Booked a table for 12 and entertained my colleagues with a top-class Indian meal. On arrival we were warmly greeted as we drank glasses of Omar Khayyam. Shown to an excellent round table in the conservatory and served us Chef's Choice. What followed can only be described as a procession of exceptional food with a variety of dishes too numerous to remember or name, washed down with 6 bottles of fabulous white wine. All who dined, thought it was the best meal they had ever eaten and would return again on special occasions – or when the company was paying!! £735 for twelve.'* DL. *'We go to enjoy the pianist as much as the food'* RCF. *'We moved to the curry desert of Devon from Berkshire and regularly ate at the Bombay Brasserie, a great exponent of the skills of cooking great Indian food.'* AF. Daily lunch buffet: £20. Min charge: £30.00. Service 12.5%. Hours: 12-3/7.30-12. (82 - 84) *See page 40*. Branch: Quilon, sw1.

CAFÉ LAZEEZ A-LIST

93 Old Brompton Road, SW7 020 7581 9993

Lazeez, meaning *'delicate and aromatic'*, describes itself as a 'new type of Indian restaurant'. It operates in true café mode, with nonstop opening hours. It has a striking frontage, with 26 good-weather seats outside. Inside are 130 seats, on two floors. Downstairs in stark, minimalist surroundings, is a short-menu café (which changes to full menu after 7pm). Upstairs is decorated with an illuminated, white, tented roof, and a full menu. Its owners are Pakistani, in the persons of the elegant Ms Sabiha Kasim and her brother Zahid. They were undoubtedly ahead of their time with their bar/new-wave concept. Despite criticism in earlier years about the evolved nature of some of their food, they've stuck to their guns. Suddenly, and at long last, we're getting the good reports we've always longed Lazeez to achieve. HC glows: *'Spicing different, and not necessarily Indian. A good place to take people who say they don't like Indian food. Succulent prawns, sizzling lamb chops, well-spiced vegetables, rich and creamy Korma, the Lamb Sag, not enough lamb, but good flavour, Saffron Rice fantastic, firm, fresh and spicy mushrooms, star dish, aubergine – superb – and the Nan, small, round, lightest and crispest I've had. Expensive, but first class. Overall, a wonderful meal.'* HC. That Korma is a good example. It's authentic, as done in the Pakistani heartlands where the meat is marinated in yoghurt to tenderise it, resulting in a mild, aromatic dish with subtle spicing, including a hint of garam masala, ergo Lazeez! *'It's a lively place. We like to enjoy the bar downstairs for an hour or so then go upstairs for our meal.'* Following Cafe Lazeez's deal with Payne & Gunter to supply Asian food for Natural History Museum catering events, Cafe Lazeez has now signed a deal to provide Asian food for similar events at Twickenham rugby Club. Average snack price £7, meal price £33, inc. service and cover charge. Hours: 11-11. (10.30 Sun.). Branches: Café Lazeez, London W1 & Birmingham B1.

DELHI BRASSERIE

134 Cromwell Road, SW7 020 7370 7617

Owner Mr A Jabber says *'shop out and pop in'* (it's near Sainsbury's). A bright comfortable spacious 60-seater. Chef Ram Singh's food and service is reported to be excellent curryhouse stuff with all your favourites on the menu. Hours: 12-11.30.

KHAN'S OF KENSINGTON

3 Harrington Road, SW7 020 7584 4114

60-seater, est. 1991 by Mr Khan (no relation to Khan's, W2). We have several good reports about this venue. It's a meat-eater's haven – scrumptious chops and tikka, tender lamb main courses, and all at a reasonable cost. Hours: 12-2.30/6-11.30; Sat. 12-12; Sun. 12.30-11.

SHEZAN INDIAN TOP 100

16 Cheval Place, Montpelier Street, SW7 020 7584 9316

This long-established (1966), very traditionally elegant 120-seat Pakistani restaurant, is in a residential street a block north of Old Brompton Road. The downstairs dining room, past the bar, is elegantly simple, with its downlighters, pewter plates, long-rolled napkins, traditional Pakistani chairs, all made theatrical by strategic lighting and candlelight. Chef Khan's food is as sophisticated as the service. It's traditional authentic Pakistani food done as it would have been for the royal courts. No innovation, no nonsense. Not even CTM (but its originator dish, Murgh Makhni) £12. The prices are Knightsbridge, but it's worth every penny just for regal service and care. Our favourite is still on: Choosa e Shezan – a chicken (whole poussin)-and-egg story described on the menu as *'a speciality of our dear old Khansama (cook)'*, and billed at a dear old £16! Set lunch £12.95. Minimum charge dinner £25. Service 10%. Cover charge £1.50. Takeaway 20% off. Shezan branches in New York

London SW8

Battersea, South Lambeth, Vauxhall

CAFÈ ZIA NEW ENTRANT

811 Wandsworth Rd, SW8 020 3202 0077

In 2002 renowned chef and restaurateur, Manju Choudhury took a sabbatical from his successful group of over 20 restaurants (the Hawelli Group, well known to this *Guide*) to explore the flavours, food, and ingredients that make up India's famously diverse culinary world. After a four-year hiatus, he has translated much of what he learned into a stunning menu at his new flagship restaurant, Café Zia. Manju's brother, Mosru Choudhury co-owns and manages the 100-seat restaurant. The contemporary design is fresh, with curtained windows and natural lighting offering a homely setting. Collaborating with his Head Chef, Govinder Prasad-Gurung, who joined the restaurant after ten years as Head Chef of Battersea's Bombay Bicycle Club (also well known to this Guide), Choudhury offers diners signature dishes like Bhuna Gosht Khybari, tender lamb flavoured with a hint of coriander and ginger cooked in a garlic and onion sauce; Chicken Aishwarya, slices of tender butter chicken breast marinated in lemon and methi leaf and cooked in a rich almond sauce; and Mala King Prawns, that are simmered in wine, garlic and almond sauce. Delivery service over a four-mile radius. *Puja Vedi, Ed, Tandoori Magazine.* .

Cafe Zia, SW8

London SW9

Brixton, Oval, Stockwell

OLD CALCUTTA

64a Brixton Road, SW9 020 7582 1415

Old Calcutta and its predecessor (Oval Tandoori) have been in this Guide from the beginning. Owner Abdul Mazid says: *'we're situated at the Oval tube end of the road (the A23) an area sometimes described as a gourmet desert.'* But not for curry gourmets who love the formula. Delivery: 3 miles, £12 min. Hours: 12-2.30/6 -12. Go on the website to hear some lyrical Ravi Shankar music. <www.calcutta.co.uk>

Chutney Mary

The elegant kebab platter

The magnificent Tokri Chaat

London SW10

Chelsea, West Brompton

CHUTNEY MARY

OUTSTANDING RESTAURANT

535 Kings Road, SW10 020 7351 3113

Chutney Mary opened in 1990. From the beginning they had a brigade of six chefs each from a different region of India, each dispensing their own speciality dishes. This was not the first to do this, but Chutney Mary did it rather well. We are proud of the fact that we gave Chutney Mary the first ever Best Restaurant Award back in 1992. And we did it again in 1999. Owners Camellia and Namita Panjabi and Ranjit Mathrani have since become well-established in the restaurant industry and have become renowned for their high quality Indian restaurants. They next bought Veeraswamy (W1) then opened one after another revolutionary Masala Zones *(See wl).* and more recently, the stunning Amaya, SW1. all Award winners in this Guide. Amaya won the ITV Tio Pepe Best Restaurant of the Year Award and in January this year it was awarded a Michelin star. Quite why Chutney Mary and In November 2005 Camellia won Best Restaurateur of the Year 2005 at the World Gourmet Summit annual awards in Las Vegas. Such awards are not given lightly, and the trio have no fear, it seems when it comes to restyling. In 2003 they shut Chutney Mary down for three months for a total refit. DBAC takes up the story: *'On a preview visit, Pat and I were treated to an exclusive dinner. The refurbishment left little trace of its pre-existence. The old colonial bar has gone, replaced by a bright and airy private dining room. Sparkling Indian mosaics (a glass ball is made, and then smashed, the pieces are then gathered to make the mosaics) take you down to the main restaurant, which is decorated with works of modern Indian art, concealed spot lights, and masses of candles held in clear crystal glass. The conservatory is still there, complete with tree and sparkling fairy lights. The water fountain has gone, but new pot plants decorate the perimeter of the encirclement. We start with Bombay Blush (Champagnoise with rose liqueur, decorated with purple orchids).'* DBAC. Those candles are in specially designed Indian glass candelabra which effectively create a romantic ambience similar to the twinkling of a Sheesh Mahal. Hi-tech lighting gives a moonlit effect to the legendary conservatory, decorated with its forest of Indian greenery. A sumptuous, thickly woven carpet and dark wood furniture swathed in silk cushions helps to create a luxurious yet relaxed atmosphere. The wine list by wine writer Mathew Jukes is definitive, and would do justice in any restaurant. It features over 100 wines, kept in a glassed-in, temperature-controlled wine room in the restaurant where customers can see the ideal conditions in which their wine has been kept. Jukes promises relatively low mark-ups on the more expensive wines – *'to encourage experimentation'*. Taj-trained Chef Nagarajan Rubinath has taken the mantle from Hardeep Singh now at the Group's Masala Zone. The menu constantly changes. although some old favourites remain constant. .Some years ago, Mathrani asked me how presentation could be improved at Indian restaurants. I recall blubbering some inconsequential answer. I know now that the Panjabis already had the issue in hand. Food presentation at Chutney Mary is revolutionary and it is still unique in the Indian market. Each dish has its own bespoke high-quality white platter or handmade glass plate chosen for shape and utility. on which it is plated with its own food-layout by the chefs. Nothing illustrates this better than the starters. For example, magnificent Tokri Chaat (*see above*); a potato-lattice basket exudes home-made imli and yoghurt-based 'street-food' studded with fresh green coriander and red pomegranate seeds. It not only looks good, it tastes good too, and this alone could be my last dish on earth. The Kebab Platter is equally elegant. There is also. But there are other favourites: Chandini Tikka (cornfed chicken breast tikka using white spices) or Konkan Prawns with asparagus.Starters (£6.25 to £9.50). Main courses (£16 to £ 20) include four different Chicken Tikkas, Duck with Apricots (a Parsee favourite – Jardaloo), fanned slices of pinky duck breast, drizzled with a spicy minced sauce with halved apricots, a fab Tandoori Crab, and other modern crab dishes that are all the rage in Bombay seafood restaurants. Wild Seabass Allepey (pan-grilled in a coconut and coriander sauce with green tomato salsa) or Mangalore prawn curry (with chilli hot sauce with tamarind and coconut). Vegetarians have a choice of two platters – one is a traditional North Indian platter of vegetables and daal. The other comprises unusual vegetarian dishes such as stir-fried banana flower with coconut, baby courgette masala, okra and water chestnut in a selection of 7 items. Desserts from c£6include the legendary Dark Chocolate Fondant with orange blossom lassi. Mains come plated, which some don't like because it makes sharing hard. There is a good selection of sides and breads, including Black Urad Dal (Maharani) – [DBAC's favourite] dark, rich, creamy, aromatic spices, swirl of cream. Suffice to say, the bold redec venture paid off. The place is more gorgeous than ever. Its regular clients are back, and loving it all the more. One way to try it all is to order the Tasting Menu of seven courses at £70 per head. Chutney Mary deserved its 1992 and 1999 Awards and it deserves it again. Nobody does it better. The Panjabis are the most innovative restaurateurs in the Indian sector. They stick to their beliefs, which is to offer Indian food done exquisitely well. Chutney Mary, their first venture got off to a slow and timid start. But that was years ago. It is now a huge success and a visionary pioneer. The team are now as confident as can be, and we can only await their future ventures impatiently. Meanwhile Chutney Mary remains my all-time favourite Indian Restaurant. 3 course set lunch £17. Service charge: 12.5%. Jazz lunchtime Sundays. 24-seat party room upstairs. Hours: Lunch 12.30-2.30, Saturday and Sunday only. Dinner 6-11, daily except Sunday - 10.30 *See page* 28. <www.realindianfood.com>

PAINTED HERON BEST CHEF AWARD AND A-LIST

112 Cheyne Walk, SW10 020 751 5232

It's between Albert and Battersea Bridges, on a corner site. Parking is difficult; there are few single yellow lines. The restaurant is tastefully decorated, under the minimalist banner – white walls with modern prints. Tables are simply laid, white linen cloths, napkins, contemporary cutlery and a single wine balloon. Rounds of moulded glass contain coloured oil with wick to light each table inadequately. Chairs are painted black wood, seated with leather and comfortable. Lumber floors are polished and the large plate glass windows are dressed with wooden slatted blinds. We perused the menu and sipped Shiraz (£17), over a large oval platter, generously piled high with fresh Popadom strips, accompanied by three chutneys – Beetroot, Coconut and Mango and Chickpea with Chilli. All hand-made and all fabulous. Staff are smilers - smart, clean and very willing. The Painted Heron's young owner decided in 2003 to get into the Indian restaurant business. It wouldn't be my advice, but he's in property and owns the building, and he seems to have an instinct for it. His ace card is his choice of chef – Yogesh Datta. He's Taj-trained, and it is amazing just how good Taj chefs are.

Painted Heron, SW 10

Yogesh has absolutely no ego (others take note). He is totally dedicated to hands-one cooking. He enjoys a challenge and he's very much hands-on. His menu, which changes every few days, has no long, meaningless narrations, just short, concise definitions, or perhaps the best explanation, honesty! And Yogesh runs the kitchen with just two other chefs. (others take note). The food sometimes has an innovative signature, but it is glorious Indian food, all carefully crafted and accurately spiced. For starters, we settled on 'Pheasant Breast with Green Chilli and Garlic' a good piece of foul, carbon-tinged from the Tandoor – tender meat on a minuscule bone, accompanied by a salad flavoured with ajwan and ginger – delicious. We also had 'Chutney-stuffed Paneer Cheese Tikka', an oblong of exquisite hand-made cheese, split into two, rather like a sandwich, stuffed with Podina (mint). As if that wasn't enough we couldn't resist Gol Goppa, a wheat-flour mini 'flying-saucer', loaded with a spicy small potato cubes drizzled with imli and a trickle of natural yoghurt. Main courses were a quarrelsome choice, with so many delectable dishes. We agreed on 'Chicken stuffed with green chilli pickle in hot Rajasthani curry', a very clever dish of chicken breast which Yogesh had lightly beaten, making it flat. Chilli pickle had been positioned and the chicken rolled in a cylinder then baked. The enrobing spicy, creamy sauce contained curry leaves with long slivers of lightly sauteed onion. Ingeniously innovative but very Indian in taste. 'Lamb Shank with aromatic spices', was served in a impressive, round, shiny, white metal bowl with a wide flat rim. The portion was so large it could have generously fed two and was so tender it literally fell of the bone. I choose side dishes of 'Wild Mushroom Pullao', Basmati rice, oval-plated, good flavour with tonnes of garlic and delicate slices of different fungi varieties. Since giving up wheat, I am now appreciating rice much more than before and can tell the good stuff from the dud! Simply described as 'Black Lentils' urid dal, well cooked, creamy, with a whirl of fresh cream decorating it surface. Quite chilli hot, but with a full, rounded flavour, not raw. Pat requested a Mint Paratha. He thought it would harmonise his meal well and he was right. It was delivered in a basket, rolled very thinly and sprinkled with finely chopped, dried, mint leaves. Pat's words 'VERY nice.' Full to the gills, we resisted Gulab jamun with chocolate ice cream £4, or Coconut tarte with coconut ice cream and chocolate syrup £4. We were delighted to give Yogesh our **BEST CHEF AWARD.** Nobody anywhere does it better. Main courses from c £10. Discretionary 12½% service charge. Garden seats. Hours: Lunch 12-2.30 weekdays. Dinner 6-11 daily. Sadly their SE11 branch did not stay the pace and is closed. <www.thepaintedheron.com>

VAMA THE INDIAN ROOM TOP 100

438 Kings Road, SW10 020 7351 4118

Vama, meaning 'womanhood', was established in 1997 by brothers Andy and Arjun Varma. Stylishly decorated with ochre walls and teak chairs, hand-made crockery from Khurja, and a fossil-stone floor. It is quite obvious to see why the 110 seat Vama is so popular. The Varmas (different spelling) are charming men, who are very relaxed chatting to their many regular clients including Lloyd Webber, Rowan Atkinson and Curry Club member Sir John-Harvey Jones. The cuisine is North West Frontier. This takes us from the Afghan border to the Punjab. Specials: Mahi (Salmon Tikka) Ajwaini £8.75. Tandoori Jhinga, Tiger prawns marinaded in yoghurt, chilli-oil and fennel, roasted on charcoal, £13.50, being the most popular dish ordered. Mains include duck, partridge or quails. And it is a venue where you get the rare paper-thin Roomali Roti ('handkerchief bread'). We certainly rate Vama's and are delighted

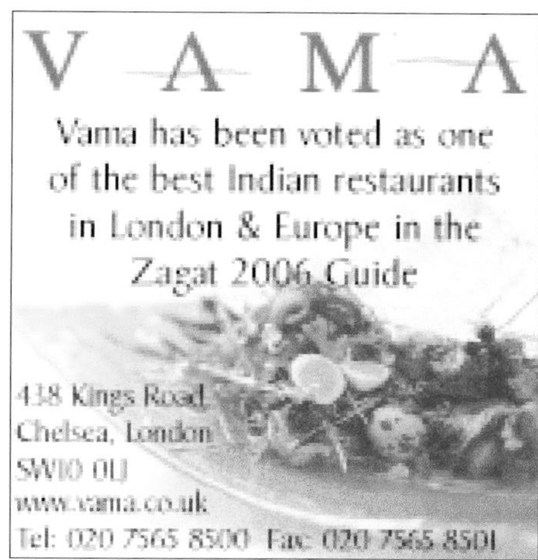

to keep it in our **TOP 100**. Good weather seating outside on the patio: four tables to choose from. Entertainments: cabaret and belly dancer. 35 seat party room. 4 patio tables. Service 12.5%. Cover charge £1. Hours: 12.30-3/6.30-11.30; 10.30pm on Sun. Vama-Ji, is the brothers' Indian cuisine delivery service. Cooked at their state-of-the-art, new Central Processing Unit in Battersea it delivers to homes and businesses within a 10 mile radius of Battersea, ring 020 7736 2300. Vama-Ji have opened four concession counters and two diners in Selfridges food halls in Manchester, Birmingham and London.

V A M A
Vama has been voted as one of the best Indian restaurants in London & Europe in the Zagat 2006 Guide
438 Kings Road
Chelsea, London
SW10 0LJ
www.vama.co.uk
Tel: 020 7565 8500 Fax: 020 7565 8501

London SW11

Battersea

BSWAYAM RUCHI NEW ENTRANT

2 Battersea Rise SW11 020 7738 0038

A Keralan restaurant. It really is such a treat to see such good regional food served here. Menu Snapshot: Achappam £2.95 - a flower shaped snack made of rice flour, coconut, black sesame, cumin; Pickles and Chutneys £2.50 - mango; lemon; garlic; fish; mixed vegetable pickle and coriander chutney; Medu Vada £3.95 - soft silky dumplings, lightly fried, crisp crunchy case, made from urid dhal, black pepper, fresh green chilli served with coconut chutney; Potato Bonda £3.95 - potato balls fresh ginger, curry leaves, coriander, black mustard, dipped in chickpea flour batter, crispy fried, served with creamy coconut chutney; Konju Varathathu £5.95 - crunchy battered fried prawn with corn flour, egg, chilli, ginger, garlic. Ruchi Kadal Soup £4.25 - £3.45 - peppery broth of lentils, garlic, tomatoes, spices, tamarind; Alleppey Konju Masala £9.95 - stir-fried prawns, ginger, curry leaves, chilli, mustard seed, crushed black pepper; Crab Thoran £12.95 (one of Pat's) - crab meat stir-fried, grated coconut, green peas, shallots, mustard seeds, served in shell. *'Rasam is of my favourites, another is Erachi Olathiyath £7.95. The first time I ate this dish, we were staying in South India, where a green lizard lived behind the bathroom mirror. The hotels' restaurant, called the Sea Shells, because of the huge shell chandeliers that hung from the ceiling, served this rich aromatic dish, flavoured with roasted coconut, turmeric, red chilli and onion. While we ate, a cockroach crawled up the wall and disappeared behind a picture. No such visitor at Swayam Ruchi though.'* DBAC. Back to their menu: Masala Dosa £6.95 - a paper thin pancake made of rice and black gram, folded in half with a filling of spicy potatoes, cooked with onions and ginger. *'If you have never eaten a dosa, I insist that you try one, share one! Some years ago, when we stayed at the Fort Aguada, Goa for a weeks holiday, I ate Masala Dosa with Sambar and Coconut Chutney every day for breakfast. We then flew to Bangalore to visit Raji and Balan of Mysore Breweries. Raji laughed long and loudly, when I told her my eating habits! Rasam is her favourite too, and she serves it from a Wedgewood Florentine teapot!'* DBAC. Back to their menu: Beetroot Pachadi £5.95 - fresh beetroot,

yoghurt, coconut, mustard seed and curry leaves; Appam £2.65 - a crispy, spongy rice pancake - delicious! Hours: 12 - 3 / 6 - 11. <www.swayamruchi.com>

London SW12

Balham

BOMBAY BICYCLE CLUB

95 Nightingale Lane, SW12 020 8673 6217

Great logo of a turbaned Raj-style waiter holding a serving dish while riding a penny farthing. Known to some as the BBC! *'Something wonderfully luxurious, elegant decor, massive vase of flowers dominates the room, charming staff, starched white tablecloths and napkins. In the winter, it's cosy and snug, in the summer the windows and doors are thrown open, the colonial ceiling fans whir, and it all looks extremely pretty.'* RL. Hours: 7-12 Monday to Saturday. Branches: SW8, SW11 and SW20.

NANGLO

88 Balham Hill Road, SW12 020 8673 4160

Fully licensed and air conditioned. One of the few Nepalese restaurants in the country actually serving authentic Nepalese food. Starters include (all £2.70): Shekpa Soup, noodles, chicken, lamb and spices. Tareko Chyau, mushrooms covered with spice lamb mince. Soaltee Alu, potato patty, lentils, onions, herbs, cooked on flat iron plate, served with sweet yoghurt. Main courses: Khorsani Chicken or Lamb £5.70, fiery dish with fresh green chillies, ginger and spices. Nepalese Sam £7.70, noodles with chicken, lamb, vegetables, served with side sauce. Fewa Fish £8.50, spicy salmon, medium hot. Pahelo Pharsi £3.50 - pumpkin, tomato and onion. *'I am a retired Major - 6th Gurkha Rifles, who lived in Nepal for 5 years. The food we had was authentic Nepalese, very tasty, large portions. Service excellent. A clean, fresh and modern decor (no garish painting of Mount Everest! All staff Nepalese. Head chef is Anand Kumar Gurung who is cultural secretary of the Yeti Nepal Association in the UK.'* JT. Hours: 12-2.30/6-11.30, Friday and Saturday to 12, Sunday to 11.

SADYA NEW ENTRY

90 Bedford Hill, SW12 020 8673 5393

South Indian cuisine is spreading northwards from Tooting. Sadya is literally a Kerala feast, traditionally served on a banana leaf *(see page 75)*. And you can get it served here in that manner if you wish; but don't eat the food with cutlery; right hand please and you will be a Kerelan through and through. Head chef Sunny Kuttan (pictured above left) with chef Jobin Tom are in charge of food. They are pictured preparing a masala dosa. Their menu is an encyclopedia of Kerelan food. And there are many non-veg dishes, cooked in the Keralan Nair style. Dishes of the day displayed on a blackboard. Here is a snapshot: Chilly Iddly, steamed rice cakes, served with chilli coconut chutney and sambar £2.95. Chicken 65, a bar snack found all over Southern India. Chicken cubes marinated in our traditional batter and deep fried, £3.95. .Meen Polichathu, King fish marinated in a paste of red chilli, turmeric, lemon juice and grilled in plantain £7.50. Chemeen Ulathiyathu, Prawns as you never seen before, presented dry, deliciously spiced with pepper, coriander and chilli £6.50. Kappa and Meen curry, a favourite after a hard day's work in the paddy fields (or the Balham offices!) – tapioca spiced with turmeric and green chillies, served with fresh water fish cooked in sautéd coconut £6.50. Lamb Porichathu, marinated with crushed garlic, turmeric & dry chilli and slow-cooked and served

Sadya, SW12

Fresh coconut; Sadya, SW12

with a generous topping of lightly brown onion and curry leaves. Delicious with Paratha Njandu Curry: Baby Crab cooked in its shell with roasted coconut sauce, onion, tomato and spices. £8 Ulli Theeyal – means Fire Dish! Shallots poached in tamarind extract in a spiced masala. to try many items order the Veg Sadya – 3 course meal with a selection of vegetable side dishes, rice and bread. Can also be served in a fresh banana leaf if you want to go truly Keralan. £8.50 Non Veg Sadya- As above, but for the non veg lovers £10.50. Main courses £4.50 --£8. Service charge: 10%. Hours: 12 - 3/6 - 11 Sun-Thur, Sun; to-midnight Fri, Sat

TABAQ — BEST PAKISTANI AWARD

47 Balham Hill, SW12 — 020 8673 7820

If the previous entry sounded too veggy for you, here is the perfect antidote. Here at Tabaq, as in Pakistan, meat predominates. A very comfortable, cosy restaurant, with pink linen table cloths and napkins and just 50 seats. Lovely stylish, traditionally hand-made embroidered wall-coverings hang all around the room, depicting scenes from Lahore. Tabaq is owned by the ex Kenyan Pakistani Ahmed brothers. Mushtaq runs front-of-house; Manoor is head chef, and the culinary magic emanates from him and his brigade. But don't expect quick food from him. He cooks everything freshly, and a 30-minute wait is not uncommon. The Tabaq (a large Pakistani serving dish) menu is pure Lahori cuisine. Lahore is famous for its cuisine and was once one of four major palace cities, resided in by rotation by the great Moghul emperors, rather in the way that QEII rotates round Buck Pal, Windsor, Sandringham and Balmoral. Agra, Delhi and Srinagar in Kashmir were the others, all linked by still-extant tree-lined trunk roads. Mansoor's cooking is typically Lahori Moghul. One technique unique to Tabaq is steam roasting (Charga). cooking which infuses the spices and makes the meat moister. Illustrated alongside Mansoor's star dish, a whole steam-roast lamb costs £140.00 with all the trimmings. (24 hrs notice, for 12+ persons). We hear good things about it, and indeed about everything at Tabaq.. *'Aubergine Pakora — that's the starter for me, I thought. Four lovely, big slices of aubergine, covered in a spicy and very crispy batter were served with a delicate julienned salad and its own little pot of yoghurt dip - delicious. Pat plumped*

for Lamb Kebabs. I had given up eating kebabs (except for my own of course), because they are invariably disappointing, being fatty and chewy, with little bits of sinews getting taught between teeth and being an irritating distraction for the rest of the meal. My own kebabs are 'Katori' meaning 'silk' which melt in the mouth and that's because I go to the considerable effort to mince my own meat and pick out by hand (a tedious job) all the gristle etc which I dislike so much. However, Tabaq kebabs, were four perfectly shaped kebabs, served from a sizzler with salad, and they were very good indeed, being well ground with unwanted matter removed. For our mains, I chose Murghi Makhani - chicken slices in a saffron coloured, creamy, butter sauce. Not my usual choice, but I knew it would be properly cooked here and I intended to spice it up with chillies (much to the dismay of the chef). It was wonderful and worked really well with my tiny slices of fresh green chilli. Pat leapt upon Palak Lamb — one of his favourites, it was exceptionally good. Very tender chunks of lamb (no chewy pieces), well cooked with spinach, lovely. We chose Jeerawallah Aloo, hot Fenugreek Paratha, thinly rolled and fried in butter — fantastic and Plain Rice. I am demanding about rice too. It has to be al-dente, not grainy, not soft. At Tabaq it is superb. Brandy and coffee finished a perfect meal.' DBAC. *'Excellent Karahi Kabab Murgh at £7.25 as a starter between two was really sharp, fresh spicy taste. Maureen had Palak Gosht-£7.25, how do they get the spinach to stay wrapped around the meat, which made the dish better than normal, I wonder.? I had Gosht Ka-Lazeez Masala (award winning dish, ginger, garlic, garam) £8.50. Not in fact "my cup of tea", but very different, and lamb so tender, well worth the experiment. The nan was good, not soggy, and the vegetables, chana masala and matar paneer at around £5 were again tasty. That seems to be a difference between good and ordinary meals, all too often the veg are just a bland "side" to the main — not at Tabaq. We were pretty full, so were startled to be given (without asking!), not one pud but 3 as tasters! Message: leave more room in future. Kulfi, Halva and Kheer Khas were all home made, and complemented the meal very well — so much for my taste buds, asking what fruit was blended for the Halva, I was told Carrots!! But there were nuts and saffron, no excuse I guess'.* C&MC. And on another visit: *'Manoor must still do the preparation I think, despite the fact he now runs a second restaurant elsewhere in Balham. Our friends have moved south from near Bradford, so know their curries, and were suitably impressed. The flavoured pullau is also sufficiently different to be a welcome change from garish colours. 10% CC discount helped with a £125 bill, but 3 hours passed in a very enjoyable manner. Mushtaq mentioned he was considering a place in Brighton. Now that would be a welcome change from our usual local bland cooking.'* C&MC. Show Mushtaq this *Guide* and you too might get a discount. Hours: 12-2.45 /6-11.45; closed Sunday. Ask about their bottled sauce range (shown below). <www.tabaq.co.uk>

London SW14

Mortlake, Putney, Sheen

SARKHELS NEW ENTRANT

199 Upr Richmond Rd, SW14 020 8876 6220

Opened 2004, chef Udit Sarkhel and chef Pradip bring homestyle regional Indian cuisine to this 38-seat. See Sarkhel's, SW19. Hours: 12-2.30 /6-10.30.

TASTE OF THE RAJ

130 Upr Richmond Rd, SW14 020 8876 8271

A typically well-managed Bangladeshi formula curry house, owned by the charming and personable Shawkat Ahmed, which has been operating for years and producing a highly popular formula at reasonable prices. Such venues form the backbone of this Guide, up and down the country, and are much-loved locals enjoyed weekly by their regulars. There is little more to say about such venues. Lunch and dinner daily.

London SW15

Putney

MA GOA TOP 100

244 Upr Richmond Rd, SW15 020 8780 1767

Opened in 1993 by the Kapoor family. Deepak looks after the diners, while Sushma is the chef. In fact she's his mum, so easy on the Ma Goa gags! The restaurant seats 50 and has had a modern-look makeover. We describe Goan food in some detail on page 65. Goa is one of India's 24 states, not a country in its own right, as some think. It is on the western coast of India and, because it was Portuguese for nearly 500 years, it inherited different characteristics from the rest of India, including a small pork-eating, Christian population. Goan cooks were prized in the Raj (because they would handle beef and pork and could cook well). Until a few decades ago, Goan cooks were frequently to be found in merchant

Ma Goa, SW15

ships. In the 1960s Goa was 'discovered' by hippies, and more recently, it has been 'discovered' by holiday companies offering the cheap package at formerly beautiful, exclusive, caring hotels. Goan food is rarely found in Britain. And what of Sushma's food? As a regular visitor to Goa, I can vouch that it's as near to home-cooking as it gets. Goan food is unique, having that Portuguese influence – any meat goes and pork is the favourite, as is the chilli. Good examples at Ma Goa are Goa Sausage £475, (Chorizo) pork meat sausage with cinnamon, cloves, garlic, palm vinegar and red chilli, topped with spicy onion salsa, and Porco Balchao, Shrimps in tomato and Goan pickling masala served with Goan steamed bread £4.50 Vindaloo £9, this is the real thing, based on the Portuguese dish, Vinho d'alhos. In the Goan version, pork is marinated with palm (toddy) vinegar, garlic and roasted spices and plenty of red Goan chillies. It is then slow-cooked to achieve maximum penetration of flavours. Ma Goa serve it in traditional earthenware. Aunty Bella's Goa Lamb Tomato, clove, garlic, ghati chilli, palm vinegar & curry leaf sauce with diced lamb £8.95. Ma's Fish Caldin Escolar steaks (white boneless fish) in a fine coconut, mustard & fenugreek seed sauce £10.50 . The daily specials board makes this restaurant an adventure. Goan delights, with unique names such as Cafreal, Balachao, Assado, Temperado, Buffado, and Recheiado all appear at one time or another. If these dishes are new to you, advice is forthcoming. Also they do cook regional dishes other than Goan, but our advice is to stick to Goan. *'If you ask for Goan heat, you'll get it hot! For loonies like Pat, look under side orders and accompaniments for Taliwi Mirch £1 (fried green chillies in mustard oil). There are even Goan puds, such as Bebinca, a heavily sugared egg layer-cake, with cashew nuts — fantastic but sickly!'* DBAC. But a word of caution. Please be patient. Sushma will not be hurried in the kitchen. Relax with their chilled Portuguese Vinho Verde wine, or Ambari beer, brewed in Goa, £2.25 and nibble something while you wait for your order to be cooked. *'Had one of the best evenings we have ever had. Definitely the sort of restaurant to enjoy the whole evening. Interesting food, good portions, well presented and fabulous. Faultless service and atmosphere. Mature clientele. Not cheap, but reasonable, superb for the value.'* HC. Service 12.5%. Takeaway: 10% discount. Hours: 6.30-11 Mon to Sat. (12.30–3, 6.30-10 Sunday). Branch: 194 Wandsworth Bridge Rd, Fulham, SW6 0207 384 2122. <www.ma-goa.com>

MUNAL

393 Upper Richmond Road, SW15 020 8876 3083

Khem Ranamagar established his 65-seater in 1991. You'll find at least 100 of your favourites here. But this is Nepalese and the 'always-polite' crew would love you to try some of chef Bijaya Thapa's few Nepalese items on the menu, such as the starter Momo, meat dumpling with tomato chutney. Or Sadheko Meat or chicken, marinated, cooked, served hot, mixed into a salad and quite spicy. Nepalese mains include Meat or Chicken Bhutuwa, a dry-fried dish. *'This restaurant is where I took my wife on our first dinner date together,'* says RAC. *'A frosty evening but welcome was as warm as ever. Chicken Pakora and Dal Soup, served hot and spicy. Butter King Prawn (huge) Masala, Boiled Rice, Tarka Dal and Keema Nan. Only grumble, Dal was cold.' 'I just thought to tell you about my daughter's wedding reception. We agreed on a three course meal with a set menu for 45 people and champagne. The starter was Chicken Tikka, Prawns and Vegetable Samosa. The main course was a buffet style serve yourself affair. The choice was Chicken Tikka Masala, Lamb Bhutuwa and a beautiful Masala Fish Curry. Also Tarka Daal, Rice and a wide selection of Naan breads. Dessert was a wedding cake provided by us but fruit salad and coffee was available. The cost of this was £650 which included all drinks from the bar and seven bottles of champagne.'* DAB. Minimum charge £10. Delivery: £12 min, 3-mile radius. Hours: 12-2.30/6-11.30 (12 Sat & Sun).

London SW16

Norbury, Streatham, Streatham Hill

MIRCH MASALA TOP 100

1416 London Road, SW16 020 8679 1828

Young Asians in here (and it was buzzing with them) told us that Mirch Masala is Bombay vernacular for 'buzzing' (with excitement) aka 'hot stuff'. Literally meaning pepper mixture, this original Mirch Masala was established in 1997, 'pepper mixture', is an offspring of the ever-popular Karahi King, where meat is king, cutlery is out (OK, limpets can have a knife and fork). This unlicensed (**BYO**, no corkage charge) café is pleasant, light and bright, air-conditioned and seats 70. Open kitchen, with unusual Kenyan-Asian specials by owner Riaz Sabir's brigade, who delight in bringing their own cooking straight to the horse's mouth – yours that is. Great theatre, enhanced by high decibel Bangra and lively diners. Cassava chips (mogo) can substitute for popadoms, Patra £2.50, and freshly made. Kebabs 70p. Wide selection of dechi (saucepan) or karahi dishes, kebabs and all the trimmings. Main course: Karahi Methi Gosht/Murgh £4.50 (lamb/chicken with fenugreek leaves) – can't imagine a Punjabi restaurant without this dish. Good veggie stuff, too. How about Karahi Valpapdi Baigan, £4, or Matoki, plantain curry. Set lunch: £5 for veg, £6 non-veg, served from 12-4. Credit cards accepted. Hours: 12-12 daily. Branches Mirch Masala Takeaway Lavender Hill sw17. 111- Commercial Road, Shoreditch, E1; 213 Upper Tooting Road, SW17; 171 Southall Broadway, Middx. See page 101. . <www.mirchmasalarestaurant.co.uk>

SHAHEE BHEL POORI VEGAN

1547 London Road, SW16 020 8679 6275

Vegan food is vegetarian without any animal products such as dairy products and honey . Lebas Miah's licensed 75-seater, opposite Norbury Station, serves Gujarati vegetarian and some south Indian vegetarian dishes, and some of which are vegan. As you can see on *page* 73, there are many goodies in this style of cooking. Thalis and Dosas are still, we hear, the most popular dishes served. Specials include Chappati Chana (hot), chick peas marinated in a balanced blend of spices and sauce, served with green coriander. Bhel poori (cold), delicious mixture of Indian savouries blended with spices and exotic sauces which make this dish unique. Dahi Vada (Bhalle) (cold), spicy black-pea-flour fritters, with yoghurt and sweet and sour sauce, all £1.75. Rava Onion Dosa, a crispy onion vegetable pancake stuffed with delicately spiced potatoes, served with coconut chutney and Sambar, £4.10. Hours: 12-2.30./6-11. Sunday buffet.

SHAMYANA

437 Streatham High Rd, SW16 020 8679 6162

Another good value Pakistani Punjabi caff, opened by Mohammed Tanveer in 1998. No frills. Seats a huge 130 in two black-and-white tiled floored rooms. Enormous menu, some 130 dishes, cooked in an open kitchen. Starters: Masala Fish (white fish in spicy sauce), Dhal Bhajia (spiced lentils deep-fried in chicken pea dough), Zeera Chicken Wings £2.50 (wings marinated in spicy sauce). Main courses: Masala Karela Gosht (lamb cubes cooked with bitter gourd), Ginger Chicken, Lamb Biriani (lamb with stock flavouring the rice). **BYO.** Daily specials. Delivery: 3-mile, £14 min. Service 10%. 50 space car park at rear. Set lunch: £5. Service 10%. Sunday buffet: 12-6, £5.50. Hours: 12-12.

London SW17

Tooting

Upper Tooting Road (UTR) has reached a maturity, though with less street (pavement) trading than Southall. For years, the area has reflected the varied roots of its Asian population. In the half a mile, between Tooting Bec and Tooting Broadway tube stations, there are restaurants serving nearly every style of authentic food from the subcontinent. Nowhere else in the world has such variety cheek by jowl. South Indian restaurants include Sree Krishna, 192 UTR, Radha Krishna Bhavan, 86, and Kolam, 58. There are now more than one Sri Lankan outlets, the best of which is still Jaffna at the Broadway. Milan, 158 UTR and Gossip, 180 are two Gujarati vegetarian havens, and largely vegetarian Kenyan Asian food is to be found at Kadiri, 32 UTR, and Kastoori, 188, while at Masaladar, 121, you get this food plus Bhel Poori and meat curries alike. Handis, 164 and Lahore Karahi at the Broadway are Pakistan and fill the carnivore gap, Southall-style. As if that were not enough there are two formula Bangladeshi curry houses, the Peacock, 242, Calcutta Indian, 116, and Raja, 169. Veggy Indian sweet and snack takeaways include Ambala, 48, and Alaudin, 98, with Royal beyond UTR (north of Tooting Bec). The shops are getting better and more varied. Competition is rife with more and more excellent rivals opening, all displaying their wares on UTR itself, many until late, every day including Sundays. Sakoni, 204-208 UTR, is still the best Asian veg shop in London and there is no better Asian grocer than next-door Dadus, 210. There are several Sri Lankan grocers too. Utensils shops, sari boutiques and halal butchers have sprung up too. My prediction that parking would become impossible has come to pass. But with the tube so convenient, UTR is an all-day curryholic's theme park. Here's more detail:

HANDIS

164 Upper Tooting Road, SW17 020 8672 6037

A 60-seater Pakistani restaurant owned by Mrs S Sheikh and managed by Mr J Sheikh. Cooking is down one entire side. The Handi, a cooking pot, and dishes are served either in this or in the karahi. It's kebabs, tikkas, tandoori meat and chicken dishes in which this type of venue excels. There are a number of Punjabi-style vegetable dishes, such as Aloo Sag, and well cooked side dishes. One correspondent loves their chupattis. CT. Hours: 11-11.

JAFFNA HOUSE BEST SRI LANKAN

90 High Street, SW17 020 8672 7786

We are often asked how do you choose a restaurant to go into the Guide. Our answer that four letter word beginning with 'C' : Care. This means the service is good and above all the food is good. Michelin have a different perspective, and good luck to them, because Jaffna house will never ever win a Michelin Star, yet they can cook better than 90% of the UK's Michelin-starred chefs. For those who must have meaty tandoori items and north-Indian curries, you've got your own side entrance and dining room, with food cooked by Aziz and Kannan. I've no idea how good it is; but do enjoy (and tell us about it, if you like). Where the serious palates boldly go (through the front door) is into K Sivalogarajah's and M Sivanandan's Tooting Broadway place, which built its name on its authentic, no compromise, chilli hot (as-it-should-be) Sri Lankan and south-Indian dishes with its particularly popular different Friday, Saturday and Sunday specials. Tastebud-tantalising stuff like Vadai – gram flour doughnut, drenched in home made yoghurt and sprinkled with garam and (if you are lucky) chopped fresh green chilli, Masala Dosa £1.50 – must be one of the cheapest in the country. Sri Lankan specials are delightful, with Pat's benchmark crab curry scoring really high because it was searingly hot, and used fresh crab. *'Wow!! this was the second* **TOP 100** *restaurant in 24 hours... lucky or what?!'* [Yes] *'and we didn't break £50! I have LOVED this restaurant/cafe for years, eight or nine at least. It remains magnificent value for wonderful food. Potato Bondas and Onion Bhajia simply the best, and this before we got to Mushroom Curry, Chana Curry, Coconut Rice – fragrant and so light, almost floated off the plate! Vegetable Kottho – substantial, full of fresh vegetables. Curries clearly freshly prepared, very chilli-hot, just beautiful. We* *were stuffed full, long before we finished the food... all for £9!! Wonderful!!!'* AG. *'We holidayed in Sri Lanka and were longing to try the food again. Starters were the best – delicious Masala Dosa and lovely spicy Devilled Chicken which was very reminiscent of the food we had sampled in Sri Lanka. Chicken and String Hoppers, but they came all mixed together, which made it taste a bit like vermicelli or chow mein – anyway I shall definitely try again.'* NP. Set lunch: £4 and £5, served from 12-3. Hours: 12-12pm.

KADIRI

32 Upper Tooting Road, SW17 020 8672 0710

A Kenyan Asian licensed restaurant, it does tandooris, kebabs, and regular curries and all the trimmings. Try Cassava chips (mogo) with imli as a good substitute for popadams, served with authentic imli, sweet and sour tamarind chutney. Fried fish Masala, Tali Hui Jinga, breadcrumbed, deep-fried prawns, and Tandoori King fish, that tasty fish so loved in south India, are three unusual starters. Jeera chicken or butter chicken are *'just like the Brilliant's'* (*see* Southall Middlesex) according to one scribe (AN), while another (BD) was *'smitten by the biriani.'*

KASTOORI PURE VEGETARIAN

188 Upper Tooting Road, SW17 020 8767 7027

The Thanki family hail from Kathiyawad in Gujarat, via Kenya and specialise in both Gujarati and Kenyan vegetarian dishes. The former include Vegetable Samosas, Dahi Vadas, Kadhi (yoghurt and besan sauce, with dumplings), and Katia Wahd, a tomato-based curry. Karela Bharah is stuffed bitter gourd. The latter gives Cassava Chips, Chilli Banana, £4.50 (green banana stuffed with chillies and served with pickle), Kasodi, £4.50 (sweetcorn in a peanut and yoghurt-based sauce), and Matoki, plantain curry. Their Bhel Poori is a crunchy snip at £2.50, but their Corn Bhel didn't work for RL: *'I hoped for a new type of Bhel Puri, but this was a salad of diced potato, tomatoes and canned sweetcorn mixed with imli (tamarind sauce).'* This is one of the few places where you can experience Bhatura, giant puri bread, £1, which puffs up to balloon-size when deep-fried. Thali curry selection is extraordinary. Vegan dishes. Hours: 12.30-2.30 (Mon. & Tues. closed) /6-10.30, daily.

KOLAM

58 Upper Tooting Road SW17 020 8767 2514

Established in 1982 by S Rajakumar. Seats 52 in one long thin dining room. The food is authentic South Indian, as they have it in Tamil Nadu, plus standard north Indian items. Service is very friendly, albeit at freeze-frame slowness. Mañana is far too fast, which reminds one greatly of India. Patience will reward you with a good inexpensive meal, and, as ever, go for the South Indian delights, which is what they know best. **BYO** allowed: £1 corkage. Hours: 12-2.30, Tues.-Sun./6-11, daily (12 on Sat.).

LAHORE DREAMS NEW ENTRANT

200 Upper Tooting Rd SW17 020 8682 9777

Average £14-£17. Unlicensed. No corkage charge. This is quite a new and up-market restaurant (for Tooting) which adds to the super local mix. The food is Pakistani and the decor evokes the Moghul Lahori atmosphere (Lahore was one of the emperor's major fortress cities). So none of your minimalist décor, hard surfaces and and lurid dayglow colours. Here it is olde-worlde Indi-pics on the walls, carved chairs and lamps and good old sensible service. But it is Tooting, so expect ridiculous prices; cheap that is! Buffet lunch £5.£8 dinner eat your fill. Even a la-carte won't set you back more than c£15, and it's unlicensed with **BYO** with no corkage. Hours: 12-11.30.

LAHORE KARAHI

1 High Street, SW17 020 8767 2477

This was the first Karahi-house on Tooting Broadway opening in 1995. It has been copied a fair bit so the formula is now quite well-known; stand at the counter and order your takeaway – or if you plan to eat in, sit down and wait to be served, with the cooking on view. Typical Pakistani Kebab House menu. Starters include: Masala Fish, chunks of marinated fish, fried. Sheek Kebabs. Main courses: Chicken Jalfrezi. Veggies might try the Karahi Karela, bitter gourd, Methi Aloo or saag Paneer. Cash preferred. No credit cards. Unlicensed, **BYO,** no corkage. Average meal £10. Hours: 12-12.

MASALEDAR

121 Upper Tooting Road, SW17 020 8767 7676

Smart frontage with its smoky plate-glass window?

Terracotta tiles on split-level floors. Plants in pots and trailing leaves. Smart up-lighters behind large halved karahis. You can sit outside watching all this through that window, at the five pavement tables. Service is slow, but they really do cook it fresh to order in the open kitchen. Many old favourites on the menu, all good. Starters include Bhel Poori, and Mandazi, samosa-shaped deep-fried bread with an African-Asian name. Mains: *'Rich, vivid Punjabi-type curries. Ginger Chicken and Methi Gosht very good. Cumin-flavoured Pilaw Rice (just like you get in Rusholme). Reasonable prices, thoroughly recommended.'* JR. Seek out the unusual: Dekchi Gosht, Halal mutton, on-the-bone, slow-cooked in a metal-waisted cooking utensil without handles. Strict Muslim rules apply: no alcohol permitted so **BYO** is not permitted. Credit cards accepted. Hours: 12-12.

MILAN VEGETARIAN

158 Upper Tooting Rd, SW17 020 8767 4347

Taj Mehta's vegetarian café is just the sort of place we like to recommend. It's unpretentious, unexpectedly licensed and air-conditioned. But for the vegetarian, what more could you ask for? If I were you, I'd ask for popadams and their adorable fresh home-made relishes. Next I'd ask for their fabulous Bhel Poori. I'd avoid the Masala Dosa (they do it better at Sree Krishna), and I'd go for its subtly-spiced Gujarati curries, made largely from besan flour and yoghurt, spiced with turmeric and curry leaves. If it's new to you, ask for help. The dish of the day is always a good option. And do try the fresh Rotla (millet bread). Leave some room for the terrific Indian sweets on display. And buy some fresh 'Bombay mix' items. For a complete filling meal, try the Thali – a good selection of vegetarian curries including something sweet for pudding – at £6 a real feast. 'Another good one' SM. Minimum charge still a ridiculous £2. Average meal under £10. Takes no credit cards so cash preferred. Sunday lunch £5.75. Hours: 10-10.

PEACOCK TANDOORI

242 Upper Tooting Rd, SW17 020 8672 8770

When this 50-seater Bangladeshi curry house opened in 1988, Tooting's current crop of fine authentic restaurants didn't exist. But the Peacock has stood the test of time. Owned and managed by Mr Yogi Anand, it does the formula to a high standard. Well, it has to being on that street! But look for the unusual, for example, Paneer Pakora (curd cheese, dipped in spiced gram batter and fried), Brinjal Pakora (sliced brinjal coated with batter and fried, served with salad) as starters. Mains: Sag Kamal Kakri (lotus roots cooked with spinach and onion), Batair e Khas £7.65 (quails in mild curry sauce with fresh coriander). Weekend buffet £8 (under 12, half price). Service 10%. Takeaway: 10% discount. Hours: 6-12.

RADHA KRISHNA BHAVAN TOP 100

86 Tooting High Street, SW17 020 8682 0969

This restaurant was opened in 1999 by H.K.Haridas, an experienced Keralan restaurateur, following a partnership row at the Sree Krishna. Haridas got the head chef and set up this Krishna down the road. It specialises in South Indian Keralan cuisine, with dishes from the cities of Cochin, Malabar and Travancore. Have the Rasam (hot and spicy soup, with floating slivers of garlic, curry leaves and a red chilli! – this is a DBAC benchmark, which if she doesn't get hiccups, it's not hot enough for her!), Masala Dosa, Sambar and Coconut Chutney are as good as it gets. Some have that choice for starters and go on to curries. I don't know how they do it. I'm too full for it. But the curries are worth trying. You can stay vegetarian if you like. All their vegetable curries are spot on. Contrary to popular belief, meat, chicken and fish dishes are commonplace. Even the Chicken Korma (if you must) is given the South Indian touch – creamy, coconut with ground almond. But don't forget the wonderful Lamb Cutlets (patties of spicy minced lamb, bread crumbed and fried, served with tomato sauce and salad), King Prawn Fry (with ginger, garlic, spices and sliced coconut), Malabar Chicken (with coconut, curry leaves, garlic and mustard), Spinach Vadai £3 (fried crunchy doughnut of channa dal, green chillies, onion, ginger, curry leaves and fresh spinach served with chutneys). And if you have any room left Banana Leaf Cake, rice with sweet filling of coconut, banana and jaggery wrapped in banana leaf and steamed – divine. Main courses from £2 to £7, Sunday Thalis, £6-£8. Min charge: £6. Service 10%. Licensed. Credit cards accepted. Hours: 12-3/6-11 (Fri. & Sat. to 12am).

SREE KRISHNA TOP 100

192 Tooting High St, SW17 020 8672 4250

Pravin Pillai's Sree (pron Shree) was the the

original Tooting Krishna restaurant. And now there are three (*see* Rhada above and Vijaya below). Regular readers know it's a regular haunt of ours, involving a round-trip of 90 miles. Watch out for the corner site on the left (coming in to London). Parking is usually OK in the evening. Despite a redec it retains all the old charm which lets you pretend you are in India while you indulge in no-nonsense, efficient and friendly service., and they're used to full houses (120 seats). The menu offers all the same south Indian items as Rhada, and this Krishna cooks them just as competently and accurately. To me there's too much curry house food being dispensed. Blame the customers for demanding it, I suppose, but they should go the the Peacock, and leave the Krishna to do what they do best, which is anything South Indian, and preferably vegetarian. It's more satisfying than any carnivore realises. So read the caveat, and note we retain its **TOP 100** cachet. Set thalis, Sun lunch, £5.95-£7.95. Service 10%. Credit cards accepted. Hours: 12-3 Sun.-Thurs.; 6-11 Mon-Thur; (to 1145 Fri. & Sat).

VIJAYA KRISHNA

114 Mitcham Road, SW17 020 8767 7688

The third Krishna in the trilogy opened in 1995 by Vijayan Mullath who also manages front of house at his 40-seater and keeps a watchful eye on the kitchen, where he poached the sous chef from Sree Krishna at the time of the partnership row. His restaurant is decorated with scenes of South India. The Keralan specialities don't disappoint. Popular authentic dishes such as Masala Dosai, a light rice flour pancake, rolled over a firm, gently spiced potato curry, Avial, a fluid curry made with yoghurt and mixed vegetables, and Sambar, a runny lentil curry containing, if you are lucky, many drumsticks, with which you are to scrape the flesh off with your teeth – lovely says DBAC, who also enjoyed Kozhi Varutha Curry, chicken in garlic and coriander sauce, and Green Banana Bhajia are served. PS: please ignore the curryhouse favourites and enjoy Kereal! Delivery: 2-mile radius, £12 min. Service: 10%. Hours: 12-3/6-11 (Fri. & Sat. to 12).

London SW18

Earlsfield, Southfields, Wandsworth

KATHJMANDU VALLEY NEW ENTRANT

5 West Hill, Wandsworth, SW18 020 8871 0240

Owner Uttam Basnet, took over the reigns of this very cosy 38-seater in 2005 and serves Nepalese delights. Remember that Nepal boarders India and China, so don't be surprised to see Spring Rolls £2.25 on the menu. Menu Snapshot: Kalejo Bhutuwa £3.25 - chicken livers fried with Nepalese spices - a favourite of mine; Lamb Sekuwa £6.25 - Nepalese spiced tandoor lamb chops; Chicken Chitwan £6.95 - spicy hot; Gurkha's Lamb £7.50 - with tomatoes; Nepalese Murgh Masala £6.95 - spicy sauce, mushrooms and peas. Licensed: stocks Cobra £3 a bottle, house wine £8.95. Delivery: 3 miles, £7 minimum. Price Check: Popadom 50p, CTM £6.50, Pullao Rice £2.50. Hours: 6 - 11.45, Saturday to 12. <www.kathmanduvalley.com>

SARKHEL'S A-LIST OUTSTANDING RESTAURANT AWARD

199 Replingham Road, SW18 020 8870 1483

Udit Sarkhel was, for over a decade, Exec Chef at the BB, SW7. He wanted more freedom and was prepared to take the risk. In 1997, he opened in what was then an. unfashionable part of SW, in a tiny shop front on a double-yellow-lined, outside curve of a bend on a busy road. Within a year, the business was solid enough for them to get the two

Sree Krishna, SW17

units next door doubling the seating to 72. We continue to get numerous good reports about Sarkhel's. Udit changes the menu all the time and he often has specials on the brew, so ask for them, if you want a a change. Also look put for Udit's themed food festivals where the menu is devoted top one or another region. '*Outstanding in every respect. The management were on hand and gave us an extra dish on the house for us to try, which was a very nice gesture.*' CC. '*Proving that Udit is a cookaholic, the regular menu is frequently augmented with one of his regular food festivals, examining the regions of India. We went for the Hyderabad festival. We ate lightly fried plain Popadoms with three small pots of Chutney – including chilled concoction of smoked aubergine and coconut – deliciously different. Pat always enjoys Udit's Chettinand Shrimps. More up my street are Shrikampuri Kebabs – two melt-in-the-mouth round patties of minced meat, stuffed with slices of boiled egg, served with onion rings, wedges of lemon and an ample pot of Podina Chutney – wonderful! You don't see 'billy-goat-gruff' on the menu often – but that's what we ate for main course, Goat Curry, on-the-bone, with another unusual curry, rabbit, served with scrubbed new potatoes and baby carrots, large joints of delicious juicy white meat, again on the bone smothered in a rich spicy sauce. We decided against rice, and ate Roti and Potato stuffed Paratha – fantastic.*' DBAC. Essential to book. Continues with its **TOP AWARD** winning status. Hours: 12-2.30 / 6-10.30, Tuesday to Sunday. Closed Monday. Branch SW14. *See page 87.*

London SW19

Wimbledon

DALCHINI — TOP 100

147 Arthur Road, SW19 — 020 8947 5966

Almost opposite Wimbledon Park Underground station (so parking difficult) this is a Chinese restaurant, but it's no ordinary Chinese. Dalchini (meaning Chinese cinnamon) serves Indo-Chinese. If you've never experienced Bombay's most popular dining-out food, you must do it. Called Hakka Chinese cuisine, this is where you'll find it and it is Britain's only restaurant serving it. Hakka means 'Guest People.' As with everywhere else in the world, there have been Chinese living in India for over two millennia, but Indian civilisation predated that, so the new immigrants were guests. Cochin, that beautiful Keralan seaboard town means 'Chinatown', and uses its famous Chinese fishing nets to this day. Cochin was the major port for Indo-Chinese trade from Roman times and for centuries until the demise of the Silk route. Over time, these Chinese settlers, merged their Oriental style of cooking with Indian ingredients. Owner Veronica Sarkhel is herself Hakka Chinese and raised in Bombay. So is her uncle, Johnny Chang, who is the super-smooth front of house manager (he managed Mumbai's top Chinese, China Garden until he came here). The three chefs are also from Bombay. Hakka, led by Steven Lee. At it's really impossible to recommend dishes; they are all so good. Everything has a light Indian spicing. To me this brings Chinese food to life. Ask Johnny or the staff for advice. They are happy to help. Or else just dive in. Dishes to savour include Spring Chicken Lollipops – cute name, in fact pretty little chops dusted with a Hakka spice mix, or Red Pumpkin Fritters (starters). Mains we like include Hakka Chilli Chicken cooked with five spice and green chillies, Prawn Manchurian cooked with coriander, ginger and garlic and Crispy Okra, smothered with hot garlic sauce; Hot Garlic Paneer Szechuan, or Moi-Yan aubergine, folded with minced chicken and shrimp. Because Indians don't eat beef, Hakkas created a range of goat dishes, translated at Dalchini into lamb. I suppose today's celeb chefs who believe in their arrogant fusion foods should come here to find out just how to mix Indian spices with soy. Dalchini is the only place in Britain which does it successfully. Welcome to a position high up on our **TOP 100** list. Lunch & dinner daily except closed Mondays.

HOUSE OF SPICE

Kingston Road, SW20 020 8542 4838

SUVAI ARUVI — NEW ENTRANT

96 High St, Colliers Wood, SW19 020 8543 6266

For such a small venue, the range of Sri L:ankan food on offer is impressive. Devilled dishes (prawn, meat and chicken are suitably hot, and the Kotthu Roti (slices of SriLankan flatbread, chopped up with curry), is light and moreish. Sambols, such as Sambol (coconut or onion chutney) are a must, as are Hoppers (noodles). The takeaway trade is brisker than the sit-in. No credit cards. So inexpensive that cash is best. Hours: 11am-midnight daily.

London SW20

Raynes Park

COCUM — NEW ENTRANT

9 Approach Rd, SW20 020 8540 3250

Cocum or Kokum is a plum-like, dark, purple-black fruit, dried by wood-smoking. Also called Fish Tamarind, Kodam Puli, Kudam Pulli, etc. the words Kodam Puli are Malayalam (language of south India) for 'fish' and 'tamarind' (puli). However it is neither, but it gives us the clues that it is sour and used with fish. It is used by Kerala's small Syrian Christian community at Travancore Unlike most Keralans they eat offal, chicken, duck, fish, shellfish, beef, and wild boar. 'So what do we find at Cocum, SW19? 'No glamourous decor, but a friendly welcome and swift seating and advice to try the fish and prawn pickles with Achappam (flower-shaped wafers made of riceflour and coconut with black sesame, soonf and cumin seeds). Their fish dishes included Meen Vevichadu, red in colour and flavoured with cocum and chilli. Vevichathu Surmai (Kingfish) also uses cocum. Meen Patiichadu with mango and coconut chippings. There are plenty of vegetable dishes and we had Thoran and Lemon Rice. Again taking advice we had Payasam, rice-pudding boiled with coconut milk and jaggery and garnish with fried cashew nuts. Main courses £4 - c£8. Service charge: 10%. Open slip noted. Takeaway and delivery (3-mile radius over £15) Hours: 12-2.30 Sat-Thur; 5.30-11 Mon-Thur; -11.30 Fri, Sat; -10.30 Sun

London W

Area: West End
Postcode: W1
and West London
W2 to W14
Population: 630,000

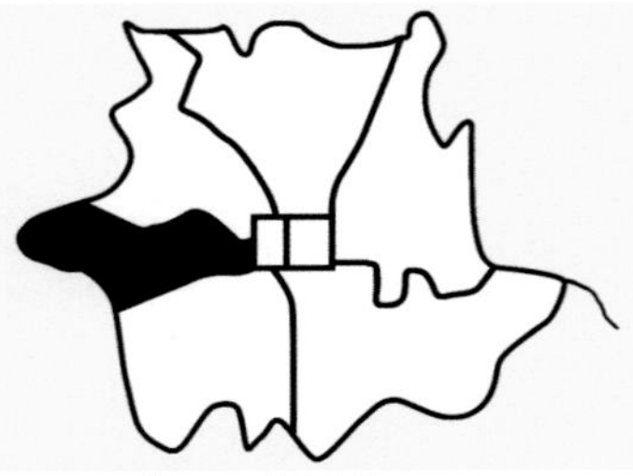

See page 109 for key to this map.

London W1

The West End

ANWARS — TOP 100

64 Grafton Way, Tottenham Court Road, W1
020 7387 6664

Treat Anwars as the forerunner to the numerous successful Lahore Kebab Houses. It opened in 1962 as a 52-seater to serve local Asians, drawn to the area to buy spices next door at the then renowned Bombay Emporium, which later closed and went on to become BE International (Rajah brand), which is now owned by HP foods. Anwar's itself was taken over in 1985 by Muhammad Afzal Zahid. who keeps to the old ways. It serves gutsy, spicy Pakistani food. You walk in, make your choice from the dishes of the day (no menu as such) on display in the serving counter, pay – they do accept credit cards – then carry your tray to a formica table, jugs of water in place, and enjoy it. *'Everything, including bhajis and naan bread, is microwaved. Seekh kebabs, Karahi Gosht was really tasty. ambience and, more importantly, the food all remain unchanged. Set lunch, £6 for Chicken Curry, ladle of mixed vegetables, ladle of Chana, ladle of Sag Aloo over a mound of rice, with a Puri and a cup of tea.'* MW. The vegetarian version is £5. Unlicensed, **BYO** no charge. Hours: 12-11, daily.

BENARES TOP 100

12 Berkeley Square, W1 020 7629 8886

Benares is named after India's holiest city (formerly Varanassi). Upstairs to an expensive, architect-designed shiny black granite bar area, with smart Indian furniture hidden between ornate wooden partitions and the water pool with floating candles and petals. The Benares Bellini mixed with liqueur mango, passion fruit or strawberry-topped, with prosecco, is very popular. They serve bar snacks such as mini vegetable parcels with mint and tamarind chutney and crisp fried cod in a spicy batter. There are three private dining rooms off this area. The main dining room has polished grey limestone flooring, textured and sculpted white walls, and interspersed with artifacts, and is undoubtedly expensive but unexceptional. Chef Atul Kochhar is Oberoi-trained and worked at their Delhi Hotel. He was poached by an Indian magnate who opened Tamarind in 1994. At first Atul was understaffed and produced timidly spiced dishes for an underwhelmed clientele. But we saw the talent and awarded Tamarind our **MOST PROMISING NEWCOMER AWARD** in its first year (1995), **BEST INDIAN** 1998 and **BEST CHEF** 2000. *'As part of his culinary exploration Atul's menu has a monthly regional menu. Starters such as Makali Sukhem (squid salad with coconut shavings, coriander leaves and tamarind) and Jal Tarang (a salad of scallops, prawns and oyster fritters with grapes-ginger dressing) are unmistakably Indian dishes presented in a modern European style. Main courses range from the traditional Murg Makhani and Rogan Josh to Lagosta Xec Xec Goan lobster and prawn masala, served with tomato and red onion salad. The restaurant also holds regular master classes, where groups of between four and six are invited into the kitchen for two hours at a time, where they can be privy to Atul's kitchen secrets'. Puja Vedi, Ed, Tandoori Magazine.* We still get mixed reports about Benares. Some dishes are as good as they get, and others are bland and uninspired. It is simply inexplicable, but considering the Mayfair prices and that Michelin Star, so badly deserved by a good number of unfalteringly good haute-cuisine Indian restaurants it is inexcusable too. Main courses c£16-£2s. 2 course set lunch £15 Set dinner £55.Service charge 12.5%. Hours: 12-2.30 weekdays / 5.30-10.30 Mon to Sat; 6-10 Sun. <www.benaresrestaurant.com>

CAFÉ LAZEEZ TOP 100

21 Dean Street, W1 020 7434 9393

See SW7 for menu details. This newer venture has outside tables, a bar/brasserie and a huge restaurant. *'Ignore the non-Indian snacks downstairs and upstairs perhaps avoid their pan-Indian inventions and pick some authentic Pakistani haute-cuisine'.* JGS. *'Really excellent.'* KB&SS. Hours, Brasserie: 12-1AM, daily. Restaurant: Lunch 11-3/5.30-11.45, Mon to Sat. Branches: SW7, & EC1.

CAFE T NEW ENTRANT

Asia House, 63 New Cavendish Street, W1 0207 7307

Asia House promotes the arts and cultures of countries from Iran to Japan and from the Central Asian Republics to Indonesia. It stages talks, events and conferences, lectures and performances and regularly changing art exhibitions. Cyrus Todiwala's' new venture opened in 2006. The name Café T comes from the wide range of teas offered as well coffees, a light lunches with wine or Asian beers or afternoon teas. It serves pan-Asian snacks curries sandwiches and soups. For example: Thai prawn & coriander baguette, £4.45, prawns, tossed with Thai green curry mayonnaise; Frango Espeto Peri-Peri, £4.45,Chicken marinated in Goan style peri-peri masala, chargrilled, sliced and filled with sliced cucumber, tomato & coriander. Country Chicken, £4.25 from the Taj Mahal Hotel, chargrilled chicken tikka finely diced blended with mayonnaise, finely minced chilli,mango chutney, mustard & fresh coriander. Mains include Parsee Lamb Dhaansak, £9.25 served with brown onion & star anise flavoured rice and a meatball kebab and Vindalho de Porco £7.75 the classical Goan version. There is even Bento Box £13.95. Hours: L1-5, Mon-Sat - 1pm. Closed on Sundays & All Bank Holidays

CHAI PANI BEST VEGETARIAN AND A-LIST

64 Seymour Street, W1 020 7258 2000

Rajasthan, the land of the kings, is arguably India's most colourful state, renowned for its palaces and forts, charismatic cities, sparse jungle and lakes which make it India's top tourist state. Ironically, Rajasthani cuisine is India's least known, and tourists to Rajasthan are unlikely ever to try it. Despite there being a few restaurants named

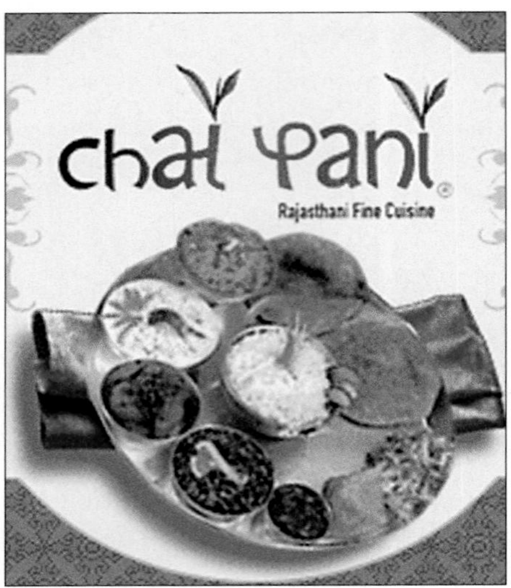

Rajasthan up and down the UK, none serve real Rajasthani food. Others stage Rajasthani festivals, although again, their accuracy may be adrift of the real thing. Consequently few British devotees of real Indian food will have tried Rajasthani food. There are in fact two distinct Rajasthani cuisines, one meat-based the other vegetarian. Hunting has always been a Rajasthani way of life providing wild meat and poultry, cooked on the spot, examples of which are Jungli or Lal Maas and Sufaid Mass, red, very hot curries and white, mild curries respectively. Chai Pani does not serve meat-based food. It specialises in Marwari cuisine, a merchant community living in the Shekhawati area of the Thar desert, where it is not unknown for rain to be absent for years. Consequently no wheat, rice or root vegetables grow there, and such harsh conditions result in Rajasthan's unique cuisine being largely, but not entirely vegetarian. Specialised crops which do grow in this region include kair or ker (a small berry), sangri (Rajasthani string-bean), guar (cluster beans), bhajra (millet) indeed there is a popular millet porridge called Bajra Khichadi, often eaten with pure ghee alone. Raabri is a traditional Rajasthani millet soup. Gram is made into rissoles or sauces akin to the dishes of neighbouring Gujarat, although lacking the sweet taste so beloved by Gujaratis. Other lentils used are mooth, moong and the indigenous arhar dahl.

And so to Chai Pani (literally Tea-water, but implying a warm welcome). The restaurant is owned by Rajasthani sisters Joti and Sandhya Goenka. The restaurant is small and plainly decorated, but sprinkled with Rajasthani objects d'art (peacock feathers, puppets, and artifacts, which are for sale. The charming waiter/manager is from Bombay. The sisters are the cooks and their empire is 'down in the basement'. From there emanates superb food. And the advice on what is what is fluently helpful. A-la-carte, brings you several items at £5.50; a number of Bhel Puri items, Daal aur Kadhi, lentil / yoghurt soups; Panchmela Daal, a slow-cooked five -lentil mix and Besan Chilli Kadhi - Mini Gramflour Pancakes (Besan Chilli) in a yoghurt and gram flour based sauce. Mung Daal / Bajra Khichadi is savoury rice and lentil or millet and lentil casserole, similar to kedgeree, best eaten with kadhi, the Gujarat-style curry. The range of breads is encyclopedic, and as far as we know unique to Chai Pani. Here are a few examples: Missi Roti is spicy gram and wheat flour bread, Bajra Roti, traditional Rajasthani millet and wheat bread ,both £4. Besa Kuttu Chilla are gram flour / buckwheat flour pancakes, while Urad Matar Kachori are puffed bread stuffed with a choice of lentils or peas, both £4.50. Batti is a Rajasthani rural bread roll, £5 and for £8 you will get the Bread Basket containing a selection of these fine breads.Daal aur Kadhi - £5.50. If you are new to Rajasthani food, try one of their extraordinary range of Thaalis (sic). The one which gives you, in effect a tasting menu of starters to dessert is the Royal, £25. Of interest is the wheat-free Thaali, £16 with salad, starter, bread, rice, daal/kadhi, 2 curries, yoghurt and a dessert. The most specialised Thaali, and therefore one which will be totally unfamiliar to most diners, is the Desert Thaali, £10, consisting of a choice of Bajra Roti, Bajra or Moongdal Khichadi served with kadhi, ghee, jaggery, salad and curries. Whether you are vegetarian or not, we commend this venue to you. Hours: 12-2.30, (set buffet £6) Mon-Fri; 12-4.30 Sat, Sun and Bank Hols. 6-10.30. <www.chaipani.co.uk>

CHOR BIZARRE

PREVIOUS AWARD WINNER AND A-LIST

16 Albemarle Street, W1 020 7629 8542

Delhi's Chor Bazaar is a kind of permanent cart-boot-sale, where you can buy anything at knock-down prices. Meaning 'thieves' market' it was originally the place where the villains pushed stolen goods. Entrepreneur Rohit Khattar, owner of Delhi's 32-room Hotel Broadway, hit on the idea to exploit this image. The hotel restaurant needed a revamp, and he cannily renamed it Chor Bizarre exploiting the linguistic twist from 'Bazaar' to 'Bizarre'. The spin told Delhi it was furnished from the real Chor Bazaar. No two chairs of tables were the same. It took Delhi by storm. Mr Khattar set his eyes on Mayfair. When Mahendra Kaul's 85-seat Gaylord site became available, in 1997, it was perfect. 'Antiquities' abound and one table, for example, is encased in an '18th-century four-poster bed' from Calcutta. Chefs Deepinder Sondhi and Manpreet Ahujas major on Kashmiri dishes which include: Goshtaba, a Kashmiri speciality of minced lamb balls cooked in a yoghurt gravy, Nadroo Yakhani, lotus stem in spiced yoghurt gravy. Gilauati Kabab, lamb kebab flavoured with saffron served with tomato and white radish salad and mint yoghurt chutney and Marz Wangun Korma, lamb cooked with Kashmiri chillies with cardamom and cloves, Haaq, spinach cooked with aniseed, Rajmah, red kidney beans and Chaaman, (lotus stem). A neat way to try these and other Kashmiri dishes is to order the Tarami £24. There are many other dishes on the menu from other Indian regions, and all are expertly cooked. For example Soups, Chaats, Tikka and Tandoori starters, and from Pakistan, Tak-a-Tak. After the chef starts frying the dish, he takes the two steel, flat-edged spatulas and rapidly bangs them one after the other on to the pan to chop, mash and mix the ingredients. The dish gets its name from the noise made – taka-taka-taka-taka. Try Kalaji Tak-a-Tak, chicken liver tossed on a high flame with coriander. Our benchmark Dal Makhni, thick black lentil flavoured with tomatoes and cream, immersed overnight on the tandoor; here it's masterly. The Tamil Nadu speciality, Chicken Chettinad, £ 13 (*see page* 75) is turning up on many a menu, usually cooked totally incorrectly. But here it's perfect, cooked in a hot sauce with a predominant flavour of pepper, aniseed and curry leaves. And if you want a good southern taster, the South Indian Tiffin, brings you (in typical office Tiffin carrier) Orange Rasam, Chicken Chettinad, Malabar Prawn Curry, Avial, Sambhar served with Rice and Malabari Parootha on a ceramic banana leaf platter. We like this report: *'We probably spent more time standing outside deciding whether or not we could afford to go in than actually eating! Once inside, it didn't disappoint. Bizarre is certainly the right word, the mismatch of chairs, tables, ornaments actually works well. Food, it has to be said, was fantastic. Started on the right track with bowl of mini pops and excellent pickles, left on table for us to devour. Maggie ordered the Maharani (Vegetarian) Thali consisting of Pakoras, Kurkuri Bhindi Nadroo, Wild Mushroom Mattar, Palak Makkai, Zeera Aloo, Dal Makhni, Cucumber Raita and Zafrani Pulao £22. I had the Maharajah (meat) Thali, with Gazab Ka Tikka, Sharabi Kababi, Tikka Masala, Mirchi Korma, Palak Makkai, Zeera Aloo, Dal Makhni and Cucumber Raita and Zafrani Pulao £24. As if this wasn't enough along came unadvertised mini Nan. Superbly fresh and nicely spiced. Exquisite Mango Kulfi. A really good meal. However, at £40 each, including service, it was baked beans on toast for the rest of the week.* AR. *'Had not been since it opened, wonderful to find it just as good, probably better. Fantastic decor, friendly service, cheerful and efficient. Absolutely superb food, well spiced, good initial ingredients in good portions. A first class lunch – lucky that my new office is in the same street!* [Danny, do you need an excuse?] £97 *for two, very typical for lunch in Mayfair.'* DRC. Wines matched to each dish by Charles Metcalfe, available by the glass. Culture evenings: e.g. book readings, comedy evenings, creative writing workshops to theatre/movie festivals. Food festivals. Private room downstairs, seats 30. Service charge 12.5%. 12-3/6-11.30, Monday to Saturday. (6-1130, Saturday).

CHOWKI TOP 100

2 Denman Street, W1 020 7439 1330

Chef Kuldeep Singh has spearheaded a valuable group of restaurants. Valuable because their food is expertly cooked, and is real Indian food. He opened Mela in 2000, and to prove its success Chowki opened in 2002, in a short street behind Eros, better known for its formula curry houses. But Chowki isn't one of those. Indeed Kuldeep's mission is ' to return to the roots of India's culinary tradition.' Operating with 120 seats in three areas, it changes parts of its menu monthly, with food from three different Indian regions at a time. And with the chef brigade all being Taj-trained it's well within their capabilities to cook highly accurate dishes. For example it's Punjab, Sikkim and Keralan food one month, then Pakistan, Calcutta and Coorg another, and so on. The format is three starters and four mains from each region, all available a-la-carte, or priced at £11.95 for three mains and any four starters, and with lunch from £6.50, you can't complain (except you do, about the uncomfortable seats mostly). It's cheap and cheerful. Busy at peak

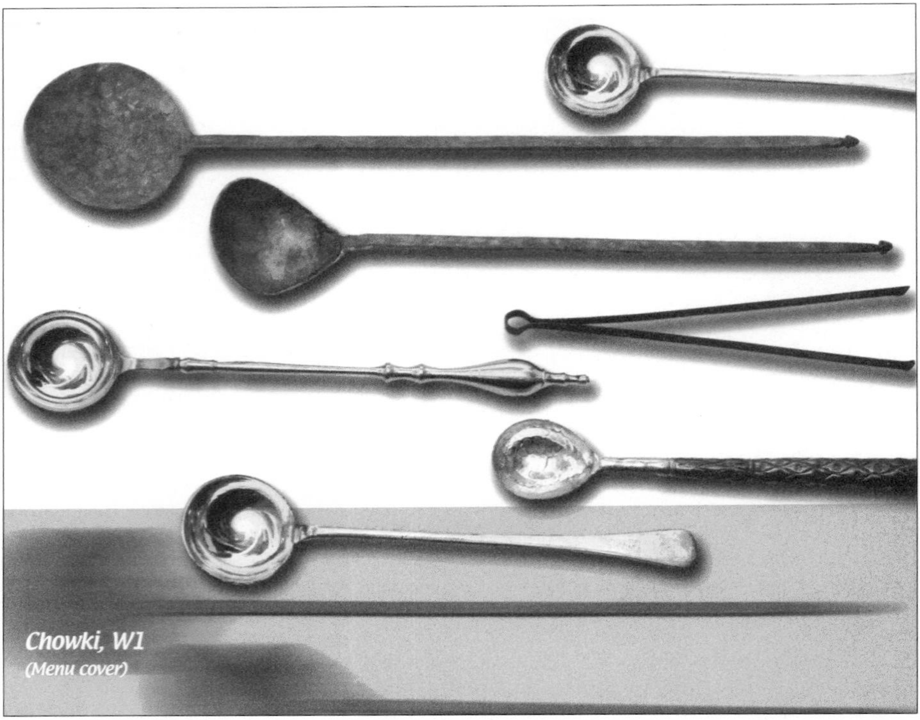

Chowki, W1
(Menu cover)

times but usefully open all day: 12-11.30 daily except Sunday to 10.30. Branches: Dilli Manchester, 3 Monkeys, Croydon, Surrey, Mela, WC2, Soho Spice, W1. <www.chowki.com?

DEYA — NEW ENTRANT

34 Portman Square, W1 — 020 7224 0028

Along with successful restaurateur, Claudio Pulze and his business partner Raj Sharma, Sir Michael Caine, has opened his first ever Indian restaurant, . The 70-cover Deya, meaning 'lamp' boasts traditional Rajasthani style paintings, wall sized antiquated mirrors, opulent high ceilings, chandeliers and richly hued curtains, which are harmonised with dark floors, high rise windows and a glamourously elaborate wire light fixture atop the modish dark wood framed bar. It was Caine, no stranger to running a restaurant, who said, *'when you enter a restaurant, you are on stage. Once you are seated, you are the audience.'* As you enter, the feature which grabs you in is the mural. It is typically Rajasthani, ie a cross between Guernica and Muffin the Mule, with an incongruous bar projecting out of it, it is to say the least, different. Head Chef, Sanjay Dwivedi, previously of Zaika (owned by the Group) serves a traditional Indian menu. Signature dishes include Murghabi Mussalam, duck leg cooked gently in spices served in a rich black lentils sauce and masala; Bhune Rattan, blue fin tuna marinated in chilli and ginger served with mustard seeds and spicy cabbage vada; and Grilled aubergine, stuffed with paneer, green

Deya, W1

chillies, ginger, red onions and chat masala, topped with spicy tomato chutney. The dessert menu includes Mango and Coconut Rice Pudding with Lychees - basmati rice cooked gently in coconut milk finished with fresh mangoes served with caramelised lychees filled with peanuts and Rosewater Panacotta - fresh petal cream served with black pepper tuiles. Indian tapas, like crispy squid fritters and light bar snacks are also on offer. The menu is changed seasonally. Main courses £10 -£15. 5 course set meal £25 - £45. Service charge: 12.5% Hours: 12-2.45, Mon-Fri. 6.30-10.45 Mon-Sat. <www.deya-restaurant.co.uk>

GAYLORD TOP 100

79 Mortimer Street, W1 020 7580 3615

When it opened in 1963 Gaylord was not only Britain's first upmarket Indian restaurant, it also pioneered the Tandoori oven in Britain. The name is a play on the names of the original owners Gai and Lamba, who had opened one of Delhi's very first Indian restaurants called Kwality in 1948. By the 50's there were Kwalities all over India. But they were little more than caffs. Having made a fortune producing ice-cream, the pair decided to go upmarket, with their first Gaylord which opened in Delhi in 1958. Other branches followed soon after in Bombay, San Fransisco, Kowloon, Kobe Japan, Bahamas and Manchester. *'Our friends, Andrew and Diane, my husband Rob and me are regular curry eaters and we love to try somewhere we haven't been before. We enjoy excellent quality curries and the dining experience is very important as we make a night of it. So with the crew and our aims named let me tell you about the Gaylord. All four of us agreed that it was a wonderful curry with such different tastes. We started with tandoori fish, onion pakora, vegetable samosa and chicken chat. The starters were good quality with the chicken chat being made up into a salad, very interesting and quite spicy, but not too spicy. Chutneys were good with an especially hot green 'harassi like' substance the favourite of us all, though to be used with caution. Diane had to wait for her starter of samosa a bit longer than the rest of us because according to the waiter the chef had discarded the first lot because they were not up to standard!!! (A good sign I think) Main courses were superb, sag chicken – the best we have ever tasted! Chilli chicken tikka had an excellent char grilled flavour, chilli lamb was some of the tenderest lamb ever in a curry and my channa kabuli was stunning, very hot with lots of taste and small pieces of raw chilli...all excellent. The side dishes were good too, with Aloo Zerra being our favourite. The rice was good but nothing spectacular. Plain naan was good, stuffed paratha a little too greasy for my liking and the missi roti competent (Taste of Raj in Sandbach do a much better one). We were all very impressed with the food and will certainly return. The service charge is included automatically and while I understand that many people don't tip realistically, we do and use it to tell the restaurant that the experience has been good. The service was fine though there was a wait for the food, which you don't object to when you taste the quality and you realise that it has all been cooked from first principals and not the same sauce-base with different ingredients..* KW. Service 15%. Cover charge: £1.20 – includes a Popadam and pickle. Delivery. Takeaway: 10% discount. Hours: 12-3/6-11.30 ; Sun. to 11.

GOPALS OF SOHO

12 Bateman Street, W1 020 7434 1621

Gopal, real name NT Pittal, earned his spurs building Amin Ali's part, by cooking superb food, first at the Lal Qila, then at the Red Fort. Feeling his career was going nowhere, he opened his own restaurant in 1990, and the accolades poured in. We got a dip for a few years, but now you like it again. Mr Pital jnr, Gopal's son, runs the place while Dad competently cooks classic Indian food to the standard menu, with the full range of starters from bhaji to kebabs, tandoori and curries, but a closer look reveals specials from Goa to Kashmir, Lucknow to Hyderabad: *'Father of a French student came over for a conference at OFSTED Headquarters. I rolled up to meet him at the appointed hour, to be faced with the prospect of an evening with not one, but six Inspectors, his colleagues coming along as well!!! I had done by homework the night before. I called up Gopal's on my mobile – I had stored the number – reserved a table and whistled up a couple of cabs. Gopal's was very good indeed, helpful with the menu, and very tasty indeed.'* JGR. Hours: 12-3/6-11.30

IMLI AWARD WINNER BEST INDIAN

167 Wardour Street, 1 020 7734 5959

'Imli' in Hindi means 'Tamarind' and this gives you the clue that Michelin-starred restaurant, Tamarind has branched out with a new baby, a casually sophisticated eatery in London's West End. Spread across 2,000 square feet over two floors, Imli is a 124-seater casual and informal all-day diner. To decor delicately blends the simplicity of the modern world and combines it with traditional Indian elements including an eclectic mix of Indian art and artifacts. Modern characteristics of bold form, colour and scale are mixed and layered with traditional Indian elements of craft, pattern, and texture to create a unique and inspiring culinary experience. Tamarind's Sous Chef, Samir Sadekar was promoted to the role of Executive Chef at Imli. Originally from Goa, Samir studied Hotel Management at India's prestigious Institute of Hotel Management in Bombay, and then spent two years training at the Maurya Sheraton, where he worked in the world-renowned kitchens of Dum Pukht and Bukhara (see end pages). Samir has created an exciting menu, taking influence from India's dabbas (roadside stalls) that serve the middle class in the coastal areas of southern and western India, but with a stroke of contemporary

genius. but the staple menu is divided into four sections: 'Light and Refreshing'; 'New Traditions', 'Signature Dishes and 'Desserts' Examples: 'Light and Refreshing': Spiced potato cakes £2.95, with ginger, chilli and tamarind sauce (similar to alu tikkas), Papdi Chaat, £3.25, Whole wheat crisps and bean sprouts with vermicelli, sweet yoghurt and mint chutney and Banana Dosa – sweet banana pancakes served with a savoury chutney, £3.50 give traditional street food a refined and modern touch. 'New Traditions', eg: Fenugreek Wraps £4.95, chicken tossed with julienne vegetables in fenugreek bread with a yoghurt mint sauce. 'Signature Dishes', eg Aubergine Masala £4.75 – diced aubergine sautéed with fresh curry leaves and tomatoes served with paratha or rice, Adraki Fish, £5.25, coley sautéed with ginger and tomato and tempered with mustard seeds and ajwain served with paratha or rice. 'Desserts', eg: Indian Caramel Custard £2.95, coconut milk and jaggery crème caramel, and the unusual, but tempting Indian Cardamom Caramel Custard. £2.95. .Formidable value are the 'tasting' menus starting at £15. At affordable prices, even with the service charge of 12.5%,.Imli proves that London's west end need not break the bank. Puja Vedi, Ed, Tandoori Magazine. Take-away available. On Friday and Saturday nights bookings are only taken for 4 or more people. They claim max wait time, if any, is 10 minutes. Hours: daily 11.00 - 11.00. <www.imli.co.uk>

INDIAN YMCA CANTEEN

45 Fitzroy Street, W1 020 7387 0411

Like this place this entry hardly changes, though the acceptance of credit cards, a longer lunch time and non-resident access to dinner are new, as is the price rise – up by an inflationary 10 pence per curry. To find it, follow your nose north up Fitzroy Street – the large modern block on your right may already be permeating curry smells from its basement kitchen. Enter, and out of courtesy, please ask at reception, (manned by gentle young Indians) if it's OK to use the canteen. The canteen, on your right, is clean, with brown functional formica-topped tables. It's deserted 5 minutes before opening time, then as if the school bell's rung, it's suddenly packed full with Asians, many of whom are students, and this is their residence. (Like all YMCAs, residency is open to anyone, though officially this one is subtitled Indian Student Hostel.) All students of good curry, should visit here before they can graduate as aficionados. These are the rules: Be punctual, (opening and closing times and rules are as sharp as the Post Office); no bookings, no smoking, no license, no alcohol, so no **BYO,** and no nonsense! Unlike the Post Office, everything else works, and the staff care. Take a plastic tray, join the always-busy queue at the stainless-steel servery. It's basic, and unsophisticated but authentic expertly spiced and cooked Indian school-dinner-style – food, like you get at streetside Dabbas the length and breadth of India. Chicken and fish curries, lamb curry from £2.50, vegetable curries all £1.50 and lentils £1. Your choice handed to you in bowls. Top up with chupatties, tea or coffee, and pay at the till. It's absurdly cheap – hard to exceed a fiver, and it's remarkable that they now take credit cards. Then jostle for space at a shared formica table. The food may not be five-star but the company can be, when you share your table with talkative, friendly students. Men in white coats tidy up after you. *'Marvellous.'* MW. Set lunch £5 two courses, Sat. & Sun.. Two function rooms seat 30 and 200.Hours: 12-2 daily, except Sunday 1230-1.30 and dinner 7-8, daily.

THE KERALA

15 Great Castle Street, W1 020 7580 2125

This 40-seater is decorated in a very Indian way, with artifacts hanging off the walls including golden umbrellas used by temple elephants. Owner's wife Mille is in charge of the cooking. The food is pure south Indian, with a full list of protein and vegetable dishes. And for the most part it's reasonable, but it's not memorable. *'It was, I feel, very authentic, but not particularly good. We shared a Dosa – spicy potato in a wrap – fabulous! But Vardi – lentil cake in yoghurt is probably an acquired taste. Prawn Biriani was ridiculously hot, nice rice, fabulous Paratha. £33 for three courses including lager – very reasonable.'* MG. Hours: Lunch 12-3/5.30-11, daily.

MASALA ZONE

AWARD WINNER – A-LIST

9 Marshall Street, W1 020 7287 9966

This, the first of five Masala Zones was established in 2001.The concept is to serve real Indian food cooked by a fresh new wave of young Indian chefs at a price point of around a tenner, which will appeal to a new young wave of customers. It's a concept so simple that one is unaware, perhaps of just

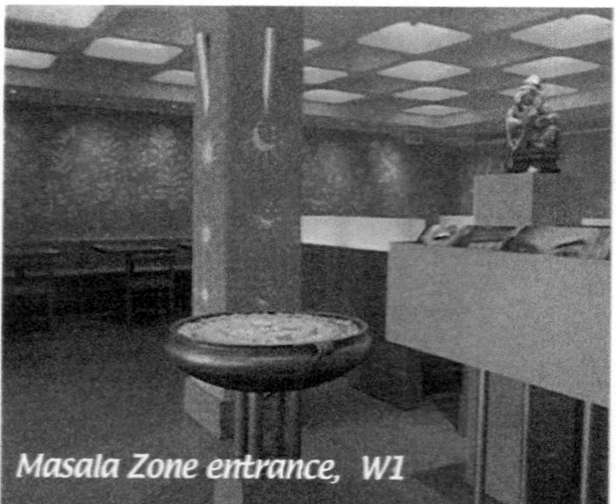
Masala Zone entrance, W1

how brilliant it is. As you approach the interior is revealed behind full-length, full-width plate glass windows. There are 160 seats, some at street level, and the remainder a few steps down on a lower lever, overlooked by the higher level, giving the venue character. Chairs and tables are light and modern, on a wooden floor. Wall decor is inspirational, and deserves your attention. It was painted on a mud-like terracotta background by Indian tribal artists, who paint cartoon-like line-drawings in white with sticks. They'd never been outside their village, let alone to London. Doing what the tribe has done for centuries, they tell the history of mankind, in a series of episodes. The drawings carry humour, pathos and perception. And the artists were so awe-struck with the capital, that they added a new penultimate episode – scenes of London, including some things they'd not seen before – Buck House, some guardsmen, the Tower, and their favourite – a stretch limo. Their final episode is drawn around the restaurant's bar servery hatch and depicts mankind getting drunk and falling over. There's not much chance of that at Masala Zone, only soft drinks, wines and beers are sold, and customer turnround is fast. This is because service is fast, from smartly uniformed young men and women and the kitchens are fast too. But this is no criticism. It's fast if you need it, but if you want to dwell, we've never noticed pressure on you to leave, no matter how busy it gets. The actual cooking takes no shortcuts – curries are slow-cooked to maximise flavours in the large kitchens behind, which includes a completely separate vegan kitchen, with its utensils coded so that they never touch meat. There is a further kitchen in view, with a series of smallish warmers containing ready-cooked food, which are constantly refilled by the chefs behind. Cold food emanates from one side of the kitchen, hot on the right. You place your order, and it's immediately doled out to the waiter . This leads to what some reporters complain about as being chaos. This is because dishes arrive to your table as soon as the chefs issue it. Some things take longer than others, and your order may arrive mains first, starter last, in any order. Masala Zone has been likened to Wagamama. A few other aspects of Masala Zone already noted: price, queues, youth and fun may be likened to Wagamama But the resemblance is skin-deep. Service, rather than self-service is an obvious difference, as are comfortable chairs. Most importantly, Masala Zone's food is much more complex. Wagamama's is noodle nosh doshed out by non-skilled cooks. All Masala Zone food requires very high skill levels to cook. Snacks (or starters) include several types Bhel *(see page 75)* – Bombay street food. Chicken Samosas, lightly spiced, finely minced chicken with green peas; Shikampuri Kebab, melt in the mouth, aromatically spiced, minced lamb croquettes. Malabar Seafood Bowl, prawns, calamari, fish kofta with flat noodles in a richly curried soup. Everything is available a la carte., but way-to-go is with the Thalis *(see page 99)*. Items do change weekly, but this is an example — snacks of Khandvi, Dhokla (a pancake of besan flour, spiced and rolled up like a swiss-roll and cut into slices, served chilled). Yoghurt Curry, Potato Curry, Dal, Aubergine and Plantain Curry, Rice and Chuppatis served with chutneys of Mango and Coriander. Add to that your choice of Achari Chicken Curry or Prawn Curry or Lamb Curry . There is a vegetarian Thali, and a weekend children's Thali. Noodle Bowls with Bombay-style Indianised Chinese is a spicy take on regular Chinese cuisine. Desserts: Caramel or Mango Kulfi, Shrikand with Fresh Fruit, Gulab Jamun with ice-cream, Caramelised Carrot with ice cream all priced at £2.50 each. '*Fantastic concept. A top quality Indian meal cooked in front of your eyes for less than a tenner in a prime West End location! It is a large split-level, modern café-style restaurant with the cheerful and confident chefs practising their art with a flourish in full view at the back of the establishment, as you dine. A nice piece of theatre for the West End! Food quality was first class. Minced Chicken Kebab, Chana Jabal Roti (chick peas) was particularly good, as were the Chicken Mangalore, Rogon Gosht and Chicken Vindaloo (one of our party was feeling brave!). The Thaliís looked particularly good with a choice of meat or vegetarian, and appeared to be the most popular items on the menu, being ordered by every second diner in the venue. The great thing about their Thali's is you get to choose the main dish(es) and the smoked clove lamb dish was truly sensational. The accompanying vegetable dishes and the mixed meat starter were also excellent, as was Anita's vegetarian thali. The dishes were all characterised with excellent flavours although they did tend to err on the hot side of spicy (which was nice). Good-sized portions and outstanding value for money. Service was efficient. Overall opinion — very good even without the exceptional prices. Factor in the prices and location as well and it would be daft not to return (and I will!). Would highly recommend. This establishment truly is a gem.'* SO. Lunchtime treats also include spicy sandwiches. Spend between £8 and £15 plus drink. No reservations, so queueing is possible at peak times. Takeaway menu offers a good selection of street food and curry and rice dishes. Delivery free over £10 and covers the many central and west London postcodes. 25% discount is also available for delivery lunch orders over £40. Service: 10%. Hours: 12-3/5,30-11 Mon-Fri. Sunday 12.30-11. We are so delighted with the concept that we must give Masala Zone a special award. **BEST** *See page* 28. *See page* 28, Branches:N1 & W1, WC2. <www.realindianfood.com>

PALMS OF GOA

12 Charlotte Street, W1 020 7636 1668

'After lubrication in the Bricklayers Arms round the corner, Palms of Goa is the usual destination. Rapidly becoming one of my favourite haunts. Lamb Xacutti is very good, as is the Goan Chicken and fish dishes. Not as authentic as Ma Goa, SW14 but very tasty. Good rice and breads, excellent attentive service and the best Tarka Dal I've had in a long while. Good value in the heart of London.' AR.

LA PORTE DES INDES
OUTSTANDING RESTAURANT

32 Bryanston Street, W1 020 7224 0055

Owned by the Blue Elephant Group (*see* sw6) it opened in 1997, under the management of Sherin Modi Alexander with her husband, Mernosh Modi, in charge of cooking. Both Taj-trained they have really grown into the role. Their professionalism cannot be bettered. Once a ballroom which blossomed in the wartime 1940's, and lying derelict by the 1980's, owner Karl Steppe applied his Blue Elephant decor yardstick here, and went all-out with a £2.5m spend. Unlike others whose budget claims are greatly exaggerated, you can easily see how transforming this vast place cost all of that, particularly since its layout isn't an easy one to deal with. Features include a sandstone arch, a 40-foot waterfall, a sweeping staircase made of white marble with pink sandstone balustrades, imported especially from India's pink city, Jaipur. Airy, domed skylights enhance La Porte's daytime atmosphere, making it a different place in darkness. There is a forest of jungle plants, a wealth of Indian artifacts and antiques, and the range of eating rooms, including the tiny private dining rooms seating 12 and 24 respectively, and three more dining areas bringing the total seating up to 300. The lunch presentation of food on raised copper salvers is opulent and attractive, and you can e-a-m-a-y-l for £19.90. *'We've eaten lunch here many times and have not been disappointed'* RL. *'I love this restaurant. From the welcome at the door to the presentation of the bill. The food, is just superb. Murgh Makhani (CTM) is just how it is in India and just how it should be. Flavoursome chicken pieces from a whole chicken — not the usual chunks of tasteless chicken breast — are smothered in a delicious, creamy, delicately spiced crimson gravy. Potato-stuffed parathas are buttery and light. You will want to eat them even if you are full to bursting. Big, fat, juicy King prawns floating in a light, mustard seed, turmeric coloured, coconut milk sauce. The puddings will not disappoint. The frequently held themed food festivals are a remarkable eduction in Indian regional food.'* DBAC. *'Deservedly* **TOP 100**, *my all-time favourite restaurant.'* SO. We continue to remain impressed by La Porte. La Porte's ambience, decor, service, food is all as good as it gets. La Porte has become an

La Porte des Indes, W1

Indian's Indian, with an ever-increasing clientèle from the subcontinent. We gave it our **BEST IN UK AWARD** in 1998. This Award is a permanent accolade, and does justice to Mernosh's fabulous food and Sherin's tight management. Average spend £50. Service discretionary. Cover charge £1.50. Hours: 12-2.30 Mon.-Fri (to 3pm Sun)/7-11.30 Mon.-Sat. (Sun. 6-10.30). Branches: Blue Elephant Thai, sw6, and others in Europe.

RAGAM SOUTH INDIAN — TOP 100

57 Cleveland Street, W1 — 020 7636 9098

Established in 1984 this cosy restaurant seats 34 upstairs, 20 downstairs, and has a strong following. Chef Nair cooks standard curries and, being from Kerala, authentic south-Indian food. All the south Indian favourites are there, and we recommend the Fish Mooli, white fish simmered in a sauce of garlic, mustard seed, curry leaf and coconut milk.. It remains in our **TOP 100** because you say it should. Don't forget the lunchtime 'quick meal' £5 for curry, rice and bread! Service, 10%, not included. Delivery: min £10, local area only. Hours: 12-3 Mon - Thurs & Sat; 6-11.15 Mon - Sat; Sun. 6-10.30.

RAJ TANDOORI

72 Berwick Street, W1F 8TD — 020 7437 2897

This old-hand opened way back in 1969. Abdon Noor serves Northern Indian food, all the usual curry favourites, plus some Bangladeshi specials including Ayer Bhuna (Bangladeshi fish) and Satkora (Bangladeshi citrus fruit) Gosht. Seats an intimate 36. Air-conditioned. Takeaway: 10% discount. Show Mr Noor this *Guide* and you may get a discount. ours: 12-2.30/5.30-12.

RASA — A-LIST

6 Dering Street, W1 — 020 7629 1346

Opened in 1998, this is the second of three restaurants established by Shivadas (Das) Sreedharan and his wife Alison. As with the original Rasa (London N16), they specialise in southern-Indian vegetarian cooking from Kerala, south India's richest state. Superb cooking by Chef RS Binuraj and his team. Nibbles include Pappadavadai (paps dipped in batter and sesame seeds and deep-fried) and Acchappam – rice batter crisp made from a mould (acch). Starters include: Banana Boli (ripe plantain dipped in besan flour and black sesame, fried, served with peanut and ginger sauce), Vadai Selection (fermented lentil soft dumplings, deep-fried to give a crisp outside). Main course curries (all at c£7) include Moru Kachiathu – sweet mangoes and green bananas cooked in yoghurt with green chillies, ginger and fresh curry leaves, Beet Cheera Pachadi – fresh beetroot and spinach in a yoghurt with roasted coconut, mustard seeds and curry leaves, and the house signature dish Rasa Kayi (minced vegetables, ginger, garlic and fennel seed). To experience several of these try the Travancore Feast £22, Tamarind, Lemon and Coconut Rice (with fresh coconut and black dhal) £4 each. During the evening all main courses are traditionally served on banana leaf. Prices are a bit higher than N16. Like its sister restaurants, the place is very tiny with seating on two floors packed into the narrow rooms. It does two full sessions every night, plus a full week-day lunch trade. So book and go early. Service 12.5%. Hours: 12-3/6-11. Sunday dinner only. Branches: Rasa, N16 Rasa Express NW1 & N16 and next entry. <www.rasarestaurants.com>

RASA SAMUDRA A-LIST

5 Charlotte Street, W1 020 7637 0222

Outside it has the same blackcurrant-yoghurt-pink paintwork, shown below. And if you have déja-vue from page 128, all Rasas are the same colour; this is Das' house colour and he loves it. Lovely hanging baskets burst with red flowers. Inside wooden carvings hang on pretty Wedgewood blue walls. Dining is on two floors, and the regulars tells me they prefer quieter, more spacious upstairs. If you wish to understand Keralan food, all Rasas are encyclopedic in the subject. The menu includes many of Rasa's signature vegetarian dishes (see entry alongside). But here Das uniquely specialises in Keralan fish and seafood (Samudra means 'of the sea'). Special seafood starters: Rasam (consommé with prawns, crab, mussels, squid and tomato), Crab thoran, – fresh crab meat stir-fried with coconut, mustard seeds and ginger. Main courses include: Meen Elayil Pollichathu (pomfret marinated in paste of Kanthari chillies, curry leaves, green pepper and fresh coconut slices), Crab Varuthathu, crab dish cooked dry with ginger, curry leaves, chilli and mustard seeds, Konju Manga Curry (king prawn, green mango and coconut sauce), and Varutharachameen curry, , tilapia fish in a sauce made with roasted coconut, red chillies, tomatoes and tamarind. Puddings: Pal Payasam £3.50 (spiced rice pudding, cashew nuts and raisins). Set menus: £22.50 vegetarian, £30 seafood. Lots of different types of funny-shaped Pops and numerous delicious chutneys are a meal in themselves including the remarkable Meen Achar fish pickle) and Konju Achar (prawn pickle). Fantastic Fishy Broth to start (Meen Rasam). We get reports of curt service at Rasa and indeed had experience of it ourselves. 12.5% service charge and expect to pay above average prices. Main courses £7-£15. Set meals (both highly spoken of) c£24 (veg), c£32 (seafood). Hours: 12 - 3 /6 - 10.45. Sunday dinner only. Branches, see above. <www.rasarestaurants.com>

RASA EXPRESS W1 NEW ENTRANT

5 Rathbone Street, W1 020 7637 0222

The second Rasa lunch-time, inexpensive, no-fuss outlet, and clearly the pilot for a nationwide franchise operation. See Rasa Express NW1 for details. Limited hours: 12 - 3 Mon-Fri

RED FORT A-LIST

77 Dean Street, Soho, W1 020 7437 2525

This venue is in the hands of the very capable Amin Ali. He has already built his name by securing Camden Council grants to open restaurants, which at the time achieved much acclaim such as the Last Days of the Raj and Lal Qila. They were co-operatives in that the work force shared in the work and the profits. But Ali had more ambitious ideas, and his Red Fort opened in 1987 claiming it was it was the first to offer the real cooking of India. This is not the case, of course, (see Veerawamy and Gaylord, W1. but a lot of people believed it. At first it was nothing more than curryhouse food, although it was done well. Then Amin got his ace card in the form of chef Mohammed Rais, a Delhi-trained master chef par excellence. Then came a controversial fire which destroyed this iconic venue. Rias went off to the Darbar, SW6 and the place lay dormant. Eventually a £2m rebuild took place and the Red Fort reopened in late 2002 to a fanfare of publicity, something Amin is adept at. The exterior is modernised but still recognisable. Inside 85 seats reside in a modernist Mughal setting with sand-coloured walls, Indian trimmings, slate floor with a red path, dotted with mosaics leading you to the back where water drizzles down the wall. Nearby, Tandoors are in view (behind glass). The drama continues in the toilets, where no expense has been spared. Neither has it backstage where there is a space-age, rarely-found air-conditioned kitchen. Rias returned to the fold and brought back his expertise in Dum Pukht cuisine (see page 69). Rias mastered Dum under the legendary Lucknowi Chef Qereshi, the Exec at Delhi's Mughal Sheraton Hotel Dum Pukht restaurant. His specialities include starters such as Galauti Kebab – the smoothest patties of minced lamb and spices. Teetar Gilafi Kebab – spiced roasted minced partridge or Monkfish Tikka – chunks of monkfish smoked with ginger. For main course, the Dum Pukht cogniscenti go for Dum ki bater (quail in a creamy yoghurt, almond and cashew nut sauce) or Aromatic lamb shank or any of Rais' Birianis, each cooked in a sealed pot: Avadhi Gosht Biryani – Rais' 300 year old family recipe of lamb and rice. Samudari biryani – scallops, squid, prawns and rice. Subz biryani – moist basmati rice, vegetables and spices. Other dishes include Mahi

Red Fort's air-conditioned kitchen

Anaari, succulent king prawns with saffron sauce; Bhuni Duck, in a dry sauce; Lamb chops marinated in pomegranate juice. *'The food is really superb, service good and the whole lunch a very enjoyable experience. I did notice the the menu is very small but I am sure all diners would be delighted with anything they choose.'* DC. The venue's basement never worked well in its previous incarnation. But it does now in the form of Akbar a 'sexy' bar, seating 75 which can be used before or after dining upstairs or for lighter meals. Natural stone floors, with luxurious rugs, leather armchairs and low tables a an eclectic mixture of art and sculpture and an extensive bar serves everything including Indian-style cocktails which runs to 1am deep in the vaults). It was good and the restaurant has plenty of charisma, just like its owner. Service charge 12.5%. Table d'hote lunch and pre-theatre specials from £16 for 3 courses. 12-2.15 Mon-Fri; 5.45-11 Mon-Sat; Sun 6-10. <www.redfort.co.uk>

REGENT TANDOORI

16 Denman Street, Piccadilly, W1 020 7434 1134

Long-established standard curry house waving the flag for the formula. Good for a fix at sensible prices. Lunch and dinner daily.

SOHO SPICE TOP 100

124 Wardour Street, W1 020 7434 0808

Owner by chef Kuldeep Singh, Asraf Rahman and Dinesh Mody who jointly run Shaftesbury Avenue's Mela WC1 and Chowki W1. The menu features an extensive and intricate range of kebabs which change on a daily basis and are cooked in the show kitchen. Raminder Malhotra, Executive chef says he takes inspiration from chefs with royal pedigree including Tundee Main, a prominent craftsman of the 19th century. Chef Raminder highlights the fine line in the art of kebab making, *'What differentiates a great kebab from an indifferent roast is that it should be crisp on the outside and soft and succulent on the inside.'* He also offers his signature 'hook kebab', a leaf-wrapped meat attached by hooks linked to one another and cooked in the tandoor. Other menu examples include steamed sea bass with raw mango, topped with kokum and coconut-tempered shrimps, wrapped in banana leaf; and Tandoori pheasant breast marinated with orange rind, roasted cumin and rock salt. The menu also includes vegetarian options such as potato kebab with sweet and sour fruity filling, grilled over charcoal ambers. Alongside the kebab menu are sections offering more traditional Indian choices of favourite curries such as spicy chicken curry or Konkani prawn curry. The late night basement bar/ night club opened in 2005. The combination of rich and warm colours, together with retro furniture, results in a stylish and contemporary room that features dark wood walls and plush roomy red leather banquettes. These double up as booths, ideal for groups or parties. An archway leading from the edge of the bar leads towards the DJ booth and dance floor, illuminated by disco lights. The range of drinks include speciality cocktails produced by Head Bartender Francis Lama and his team. Bar snacks are served until 3am, include kebabs, tawa grilled halibut steak, lobster barbeque, plain or flavoured naans and squid with pepper, garlic, tomato and ground spices. PV.

TAMARIND AWARD WINNER & A-LIST

20 Queen Street, W1 020 7629 3561

Opened in 1994, This *Guide* gave it **BEST NEWCOMER AWARD** in 1995 - 97, **BEST INDIAN**, 1998-9 and and **BEST CHEF** 1999-2000 becoming the only Indian restaurant to be so awarded It won its first Michelin star in 2001 which it continues to retain Owners Leader Wick Services, a family owned business in India are immensely proud of the success of Tamarind. Internationally the restaurant has been given recognition by New York Times Golden E Award for Excellence, which is given only to five restaurants worldwide. General Manager Rajesh Suri (formerly with Red Fort and Veeraswamy) joined in 1998 and is in no small part responsible for this success. Atol Kotchar was the original chef, and when he left in 2002 (to open Benares, W1), Sous chef Alfred Prasad (ex Delhi Sheraton and Veeraswamy) took on the mantle of Head Chef. He graduated from the Institute of Hotel Management, Madras in 1993 and completed his advanced chef training at the 'Maurya Sheraton' in Delhi, working at the legendary 'Bukhara' and 'Dum-Pukht' restaurants *(see end pages)*.then to the Madras Sheraton Hotel where he was Executive Chef at 'Dukshin'-one of India's premier south Indian restaurants. Alfred finally moved to London in June 1999 where he worked as Sous Chef at 'Veeraswamy'. The original Emily Todd Hunter, decor included an array of gold and copper and Indian antiques. Handmade cutlery, copper pots

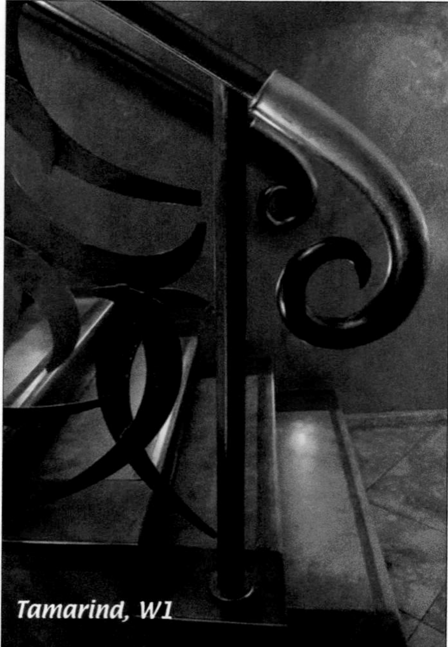
Tamarind, W1

and papier maché menus set off the concept. Since our last edition there has been a redesign by Charles Leon which changed things quite a bit. The wall with saris has been replaced with antique mirrors with the Tamarind logo running through it. The staircase now gleams with hand-blown crystals and the bar has also been extended . he restaurant is one big well-spaced room with 26 tables that seat up to 90 seats. The preconceived notion of being unable to match Indian food and wine is dismantled here with the help of an experienced sommelier, who assists the customers in choosing the right drink. He in turn is assisted with a choice of 140 different wines, mainly from France, and the New World. Prices range from £15 to £1500 per bottle. Rajesh says, '*Over the years we have learned to change 2-3 different wines each month. Every fortnight we have a wine tasting for the staff. We have a really good sommelier, so the customers can trust his judgement'*. Prasad has maintained the Tamarind tradition on the new menu, with old Tamarind favourites, but has put on new dishes as well. The the open-view kitchen is the location for the Tandoors and kebab-making. Here are some menu examples: starters include Saag Aloo Tikki, spiced potato cakes with a spinach filling, served with tamarind chutney, Tandoori Subzi, grilled broccoli and paneer in spicy marinade, Murgh ka Chat, smoked chicken salad with red onions and peppers in a spiced avocado dressing. interesting mains include: Seafood Moilee, scallops, squid, mussels and kingfish in a mild coconut sauce, £16.50, Lamb Chettinad, cooked with Chettinad spices, £16.50 and Bhuna Achari Khargosh, rabbit cooked with pickling spices. Our benchmark dal Makhni, low-cooked black lentils was perfect. Roomali Roti was handkerchief-thin and soft. Some things are just brilliant, but some of the slightly unconventional experiments are less so. *'With a huge reputation to live up to as outlined in the Guide, I chose to meet a business associate for a 'working lunch.'* [Really David, those 'working lunches' always seem to take place at a luxurious Indian restaurant]. *'Booked in advance, warmly greeted, shown to table and offered Kingfisher and Popadoms as I waited – excellent. Each dish was fabulous, definitive spices and flavours that did not overpower. Fabulous service, from booking to bill. Many will be put off by the prices but should not be. Whether impressing clients or celebrating a family occasion, a visit is highly recommended. £182.31 for two.'* DL. *'We will be down in London this weekend. You will not be surprised to learn we will be taking the opportunity to visit our favourite establishment, The Tamarind in Queen Street. Our daughter is coming over for a few days from Greece and it will be her first visit to the restaurant'.* SC. Tamarind remains an **A-LIST** restaurant in our Guide. Then it always was. Main courses £15-£30. 2 course set lunch £18, 3 course £20. 2 course set meal (6-7pm) £23. Service charge: 12.5% Delivery. Hours: 12-3 Mon-Fri; -2.30 *(See Imli W1 and pages 14 & 15)* <www.tamarindrestaurant.com>

TASTE OF MUGHAL

29 Great Windmill Street, W1 020 7439 8044

Long-standing Piccadilly curryhouse, a much-needed venue for some who love the formula. Seats 50 diners. *'Never varies after all these years of visits.'* RW. Takeaway: 10% discount. Hours: 12-11.45.

VEERASWAMY

OUTSTANDING RESTAURANT AWARD

99 Regent Street, W1 020 7734 1401

2006 marked the 80th birthday of this venerable institution and owners Ranjit Mathrani, Namita and Camellia Panjabi, the trio behind Chutney Mary, Amaya and Masala Zone marked the occasion by transforming the already gorgeous venue into a truly stunning ninth decade. As they put it *'the restaurant now reflects the glamour and glory it exuded*

in the 1920s'. But this is not 20s décor it is strictly 21st century. Mind you the pedigree is never forgotten. Established in 1926 and for many years, Britain's only Indian restaurant, its founders were an Indian princess and her husband, the great grandson of an English General in the Bengal Army. Customers included Edward, Prince of Wales, King Gustav of Sweden, Pandit Nehru, Indira Gandhi, Charlie Chaplin, King Hussein of Jordan, and Marlon Brando. You will notice picture of the rich and famous devotees of Indian food. t whose rendezvous it has always been. Most definitely not the former, but decidedly the latter, one customer was also my mother, who saved up here nurse's money for an occasional visit in the 1930s to satisfy the fix she had acquired in the Raj. The entrance then as now is on the aptly-named Swallow Street. Go up the stairs one floor or take the lift. As you enter the main room, the wall-to-wall picture windows at first dominates with their great view of Regent Street. But you are soon spell-bound with the interior. The silver painted ceiling. the dark wooden floor, the handmade Moghul floral-design carpets and Indian black granite speckled with gold. On one wall, vividly coloured turbans remind one of the Indian Maharajas who once frequented the restaurant. Century-old Kalighat-style Bengali paintings adorn the

restaurant. The tiled mirror wall (at the cute booth called the honeymoon table) is a good idea but who cracks the tiles? The lighting combines primary-coloured glass shades redolent of handis, exorbitant chandeliers, and LCD lighting colour-changing the fretwork screens. The short menu includes classics from throughout India and contemporary creations produced by a brigade of specialists from different Indian regions. Items from bhel, to dosas and lamb shank to lobster from Hyderabad to Chowpatti beach, and Goa to Delhi. This is not to everyone's liking, since it's far removed from curry house stuff and it's in the higher price range. Caveats issued, let me now tell you why this restaurant is so high in our estimation. We have always found the starters to be par-excellence, sometimes delectable, sometimes transcendent and the protein dishes too. On our recent visit we had Raj Kachori (a giant pani-puri filled with dahi and bhel street food, quite divine and much better than its description in the menu.) and green vegetable kebab. Our mains were a delectable Lamb Biriani with a smooth pink Mirchi Salan sauce (chilli curry - delicious but very mild) and Syrian chicken stew, pink sauce again, but spicier and quite outstanding. We had Sukhe Aloo potatoes, great and green Romali Roti (food colouring) disappointing.. Desserts at the Panjabi establishments have always been way above average, partly because they are made on site and not bought in. I am indebted to Sejal Sukhadwala, whose Time Out Indian restaurant reports are always perceptive and very witty, and who wrote of US food writer Jeffrey Steingarten, *'he once memorably described Indian desserts as tasting of face cream. - but here the own-made kala jaam (semolina and milk dumplings in rose-scented syrup) and rasgollas (poached paneer dumplings) were fabulous.'* I can add to that: for it was at Veeraswamy that I first had hot Gulab Jamun, *(see page 89)* flambéed in Cognac. Some face cream! One more thing: the wine list is an exemplary selection. Mr Mathrani is a connoisseur, and it shows. If ever there were a time to convert from beer to wine, this is it. As for price. It's not always out of reach. True a meal for two will be c£80 + booze.. But the 3 course set lunch is just £17, and there are good-value set dinners too: 5.30-6.30pm and 10.30-11.30pm, £12 two courses, £15 three courses. Service 12½%. Upstairs the Palmer room (named after the founder) takes 36 seated and 60 standing. When we started the Curry Club in 1982, we used this room to hold our monthly meetings. It was then rather tatty. Not now: it is transformed with more turbans and is invitingly laid out for dinner for 18. And there are a number of framed prints up there which deserve attention. Our £89 meal was too much for us and it was willingly packed to take away, and would have made the cost more bearable to get two meals out of it. Sadly when we unpacked next day they had failed to pack the main courses and out much anticipated dinner went out of the window. If you phone in to book, beware the uneccesarily endless recorded message, and when you do press 3 to reserve, you may have to listen to an entire Brandenburg concerto before anyone answers. you. Hours: 12-2.15 (Sat & Sun. to 2.30) 5.30-10.30. (Sun. 6-10.30). *See page* 28.

WOODLANDS — TOP 100

77 Marylebone Lane, W1 — 020 7436 3862

A branch of Mr Sood's well-liked, small chain of southern Indian vegetarian restaurants. See SW1 branch for details.

YATRA

34 Dover Street, W1 — 020 7493 0200

Opened in 2000 by Sonu Lalwani with his wife Liah. Yatra, meaning *'pilgrimage'*, or *'journey'*, is so called because the couple's concept is that their diners *'journey into India and beyond'*. Beyond might be their highly profitable basement Bollywood bar of which more below. Said to be Marco Pierre White's favourite Indian restaurant, the recent redec is sleekly attractive. with ivory and deep red walls, alcoves, wood carvings, a dark shiny floor, black chairs with gold upholstery and inviting tables Head chef, Sam Seghal's menu is more pan-Asian and less Punjabi than his predecessor's, and it is a bit spiced-down for the true aficionado. Yet it does contain some juicy items for the curryholic. Starters include Burmese lamb kebab (griddled patties of minced lamb, potato, roasted cumin and fresh coriander) and Achaari chicken tikka (marinated in pickling spices). Mains are all served with a portion of steamed rice or naan bread and include Meen Moilee (monkfish tempered with shallots and curry leaves, cooked in a fenugreek and red chilli spiced coconut sauce), and Yatra's special chicken (tender morsels of chicken tikka cooked in ghee and sun dried tomato cream sauce). Vegetable dishes include Achaari Paneer (infused with pickling spices and mustard oil,

cooked with fresh tomatoes). Average spend £45. 2 course set dinner £32. 12.5% service charge. Private dining area, 26 seated and 45 standing. Hours: Mon to Wed 6.30-11. Thu to Sat 6-11.30. Note,lunch is only 'European' food. The basement Bollywood Bar runs on Fridays and Saturdays 7pm-1am, during which hours it heaves with young and not-so-young Asians Bangra-ing the night away at £10 entry and £7 a cocktail. This popular Bar has two USPs. It is a London waterhole for Bombay Bollywood movie stars, and being the first such bar, it is often packed to the gills (190 people standing, or 100 seated). Indian bar snacks. Bar: <www.barbollywood.net> Restaurant <www.yatra.co.uk> Branch: Yatra Club Manchester.

London W2

Bayswater, Edgware Road, Paddington, Westbourne Grove

BOMBAY PALACE TOP 100

2 Hyde Park, 50 Connaught Street, W2
020 7258 3507

In the late 1970s, Mr SS Chatwell was a successful Indian restaurateur in Ethiopia. Then a regime-change left him fearing for his life. He packed his bags and left for the USA. Luckily he'd packed his many bags full of dollars, and I mean FULL. I know because I met him in NY and he told me. It was not long before he opened Bombay Palace London opened in 1983. The 135-seater is: *'Top notch restaurant, impeccably appointed in bright and airy single room. Smart polite and efficient staff. Real tablecloths and napkins. Engaging if not extensive menu offering mostly North Indian dishes. Complimentary Popadoms and small tubs of sauces. Very nice starter of Bombay Tiffin Vegetarian £7.90 - a selection of Aloo Tikka, Aloo Paratha, Onion Bhajia, Bhel Puri and Samosa ... all distinctively different and very tasty, served with lettuce leaves and sliced giant radish. Balouchi Raan £14.60 - outstanding, exquisite, beautifully tender cut of lamb leg, partially sliced of the bone. Had been marinated and slow cooked, with a hint of char - fabulous, subtle, varied flavours, a little sauce. Peshwari Naan £2.45 - light, fluffy, aromatic and tasty with a smattering of nuts and fruits. However, service charge rather steep at 15% and automatically added.'* RW. Menu Snapshot: Bombay Fish Curry £9.70, kingfish fillets simmered in a spicy curry sauce with mustard and turmeric; Murgh Kaleji Masala £5.30, chicken livers sautéed with onion, tomato, cumin and coriander; Anarkali Chaat £4.60, fresh pomegranate seeds, goats cheese, watercress, grapefruit and walnuts; Dahi Batata Puri £4.50, crisp lentil puffs with tangy mixture of bean sprout and coriander, finished with hung yoghurt, mint and tamarind chutney; Batak Pepper Fry £9.70, duck with roasted onions, crushed peppercorns, lemon and bell pepper. Service 15%. Cover charge £1 Takeaway: 10% discount. Hours: 12-2.45 (Sun. 12-3pm)/6-11.30. (Sun. 6- 11). Branches: Beverly Hills, Budapest, Houston, Kuala Lumpur, Mississauga, Montreal, New York, Toronto, Washington DC . <www.bombaypalace.co.uk>

CONNOISSEURS INDIAN

8 Norfolk Place, W2 1 LQ 020 7402 3299

Bright, cosy 46-seater which Chef Kabir Miah adds authenticity to the formula with interesting appetisers such as Bombay Roll, ground steak coated in potato paste and deep-fried, and Ayre Cutlet, Bangladeshi fish pan-fried with onion. Main-course dishes include Hass Baas (spicy duck cooked with bamboo shoots), Potato Tilli (lamb kidney cooked with potato), Khashi Gazar, goat's meat cooked with baby carrots, Parrot Fish, in a thick spicy sauce,, Shorisha Ayre, is spiced with mustard paste, or Venison, pheasant, grouse and quail Bhoona. The Meat Thali was excellent value, good quality, nicely presented and very filling. Set lunch: £7.95 three courses, set dinner from £8.50. Delivery: 5-miles. Hours: 12-2.30/ 6-12.

DURBAR NEW TO OUR TOP 100

24 Hereford Road, W2 020 7727 1947

Opened when time began in 1956, by Shaimur Rahman Syed. Seats 60 diners – wicker chairs, arches, plants, Indian art, brass coffee-pots. Serves Northern Indian curries with a handful of specials which include: Chicken Xacuti, very hot with dry chilli and coconut and Chicken Silla, shredded chicken tikka. Good-value are the Thali set-meals from £8.95. Co-owner Chef Shamin Syed won the International Chef of the Year Contest in Feb. 2000. He says of his winning dish – Oriental Chicken *'it's been on the menu for over 24 years'.* What more can we say about one of London's most stable and experienced venues? Well there is a bit more. RCF says *'it's one of our regular haunts. Whenever we go it is without fail packed full of Indians and Arabs. That says quality.'.* Hours: 12-2.30/6-12. Branch: Greenford Tandoori, Ruislip Road East, Greenford, Middlesex

Co-owner Shaimur Rahman Syed serving customers in 1956. (note the white coat). If you can recognise yourself (or your relatives) here and can prove it, the Good Curry Guide will treat you to a free dinner with the editor at Durbar.

GANGES

101 Praed Street, W2 020 7723 4096

It's just a curry house, but it's very popular and it's been with us since our first *Guide*. Hours: 12-2.30/5.30-11.

GINGER

2004 AWARD FOR BEST BANGLADESHI CUISINE TOP100

115 Westbourne Grove, W2 020 7908 1990

Bangladesh's top chef, Albert Gomes was Exec at Dhaka's five-star Sonargoan Hotel when we met him there in 1996, and were stunned by his cooking. He was frankly surprised at our enthusiasm, under the impression that the UK's 7,000+ Bangladeshi-owned restaurants would offer their own food. We urged him to get a posting in London, and put Bangladeshi cooking on the UK map. And he did. Firstly with a short festival at the Red Fort, then hooray, in a permanent position at the new Ginger, in 2001, and he brought his chef son. His style is upmarket home-cooking, and at Ginger he was given an upmarket new venue (modern wood floor, cyan chairs and white walls). I'd have preferred a more upmarket location, but it's there, and we should rejoice. Bangla cooking (*see page* 50) majors on fish, the bonier the better, shrimps, and a wealth of fresh vegetables, many only recently seen in the UK. Banglas love sweet, bitter, sour and hot. Curries are generally thinner than we get at the curryhouse, and beef, chicken, mutton are eaten on the bone. That said, the Brits are not yet ready for bones or bitter or very sweet desserts, and Gomes uses fish like Bekti, a favourite Bengali fish, which is relatively bone-free, with firm, white flesh. Even so the menu produces unfamiliar dishes, starters such as Bekti Macher Kebab, tandoor-baked. Gomes develops this further with Stuffed Squid, yoghurt-marinated squid stuffed with the same tandoori Bekti, both £4.50. Singara is the Bangla Samosa, using spiced vegetables stuffed into short-pastry, and made into a pyramid shape. Pyazi, the Bangla bhaji, their favourite street snack, both £2.95. Katti Kebab Calcutta's favourite snack, shredded pieces of spicy roasted leg of lamb served in a whole wheat wrap, £3.95. Mains do include CTM and it's done well (and yes it IS available in Sylhet's Polash hotel, no 100 on the menu!. But, please, try something new. Kashi Bhuna is a boneless goat curry, spiced hot, Kacchi Biryani, delicately flavoured, aromatic Moghul lamb biryani with dried plums and flaked almonds, Papaya Gost, aromatically spiced lamb cooked with green papaya, all £7.95. Dab Chingri is made by mother-in-laws when the son-in-law visits, using king prawns, cooked with fresh coconut milk, cardamom and a bit of saffron then served in a tender green coconut, £11.95. Surmai Macher Biryani, unique to Bengalis – fish biryani, £8.95. Raj Ash Kalia, a Bengali stir-fry of duck, capsicum and onions, lightly spiced. Moni Puri Prawns, a classic dish from the moni puri tribes people of Bangladesh, which consists of juicy king prawns cooked with ginger and light spices in a mellow sauce, £13.50. Bangladeshi vegetables appear on the menu when in season. Look out for chichinga, potol, kakrol, karela, doodi, mooli, lau, and more appearing in expertly cooked classics such as Pumpkin Bhaji, fried red pumpkin in a mild sweet and spicy taste, Green Banana Curry, fried plantain in a thick sauce, Baingan Borta, puréed smoked aubergine with ginger and garlic, Potoler Dolma, a Hindu dish from West Bengal, small gourd-like vegetables stuffed with paneer and golden sultana, Lau Dal, moong lentils and white pumpkin. No Bangladeshi meal is complete without their beloved bitter tastes. Shukto combines karela (bitter gourd) with aubergine, potato, green papaya, carrot, sweet potato, green banana and mooli cooked with a little bit of milk. All around a fiver each, and you can do no better than choose an all-veg meal at Ginger. Desserts are equally classical: Mishti Doi, a sweetened set yoghurt resembling shrikand, and Payesh, a jaggery-flavoured rice pudding. This is the break-through the UK has been waiting for. Our 7,000 Bangladeshi restaurateurs must take note. We the critics and gourmets have been saying it to you long enough; it's time to stop being complacent by coining it by doling out curryhouse pastiche. You may be right; middle England isn't ready for you to throw out the lucrative CTM/Korma/Vindaloo baby with the bath water. but if you want your industry to be taken seriously, it's time to see why Ginger much deserves our **BEST BANGLADESHI AWARD.** Takeaway 20% Discount. Hours: 5.-11,

JAMUNA

NEW ENTRANT

38A Southwick St, Paddington, W2 020 7723 5056

Jamuna opened in 2005. The decor of the 50-cover restaurant, found off Edgware Road retains

Jamuna, W2

simplicity, with bare wooden flooring, blond wood furniture, yellow and mustard walls and soft lighting giving it an inviting ambience. Head Chef, Jasbinder Singh has an impressive track record. After having trained at the Oberoi in India he joined London's elite with restaurants like The Cinnamon Club and Mint Leaf on his CV. His cooking style takes traditional dishes and gives them a modern twist, with a focus on using fresh ingredients and even some organics thrown into the mix. Starters like Spinach Cake served with homemade tomato and raisin chutney £5.50 and Samundri Tikka £7, made with corn-fed chicken marinated with orange zest, chilli and honey and Murgh Bemisa, £7, pan fried chicken cakes flavoured with garlic, basil & lemon leaf. Mains include Adraki Chaampen, Lamb cutlets from the tandoor, marinated in ginger, peppercorn, mint and yoghurt £24; Spinach and Cottage Cheese Dumpling, with garlic & served with tomato gravy £12; Baigan Bhartha, aubergine cooked in the clay oven with ginger, coriander & tomato £12 or Lobster with saffron and garlic £36. Rajasthani Venison, is marinated with Rajasthani spices in sesame and tamarind sauce. Freshly made desserts and a global selection of wine.. *Puja Vedi, Ed, Tandoori Magazine.* Party room, seats 25. Service charge: 12.5%. 12-2.30/6-11 daily <www.jamuna.co.uk>

KHANS TOP 100

13 Westbourne Grove, W2 020 7727 5420

Khans was opened in 1977 by Mrs QN and Salman Khan. It seats an enormous 280 diners in two rooms (180 seats upstairs, plus 100 in the basement). The main room's high, cloud-painted ceiling is supported by a forest of gilt palm trees. There is a huge Hindi-arched mahogany bar and countless tables with pink cloths and black bentwood chairs. Here's the usual caveat: it's a love it or hate it place. They claim it is not unusual for them to do 1,000 covers a day. And therein lies the

Khan's, W2

problem. This sheer volume results in a New York-style 'have-a-nice-day/take-it-or-leave-it/don't mess with me' service attitude. You'll either love that for a kind of perverse entertainment value, or you'll hate it. As first impressions count, we would not recommend it for a curry first-timer, nor to demure foreign tourist groups. Even Americans are shocked. Despite these caveats clearly written in each Guide, we still get the hate it reports: eg: *'Dear Sir/Madam'* (!!! Ed) *'I am amazed to find that you include Khans. My experience is that it is a bottom-of-the-league, fast-food outlet. I am convinced their motto is 'pack-em-in, serve up some mediocre food and get em out as quickly as we can!'* CJ. Ah me! What would this *Guide* be without such letters. But, for seasoned curryholics, it is an institution and decidedly not to be missed. Indeed, Khans has built up a very large customer base of frequent (some-three-times-a-week, apparently) regulars from far and wide, who certainly love Khans, and especially its Punjabi/north Indian food. Meat and Chicken dishes are all sensibly priced at £4.25. It's all robust and expertly cooked. Prawn Curry £5.15, A few house specialities include Fish Curry, £5.55,slices of fish cooked in a medium spiced sauce, on the bone. Methi Gosht, Chicken Tikka, Butter Chicken, Bombay Aloo and Mutter Paneer. Chana Masaladar £3.05, chickpeas spiced in garlic, ginger, chilli paste, lime juice and onions. Khan's has settled down to its alcohol-free regime, and we continue to get plenty of reports from the old-hands, (who now tank up in the pub, then snatch a quick Khan's before returning to the tank), to bemused newcomers, who find it all a bit strange. What they have in common (well nearly all, not everyone reads the caveat), is praise for the food, and a kind of delight in the charsima which is every day Khan's. It stays in our **TOP 100.** No alcohol permitted, but Khans sells non-alcoholic Cobra, which is not at all bad. Service: 10%. Set lunch: £5.99. Hours: 12-3/6-1030, Monday to Thursday. 12-12, Friday to Sunday. <www.khansrestaurant.com>

MANDALAY BURMESE A-LIST

444 Edgware Road, W2 020 7258 3696

This restaurant has the distinction of being the UK's only Burmese restaurant. Located at the moment in the unfashionable end of Edgware Road, it seats just 30 and is run by the Ally brothers, Dwight (front) and Gary (cooking) Burmese-born and Norwegian-educated. We say at the moment because we're told of plans afoot to relocate. Mum and Dad were on duty when I dropped in for lunch. She was busy cooking, and he busy chatting to a regular customer. I asked for a beer and got it at once, suitably cold, from the Fanta-packed cabinet, as much part of the décor as the oil-cloth table covers. This place is a must for foodies. It will never get a Michelin star, thank heavens – it is far too scruffy and in the wrong location! But for an utterly honest, non-rip-off, inexpensive, hard-working, sensibly operated,clean and simple gaff, this is it, above all reeking with **CARE** from top to bottom and sumptuous food.

Burmese food is a cross between Chinese and Indian cuisine with a slight influence from Thai food. Rice and noodles are the most important staple foods. Fritters, soups, salads and main dishes such as stir-fry and curry dishes make up every day meal. Many interesting meat and seafood dishes and a variety of exotic vegetable dishes can be found in the cuisine. Ingredients such as garlic, turmeric, tamarind, coriander, mint, tamarind and chilli show the Indian influence; fish sauce, shrimp paste, dried shrimps, lemongrass and coconut milk., its Thai influence and soy sauce, noodles, rice flour and ginger, Chinese. Whoever is on duty will give good menu guidance.

And here is a Snapshot from it: A-Kyam: fritters from £2.30, Bean Sprout; Calabash; Leafy Green; Shrimp and Bean Sprout; Shrimp and Vegetable. A-Thoat: salads from £2.50, Vegetable Samosa Salad, Raw Papaya and Cucumber, Chicken and Cabbage, Shrimp and Lettuce. Hin-Cho: soups all £2.50, Red Lentil; Bittle Gourd; Chicken, Shrimp and Lime. Main Courses: Spicy Lamb Curry £6.50, Pickle style Lamb – all £6.50. Chicken with Lemongrass, Chicken in Tamarind and Chilli Chicken all £5.90. Noodle Dishes: Mokhingar £6.50, rice noodles in fish soup, Noodles Coconut and King Prawns £6.90, Spice Rice and Lamb or Chicken £6.90. Desserts such as Banan Fritters £1.90, Coconut Agar-Agar Jelley and Faluda (milk, ice cream, jelly and Rose syrup £2.90. Dad told me to try the Tea-leaf salad. It uses leaves he says are imported from Burma (I didn't ask how) which Mum had made that morning just for him. I protested saying I couldn't eat his lunch. He said *'no worries she's made enough for an army.'* It consisted of fried moong lentils with the texture of rice crispies, loads of chilli (great) something fishy and salad and tea leaves. Amazing!. *'We started with Shrimp and Vegetable Spring Rolls and Egg and Potato Samosas £2.10 served on a single plate in anticipation (correctly) of them being shared, accompanied by bowls of chilli, tamarind and soy – delicious. Lamb with Ginger £5.50, extremely tender lamb, in a thick, tasty sauce with right amount of ginger. Chicken Curry with Tomatoes – spicy tomato based thin curry sauce akin to Thai curries. Noodles Coconut and Chicken £5.90, a heap of soft and crispy noodles with plenty of chicken intermixed, all in coconut juices. Vegetable Rice, Chinese style with texture. All dishes were excellent, each tasting very distinct, fresh, lively, and agreeably flavoursome. Wonderful food, value tremendous. Highly recommended.'* MW. That was mw's first visit. Here's what he has to say three years on, now as a regular: *'Had one of my regular visits last week. As always, wonderful food. It's certainly my sort of place, and as it's always good there's little to add'.* MW. Licensed. Despite being inexpensive, they sensibly take credit/debit cards. Essential to book evenings. Takeaway service. Babies and children welcome: with high chairs on offer. Hours: 12-2.30/6-10.30, Monday to Saturday. Closed Sundays and bank holidays. Just round the corner is the Ally family's hotel, also called the Mandalay (per En-suite room double/twin inc breakfast.) - £59.00. <mandalayway.com>

NOOR JAHAN 2

26 Sussex Place, W2 020 7402 2332

Opened in 2002. MD Aziz Ahmed serves the formula in 90 seats on two floors in trendy Lancaster Gate. A three course meal with wine is approximately £30 per person. Hours: 12-2.30/6-11.30.

SITARA

228, Edgware Road, W2 020 7723 1101

At Sitara, meaning 'star', chefs, Hitender Trikha and Rajesh Sharma have taken a modern interpretation on classic pan-Indian cooking and devised a menu that features dishes such as tandoori-style lobster flavoured with fenugreek, Roghan Josh, Bhel and Kadhai Murgh, and coupled it with innovative ideas like Indian-style dim sum. Run by manager, Dal Lall, the restaurant has a 6am entertainment license offering live Indian and Arabic entertainment, on its small dance floor in this elegant contemporary restaurant. Average Price £50. Mon -Fri 5.30-late, weekdays. 6-late. Closed Sundays.

London W4

Chiswick

WOODLANDS TOP 100

12 High Road, W4 020 7994 9333

A branch of Mr Sood's well-liked, small chain of southern Indian vegetarian restaurants. See SW1 branch for details. Party room seats 40. Two pavement table. Service charge: 12.5% Hours: 12-2.45/6-10.45.

London W5

Ealing

MONTY'S NEPALESE CUISINE

There are enough Monty's in Ealing to form a Gurkha regiment. Three Nepalese chefs Hari Thapa, Bisnu Karki and Mahanta Shrestha, set up originally in the incredibly popular Ealing Broadway venue (now closed) in 1980. They relocated to South Ealing. Since then, the original group split, but they all still use the original name, logos, spin, menu and they all have Nepalese cooks. So because we have as many raving reports about any of the four venues, what we say is that all the Monty's do all the formula curries (which the cook well). And they all have a Nepalese specials list with items such as: Kathmandu Dal £4.35, lentils with ginger, onion, green chillies, tomatoes and cumin; Aloo Bodi, £4.35, potato with black-eye beans; Chicken Dilkhoosh £9.75, chicken breast in a creamy sauce with rice and mushrooms to mention just three. Our advice is that you go for the Nepalese items. *'Monty's provides excellent value for money and are a haven of quality cuisine, exquisite Nepalese spicing and caring service.'* AIE. Take your pick of which Monty's you prefer, and frankly any one is as good as any other. Here they are:

Monty's, High Street, W5

MONTY'S NEPALESE CUISINE BEST UK NEPALESE

4 Broadway Centre, High Street, W5 020 8579 4646

Young blood Dipender (Bishnu's son) converted an Italian restaurant next to the Post Office and Club Boulevard in 2000, and refurbished it to be the most spacious, and most modern Monty's. It's a light and airy restaurant with wicker furniture, layers of fresh linen and attentive, smiley waiters. *'We are named after Sir Montgomery'*, he says, but doesn't expand on this elusive explanation. Hours: 12-3/6-12. (to 11 Mon). Branch: Monty's, W13. <www.montys-restaurant.com>

MONTY'S NEPALESE CUISINE

1 The Mall, Broadway, W5 020 8567 5802

Mahanta Shrestha took on this 68-seater venue, *'Monty's came from my name, Mahanta'*, he says. Details, see above. Hours: 12-3/6-12. Branch, Monty's, 53 Fife Road, Kingston. Run by Kishore Shrestha.

MONTY'S NEPALESE CUISINE

224 South Ealing Road, W5 020 8-560 2619

The reincarnation of the first Ealing Monty's opened here years ago. Still going strong with Hari Thapa in charge. *'The name Monty's,'* he says, *'is a tribute to Field Marshal Lord Montgomery, of ww11 Romell and Tobruck fame, and many Gurkhas fought under him.'* Hours: 12-3/6-12am. Details, see above.

ZAYKA INDIAN CUISINE

8 South Ealing Road, W5 020 8569 7278

I'd love to say that Ealing has the best Indian

restaurants in the area. It was where I was born, and it had curryhouses in the 1960s. Sadly, they come and they go. We rate them, you hate them. But the one which you all praise is Zayka I Admittedly, the decor is basic despite the redec *'but the food (and the prices) excellent as is the service.'* AR Zayka opened in 1990 and has established itself as one of west London's favourites, serving all the popular tandooris, starters, curries and accessories including fish specialities and an extensive vegetarian menu. Sunday e-a-m-a-y-l. Takeaway. Free local delivery on orders over £5. Hours: 12-2.30 (Sun to 3)/6-11.30 (Fri & Sat to 12am).

London W6

Hammersmith

AGNI NEW ENTRANT – TOP 100

160 King Street, W6 020 8846 9191

Agni is the Hindu fire God whose qualities include a 'burning passion'. Two men had that passion – to open their own restaurant, after slogging out out for others. Gowtham Karingi was a Veeraswamy Head Chef and Neeraj Mittra, managed Chutney Mary and Zaika. Gowtham Karingi and Neeraj Mittra achieved their dream in 2005 in a location full of competition, Curry alley, aka King Street, Hammersmith, opposite the Townhall, But Agni has its USPs, not so much the fact that the menu is based on Ayurvedic principles, something on offer at other venues, but because Gowtham had been cheffing at Zaika and Veeraswamy and before that at Delhi's Bukhara *(see end pages)* and Neeraj had managed at Chutney Mary, Café Lazeez and Zaika. With pedigrees like that many of King Street' curryhouses can quake in their boots. Because for the same money, you can get Indian food as good as it gets – West End food at suburban prices. Udit Sarkhel did it in SW18, and Agni are doing it for lucky Hammersmith. As for all the spin about Ayurveda, it is poo-pooed by many Indians, and it can even can put some potential diners off trying the venue. They wrongly expect a kind of happy hippy commune, joss sticks and mantra-singing. Agnis is far from that, the tiny restaurant (45-seats on two floors) is very minimalist with pinky-peach walls, bare boards and the chairs and tables as spartan as those you find at the GCSE exam hall, though doubtless costing oodles more. But we don't come to eat the furniture, besides the cogniscenti prefer the marginally quieter upstairs, with its on-view kitchen. So does Agni live up to more of their spin? *'Great tasting food, exotic presentations, friendly-efficient service, comfortable surroundings and no-frill prices'* Answers, yes, yes, yes, no (those chairs!) and yes. The welcome from the waiters in smart red-tunics is indeed spot-on and informative. The whole menu is imaginative and in some parts original, yet true to India, and as you'd expect, very good indeed. Here are some Snap-shots: Papri Chaat £2.95, crisp whole-wheat biscuits dipped in yoghurt, with potatoes, chickpeas, tamarind and herb chutney; Maro Bhajiya £3.50, a Gujrati snack of slivered vegetables in a bishop's weed spiked gram flour batter.; Mumbai Bhel £3.25, snack of puffed rice, bombay mix, peanuts, potato, salad, fresh lime & chutneys; Chicken Tikka £4.50, 3 flavours, green herb, red spices and malai (cream & herbed yoghurt); Chicken 65 £3.75, south India's current favourite bar-snack, spicy-marinated chicken wings, with coriander, cumin, red spices, star anise, golden fried; Calamari Vepudu £4.50, crisp-fried calamari coated with black onion seeds and rice flour, served with a chilli chutney . Mains include Kolhapuri Chicken £7.50, a curry from Kolhapur near Mumbai with ginger, garlic, red chilli, coriander and coconut; Seafood Moilee £8.50, from Kerala's coast, with salmon, prawn, squid, mussels, coconut milk, flavoured with curry leaf, stem ginger, turmeric and lime. Several Thalis are on offer from £7.50 and the Hyderabadi Biryani is a which derives its name from the Persian word "Birian" meaning (Basmati) rice fried with rose petals, saffron, vetivier, cardamon and sweet spices before adding layers of Chicken or Lamb or Vegetables, or Prawns and slow-cooking in a sealed pot, also from £7.50. The desserts all £3 are truly imaginative, and why not? Try home-made "Paan" Kulfi, made from fresh betel leaf kulfi with fennel, betel nut, dill seeds, melon seeds, rose petals and coriander, or the super-coloured Beetroot Halwa, slow-cooked with butter ghee, jaggery and cardamom. Or there's Red Chilli Ice Cream, *'not at all spicy ..... just naughty'*, the menu says! or Rose Petal & Pepper Kulfi £3. Finally we give Gowtham and Neeraj top marks for an informative website. It carries the usual info, plus Gowtham's and Neeraj's 'Cooking Portal' where they offer their recipes, cooking techniques, and lessons *'cheats and kitchen speak'*, encouraging 'members' to blog.. I love the fun and random bits of information and I simply cannot resist passing one bit on to you.

Clicking the button for more information on 'Tandoori', we learn the following astonishing fact: *'On July 2, 1995, the Indian politician Sushil Sharma was accused of murdering his wife, chopping up her body and burning the remains in a restaurant's tandoor oven. This grisly episode came to be known as the Tandoor Murder case. A court found the accused guilty on November 7, 2003, and he was sentenced to death.'* Something to contemplate when enjoying your mixed platter? Joking aside this is a seriously good restaurant reflecting in all departments the passion which' Agni' Hours: Delivery Deservedly enters our TOP 100. Hours: 12 -2.30 / 6-11 Mon-Fri; 4-11 Sat. / 12-10.30 Sun. <www.agnirestaurant.com>

GREEN CHILLI NEW ENTRANT – TOP 100

220, King Street. W6 020 8748 0111

Business partners Head Chef Rajender Kumar, ex Maurya Sheraton Delhi's and Dubai's Kwality Hotel, G.M. and business partner Amit Dua ex Indian Taj and Oberoi 5 star hotels and Arif Khan., ex Baylis House, Slough opened Green Chilli in 2006. Light hues and 70 high-backed leather seats airily grace the venue. The cooking is mostly Punjabi with some specials from around India and a little innovation. Menu Snapshot: Kurkure Mushroom £3.95 Chef's original, fresh button mushrooms, deep-fried with a stuffing of fruity vegetable pickle and paneer. Mixed Pakora £4.25 shredded potatoes, spinach and onions, spiced with fennel, coriander and ginger, deep fried and served on a bed of sago poppadoms. Butter chicken £6.50, on-the-bone chicken, marinated in butter and yoghurt roasted in a tandoor; Lamb chops £6.50 , soaked overnight in dark rum marinade, spiced with crushed garlic, pounded chillies, cloves, coriander, mustard and yoghurt, cooked over live charcoal; Chicken Duck Shaslik

Chef Kumar 'throwing' a Roomali Roti (thin flatbread) at Green Chilli, W6

£10.50, marinated overnight in a spicy yoghurt marinade, skewered with onion, courgettes, tomatoes and peppers.Main course dishes: Vegetable kofta £5, vegetable dumplings served in rich curry gravy. Dal Makhani Side £4, Main Dish - £6, black lentils, slow -cooked overnight on a resting tandoor and finished with home-made butter. Kori Gassi Chicken £7.25,on-the-bone in a thin, spicy curry flavoured with roasted and ground red chillies, coriander seeds, pepper corns, cumin, coconut and garlic, finished with tamarind pulp. Laal Maas £7.50, lamb shanks cooked in hot Rajasthani masala. Bombay Fish Curry £8, simmered with doodhi (gourds), pounded cumin, coriander and aniseed finished with a tang of tamarind. Jumbo Pepper Masala £10 prawns stir fried with curry leaves, roasted moong lentils, freshly crushed black peppercorns, onions and bell peppers, topped with grated coconut. Breads include Roomali Roti £2.25, whole wheat very thin bread made from unleavened dough. The desserts list is conventionally Indian: Ras Malai £3.25, Gulab Jamun with Ice cream £4, Maal pua with rabri £4, and Gajar ka Halwa £3.50. Hours: 12-3 / 6-12 Mon to Sat; 12-3 / 6--23:30 Sunday. <www.greenchilliltd.co.uk>

INDIAN ZING NEW ENTRANT – TOP 100

236 King Street, W6 020 87485959

Another stunner with an Indian Chef patron on this celebrated road, Indian Zing opened in 2005. Head Chef and proprietor Manoj Vasaikar has been associated with some of the most successful Indian restaurants in Mumbai and London, including Deputy Head Chef at Chutney Mary and Head Chef at Veeraswamy. In India he worked for Taj and Oberoi Hotels. His more recent opening, Just India, in Putney, attracted a number of awards in national and industry press and a nomination for The London Carlton Restaurant Awards in its first year of operation. Food at the restaurant is inventive, fresh and healthy. Starters such as Green Peppercorn Malai Tikka £4.50, chicken chunks marinated with fresh peppercorns and cheese and cooked in a clay oven, are a 'must try'. Main courses are equally enticing with dishes such as Monkfish Tikka £10.50marinated in a green masala of coriander and mint, griddled in a clay oven, served with a tamarind relish and Tandoori Artichoke and Paneer, £9.50, in a cashewnut and tomato sauce; Ghatti Lamb £8.60,

Indian Zing, W6

from the Sahyadri Ranges with herbs and black pepper; Malvani Lamb Curry £8.60, from coastal Mahrashtra using black pepper and dried coconut. In Indian Zing's decor, the ethos is comfort and quality, with a simple and elegant finish. The restaurant was designed on the principles of Hindu mythology: Vastu Shastra. Vastu means 'house' or dwelling place and its traditions create a harmony between the five elements of earth, sky, fire, water and air in the environment. Indian Zing has all the ingredients of a successful restaurant. Great service, inventive food, and relaxed atmosphere. This is somewhere I would visit for a light Indian lunch or for a relaxed evening with friends. With future plans of introducing an Ayurvedic Doctor to help customers choose the 'right' food for their unique body make up and holding regular food festivals, Indian Zing is a promising entry for everyone's diary. Puja Vedi, Ed, Tandoori Magazine. Hours: 12-2.30 and 6 - 1030. <www.indianzing.co.uk>

LIGHT OF NEPAL

268 King Street, W6 020 8748 3586

Jaya K Tamang and KC Druba Have lit up King Street for decades. '*When did this one open? I remember my parents taking me there when I was what? four? five?* ' [1979, Ed] *'and now I take my kids. Great.'* CP. This popular, long-standing restaurant does the 'Nepalese' curryhouse formula, which is mostly the old curryhouse favourites. JL still reminds us *'My favourite is still the Butter Chicken. It's chunks of chicken, resembling tikka, red and tender, but with a garlicy taste. With it you need their coriander dip – a pureé of mint, coriander, onion, pepper, chilli and lime juice.. After that I don't need anything else, well a roti goes well, and Cobra.'* JL. We like the Sak-su-ka, minced lamb with egg, tomato and Nepalese spices. Hours: 12-2.30/6-11.

SAGAR

NOMINATED BEST VEGETARIAN

157 King Street, W6 020 8741 8563

It is a pleasure to see the first South Indian in Hammersmith thriving. And you can tell it is because it is now open all day. Sagar and the other 'new' boys on the street are a pointer to the way things are heading. The public are tiring of formulaic curryhouse food and once they taste the real thing, there is no going back. Let us hope King Street is the fore-runner to such superb venues nationwide. Sagar's small interior is modern with the right amount of south Indian knick-knacks. Owner: S Sharmielan cooks food from Udipi, a small coastal town, north of Mangalore in the south-western state of Karnataka, celebrated for Bramin temples and cuisine. Masala Dosa originated here. By the sixth century AD, they were being made as temple feedings for thousands of worshippers. Udipi dosas are made from a thin batter cooked very thin and crisp in Karnataka and thick and small in Tamil Nadu. Also on the menu are Rasam, Sambar, Uppuma, Uthappam (*see p* 75). Curries include Kootu, a typical Madrassi dish as found in the local homes, where it is slow-cooked in a mud pot over wood fire. It's a hot and sour curry, containing gourd, chilli, tamarind, sesame and coconut. Traditionally it's served with Kazhani meaning 'rice-washed water'. Kootu is traditionally served with that rice. At Sagar, you can order Bakabhat, a yoghurt-based rice, or Lemon rice, with cashews and curry leaves. The menu is a glossary in itself. Two temple puddings traditionally served to the public (by the thousands) at festival time are Payasam, made with vermicelli, sugar, condensed milk and cashews and Sheer,a wheat-based pudding with ghee, raisins and nuts. The staff are ever-helpful if you need menu translations. Hours: 12 - 11..every day. Branch: Twickenham, Middlesex.

TANDOORI NIGHTS — TOP 100

319 King Street, W6 — 020 8741 4328

Mr Modi Udin's venue is one of the longest-standing on Curry King Street. It is pure Bangladeshi curryhouse and Modi is proud of that. He as friendly as they come, as are AB Choudhury, and his staff made the more confident with chef Mabul Miah's food. Fully licensed and air-conditioned. *'Extremely well laid out and furnished restaurant on the busy King Street. Seating for 100 with several discreet areas. Very attentive, efficient and knowledgeable staff. Succulent pieces of Tandoori Chicken with those small crispy cinders that you get on the best cooked meat. Equally enjoyable and freshly cooked Seek Kebab with just the right balance of heat and spice. Cool and fresh Cucumber Raitha with a subtle sour bite. Exceptional Rogan Josh with tender chunks of lamb in an exquisite and quite the best sauce I have had to date. Mould of aromatic, al dente Pullao and a soft, fluffy Nan. Very enjoyable.'* RW. Specialities: Bataire Masala £9.95, two quails barbecued and cooked in sauce. Sunday Buffet: £10, families welcome, concessions for children. *'Deservedly* **TOP 100.'** SO. Hours: 12-3/6-12. Branch: Twickenham, Middlesex.

London W8

Kensington High Street, Notting Hill

MALABAR — TOP 100

27 Uxbridge Street, W8 — 020 7727 8800

Jo, Sophie and Tony Chalmers' and Anil Bis's three-floor 56-seat Malabar has quietly gone about its business since 1983. and it is a Notting Hill fixture, largely enjoyed by its clutch of locals. It is not expensive, and the care is comfortable and assured, from the cooking to the service. Despite its name, with dishes like *Murgh Makhni, butter chicken, Gosht Masala –*

plenty of fresh mint, both c£8, and delicious. BH *Five Lentil Dhall – less convincing, more spices needed.* the food is more north Indian than south. Chilli Bhutta starter £4, a take on sweetcorn, is unusual *'A likeable restaurant with food quite different in spicing and presentation. I wish this were in my hom,e town, Berlin.'* BH. Remains secure in our **TOP 100.** Hours: 12-2.45/6-11.30 Mon-Sat; 1-2.45, 6-10.45 Sun. Closed one week in Aug.

UTSAV

17 Kensington High Street, W8 020 7368 0022

Entrepreneur owner of Malabar Junction, WC2, Ashok Modi launched Utsav, meaning 'festival' in 2003. It has 150 seats on two floors, almost opposite the Royal Garden Hotel. Architects Astore Harrison have designed contemporary decor, outside (striking glass, and blues, and a cute use of the first floor bay window. Inside an attractive wooden bar, white walls, creative lighting, theming blues and blondes. The food by chef Gowtham Karingi, ex Zaika sous chef (*see next entry*) is pan-Asian, a bit from here and a bit from there. OK if the chefs understand regional spicing immaculately, and that they can get difficult ingredients. We felt perhaps the Goan Prawn Balchao lacked that sourness only achieved from toddy vinegar, while Kashmiri chilli would have helped the Roghanjosh. And there were too many squiggly dots and squirls (a Ziaka trick, passée in our opinion). That said, the Tirangi Chicken Tikka, marinated in saffron, cheese and coriander, was masterly. The Chicken Varutha in tamarind, red chilli, shallots, curry leaves & tomato sauce had spot on south Indian tastes, as did the fine Dosa and chutneys. The Paneer was fresh and juicy. Service charge 12.5%. Hours: 11.30-3 daily, 6-11. Mon - Thurs; to 11.30 Fri & Saturday; -10.30 Sunday.

ZAIKA A-LIST

1 Kensington High Street, W8 020 7795 6533

This was Claudio Pulze and Raj Sharma (owners of SW1's celebrated Al Duca and Fiore Italian restaurants) was their first Indian venture (with Vineet) before Deya. Set in a former bank, which bestows on it carved high ceilings and double height windows, with their crimson swag curtains.. The interior is elegant with ivory and buff paint scheme and wood panelling. Seats have various coloured backs. Delhi-born Sanjay Dwivedi is probably the brightest star to have qualified as a chef via the celebrated Ealing's Thames Valley Catering College's Asian course. At first he practiced his continental skills, but his Indian roots soon came to the fore and he joined Zaika when it first opened in 1999 as Vineet's deputy. After a short secondment to open Deya W1, he returned to Zaika as head chef when Vineet departed to open his own venue (Rasoi Vineet Bhatia). Head Barman Davide Farchica residing in his 'Bedouin-style' 25-seat cocktail bar 25 guests has cocktails from £7 to £36 and if you think that's expensive, how about the Louis Roederer "Cristal" 1989 champagne at £700.00, which makes an n/v glass at £12.50, or a glass of Colombard Chardonnay General Bilimoria white wine at £ 5.50 seem inexpensive!, which are just three of the items on Luigi Gaudino's constantly changing wine list. Food prices range from £6.25 to £9.50 for starters and £12.50 to £21.50 for main courses. The 6-

Zaika, W8

Zaika, W8

course 'Jugalbandi' tasting menu consisting of 1) scallop; 2) duck kebab;3) seabass with 'dosa' potatoes served with 'sambhar'- lentil and vegetable sauce; 4) Spiced wild mushroom rice, mini papadum & tomato 'makhni' ice cream; 5) Roghan Josh cooked in a rich onion & tomato sauce served with saffron rice; 6) Kulfi at £38 and with 5 glasses of different wines £58. A Vegetarian version is available at the same prices and there is a bigger version at £58/£87, though we think you'll need a huge appetite and/or a doggy bag to get through it all! The pre-theatre dinner (6 - 6.30) is a reasonable £15 for two Courses and £18 for three. (good for the Albert Hall). Dwivedi's continental hand and his time with Vineet shows through with flavours and ingredients which are not Indian. Ingredients such as rosemary, basil and olive oil are distinctively European and do not sit easily on my Indian palette. That said Zaika is a well-oiled, competent venue, usefully placed for the Albert Hall and the Royal Lancaster Hotel. Service 12½%. Hours: Lunch: 12-2.45, Sunday to Friday. Dinner: 6.30-10.45, Monday to Saturday, to 9.45 Sunday. <www.zaika-restaurant.co.uk>

London W13

West Ealing

LAGUNA — TOP 100

1-4 Culmington Pde, 123 Uxbridge Rd, W13
020 8579 9992

You cannot miss the huge frontage, decorated with individually planted conifers in square wooden tubs. And you should not miss going in to this 120-seater restaurant with its stylishly decorations in pastel shades, with arches and ceiling fans. Established in 1984 by Sunil Lamba, (with relations to London's Gaylord) and it's been in this *Guide* since then, serving competent north Indian formula food. It's built up a large local following, and in its time it's seen so many new Indian restaurants come and go in Ealing, and even now it stands out above the 25 or so competitors, a chupatti-throw away. Laguna Special Butter Chicken £5.95 is the most popular dish. Service 10%. Sun. 12-12. Mr Lamba is proud of his outside catering department, and what a party with a difference it will make when you use the service. <www.lagunarestaurant.com> Branch: Laguna Banquet Hall, North Acton Road, NW10.

MONTY'S TANDOORI

54 Northfields Avenue, W13 020 8566 5364

'My curryholic daughter moved to Ealing last year and sussed Monty's out pretty quickly and invited me their on my previous visit. Lovely decor, swift service, fresh salad and yoghurt dip. Popadoms and pickles were served while we ordered and this immediately relaxed us for a pleasant evening. Spicing and quality subtle and superb. We were stuffed, enough left for a meal for two in the freezer. Why black ceilings in the toilet?' AIE. *'Highly recommended. The bill for three people with drinks was £52.* so. Hours: 12-3 and 6-12. Branch: Monty's, Broadway Centre, W5. (and more details).

CARDAMOM INDIA — NEW ENTRANT

86 Northfields Ave, W13 020 8840 1634

Opened in 2003, Shipu's Cardamom has built itself a good reputation, thanks to its friendly service, modern music, a comfortable, modern restaurant. Shaikh manages Cardamom, and has previously run restaurants in the City and the West End. He says he likes to treat customers as friends and his regulars agree. The food is Bangladeshi curryhouse cuisine, prepared by Chef Khan and his team Menu Snapshot: Jhing - a nehari jumbo prawns marinated in mustard, fenugreek, ginger, yoghurt, lime juice and saffron; Maach Citrus, a fillet of white fish which is cooked with citrus, tamarind and fresh herbs. plus all your favourite curries and vegetable side dishes, rice and bread. Hours: 12 - 2.30/5.30- 11.30.

London W14

Olympia, West Kensington

AL'INDIENNE

197 North End Road, W14 020 7610 2020

It's maybe not quite the best end of North End Road, but it does a good job. The frontage isn't that interesting, but inside it's a forest of palms, and foliage, wooden floor, colonial chairs, Indian artifacts and crisp, white linen. Owner MJ.Arshad and his personable staff make it a welcoming occasion. Chef Raja cooks all the favourite curries, but his specials are worth noting. For example, try his Kunkry Bhindi starter, okra fried with poppy seeds and basil, or the mains: Guinea Fowl Tendary, smoked breast flavoured with black cardamom, and cinnamon, served with dal and lemon rice . Lobster ke Mezay, with poppy and dill, Nan A Magajia – stuffed with soft curd cheese, onion and chillies. *'Good welcome and cuisine excellent. Service with smiles and food in abundance.'* JL. Delivery. Hours: 5.30-12, daily. Sunday buffet: 5-11.30.

London WC

Area: West End .
Postcodes wc1, wc
Population: 165,000

See page 109 for key to this map.

London WC1

Holborn

HASON RAJA NOMINATED BEST BANGLADESH

84 Southampton Row, WC1 020 7242 3377

This 150-seat Holborn restaurant is named after a 19th century Bangladeshi poet-playboy who led a life full of drama, colour and romance. Established in 2003 its owner Rafu Miah, has put his 30 years industry experience into creating an venue with elegant surroundings, adorned with immaculate suede Italian furniture and fresh flowers, an exotic feel, which complements its theatrical inspiration. The menu is Indian and Bangladeshi. Signature dishes include the Shathkora Mangsho, a traditional Bangladeshi dish of diced shank of lamb cooked with wild Bangladeshi lemons; Anari Chaamp, tawa grilled lamb in a star anise and pomegranate sauce; the innovative Goose Ki Parchy, french goose in an aniseed and poppy seed blueberry sauce and the chef's special recipe Garlic Murg Tawa, tender chicken cooked with tomatoes and green peppers with a touch of ginger and garlic. The vegetarian options are equally appetising with Tandoori Phool, roasted broccoli with olives and crushed peppers and Kumbeki Sheek Kebabs, an outstanding dish of mushrooms, yam and paneer with mixed spices. Service is spot-on at affordable prices. If your favourite dish doesn't appear on the menu then the manager will ensure that it is prepared for you. Nominated as Best UK Bangladeshi restaurant by this *Guide.* Private room 20 plus another area in the basement for overflow or special functions. At lunchtime there is a 12 dish buffet for just £10

MALABAR JUNCTION TOP 100

107 Great Russell Street, WC1 020 7580 5230

Light, bright and airy restaurant with Victorian-styled glass sky-light giving a good summery feel. Bamboo chairs, palm trees in polished brass pots, original paintings, a marble fountain and smiling Keralan waiters complete the scene. The menu specialises in Keralan cuisine, with dishes from the cities of Cochin, Malabar and Travancore. Hot is the norm in Kerala but they cool it for *'western tastes'*! If you want it hot, tell them, the kitchen are happy to accommodate. Contrary to popular belief, meat, chicken and fish dishes are commonplace in south

India, and here they do everything well. Pick from such starters as Lamb Cutlets, £5, patties of spicy minced lamb, bread crumbed and fried, served with tomato sauce and salad, King Prawn Fry £8.50 (with ginger, garlic, spices and sliced coconut), Malabar Chicken £8.50 (with coconut, curry leaves, garlic and mustard), Spinach Vadai £3 (fried crunchy doughnut of channa dal, green chillies, onion, ginger, curry leaves and fresh spinach served with chutneys). And if you have any room left Banana Leaf Cake £4, rice with sweet filling of coconut, banana and jaggery wrapped in banana leaf and steamed – divine. The bar and further dining facilities are downstairs. *'Very courteous and hospitable. Clean, good vegetarian and non vegetarian food, prepaid in separate kitchens by different chef's. Quantities of food more than enough. A pleasant experience.'* NR. Hours: bar – 11-11, except Sun: 12-10.30; Restaurant: 12-3/6-11.30.

RASA MARICHAM NEW ENTRANT

1 Kings Cross Road, WC1 0871 0757217

Located in the 405-room Holiday Inn which opened a 160-seater 'Indian' at this venue in 1998. It had Goan chefs and lasted a year or two. In our last Guide it reopened as a branch of the Original Lahore Kebab House, serving really gutsy carnivorous Pakistani food. That lasted a couple of years. For its third incarnation, it has turned to the Keralan Rasa restaurant group to make it work. Maricham means black pepper, and pepper, particularly Keralan pepper is India's king of spices, her biggest spice export. This major spice was the heat-giver before chillies arrived from Brazil in the 16th century. Keralan food had been developed centuries before Christ, and pepper was and still is a big player in recipes. Take Muligatawny. It literally means 'pepper water'. Das's spin told us that the menu would be 'showcasing' black pepper'. I am sure there isn't a [person in the world who does not adore pepper, but overuse can be detrimental, and here its use can be rather heavy-handed. It appears in many items, and it is emphasised rather childishly by highlighting the word in the menu, on the front of which is given an explanation of ayurvedic philosophy, which originated even earlier. Pepper, it tells 'is used to cure digestive problems such as wind, constipation ,nausea and diarrhoea.' Hmm! Just what we need to read in an upmarket restaurant. But if it hasn't got you on the run (to the exit), stay. Keralan food doesn't get any better in the UK. True pepper does make abundant and contrived appearances, for example pre-meal Snacks include Pepper Potato Chips, batter-fried potato wedges, laced with lashings of crushed black pepper., There's Green Pepper Pickle; Prawn Pepper Masala £8.50, a stir-fry of prawn with ginger, curry leaves, chilli and mustard seeds, tempered with crushed black pepper and fresh lemon juice; Cheera Parippu Curry £5.95, spinach and toor dal cooked in a thick sauce of garlic, tomatoes and green peppers, flavoured with curry leaves; Lamb Puffs £4.75, baked puff pastry covers black pepper marinated lamb and vegetables. These are superb as are these other snapshots from chef Prasad's menu: Lamb Maricham Fry £6.95, with or without coconut toddy, a favourite dish in achayan (Christian) homes and a wedding would be unimaginable without this lamb dish cooked in chilli and turmeric water and then stir-fried with Indian shallots, ground pieces of black pepper and fine coconut slivers; Malabar Erachi Chaaru £6.50, or Aattirachi curry. Lamb cooked with aromatic spices, turmeric, red chillies and onions. 4 course non veg meal, £20. Vegetarian £15.00. The ideal way to get a taste of Kerala. 12% service charge. Hours; 12.30 - 2.30 /6 - 10.30.. Branches: See Rasa London N16 for descriptions

London WC2

Aldwych, Covent Garden

BHATTI

37 Great Queen Street, WC2 020 7405 5222

Taken over in 1990 by N. Ruparel. The restaurant seats 95 in two rooms and serves formula northern Indian food. It is situated in a 17th century listed building. *'Great for the theatres, and really pleasant experience here. So we go back regularly'.* HEG. Delivery: £25 minimum, 4-mile radius. Hours: 12-2.45 (2 on Sun.) / 5.30-11.45 (10.30 Sun.).

INDIA CLUB A-LIST

143 The Strand, WC2 020 7836 0650

This time we'll leave it to you to explain. *'Previously we had visited during the week, so was quieter on Saturday lunch. Warm welcome. Soon settled with an excellent bottle of chilled white wine which we had managed to extricate from 'the lady down stairs!'* [Doris: Ed] *'General Bilimoria £6 with an interesting story on the label. We were offered and accepted the set meal £11 a head, pointing out that one of our number was vegetarian. This included Popadoms — excellent with chutneys and pickles. Chilli Bhajias, Onion Bhajias, Masala Dosa and Tandoori Chicken. After a pause Lamb and Chicken Curry, Dall, Aubergine, Mixed Vegetable Potato and Chickpea, rice — plenty! Really too much for even us... but all hot, fresh and tasty. Only one waiter, even when four other tables were occupied, but he was very cheery with repeated assurances that he would bring anything else we required! Not sure about the repainted walls, glad about the retained pictures and ancient stair carpet!'* GM. *'What can you say about The India Club. The same unsmiling welcome greets you — the head waiter being the same misery who served us on our last visit. Neither the ladies nor the gents had lights, there was still no Lassi (there never is!), the chutney and onion salad were both served piled up in saucers, there was no attempt at presentation but the food was sublime and what value for money with the quantities just right.'* G&MP. And what's left to say about this much-loved venue? Plenty: *'Hi, I would like to add some comments of my own which may be of interest to you and your readers. I first came across this restaurant in the early 1970s when I worked for the London offices of an Indian newspaper chain in Carmelite Street, London. The India Club was a regular haunt of the Indian journalists based in London and home to an institution called 'the India League' an organisation that promoted Indian business and cultural interests in Britain. The restaurant may have been established in 1950 but I was told that its roots went back much further to the Indian Independence movement. I first dined there at a reception held for the Indian statesman Krishna Menon a contemporary of Jaharwal Nehru the first prime minister of Independent India. On crossing the threshold again in 2004 was just like being in a timewarp; everything seemed to be the same. Walking up the steps past the hotel reception desk which used to be called 'The Hotel Strand Continental'. The manager of the Hotel in the 1970s had I seem to recall managed to install almost his entire family who occupied half a dozen rooms at one time. It turned out that he had been fleecing the place for years before someone actually checked the books and sacked him. I peeked into the same bar and the same lounge and then walked up the same stairs to the same restaurant. When I first went there all those years ago no-one could ever remember a time when the lift was in use. It had worked once apparently but the management had forgotten to renew the guarantee and the parts were all out of date, even in the 1970s. The woman at the bar I think you are referring to has to be called Doris and has been there since forever. There used to be a legendary eastern european woman called Christine who waited at tables in the restaurant. I first took my fiancee to eat there in the early 1980s and it hadn't changed in ten years and I suppose I had got used to the slow service and taken the luke warm food for granted but my fiancee was very keen on hot food and trying to impress her I asked Christine if she would mind heating it up a bit. Christine gave me a look of daggers and said 'I try' and emerged ten minutes later 'wiz warmed plates - okay is better?' It made absolutely no difference of course but then I wasn't personally that bothered. Returning in 2004 I noted the same pictures on the wall; one of Krishna Menon, one of Gandhi, one of the Indian poet Tagore and the same funny cubist paintings that must have once been daring but just look very dated now. The food though is just as you describe it, very basic and totally different to the average fare you can expect in your average Indian restaurant. When I say basic I don't mean to be insulting to the chef as this is high praise indeed. Try the Masala Dosa that come with coconut sauce; out of this world. As you rightly say probably not the place to take someone you are trying to impress. It worked for me though as my fiancee became my wife and we have been married for nearly twenty two years so it can't have been that bad. I used to regularly dine there in the 1970s and early 1980s with a couple of work colleagues but some people will undoubtedly be put off by the funny decor and the almost standoffish nature of the waiters. They don't keep you waiting for that long but don't go over the top in trying to please you either like they do in your average high street tandoori. Oh by the way did I mention that the fire escape out the back that can be seen from the rear dining room and men's toilet windows which is also 'just the same?'* BB. Inexpensive, charming slightly bumbling service; super food, never a Michelin-star winner, so virtually devoid of posers and high on our **A-LIST** Although it is unlicensed, you can buy Cobra, wine etc on the premises, or you can **BYO** no corkage charge. Hours: 12-2.30/6-10.50; closed Sun.

MELA TOP 100

152 Shaftesbury Avenue N, WC2H 8HL
020 7836 8635

When ex-Soho Spice chef Kuldeep Singh, with Sanjay Singh Sighat and Surinder Kumar Mehra (all Taj-trained chefs) opened Mela (meaning 'festival') in 2000, they pioneered an original idea to capture a vast potential lunch trade, always illusive at the Indian restaurant. Under the spin of 'dhaba' (stall) serving 'street food' and named 'Paratha Pavilion', it's the Indian equivalent of a sandwich bar. Instead of sliced loaf, choose naan, roomali, paratha, roti, puri and bhatura, appam, uttapams (served with coconut chutney), or dosa with a topping (filling) choice of as many curries as you can imagine, dozens of them. There are, it seems, over 500 combination options. Prices range from £1.95 for a simple choice to £4.50 for a Gourmet Snack Lunch. It was an instant success. The restaurant is open all day (useful to know), but it changes atmosphere in the evening. It's somehow more relaxed allowing time to inspect the decor, rather than choke on a chupatti. Clean lines of white washed walls, large seemless mirrors and a few embroidered cushion covers, from Orissa. Square terracotta floor tiles, plastic wood-effect tables (sounds horrid but not), simple wooden chairs upholstered in spicy coloured fabric. The menu describes itself as 'Indian Cuisine – Country Style', which we interpret as Indian home-cooking. Kuldeep says "*ingredients here in England are much better than back home. This is a chef's paradise.*" And he proves it with dishes such as Bater Khada Masala, marinated quails roasted in a spicy mango masala, and Malabari Seafood Stew, mixed seafood with turnip, cauliflower, coconut milk and coriander *'I decided to start with Gosht Utthapams – fluffy rice pancakes topped with diced, chargrilled lamb, onion, pepper, freshly grated coconut and served with minty coconut chutney. A monogrammed square plate arrived with the promised two pancakes and a small salad of carrot, beetroot, cucumber and green leaves tossed in a lightly spiced dressing – delicious. Pat decided on a Raj Kachauri, mini puries stuffed with seasoned potato, chick peas, onion and topped with mint and tamarind chutneys. What arrived was one large stuffed puri, in a bowl, which looked as impressive as it tasted. Mains were Khatta Khargosh, curried rabbit and Kori Gassi, chicken on the bone in a thin, spicy curry flavoured with chilli, spices, coconut tamarind. We accompanied our dishes with Plain Rice £1.95, Roomali Roti – better than the offering at Benares – and Mirch Baingan Ka Salan, baby aubergines in peanut-flavoured yoghurt gravy, which never arrived and I decided not to remind them. Mela is a lovely restaurant, with cheerful waiters, serving lovely Indian food.'* DBAC. This is echoed by HC: *'Charming and authoritative person in charge. Whole place was running well. Food, again outstandingly good, definitely a very good restaurant – amazing menu..* HC. It remains high in our **TOP 100.** Hours: 12-11.30, daily. Sunday to 10.30.

MOTI MAHAL

MOST PROMISING NEWCOMER AWARD

45 Great Queen Street, WC 020 7240 9329

It is about time that that this restaurant opened in the UK (in 2005) and I am truly delighted. It has a remarkable pedigree, the story of which which I will share with you. The tandoor, the ancient clay oven, and its offspring tikka, meaning 'a little piece', had been an unintentionally well-kept secret

Moti Mahal, WC2

in its place of origin, the rugged, inhospitable, mountainous area of Pakistan/Afghanistan for centuries, When Kundan Lal Gujral opened Moti Mahal to serve tandoori dishes in 1920 in Peshawar it was the only such restaurant in the world. Then in 1947 along came partition, the separation of one nation into the states of India and Pakistan. One of the unforeseen effects of partition was the fleeing of population who being of the 'wrong' religion feared persecution. Hindus fled from what became Pakistan into India and vice versa. One such Hindu political refugee, that restaurant owner, fled from Peshawar taking his tandoors with him. In 1948 he established Moti Mahal in Daryaganj, Delhi making it not only India's first tandoori restaurant, but one of India's very few restaurants of any kind. It remained the place to go for decades. I was taken there in 1984 by a Delhi friend of mine, who remarked, *'Visiting Delhi and not eating at Moti Mahal is like going to Agra and not seeing the Taj Mahal'.* Tandoori in Britain was in its infancy at that time, and I can truly say I had never tasted Tandoori items as good as there. So successful were they that Moti Mahal embarked on the franchising route and now have over 30 franchise Motis' many in Delhi and they are looking for more franchisees all over India. So Moti Mahal finally opened in London on the former Covent Garden site of Zilli 2 under the ownership of the founder's grandson. Monish Gujral. You will be forgiven for finding it hard to find. Its signage is tiny and high up and the full-length, full-height glowing window display of bottles looks like an extension of the pub next door, but it is the Moti. The 85-seat restaurant spans two floors. Guests can join the bustling ground floor bar and dining area. The main interior is raw-stone-walled, while natural linen and cotton cloths and upholstery give the Indian feel. Dark heat-treated oak floors are offset against the orange silk wall hangings. The copper-backed open kitchen is busy with chefs at their the tandoors. Candle lanterns lead you downstairs to a more intimate dining room and another bar where 80 different whiskeys are displayed on illuminated glass shelves. There is also a private function area with a capacity of 100 standing. But decor is not the main selling-point here. It is the food. Moti selected Anirudh Arora, formerly sous chef at Benares, as exec. His menu reflects a wee bit of new-wave but it remains true to the original Moti with the meats of the Northwest Frontier high on the agenda. Moti claim to have invented the Tandoori Chicken, Murgh Makhani (Butter Chicken) and the famous Dal Makhani. They did not, but they do these dishes to perfection. As you might expect, their Tandoori dishes feature large and include Murg ka Soola (grilled supreme of chicken with cracked pepper and dill), Ajwain Aur Pilli Mirch Ki Machhi (organic salmon in carom seeds, yellow chillies and yoghurt) and venison kebab. Appetisers include dishes such as Sagar Rattan (scallops tossed with tamarind and baby tomatoes and pan fried crab cakes) and Shammi Sheekapur (ground lamb kebab from the erstwhile kitchens of Awadh"lamb patties filled with yoghurt, mint and onion) and Pan-fried cakes of corn, spinach and lentils. Main course dishes include Kadal Muthu Mappas (mussels, squid and monkfish simmered in coconut and curry leaf), which can be had with variety of accompaniments. Meal with wine and service charge: around £45. We are pleased to give it our **MOST PROMISING NEWCOMER AWARD.** Hours: Monday to Saturday, 12:00 - 15:00, 18:00 - 12.

PUNJAB — NOMINATED BEST PUNJABI

80 Neal Street, WC2 — 020 7836 9787

The Punjab opened in 1947 in Aldgate and moved to its present site in 1951, making it the oldest UK Punjabi restaurant. For its entire life it has been in the capable hands of just two men, the late founder and now his son Sital Singh Maan. The venue has several areas. Some prefer the rear room with its more modern looks. Others prefer the side room which seems to retain its Indian looks. The Punjab was one of the original pioneers of the curry formula. Only here it is done as it has always been done, and as it should be. The result is unlike the newer Bangladeshi clones, and is probably what old farts think they remember when they say *'curry isn't like it used to be'*. CT is a bit suspicious if the redec; *'the wooden tree is quite striking. Seems not to have weakened the food.'* CT. The food is meat-orientated, spicy, savoury and very tasty. Specialities: Anari Gosht £7.50, pomegranate and lamb, Benaam Macchi Tarkari £7.50, nameless fish curry, Acharri Murgha £7.80, pickled chicken. Also try the Vegetable Koofta £4.70, diced pumpkin with spices and herbs made into balls. *'A year ago we had an outrageously mediocre meal. Decided to give it another go. This time Chicken Methia – beautifully flavoured and chicken was real quality. Linda had Chicken Tikka flambéed with brandy at the table – spectacular.'* MG. Regulars have their own club, the 'Punjabbers'. High in our **A-LIST.** Service 10%. Lunch and dinner, daily. <www.punjab.co.uk>

Punjab, WC2

SITAR BALTI

149 The Strand, WC2 — 020 7836 3730

'Can confirm that food is as good as ever and the one grumble on several earlier visits, the mean size of portions, seems to have been rectified, long may it continue. Service always friendly and generally good.' HC. *'Now opens at 5.30 so we can get to the theatre by 7.30pm without a rush. Prices are a little higher than average, but food warrants every penny. Fried King Prawn for starter – prawns coated in crunchy vermicelli, very good, served with spicy dip. Special Starter turned out to be a giant king prawn, opened out and served tail up, very eye-catching, with most wonderful mustard sauce – outstandingly good, will have main course version next visit. Brinjal Bhajee – large chunks, very good. Gulab Jamun – wonderful to have it offered and they were superb. All waiters were smiley and helpful – a most enjoyable dinner.'* D&HC.

TANDOORI NIGHTS

35 Great Queen Street, WC2 — 020 7831 2558

Owner Mrs Yasmeen Rashid opened her first Tandoori Nights in Cockfosters, Herts, in 1988, and her second in NW1 months later. In 1993 she opened this branch with Manager Salil, and chef Waris Miah. Anyway, the delectable Yasmeen bumped into your editor at an Asian industry do recently. *'Why have you delisted me', she squealed and peeled?* To avoid funny looks at functions, she's back. Also to avoid future squealings, Yasmeen is also running a curry ready meal company called *Organic India*, which can be contacted on 020 8805 2223. Service (at the restaurant) 12½%. Lunch and dinner, daily.

ENGLAND

The entries in this Guide are recorded in alphabetical order: first the county then, within that, the town, then the restaurant. With the demise of Avon, we now start with Bedfordshire, the first town we record is Arlesey, and its first restaurant is Raj Villa, and so on. Our last English county is Yorkshire West, and Wakefield is the last recorded town.

BEDFORDSHIRE

Area: East of England.
Population: 580,000
Adjacent Counties:
Bucks, Cambs,
Herts and
Northants.

Arlesey

RAJ VILLA

27 High Street, Arlesey 01462 835145

70-seater owned and well managed by Akthar Ali since 1996. Branches: Raj Gat, Bedford Street, Ampthill, and Raj Moni, Upper Street, London, N1.

Bedford

ALAMIN TANDOORI RE-ENTRANT

51 Tavistock Street 01234 330066

Gulzar Miah's corner building stands out especially at night time. The 42 seats are of pale-wood in a classical design, yet the place has a modern feel. Gulzar Miah promises less fat content in his typical menu, containing all the favourites. Hours: 12- 2/6 -12.(12.30 Saturdays).

CHOUDHURY'S OPEN KITCHEN

2 The Broadway, Bedford 01234 356162

'*Choudhury's is the best and largest restaurant in Beds. It's been beautifully refurbished, bringing it bang up to date. It has a new menu with some tasty new and exciting dishes including fish. You can watch your meals being prepared in uncompromisingly modern surroundings: hence the new name "Choudhury's Open Kitchen". We have travelled quite extensively in India and Sri Lanka and all the Indian restaurants in the south of England and we have come to the conclusion that Choudhury's is best.*' PE.

GULSHAN

69 Tavistock Street, Bedford 01234 355544

Chef Shanu Miah cooks Pakistani and North Indian at S and Mrs BK Nijjer. '*Try Lamb Sharab (lamb tikka cooked in cream and almond liqueur) served with Pullao Rice.*' BB Show them this Guide and you might get a discount. Hours: 12-2PM/6-1AM.

Luton

ALANKAR

276 Dunstable Road, Luton 01582 455189

'*Took advice from the Guide and was very impressed. Looked, from outside rather peculiar for a curry house. However, the food was of excellent standard. Reminded me of Madhu's, Southall.' Not quite as good (is there better?) ..but the menu was vast. Had Kebabs and Lamb Chops, all came sizzling. Fish Masala very enjoyable. I must also say the spicy Popadoms were the best I've had, full of flavour. Well worth a mention, would go again without a doubt. Nearly forgot, they served a beautiful dish called Begun Bortha, which is mashed aubergine. It was wonderful, trust me*'. LH.

MEAH TANDOORI

102 Park Street, Luton 01582 454504

'*Delightful.*' DS. '*Very impressed with the personal service and the splendid chicken shashlick.*' AW. '*A good restaurant*'. TK.

BERKSHIRE

Area: South East
England
(west of London)
Population: 806,000
Adjacent Counties:
Hants, Surrey,
Middx,
Oxon, Wilts

Cookham

MALIK'S TOP 100

Royal Exchange, High St 01628 520085

Set in a former country pub, complete with clinging ivy, and olde beams, this restaurant takes its name from Malik Ahmed, who, with partner Mujibur Rahman, runs front of house. He promises to give you food cooked to the highest standards, along with good wines, elegant surroundings and a wealth of atmosphere. And from reports received, he does it. Sunday buffet lunch e-a-m-a-y-l Adult - £9.95 Child - £6.95. Super banquet (evenings) £18.95 per head (minimum of four) as follows:: Murgh Satta (Chicken with ginger and mushroom), Murgh Tikka Masala (chicken) Chingri Saag (King Prawn with spinach), Lamb Pasanda (Very mild lamb) Accompanied by:Bengali Vegetable, Special Egg Fried Rice and Basmati Rice, Peshwari & Plain. Hours: 12 noon to 2:30 / 6-12. Branch: 14 Oakend Way, Gerrards Cross, Bucks 01753 880888. <www.maliks.co.uk>

Crowthorne

VILLAGE TANDOORI

204 Dukes Ride, Crowthorne 01344 780118

Good formula house where you may get a discount if you show the manager this *Guide.*

Eton

GOLDEN CURRY NEW ENTRANT

46 High Street, Eton 01753 863961

'Still there and very good.' BT.

TIGER GARDEN NEW ENTRANT

47 High Street, Eton 01752 866310

Situated in 'The Cockpit', built in 1420, where Charles II was a spectator. Note the stocks outside for ancient punishment. Menu Snapshot: Dall Pakora £3.50 – lentils mashed with onion, coriander, battered and fried. Enda Bhunjon £4.95 – spiced egg halves in aromatic onion sauce. Mass Biran £15.95 – boal fish steak, pan fried with green chillies. Takeaway: 15% discount. Price Check: CTM £7.95, Tarka Dal £3.95. Hours: 12-2.30/6-11. Branches: West Street, Marlow. 01628 482211. Tiger Cub: 29 Station Rd, Marlow. 01628 482020. <www.tigergarden.co.uk>

Hungerford

MOONLIGHT

43 High St, Hungerford 01488 685252

Good formula house where you may get a discount if you show the manager this *Guide.*

Reading

GULSHAN TANDOORI

Wokingham Road 0118 966 799799

Mr Raja's Gulshan, opposite Reading Railway station is popular with the locals. *'I would like to bring a good restaurant to your attention. This restaurant has always delivered what it promises in their menu. The food is nice and consistently nice, it is always my first choice to recommend to anyone as I only received good feedback. The owner, Mr Raja, always looks after us, not just because we are regulars there, but also eager to hear our views with a view to improve. Our answer is always same, food is nice - keep it that way. What is amazing is his enthusiasm to provide a good service to everyone and you can see him running around to personally cater every table.'* HBR. *'I would just like to add that as a regular to the restaurant, the good food and the atmosphere is very warm and I will not hesitate to recommend this Restaurant to anyone interested in experiencing the best in Indian Cuisine.'* SSJ.

THE GURKHA INN

64 George Street, Caversham 0118 948 3974

Popular 42-seater. Car park nearby. Delivery: £12 min 3-mile radius. Hours: 12.30-2.30/6-11.30.

KATHMANDU KITCHEN NEW ENTRANT

59, Whitley Street, Reading 0118 986 4000

This 90 seater opened in 2001 and changed ownership to Nikul Patel in 2005, after which we received several favourable reports on Manager Navib Thapa's service and Chef Purja's food. True it has only a few Nepalese dishes on the otherwise standard menu. Try the Momo, or special Noodles, or the underrated Shak-Sukha, a Nepalese mince dish. Our our Indian friends like the place. *'It fairly recently changed hands and you can see a great deal of improvements in the service at this big restaurant. You will notice that the restaurant is getting fuller every week. By contrast, the owner, Nikul Patel, is a young chap and he is equally dedicated to this new business, enthusiastic and eager to improve. Although he appears new in the business and in the area, with his talent, he is learning the ropes pretty quickly. You see constant improvement inside and outside and a great deal of improvement in the taste of food with the same chef working there. I wrongly judged him first by his lower prices but then realised that he has to do that, being right in the middle of the most deprived ward in this country! We all admire the food, service and personal touch at this restaurants and would like to recommend you to feature it in your Guide.'* HBR. Good Gimmick: If you live within 3 miles, and spend £80 or more (maximum 4 diners) you get a chauffeur service. Price check: CTM £6.90, Tarka Dal £3.45, Pullao Rice £2.25, Naan £1.75. Hours: 11-2.30/5 -11.

SPICE OVEN — NEW ENTRANT

4 Church Street, Caversham 0118 948 1000

Fully Licensed. Air conditioned. *'Very impressed by quality of decor, feeling of spacious seating. Service very friendly and prompt. Waiters' uniforms modern, tasteful. Number of starters comparatively small compared to many restaurants, but quality very high. The 2004 GUIDE describes food, spicy and not for the faint hearted - certainly true. Started with Chicken Tikka Malai - flavour absolutely heavenly! Flavours of Chicken Tikka Biriani, Chicken Ajwaini, Dal Kabila, Pullau Rice and Roti - intense, bursting into a play of sensations across the taste buds, a well planned melody. Minor complaint, Biriani - over-powering cardamom.'* R&NT. Price Check: Veg Samosa £3.25, CTM £6.75, Pullao Rice £2.25. Hours: 12-2.30/6-11.

SPICE OVEN

2 Church Street, Caversham 0118 948 1000

'The food tends to be on the spicy side and not for the faint hearted. The restaurant is large, luxurious with wood carved fittings. The Taj-trained Indian chef produces authentic regional food. The prices reasonable. One of the best. A great addition to the Reading curry scene.' GP.

STANDARD NEPALESE

141 Caversham Road, Reading 0118 959 0093

Established 1980. Seats 140. 8 parking places at front. Pond and fountain as centrepiece. Nepalese specials include Katmandu Aloo. *'Three of us descended on this very spacious restaurant at 6pm on a Wednesday evening; by 8pm it was packed and queuing! Delicious spicy hot carrot chutney. Chicken tikka cooked in a specially prepared mild tomato sauce was out of this world. Chicken shashlick was brilliant. Absolutely nothing standard about this restaurant at all.'* MB. Takeaway: 10% discount. Free delivery, 10-mile radius. Hours: 12-2.30/6-11.

Slough

BAYLIS HOUSE — NEW ENTRANT
A-LIST — NOMINATED BEST INDIAN

Stoke Poges Lane, Slough 01753 555 555

Club Baylis opened in 2003 and *'It should definitely be in the guide.'* S.O. Agreed, Steve, and since you kindly came on one of our cookery courses The Curry Club holds there, it gives us both the chance to tell all. Baylis pronounced Bay-lees is an exciting new venue. Actually the main house is quite old. Set in a five acre garden, it was built in 1697 by Sir Christopher Wren. It lay derelict for decades until it was bought in 2002 ago by an enterprising team. At once they restored the house and built a huge modern conference and banqueting suite which can hold more than 400 guests alongside. This marriage of old and new is striking and exciting. Alongside is a 16-bed hotel with en-suite bedrooms, and there is also a restaurant and bar, called Club Baylis, open to all. But the beauty of Baylis is that it is Indian-owned, Indian-managed and has Indian chefs led by Ashwani (Ash) Kumar. The venue handles a large number of Indian weddings, but more than that, it is a perfect venue for The Curry Club's Residential Cookery Courses. But that's another story *(see pend of the book).* so.. goes on: *'It is a bit cheeky to put this in as a review as the only time I have visited Baylis was during Pat's excellent curry course here. Shame on me for not going back with a big capital S! As the course progressed the manager and chefs became more and more fascinated with what Pat and Dominique were doing, and ended up inviting all of the participants to visit the kitchens of this fine complex. The banqueting kitchen makes you feel like you have just stepped onto the set for 'Land of the Giants'; the pilot lights on the gas burners alone being more powerful than my own stove — nuke setting! Head chef Ash took time out from preparing 400 covers for a wedding that night and 40 covers for the restaurant's busy Saturday lunchtime. He not only proudly showed us around, he prepared some stunning dishes right in front of our eyes. On the evidence of the dishes that we tried in his kitchen, I fully expect that this restaurant will figure prominently in future guides. Particular favourites tasted were his Monk Fish Moullee (cooked in Coconut Cream, Pepper and Curry Leaves), the Bombay Potatoes, Chicken*

Methi and Spiced Pan Seared Salmon, but all of the dishes (rustled up effortlessly in front of our eyes) were superb (as of course were the banquets lovingly prepared by Pat and Dominique's own fair hands!). Overall opinion – excellent, would definitely recommend and I really must make the effort to return.' S.O. We can endorse this. The food is gloriously cooked by Ash and his brigade of Indian chefs. Service is like you get at 7-star Indian hotels – discrete yet attentive and very accurate. Menu Snapshot: Tandoori Mixed Grill £9.50, king prawn included, but Naan Bread must be ordered separately; Goan Style Gilthead Bream £7.95, the whole fish cooked in the tandoor; Hara Channa Kebab £4.95, chickpeas, potatoes, spinach and garlic tempered patties – delicious!; Phal Dari Kebab £4.95, minced banana cake; Chicken Tikka Lababdar £6.25, onion, tomatoes, fenugreek; Prawn Moilee £9.95, coconut curry sauce; Paneer Taka Tak £5.50, stir-fried cheese, red onion, peppers, chilli; Dal Makhani £3.95 - black lentils in tomatoes and garlic *('yum yum!!'* DBAC).One of our Indian reporters sums it up: *'I regularly visit here and there is no doubt that this restaurant has maintained its level of service with the ever-excellent food quality as good as we experienced at the opening.'* H.B.R. Bar Menu: small portions (and prices!) of snacks including: Cocktail Samosas £2.95; Vegetable Pakora £2.95; Malai Kebab £3.95; Prawn Chilli £4.50 - wrapped in filo pastry. Hours: Lunch Buffet: 12 - 3, Monday to Friday, £12.95. Dinner, 6 - 10.30. Sunday Dinner Buffet: 12 - 3 / 7 - 11, adult £7.95 and children £5.00. <www.baylishouse.co.uk>

BARN TANDOORI

Salt Hill Park, Bath Road, Slough 01753 523183

It's in a rather grand, ex-cricket pavilion in the middle of nowhere – well, a park, actually, and next to the tennis courts. Taken over in 1996 by Messrs Mehbub, Rahman, Alam and Kandakar. Serves formula curries. *'I have revisited this excellent Indian restaurant in the park twice with large business parties at very short notice. The staff copes admirably, delivering many different orders at the same time, maintaining high-quality cuisine with superb service.'* TE. *'Masalla dosa was a great mixture of vegetables in a pancake. Chicken dhansak was tasty with an excellent balance of spices and chillies with the lentils. Worth a return visit.'* RH.

SKYWAYS HOTEL AND BRASSERIE

19 London Road, Slough 01753 522286

And if a curry barn isn't enough excitement, how about a curry b&b in the same town? Skyways is a family-run hotel offering an excellent 'home from home' service with lovely warm rooms, satellite television, and full English breakfast. All at half the price of the larger hotels around Slough. Nothing unusual in that, you say, but what about the restaurant? Says TE: *'It has retained the same Nepalese chefs and waiters whose excellent cuisine and efficient service put Skyways 'on the map'. New manager is Ram Panwar, from the Cookham Tandoori, who has a long track record of success in cooking and managing tandoori cuisine. Revamped menu offers a wider variety of dishes and 'special dinners'.* TE. *'I stayed here and enjoyed an excellent meal at a reasonable cost. Chicken Patia was excellent, generous naan breads and free pickles and popadoms. I would recommend this hotel and restaurant to curryholic business travellers and regular diners.'* RA.

Suningdale

TIGER'S PAD TOP 100

3 Station Parade, London Rd 01344 621215

Richard Green's Tiger's Pad is set in expensive, minimalist, open-plan decor with satisfying tables. They have Indian chefs, led by Chef Ajoy Sachdev and it is great to find the real delicious thing, rather than another formula curry house. We get many satisfied reports on the place, for example AF has consistently commented the likes of: *'Gets better and better. They continually refine and change their menu. Sikadari Badi Lamb is out of this world. I'm convinced it is the "find of the decade"'.* AF. DBAC.says: *'it is a gem of a place and the sort of pad anyone would wish to find as their local.'* And then we got this poignant note from Alan: *'We moved to the curry desert of Devon from Berkshire and can find no equal to the Tiger's Pad in Sunningdale, a great exponent of the skills of cooking great Indian food.'* Sunday Buffet £10.95 from 12 - 5pm.

Thatcham

KAILASA

35 High Street, Thatcham 01635 862228

'There are some restaurants which give you a good feeling as soon as you walk in - the Kailasa is one. Inviting eatery with white wood tables, royal blue napkins and fan shaped wall hangings - flock wallpaper enthusiasts would probably have a fit! Chefs Specials include: Boal Kofta, Sabji Bangla, Shatcora Gost, Sylheti Akni, Chingri Anana. Tandoori Chicken - seriously tender and seriously large. Excellent King Prawn Puree - juicy, tender, well spiced

beasties. Chingri Ananas - chicken with pineapple, served in half a shell, with loads of fresh coriander - delicious. Sylheti Akni - kind of mixed meat biryani with a proper vegetable curry. A special mention to Sag Bhajee, obviously made from fresh spinach - a really nice change. Nan and Popadoms were, respectively, light, moist and warm, non-greasy. All in all a very pleasant lunch.' S&ZM.

Theale

CAFE BLUE COBRA — TOP 100

20 High Street, Theale — 0118 930 4040

Blue Cobra pioneered a dual menu restaurant serving Thai and Bangladeshi cuisine under one roof in 1999 Abssar Waess. The first-timer is struck by the coolness and fresh cleanliness of the decor. The bar area, with its marble and cane furnishings, seats 30. It leads on to the main dining area, whose 60 ormolu seats are designed to evoke airy oriental verandas. The light walls are a regularly changing 'gallery', home to the works of local professional artists. Cuisine is under Ana Austin leads two separate chef teams. Diners can order one cuisine or the other or they can mix and match. *'I generally prefer to stick with one cuisine, so I often make two visits in a week, having Indian one day and Thai the next'*RL There is a wide range of Bangladeshi and Bengali dishes, some of which will be familiar to the curry aficionado. Delights include Shingara 2 veg & Ponir Pastries, £3.25; Garlic Calamari Served with herbs tossed on sweet potato £4.95, or Skewered Chicken Pakora Battered and deep fried £3.50, Onion Bhajee Deep fried, chopped onion cluster £2.95. Mains include Grilled Duck Breast Tandoori Tikka Masala with sweet peppers £7.75 and Skewered Vegetables Grilled £5.50. Thai Appetisers include Siam Delight (a selection including):Thai Prawn Toast (4), Deep Fried Tiger Prawns (4), Veg Springroll (2) and Spicy Chicken Niblets (4) all for £9.85. Thai Mains include: Chicken Curry Green Style £6.50, Duck Pad King Stir Fry £7.25 and Prawn Pad King Stir Fry £6.50. *'What a dilemma - should I choose from the Indian menu or to select from the Thai? Food was sensational, unique and exquisitely presented, very different to the average formulation curries. Playing contemporary blues music made a nice change.* SO. Price Check: Popadom 50p, CTM, Regular £6.95, Large £8.25 Tarka Dal £3.50, Pullao Rice £3.50. Bengali or Thai Banquet For 2 £15.95. Hours: 12-2.30/6-11. Closed Sundays. <www.cafebluecobra.co.uk>

Twyford

HAWELI — NEW TO OUR TOP 100

15 Church Street, Twyford — 0118 932 0939

Raj.Sattar runs a very good establishment as is recorded by our reporters. *'Further to my last report on the Haweli, of Twyford. They have stopped using artificial colourants, which is wonderful. Back to good natural flavours and colours. Nicki and I have had several takeaways since and the food has been very good. Business is absolutely booming - I have never seen it so busy! Must be the success to be reaped from being entered in the GUIDE.''A couple of weeks ago we had our young nieces over for 5 days and treated them to a meal from Haweli. The youngest (only 9!) came with me to collect the order and the staff treated her like a little princess - which she is, of course. She was much impressed! Last night I tried something a little different - Khulnar King Prawn... baby lobsters barbecued in the shell then served delicately spiced with herbs in a Bangladeshi style sauce. Very nice. I must get the nieces over at Easter so that I can take them there for a meal out.* RT. And again: *'The food and service was impeccable as always. I telephoned for a collection as my wife wasn't feeling up to going out. We ordered a Chicken Tikka Biriani £8.95, a Murgh Mowchak £6.95, a Pullao Rice, a portion of Niramish £2.95 and a Plain Naan £1.65. The telephone manner was very friendly (I think they are beginning to remember me) and the food was ready when I arrived. The friendly greeting at the door made me feel like a sultan! The meal was carried to the door for me and contained two Popadoms and a rose for my wife. The food was excellent as usual. This restaurant is really blossoming more each month - well worth a visit.'* RT. Menu Snapshot: Reshmi Kebab £2.95 - minced lamb burger spiced and cooking in butter served with a fried egg; Sulimoni Kebab £3.25 - authentic Bengali kebabs served with melted cheese; Aloo Bora £3.95 - potato cake made with mashed potatoes, seasoned with mint and ginger, served with tamarind sauce; Lamb Pasanda £6.95 - cooked in yoghurt, cream, ground almonds, fragrant spices and red wine; Tandoori Mixed Grill £9.95 - Tandoori Chicken, Chicken and Lamb Tikka, Sheek kebab, King Prawn and Naan bread, all Balti dishes include a Naan. Takeaway: 15% discount - quite a saving! Delivery: 5 miles. We have enough satisfied reports to say welcome to our **TOP 100**. Hours: 12-2.30/5.30-11.30. <www.hawelitwyford.co.uk>

THE MITA'S

37 London Rd, Twyford — 0118 934 4599

M.Quayyum and Chef Shilu Miah's 38 seater, has its regulars who tell us they have dined here at least once a week since it opened in 1994. House specials are the Bangladeshi Hundee Dishes, (the special pot) from £5.25. Takeaway: 15% discount. Car Park at rear. Hours: 12-2.30/6-11.

Windsor

SPICE ROUTE — TOP 100

18a Boots Passage, Thames St 01753 860720

Last Guide we reported that Mridula Baljekar a prolific Indian cookbook writer, confided in us that she wanted to run a restaurant. As we said, we were surprised. She'd never done it. But after a number of ups and downs, she has one of the best restaurants in Windsor, and certainly the best Indian. The site is not hard to find, but parking is. Once inside, bar on the left, and a long narrow room opening out at the end. You'll observe the glass-fronted kitchen and maybe the aptly named chef Tika Ram (formerly chef to the Oberoi family who own the Indian Hotel chain) hard at work in it. The cooking brigade produce solid confident work. The menu is a combination of Mridula's own recipes and the chefs, and it is gourmet home-cooking. PS: As we go to print it has been sold. It remains to see whether it stays in our **TOP 100.** Lunch 12-2. Dinner 6-11, closed Sunday.

Windsor's best curryhouses, Red Rose, Sharmin and Viceroy Premier are '*Still there and very good.*' BT

Wokingham

ROYAL INDIAN TANDOORI

72 Peach Street, Wokingham 0118 978 0179

A 70-seater established in 1978 by T Ali, serving excellent Bangladeshi and Kashmiri-styled curries by chef M Miah. Banquets on Sundays. Takeaway menu 15% discount. Hours: 12-3/6-12am.

SULTAN BALTI PALACE — TOP 100

7 Market Place, Wokingham 0118 977 4397

In the middle of the pretty old town, upstairs, low ceilings, black beams, white washed walls, several small dining rooms make for an intimate and upmarket dining experience. Downstairs is modern, cafe -style, with its own menu, for light snacks while out shopping or between office meetings. Good Pakistani cooking. Branch Originasia, Richmond, Surrey.

BRISTOL

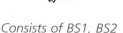

Area: South West England
Population: 410,000
Adjacent Counties: Glos, Soms

Bristol Centre

Consists of BS1, BS2

RAJDOOT

83 Park Street, Bristol BS1 0117 926 8033

Established in 1966 by Indian architect Des Sarda and now is owned by V. Pathak and managed by Biju Mulavarikkal. It pioneered the up-market look at Indian restaurants with its attractive, very Indian decorations eg: beaten copper tables in the bar area and bronze statues. The new ownership seems to have brought a stability in food quality over the last 2 years. Here is a Menu Snapshot: of Chef Bharat Bhusan's offerings: Paneer Tikka £3.95 - cubes of Indian cheese marinated with yoghurt and spices served with onions and capsicums; Makhan Chicken £8.95 - tikka cut from chicken supreme, simmered with butter, yoghurt, onions and puréed tomatoes, flavoured with cinnamon, cloves and a touch of fresh cream; Bombay Aloo Jeera £4.50 - potatoes tossed in cumin, ginger and garlic; Onion Kulcha £2.70 - bread stuffed with onions and herbs. We no longer get complaints that it was insipid. Price Check: CTM £7.95, Tarka Dhal £4.50, Pullao Rice £2.10, Naan Bread £1.95 Hours: 12-2.30/6-11. Branches: Manchester, Birmingham, Dublin and Fuengirola, Spain. <www.rajdoot.co.uk>

KATHMANDU — NEW ENTRANT

Colston Tower Colston St Bristol, BS1 0117 929 4455

Ashok Mali's 100 seater opened in 2003. Here is a menu snapshot from chef Nepalese Kancha Mali's repertoire: Kancha Kukhura Special.Tandoori chicken cooked in Nepalese spices. Chhoyla Lamb cooked on charcoal with ginger and garlic and served in a 'hot' sizzler.

Chicken or Lamb Kritipur, with whole spices in the curry. Sea Bass Nani, fillets cooked in a creamy Nepalese sauce, served with butter beans and asparagus. Chicken or Lamb Natapole, with tomato, coriander and ghee. Duck Makalu, strips of duck breast cooked with coriander, peppers and onions in a truly Nepalese style. Price Check: CTM £8.95, Tarka Dhal £3.25, Pullao Rice £2.20, Naan Bread £1.95. Set Lunch £6.95, Set dinner from £14.50. Hours: 5.45-11 (12 Sat, 10.30 Sun).

Bristol North East

BS5 *Easton,* BS16 *Redfield*

(for adjacent Staple Hill see Glos)

OH CALCUTTA! NEW ENTRANT

216 Cheltenham Rd, BS16 0117 924 0458

Oh Calcutta is a partnership of Simon Perry, his brother Matthew and Jullu Miah, who is also head chef. Oh! Calcutta is influenced by the contemporary styles and vibrant colours of Barcelona. Built-in lighting in the seats and an exposed air conditioning unit, create a freshness throughout the restaurant. An 8ft x 4ft projection screen shows 'visual music', playing chilled lounge sounds with random arty images giving customers an added dimension. Trained in the Midlands and specialising in Bengali cuisine, Jullu has drawn up a menu of some of Bengal's favourite dishes. Each order is cooked fresh upon request, using small amounts of oil, bearing in mind how important healthy cuisine is to consumers. The 52 cover venue ensures that they are able to give their customers time and offer a good dose of friendly service, just like in Spain. For take-away prices, please deduct 20% from listed prices on orders placed between 6 - 7pm and 10-11pm, 10% at all other times. Price Check: CTM £9, Tarka Dhal £2.95, Pullao Rice £2.10, Naan Bread £2.20. Hours: 6-11.30. <ohcalcutta.co.uk>

SPICE OF NEPAL TAKEAWAY

245 Lodge Causeway, Fishponds, BS16
0117 965 0664

A Nepalese takeaway opened in 1997 by head chef Pradeep Karki. Dilip Karki manages front of house. Momo, dumplings filled with mince, steamed, served with Nepalese Tomato Pickle. Kastamandapa, a mild dish, flavoured with ground nuts, cream, with a hint of garlic, good. Del £10 min 3-mile radius. 6-11.30pm; closed on Sun.

Bristol North West

Consists of BS6 to BS11

BS7 *Bishopston, Horfield*

GHURKAS TANDOORI

403 Gloucester Road, Horfield, BS7
0117 942 2898

A popular 46-seater local with some Nepalese dishes. . Delivery. Hours: 12-2p/6-12.30am.

BS9 *Westbury-on-Trym*

BRITISH RAJ

1 Passage Road, BS9 0117 950 0493

Some of our scribes say this classical, upmarket restaurant, open since 1973, is one of the most highly respected in the south-west.

BUCKINGHAMSHIRE

Area: South East England (west of London)
Population: 696,000.
Adjacent Counties: Beds, Herts, Middx, Northants, Oxon

LEMON GRASS NEW ENTRANT

17 Hill Avenue, Amersham 01494 433380

Golam Sarwar opened this 38 seater in 2005. Its name might make you think Thai not Indian, but in fact it is a regular curry house with all the favourites. It is **BYO** making it attractive, price-wise. Some of chef Islam's specials have curious names too: Flamingo is not, presumably, that pink bird (though it might make a great alternative name for CTM), it is chicken or lamb cooked with herbs, yoghurt and, yes, lemon grass!. Juliet Roman sounds like a Shakespearean TV police series, but is in fact Chicken Tikka with minced meat, capsicum, tomato and saffron, both £8.95. Chicken Sandeman is not to do with wallpaper, it is Tikka cooked with garlic, yoghurt, cheese and mushrooms, etc at £7.95. Good fun, eh? Price Check: CTM £7.50, Tarka Dhal £3.20, Pullao Rice £2.30, Naan Bread £1.85. Hours: 5.-11.

SANTHI — NEW ENTRANT

16 Hill Avenue, Amersham 01494 432621

The 90-seater Santhi was opened by Rashid Miah in 1992. .Chef Shotul Miah recommends his Anarkoli Chicken or Lamb (£7.95), cooked in a creamy sauce, or Santhi Special Beef (£11.95), fillet steak in a mild creamy sauce. Price Check: Tarka Dhal £3.35, Pullao Rice £2.30, Naan £1.95. Hours: 12-2.30/6-10.45. <www.santhirestaurant.co.uk>

Aston Clinton

SHAAD — NEW ENTRANT

132 London Road 01296 630399

Fully licensed. Opened in 2004 in a former pub. *'Friendly welcome with modern crockery. Attractively refurbished, pub interior with large conservatory at rear and car park. Generous portions of usual formula curries. Service, on the whole good, but bar slow on this occasion. Clean toilets.'* CL. Always good to hear about the loos! Takeaway: 20% discount, £15 minimum order. Sunday Buffet: 12 to 3 - £9 adult, £5 child. Banquet Night: £10.95, every Thursday. Price Check: Popadom 70p, CTM £7.95, Pullao Rice £2.15. Hours: 12-2.30/5.30- 11.30.

Aylesbury

THE CHADNIS

43 High Street, Waddesdon 01296 651255

Established in 1999 by Mr Shah. Seats 70. Fully licensed and air-conditioned. *'Nearly a year since I last visited, a mate and I decided to see if the place still 'lived up' to it's GUIDE entry. Were offered a small table for two, but opted for the larger four seater in the window. Popadoms and pickles were excellent and hot! Non Vegetarian Thai - fantastic, generous portion, Nan - excellent, Lamb Pathia - the best I've ever eaten. My mate said the Pullao Rice, Onion Bhajia and Tarka Dal - all super, could not be faulted. Plenty of staff, service attentive. As were left, the place was getting busy, good sign for a Monday night. Toilets clean but had an odour!'* DL. Price Check: Popadom 50p, CTM £7.20, Pullao Rice £1.95. Hours: 12-2.30/6-11. (Friday/Saturday - 11.30)

HOUSE OF SPICE

19 Fort End, Haddenham 01844 299 100

Situated in a former public house, nicely appointed with good ambience, very good quality food and service. Varied menu showcasing some interesting new dishes. Good to see it in the GUIDE 2004, if it carries on like this it will definitely be in the next one!' (My pleasure, Steve). *'Recommended.'* SO. *'Two further visits since my above review but can't recall the dates. Very good quality food and service. Would reiterate what I said before that this successful restaurant offers a varied menu, showcasing some interesting new dishes alongside some old favourites.í Nicely appointed with good ambience. Very good quality food and service during each visit. Didn't disappoint this time either. Benchmarking dishes passed with flying colours along with some new offerings. Overall opinion: very good. Would return again and recommend.* SO. Price check: Popadam 60p, CTM £7.95, Pullao Rice £1.90, Peshwari Nan £2. Hours: 12-2.30 / 6 - 11.30. Branch: Chinnor Indian, 59, Lower Rd, Chinnor, Oxon.

Bourne End

ALY'S TANDOORI — NEW ENTRANT

at Heart in Hand,Cores End Rd, Bourne End , 01628 531112

Mohammed Hussain doesn't mind if you call him Aly, nor does his manager Jala Uddin. Its location is in a rather tempting-looking former pub, with a pretty front 'awning' and hanging baskets. This 70 seater opened in 1999, though it it didn't change its name to Aly's until recently. and *'it's about time it appeared in the GUIDE.'* RL. Price Check: CTM £6.95, Tarka Dhal £3.75, Pullao Rice £2.75, Naan Bread £.1.95. Hours: 12-3/6 -11.30. Sunday: 1- 1.

High Wycombe

CURRY CENTRE

83 Easton Street 01494 535529

'Haven't visited for a while as I'm not often in the right place at the right time so to speak. Consequently, when an opportunity to meet up with some business colleagues presented itself, I decided to stick my neck out in the hope that it was still as good as it was last time that I visited. I'm pleased to say that my two colleagues and myself were

not disappointed. The Tandoori Chicken was excellent, with perfectly cooked, succulent chicken, which was beautifully spiced with just the right amount of heat. For main course I had Lamb Achari that was also very good with nicely spiced lamb in a very tangy Indian Chutney sauce. My colleagues also seemed to fare very well with Chicken Tikka and a mild creamy chicken dish, which I've forgotten the name of. Also on the menu were a number of new and different dishes that I have not seen before including a mango and chicken dish for which they won an award. I can't lay my hands on the takeaway menu at the moment but I'll send you more details if I come across it! Service was also good and the staff were all very friendly. Prices also seemed very reasonable for this area. Overall opinion – very good and will come back to try some of those other dishes. So may curries, so little time! S.O.

Milton Keynes

(Includes Bletchley, Stony Stratford, Woburn Sands and Wolverton)

JAIPUR **AWARD WINNER**

599 Grafton Gate E, MK 01908 669796

Known only by his surname, Ahad had a dream to construct a new fantastic new restaurant, in white marble – a Taj Mahal complete with dome. We all have dreams. Few of us realise them. He spent years planning and once he decided to proceed he took a financial risk the like of which is no dream ... nightmare rather. Even his banks were dubious. But Ahad started to build. MK's residents thought he was building a mosque, which Ahad thought hilarious, as he is firmly a restaurateur. It was opened in 2004. We believe the resulting free-standing restaurant is unique in the world. See the picture on page 28. The inside is just as plush and it cost Ahad a cool £4m. 'You can spot the Jaipur from some distance away, it really does stand out. Through double glass doors is a large circular reception. A young man takes coats, umbrellas etc.Photographs and awards adorn the walls, a sweeping staircase or a lift takes you upstairs to Ahad's new Thai restaurant, the story of which appears below. There is a sign on the restaurant door, which politely requests smart dress, no trainers or jeans. (Hooray for that). A grand, well-stocked bar, is located on your right and is for drinks service only. If you have arrived early or are waiting for a table, you on the side of the main eating arena, behind very beautiful and high, turquoise glass screens. The dining area has been divided into three spaces. The main area isencircled by more turquoise screens, which in turn encircle a lavish, four-faced, three-tiered waterfall, made from beaten copper cubes. Sparkly glass coins, in different hues of blue share the tiers with fresh orchids. The walls of the other two dining spaces have huge, tasteful, hand-painted murals of Maharajas in howdahs on elephants. Menu Snapshots: Dahi Papdi Chat £3.25 - tangy mix of flour-crisped, potatoes, chickpeas tossed with yoghurt and tamarind sauce. Squid and Avocado Salad £4.95, served on a bed of sliced mango. King Prawn Puri £6.95, sweet'n'sour spiced prawns rolled into a spinach flavoured bread. Sula Salmon £6.95, smoked Rajasthani speciality, marinated with honey and dill leaves. Dum ki Nalli £8.95, delicately spiced Avadh's lambshank. Lal Mas £7.95, lamb cooked with red chilli.

Ahad has a huge following of sophisticated diners, who love it. As last time, we've had loads of reports about the Jaipur and there isn't a bad one amongst them. Indeed have had more delighted reports about the Jaipur than almost any other restaurant. Here is the pick of them, from a one-liner to an essay: *'One of my favourites'* R.A.C. *'Truly outstanding. The Swordfish tikka starter was superb and the second time I visited and asked why it was no longer on the menu they said no problem and made it especially for me. That is the quality of service you get here. The Lamb shank was tender, falling off the bone and the spices it was cooked in were sensational. You may have guessed; I like this place.'* so. So much so that Steve went back: *'Two more great evenings at this excellent restaurant, creating a further four new converts to this fine establishment. It's good to see that the consistently high standards are being maintained. During the first visit with a colleague from Australia, we enjoyed the excellent Kashmiri Rogon Gosht and Tandoori Swordfish amongst others. During the most recent visit with a party of four, we tried the Tandoori Sea Bass which was very succulent, perfectly cooked and with a very delicate and flavoursome, but complimentary spicing; Chicken Korai does what it says on the tin!í - an excellent example of this old favourite. Chicken Paneer had very delicate spices but without any single one dominating; excellent texture to the cheese (firm but not rubbery). Vegetable Kebabs were also much enjoyed. Overall opinion – Excellent, would continue to recommend and this restaurant and it should continue to maintain its Top 100 position and award as Best outside London..í Shame they no longer seem to do the Tandoori swordfish but even so, as Arnie so eloquently put it I will be back!'* S.O. You can understand Ahad's problem, Steve. If customers do not order it, it is not possible to keep it on the menu. *'Hi Pat, Looking forward to your new good curry guide, take old copy where ever we go. Tried at least 35 restaurants from it. Our favourite is Jaipur in Milton Keynes. We stay in the Hilton for the week-end and always visit the Jaipur Saturday night. A place to dress up for.'* D.V-W. *'I have visited this restaurant on many occasions and aside from the outstanding quality of the food, the other most noteworthy element of this establishment I would like emphasis is its consistency. The ambience of this restaurant and service is also spot on. It is probably my most visited restaurant; whilst by no means the closest to home (it takes between 45 minutes and one hour to get there). The reason that I keep coming back is that the quality of the food is outstanding and it has never let me down. I have taken friends,clients and overseas visitors there on numerous occasions and it has always consistently been exceptional. On one particular visit, I took along a friend who was visiting from Australia. He had originally lived in the UK and has been visiting Indian restaurants for as long as I have. He mentioned to me that he had always been intrigued by the dish called Kurzi lamb. Since this is marinated whole leg of lamb, it needs to be ordered at least 24 hours in advance which meant that neither of us had tried it before. Despite the fact that the only date we could all meet up was a Sunday – Reeder (maitre d') arranged for their own version of this legendary dish to be served to us alongside the normal Sunday buffet. The buffet itself was excellent, including their wonderful Tandoori Swordfish,'* (see Steve you are not alone!) *'but the lamb was truly outstanding. Our party consisted of four adults and four children and everybody went home very satisfied. On another occasion Jaipur kindly hosted a farewell event for a colleague and good friend of mine, catering for around ten, including a number of important clients. Needless to say there were a number of new Jaipur converts that day. Overall – an excellent top quality restaurant! They'll have to change the locks of the door is they want to stop me coming back! I will continue to recommend it.'* B.P. Price Check: Popadom 60p, CTM £8.95, Tarka Dhal £3.75, Pullao Rice £3.00, Naan Bread £2.75. Takeaway: 10% discount. Sunday Family Buffet: 12 to 4 – £12 adult, £6 child. Hours: 12 to 11.30 (Sunday to 10.30). Snacks and beverages only between pm and 5pm, except Sundays. <www.jaipur.co.uk>. *See also inside front cover.*

LA HIND

502 Elder Gate, Station Sq, MK 01908 675948

MK is well endowed with Indian restaurants, and you would imagine that La Hind, formerly Mr Ahad's Jaipur, now run by Suhel Ahmed, would be as full as it was in its Jaipur days. But it is, well almost. It is a fairly standard menu, with Duck appearing here and there. Specials include Duck such as Duck Tikka Jalfrezi, £6.90.Price Check: Popadom 50p, CTM £6.50, Pullao Rice £1.90. Sunday Buffet: £7.90 adult, £4.90 children, 12 to 4. Hours: 12 to 2.30 (Friday closed) and 5.30 to 11.30 (Sunday 12 to 11pm). <www.la-hind.com>

JALORI — TOP 100

23 High St, Woburn, MK 01908 281239

M.A. Hai (Ahad's brother – see Jaipur, above) is known to all simply as Hai, and like his brother he is a very successful restaurateur. He established the the 80-seater Jalori in 1994. It's bigger than it looks, and has a loyal following that includes Johnny Dankworth and Cleo Lane. It is really pretty inside and out as the picture overleaf an on page 200 show. Chef Abdul Quayam prepares food that is *'First class.'* B.G. Starters include Kebab-e-Aloo Palak £3.75, a crisp rissole of potato and spinach served with sweet & sour sauce. Spicy Tandoori Wrap £3.75, barbecued spicy sweet and sour chicken served in a pocket of thin Indian bread. Some mains: Elaichi Duckling £8.95, roasted duck breast cooked with spices, dried apricot, pepper, tomato and fresh herbs. Chicken or Lamb Peri Peri £7.25, chicken or spring lamb cubes, spiced with peri peri sauce,(chilli) and finished with sun-dried tomatoes. One English dish roosts uneasily on the menu: Roast Chicken with chips peas and mushrooms. £8.50. Get rid of it please Hai. If your diners don't like Indian food, why are they there? You do not often find Indian Desserts at Indian restaurants (no demand they tell us) but at the Jalori you will get Gulabjaman £3.25, small cake-like fried spheres in sweet syrup and Rasmalai, ditto, not fried, in a milky sauce with pistachio nuts, both £3.25. They are divine ! Try them, or else it will be '*no demand!*' *'I would like to tell you how much we always enjoy eating at Jalori Indian Cuisine in Woburn Sands, Milton Keynes. Mr Hai and his staff are always very welcoming, the restaurant is always immaculate and popular with other diners. They have a wide range of choices, all well described on the menu and although there is always something we haven't tried before, the Onion Bhajees always get my vote as the best I've ever tasted. We do try other Indian restaurants, but the Jalori is the one we keep coming back to.'* M. A. Licensed but, unusually you may **BYO**, corkage charge £2. Every restaurant should do that. Indeed the Jalori deserves its **TOP 100** rating for that alone, but it also deserves it for Hai's attention to detail and care. Min charge £15 per person, but no service or cover charges, and the prices are reasonable. Price Check: Popadom 60p, CTM £7.50, Tarka Dhal £3.10, Pullao Rice £2.40, Naan Bread £1.90. Hours: 12-2.30/6-11.30. (Sunday e-a-m-a-y-l buffet till 3pm, £8.95). <www.jalori.co.uk> *(see overleaf and page 220).*

Jalori, Woburn, see previous page

MOGHUL PALACE TOP 100

7 St Paul's Court, High St, Stony Stratford, MK 01908 566577

'It's an old monastery school where monks once beat knowledge into the sons of local gentry.' LT. Now the local curryholic gentry beat a path through its Gothic arch, complete with wrought-iron gate, beyond which stands the imposing clerestoric building. Owners Monowar Hussain and Anfor Ali greet you and, given a chance, will tell you how much they spent in 1994 converting this Victorian former cigar-factory-cum-orphanage-cum-school into their 100-seater Palace. And impressed you will be, with the spacious reception area with its armchairs and comfortable sofas where you wait to be seated, and the scale, height, tiled floor, stonework and wood panels of the dining room. Be nice to the gargoyles, they're there to ward off bad vibes! And wonder what the monks would think of the menu offering all the familiar curry items.. *'Original wood panelling still in place, very high domed ceiling over half of restaurant - with mock stars in the deep blue sky and a mural copying Michael Angelo's Sistine chapel ceiling at the non-smoking end, which is raised up two or three steps. Food superb. - delicious, but no salad which I thought a bit mean, however, contents of the thin pancake included lots of coriander, sauce and prawns of course. Regretted choosing Chicken Tikka Bhuna when I saw my companion's Chicken Shashlik, which he said was the best ever, anywhere. Service good and friendly - I'll go again.'* MS. *'we perused the menu in the lounge, where the conversation ranged from church to curry.'* DL. Takeaway: 10% discount. Hours: 12-2.30/6-11.30.

ORCHID LOUNGE AT JAIPUR

BEST UK ORIENTAL ASAIN RESTAURANT

599 Grafton Gate East, MK 01908 669 811

It has been a long time coming. Even before Ahad opened his Jaipur *(see earlier)*, he had plans to turn the first floor into a Thai restaurant. I remember walking over the empty space with him. *'What do you think?'*, he asked, something he does to everyone. Well now it has opened and it is a sumptuous, astonishing venue, worthy of anything in the west end. The cooks and waiting staff are Thai and the food is authentic and served beautifully. We have had several reports which cannot fault the place, but so. one of our prolific reporters found it a little wanting on a quiet day. *'Situated upstairs in the excellent Jaipur restaurant in Milton Keynes, this restaurant oozes class from the moment you get through the door. The interior is exquisite and the ambience was excellent, a bright and airy outlook with access to balconies which boasted 'stunning' (I quote) views of Milton Keynes. The waiters/waitresses also looked the part, being dressed in regional costumes, and there was a lady playing traditional dulcimer as you entered. The service was spot on, as it should be considering there were only two other tables occupied. The food though was sadly quite variable. Presentation was very classy though. Starters: Prawn Crackers with tasty dips including roasted chilli and garlic plus spiced soy and red chilli were delicious. Tord an (fish cakes) were ok but not the best execution I have seen. Peek Gai Yud Sai (stuffed chicken wings) was pleasant enough. Poo Nim Gratium (soft-shell crabs) – very strong garlic character dominated; not a favourite. Gai Hor Bai Toy (Chicken in Pandang Leaves) – overcooked and dry, leaves disintegrated in your hand leaving black smears. Main Courses: Tiger Cry Steak (barbecued sirloin with salad and spicy dip) steak was overdone and the chilli sauce that came with the fish worked better than the one provided. There is a Thai Pub/Restaurant called the Greyhound in Marsh Gibbon that does this sooooo much better! Salmon Choo Chee (Salmon in Red Thai Curry sauce) – exquisite, excellent balance and cooked to perfection. Pla Yang Bai Tang (Sea Bass with Chilli Sauce) also exquisitely presented and cooked; accompanying chilli sauce was delicious. Ped Gration (Duck in sweet and sour sauce) – very clean sauce which didn't drown the flavour of the duck. Overall opinion was that it seemed as though it should be excellent. I was disappointed that some of the dishes had not been better prepared considering how quiet they were. When the new area upstairs was due to open guests of Jaipur were canvassed for their opinion as to what it should become. My view was predictably – more of the same! I would like to try this place again but probably won't get around to it as I would be naturally drawn to the Jaipur downstairs (being a fierce creature of habit).* so. We publish it in full although we and other reporters have not experienced the same food problems. In fact we are so happy with all that Ahad has achieved with this venue that we have made it the unique **AWARD OF BEST ORIENTAL ASIAN RESTAURANT** and that includes Malaysian, Thai, Indonesian, Burmese and Japanese *(see pages 37 and 77)*.

THE SILK ROAD

151 Grafton Gate E, MK 01908 200522

This is first venture of owners, Adbus Samad, who also lectures on Pan-Asian food at Birmingham City College and Subhojit Chakravarty, who is also Head Chef, who trained as a chef in Calcutta then worked in top 5 Star hotels, including Delhi's Orchid. The menu is largely Indian regional cuisine, rather than curryhouse, and there is a hint of fusion in some dishes. The menu is described as *'contemporary in style yet maintaining the traditions of authentic Indian cooking'.* Presentation is in the plated style rather than served in a pot or karahi. Many diners dislike this style, because it determines your portion size and it makes sharing difficult – a technique done at a number of trendy London westend Indian restaurants. Some menu snapshots: Rajasthani laal maas £7.95, lamb braised with aromatic spices, chilli, ginger and garlic. Chennai ka Chettinaad, £7.95, a south Indian chicken curry fried with spices, crushed peppercorns and curry leaves. Thai Red Curry (Gaeng Phet) flavoured with bamboo shoots, coconut cream, lime leaves and fresh chillies, chicken/beef £7.95 king prawns £8.95. Malaysian spicy king Prawns £12.95 King prawns simmered in coconut milk, lemongrass, chillies and roasted mustard with cucumber and mange tout. Lamb Shank Masaman £12.95, Thai-style Lamb Shanks cooked with coconut milk, roasted peanuts, lemon grass, cassia bark, hint of fish sauce and cardamom pods. Vegetable dishes can each be ordered as a side dish £3.25, or a main course £5.95. Notable are Punjabi Chole: chick peas cooked traditionally like a north Indian-style with yoghurt and special Chana Masala and Dahl Panchmel, a mixture of five different lentils cooked slowly in a pot and then tampered with whole cumin. Indian Banquet £14.95 pp (min 2) and Oriental Banquet £15.95 pp (min 4). Hours: 12-2.15 /6-11. All day Sunday Buffet 12-9.30 pm. Reports please. <wwwthesilkroadrestaurants.co.uk>

Newport Pagnell

MYSORE TOP 100

101 High St, Newport Pagnell, Milton Keynes 01908 216426

Another high-standard goodie from the Ahad stable, this one operated by brother M Abdul Odud. *'The dining room, cleverly housed within two cottages, seats 98, yet provides a number of secluded areas, which 'give a good feeling of privacy'* HG. *'We were unsure of arrangements and numbers for a special charity dinner, so Mr Odud gave us a selection from the menu at a fixed price. Lamb Dhansak with Sag, Mixed Raitha, Pullao Rice and Paratha, all very good. The complete meal and decor (small corners and niches, then a large area with skylight, a bit colonial and glorious at full moon) to be recommended.'* BG. *'Colleague prefers the Mysore to Jaipur. He had Chingri Puri – KP's served in a thick sauce on thin deep-fried bread. I had, Jhinga Puri – KP's in a sweet and sour sauce, served on a puffed bread. Both went down a treat. Followed by Chicken Zallander, Chicken*

Delight, Vegetable Pullao, Bhindi and Naan. I have to admit that it was better than the Jaipur, which is not exactly a slouch in the curry stakes. I guess when you are choosing between very good restaurants, personal taste has to come into it and I like the cosy feel of the Mysore. I have been to the Jaipur and had just about the best meal I have had, but it is a bit formal. I like places that are more laid back and the Mysore is that' MW. 10% discount for takeaways. Hours: 12-2.30/6-11.30pm.

Princess Risborough

COCO TAMARIND NEW ENTRANT

Aylesbury Rd, Askett 01844 343111

Situated in a former pub, this classy restaurant seems to have got it right compared to the Indian restaurant that occupied these premises previously since the pub closed some years ago. The decor is modern and stylish with elegant, high backed chairs, white tablecloths, recessed spotlights in the ceiling and a pretty blue teardrop-shaped oil lamp and a rose bowl containing a contemporary flower on each table. There was a wooden display cabinet at the far end of this 70-seater restaurant, housing traditional Indian themed ornaments including wooden elephant bookends, spice collages and a pestle and mortar. The effect was finished off with solid, nicely weighted cutlery next to large, square, white 'welcome plates' which remained on the table during popadoms. Service was fairly efficient, attentive and friendly with a separate drinks waiter and the maitre d taking the food orders. The wine list was of modest size but with a thoughtful range to suit most pockets. Food was beautifully presented and of excellent quality with many new dishes sitting happily alongside old favourites. Prices were on the high side but then so was the quality. Portion size was excellent for the starters but then of a similar size for the main courses (I know what you're thinking but they have a policy of not serving starters on their own!). Starters: Scallops Masala (£7.95), Salmon Tikka (£7.95), Vegetable Pakora (£3.95): with delicious red onion, tomato, mango and sweet chilli chutney, Murg Chat (£5.25) and King Prawn Puree (£7.95) were all excellent. Main courses: It was great to see a range of different fish options: Tandoori Monk Fish (£15.95) was truly delicious as was the Goan Fish Curry (£12.95), cooked with curry leaves, pepper and coconut milk. The Sea bass was also good but lacked any real wow factor. Chicken Pathia (£7.95) was very hot but tasty; Flattened Chicken with Spinach and Cheese was sweet, spicy, well balanced and delicious. Another interesting item was whole Lamb Shank, deliciously spiced but again a little on the hot side. Dal Samba (lentils with vegetables) was also excellent with perfectly cooked al denté vegetables, served here as a main course. Service was overall very good for a full and busy Saturday evening, taking around 3 hours to serve our large family party of 9 with drinks, popadoms, starters and main courses. There was an oversight on the main courses, which could have spoilt the evening for one member of our party had there not been such a good selection of alternatives amongst the rest of the party. The incident was dealt with very professionally though and to our satisfaction. Overall opinion: very good, would definitely return and would recommend for those who would like to try some different Indian dishes and are prepared to pay more for the quality.' SO. Price check: Chicken Tikka Masala (£7.95), Vegetable side dishes: 12 at £4.95 and 8 at £3.95; popadom (£0.70); chutney (£0.70); Naan (£2.50); rice (£2.95). Hours: 12 -2.30/6 -11.

JAFLONG

16 Duke Street 01844 274443

SO. has formed his opinion over a number of visits. *'Very competent, reliable and reasonably priced formula curry restaurant. Bright interior with good amount of space for a fairly small establishment. Very friendly, welcoming staff. Good quality food with the Prawn Puri, Tandoori Trout starters and the Achar Lamb (cooked with Indian Pickles), Chicken Pathia and Korai Lamb being particularly good. Overall opinion – very good. Would continue to recommend as being the best in the immediate local area.'*

Stokenchurch

MOWCHAK PUB & RESTAURANT

Wycombe Road 01494 485005

Good because it's a proper pub serving English real ales, (and everything else a traditional pub serves) and the restaurant does good quality formula curries. *'It's a dream for a CAMRA lover and Curryholic, and we find it worth travelling a long distance at least weekly, just for this delightful combination'.* RL. *'Have enjoyed this establishment on a number of occasions. Bland exterior of pub belies excellent restaurant - clean, bustling and modern in style, everything nicely presented. A rare pleasure to sample fairly well-kept English ales such as Fullers London Pride and Adnams in the same building.*

Very tasty chutneys, particularly good mango, are presented in attractive wooden dishes. Prawn Puri – excellent execution, one of my benchmarks. Chicken Tikka - flavour a bit sweet and mild for my taste. Lamb Korai – possibly the best I have tasted, a lot of fennel and cardamom – loved it! Vegetarian Thai – quality but quite pricey. Chicken Balti – spicy, tangy with large pieces of chicken, very good.' SO.

Wendover

RAJ

23 Aylesbury Rd, Wendover 01296 622567

A 300-year-old listed building in a beautiful old street, in a picture-postcard town. Exposed beams, with walled partitions, dividing the 60 seats into almost separate rooms, creating agreeable ambience and comfort. *'Busy Friday evening but still service very good with a bit of joyful banter with the staff. Chicken Zafrani , good, Chicken Pathia , very tasty. One of our party changed order to Chicken Tikka once seeing one arrive on next table ; never seen one like it and wonderful flavour! Light and fluffy Nan breads. Very enjoyable experience in a 'not too cramped' atmosphere.'* JH. *'Very tasty, high quality, formula curries with good service. A little cramped. Still serves their famous Balti curry in a bucket! I have been there on a couple of occasions now and look forward to my next visit.* SO.

Winslow

MAHABHARAT

25 Market Square, Winslow 01296 713611

First opened in 1979, taken over by Nurul Islam in 1990, the ground-floor restaurant seats 44 diners, plus private room for 26. Show the manager this *Guide* and you may get a discount. Takeaway: 15% discount. Hours: 6-11.30 (Sat. to 12).

WE NEED YOU!!!

Please tell us everything you know about the curry restaurants you visit.

Simply use the forms on pages 465 and 466

MANY THANKS!

Jalori, Woburn, see page 215

CAMBRIDGESHIRE

Area: East of England
Population: 740,000
Adjacent Counties:
Beds, Essex, Herts,
Rutland, Lincs,
Norfolk,
Northants,
Suffolk

Cambridge

CAFE NAZ — AWARD WINNER & A-LIST

47 Castle Street, Cambridge 01223 363666

One of the very successful restaurants in the bright, well-run chain. It is in our **A-LIST** as Nominated Best Bangladeshi and Winner Best Chef Award. (see pages 30 and 40). See also Branches at Cafe Naz, Brick Lane London, E1 and Cardiff. *'One of the best meals that I have had.'* JP.

GOLDEN CURRY

111 Mill Road, Cambridge 01223 329432

Safe-bet curryhouse. Show the manager this *Guide* and you may get a discount.

GULSHAN

106 Regent Street Cambridge 01223 000000

'A welcoming interior, friendly, polite staff – handshakes by five of the staff!. Good, subtle Indian music. Good, thick, pink carpet. High level of cleanliness. Cosy bar, no smoking, cool atmosphere. Ordered Prawn Ceylon – hot and spicy. The flavours overlapped, and the rice was smooth! I was not given huge amounts, but I was still full after the meal. A good restaurant.' DW

INDIAN GARDEN

13 Victoria Street, Littleport 01353 863642

Air-conditioned, non-smoking restaurant. Price Check: Popadom 50p, CTM £7.50, Pullao Rice £2.10. Takeaway: 10% - under £20, 20% - over £20. Hours: 5.30 to 11, Friday and Saturday to 12.

INDIA HOUSE

31 Newnham Rd, Cambridge 01223 461661

Safe-bet curryhouse where you may get a discount.

KOHINOOR

74 Mill Road, Cambridge 01223 323639

It's been there for donkey's years. Show the manager this *Guide* and you may get a discount.

PIPASHA — NEW ENTRANT

529 Newmarket Rd 01223 577786

Manager: Abdul Hye. Seats 60 diners in two rooms. Menu Snapshot: Ayr Biran £3.50 - gently spiced Bangladeshi fish, fried with onions, green peppers (contains bones); Bhegoon Chop £2.40 - aubergine dipped in spicy flour, fried in ghee; Shabji £2.65 - sweetcorn, broccoli, beans, carrot, potato and cauliflower in mustard paste; Lemon and Coriander Rice £2.20. Stocks: Cobra. Delivery: £2.50 charge, 3 miles radius, £10 min. Price Check: Popadom 50p, CTM £7.40, Pullao Rice £1.90. Hours: 12-2 /5.30-11.30, Sunday to 11. <www.Pipasha-restaurant.co.uk>

TAJ TANDOORI

64 Cherry Hinton Rd 01223 248063

Safe-bet curryhouse. Show the manager this *Guide* and you may get a discount.

Ely

SURMA TANDOORI

78 Broad Street, Ely 01353 662281

Safe-bet curryhouse. Show the manager this *Guide* and you may get a discount.

Peterborough

BOMBAY BRASSERIE

52 Broadway, Peterborough 01733 565606

Safe-bet curryhouse. Show the manager this *Guide* and you may get a discount.

INDIA GATE

9 Fitzwilliam Street, Peterborough 01733 34616

Safe-bet curryhouse. Show the manager this *Guide* and you may get a discount.

TAJ MAHAL

37 Lincoln Road, Peterborough 01733 348840

Equally safe-bet curryhouse. Show the manager this *Guide* and you may get a discount.

St Neots

JONONI

12 High Street, St Neots 01480 219626

CHESHIRE

Area: North West
Population: 1 million
Adjacent Counties: Clwyd, Derbs, Greater Man, Mers, Shrops, Staffs

Chester

RUAN ORCHID NEW ENTRANT

14 Lower Bridge Street, Chester 01244 400661

'I have a weakness for lunch time curries. Quality of food magnificent. First and second visit, had Chicken Curry with Kaffir lime leaves, and after a lengthy discussion on merits of hot and Thai hot - settled on hot. (David - Pat and I always settle for Thai hot!) First mouthful was sublime, like having the whole of the Rio Carnival dancing on my tongue.. Flavours were exquisite, tamarind coming through - superb. In the end even my little toe was sweating, but what a great meal. Had the same dish on my next visit - again brilliant. Chicken in Hot Thick Curry and Beef in Red Thai Curry also magnificent. Producing some of the best curries I have ever eaten, flavours shine through.' DB.

GATE OF INDIA NEW ENTRANT

25 City Road, Chester 01244 327131

Established in 1973 and taken over by Moinuddin Ahmed in 1992, seats 64 diners in two rooms. Takeaway menu states that, "Starters, side dishes and beverages will not be served unless accompanied with a main meal." This seems rather outdated, after all we have just experienced a extremely hot summer, and trade has been down (we are all on ours hols or have dusted down the barbecue). I suspect, if we could eat JUST starters eg: a plate full of Samosas and Bhajias, with salad and Mint Raita, then the curry house would be full. The menu contains all your curry house favourites, that you would expect to find, however, the Tandoori Mixed Grill £8.70 has no Nan! Stocks: Cobra, Kingfisher and Lal Toofan. Takeaway: 10% before 11pm. Price Check: Popadom 70p, CTM £7.40, Pullao Rice £1.95. Hours: 6 to 2, Saturday to 2.30, Sunday to 1.

Crewe

EVENING SPICE NEW ENTRANT

Poolside, Madeley, Nr Crewe 01782 750088

Situated in a former pub, The Bridge Inn, which proprietor Nasir Miah purchased in 1998. GA Choudhury, chef's Menu Snapshot: Tandoori Scallops £5.95; Tinda Mache £8.95 - boned fish, baby pumpkin; Duck Pilli-Pilli £8.95 - spicy sauce, barbecued tomatoes, onion, capsicum; Banana in Ghee £3.45; Pea and Egg Rice £2.80; Chilli and Cheese Nan £2.80. Takeaway: 20% discount. Price Check: Popadom £1 for two, CTM £7.95, Pullao Rice £2.50. Hours: 5 to 10.30, Monday closed, except Bank Holidays. <www.eveningspice.co.uk>

Ellesmere Port, Wirral

The Wirral is neither a town nor a county and until 1965 was part of Cheshire. Since then the northern part (a small, digit-like, curry-rich peninsula between the rivers Mersey and Dee) has been part of Merseyside. Ellesmere Port remains in south Wirral but is in Cheshire. See also Merseyside.

MUJIB

Viscount Hotel, Whitby Rd, Ellesmere Port 0151 357 1676

Chef Proprietor Nazrul Ali has created a fusion menu laid out in 22 sections, with unique dishes such as Chittagong crab salad served with garlic croutes and mango dressing, organic vegetarian dishes, Atkins dietary dishes and classics like Korma, Madras and Vindaloo. *'I wish to recommend a new Indian restaurant - the Mujib - which is aiming to 'beat the*

Birmingham Balti of the fusion of the North'. With restaurants in Harrogate, and now Ellesmere Port, Cheshire, the Mujib specialises in 'Indian fusion' - a unique culinary experience that 'merges' Indian and cosmopolitan fayre. Proprietor and chef Nazrul Ali has drawn on his experience of Indian, French Provencale, Italian, Oriental and Thai cuisine to create the original menu. The dish Joi Yorkshire, created by Ali, is typical of the fayre on offer, mixing traditional English roast lamb and light spices with Yorkshire pudding and Bhuna sauce. Let your Curry Club members know about the unique experience that is the Mujib.' KC. 12-2 (M-Sa)5.30-11.30 (M-Th) 5.30-12 (Fri-Sat) 12 -11 (Sun). Branch: Harrogate. <www.mujibrestaurants.co.uk>

SHERE KHAN

26 Cheshire Oaks, Outlet Village, J10-M53 0151 355 5150

'An upmarket version of the Rusholme Kebab shops, modern furnishings, well lit and tidy. "A new concept on dining - Freshly prepared Indian food," I asked for Chicken Tikka with a Madras sauce, but they were unable to do it. The food arrived within two minutes, so is already prepared, waiting to be served. Opted for Chicken Jalfrezi, instead, served with Pullao Rice. Decent portion, tender chicken, very wet sauce, very few peppers or onion and only one chilli. Served in a bowl, around an island of rice. Whole experience lasted just 15 minutes. Cost is reasonable and OK for a quick fix.' DB. (I know, Dave, it wasn't the greatest meal, but it is an interesting idea. – Ed).

THE TAJ OF AGRA FORT

PREVIOUS AWARD WINNER TOP 100

1 Cambridge Rd, Ellesmere Port 0151 355 1516

Spacious, clean and welcoming restaurant owned by Shams Uddin Ahmed. *'A couple of nice touches set it apart – the waiters, in their Agra Fort jackets, ask you how long you want between starters and main courses and give you the time requested, and slices of orange were delivered with the hot towels after the main course, whether desserts were ordered or not. Pepper stuffed with small pieces of tandoori chicken and lamb, as mentioned in the guide, was excellent. Paratha was one of the best I've had. A very good evening and I look forward to visiting again.'* OC. *'Heartily recommended.'* RW. *'We totally recommend this restaurant to you.'* MB and friends. *'Decor and service top drawer. Popadoms – warm and crisp, lime pickle needed replenishment, garlic and ginger chutney (a new one to me) was excellent. Tikka melt in the mouth, Bhajia size of tennis ball. CTM – too red, Jalfrezi – drier than normal, both excellent. Naan warm and moist. Top rate.'* DB. Hours: 12-2/6-11.30 (12.30am on Sat.). Sunday buffet 1pm-11.30pm.

SPICE GARDEN

338 Booth Lane, Middlewich 01606 841549

'New restaurant in strange location - you need a car to get there! Quite surprised to see a number of people eating at 5.45pm. Ordered Popadoms 50p, and Chutney Tray £1.50 - fresh and good. Chicken Tikka Biryani - good portion of rice with a fair bit of flavour. A good amount of tikka tended to lack flavour, but was moist and tender. Madras curry sauce thick and spicy. Service pleasant.' DB.

Northwich

BENGAL DYNASTY A-LIST

Rear of Black Greyhound, Hall Lane
Wincham, Northwich 01606 351597

The interior of this 150-seater is an absolute dream. with white walls, blonde floor boards, original hanging art and suspended lights over each table. Running down both sides of the restaurant, are comfortably upholstered, semi-circular booths, encasing round tables, very stylish and enough space for six. Square tables, two lines of them, run parallel to the booths, giving great flexibility for dining. *'Impressed.'* DBAC This is the third of a small chain of excellently managed restaurants. *For more information see Bengal Dynasty, Deeside, Clwyd, Wales and see p 6.*

Sandbach

THE TASTE OF THE RAJ

11 High Street, Sandbach 01270 753752

Anam Islam's 38-seater safe-bet curryhouse is opposite the cobbled square with the Sandbach Cross. Show him this *Guide* and you may get a discount.

Upton

Adjoined to north Chester, but is part of the Wirral; see Ellesmere Port, above.

UPTON HALAL BALTI HOUSE

167 Ford Road, Upton , Wirral 0151 604 0166

Shofiul Miah's venture opened in 1996 and is not licensed, so **BYO** is a big attraction. And it's relatively cheap. Open daily except Tues, 5-11.30.Branch: Manzil, 73 Grange Rd East, Birkenhead. Show him this *Guide* and you may get a discount.

JAHAN

Chester Rd Walton Warrington 01925 860 86

Previously 'The Ship Inn.' *'Just happened to be driving past, noticed this relatively new restaurant open for lunch. Out of the way for passing custom, so surprised to be joined by a group of twenty others. Nicely decorated, modern style, light and airy. Popadom, Onion Bhajia, Mango Chutney and Yoghurt arrived well presented, nice and fresh. Chicken Tikka Biriani - not the biggest portion, but sufficient with decent proportions of chicken, garnished with omelette, cucumber, tomatoes and served with a very healthy portion of curry sauce. Rice nice, fluffy with good flavour, chicken subtly spiced, curry sauce was rich with a kick, not quite hot enough. One of the best Birianis I've had over the last year. Service wasn't the best, but I will give it another try.'* DB. Sunday Buffet adult £9.95, child £5.95. Secure parking on site. Hours: 12 to 2.30 and 5 to 11 (Saturday and Sunday 12 to 11).

CORNWALL

Area: West Country
Population: 517,500
Adjacent County:
Devon

Bodmin

VIRAJ INDIAN CUISINE

50 High Bore Street, Bodmin 01208 73480

'Food surprisingly good. Prices average, portions ample, service good.' MW.

Callington

PREETI RAJ

5 New Road, Callington 01579 383818'

Competent curryhouse. Hours: 12-2.30/5.30 - 11.30.

Newquay

INDIAN SUMMER

20 East Street, Newquay 01637 872964

Curryhouse menu. *Waiters all bored and disinterested . Average prices, plentiful portions.'* MW. This is a comment we receive a lot about Cornwall. Must be the air! Or do you know better?

Padstow

THE JOURNEYMAN

Mellingey Mill, St Issey, Padstow
01841 540604

'Hi Pat Have been a big fan of your club for several years now, (your balti cooking book was the first curry recipe book I bought) so much so in fact that in three weeks I'm opening my own restaurant serving Indian, Thai, Chinese and traditional English fayre in the middle of rural Cornwall. After years of coming here on holiday from the midlands I just got fed up with not being able to get a decent curry and so decided to do something about it. If you wish you can mention it in your magazine I'd be glad to help, in any event it would be a pleasure to see you if you're in this neck of the woods. Kind Regards' Steve Lloyd, head Chef & Partner. *'First impressions: very friendly, cosy, tasteful decor, original features in keeping with the buildings original function as a watermill. Friendly welcome, homely, felt comfortable straightaway. Well presented and varied menu - including Beef Wellington. Good quantities, excellent Balti Jalfrezi - very tasty. Very impressed all round.'* DR MO. OK so it does English food. but in the curry desert of Cornwall, it makes a change not to be a Rick Stein fish operation. Oh and yes, the Balti should be good – I know the recipe!! – Ed.

Penzance

GANGES BALTI

18 Chapel Street, Penzance 01736 333002

'A large restaurant. Superb quality Chicken Kahlin, huge chunks of chicken, the largest I've ever seen. Many different flavours in the meal, top quality stuff.' GGP. *'Chicken Karahi, cooked with black pepper, attractive sour taste. Egg Bhuna, very good but slightly greasy. Very prompt, efficient service.'* MP.

St Austell

TAJ MAHAL

57 Victoria Rd, Mount Charles 01726 73716

Established 1985. Fully Licensed and air conditioned. *'Our GUIDE has proved a great source of information and we have particularly enjoyed our visits to the Taj. Prompt, courteous and attentive service. Onion Bhajias £1.95 - crisp and tasty. Garlic Naan £1.90 - large, probably the best we have tasted in the last few years. Vegetable Dupiaza £4.95 and Chicken Tikka Masala - well spiced, generous portions. Unlike other restaurants the rice was light, with pleasant flavour. Clean if basic toilets. (Good to hear! - The Ed). Looking forward to visiting once more.'* N&JG. Price Check: Popadoms 40p, CTM £6.30, Pullao Rice £1.80. Hours: 5.30 - 1.30.

St Ives

RUBY MURRIES TAKEAWAY

4b Chapel Street, St Ives 01736 796002

Takeaway only. *'Punjabi proprietors, moved from Leicester and offers Punjabi cuisine. Virtually impossible to park outside. Have arrangement with pub up the road you can eat your takeaway with a pint – an admirable arrangement.'* MW.

Truro

GANGES

St Clement Street, Truro 01872 24253

Mohammed Udin's Ganges is Truro's first (1987) and biggest restaurant, seating well over 100. *'Good sized portions, average prices.'* MW. Takeaway: 25% discount, min £10. Hours: 12-2.15 and 6-11.15, Fri / Sat 11.45.

GULSHAN

Fore Street, Probus, Truro 01872 882692

'Run by Alom Ali (from Chittagong) and his English wife Sue, ably assisted by son in kitchen and daughter in restaurant. A pleasant, airy restaurant, plain white walls. Marginally, above average prices, portions extremely generous. Good quality succulent, pieces of chicken. Service efficient and friendly. A nice little gem in the Cornish countryside.' MW. Alom and Sue also provide frozen curries to locals pubs, campsites etc. Takeaway: 10% discount. Hours: 5.30-11. Monday closed, except Bank Holidays.

SHANAZ

1 Edward Street, Truro 01782 262700'

Karim Uddin's popular Shanaz is in its 12th year. *'Our Truro favourite. The food is essentially Bangladeshi formula, but extremely well done and well presented. I recommend their Chicken Paneer, and Chicken Jalfrezi, the chillies being just the right heat, and their naan is the best I've tasted.'* GP.

CUMBRIA

formerly Cumberland and Westmoreland
Area: North West England (Lake District)
Population: 496,000
Adjacent Counties: Borders, D&G, Durham, Lancs, Yorks

Barrow-in-Furness

MITHALI

252 Dalton Road, Barrow 01229 432166

'Drove around town and discovered Mithali by accident. Wednesday night and parked right outside.' (Tony, you always manage to park outside the door! how do you do it? – Ed.) *'Met a man outside, carrying his takeaway, said it was his regular haunt and the curries were very good. So, in we went! Two elderly waiters seemed to know all their regular diners.* (Show them this *Guide* and you may get a discount). *'Mushroom Pakora - dipped in a light besan batter, slightly spiced, then deep-fried -very, very good. Sheek Kebab - OK. Mithali Special Curry - lamb and chicken in hot sauce with huge lightly battered (unshelled) King Prawn on top eaten with Nan bread - couldn't fault it. A little on the expensive side, but we came away extolling the virtues of the place.'* T&MH.

Carlisle

DHAKA TANDOORI

London Rd, Carleton, Carlisle 01228 523855

Off at J42 of the M6 and you'll find A Harid's 100-seater smart, up-market restaurant. Est in 1995, the 100-seater has car parking for 100 at rear and a new large front conservatory. *'Comfortable seating and pleasant decor. Good, friendly service. Large portions of lovely food reasonably priced. Much better than motorway services!'* IB. *'Consistently good. Try Chef M Ali's Kebab Kyberi, diced chicken in mild spices with fresh tomatoes, onions, served sizzling in iron karahi.'* AY. Show them this *Guide* and you may get a discount. Delivery: £12 min. Hours: 12-2/6-12am.

Cockermouth

TASTE OF INDIA

4-5 Hereford Ct, Main St 01900 822880

F Rahman's 60-seater is divided into two rooms with a 44-seat private room. Show him this *Guide* and you may get a discount. It's *'nicely decorated, and Chef NI Khan offers good choices. Judging by the number of takeaways being collected the place is very popular with the locals. All curries excellent, if slightly milder than usual. Excellent flavours/use of spices.'* AY. Hours: 12-2.30/5.30-12am. Branches: Red Fort, Keswick *'excellent meal.'* DH, and Emperor of India, Bowness.

Kendal

FLAVOURS OF INDIA

20 Blackhall Road, Kendal 01539 722711

Yaor Miah's 95-seater – a competent curry house.

Penrith

CAGNEYS TANDOORI ©

17 King Street, Penrith 01768 867503

'Took a welcome caravan week to Penrith on the edge of the Lake District to resample Cagneys. A very unusual restaurant with a wall separating the 'u' shape. Parking easy. Shown to a window table for four, which overlooked the main street of the town. Kingfisher and Bangla only came in bottles and expensive. Northumbrian Bitter (I'm a real ale man) was a reasonable £2.40 a pint. Please decor, service OK, waiters smiled. Garlic Mushroom Puri £3.35, coloured orange, not impressed. Sheek Kebab £3.25, Lamb Tikka £3.25, Fish Tikka £3.35, enjoyed by all. Chicken Jalfrezi £7.95 (my usual), OK, sliced chillies, hot. Monika had Karahi Gosht £7.95, tasty, large and flat pieces of exceptionally tender lamb. Plain Nan – superior.' T&MH. Half portions available for children. Price Check: Popadom 60p, CTM £7.95, Pullao Rice £1.85. Hours: 12 to 2 and 5 to 11.30.

RAJINDA PRADESH

Oasis, Whinfell Forest Penrith

'Only open to holiday makers at this Centre Parks location and is highly recommended. Nicely decorated, light and airy, lovely relaxed atmosphere. Booked and glad we did, (seven of us) place quite full. Started with Popadoms, excellent value 70p including chutneys (that is good to hear, can anyone else do better? – The Ed.) Onion Bhaji – two tennis balls, crisp on outside, moist on the inside, nicely spiced and garnished only with lemon and tomato. Meat Samosa – crisp and nicely spiced, again with paltry garnish. Chicken Chat – not the biggest portion in the world, buy accompanied by a decent amount of salad garnish. (Dave, you are obsessed with size! – The Ed.) Chicken Chilli balti – excellent, good heat, superb flavour, not the biggest portion, but adequate. (There you go again! – Ed.) Jacs – she who doesn't eat Indian food any more, had the spiced chicken breast with boiled rice, which she said was excellent. Chicken Dhansak – good portion, plenty of pineapple and chicken, but could have been hotter. Pullao Rice – good, light and fluffy. Breads – very good. Highly recommended. £125.00 for seven.' DB.

CHUINI'S

19 King Street, Penrith 01768 866760

Safe-bet curryhouse. Show the manager this Guide and you may get a discount. Hours: 5-12.

TASTE OF BENGAL

60- Strickland Gate, Penrith 01768 891700

Established 1994. Fully licensed and air-conditioned. *'Sunday night at 7.45pm: waiters not geared up for a rush, because two other parties arrived at the same time. Nice to see families with children enjoying a curry experience. Parking difficult, fairly good 'chippy' across the road. Drinks served promptly, but waited for starters. We shared a Mixed Kebab – not really big enough for two, too much for one. Friends ate Onion Bhajia £2.20 and Sheek Kebab £2.70, OK, enjoyed. Naga Curry Masala – based on a special Indian chilli'.* (Actually, Tony, Naga is unique to Bangladesh and VERY hot, rather like a Scotch Bonnet - Pat loves them! Ed) Tony continues: *'I ate the chicken version, marvellous. Lamb Tikka Roghan Josh £6.50, lamb slightly chewy, but not gristly bits. Lamb Pathia £7.50, definitely the hottest dish between us, enjoyed it nevertheless. Chicken Tawa £9.95, expensive, but Nan included, very impressed, very tasty, slices of chicken, served on griddle. Our friends, Julia and Peter, have a spoilt Jack Russell, they always take a couple of pieces of lamb or chicken back it him – but not today, they didn't. Highly recommended.'* T&MH. Thursday Night: choice of starter and main course set meals for £10.95, including Popadoms and Chutneys. Takeaway: 20% discount. Price Check: Popadom 50p, CTM £6.95, Pullao Rice £1.90. Hours: 5 - 11 (Friday / Saturday to 11.30).

Whitehaven

AKASH

3 Tangier Street, Whitehaven 01946 691171

Owners Abdul Karim and MK Rayman and Nurul Hoque's cooking attract a loyal following. Show them this *Guide* and you may get a discount. Takeaway 20% discount. Hours: 12-2.30/6-12.

ALI TAJ

34 Tangier Street, Whitehaven 01946 693085

'This long established curry house gets better with age. Still very good value and excellent food. Good selection of dishes. The service is friendly and good. It is still the best curry house in the area. Very consistent.' RE.

DERBYSHIRE

Area: East Midlands
Population: 980,000
Adjacent Counties: Cheshire, Leics, Greater Manchester, Notts, Staffs, S Yorks

Allestree

EDEN GARDEN NEW ENTRANT

Unit E1, Park Farm Centre 01332 558 555

Restaurant and wine bar (how nice!), with Tapas menu, serving Tikkas, Kebabs, Bhajia and Samosas - delicious! *'The very best, you could taste all the different spices. Relaxed atmosphere.'* L&ST. *'Impressed with the decor, friendly and well informed staff.'* AB & BJ. *'Friendly people, fantastic food with great service.'* M&PT. Menu Snapshot: Harin ke Khazna £13.95, grilled venison, pan fried, garlic, pepper, crushed tomatoes, bay leaves, methi, served with vegetables and rice - one of Lord Mountbatten's favourite dishes, while he was a viceroy; Mumbai Machli £12.95, monk fish, onions, garlic, ginger, tomatoes, whole red chillies, fresh lime leaves, served with rice; Zeera Has £12.95, strips of duck, stir-fried with potatoes, black cumin, curry leaves, twist of orange and lime; Vegetable Makhani £7.95, cauliflower, courgette, aubergine, carrots, peas, turnip, capsicums, sultanas, almonds, pineapple, green chilli and fresh cream; Garlic Tomato Nan £2.30. *'Excellent food, wonderful staff and service. Presentation perfect, tops for ambience.'* JB & TN.. Stocks: Cobra. Price Check: Popadom 60p, CTM £9.95, Pullao Rice £2.30. Hours: 5.30 to 11.

Alfreton

NEW BENGAL

3 King Street, Alfreton 01773 831620

Show F Ahmed this *Guide* and you may get a discount. Hours: 6pm-12am (1am Sat.).

Burton-on-Trent

SPICE OF ASIA

99 Station Street, Burton 01283 517799

'Food of high quality and served by very obliging staff, clean table layout, quality cloths changed between courses, nice flower decorations, comfortable seating with sufficient space between tables, pleasant background music. You can bring your own drinks, with no corkage, hygienic toilets.' BM. Takeaway: 15% discount. Delivery: 5 miles £10 minimum. Hours: 5.30-12, Fri/Sat to 12.30.

Buxton

INDIAN PALACE

5 Cavendish Circus, Buxton 01298 77260

Competent curryhouse. Hours: 5-1130

TAJ MAHAL

35 High Street, Buxton 01298 78388

Mr Koyes Ahmed's Taj Mahal continues to be a popular local venue. *As Buxton is the highest town in England, the Taj Mahal must be a contender for the highest curry house in the country.'* RW.

Castle Donnington

CURRY-2-NIGHT

43 Borough Street 01332 814455

The former Village Tandoori now basks in the new

name Curry-2 -Night. *'Very courteous and attentive service in newly refurbished premises. Onion Bhajia and Chicken Tikka - well presented and Garlic Nan probably one of the best tasted in a long while. Particularly generous Vegetable Balti and Chicken Tikka Masala, good quality and well presented. Will definitely return.'* N&JG. All Tandoori or Tikka Masala dishes are served with Pullao Rice and range in price from £7.80 for chicken to £8.95 for king prawns - good value, I think we all agree! And if you are feeling like a saucy curry, you can order extra portions for as little as £2.50. Price Check: Popadom 50p, CTM £7.80 (inc Pullao Rice), Pullao Rice £1.80. Takeaway: 10% discount, £10 minimum. Delivery: £10 min, 5 miles. Hours: 5.30-11.30 (Friday / Saturday to 12).

Chesterfield

GULAB

207 Chatsworth Rd, Brampton 01246 204612

R Miah and A Rahman's Gulab seats 40 and serves formula curries. Show them this Guide and get a discount. Hours: 6-11.45 (12.45 Fri. / Sat.).

INDIAN BLUES

7 Corporation St, Chesterfield 01246 557505

'Colleagues had praised it. Fairly busy, bar with a handful of drinkers looking as though they had no intention of moving to a table. Usual versions of everything,;not a modern style menu. The candle on the table was lit when we asked but blown out when the food arrived! Brinjal Bhajee £1.85 - disappointing, very undercooked, all other dishes good. Nan £1.30 - excellent, light, crisp and well charred underneath. Food was very good, very reasonable and we really enjoyed the meal.' HC. *'Recommended by 'locals'. Despite not booking, were shown to an excellent window table, offered drinks and popadoms straight away - fresh and excellent. Very good and hot Shami Kebab £2.50. Chicken Pasanda - enjoyed. Mama Halimas Biriani £7.90 (lamb tikka, chicken tikka, king prawn served with chilli and tomatoes, hot and spicy) - served on a silver platter, really excellent, hot, spicy - fabulous! (garnished with enough salad to feed a platoon.) Not exceptional service.'* DL. Price Check: Popadom 40p, CTM £4.50, Pullao Rice £1.20. *'You are immediately struck by the 'accuracy' of this restaurant's name when you enter and are faced with the striking red walls! Mixed Kebab starters very good as was Tandoori Trout. Prawn Puree was slightly odd though with a creamy coconut Korma style sauce, although I think this dish seems to be popular in this region (see also Kaash, Chesterfield). Service was good. Overall opinion – very good, would recommend and return here.'* SO.

KAASH NEW ENTRANT

375 Sheffield Road, Whittington Moor, Chesterfield 01246 261655

'Competent formula curry restaurant almost next door to the excellent Derby Tup pub. Ambience and service good: including an immediate, no-nonsense swap for a dish that I had wrongly ordered and didn't like (there were two very different Prawn Purees on the menu). A pigeon could have figured this out faster than I did (see Indian Blues above)! The quality of the food was also very good including the Karai Gosht and the Balti Chicken Rezala. Overall opinion – very good and would visit again.' SO.

Derby

ABID TANDOORI

7 Curzon Street, Derby 01332 293712

Mohammed Ilyas' 90-seater serves Pakistani and Kashmiri curries. *'This particular evening the food was delicious; it always is. The dishes are always very generous and the service is always quick and the waiters are helpful. It's comfortable but by no means up-class, just right 'but you can BYO, £2.50 a cork.'* NH. Hours: 5.30-3. Branches: Abid, Matlock. (see below) Abid Balti, Causley Rd, Alfreton.

ANOKI NEW ENTRANT & TOP 100

129 London Road Derby 01332 292 888

'Uses high quality tableware and crockery which would not look out of place in any Michelin star establishment. Enter and ascend the stairs, where you are warmly welcomed by your host in traditional dress. Luxurious and very tasteful surroundings, very comfortable high backed chairs with beautifully decorated tables including white linen. On the rear wall, Bollywood movies are projected, but this is not disturbing. Complimentary Popadoms are served, neatly cut into triangles, with a selection of pickles. Menu quite limited, but varied enough, daily specials add variety. Thoroughly enjoyed starters of Paneer Kebab – excellent; Prawn Puri - best I've tasted. Lamb Haandi, Dal Makhani, Pullao Rice and Nan - perfect presentation and exceptional taste. Extensive but pricey wine list. A TOP 100 restaurant.' D&VH. Agreed Ed.

SHABUZ BAGAN

80 Osmaston Road, Derby 01332 296887

Competent curryhouse and *'very friendly'* GAM

Glossop

BULL'S HEAD ALE & CURRY HOUSE

102 Church Street Old Glossop 01457 853 291

There are other curry-serving pubs in this *Guide,* but this one is in *CAMRA's Good Beer Guide* and now in ours. This marriage made in heaven is a first. Old Glossop is a village in the Peaks at the foot of the Penines. The Bull's Head was built in 1604, with stone floors, low beams and open log fire. 390 years later publicans Thea and Steve Hakes moved in and brought with them curry chef, Fais Ahmed. A full curryhouse menu is served evenings only. Price Check: Popadom 75p, CTM £6.20, 1Pullao Rice £1.20. No Juke box or gaming machines. Specials board. Takeaway: 10% discount. Hours: 5.30-10.30 (Sunday 4-10).

Ilkeston

SHAH JAHAN

1 Awsworth Road, Ilkeston 0115 932 3036

Abndul Aziz's restaurant seats just 34 diners and was established in 1984, so please book. Menu Snapshots: Hot Meat £1.90, coconut, garlic, ginger, coriander leaves; Tandoori Mixed Grill £14.95; Keema Biriani £5.25 – keema is one of Pat's favourite curries – big secret!; Cheese and Tomato Nan £1.60. Delivery: 3 miles, £4.95 minimum. Price Check: Popadom 35p (one of the cheapest we know of), CTM £7.60 (inc rice and salad), Pullao Rice £1.50. Hours: 6-12.30, Fri/Sat to 1.30. Branches: Multan, Pakistan; Germany and Australia.

Matlock Bath

ABID TANDOORI

129 Dale Road, Matlock Bath 01629 57400

Mohammed Bashir's 70-seater is in this delightful Peak District spa town, nestling on the River Derwent, with its many pleasant walks and even a cable car to take you to the top of the cliffs. Just the thing to work up an appetite for Chef Maroof's Pakistani and Kashmiri cooking. *'The Lamb Bhuna was huge and excellent. The rice was a little al dente and the Sag Aloo was a disappointment. Massive menu.'* AGR. Delivery: £20 minimum, 5-mile radius. Hours: 6 - 12 (1am Fri./Sat.). Branches: Abid, Derby. *(see above)* Abid Balti, Causley Lane, Alfreton.

Ripley

SHEEZAN II ©

11 Church Street, Ripley 01773 747472

Pakistani and North Indian-style curries in the capable hands of N Hussain (head chef) and M Sharif (manager) since 1983, who may give you a discount if you show them this *Guide.* A/c, 42-seater. Hours: 6-12 (1am weekends).

DEVON

Area: West Country
Population: 1,102,000
Adjacent Counties: Cornwall, Dorset, Somerset

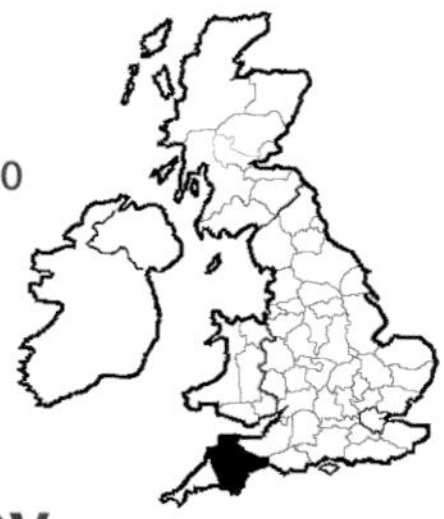

Bovey Tracey

SPICE BAAZAAR

38 Fore Street, Bovey Tracey 01626 835125

'I guess it's pretty well bog-standard, but round here it's gold dust' TR. Hours: 6-11.30.

Exeter

GANDHI

7 New North Road, Exeter 01392 272119

'Remains reliable; friendly staff, tasty. food Keep it in the guide!' CS.

JAMUNA NEW ENTRANT

9 Market Street, Eyemouth 01890 751007

40 seater est 2006 by Humyune Khan. Takeaway: 10% discount. Menu Snapshot: Sag Paneer of Puri £3.95, spinach and cheese on fried bread; Chicken Malaya £5.95, banana, pineapple and almonds; Tandoori Mixed Grill £11.95 - served with salad, but no Nan; Pineapple Curry £2.95. Price Check: Popadom 50p, CTM £7.45, Pullao Rice £2.00. Hours: 12 - 2 and 5 - 11.30.

GANGES

156 Fore Street, Exeter 01392 272630

'This was excellent with a starter of Scallops Masala - something I have not seen before. The remainder of the meal was also good.' JAP.

TAJ MAHAL

50 Queen Street, Exeter 01392 258129

'On a Sunday evening, I expected to find this reasonably empty. It was in fact busy, to their credit, I was found a table - and more importantly was not rushed. The meal was very good, the side dish of dry vegetables was genuinely dry and very tasty.' JAP.

Ilfracombe

BOMBAY PALACE

36 Green Close Road, Ilfracombe 01271 862010

Fully licensed 60 seater owned by R.Miah and family. Show him this *Guide* and he may give you a discount. Offers a variety of curryhouse dishes, with specialities of duck and salmon. Menu Snapshot: Nargis Kebab £2.50, spiced minced meat, wrapped around hard boiled egg; Tomato Bhajee £2.25; Jamdani Biriani £7.50 - chicken and minced meat; Cheese and Onion Nan £1.95. Delivery: 2 miles, £15 minimum. Takeaway: 10% discount. Price Check: Popadom 50p, CTM £6.25, Pullao Rice £1.95. Hours: 5.30 - 11, Saturday to 11.30. Branches: Barnstaple and Exeter.

ILFRACOMBE TANDOORI

14 High Street Ilfracombe 01271 866822

Est 1987. Head Chef: Jamal Miah. Birthday Parties enjoy a complimentary cake. Min Charge: £9.95. Price Check: Popadom 50p, CTM £6.95, Pullao Rice £1.95. Hours: 6 - 11 (Sunday to 10.30). <w:www.ilfracombetandoori.co.uk>

RAJAH TOP 100

5 Portland Street, Ilfracombe 01271 863499

'We stumbled across what can only be described as a piece of curry heaven. Welcomed you into atmospheric surroundings via a very comprehensive and reasonably priced menu. Good ambience and helpful waiting staff. Tantalising smell of orders being prepared was almost too much to bear, but in no way prepared for the cuisine placed in front of us, nothing short of perfect. Having eaten our way through half the meal, we ordered another Nan. This was speedily placed in front of us and just as speedily demolished. Shame we found this piece of heaven on our last day in Ilfracombe. Wish they could post their curries to Hull.' M&JR. *'I and my wife, first went there in 1993 and found it a pleasant, friendly restaurant with attentive and knowledgeable staff. We have visited it once or twice a year most years between then and now, albeit sometimes for takeaways as my young son wouldn't sit still long enough to risk it. Both takeaway and restaurant meals take a while to be prepared they are worth the wait. However, I have tried Chicken Dopiaza and Lamb Rogan Josh and both are different to the 'traditional' fare found where we live in Sutton Coldfield. That said these interpretations are nice in their own way, but do not expect lots of tomatoes in the Rogan Josh. The meat in all the dishes is nice and tender. On our last visit we tried some ribs as starters, unusual for an Indian restaurant. These were I think in a honey based sauce I can't remember exactly. They were delicious and there was a lot of them. The menu is short but includes some dishes not found where we are. The décor of the restaurant lends extra charm and the restaurant when busy seems cosy, comfortable and relaxing, never overcrowded. The standards have remained high on each visit. Finally I must mention the Peshwari Naan, the best I have had.* RGC. Mr Chapman (RGC above. and no relation) has put his finger on why some people like Ralph and Janet Wild's restaurant while a few seem less keen. Put simply it is NOT curryhouse food. For example, there should not be tomatoes or red peppers in the authentic, aromatic Roghan Josh. The dish originated in Moghul Kashmir before such ingredients were 'discovered' in the Americas. See page 96. I used to run this kind of caveat a lot when discussing the food cooked to authentic recipes at our better restaurants. Seems I have to do it again! I for one am happy to keep the Rajah in out elite **TOP 100** slot.

Newton Abbot

PASSAGE TO INDIA

137 Queen Street, Newton Abbot 01626 688443'

Much-liked competent curryhouse.

EASTERN EYE NEW ENTRANT

120 Queen Street, Newton Abbot 01626 352 364

Established 1990. *'Good formula curry restaurant. Some of the food was on the sweet side and slightly heavy on garlic but very enjoyable all the same. Service was first rate with friendly, good-humoured waiters who kept up a good rapport with customers. When complimented on the food, one replied, "It's Indian!" mimicking Sanjeev Baskar from the TV series Goodness Gracious*

Me. It was a good evening.' SO. Delivery: £2, 4 miles. Price Check: Popadom 40p, CTM £5.35, Pullao Rice £1.65. Hours: 12-2 and 5.30 (Friday and Saturday from 5.15) - 11.30 (12 Fri /Sat).

RAJ BELASH

41 Wolborough Street 01626 332057

'Advertises itself as a Nepalese restaurant, yet there are few Nepalese dishes on offer. Never the less, the food was good – Mussels Masala to start with – a pity the mussels had been shelled, with Elaichi Duck, also very good.' JAP. Sunday Buffet: 12.30 to 8, £7.90 adult, £4.50 child. Set lunch: 12 to 2 - Monday to Saturday £8.90 adult. Price Check: Popadom 50p, CTM £6.90, Pullao Rice £1.90. Hours: 12-2.30 (Fri / Sat closed) and 6-11.30 (Friday and Saturday to 12).

Penzance

TAJ MAHAL RE-ENTRANT

63, Daniel Place, Penzance 01736 366630

'Tucked away in a side street off the seafront on the Western side of Penzance, this little gem of a restaurant is extremely hard to find. We had visited here once about 8 years ago but had never been able to find it again in several more visits here. Although well served for eateries, Penzance is gifted with many Indian Restaurants (there are 3). Some unusual choices and a wide range of fish dishes; quality outstanding; quantity more than adequate Decor contemporary. Understated but effective lighting Service prompt, polite if deferential. No request about popadoms when we arrive Comfort: stylish, comfortable chairs, some partitioning, although rather close together. Comments Starters: Lamb Tikka £2.85 well marinated, very tasty. Best I've ever tasted. Taj Mahal Mixed Special £3.45 (Sheek Kebab, Onion Bhaji and Chicken Tikka) all well marinated, deliciously light, well presented and tasty. Main Course: Aman Bujin £7.35 (Chicken Tikka cooked with almond, coconut and mango in a sweet honey sauce. This was well marinated and very sweet and korma like.) Lamb Tikka Marichi £7.35 sizzling hot, very spicy and well marinated. Side Dish: Matar Paneer £2.60 OK but nothing to write home about. Accompaniments: Pullau Rice £1.90 very nice; Peshwari Nan £2.20 a doughy and no syrup; Drinks 1 pint Kingfisher £3.20 and Sparkling Water £1.70 Bill: £32.30 Tip £3 Total £35.30 Mark: 8/10. G&MP.

Plymouth

JAIPUR PALACE

144 Vauxhall Street, Barbican 01752 668711

Syed Wahid's air-conditioned and licensed restaurant, seats 70 diners in two rooms. Menu Snapshot: Chicken Pakoras £2.65 - fried with lentils and green chilli; Chicken Laflong £6.10 - barbecued chicken, Satkora (Indian citrus fruit); Egg Bhuna £3.10; Coconut Rice £2.40. Takeaway: 20% discount. Delivery: 4 miles, £10 min, Mon - Sat, 6.30-11.30. Price Check: Popadom 50p, CTM £7.75, Pullao Rice £2.60. Hours: 12-2, Fri/Sat closed and 5.30-12. Sister takeaway to Jaipur Palace in the Barbican. The menu the same, but the prices are not. Price Check: Popadom 50p, CTM £5.95, Pullao Rice £1.95. Hours: 5-11, Fri / Saturday to 11.30. Branch: Meghna Takeaway, Fore Street, Ivybridge. 01752 698138

MAHA-BHARAT NEW ENTRANT

52 Torwood St, Torquay 01803-215541

'In the three years, that we have lived in the quality-rich but curry-free-zone that is South Devon, w have tried somewhere in the region of 25 restaurants from Plymouth to Teignmouth to Paignton to Torquay. Sometimes we have stuck with a particular restaurant for 3 or 4 months, only to find that the chef leaves and it all goes downhill. We have eaten some of the worst curries ever cooked and we've eaten some pretty good (but never great) curries. You have to understand that we moved here from Berkshire and regularly ate at Madhu's Brilliant, Bombay Brasserie, Madhuban in Liss, Viceroy-of India in Virginia Water and Tiger's Pad in Sunningdale - all great exponents of the skills of cooking great Indian food. Devon was a desert! .... but now we have found an oasis. The restaurant is called Maha-Bharat. It's plain ugly to look at from the outside. I got a recommendation to try it and was surprised to find that inside it's great. The staff are wonderful. They remember my name after only 3 visits. But the food - oh the food is wonderful. We went there last weekend with a group of 9. The waiter looked after the children (3 x 5 year olds - entertaining them with the HUGE fishtank) while we revelled in dhansaks, vindaloos, jalfrezis and bhunas with wonderful naans & parathas. Then the kids were served terrific (unspiced) chicken tikka which they all thought was very grown up. All in all a tremendous restaurant with a great chef and staff that recognise what customers are all about. Up there with the best and after trawling through dozens & dozens of restaurants in South Devon I'm pleased to report that there IS somewhere where it is worth eating Indian food in this part of the world.' AR. *'PS:..just don't be put off by the outside decor! I was ~ BIG mistake!'*

SAJNIZ NEW ENTRANT

487 Christchurch Rd, Boscombe 01202-391391

Situated on a corner premises, Sajniz is long and spacious. It is newly opened and well appointed. The refurbishment is impressive and puts the customer at ease. The furniture is elegant and comfortable and there's plenty of space in a lengthy restaurant with a classy bar. The menu has all your favourites and some new things to try. The following are all worth a try at £8.50: Sajniz Oriental Express, sliced chicken tikka and egg noodles is medium curry and very acceptable; Their Bonnani Chicken, chicken breast with slices peppers, mushrooms and chillies is hot and racy; Asary Lamb is lamb and pickle curry has oomph and good edge and Taal Chicken mixed masala and buna styles to give a warm but mild curry. From the high street standards their Butter Chicken, Dhansak and Ceylon are worth considering and are nor ferociously hot. Sensible variety of vegetable side dishes including Kala Bajee (kidney beans). Be warned, Nan at Sajniuz comes the size of medium blanket and will easily do for two people. They do Banquet Nights on Tuesday and Wednesday and a really fine set meal for two £21.50, four £42.50 and six £55.50. Service is genial and welcoming if a bit slow the night we were there. Very busy at weekends. All told an experience that will make you feel thoroughly spoiled. One feature deserves a double plus – they have a custom built disabled toilet. You feel trouble is taken to please.' RG.

Seaton

RAJPOOT

41 Harbour Road, Seaton 01297 22223

Fully licensed and air conditioned. *'The lights of the Rajdoot, shining like a beacon through the mist and rain, in this quiet, little town. Warm welcome from proprietor brothers Mizzen and Azziz. Comfortable restaurant. I don't know what we did without them!'* JB. Hours: 12 to 2 and 6 to 11.

DORSET

Area: South West
Population: 701,000
Adjacent Counties:
Devon, Hants,
Soms, Wilts

Bournemouth

ANGLO INDIAN

223 Old Christchurch Rd 01202 312132

Runu Miah stocks: Cobra at his Anglo Indian.. Takeaway: 15% discount. Minimum Charge: £8. Price Check: Popadom 50p, CTM £7.15, Pullao Rice £2.15. Hours: 6 to 12. e: runimia@aol.com

Christchurch

STARLIGHT

54 Bargates, Christchurch 01202 484111

Ian Clasper and Abdul Hai might give you a discount if you show them this *Guide.* 12-2/6-12.

Poole

THE GATE OF INDIA

54 Commercial Rd, Lr Parkstone, Poole
01202 717061

Messrs Choudhurys' Gate, established in 1993,

seats 80 in two rooms and is a very popular venue. *'The very posh Poole Yacht Club is not far away and their membership is noticeable here. Poole Hospital doctors and medical staff frequently make up parties and 'The Gate' do a fair number of charity events. Spacious (free in the evening) parking accommodation at the rear. Each visit is a delight. Consistently high standard menu. Long may they prosper.'* RG. Takeaway: 10% discount. Hours: 12-2.30/6-12.

MOONLIGHT

9 Moor Rd, Broadstone , Poole 01202 605234

Reliable house where A.Malik might give you a discount if you show him this *Guide.*

SAMMY'S NEW ENTRANT

193 Bournemouth Rd, Lr Parkstone, Poole 01202-749760

'Sammy's previously trading as the Royal Lahore, offers an enjoyable night out with memorable food. The service, menu and cooking are of a very high standard. But there's much more to it all than that. We visited during the Easter holiday and the place was packed to the ceiling. It was noticeable how many family parties there were; all with children – all having a great old time. This was clearly Sammy's policy, encouraging family visits, parties and children. It pays dividends. The staff are vociferous, jolly, vigorous, helpful, charming and attentive. Lights out for the cake with candles! Enthusiastic choruses of "Happy Birthday to You" with three hearty cheers! This is more than a meal. It is a night out. The menu is very fine and all dishes are cooked to order as you watch them at the grills and ovens with the occasional exciting flare-up (all safely behind glass). Among tasty starters Champ Gosh (marinated lamb chops) £3.80;Chicken Wings £3.00; Liver and Kidney £3.90. There's a goodish selection of standard curry dishes. Chef's Specials include a simply sparling Chilli Chicken (or Lamb or Prawn) laced with dynamic green chillies £6.90; a rich and subtle Tawa Chicken £6.90 and delicious Methi Lamb (or Chicken of Prawn) £6.90. A good range of Masala dishes. and Tandoori main dishes with a Tandoori Mixed Grill as a main dish comes to table at £8.90. A selection of Birianis at £7.50 and Vegetable side dishes include a splendid Muttar Paneer £5.50 and Mixed Bindhi and Karela (okra and bitter gourd) £3.50. Sammy's is to be especially commended for having a well appointed disabled toilet and although the high doorstep makes wheelchair access a bit problematic, they'll all lend a hand to get you aboard and spoil you rotten when you're settled in. Sammy himself circulates among his guests and makes you feel so much more than just a paying customer. Free delivery. Very highly recommended. Not to be missed.' RG. Sammy has another restaurant in adjacent Ashley Road, Poole.

TAJ MAHAL 2

38 High Street, Poole 01202 677315

'Lots of duck speciality dishes. Also served good formula curries. A large group of us proved no problem to the staff on a busy Saturday night. Well worth the visit.' SO.

Sherborne

RAJPOOT

House of Steps, Half Moon St 01935 81245

Bangladeshi specials such as Shatkora and fish dishes are notable as is the discount you might get if you show them this *Guide.*

Wareham

GURKHA NEW ENTRANT

Sandford Road, Sandford, Wareham 01929

Opened 2006, it is Nepalese owned and run, but offers a range of Chinese, Thai and Malaysian as well as Indian and Nepalese dishes. Although it does have an a-la -carte menu, the main theme is an buffet at the very reasonable price of £7.95 for lunch and £11.95 for dinner. *'Despite poor weather and being a Monday in January it was reasonably crowded, which was a good sign, particularly as it's a fairly large restaurant. It must seat 100+ in pleasant, comfortable surroundings, with the modern-style wooden flooring and a bar at one side. More importantly, the buffet counter offered a good selection - nowhere near the 95 of course, but about 30 including two soups, three different rice, noodles and popadoms. In addition there were various vegetable garnishes, pickles and sauces. What's more, the trays were not full so as to gradually get cold and congealed during the evening, but were regularly topped up by small amounts being continuously cooked by several chefs in the open kitchen behind. As I made a total pig of myself I can't recall everything I managed to sample, but I do recall that it was all very good indeed. Amongst the starters I found the onion bhajias excellent - small but very crispy. The Malaysian chicken satay and peanut sauce, and Chinese aromatic duck and pancakes were also very good. Of the main dishes I recall the Nepalese Lamb was particularly tasty - tender lamb in a rich dark and spicy sauce. I mixed different Oriental dishes with abandon ñ Chicken Samrod (Thai hot sweet and sour chicken) with Nepalese Lamb, Chicken in Black Bean Sauce with Gurkha Beef Curry, Nepalese Dall with Chicken Tikka Masala until I had to rest my stomach on the table in exhaustion. It was all delicious..'* MW.

DURHAM

Known as County Durham
Area: North East
Population: 872,000
Adjacent Counties:
Cumbria,
Northumberland,
Tyne & Wear,
N Yorkshire

Bishop Auckland

THE KING'S BALTI

187 Newgate St, Bishop Auckland 01388 604222

Owned by Mohammed Boshir Ali Hussan. Baltis and standard curries on the menu. Chutneys and Pickles 50p a portion but if you buy a jar from an assortment they are £2.50 a jar – brilliant idea! And you might get a discount if you show thm this *Guide.* Hours: 5-12am. (11.30pm on Sun.).

Chester-Le-Street

GOLDEN GATE TANDOORI

11 South Burns Rd, Chester-Le-Street 0191 388 2906

Established in 1993. Seats 45. Ample parking to front. House specials: Kaleeya Beef or Chicken, hot cooked with roast potatoes, marinated in yoghurt. Sylhet Beef or Chicken, strongly spiced, dry with eggs and tomatoes. Takeaway: 10% discount. Delivery: £10 min, 6-mile radius. Hours: 12-2/6-12am.

Darlington

HOUSE OF SPICE

Darlington 01235 532856

The former Prince of India (est 1976) changed hands in 2004 to Abdul Goful, also manages. Menu Snapshot: Bater-e-Masullum £7.95, quail stuffed with pistachio, almond and sultanas, sprinkled with aromatic herbs, roasted on a low heat, served with a smooth cashew nut gravy; Suka King Prawn £10.95, spicy sauce with tamarind; Goan Fried Rice £2.95, fried with prawns, eggs and onions. Takeaway: 20% discount. Delivery: £12 minimum, Abingdon and surrounding area. Sunday Lunch Buffet: £9.50. Price Check: Popadom 60p, CTM £7.50, Pullao Rice £1.90. Hours: 12-2.30/6-11.30, Saturday to 12.

SHAPLA

192 Northgate, Darlington 01325 468920

Established in 1980, SA Khan's 80-seat restaurant is *'Brilliant.'* PJ. *'Excellent.'* DMC. And you might get a discount if you show him this *Guide.* Hours: 12-2 / 6-12am; closed Fri. lunch.

Durham

SHAHEENS INDIAN BISTRO,

48 North Bailey, Durham City 0191 386 0960

'Bright and lively restaurant, pleasantly sited in an old post office on one of the side streets leading up towards the cathedral and castle. As you enter you can't miss the large painting of the Taj Mahal along the right hand wall and the backlit plastic vines, which peep through a wooden latticework suspended just below the ceiling. Sounds awful I know but actually it's OK! King Prawn Puri £5.90, had a good balance between the tomato, herbs/spices and the acidity although it seemed a bit light on the prawns for that price! Mutton Tikka Masala Balti £9.20, was perhaps angling for the most number of Indian Dishes in one name, although as it included rice they could probably have got away with chucking a Biriani in the title somewhere! However, it had a good balance between the spices, the tomato and the rich ghee sauce. The Pullau Rice that accompanied this dish was very pleasantly aromatic and flavoursome. Service was OK. Overall opinion –slightly pricey but good, would recommend and return.' SO. Opens at 6pm.

Stockton-on-Tees

MEMSAHIB'S NEW ENTRANT

Boundary Cottage Farm, Inkerman, Tow Law 01388 731818

You can purchase a whole jar or pickle or chutney at £2.70 each – probably a good idea if you are eating in a large party of perhaps eight or more. Takeaway: 10% discount. Delivery: £10 minimum. Happy Nights: six course set meal £9.50, every Thursday and Sunday. Stocks: Cobra and Kingfisher. Price Check: Popadom 60p, CTM £7.25, Pullao Rice £1.95. Hours: 5.30 to 11, Fri/ Sat/ to 11.30. Branch: Monju Stanley DH9 7OG

ESSEX

Area: Home Counties, (east of London)
Population: 1,640,000
Adjacent Counties: Cambs, Herts, Kent, London, Suffolk

Part of Essex was absorbed by Greater London in 1965. We note affected towns/suburbs.

Benfleet *(includes Thundersley)*

MUMTAZ MAHAL

10 Essex Way, Benfleet 01268 751707

Opened in 1977, Abdur Rahid's Mumtaz is well respected and well liked. Show him this *Guide* and you might get a discount. Large car park adjacent, and inside 90 seats are split over two floors and has a cosy atmosphere. It's all standard stuff, with every variation you can imagine on chicken, lamb, prawns and vegetables, and it's all done *'sumptuously'* IDB

Braintree

CURRY PALACE

28 Fairfield Road, Braintree 01376 320083^

Est. 1975 by MA Noor, whose restaurant seats 52 amidst warm, modern interior with framed canvas art imported from Bangladesh. Show him this *Guide* and you might get a discount. House specials: Balti Chicken Tikka and Chicken Dhansak. Takeaway: 10% discount. Hours: 5.30-11pm; closed Mon.

Burnham-on-Crouch

POLASH

169 Station Road, Burnham 01621 782233

Sheik Faruque Ahmed's fully licensed, air-conditioned restaurant is an old friend. Show him this *Guide* and you might get a discount. Price Check: Popadom 55p, CTM £6.95, Pullao Rice £1.95. Hours: 12 to 3 and 6 to 12. Stocks: Cobra. Branch: 84-86 West Road, Shoeburyness, Essex. 01702 294721

Chelmsford
(includes Great Baddow and Writtle)

ESSENCE INDIAN ON THE GREEN

NEW ENTRANT

30 The Green Writtle 01245 422228

You've guessed it, this huge 200-cover restaurant overlooks the village green, furthermore this is nth reincarnation of an Indian restaurant on this site.. Essence has a contemporary interior with a soft neutral background enhanced with inviting pictures that reflect the history of Writtle and the essence of India. Pre-dinner drinks are on offer in the Piano Lounge, where diners can sit back and relax in comfortable leather sofas, sipping on a cocktail and view pictures of famous patrons of the restaurant's other branches that decorate the walls. Essence serves an extensive Indian & Bangladesh combined menu, with a large choice of intriguing fish dishes and chef specials that are put together by Head Chef Jahanger Hussain. Essence is the latest venture of the Essence Group, a family run business established in 1998 and owned by Sharife Ali, Tariq Ali, Abi Kabir, Farouk Ullah and

Sam Uddin. They have three other sites - Chadwell Heath, Romford, Essex; Redhill,Surrey and Sedgley, West Midlands. Puja Vedi, Ed Tandoori Magazine.

TAJ MAHAL

6 Baddow Rd, Chelmsford 01245 259618

'Formerly Taj Mahal, when it was a fairly standard restaurant, but they have now refurbished it along the modern, trendy lines of chrome and pale wood.' MW. *'Despite the redec, the food remains the same and I like it!'* RL. Price Check: Popadom 50p, CTM £5.30, Pullao Rice £2.20. Hours: 12 to 2.30 and 5.30 to 12.

Clacton-on-Sea

EAST INDIA TAKEAWAY

182 Old Road, Clacton 01255 427 281

Manager: MA Salam. Price Check: Popadom 45p, CTM £5.60, Pullao Rice £1.90. Hours: 5 - 11.30, Sat - 12.

Colchester

SAGARMATHA GURKHA

2 St Botolphs Circus 01206 579438

Established in 1999. Formerly called Oriental House. Seats 42. There are of course many if not all your old favourites on the menu, and done well too, as they are so often by Nepalese chefs. Specialities include: traditional Nepalese 'village' meal (£9.95), the most unusual dish being Shanjali Kukhura (chicken marinated in ginger, green chilli, herbs and spinach). Two large car parks with CCTV in front and rear. Takeaway: 10% discount. Delivery: £15, 5-miles. Hours: 12-2/5.30-11.30.

Dunmow

JALSA GHAR QUEEN VICTORIA

79 Stortford Road, Dunmow 01371 873 330

Owner: Iqbal Chowdhury. Situated in a public house - Queen Victoria. Established October 1998. Menu Snapshot: Crispy Sardines £4.50 - marinated and shallow fried; Vegetable Roulade £3.50 - spiced vegetables, rolled in Indian pastry; Peanut Chicken £7.70 - lightly spiced with lime and lemongrass; Lamb Chop Bhuna £7.70 - hot; Kashmiri Rice £2.50 with pineapple; Coriander Nan £2.10. Takeaway: 10% discount, minimum order £10. Stocks: Cobra. Price Check: Popadom 50p, CTM £7.20, Pullao Rice £2.10. Hours: 12 to 2.30 and 6 to 11, Friday and Saturday to 11.30. Sunday 12 to 10.30. e: <www:jalsaghar.co.uk>

Epping

RAJ

75 High Street, Epping 01992 572193

Mumin Ali tells us his 40-seater is *'beautifully decorated with artificial plants with coziness and elegance'.* Chef Abdul Ali cooks formula curries. *'Good quality food.'* SR. Delivery: £10 min, 5-mile radius. Hours: 12-2.30/6-12am.

Gants Hill (Greater London)

KANCHANS TOP 100

53 Perth Road, Gants Hill 020 8518 9282

Location, location, location', they say. And it is almost on the roundabout, near the tube, with a huge plate glass window with large ornately carved wooden double door with brass studs. Unmissable. But is Gant's Hill in suburban Essex the right location. Only time will tell. Because this restaurant is a real cut above anything for miles around. Inside it's a beautifully decorated restaurant, with creamy walls, crystal mirrors, Indian artifacts, lavish upholstery and place settings. Upstairs is a huge banqueting suit which is ideal for large family-and-friend parties. And does well for smaller Asian weddings. The owners have run a standard curryhouse down the road for years, but they decided to do the job properly. The chefs all imported from India, cook authentic Punjabi Indian curries and accompaniments - everything wonderful from the spicy Lamb Knuckle to the Black Urid Dal. Definitely worthy of our **TOP 100**. Gants Hill is very lucky indeed. Parking at rear. Cover charge £1.50. Hours: 12-3/6-11.30.

Heybridge

HEYBRIDGE TANDOORI

5 Bentalls Centre, Heybridge 01621 858566

Abdul Rofik, Abdul Hannan and Nazrul Islam's 70-seater, decorated in bright colours with blue tablecloths, pink napkins, has a non-smoking room. The centre has ample 24hr security-guarded car parking facilities. *'Excellent. Everything well presented, fish specials were superb, attentive service. Four non-regular curry eaters have become converted.'* SJ. Fish specials include Chandpuri Hilsha, Boal, Ayre and large Chingri (prawns). Delivery: £10 minimum, 3-mile radius. Hours: 12-2.30/6-11.30 (Sat. to 12am.).

Hockley

KERALAM

200 Main Rd, Hawkwell, Hockley 01702 207188

'The only South Indian in the area. As good as those in Tooting and Kerala itself, which I know well. Dosas could not be bettered. Interesting vegetables like beetroot. Staff friendly, prices reasonable, well worth a detour.' JAR. Menu extracts: Bhelpoori £2.50, poori, puffed rice crispies, potato, green chilli, sweet and sour sauces. Squid Fried, marinated squid served with salad Trivandrum style. Cashew Nut Pakoda, batter fried cashew nuts served with Date Chutney. Masala Dosa, rice and lentil pancake filled with potato and onion masala, served with Sambar and Coconut Chutney. Malabar Meen Moli , kingfish cooked with tomatoes, tamarind, onion, garlic, ginger and garnished with coconut milk and curry leaves. Kerala Erachi Olarthiathu, boneless pieces of lamb fried with fresh sliced coconut and herbs. Fully licensed .Delivery: £15 min, 3 miles. Hours: 5.30-11.30.

Hornchurch

CINNAMON SPICE

10 Tadworth Pde, Elmpark 01708 478510

Syed Ahmed Stocks: Cobra. Price Check: Popadom 50p, CTM £6.85, Pullao Rice £1.95. Service charge: 10%. Delivery: £10 minimum, 3 miles radius. Hours: 5 to 12.

Ilford (Greater London)

(inc Goodmayes, Newbury Park and Seven Kings)

CURRY SPECIAL TOP 100

2 Greengate Pde, Horns Rd, Newbury Pk, Ilford 020 8518 3005

Family-run by GL and Paul Luther, Punjabi Kenyan Asians. They are related to the Southall Anands (*see* Brilliant and Madhu's, Southall, Middlesex), resulting in a different menu from that at the formula curry house. This is the real taste of the Punjab – savoury, powerful, delicious and satisfying, and as near to Punjabi home-food as you'll get in Britain. The family signature dishes are Karai Mexican Mixed Vegetables, and the renowned Butter Chicken, Jeera Chicken and Chilli Chicken. A full portion for four is £12-13. Half-portion £6.50-7. These are starters, and are huge. And the fun is to go in large parties and share each of these. That's the way the local Asians enjoy it, leaving lots of room and lots of choice for the main course. Clues to the Luthers' Kenyan background is also in the menu. Mogo Chips are fried cassava, £3 and Tilipa Masala is an African fish curry, starter £3, main £6.50.Try the Kenyan Tusker lager. *'Food brilliant, authentic and interesting. Service quite slow but well worth the wait. Definitely not run of the mill. Worth the TOP 100 status.'* SJ. Remains in our **TOP 100**. Hours: 12-2.30, Tues.-Fri./6-12 daily; closed Mon.

HAWA BENGAL

530 High Rd, Seven Kings 020 8599 9778

Mr Bashir Ullah is the owner-chef here, while Mr Hudda Kabir runs front of house. *'We visit regularly and find the staff very helpful, pleasant and knowledgeable and have sampled many of their dishes. We have also been guinea-pigs on occasions and had the opportunity to try new and tasty dishes not yet on the menu. Our favourites are Sag Chicken, CTM, Balti Chicken, Chicken and Mushroom Biriani and especially the Dilkush Special.'* AN. Hours: evenings only.

JALALABAD TOP 100

247 Ilford Lane, Ilford 020 8478 1285

55-seater established in 1977 by Nazrul Islam (head chef) and Badrul Islam (manager). It serves 'good-as-they-get' formula curries. Diane says it all really: *'We went there on it's recommendation in the guide. Fantastic! Excellent food, lovely people and comfortable surroundings. Prices are inexpensive and they also provide a delivery service. We haven't gone anywhere else since we discovered it. Absolutely deserves its place in the Top 100.'* DA. Stays safely in our **TOP 100**. Delivery: £15 minimum, 3-mile radius. Hours: 12-2.30/6-12 (1am on Fri. & Sat.).

JALALABAD 2 NEW ENTRANT & TOP 100

992 Eastern Avenue, Newbury Park 0208 590 00 00

New branch of the above. has attracted the likes of

world embassy champion snooker player Ronnie O, Sullivan. Menu details the same. *'My first impression was pleasant surprise. The décor was of high quality minimalism. I was greeted at the door by the waiter, who showed me to my seat, followed up by the menu. I was intrigued by the variety of the cuisine available, but could not make my mind up, so I was recommended the Chefs special biryani (£7.95) – succulent chicken, lamb, prawns and mushrooms, alongside the Peshwari chicken – cooked in an exotic sauce topped with onions and garlic garnished with fresh coriander. I also ordered a side order of Bombay Aloo (£2.50) a spiced potato, which dipped in the chef,s special sauce tasted exquisite. I was particularly taken in by the Motka Kulfi dessert (£2.50) which came in an exclusive ceramic pot filled with highly luxurious rich saffron and pistachio flavoured ice cream topped with nuts. Bollywood music videos play on a large widescreen television to depict the exotic and carry on the theme of the Indian cuisine.'* FA. Delivery: £15 minimum, 4-mile radius. Hours:6-11.

MOBEEN

80 Ilford Lane, Ilford 020 8553 9733

The owners of this chain of Pakistani caffs are strict Muslims, so BYO is not permitted and it's unlicensed. Go for darned good, inexpensive, value-for-money, Punjabi, Kebabs, tandoori items and curries of all sorts, selected from the counter, with specials varying from day to day. No credit cards. No smoking. Can be heaving with local Asians, who know you won't find better food, and which adds to a fab atmosphere. Being Punjabi, it's a bit short of vegetarian fodder, but for those, see next entry. Hours: 11am-10pm. Branches: Mobeen, 229 High Street North, London E6; Mobeen, 222 Green Street, London E7; Mobeen, 725, High Road, Leyton, London E10.

SRI RATHIGA NEW ENTRANT

312 High Road, Ilford 020 8478 7272

Treasure this one please Ilford! Raj Mohan Ramadass' restaurant specialises in Tamil Nadu cuisine – fabulous south Indian food – none of your curryhouse here. So our advise is not to ask for the kormas and the CTMs. Try things form this snapshot of what you can expect to eat: Thayir Vada £1.95 - fried doughnut made of black gram batter, ginger, onions, green chilli, curry leaves and cumin, then soaked in seasoned and tempered yoghurt; Cashew nut Pakoda £3.95, nuts dipped in spicy batter and deep-fried; Chicken 65 £4.95, fried bone chicken marinated and fried, served with cucumber, onions and lemon; Mutton Mysore £6.95, with ginger, garlic, coriander leaves and red chillies; Rasam £1.95, hot pepper soup of tomatoes, tamarind and spices; Ghee Roast Masala Dosa £4.95, crisp pancake, roasted in butter, filled with potato masala, served with sambar (lentil curry) and chutneys; Uthappam £3.50, rice and lentil flour, topped with chopped, onions, green chillies, tomatoes, curry leaves and ginger, served with sambar and chutneys; Nandu Varuval £7.95, fried crab curry; Vazhakkai Poriyal £3.25, green banana curry. Delivery: £15 minimum, 2 mile radius. Stocks: Cobra. Takeaway: 10% discount. Price Check: Popadom 50p, Chicken Chettinad £5.95, cooked with curry leaves and mustard seed, Pullao Rice £1.95. Hours: 12 to 3/6 to 11, Saturday to 12. <www.srirathiga.co.uk>. Could Ilford get third TOP 100? Reports please.

SURUCHI

506 High Road, Ilford 020 8598 2020

Cuisine is a strange combination of: South Indian and Chinese. Specialists in vegetarian dishes, Indian style, including such favourites as: Bhel Puri £2.95, Masala Dosas £3.25, Onion Uttappa £3.25, Vada (2) with chutney and Sambar £2.50. If you prefer a little Chinese delicacy, try the Mogo Chilli Fry £3.50, Spicy Szechuan Noodles £3.50, Spinach and Bean Sprouts with dry chillies £3.50. All sounds great to me!! Service charge: 10%. Takeaway: 10% discount. Lunch Special: three courses £4.99 – good value. Hours: 12 -3/6- 12.

Leigh-on-Sea

MUGHAL DYNASTY

1585 London Road, Leigh 01702 470373

Nazram Uddin's pretty, upmarket 68-seater, serves tandooris, starters, curries and all the favourites and is a popular local.

TAJ MAHAL

77 Leigh Road, Leigh 01702 711006

Established in 1973 and owned by Shams and Noor Uddin, manager and chef respectively. Seats 70; it's hugely popular. Recently refurbished. *'Wide menu, generous portions, service attentive and prompt. We have never had to complain in seven years.'* AGH. Specials include: Rason Mirchi, Chingri Ballichow, Chanda Fry, Lamb in Plum Sauce, Sweet and Sour King

Prawns, Pomfret-Fried. *'Has maintained an admirable reputation for consistency of quality. Excellent reasonably priced food, produced in visibly hygienic conditions. Friendly, efficient service to both old and new customers. I personally still find the Chicken Vindaloo my favourite.'* GSH. Hours: 12-2.30/6-12.

Ongar

VOJAN

Epping Road, Ongar 01277 362293

Proprietor Jamal Uddin's restaurant is worthy of notice. It has a separate bar area with comfy chairs. *'Bright and welcoming decor. Very clean and attentive waiters. Live music on Wednesday evenings. Adequate quantities of food, overall a good restaurant - recommended.'* DC. Menu extracts: Goan Crab and Mussel Puri £4.50, freshly cooked with garlic and medium spices, served on deep-fried bread. Sulimoni Kebabs £4.75, kebabs served with sliced herbal cheese. Lobster Delight £21.95, one big lobster, sweet and sour spicy gravy of red chilli, onions, tomatoes and garlic. Chilli Aubergine Bhajee £8.95, cooked in yoghurt, flavoured with peanuts and fresh coconut. Sunday Buffet: served from 1-10, £9.95 adult and £4.95 child. Hours: 12-2.30/5.30-11, Friday and Saturday to 11.30. Sunday 1-10.

Rayleigh

RAYLEIGH SPICY TAKEAWAY

159 High Street, Rayleigh 01268 770769

Fully licensed and air conditioned. Formerly Curry Palace. Smallish restaurant seating just 36 diners. Delivery: £10 minimum, 4 miles radius. Price Check: Popadom 50p, CTM £5.50, Pullao Rice, £1.70. Popular dishes include: Chicken Tikka Kushbu £5.95, tangy, aromatic, bhuna style. Hours: 5.30 to 11.30, Saturday to 12, Sunday to 11.

Romford (Greater London)

ASIA SPICE

62 Victoria Road, Romford 01708 762623

Originally opened in 1970 as India Garden and under the present management (Yeabor Ali) since 1975. A medium-sized restaurant seating 54 diners. Branch: Rupali, South Woodham Ferrers, Essex.

Shoeburyness

POLASH

84 West Rd, Shoeburyness 01702 293989

The Polash and its slightly younger branch have been in our *Guide* since we began, which makes them old friends to these pages. Manager SA Motin tells us his decor is 'wonderful, air conditioned, with water fountain'. But there's a third Polash in the same ownership. Not in Essex, nor even Britain. It's in Sylhet, Bangladesh, the town where so many of our curry-house workers come from. Polash is the best hotel in town, and their restaurant, the Shapnil, has an item on its 200-dish menu that amazed us when we visited. Item 95 is no less than CTM! It is the only place in the whole of Bangladesh where it is to be found. And, says owner Sheik Faruque Ahmed, 'it sells really well!!!' His UK partner, M Khalique, agrees. *'The food was beautifully prepared, tasty and the right strength. Service excellent. Atmosphere relaxed and friendly.*

Red Dragon

Coco Passion

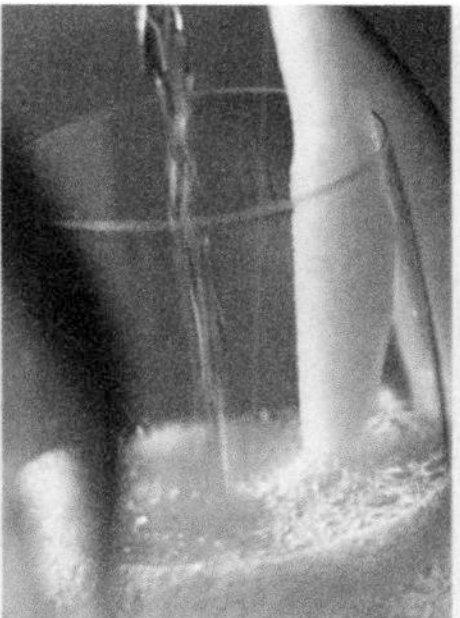
Monsoon

Indian Cosmopolitan

Delicious cocktails form La Porte Des Indes Restaurant, W1. Recipes in La Porte des Indes Cookbook.

Despite the fact that the proprietor informed us that they did not give CC discount on a Saturday, they accepted the coupon and gave us a discount of 10%.' BP-D. Minimum charge £10. Hours: 12-2.30 /6-12; Sun. 12am-12pm. Branch: Polash, Burnham on Crouch.

Southend-on-Sea

KERALAM

28 Clifftown Road, Southend 01702 345072

Said it about Ilford and I'll say it here too. Treasure this one please Southend, especially as it is easy to find, being opposite Southend railway station.! It is another south Indian restaurant, and with it. Mr Sadique's vibrant fresh food breaks away from the curryhouse mould. Don't think that all South Indian food is vegetarian or fish dishes – not true – chicken and lamb feature very nicely. Menu Snapshot: Kappa and Meen Curry £3.95, cassava, herbs, spices, served with fish curry; Kadkka Porichathu £3.25, fried mussels; Erachi Olarthiathu £5.95, lamb fried with fresh sliced coconut (one of Pat's favourites); Malabar Meen Birinani £6.95, marinated Kingfish, onion, cashew nuts, sultanas, curry leaves and rice, served with coconut chutney, raita and salad; Avial £3.25, fresh vegetables cooked with coconut, yoghurt, cumin, curry leaves and spices; Kaipanga Varatiathu £3.25, curry leaves, mustard seeds, cumin, fennel, deep-fried bitter gourd and puréed fresh coconut; Pickle Tray is expensive at £2. I hope it contains some tasty home-made delicacies! *'The food is as good as ever.'* JAR.. Stocks: Cobra. Price Check: Popadom 50p, Cheera Chicken £5.25, Pullao Rice £1.75. Hours: 12 to 2.30 and 5.30 to 11.30, Sunday to 11. Reports please.

Westcliff-on-Sea

SHAGOOR

Hamlet Court Road,Westcliff 01702 347461

'Very large and beautifully decorated. Appearance of restaurant and staff very clean and tidy. Noorandi kebab - very pleasant, chicken and vegetable patties. Garlic Chilli Chicken - good. Tandoori King Prawn Masala - excellent, not over cooked.' AS. Highly commended by SS.

GLOUCESTERSHIRE

Area: South West
Population: 821,000
Adjacent Counties:
Bristol, Gwent,
Somerset, Wilts

With the demise of Avon as a county in 1997, Gloucestershire has regained territory which was taken from it when Avon was formed in 1965.

Cheltenham

CURRY CORNER

131 Fairview Rd, Cheltenham 01242 528449

Established in 1977. Seats 40 in two rooms. Tudor style interior. Specials include: Shagar Anna, Sweet Sylheti Surprise and Mughal Shahi. Takeaway: 10% discount. Hours: 5.30-11.30.

INDIAN BRASSERIE

146 Bath Road, Cheltenham 01242 231350

A pretty 56-seater in pastel shades with cane furniture, managed by A Rakib. CS still thinks it's the best in town. *'Waiters always very cheerful and friendly; there's a nice atmosphere.'* Branch: Dilraj Tandoori, Dursley.

KASHMIR RESTAURANT

1 Albion Street, Cheltenham 01242 524288

Fully licensed and air-conditioned at Abdul Rauf's Kashmir. . Very ordinary looking establishment from the pavement, but step inside and it is a modern and stylish family restaurant. Stocks: Cobra. Price Check: Popadom 50p, CTM £6.75, Pullao Rice £1.95. Takeaway: 10% discount. Delivery service. Hours: 12 to 2 / 6 to 12.

Dursley

DILRAJ

37 Long Lane, Dursley 01453 543472

Standard menu. *'Delicious, ample portions, very relaxed and friendly. Excellent'* IB.

Gloucester

BABURCHI

42 Bristol Road, Gloucester 01452 300615

Formerly The Paradise. *'The menu is certainly very similar to what it was previously and it's still my favourite in Gloucester.'* CS. *'Better than ever (following a fire). Wide range of meals, service is good and prices reasonable eg: Onion Bhajia , CTM. I enjoy vegetarian meals on occasions and the menu has a Special Vegetarian Dishes section. Particularly like the Vegetable Jeera. Well worth a visit.'* DT.

Newent

NEWENT TAKEAWAY

34 Broad Street, Newent 01531 822748

'Murgh Jalable Jeera Gosht, Chicken Tikka Paneer, all three very good, the Murgh sweet and hot, Jeera smokey and meaty, the Tikka a strange but successful use of cheese in an Indian sauce. We'd have loved to try more! One of the best takeaways we've had. Decent sized portions, rice average, but flavours were the great attraction.' RB. Price Check: Popadom 50p, CTM £5.75, Pullao Rice £1.85. Hours: 5 to 11.30, Saturday to 12.

Tewkesbury

RAJSHAHI

121 High Street, Tewkesbury 01684 273727

'From strength to strength, that's how the Rajshahi has grown. Reputation with local, business visitors, tourists and boat people (the rivers Severn and Avon join at Tewkesbury) make it necessary to book to ensure a table. Warm, fresh Popadoms and tangy pickles. were washed down with draught Cobra, followed by lovely Meat Samosas, Chicken Tikka Roghan Josh, Sag Aloo, Pullao Rice and Nan. The Pistachio Kulfi was beautifully present, delicious and not rock hard as is often the case.' TE. Takeaway: 10% discount. Delivery: 3 mile radius. Licensed. Price Check: Popadom 45p, CTM £6.10, Pullao Rice £2.00. Hours: 6 to 12, Friday and Saturday to 12.30.pm

Thornbury

MOGHULS BRASSERIE

8 High Street, Thornbury 01454 416187

'Converted Inn, wood panelling, low beams. Waiters very smart, food formula curry house. Tasty Sheek Kebab, Ayr-Biran – colleague had to contend with bones [well, fish often do have bones!], removed the relish tray. King Prawn Dhansak, nicely sauced, prawns overcooked. Service OK.' MS. Hours: 12-2/6-11.30.

MUMTAZ INDIAN

7 St Mary's Centre, Thornbury 01454 411764

The Mumtaz is on two levels. The downstairs seating area and small bar are for takeaway customers and perusal of the menu. The restaurant is upstairs. *'Menu not too extensive, but food extremely good and large portions. Clean European-style decor and music! Very helpful staff and friendly. Would go back.'* WW. KB was less enthusiastic about the decor and other reports talk of standard curries of generous proportions. AE-J found the Phal too hot on one occasion and too mild on another, although his fiancée *'loves the Kormas'. 'good'* G & MP. Evenings only.

HAMPSHIRE

Area: South
Population:
(5th largest)
1,664,000
Adjacent Counties:
Berks, Dorset,
Surrey,
Sussex, Wilts

Aldershot

JOHNNIE GURKHA'S

186 Victoria Road, Aldershot 01252 328773

'Glad to see the restaurant is still as seedy as ever, although it's not quite so easy to accept since the prices are now as much as anywhere else. Mint sauce is excellent. Famous Dil Kusa Nan – an enormous bread topped with cherries and coconut.' PD. *'Food is very plentiful, beautifully cooked and spiced and nothing was left!'* JW.

Alresford

SHAPLA

60 West Street, Alresford 01962 732134

'A group of retired officers of The Royal Hampshire Regiment, who are addicted to curries, meet once a year as members of The Vindaloo Club (15 of us). A fortnight previously I'd

visited and explained to manager, Mr Moon, what I wanted. Much pleasure in letting you know — my instructions were carried out to the letter. Poppadoms the largest I have ever seen, extremely tasty Lamb Vindaloo and Garlic Chilli Chicken.' JK.

Alton

ALTON TANDOORI

7 Normandy Street, Alton 01420 82154

48-seater, owned and managed by M Shahid. *'Usual menu with a few unusuals. Linda's special comprising Tikka Chicken with spinach and chickpeas was underspiced and bland. Meat Vindaloo was hot and rather good. Nice dry poppadoms, flavoursome rice. Excellent service.'* MG. *'Greeted by the manager like long lost friends. Service was very good. There were 14 of us, and we were treated well. Food was excellent. Madras Chicken, Meat Rogan, Chicken Morrissa (beautifully spiced and hot, succulent chicken). Rice, Bhajis, Naans, all superb. We were very impressed.'* JW. Hours: 6-11.15.

Andover

MUGHAL

33 Andover Rd, Ludgershall 01264 790463

'A visit to the Mughal is deeply reassuring. Some things have not yielded to the modish and the silly, but have stuck to good old fashioned ways of doing things. The Moghal continues to do those things very well. Situated at the end of what is otherwise an unremarkable 1960's row of village shops, is this little gem. Pleasant staff ready and willing. Chicken Tikka Roll - chopped tikka bhuna covered with fresh Nan, delicious Chicken Chat, generous Mixed Kebabs, brilliant Butter Chicken, Shahi Lamb and Chicken Tikka Jal Frezi. Long live the Mughal.' RG.

Basingstoke

BENGAL BRASSERIE

4 Winchester Street, Basingstoke 01256 473795

Fully licensed and air-conditioned. *'The food has always been very good, but service is often slow, poor, amateur and generally inept. New manager has made a monumental different. Very "hands-on," with much flattery and chat - a marked influence for the better. Most enjoyable.'* HC. And then two weeks later .... *'On previous visits the service had improved so much, we had high hopes. Back to square one. New senior waiter did not write down order and that is probably why he brought two mineral waters instead of one, one Mushroom and one Pullao Rice instead of two Mushroom and the wrong main course. Delivery of food always been slow but this time it excelled itself for non-arrival. On the door step at 6pm, another table was served before us, we were told they were busy with takeaways, but all the time we were there, only one takeaway collected. Had to make do with my fourth choice as fish was still frozen! Surely on a Friday night they must need a small number of fish dishes, no wonder they don't sell any. All sounds very negative and depressing, but in fact the staff are so nice and the food absolutely superb, so we tend to bear it all.'* HC. Takeaway: 15% discount, £10 minimum. Price Check: Popadom 60p, CTM £6.95 Pullao Rice £2.10.
<www.bengalbrasserie.co.uk

KASHMIR

4 Church Street 01256 842112

'We're regulars here when we're in Basingstoke for concerts at the Anvil, partly because it is the nearest and luckily the best. Food always good but on the most recent visit it really hit an all time high, every dish was exceptionally good. It is a joy to find a restaurant that is not let down by its service.' HC. *'Waited for over an hour for the food (usual marvellous quality) to arrive. Busy with takeaways. Not impressed.'* HC. *'Redeemed itself on Friday, table was laid in favourite corner, even having two bottles of our usual wine. By design or accident the hopeless waiter was kept occupied behind the bar. All impressed with food, general ambience, everything about the restaurant. Can understand why we keep returning.'* HC . *'Reported previously that very disillusioned, but virtually forced to go back, as torrential rain and it was the nearest. Food as good as ever, if not better - Fish Tava - with tomato, garlic and lots of pepper, very good, but service hadn't changed - not a glimmer of recognition, not a word was said not related to order - quite extraordinary. Very great shame as kitchen obviously very competent, deserve better serving staff. £38 for two - good value.'* HC Delivery Service.. Delivery. Hours: 12-2.30 (closed Sun lunch .)/6pm-12am.

Emsworth

TASTE OF INDIA

45 High Street, Emsworth 01243 376 669

First opened in 1985, Tufail Ahmed took it in 2003 and renamed it from the Standard to Taste of India. A small restaurant (so book!), seating just 28 curryholics. Usual favourites include: Chicken Pakora £2.50, Prawn Dhansak £4.75, Tandoori Mixed Grill £7.95 - served with salad, (but no mention of bread) and Vegetable Biriani £5.75. Expensive Pickle Tray at £1.50. Price Check: Popadom 50p, CTM £5.50, Pullao Rice £1.95. Hours: 12-2 and 5.30-11.20, Saturday to 12.

Fareham

CAFE TUSK NEW ENTRANT

24 West Street Fareham 01329 235511

A new and exciting formula - the Indian Buffet - seating 170. Several display islands, each containing piping hot Indian food, from the very mildest Korma through to Vindaloo. Generous portions are assured, as you quite simply help yourself from the forty lunch and sixty dinner dishes. Prices: Lunch: £6.99 - Monday to Friday, £8.50 - Saturday, Sunday and Bank Holidays. Dinner: £12.99 - Sunday to Thursday; £13.99 - Friday and Saturday. Discounts for children. Hours: 12-3, Sat & Sun - 4 / 5.30 - 11.30, daily Sunday to 11.

Farnborough

GURKHA PALACE

78 Farnborough Rd, Farnborough 01252 51155

The home of the Gurkhas, Church Crookham, is no longer. And huge numbers of Britain's favourite warriors are being disbanded. Throwing the baby out with the bath water, we think. One legacy, fortunately for curry-lovers, is the relatively high number of Nepalese restaurants in this area of Hampshire. This is one where the food is authentic, the staff are Nepalese, and they serve a good range of formula curries too. . Branch: Gurkha Palace, Liphook, Hants. Hours: 12-2.30/6-11.

POPADOMS

33 Medway Drive, Cove 01252 376869

The 36-seater is painted cream and earthy red, the woodwork indigo blue, the furniture is simple wood giving an airy feeling. Swathes of cream, red and blue hang from the ceiling. Nepalese Bikash Devkota is manager. Sanjiv Singh's specials include: Chicken Monsourri – chicken tikka in hotsauce with chillies and soy. Delivery: £8 min. Hours: 6-10.30.

Fleet

GULSHAN INDIAN

264 Fleet Road, Fleet 01252 615910

'Greeted in a most friendly way. The restaurant appeared to be divided into two halves, one for couples and well-behaved diners, one for noisy oiks – what a good idea.' [and which are you?]. CP. *'Standard is consistently high. It has to be one of the best restaurants in Hampshire and Surrey. We use as our local takeaway and their food is of a consistently high standard and good value for money. If you spend £15 you receive a free Onion Bhajia and if you spend over £20 you receive a mystery dish which is a very tasty little chicken number! They are always pleased to see you. Sixteen of us went for a curry at 10pm. Superb food. Excellent service.'* JW.

THE GURKHA SQUARE

NOMINATED BEST NEPALESE

327 Fleet Road, Fleet 01252 810286

Of the several Nepalese restaurants in the area, reports received place this one at the top. And it is actually patronised by Nepalese. This 67-seater, owned by AB Gurung, managed by Om Gurung, is as good as you'll find. *'Rather twee and overrated.'* MG. *'Delighted to see the Gurkha Square in the* **TOP 100**. *My wife and I can certainly back this up. Perhaps slightly on the pricey side, but superb value for money. We particularly like the Mis-Mas, and the rice and naan are quite excellent.'* DT. *'Comfortable, polite service, excellent food.'* GR. Delivery: 3-mile radius. Hours: 12-2.30/6-11.30

WE THE RESTAURANT

NEW ENTRANT

333 Fleet Road, Fleet 01252 628889

Sammi Choudhury opened this curiously-named Indian / Thai restaurant in 2003. The design is by top Bangladeshi architect Enamul Karim Nirjhar with modern, clean decor, waterfalls and coi-carp pools targeted at the top end of the market, as its prices show. Sammi's claim to fame was the night Prince William booked for 40 army chums from nearby Sandhurst for their pre-passing-out blow-out. Sammi revealed to this publication that Wills ate CTM and ordered seconds, and that he drank Jack Daniels and Coke. Flushed with success Sammi placed an ad in the local rag proclaiming that *'you too eat the same food as heir two to the throne at £19.95'*. The menu(s) are comprehensive and here's a Snapshot: Indian starters: Shark Bhuna £ 12.95, cooked in a spicy thick sauce; Indian Tantaliser £5.50, including Lamb Tikka, Chicken Tikka, Chithol Koftha and Vegetable Koftha; Mains: King Prawn Roshney £ 14.95, cooked with garlic, green chilli, tomato, green peppers and onion and Chicken / Lamb Satkara £ 10.95, with a citric vegetable from Eastern Bangladesh. Thai starters: Prawn Crackers £ 2.95; Pak Tod £ 5.50, deep-fried mixed vegetables in a light batter, served with a sweet chilli dip. Tom Yum Kai £ 5.95, Chicken soup cooked in a herb broth with mushrooms, lime leaves, lemon grass, galangal, fresh chilli and coriander. Thai Main: Red Duck Curry £ 10.95, cooked in a Thai red curry sauce, coconut milk, and kaffir lime leaves. The wine list is remarkable: House whites and reds start at £10.95 but the Lafite Rothschild, vintage unknown, sells at £399.95, as does Louis Roederer Cristal champagne, billed as the *'ultimate'*. Personally I put Krug into that position, but this is a curry *Guide* and if you can afford it you , go for it. Price Check: Popadom 75p, CTM £8.50, Tarka Dhal £3.50, Pullao Rice £2.50, Naan £2.25. Hours 12 - 230/6 - 11. <www.wetherestaurant.co.uk>

Four Marks

SAFFRON

8 Oak Green Parade, Winchester Road, Four Marks, Alton 01420 561872

From mild aromatic Kurmas and Mossallas to spicy Madras, Baltis and House specialities, it's all here at the Saffron. 10% discount on takeaways, Minimum order £10. Hours: 12-2,30/5.30-11.30. Friday / Saturday -12.

Gosport

PRINCE OF INDIA

3 Marina Bldgs, Stoke Rd, Gosport 023 9271 1272

Popular curryhouse serving all the favourites. Delivery: £12 minimum, 3 mile radius. Price Check: Popadom 50p, CTM £5.95, Pullao Rice £1.70. Hours: 5 - 12, Friday and Saturday to 1

Hamble

CINNAMON BAY

4 High Street, Hamble 023 8045 2285

'Clean, modern decor, beautiful table linen, very different menu. Great place.' BF. Specialities include: Batak Biran Jalfrezi £11.50, boneless duck with fresh green chillies. Ayre Mass Jalfrezi £8.95, fillet of Ayre in

hot spicy sauce. Mahaan Shabji Kashmir £5.95, vegetables soaked in butter, cooked in creamy sauce with tropical fruits. Khasi Amchor £8.95, charcoal roasted lamb tikka, sweet, creamy yoghurt sauce, with mango slices. Expensive Chutney Tray at £1.50 – you could buy a whole jar for that! Takeaway: 20% discount. Hours: 5.30 -12.

Hook

HOOK TANDOORI

1 Fairholme Pde, Station Rd 01256 764844

Established in 1985 by the genial Syed Ahmed. All the old favourites and a large section of house specialities, which at first glance seem expensive, BUT, Special Pullao Rice is included. Also, beef curries are available, including: Handi - medium spices; Shatkora - Bangaldeshi lemon and Pathori - thin slices, hot - all £9.95 including rice. Stocks: Cobra. Takeaway: 10% discount. Price Check: Popadom 50p, CTM £9.95 (inc Pullao Rice), Pullao Rice £2.25. Hours: 12 to 2.30 and 6 to 11.30, Sunday to 10.45.

Horndean

INDIAN COTTAGE

4 The Square, Horndean 023 9259 1408

Established in 1978. Taken over by Anwar Miah in 1996. Seats 48. *'Have tried this restaurant a couple of times before and have never been disappointed. Excellent parking, tasteful decor, keen staff. Garlic Chilli Chicken was excellent and not overladen with chillies. Chicken Dorai was served sizzling with large cubes of breast chicken. Peshwari Naan very nice. Well worth a visit. Will go back again.'* DL. Hours: 12-2.30/6-12.

Liss

MADHUBAN

AWARD WINNER AND TOP 100

94 Station Road, Liss 01730 893363

Owned and managed by Lodue Miah, with help from his brothers Bedar, Didar and Dodo and some experienced waiters, all in smart blue shirts and yellow ties. You will not find better customer care anywhere. Customers names a remembered and are old friends. It has 96 seats and plans for a conservatory extension. Blue is the house colour, used on the exterior, the chairs, the decor, and even the menu. Like everything else, this eight-page document epitomises the Madhuban's attention to detail. It is illustrated in full colour and fully describes all the dishes. 'Uncle' Ahad runs the kitchen. There are 22 starters, 7 items from the tandoor, plus 5 nans. There is an ample choice of old favourites, and they are all done well. *'Given the extensive menu, it took some time to make any choices.* HC *Highly rated as a TOP 100 – long may it remain.'* J&JM. *We moved to the curry desert of Devon from Berkshire and regularly ate at the Madhuban in Liss, a great exponent of the skills of cooking great Indian food. How we miss it'* AF. One more thing: Prices here are among the cheapest in the area. This helps its appeal, but there is much more to it than that. I tis the eptome of a good house. We are pleased to keep this restaurant high in our **TOP 100.** Hours: 12-2.30pm/5.30-11.30pm. *See page 24*

PASSAGE TO INDIA

3 Romsey Road, Lyndhurst 023 8028 2099

Mr AA Kaysor (owner) tells us he has a good mix of passing tourist trade along with a good core of regulars, who enjoy this, their local curryhouse. Menu Snapshots: Chot Photi £3.25, chick peas cooked in a spicy tamarind and chilli sauce; Venison Tikka £5.50/£10.70; Batak Rezilla £10.50, duck pieces in hot sauce with green chillies; Coriander Nan £2.05. Stocks: Cobra and Kingfisher. Takeaway: 20% discount. Takeaway: 20% discount. Price Check: Popadom 60p, CTM £7.15, Pullao Rice £2.25. Hours: 12 to 2 and 6 to 11.30. <www.passagetoindia-lyndhurst.com>

Portsmouth

BLUE COBRA **NEW ENTRANT**

87 London Rd, North End 023 9266 5000

Opened 2006 as a 200 seater on two floors. Menu Snapshots: Zhal Naga (very hot chillies) Chicken or Lamb £6.95, from the Syhlet region, cooked with fresh Bangladeshi Naga chilli - hot!; Chicken Shahee £7.95, lightly spiced, tandoor, mint, garnished with grated cheese, served with salad on sizzler; Kanchi Chops £3.95/£7.95, tandoor marinated lamb chops, served with salad on sizzler; Masalas Chips £1.80; Moglai Poratha £1.50, flaky thick fried Indian bread with a spicy omelette. *Everything totally excellent. Decor, ambience, food presentation, service fine quality of dishes. They will do very well providing they can make the most of available parking spaces in the area.'* CF. Takeaway: 10% discount. Delivery: £15 minimum. Price Check: Popadom 50p, CTM £6.95, Pullao Rice £1.95. Hours: 12 12.

SAFFRON

1 Kingston Rd, Portsmouth 023 9277 9797

Sayed Khan's fully licensed, air-conditioned, modern restaurant is huge, (though it doesn't look it - clever seating!) seating over 200 diners, in two rooms, both with bars. Pat and I have eaten here, when the upstairs room was completely packed out with Portsmouth Football team and supporters. I am not a fan of football at all and didn't use this opportunity to get autographs. Back to the Saffron - food nicely presented and promptly served, by young but experienced waiters. The owner is a charismatic man, who has a very friendly and loyal following. Popular dishes include: Chicken Aloo Jhool and Chicken Shakuti. Menu Snapshots: Swordfish Bhuna £9.95; Kodu Goosth £8.95 - lamb, pumpkin, garlic, ginger, green chilli and coriander leaves; Chicken Raj Naga £8.95 - sliced chicken tikka, sauce made with Bangladeshi Naga chilli - hot!. Minimum charge: £8. Price Check: Popadom 50p, CTM £6.95, Pullao Rice £2.95. Hours: 12 to 2.30 and 6 to 12.

STAR OF ASIA

6 Market Way, Portsmouth Centre 023 9283 7906

Virtually opposite the old Tricorn site, and now easy parking, is this great little 40-seater restaurant, with a gorgeous sapphire blue, shiny terracotta tiles and blue mosaic front. Established in 1992 by Abdul Mothen, who also manages. Chef Gian Uddin cooks the curries. *'Far enough away from the circuit drinking area. Standard range of dishes. Hot and crispy Poppadoms. Excellent Rashmi with large portion of succulent kebab, topped with fluffy and tender omelette. Tandoori Chicken beautifully tender. Lovely Meat Bhuna and tangy Chicken Dhansak. Late generally means 1am, I left at 2.30am and people still arriving.'* RW. Hours: 12pm-2.15 (Fri. closed)/6pm to late; Sat. & Sun. 12pm to late.

Southampton

CAFÉ MUMBAI NEW ENTRANT & TOP 100

Lower Banister Road, Bedford Place
Southamptom SO15 023 8063 0006

A truly stunning venue, which opened in 2006 and offers fine Indian cuisine for up to 200 diners. There is a bar with an Indian 'Tapas' menu:. An informal buffet on the ground floor and a la carte dining on the first floor, overlooking the restaurant below and open style 'theatre' kitchens. *'Not located in the best area of Southampton. The surrounding streets house pubs and night clubs, which attract (on opening night) large groups of harmless, parading, howling Uni students, fortunatel off somewhere else. The building used to be a wine warehouse. It is clear that a lot of money has been spent re-modelling and decorating this impressive establishment. A well lit and full height plate glass window, let the uninvited see the 'beautiful people' (ie: S'ton Footballers and 'wags' etc) sip champagne and rub shoulders with other dignatories - including Pat and me!! Sally Taylor, from BBC South Today News, was in the upstairs gallery, wearing a pair of ill fitting, pale pink jeans, which should have seen the charity shop many moons ago (she looked as scruffy as me!), filming with the crew. I don't know if she stayed to eat, if she didn't she missed a treat. During the very busy and noisy reception, we were told to be seated, as the speeches were about to commence. I elbowed the 'wags' out of the way and bagged a table in full view of the theatre kitchen. Pat was announced as, the 'Egon Ronay of Indian Restaurants' - flattery indeed and gave a speech. Following Pat, a dreadful comedian, apparently a local, didn't entertain with his toilet humour, everyone looked suitable embarrassed. And then to finish off, the Mayor, who in usual 'mayoral-style', wittered on about nothing. I was reminded of a similar long Mayor's speech at another launch party many years ago, at which real comedian Frank Carson made a speech. He summed up the Mayor's speech by saying, 'Thank you, Lord Mayor for shortening the winter!' What do restaurants get mayor in for opening day? I have yet to find one who likes curry! Wines were poured and an assortment of starter platters were served. The kitchen brigade of an impressive ten chefs, is led by Uday Seth, in an on-view kitchen. All are highly trained and from five star Indian hotels, so no curr house stuff here. All the food was delicious and included: Fish Amritsari £5.25, gramflour battered-fried fish; Chestnut-Chard Pakora £3.75, water chestnut and crunchy chard pakoras; Chicken Shaslik £4.50; Aloo Tikki £3.95, griddle fried potato patties stuffed with gingered green peas; Shikhampuri Kebab £4.95, baby lamb cooked with cinnamon, cardamom, Bengal gram, minced, packed with yoghurt cheese, mint and onions, a delicacy from Hyderabad, all served with wonderful chutneys - Imli; Podina; Mango and Cachumber. Saint's Manager (can't remember his name and wouldn't recognise him if he walked past me in the street) was surrounded by his cronies! He cautiously bit off a piece of chicken tikka, as if not a fan of Indian cuisine. Well, that's OK, I'm not a fan of football!'* DBAC. Menu Snapshot: pepper Crab £5.95, soft shell crabs with garlic and black pepper with ginger and green mango sauce; Potli Samosa £3.50 , savoury chicken mince stuffed in crusty pastry, deep-fried and served with tamarind chutney; Masala Vada £3.50, coarsley ground lentils blended with fennel, ginger and green chillies, deep-fried; Machali Neelgiri £11.95, monkfish simmered in a green herb curry of coconut, chillies, coriander and roasted spices; Murg Tikka lababdar £8.5 , chicken tikkas in creamy tomato-based onion gravy, flavoured with grated ginger and an abundance of fresh coriander; Dhungaar ka Saag Gosht £10.95, sliced lamb chargrilled, smoked and tossed with spinach and garlic; Bhindi do Pyaza £6.50, green okras sautéed with onions, tomatoes and a touch of spice; Pudhina Paratha £2.50, mint flavoured, crispy layered refined flour bread. Another hgh quality curry venue for Southampton. Goes into our **TOP 100.** Hours: 12-2.30. & 5.30-11 Mon-Tue; 12-11 Wed-Sun. <www.cafe-mumbai.co.uk> *See page 43.*

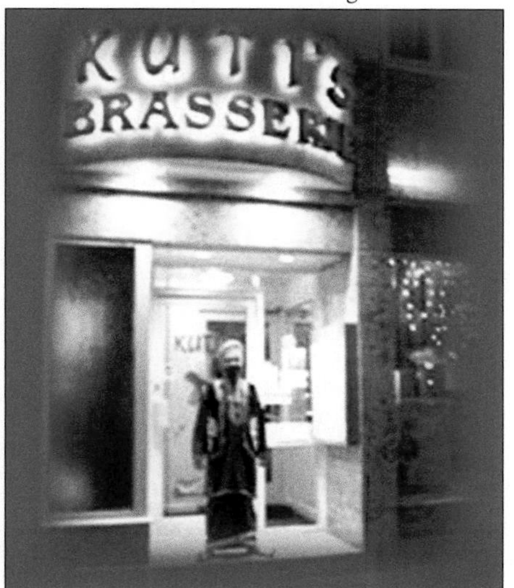

KUTI'S BRASSERIE

BEST BANGLADESHI RESTAURANT 2007/8

37 Oxford Street, Southampton 023 8022 1585

It's hard to miss Kuti's purple exterior used since they first opened in 1985 on London Road. and their relocation in 1994. Owner Mr Kuti has financed a recent major refurbishment includes hand-painted designs straight onto the walls, using a central theme of lotus flowers contrasted by silver finishing. The reception area is now styled as a lounge with a Bedouin feel again in a myriad of colours, while retaining the original purple as the core shade. Upstairs is the Francis Benali suite, named after Mr. Kuti's ex-business partner then captain of Southampton Football Club, and used for private parties. Kuti's serves Bangladeshi and Indian cuisine and there is a Head Chef for each region. Romis Miah, who has been at Kuti's for 20 years is in charge of the Bangladeshi cuisine while India-trained Kamal Kishore formerly at Delhi's Hyatt Regency, heads the Indian cooking specialities. Menu Snapshots: good fish dishes, including: ayre, sea bass, sole and trout (good news for correspondent HC); also a good selection of popular curry house dishes made with beef; Bonhoor Delight, diced venison, served with a rich orange-flavoured Grand Marnier-based sauce. £8.95, Paneer Shashlik £4.50, cubes of cottage cheese, green chilli, ginger and coriander; Kerala

Chicken £7.95, coconut, chilli; Lobia Dhal £5.95, black eyed peas, onions and tomato. We have had a lot of correspondence on this, and here is some of it. *'This upmarket establishment features a doorkeeper in traditional dress, novel presentation of mixed warm and crisp popadums in a basket, and a varied menu that is proud of Bangladeshi/Sylheti cuisine and meats not regularly encountered such as Venison, Duck and Beef. The 'Beef Bangla' is very tender and almost melts in the mouth. Expect to pay £20 per head for popadums, slightly adventurous main course, and a large 'Cobra'. The Waiters will put out balloons on the tables for birthday parties. Toilets are clean and tidy, but those easily embarrassed by "personal noises" will be pleased to learn that the piped music is at its loudest levels in the loos.'* GR. *'On two or three occasions, the quality of the food has been excellent. On my most recent visit, very much enjoyed Bonhoor Tikka, tandoor marinated venison, served with a delicious sauce. I like the way this restaurant has managed to establish itself with some signature dishes. Tandoori Quail, particularly noteworthy. Service can vary, from slow during very busy periods to slightly over-pushy on the alcohol front, but generally good quality. Unconditionally recommended.'* SO. Fully licensed and air-conditioned. Daily Buffet lunch: £8.50, dinner £14.50. Takeaway: 10% discount. Price Check: Popadom 60p, CTM £7.75, Pullao Rice £2.50. Hours: 12-2.30 and 6-12. *See also Wickham, Hants, below. and page 47.* <www.kutis.co.uk>

NATRAJ BALTI

3 Winchester St, Southampton 023 8036 6344

'I am vegetarian and the Vegetarian Baltis are very good. Also, according to friends that eat meat, the other Balti dishes are excellent too. The building was once a night club and the owners have kept the dance floor and they play live Indian music on Fridays and Saturdays.' MD.Commended by ss. Hours: 12-2/6-11.30.

MIRCHI NEW ENTRANT

4 Bedford Place, Southampton 023 8033 8800

Formerly Raj Duth. Fully licensed and air-conditioned. Menu Snapshots: Salmon Tikka £3.75; Bhatak (Duck) Roshuni £7.95 - tamarind, garlic, mild sauce; Mixed Grill £10.45 - no Nan!; Masala Chips £1.50. Vegetable dishes can be ordered as a side or main dish £2.95 / £4.95. *'Very good curry house with first class service and good value for money. A smallish curry house that gets busy so make sure that you book. Chicken Tikka Pasanda was excellent! Cheers'* RE. Student discount: 10% discount, ID must be shown. Delivery: 3 miles, £10 minimum, evening only. Takeaway: 15% discount. Stocks: Cobra. Price Check: Popadom 50p, CTM £6.55, Pullao Rice £2.15. Hours: 12 to 2, Friday lunch closed and Daily 5 to 12.<www.mirchitandoori.com>

POPADOM EXPRESS TOP 100

48 Oxford Street Southampton 023 8063 2444

This 140-seater is M.D. Aazaz Khan's second outlet, whose theme is a combination of traditionalist cuisine and modernist decor with a signature maroon colour The bar staff, who boast that there isn't a cocktail that they can't do, also offer tea, coffee, smoothies and fruit juices. The choice of name sounding more like a crisp fast-food outlet perhaps does not give potential diners the real feel of the cuisine. Khan's USP is his on-view kitchens containing no less than seven different cooking units used in India for thousands of years such as Sigrhi (open fire grill), Tawa (griddle), Mahi Tawa (walled griddle), Kadhai (wok), Lagan (steam pot) Shilajit Stone (special stones from Hyderabad, with aphrodisiac properties) and of course the Tandoor. All of this is managed by a team of highly trained Indian chefs, led by Ishtyak Ahmed. Born in the culinary heartland of Awadh (Lucknow) he learned his trade from the legendary chefs Ustad Abdullah Khan and Ustad Zaiki the was exec at Lucknow's Taj Mahal Hotel. Ram Kishore also from Lucknow is sweet maker. Ahmed uses different sauces to give every dish a completely different taste and texture and the open-plan kitchen allows diners to watch the chefs in action. The menu travels around India's different regions as well as including favourites like Chicken Tikka Masala and chef's specials like Lamb Mughlai. Main courses start at £7.95 and a selection from the more hearty set-menus are priced £15.95 upwards. Aazaz recently sold his Basingstoke branch. Take away and delivery service. Puja Vedi, Ed Tandoori Magazine.. Branch: Popadom Express 40 Woburn Place, Russell Square, London WCI <www.poppadomexpress.co.uk>

P.O.S.H.

1 Queensway, Southampton 023 8022 6377

Established 1991. Upstairs to find inviting armchairs in a comfortable lounge. Go through to

a huge nautically-themed restaurant, seating 150 diners, with bar, grand piano, band stand and a dance floor - quite a place. A FAQ: what does P.O.S.H mean?. And Port-Out Starboard- Home! And what did that mean? In the old days when ships were the main transports to India, the experienced travellers chose their cabins to be 'POSH' to avoid the hot sunshine flooding through the porthole. Menu Snapshots: Paneer Tikka £4.95, curd cheese, flavoured with ginger, garlic, coriander and lime juice; Honey Glazed Salmon Tikka £5.95; King Prawn Toast £5.95, round of toast, smothered in an olive and anchovy butter, topped with garlic and chilli stir-fried king prawn; Duck with Mushroom in Red Wine £5.95, duck, onions and mushrooms sautéed in rich creamy sauce. *'It is well decorated though its size gives it an empty feel. The dodgy middle-of-the-road music being played as you were seated did not bode well, although the restaurant itself did have quite a good ambience. Service was average to poor. The food is variable. I have eaten there and been very pleased, swordfish and salmon tikka starters, and other times it has been very average. The Baked Sea Bass was very delicate and succulent and the Sea Bass in Red Wine was also very pleasant, rich and spicy. Duck Bhuna was tender with a very nice spice balance but was too salty. The Chatt, which was chickpeas in a pleasant, tangy sauce, had a nice heat and clean coriander leaf finish. However, the Chicken Korma was poor and the Rogon Gosht quite average. Overall opinion – OK, with reservations but would probably give it another try'.* SO. Delivery: 3 miles, £15 minimum. Stocks: Cobra. Price Check: Popadom 50p, CTM £7.75, Pullao Rice £2.95. Hours: 12-2 / 6-11. <www.poshrestaurant.co.uk>

Southsea

BOMBAY BAY NEW ENTRANT & TOP 100

Fort Cumberland Rd, Southsea Marina 023 9281 6066

In 2005, Southsea Marina handed the operation of its all-day bar and restaurant to the Pompey Gandhi Group (twelve brothers and cousins, surname Karim) based in Kingston Road and who already operated two other restaurants. Parking is usually sufficient. The exterior is rather utilitarian, and the actual restaurant is up a flight of stairs, above the Marina offices. The restaurant has a two-aspect panoramic view of the sea, the 'mainland' and Hayling Island. See previous page.. After you have taken in the views, you notice the primrose yellow and burgundy walls with wall mounted seafaring artwork. The window seats, with their views are the most popular, especially in daylight. On a good day, the large outside terrace area with several steel table and chairs is a magnet, and a full service is available there. Even on a coldish day heaters make it a relaxing place to be. Exec chef Lahin Karim oversees the kitchens, and has aimed his menu at healthier food *'with less ghee and crunchy vegetables'.* He also presents his food on rather smart white china plates. It has smart pale yellow and burgundy walls with muted modern seafaring artefacts. Menu snapshot: Starters, which come with a splendid salad include Mussels £45, stuffed with rice, served with garlic and coriander sauce; Bombay Missali: Chicken tikka, lamb tikka, sheek kebab and squid orHush Tikka, duck fillets marinated in spices in orange flavoured sauce both £6. Mains include (all £9) Goan Chicken or Lamb Tikka, cooked with red goan chilli, garlic, green peppers, coriander, coconut milk and fine spices, fairly hot. Vegetable dishes (£3.20) include Broccoli Bhajee and Niramish. Set lunch menu between 12pm & 5pm is good value at £7.95. And for Sunday lunch they do a carvery roast with all the trimmings. They are usefully open all day (the only venue in the area to do this) mainly to offer a bar and snacks service for the marina boat owners, and anyone else who wants to avail themselves of this service. 12 - 11 S unday - Thursday; 3 - 12 Friday 12pm - 12am Saturday Open Bank Holidays <www.bombaybay.co.uk> *(see previous page)*

GOLDEN CURRY TOP 100

16 Albert Road, Southsea 023 9282 0262

Some years ago, I was interviewed here,by the then local TV station Meridian, and I sampled many dishes from the korma to the phal. As a definition

of the formula, they were spot on. Colours, aromas, tastes, textures, service and price – all done right by experienced 'old hands'. In fact the 52-seater has been owned by Salim Hussein (manager) and Razak Ali (head chef) since 1979, and has a justifiably loyal following. I am often sent letters & emails by people bemoaning the loss of taste these days compared with 'the good-old-days' Well here you find it, done as it used to be. One secret is that they cut no corners. Never mind that patronising phrase often overused by over-priced fancy restaurants: '*we use only the foinest and freewshest ingredients*' What else would you use? The worst and stalest ingredients? Golden Curry don't need to say that because you can taste fresh and finest. Whole chickens, for example are pot-simmered in light spices, then boned and cooked off in your curry dish, with the resultant great flavour to match. (As opposed to tasteless pre-boned breast). It has a huge local following all of whom know the waiters by name, and vice-versa. It is common to see three generations at table, all of whom have been regulars almost since birth!. This is what a decent curryhouse is all about: a friendly home-from-home, where you get cared for with decent food, secent service and an unpretentious price tag

Genial host Salim, Golden Curry, Southsea

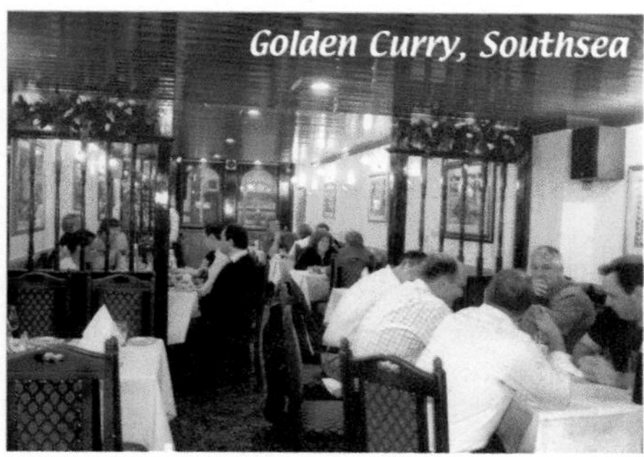

Golden Curry, Southsea

which doesn't require a new mortage. Menu extracts: Chicken Tikka Chilli Masala £7.05. Special Mixed Fried Rice £2.75, with prawns and cabbage, garnished with omelette. Vegetable Thali £7.30, Vegetable Bhajee, Brinjal Bhajee, Cauliflower Bhajee, Tarka Dal, Mushroom Bhajee, Nan and Pullao Rice – great value! *'An excellent restaurant which my husband and I go to for a "curry fix". Salim is a wonderful host, greeting his clients with courtesy and friendliness, the waiters follow his lead. Ali runs a wonderfully efficient and clean kitchen.'* C&CH. *'Excellent food and service. Our regular curry restaurant.'* DKM. *'Staff always friendly and attentive. Extremely clean and cosy restaurant. Meals range from very good to superb!!. Good sized portions which are very filling.'* GB. *'An excellent restaurant. Received a nice welcome. Table, decor– clean and tidy. Meal was as I ordered it– HOT! I have been all over the country but it would be hard to beat this curry house.'* EC. PS: The locations is great if you have a night out at the gorgeous King's Theatre, next door, and they do a quick meal if they know your plans. Delivery free, 2 miles over £20 (under that £2.50 charge made). Hours: 12-1.30 Sun to Thur / 5.30-12.30 Mon to Thur; 5.30-12am, Sun..

T & J MAHAL

39 Elm Grove, Southsea 023 9281 5824

A restaurant with two head chefs – Kalam Khan, specialises in Bengali and Goan cuisine and Joshim Ahmed, whose talents lie with authentic and contemporary cuisine. Superior formula curries served here, in this smart restaurant in Southsea, where there is is quite a choice of eateries. Menu Snapshots: Achari Chingri £4.95 - tandoor cooked, tamarind flavoured tiger prawns; All Bora £3.25 - fried mashed potato, stuffed with mint, ginger, flaked almonds and spicy peas; Mixed Grill £7.95 includes a Nan. Stocks: Cobra and Kingfisher. Price Check: Popadom 50p, CTM £6.95, Pullao Rice £1.95. Hours: 5 to 12.

Stubbington

STUBBINGTON TANDOORI

35a The Green Stubbington, Nr Fareham 01329 664615

Mr Rahman's 40-seater. Specials include: Balti £6.50, Murag Makhan £6.50, chicken cooked with butter and fresh cream.Takeaway: small discount. Delivery: £12 min, 4-mile radius. Hours: 5.30-12.

Waterlooville

INDIAN COTTAGE

51 London Road, Cowplain 01705 269351

D&BR and L&AC have been coming as a foursome for many years to Sheik Shab Uddin's tiny 30-seater (exposed oak beams, blue walls and tablecloths, red velvet chairs) because chef AH Khan's *'food is excellent and the staff always attentive'*. Hours: 12-2.30/5.30-12. Branches: Indian Cottage, Port Solent, Gunwharf Quays and Horndean.

PURE ZING NEW ENTRANT

1 Purbrook Chase Precinct, Crookhorn Lane, Waterlooville 023 9224 0066

At the time of writing it is a takewaway only, but has space and places for dining in. Owner: Hab Rahman has produced a very amusing menu, with funny little names for popular dish. Menu Snapshot: Aloo Paneer Wrap £2.55, potato and cheese filling, lightly spiced, wrapped in soft bread; Parsee Style Salad £2.45, Goan green salad of lettuce, cucumber. tomato, feta cheese, stuffed olives, sweet red chilli in spicy garlic and herb dressing; Char Grilled Chicken with Noodles £5.35; Grilled Fish £7.95; Mixed Grill £8.95 - no Naan!. Branch: Tamarind & Moonlight Express, Nutbourne, Sussex.

SHALIMAR

9 Hambledon Pde, Hambledon Rd, Waterlooville 023 9225 1565

56-seater, with smoking and non-smoking sections, managed by Mujib.*'Shalimar's greatest asset is that it does the simple things well. The Lamb Jalfrezi is a little hotter and more adventurous than usual, and the Chicken Shaslit is another highlight. A quiet, friendly establishment with young staff who are both polite and efficient.'* GS. Hours: 12-2.30/5.30-11.30.

Wickham

STAR CORNER NEW ENTRANT

Fareham Road, Wickham 01329 835353

A new venture from Kuti Miah opening after we got to press, but should be good. Reports please. *(see Kuti's Southampton, Hants)*

Winchester

BALAKA

75 Stoney Lane, Weeke 01962 855118

Ali Forid Miah's Balaka is modern and clean-lined inside. It is in all respects an good formula curry house, where you will be able to find all your favourite dishs. Cooking is, we hear, well up to scratch,a dn the venue has many regulars. Hours: Lunch and dinner, daily.

HEREFORDSHIRE

Area: Welsh Border
Population: 220,000
Adjacent Counties: Gwent, Powys, Shrops, Staffs, Worcs

Bromyard

TASTE OF INDIA

22 High Street, Bromyard 01885 488668

Fully licensed and air conditioned. *'Had a good sit down meal in here. Waiters very friendly although three other tables taken at about 8.30pm on a Friday night. Goa Murgh £5.95 – not particularly hot, although colleagues at work call me 'Asbestos Gob'. Decor– typically small town curry house.'* ANON. Hours: 12-2.30/5.30-11.30, closed Tuesday.

Hereford

KAMAL

82 Widemarsh St, Hereford 01432 278005

'A narrow-fronted and impressively named enterprise that fronts a surprisingly long and capacious curry house. Helpful and friendly staff. Menu contains usual suspects, plus specials. Real cloths and hand towels. Jangra Purr – unusual, almost spring roll, delightful chat style curry with salad and sweet sauce, enjoyable. Lamb Tikka Biriani – very good, well cooked, a shade greasy, boiled egg rather than usual omelette topping. Lamb absolutely top quality, mouth watering. Recommended.' RW. 3 course Sunday Lunch: £8. Deli: £14 minimum. Menu Extracts: Chicken Pakora £3, Stuffed Mushroom £2.50, Garlic Chicken Jalfrezi £7.50, Tarka Dal £2.50. Hours: 12-2/5.30-12.

KHAN'S

Plough Inn, Canon Pyon, Hereford 01432 830577

'Curry restaurant in a pub! Excellent food at very reasonable prices– best in hereford. Portions good, Nan too big for one person. Jalfrezi – excellent fresh chillies. Specialities: Lamb Paprika £7.25. Well worth finding.' PJM. No credit cards. Hours: 5.30-12.

JALALABAD

33 Etnam St, Leominster 01568 615656

Well promoted by the ebullient owner-manager Kamal Uddin Owner-chef Abdul Mukith's food menu attracts regular praise from Leominster locals. *'Menu Conventional Quality Excellent Quantity Very generous Decor Obtrusive peacock feathers arranged around the wall - disturbing for some Service On the slow side Comfort Good, not too close seating Comments Starters: Popadoms 50p x 2 plus £1.20 chutney; Onion Bhaji £2.25 – taste good, texture fine; Tandoori Mix £3.95; Presentation good, slightly small portions. Main Course: Chicken Keema Mattar £6.95; Garlic Chicken £6.95. Accompaniments: Mushroom Pullau Rice £2.15; Peshwari Nan £2.15. Drinks: Tiger x 2. Bill £31.40. Mark 8/10.'* G&MP.

TASTE OF RAJ

67 St Ownens Street, Hereford 01432 351075

'Plainly decorated, attractive establishment, bustling corner of city. Policed by efficient, almost surly staff. Good menu to tempt the palate. Reshmi Kebab £3.75, slightly dry, nicely hot, excellent texture, crisp salad, lurid green yoghurt sauce. Lamb Tikka Biriani £8, mouthwatering, well cooked, greaseless rice, packed with vegetables, accompanying vegetable curry better than 'bog standard' house curry sauce. Very good Garlic Nan £1.95, light and fluffy, plenty of finely chopped garlic. Tarka Dal £2.45, unusual, pieces of tomato and cucumber, thick, subtle flavours. Very enjoyable overall, definitely recommended.' RW. Takeaway: 10% discount. Delivery: £14 min. Hours: 6-11.

Ross-on-Wye

OBILASH

19a Gloucester Rd, Ross-on-Wye 01989 567860

Janu Miah's Obilash was established 1985. A smallish restaurant, seating just forty, so book your table on any night. Menu Snapshots: Tandoori Mixed Grill £9.95, no King Prawn and Naan cost extra! *Menu Extensive with a few more unusual choices Quality Very good Quantity Generous Decor Blue wooden panelled ceiling. Soft lilac and cream wallpaper Service Attentive, polite, making all the right noises Comfort A fairly small restaurant with only 40 covers but reasonably spaced Comments Starters: 2 x 85p – freshly produced; mixed starter for 2 £5.25, the stuffed pepper was boring but the sauce and chicken tikka delicious. Main course: Keema Peas £7.55 – extremely tasty; Tandoori Chicken £6.95 – could have been better marinaded. Accompaniments: Pullau rice £2.35 very good; Peshwari Nan £2.95 good; Bombay Potatoes £3.65 reasonable; Drink: bottle of House Red £10.95 very good. Mark 7/10 Bill £41.35'.* G&MP. . Delivery: 3 miles, £25 minimum. Takeaway: 10% discount. Price Check: Popadom 85p, CTM £8.45, Pullao Rice £2.35. Hours: 6 to 12.

HERTFORDSHIRE

Area: Home Counties, (north of London)
Population: 1,042,000
Adjacent Counties: Beds, Bucks, Cambs, Essex, London

Part of south Herts was absorbed by Greater London in 1965. We note affected towns/suburbs.

Abbots Langley

FOREST OF INDIA

39 High Street 01923 27007

Established 1996. Owner Chowdhury runs this large restaurant, seating 120. Menu Snapshot: Tandoori Pomfret £7.50; Tandoori Mixed Grill £7.95, including King Prawn and Naan bread – great!; Rupchanda Bhuna £7.95, lightly fried pomfret, medium sauce; Murgh Nawabi £6.75, marinated chicken, mushrooms, onions, tomatoes and brandy – fit the a King or even a Nawab! Delivery: 2 miles, £12 minimum. Takeaway: 10% discount. Service charge: 10%. Stocks: Cobra. Sunday Buffet: 12 to 5, £7.95 adult, £4.00 children, coffee and mints included. Thursday Banquet Night: £9.95. Price Check: Popadom £1, CTM £6.55, Pullao Rice £2.45. Hours: 12 to 2.30 and 6 to 11.30. Branch: Sema, Whitcross St, WC1.

VICEROY OF INDIA — TOP 100

20 High Street, Abbots Langley 01923 262163

Established in 1989 by Ronney Rahman. *'Food delicious, always fresh and elegantly presented. Waiters friendly and attentive.'* D&PM. *'Menu was full and standard with the unique addition of a number of hash (duck) dishes. Makhoni Hash – wonderfully flavourful, distinctive but mild spices in a cream and tomato sauce.'* RH. House specials: Makhoni Hash (mild) tandoori grilled duck, tossed in butter, cultured yoghurt, fresh cream and mild spices and Karahi Jhinga (hot), jumbo prawns cooked with a medium dry gravy, herbs, tomatoes, onions and green pepper, served from a iron karahi. Hours: 12-2.30/6-11. *See previous page.*

Barnet (Greater London)

(inc East Barnet and New Barnet)

SHAPLA TANDOORI

37 High Street, Barnet 020 8449 0046

Established in 1981. SI Ahmed's smart restaurant seats 50 and is popular. *'My local, always very reliable. Standard menu. Excellent Dhansak, generous Shashlik and very good side dishes. A clean, cosy restaurant.'* CT. Delivery: £1.50, 4-mile radius. Hours: 12-2.30pm/6pm-12am.

Berkhamsted

AKASH

307 High St, Berkhamsted 01442 862287

We particularly like owner Foysol Ahmed's service – greeted at the door, coats taken, napkins placed in your lap, staff are attentive without hovering.' LB. Hours: 12-2.30/6-12am.

CURRY GARDEN

29 High Street, Berkhamsted 01442 877867

'An old converted pub, lovely low beams and cosy booths. Very impressed. Will most definitely be back.' SW..

Bishops Stortford

SHADONA

High Street, Bishops Stortford 01279 508149'

'In centre of BS. Looks fabulous, rather crisp, almost Scandinavian. Excellent cuisine and sharp service. Enjoyed Cobra with fresh Poppadoms and Pickles. Shared different starters of Meat Samosas – lean and crisp, Bhajis – great, Sheek Kebab – beautifully cooked. Mains curries – Bhuna, Tikka, Korma were all served with Pullao Rice. Sag Aloo, Nan and Chapatti . Quantity and quality outstanding, we were all stuffed! Prices above average. Fabulous experience.' AE. Hours: 12-2.30/6-11.

Boreham Wood

ARGEE BARGEE — TOP 100

Albert Square, BBC Elstree Studios 01234 987654

Eastenders designers asked us to produce a **TOP 100** certificate for a curryhouse in the Square. We obliged and called it Argee Bargee. The set complete with certificate duly appeared in 2005 and has reappeared a few times since. Watch out for it, but we can't vouch for good customer behaviour.

Cheshunt

RAJ VOGUE

48 High Street, Cheshunt 01992 641297

82-seater est 1991 by Khalek Quazi. Room for 50 cars at the back. GR likes the Nawab Nargis, cooked with spicy minced chicken and fresh mint. Takeaway: 10% discount. Delivery: £15, 3 miles. Hours: 12-2.30/6-11.30; Sat. 12-2.30 (Sun -2pm) /6pm-12am (Sun. to 11pm). Sun lunch buffet £6.95.

Hatfield

PRINCE OF INDIA

10 Market Place, Hatfield 01707 265977

Established in 1993, managed by SF Ali. The restaurant seats 48 diners, and is a romantic and pleasant atmosphere. Delivery.. Hours: 5.30-11.30.

Hemel Hempstead

CHUTNEYS

79 Waterhouse St, Hemel 01442 243 595

Owning manager, Saber Khan. Seats 70. Menu Snapshot: Noodles £2.95, stir-fried, spicy minced meat, egg, coriander leaves; Pistachio Chicken Korma £5.95; Special Beef £9.50, tandooried fillet steak; Chilli and Coriander Naan £1.95. Stocks: Cobra and Kingfisher. Delivery: 4 miles, £15 minimum. Sunday lunch buffet: £7.95. Price

Check: Popadom 50p, CTM £6.50, Pullao Rice £1.90. Hours: 5.30 to 11.30.daily, 12 to 2, Sat & Sun only. <www.chutneys.biz>

GURU TANDOORI

5 Bridge Street, Hemel 01442 254725

Owner SM Rahman. Chef S Uddin. 36 seats. MBS says he has eaten here twice a week for over twenty years, and that he always recommends it to his friends, who in turn have become satisfied customers. *'The only Indian in Hemel in bad need of a refurb– including the toilet! Food, however was great and good portions, Chicken Tikka Garlic Balti – fantastic. Prawn Vindaloo – wow! Tandoori Mixed Grill– how much meat! Cramped– next table almost joining!'* JH. Justin's next visit: *'Good service, good food. Chicken and Lamb Bormani served piping hot on a skillet was fantastic. Chicken Tikka Garlic [you had that dish last time] also well worth a return visit! £57 for four.'* JH. Delivery: £15 minimum, 5-mile radius. Hours: 12-2.30pm/6pm-12am. Branch: Guru, 630, Uxbridge Road, Hayes, Middx.

MOGUL

91 High St, Old Town 01442 255146

'I feel this is the best in Hemel– beautifully decorated and always good food and service. 'Took two work colleagues and two customers – all agreed the best meal! Chicken Roushini, Chicken Rezala and Mogul Special Masala– all fantastic. Side dishes and breads– all very good.'Takeaway for two.' [and JH returns]: *'Phoned and collected within half an hour, all hot plus free Poppadoms!'* [and JH keeps returning]: *'Busy Saturday night, party of nine. Table booked for 9.30pm, sat down at 10pm. Main courses at 10.45pm, no starters. Food as good as ever– well loaded chicken and mushroom Rizato, thoroughly enjoyed by two. Only let down was Tandoori King Prawn looked great but lacking in flavour. Bill at 12.20am. An enjoyable night but too long!* [and JH keeps returning]: *'Busy Thursday night. Deep fried aubergines on the house to start absolutely gorgeous. Roushini seemed a but rich. Mushroom Rizoti and Chicken Gastoba– as good as ever.!'* JH. Takeaway: 10% discount. Hours: 12-2.30 and 5.30-11.30, Friday and Saturday to 12.

Hitchin

INDIA BRASSERIE

36 Bancroft Road, Hitchin 01462 433001

M Chowdhury's restaurant seats 32. The menu is a good example of the curryhouse method, with all your favourtites at reasonable prices. Specials: Chicken Makhani Tikka, Rezala Chicken and Fish Bhuna5. *'The best in Hitchin.'* SW. Hours: Tues.-Thurs. 12-2.30/5.30-12; Sun. 1-11pm, buffet £7.95.

Letchworth

CURRY GARDEN

71 Station Road 01462 682820

Afiz Ullah is the head chef and owner of this 72-seater, which has a *'huge friendly menu.'* MT. Hours: 12-2.30pm/6pm-12am; Sun. 12pm-12am, buffet 12-5.30pm. Branches (all named Curry Garden) at: Berkhamsted; Rickmansworth; Dunstable, Beds; Hornchurch, Essex.

SAGAR

48 The Broadway, 01462 684952

Motiur Rahman's *'Trout Masala is one of the best.'* LV. Service 10%. Lunch buffet, weekdays £5.50, Sun. £5.95. Branches: Aashiana, Broadway, Beds; Ahkbar Takeaway, Abbot's Walk, Biggleswade, Beds.

Royston

BRITISH RAJ

55 High Street, Royston 01763 241471

Established in 1976 by Nazir Uddin Choudhury, an old hand a wicked sense of humour. Sadly since his departure we have not heard a peep. Reports please. Takeaway: 10% discount. Hours: 12-2/6-12.

Sawbridgeworth

STAR OF INDIA

51 London Road 01279 726512

Established 1981 by Dilwar & Jamal Ahmed. 2 room seat 70. Free car park opposite. Specials include: Kurzi Lamb and Kurzi Chicken. Takeaway: 10% discount. Delivery: £12 minimum, 5-mile radius.Hours: 12-2/5.30-11.30.

TANDOORI NIGHT

Knight St, Sawbridgeworth 01279 722341

'We had our wedding reception in this great restaurant. Food and service excellent.' JP. *'Chicken Tikka, excellent huge pieces, very tasty. Onion Bhajis size of tennis balls. Very hot and tasty Madras, plenty of Vegetable Biriani. Friendly staff.'* JP. Hours: 12-2.30/6-11.30 (12am on Fri. & Sat.).

St Albans

MUMTAJ

NOMINATED BEST IN THE SOUTH

115 London Road 01727 858399

Originally opened way back in 1962. Present owner, Muklasur Rahman Mojumder took over in 1983 and has established himself as a highly regarded source of Indian cuisine. Seats 44 diners in two rooms partitioned by an archway. The owner's son Chad Rahman now runs the kitchen. He loves to try out new ideas, some of which are superb.. He worked some time in curry houses in Houston Texas. More recently he entered the Curry Chef of the Year competition, run by the Chartered Institute of Environmental Health. (CIEH). I wouldn't enter a cooking contest myself. What if you loose? Chad entered and won in 2002, and bless me he did it again in 2003, and again he won. St Albans ex MP Kerry Pollard loves the place but agreed with me that Chad is 'a brave man, and a brilliant chef'.*'I am lucky enough to travel widely on business, and never travel without your Guide. I aim to visit every TOP 100. I agree with all but one of those visited. Having visited many, many U.K. curryhouses in the U.K, as well as in Brussels (ugh), Amsterdam (great), Stockholm (ugh), Riyadh (ummm), and the USA (hmmm), I am always pleased to get home to St Albans, and eat at my local, the Mumtaj.'* PFM. *'Smart, elegant restaurant just outside historic St Albans. Fairly small, intimate, air of refinement. Attentive and friendly service. Excellent Prawn Puri, really aromatic sauce, plenty of prawns, slightly crisp, oil–free puri. Lamb Nashilee 5, very good combination, robust spices, plenty of ginger, texture added by peppers and chillies, good cuts of gristle-free lamb, very enjoyable. Peshwari Nan, moist, well cooked, too much filling, sweet and delicious..'* RW. We have much pleasure in decalring Mumtaj the best in a very wide area of the South of England. Delivery: 2 miles, £15 minimum. Hours: 12-3/6 -12. Branch: Chez Mumtaj 136 London Rd (opening after we go to print) .

Stevenage

GATE OF INDIA

20 The Glebe, Chells Way 01438 3176195

Abdul Salam owns this 57-seater, divided between 4 rooms. Chef Arosh Ali cooks all the favourites. Delivery: £10 min, 4-mile radius. Hours: 12-2.30pm/6pm-12am

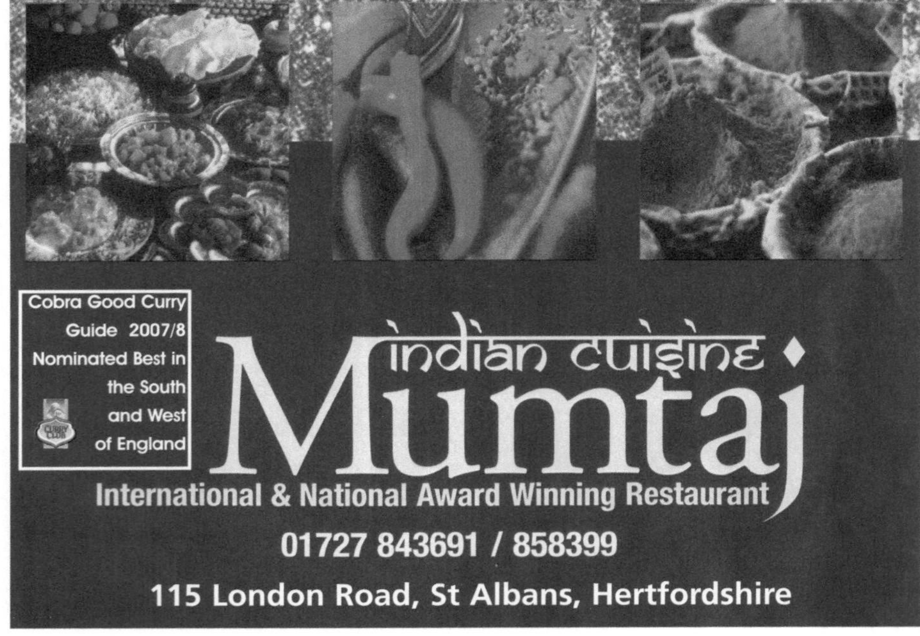

Waltham Cross

CAFÉ SPICE NEW ENTRANT

63 High Street 01992 717 546

Rezaul Huq Syed can sit 48 curryholics in his restaurant. Menu Snapshot: Chicken Chauk £3.50, chicken in batter, breadcrumbs, deep-fried, served with mixed vegetables; Chilli Paneer £5.70, cheese with spring onions, capsicum, tamarind, green chillies and garlic; Labra Rice £2.50 , baby carrots, beans, corn and asparagus. Sunday Buffet: £6.95 per person. Delivery: 3 miles, £10 minimum. Takeaway: 10% discount. Price Check: Popadom 50p, CTM £6.95, Pullao Rice £1.95. Hours: 5.20 - 11, Frid and Sat to 11.30. Sunday 12.30 - 3.30 / 5.30 11.

KENT

Area: South East
Population: 1,612,000
Adjacent Counties: Essex, London, Surrey, Sussex

Part of Kent was absorbed by Greater London in 1965. We note affected towns / suburbs..

Ashford

KENNINGTON TANDOORI NEW ENTRANT

158 Faversham Rd, Kennington, Ashford 01233 650 350

Licensed and air-conditioned. Mohammed Miah took over ownership of this 38 seater in 2006, a year after it opened. Chef Shofique Uddin would like you to know about his midweek platter (Monday to Wednesday) of a starter, a main, rice or Naan for £7.95. Delivery: 4 miles, £15 minimum. Price Check: Popadom 50p, CTM £6.95, Pullao Rice £1.90. Hours 12 to 2.30, not Friday and 5.30 to 11, Friday and Saturday to 11.30.

ZARIN TOP 100

31 Bank Street, Ashford 01233 620511

You're on your way to of from the Channel Tunnel and you need a fix. Here's your answer. The former Curry Garden (a long-term entrant to this Guide has achieved modernisation at its best. The frontage is inviting and you want to enter. In front of you is the bar area, immediately to your left the dining area. The modern interior is in shades of peach and terracotta, enhanced with tall black chairs and crisp white table linen.. Asian-inspired art adorns the walls, but what draws your eye is the water feature at the end of the room. One highlight enjoyed by the regulars is the monthly Elvis Nights. But this is no ordinary Elvis. He's Asian with a stature more like Sammy Davis Junior that the King. But he performs with a zest that makes the evening unmissable. Lunch specials: Chicken Rasili: chicken cooked with broccoli and cashew nuts and served with pullao rice and salad. Vegee Noodle: fresh seasonal vegetables cooked with noodles and served with salad. Wrap Chap Chicken: lightly spiced chicken mixed with fresh vegetables and noodles and wrapped in a chapatti. Hasin Chicken: succulent pieces of chicken cooked in light, medium hot spices; served with rice and salad. Chicken Rasili: chicken cooked with broccoli and cashew nuts and served with pullao rice and salad. Sunday e-a-m-a-y-l buffet £7.95, kids £4.95 chosen from over eighteen house

Zarin, Ashford

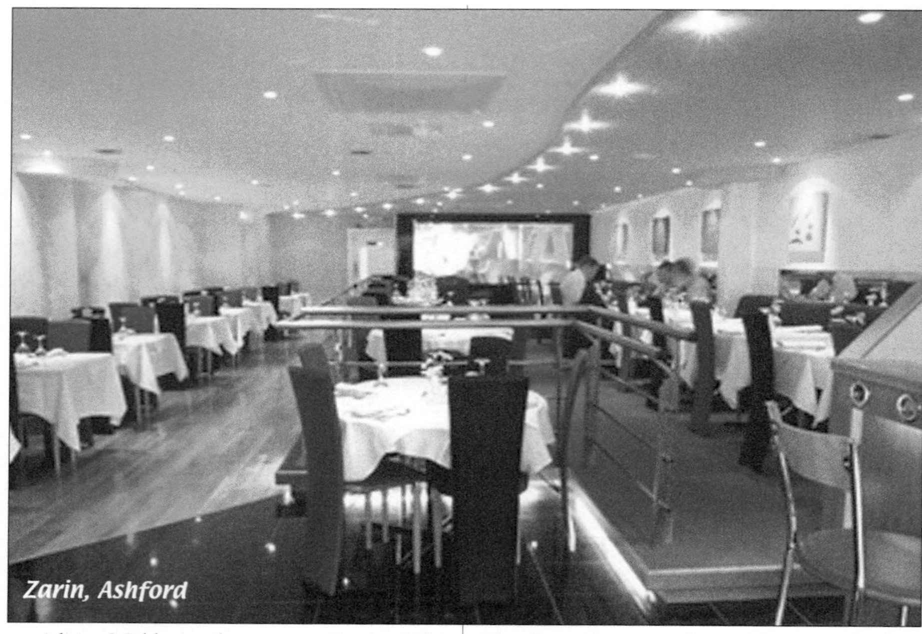
Zarin, Ashford

specialities. Midday until 10pm every Sunday. 20% Discount on Takeaway Meals. <www.zarinrestaurant.co.uk>

Barnehurst (Greater London)

JHAS TANDOORI

158c Mayplace Road East, Barnehurst 01322 555036

Est.1989 by Kuldip Jhas, who is also head chef; Robinder Jhas is the manager – a family business. Seats 50. Recently refurbished. Punjabi style Chicken and Lamb Balti is a house special and most popular with customers. 10% discount on takeaways. Hours: 6-11.30 (Fri. & Sat. to 12am); Sun. closed.

Bexley (Greater London)

CURRY HUT TAKEAWAY

166 Mayplace Road East, Bexleyheath 01322 550077

Established 1995 by Muhammed Jahangir Alam. He tells us it's very modern, with an open kitchen. Set dinner £12.95 vegetarian, £14.95 non-vegetarian. Delivery: £10 minimum, 3-mile radius. Hours: 5-11.30.

RUCHI NEW ENTRANT

56 Steynton Ave, Albany Pk 020 8300 0200

We occasionally get grumpy communications likew this one: *'Sir, I am writing to ask why we have not been included in last year's curry guide, and why we did not receive the certificate. We have been established for the last 20 years. C ould you please give me the reason for this. Thank you prashar@hotmail.co.uk.'* And we answer in the same grumpy tone! *'Sir, We cannot enter into the Good Curry Guide a restaurant we have not heard from, and despite sending you our forms each year, my database shows that you have not returned any to me before, and neither have we heard form any customers.'* The forms were duly returned and this is what we can say: Madan Prashar opened this 130 seater restaurant, decorated with ornate plaster work and chandeliers in 1986. Menu Snapshot: Punjabi Macchi £3.50 , yoghurt marinated fish, gram flour, green chilli, ginger, deep-fried; Aloo Pappdi Chatt £3.25, chickpeas, potatoes, coriander leaves, mint, yoghurt, tamarind sauce on crispy bread; Royal Chicken £10.95, chicken breast stuffed with mince lamb, almond, cashew cream sauce; vegetable dishes are £3.95 each, but you can have a tray of three for £8.95, what a good idea! Takeaway: 10% discount. Stocks: Cobra. Price Check: Popadom 65p, CTM £7.95, Pullao Rice £2.50. Hours: 12 t- 2 and 6 - 11.30, Sunday to 11. Reports please.

SAGGOR

145 Blendon Road, Bexley 020 8303 7549

Ali Uddin's *'pleasant restaurant, had a nice ambience, appetising smell as we entered – always a good start. Good menu featuring all the usuals plus a few less common names, particularly one or two interesting looking fish dishes. One of the most tasty Chicken Chats I've had for some time. Prawn Puri also unanimously approved. Subze Tandoori – a mixture of vegetables either whole or large slices, was very different. Certainly worth going to again.'* MW. Hours: 12-2.30/6-11.30.

Biggin Hill

RAJ

187 Main Road, Biggin Hill 01959 572459

70-seater, managed by AM Crorie, decorated in an 'olde worlde' style. Delivery: £10 minimum, 3-mile radius. Hours: 12-2.30 (3.30 on Sun.)/6-11.30 (12am on Sat.).

Bromley (Greater London)

CAFÉ EAST

123 Masons Hill, Bromley 020 8460 5452

Part of the Tamasha Group, owned by Shekor Tarat and Anil Deb, seats 76 diners. Brightly coloured menus, turquoise with orange for the food and fushia with orange for the wine list. Somebody has rather a *'Carry On'* sense of humour with starters like Tossing the Kyber, (Scottish salmon marinated with ginger and garlic, flavoured with caraway and char-grilled on the tandoor), Hey Griddle, Griddle, (chicken cooked on the tava with green peppers, onions, tomatoes and fresh herbs), Goan, Goan, Gone! £10.95 (in a trice, these Goan prawns with a Portuguese influence – hot and spicy!), It's all Fenugreek to Me, (nuggets of soya delicately spiced with garam masala and cooked with fresh fenugreek), Kebab's your Uncle! £6.95 (potato, cauliflower and paneer chunks skewered with green peppers, onion and tomatoes, then popped in the tandoor to char grill, and, probably the worst joke of the lot, Grandma, we love you! ,(she may be plain, nutty or even highly scented, but we know you all love your nan). I can hear the groans [gro-naans?] already! It's perhaps not the longest menu in the world, but there are some great dishes for everyone. Sunday brunch: three courses, £10 per person, live jazz band, 12-3pm. Hours: 1-2.30/6-11.00. Branch: Tamasha, Bromley.

HOMESDALE TANDOORI

28 Homesdale Road 020 8290 0671

Established in 1986. Seats 60. Undergoing redecoration. House specials: Haryali Chicken Masala £7, baked chicken in a marinade of spinach, mint and coriander puree, served in a creamy sauce. Takeaway: 10% discount. Delivery: £10 minimum, 3-mile radius. Hours: 12-2/6-12am.

KOSTURI NEW ENTRANT & A-LIST

18 Station Approach, Bromley 020 8462 8594

Kosturi seats 82 and is rather tastefully put together, with a clear vision of vibrant minimalism. Lavender walls are accented by strategically positioned spotlights that are installed in a hanging wooden beam, and merge into the naturally hued tiled flooring in the non-smoking section. The carpeting in the smoking section adds to the mix, while long-shaded contemporary lighting hangs over the rest of the restaurant, adding to the natural light that pours in from the large glass window at the entrance. Bangladeshi Head Chef, Sarawar Uddin Khan has been with Kosturi since

Kosturi, Bromley, Kent

Kosturi, Bromley, Kent

it first open in 2003, but who has been in the business for 17 years. His menu ranges from Goa to Lucknow and Punjab for which he has picked up the Bromley's coveted Best Curry Restaurant award in 2003 and 2005. Specialties are numerous and include, Chicken Capasilla, chicken off-the-bone, cooked with crushed cashew nuts, almonds and green peppers; King Prawn Kornofuli, Bay of Bengal tiger king prawns tossed in butter and garlic and cooked in a special blend of herbs and curry leaves. The most exclusive specialty on offer is the dish for which Khan won his 2005 award is Juje Limu. For this exceptional dish he marinates a chicken breast with ginger and garlic and then stuffs it with paneer, chopped onions and fresh mint. It is served with yogurt and lemon sauce and is only available on Friday and Saturday, upon request. The impeccable service is another reason for Kosturi's incredible success. Restaurant Manager Bhim Singh can take much of the credit for that. With a striking CV that charts back 25 years to Delhi's Maurya Sheraton hotels with its celebrated Bukhara *(see end pages)* and Dumpukht restaurants, for which he picked up the Best Beverage Manager Award in Asia at the 1985 Hotel and Food Service Awards. Bhim was also served President Bill Clinton. He is awarded this Guide's prestigious **MANAGER OF THE YEAR AWARD.**<www.kosturi.co.uk>

TAMASHA — AWARDED BEST IN THE SOUTH

131 Widmore Road, Bromley
020 8460 3240

Established in 1993. Owner is Shekor Tarat. Attached to a small hotel, so if you need a decent curry followed by a bed for the night, now you know. Tamasha means *'something worth seeing'.* And it is! There is ample car parking, and you enter past a smartly saluting geezer, via an awning flanked by tub plants. Inside, there's a well-stocked bar. The dining room, in two parts, seats 120 in seven rooms, and is superbly decorated like a British Raj Club, with polo sticks and hats, black and white photos of polo teams, Maharajas and sumptuous banquets. Cane furniture with palms in copper planters. Head chef Rajinder Kumar cooks food from north and south India, Goa and Kashmir. Curry house formula, it certainly is not. Favourite starters include Bhajis (Pakoras), Kebabs and Tikka, and main courses Jalfrezi and Chicken Tikka Masala. Good they are, too. But a little exploring can yield some treasures: Chicken Nilgiri Tikka, boneless chicken marinated in spices, fresh coriander and mint, cooked in the tandoor. Goan

Fish Curry, fish cooked in coconut and red chillies and garnished with fresh coriander leaves. Dum Pukht Gosht, marinated sliced baby lamb in a variety of spices and then steam-cooked in sealed earthenware, and Chicken Mirchi Wala, boneless chicken cooked in strongly spiced red chilli curry with potatoes, is popular, and Abrakebabra! so is the table magician who entertains the kids during Sunday lunch buffet. *'Crowded right through the evening and booking in advance whatever the night is to be recommended. Real orchids on the tables and everything about it shouts quality. Many unusual and imaginative dishes. Chicken Nilgiri Tikka was an intriguing shade of green, caused by being marinated in mint and coriander, flavours came through as I ate. Fish Punjabi crisp and spicy, Aloo Tikki very tasty. Raan Jaipuri and Rara Gosht equally tender and delicious. The only thing that did not suit our taste was the Peshwari Naan which was very sweet and overloaded with ground almond, but no fruit. Portions ample, service efficient and polite (but not particularly friendly, except for welcoming doorman). Prices above average, but not excessive for quality of restaurant and location. Well deserves its* **TOP 100** *status.'* MW. Menu Extracts: Malai Tikka, chicken marinated in cream cheese, cooked in tandoor, Aloo Tikki £3.95, minced potato burger, filled with lentils, served with mint and imli chutney, Aloo Pappri Chatt, chick peas, potatoes, coriander leaves, mint, yoghurt, imli sauce, crispy puri bread, Murgh Nawabi, chicken marinated in white wine, rich sauce of onion, tomato and saffron (sounds delicious!), Goan Chicken Xacuti, with coconut, Jhinga Tariwala, King prawns, spicy, tangy, red chillies, turmeric, bay leaves, Banarsi Dum Aloo, new potatoes stuffed with mint, cheese, tangy dry gravy. The annual Tamasha birthday party, held in Marquees on the grounds is amazing, and is one of Bromley's most-loved events, with unlimited food and drink , music and dancers, and a massive 600 guests. To get onto the invite list, you need to become one of Tamasha's regulars and go on their mailing list. Service charge 12.5%. 20 car parking spaces. Live jazz and blues on Sun., Mon. and Tues. evenings. Sunday lunch buffet with in-house magician for children. Takeaway: 10% discount. Hours: 12-2.30/6-11pm. *See page 12.*

ZANZIBAR

239 High Street, Bromley 020 8460 7130

Ebullient owner Ken Modi opened his Carioca in 1971 but changed its name because 'I got fed up with Karaoke requests'. The main room seats 50, its walls and ceiling decorated with coconut matting, giving the feeling of being in a fisherman's hut '– a very glamorous one' according to Mr Modi. The party room, which includes a mock Pullman railway carriage, seats 70. The menu contains the

Shekor Tarat, Tamasha, Bromley Kent

regular favourite tandooris, baltis, curries and accompaniments. *'After a morning shopping on a Saturday, we headed to the Zanzibar for a lunchtime buffet. The food is on view from the outside, as it is displayed on a warming table in the window. This sounds awful but it's actually well done, the dishes, polished and spanking clean, the food, fresh. We were politely served our starters first: a fresh, crisp salad with flat Onion Bhajis and half a Nan with chutneys, raita and a Coconut Chutney which was incredible, with a slight hint of heat from its mustard seed. The service became very friendly and helpful when we were given huge warm bowls for the self-serve buffet. The dishes were explained to us: Chicken Tikka Masala (smoky flavour – great), Bhoona Gosht, Mild Chicken Curry, Meat Madras, Bombay Aloo (excellent – new potatoes), Cauliflower Bhajee, Dal Makhani, Brinjal Bhajee, Plain and Pullau Rice and Nan bread. After two visits to this array of food, I was stuffed and delighted. Good food from a clean, well-decorated restaurant.'* MPW. Hours: 12-2 (Sun. 12.30-3.30)/6 (Sun. 6.30)-10.30.

Canterbury

SILKA — NEW ENTRANT

Canterbury Road Nr Charing — 01233 713883

'We've just got home from another Kentish newbie. On the Canterbury Road between Charing & Challock lies Silka - the sister restaurant of the one in SE1. It occupies a large building (I think it used to be the hq for the local gliding club) that is set back from the road. On the subject of location, this is very out of the way. Its about 30 mins from Canterbury and Maidstone and 15 from Ashford. It is very close to where we live but we had no idea it had become a restaurant until I spotted it on my motorcycle one day. Needs marketing badly..... The road is quiet even at busy times - you only use it if you are local or are travelling between Canterbury and Maidstone. I am frankly stunned that they have chosen this location – very pretty, right in a wood – because it really is on a road to nowhere. Anyhow, we decided to forgo our fave local in the town centre and give it a go. Having looked at the review of the London restaurant, the menu seems identical. We certainly liked the look of it but it maybe a little ambitious for the more neanderthal of local residents.' (Woops Howard, you've nearly told 'em where you live! Ed) *'For starters we went for a portion of the Tikka Paneer - which we both loved but thought the sweet sauces it was served with were just TOO sweet - and the Baby Squid - which had FIERCE green chillies and was just lovely. Almost Thai in style, I thought. I went more conservative next. A Shaslik chicken - lovely but with those same sweet sauces - while my wife went for the truly excellent Lamb with green herbs. Very sour with tamarind. Mouth watering. On the side were a Sag Bhaji - fantastic, with that lovely toasted flavour - and an average Mushroom Bhaji. We also had 2 chapattis, some sparkling water and my wife had some dry white wine. The staff were superb. Friendly without being overly so and they seemed genuinely pleased to see us - which is always nice ! The chap in charge told us all about the plans we saw the huge room at the back which they are going to turn into something very special by the sound of it. I am just concerned that they are in the completely the wrong location for the target audience. I hope I am wrong, this place makes a nice change from our lovely local.* HW.Hours: 12 to 2 and 5.30 to 11. <www.silka.co.uk> Branch: Silka, 6 Southwark Street London, SE1..

Chatham

THE ROYAL

50 New Road, Chatham — 01634 827799

'Situated in a former pub, seats forty, fairly comfortable. Surprisingly crowded on Thursday night. Interesting menu – expensive Poppadoms 75p plus 75p for a small portion of pickle. Excellent starters, my wife's favourite Onion Bhajia – four bhajis, very crisp, tasty, a better version. Chicken Tikka Chat – extremely tangy. Tandoori Mix – tasted good. Mains – Chicken Bhuna – medium strength, good well rounded flavour, very moist, fresh coriander leaves. Chicken Tikka Chilli Masala – rather rich red colour, very spicy, plenty of green chillies, pleasingly hot for my tastes, although too much for my wife (all the more for me!) Buttery Chana Masala, melting in the mouth.' MW. Delivery: £10 minimum, 4 miles. Takeaway: 10% discount, £20 minimum. Hours: 12-2/6-2 Fri closed lunchtime.

ACE OF SPICE — NEW ENTRANT

Watling Street, Chatham — 01634 578400

Ali and Mukid Choudhury have built a good reputation for their Ace of Spice, which they describe as their traditional Indian restaurant on Watling Street, serving good Indian fare. Hours: 12 to 2.30 and 6 to 11. Branch: Lily Spice, A249 at Detling Hill, Stockbury. 01795 844628.

Crayford (Greater London)

GHANDI SPICE

108 London Road, Crayford — 01322 559191

A standard curry house, established in 1997. Seats 40. Parking at front. Sunday buffet. Takeaway:

10% discount. Delivery: £10 minimum. Hours: 12-2.30/5.30-11.30; Sun. 12-11.30

Dartford

GREEN SPICE

Green Street, Green Road, Darenth, Dartford 01474 708855

Abdul Bari opened his restaurant in 1996, it seats 120 and Chicken Tikka Masala is the most ordered dish, surprise, surprise! Specials include: Fish Lazeem – Scottish salmon, medium sauce, orange zest; Kaleji Bakakara: liver, Bhuna style, hot and tangy; Silsila Chicken - marinated, cheddar cheese, mild and creamy sauce. Takeaway: 10% discount. Stocks: Cobra. Price Check: Popadom 50p, CTM £6.25, Pullao Rice £1.90. Hours: 12 to 2.30, Sunday to 3 and 5.30 to 12, Sunday to 11.30. Branch: Zara, Canterbury.

Downham (Near Bromley)

ROYAL GURKHA NEW ENTRANT

419 Bromley Rd , Downham 020 8461 4819

Originally opened in 1987 under the name Santi, taken over by JP Gautam in 2006 and yes, again CTM is the most ordered dish. The Royal Gurkha seats 48 and has a loyal following, here is just a snippet of what they have to say ... *'Excellent food and service friendly. Don't change a thing!'* JB. *'Chicken Korma and Chicken Biriani thoroughly enjoyable.'* E&PM. *'Lovely meal, bring back the Red Onion Chutney!'* MRS L. The Chutney sounds lovely - so JP, bring it back! Delivery: 4 miles, £10 minimum. Stocks: Cobra. Sunday Buffet £6.95. Price Check: Popadom 50p, CTM £6.25, Pullao Rice £1.95. Hours: 12 to 2.30 and 6 to 11.30, Saturday to 12.

SURUCHI

466 Bromley Road, Downham, 020 8698 8626

Fully licensed and air-conditioned. Istab Uddin Ahmed's popular dishes include: Tom Yum Soup £2.75, hot, famous Thai soup with mushrooms, lemon grass and prawns; Goan Chingri Palok £4.05, king prawn, spices, wrapped with fresh spinach and deep-fried; Chicken 65 £2.75 - Hyderabadi style with green chillies and curry leaves. Delivery: 3 miles, £12 minimum. Sunday Buffet: £6.95 adults, £4.95 children. Stocks: Cobra, Stella. Takeaway: 10% discount. Hours: 12.30 to 3, Sunday only and 5.30 to 12. <www.suruchiindia.co.uk>

Farnborough

VILLAGE CUISINE

145 High St, Farnborough 01689 860077

Modern decor and wooden floors at the Village. Established in 1991, it seats 40 and is not your run of the mill curry house – check out some of these fantastic dishes on the Summer Set Menu. Samosa – choose from meat, vegetable, coconut or fish. Creamed Mussels – served in their half shells, lightly spiced with saffron cream sauce. Murg Khasthri Kebab – chicken marinated overnight in yoghurt and herbs, skewered and cooked in tandoor. Hariali Lamb – boneless meat marinated in freshly ground coriander, spinach, mint and green chillies. Cucumber Rice, Spinach Nan, Mint Paratha and this list goes on! If you are not tempted by this extraordinary menu then there are of course the usual curry house curries. Proprietor Mr Fahim Maksud has promised to give a discount of 10% to *Guide* readers, please ring him for booking confirmation. Takeaway: 10% discount. Delivery: £10 minimum, 4-mile radius. Hours: 12-2.30 / 5.30-10.30; Sun. buffet 12-6.30pm.

Faversham

INDIAN ROYAL

16 East Street, Faversham 01795 536033

'Faversham's first Indian restaurant, opening in 1991 in an older Tudor style building. Probably seats forty comfortably in pleasant wood beamed restaurant – nice ambience. Standard menu, plus interesting additions such as Malai Kasa, cooked with coconut, almonds and chilli, Makhoni, cooked with mangoes, Manchurian, sweet and sour. However, I was told it was less hot than Pathia, I had visions of Chinese sweet and sour dishes so stuck to Chicken Tikka Pathia. This was very good – a nice thick hot and tangy sauce. Cauliflower Bhajee, a bit salty, but Vegetable Sambar, with lentils was excellent, delicious. Efficient and friendly service. Sufficient portions with average prices.' MW. Tuesday Night Special – £10 for starter, main, side and sundries– booking advisable. Sunday Buffet – £7.50 adult £4 children from midday to 5. Hours: 12-2.30/5-11.30.

Folkestone

GURKHA PALACE NEPALESE

NOMINATED BEST NEPALESE

97 Enbrook Valley, Folkestone 01303 257700

Kishore Sapkota is owner of this sixty seater, Nepalese restaurant. Menu Snapshot: Kalejo Bhutuwa £2.85, stir-fried chicken liver; Sinka Prawn £3.25, yoghurt marinated prawn, fried and served on bamboo skewer; Tama Bodi £2.90, bamboo shoots, black eyebeans, potatoes' (I have eaten this dish many times and can confirm that it is delicious – Ed); Chukauni £2.90 ,spicy potato salad with sesame seed; Staff Curry – Lamb £7.00; Momo £5.50, warm chicken dumplings served with Nepalese spicy chutney. Stocks: Cobra, Gurkha beer. Do try the Nepalese specialities, we have many happy reports about them, enough to Nonimate the Palace for Best Nepalese. Delivery: 3 miles, £12 minimum. Takeaway: 10% discount. Price Check: Popadom free - how generous! CTM £5.95, Pullao Rice £2.25. Hours: 11 to 2.30 and 6 to 11. <www.gurkhapalace.co.uk>

INDIA TOP 100

1 The Old High St, Folkestone 01303 259155

Mr Ali Ashraf chose Folkestone to establish his 42 seat India in 1985. Being a French-trained Indian chef and speaking French too, perhaps he felt being close to France would be *au fait*. In some cases he combines French methods (cream, wine and brandy) with Indian spices to provide an original interpretation of his Indian dishes. Since being a little critical last time (and we are just the messenger) we've been inundated with letters praising the India, strangely though, some typed by the same type-writer arrived in same-type envelopes. But we like the ebullient Ashraf, and it's great to hear from new reporters (but let's also hear from our old hands next time, please). So here are some examples: *'My first impressions were that the restaurant was mixed. It was only subtle clues that gave away the fact that this was something else. A fact I can not help feeling would be overlooked by a casual observer. The building fabric may be faded, but the table presentation and service was impeccable. My main basis for visiting the India was your books recommendation on the basis of food, and I can confirm reports that this was exceptional. I had the Crab in White Wine for My entrée (£4.95) followed by Chicken Jalfrezi*

(£5.95) and Special Fried Rice (£2.75). I have never before experienced such exquisite flavours. Every morsel exploded with new surprises and made the experience one that you wished would never end. Anything you believe you know about curry is turned on its head and it was a truly culinary experience. Having dined at the India for the first time last evening I shall certainly be visiting again and can whole heartedly agree that this establishment deserves its listing in your top 100.' DTH. 'Six of us ate there last Saturday and it was excellent. My favourite Chicken Jalfrezi was superb. We paid less than £20 a head including Popadoms, starters, main courses with vegetables, breads and drinks.' BT. Hours: 12-2 / 6-10.30.

Gillingham

50 Twydall Green, Gillingham 01634 386 110

S Rahman's curryhouse *'does some nice things'* RL. Menu Snapshot: Lamb Albadami £6.50, mango, creamy, mild sauce; Tandoori Mixed Grill £8.50, served with Nan bread. Banquet Night: Tuesday £11.95 per person. Air-conditioned. Stocks: Cobra. Takeaway: 10% discount. Price Check: Popadom 50p, CTM £6.50, Pullao Rice £1.90. Hours: 12 to 2.30 except Friday and 5.30 to 11.30, Sunday to 10.

Gravesend

(inc: Meopham)

GANDHI BALTI HOUSE

66 West Street, Gravesend 01474 536066

Owned by Abdul Basith Khan, serves Bangladeshi-style curries. Restaurant decorated in light pinks and light green, seats 60. *'Standards as good as ever. Chot Pote (spiced chickpea and egg mixture) tasty, Chicken Pathia always good, Vegetable Pullao had plenty of vegetables and nuts, a was an excellent value alternative to plain pilao rice. Service friendly and efficient and 10% Curry Club members' discount given without hesitation. Price average, portions ample. Usually fully booked in advance Friday and Saturday nights!'* MW. Sunday lunch buffet £7, children £6. Hours: 12-2.30/5.30-11 (11.30 on Sat.).

Halstead

BENGAL MANGROVE

London Road, Halstead 01959 534688

At the Bengal Mangrove you will not find your average curry house food – of course, they serve CTM etc, but why not try some of the other, perhaps, more unusual dishes. *'Took my son who although only eighteen, is a confirmed curryholic. Food was superb. Greeted by polite waiter. Drinks bill seemed a bit hefty, however, for the quality of restaurant and food, prices were reasonable. manager gave me guided tour of conservatory area (seventy seats), showing me the vast alterations to the place (I used to eat here when it was a Spanish restaurant). Interesting to see 25% discount on takeaway - I shall be back in the near future with this in mind.'* CO. Menu Snapshot: Chingri Tali Baja £3.95, tiger prawns seasoned in light spices, deep-fried in breadcrumbs; Crab Piri Piri £3.95, fiery red hot chillies, rice vinegar, spring onion and Goan spices; Mysore Bondi £2.95, mashed potato balls, ginger, curry leaves, black mustard seed, deep-fried – all starters are served with salad and homemade chutney. Badami Stuffed Murgh Masala £8.95, chicken stuffed with vegetables, cream, almonds and pistachio; Sathkari Gosht £6.95, lamb, wild lemon, naga chilli, lemon leaf; Dahi Dover Sole £11.95, pan-fried in yoghurt sauce; Salmon Tikka £7.95; Vegetable Milijuli £4.95, baby potatoes, mange tout, stir-fried in garlic oil; Nilgiri Korma £4.95, paneer, cabbage, beans, carrots, mint, sweet and mild sauce.

Maidstone

BENGAL DINER

98 King Street, Maidstone 01622 756094

'This is the site of the The Curry Inn, Kent's first Indian restaurant, founded 1965 by Mr S Meah and run by him until the summer of 2003 when he retired. It has now had a change of ownership, being run by the same people who own the Shamrat in Maidstone, and a change of chef. I wish Mr Meah a long and happy retirement and went to try out the new restaurant. At first sight it is little different that before. Still the long line of tables set closely together along each wall and seating about 50, and the furniture looks the same. And it was just as empty. However, the imitation flock wallpaper has been replaced by plain cream paint and the pictures are gone. The service was also sharper and more friendly (Mr Meah apart, of course). The menu largely followed the same extensive pattern as before, as did the prices. We had the same meal for comparison purposes. The starter of Onion Bhajia showed there was a different chef. Previously it was four large (and I mean large) round type without salad garnish, while this time they were two large flat type with salad and raita. They were fairly solid but with plenty of onion and tastily spiced. Chicken

Tikka Pathia, which as before included a full portion of rice, was fairly spicy although not quite so hot as previously (I described it a year ago as having 'a strong, gutsy spicing and hotness which set the mouth a-tingle'). Nevertheless, it was quite acceptable. The Tandoori Chicken was a standard version – probably not quite so tasty as previously (reported as being 'darkly coloured and marinated to impart a char-grilled effect in places') It seemed a typical high street tandoori chicken although my wife – the main recipient – felt there was an unidentifiable underlying taste which she could only describe as rather cheesy. She felt it was below the average offering, and who am I to argue? However, we both agreed that the Dry Mixed Vegetable was very good, with large pieces of vegetables lightly cooked and very pleasantly spiced, and better than average (last time was a pretty standard version).' MW

Marden

MARDEN TANDOORI

Albion Rd, Marden 01622 832184

Well, which do you choose? This well-established venue or the Royal? MW finds both are to his liking, so please read both Marden entries. *'All in all the people of Marden are lucky to have two Indian restaurants in such a small village, and two that provide a good standard of formula curry is a bonus. It makes for a difficult decision next time I am in Marden !'* MW. Hours: 12 -2.30/6-11.

ROYAL NEW ENTRANT

27 High Street, Marden 01622 83

'Residents of this small village can think themselves very fortunate, as this is the second Indian restaurant to be set up in the village, opening about five years ago in competition with the much longer-established Marden Tandoori (see above). The Royal is a pleasant-looking restaurant seating about 65 in two comfortable sections (and they tell me they also have a garden which can be utilised in good weather if need be!). Good menu with all the favourites plus one or two different names. Overall the food was a good formula curry standard. Tandoori Chicken well marinated and very tasty, Chicken Tikka Dhansak delicious in a thick, spicy and hot sauce, Tarka Dall a good version of the dish and just the right consistency – not too thick and custard-like, but not too thin – and the Niramish again a pleasantly spiced, good selection of vegetables (which unusually did not have any potato amongst it). Standard rice and accompaniments, although I did think the popadoms seemed particularly crisp and pleasant. Perhaps imagination, as providing they're crisp there is not usually much to comment on, but I was conscious that these seemed a touch above the average. Prices about average and plentiful portions. Service friendly and efficient' MW.

Minster

SHERAZ

10 High Street, Minster 01795 876987

'Interior looks like a Kebab House. Punjabi cooking. Friendly service. Food surprisingly good. Nappali Chicken – good, hot, chillies. Dhal Samba – tasty. OK, but oily Cauliflower Bhajee. Prices average, portions good.' MW. Delivery: £12 minimum, 3 miles. Credit cards accepted. Menu Extracts: Kofta Masala – meatballs, cooked with yoghurt, spicy sauce and egg, Bindi Ghost – orka, lamb, rich spicy sauce, onions, Peas Potato £2.60, Butter Chapatti or Onion Nan £2.25. Hours: 11-11.30, Fri and Sat to 12.

Orpington ((Greater London)

CURRY HOUSE

24 Station Sq, Petts Wood 01689 820671

Basth (Baz) Wahab runs 42-seater. *'Food good but atmosphere non-existent. Eventually won the waiters round and managed a laugh and a little conversation. Flavoursome fish tikka. Main dishes were well up to expectation.'* C&GM. Hours: 12-3 (not on Fri.) and 6-12; closed Mon.

RAJ OF INDIA

4 Crescent Way, Green Street Green, Orpington 01689 852170

Established 1987. Owner-manager Muzibur Rahman. Seats 72. Chef recommends: Akbori Lamb, cooked with sultanas and almonds in a yoghurt sauce. Takeaway: small discount. Hours: 12-2.30/6-12am. Branches: Raj of India Sheerness, Swanley and Sittingbourne; Raj Bari Sevenoaks; Maharajah Bexley; Juboraj Brentwood, Essex.

Ramsgate

RAMSGATE TANDOORI

17 Harbour Street 01843 589134

70-seater, owned by Rezaur Rahman, managed by Mrs Rahman. Bangladeshi and Pakistani curries cooked by head chef Joyanti Mendas. Sunday buffet. Delivery: £10 minimum. Hours: 12-2.30/6-12.

Rochester

BENGAL BRASSERIE

356 High Street, Rochester 01634 841930

We received a letter from the manager worried that what he called *'a mad women'* would destroy his business. She ate her meal, the said it was awful and that she would complain to us here at the Guide. She never did of course, but it is one of those horrid things that happen to restaurateurs. Our advice to them as always, is not to pay out compensation when the whole meal is consumed before the complaints begin. There are professional complainers – they can eat their fill and earn a living at it –and she was one.. Nothing wrong with The Bengal Brasserie. It is an old friend of this Guide and has many other friends. <www.bengalbrasserie.com>

SHOZNA — NEW ENTRANT

153 Maidstone Road, 01634 847 847

Jamal Udin Ahmed's Shozna is a popular venue. Menu Snapshot: Chicken Cutlet £3.50; Stuffed pepper (meat or vegetable) £3.70; all starters served with salad and mint sauce. Monchorian Chicken £7.50, chicken fillet, mango, cream; Badami Chicken £7.50, roasted cashew, butter, medium spices; Naga Chicken or Lamb £7.50, Vindaloo hot (I think you will find it hotter than that!); Bengal Pemisal £12.50, ayre fish fried in olive oil, medium spices, served with Onion Rice; Egg Nan £2.50. Stocks: Cobra and Kingfisher. Price Check: Popadom 60p, CTM £7.50, Pullao Rice £2.40. Hours: 12 to 2 (table reservation only) and 5.30 to 12. Branch: Shozna, 18 High Street, Stroud, Kent.

SINGAPORA

51 High Street, Rochester 01634 842178

Dr and Mrs Shome's 150-seater spreads over three floors, with tables in odd alcoves. Specialising in Malaysian, Chinese, Indonesian, Thai and Japanese cuisine. *'Cosy, but deceptively larger with upper floors and basement. Aromatic Duck, shredded with sliced spring onions, cucumber and plum sauce rolled in pancakes. Udang Roti, King prawns on sesame toast – substantial flavour. Ayam Penang, Malaysian dish, crispy chicken with ginger and onions, tasty. Ayam Iblis, sliced chicken, chilli and ginger, very tasty. Washed down with red house wine £8.95, smooth and excellent value. Portions a little on the small side. Efficient and friendly service. Pleasant alternative.'* MW. Delivery. Hours: 12-3pm/6-11pm (Fri. & Sat. to 11.30); Sun. 12-10.30. Branch: 73, Brewer Street, Maidstone.

Sevenoaks

ASIA CUISINE

107 London Road, Sevenoaks 01732 453153

'My local. Does a brilliant CTM with rice and always friendly service.' kt. *'Nice place, very cosy, love the Indian music. Portions more than ample and prices just right.'* RL.

SPICE CLUB

57 High Street, Sevenoaks. 01732 456688

'First class Indian restaurant. Staff smartly dressed in black, very helpful. Food is outstanding. Connoisseur starter section along with traditional Fish Pakora £3.25 very light. Lamb

Boti Kebab, very succulent. Boal Malchi, very good (Gourmet). South Indian Garlic Chilli Chicken, very popular. Sevenoaks best!' KT. Hours: 12-2.30 / 6- 11.30.

Sidcup (Greater London)

BLACKFEN BALTI

33 Wellington Pde, Blackfen Road, Sidcup 020 8303 0013

A friendly, pleasant, competent 48-seat curry house, owned by Muzammil Ali since 1983.

OVAL BRASSERIE

49 The Oval, Sidcup 020 8308 0274

Ansar Miah has owned and managed the aptly-named Oval since 1988 (head chef Mohibur Rahman). Monday and Tuesday £7.95, starter, main course, side dish, rice or Nan – excellent value. Delivery: £10 minimum, 3-mile radius, free Poppadam. Hours: 12-2.30/6-11.30. All-day Sunday 12-11.30, buffet £6.95, £4 for kids.

Stockbury

LILY SPICE NEW ENTRANT

A249 at Detling Hill, Stockbury 01795 844628

Ali and Mukid Choudhury's new destination restaurant for curry aficionados, Lily Spice, opened in July 2006. Yes that is the correct address and it is in a former a Little Chef and then the transport café Porkies on the main route between Medway and Maidstone. Plenty of free parking and say the Choudhurys, it beats town centre venues and creates a relaxed meeting environment. True? Reports please. Hours: 12 to 3 and 6 to 11. Branch: Ace of Spice, Watling Street, Chatham 01634 578400

Strood

SHOZNA INDIAN CUISINE

28 High Street, Strood 01634 710701

As at his Rochester branch, Jamal Udin Ahmed's Shozna is a popular venue. Hours: 12 to 2 (table reservation only) and 5.30 to 12. Branch: Shozna, Rochester. Established in 1978. Taken over by J Ahmed in 1996. Seats 38. Parking at rear for 50 cars. Chef Jamal Uddin Ahmed was the 2003 runner-up winner of the Curry Chef of the Year contest run by the CIEH, (Health officer's institute) and the food is good. *'Does not look much from the outside, inside pleasantly cosy. Relatively small, seating 48. Custom made furniture, all good quality. Started with my benchmark – Onion Bhajia. Four, small, round, plenty of onion, crisp outside, moist inside, excellent. Bhari Kebab – small pieces of kebab, spicy, rich sauce, extremely tasty, first class. Long debate over mains, chose Badami Chicken – delicious full bodied sauce, chopped cashew nuts, slightly herby. Dhansak – included Pullao Rice, well spiced lentil sauce. Smart, clean toilets. Portions just right, prices average. The car park is behind the restaurant, up a small alleyway, easy to miss. An excellent little restaurant, packed on a Thursday night.'* MW. Menu Extracts: Monchorian Chicken £6, chicken fillet, mango, cream. Naga Lamb £6 – garnished with Naga chillies. Naga chillies are incendiary – so be warned! Takeaway: 10-15% discount. Hours: 12-1.30/5.30-12am.

Swanley

RAJ OF INDIA

23 High Street, Swanley 01322 613651

'Popped into the Raj of India, on mentioning The Curry Club and the possibility of a discount (I always ask - even if it not shown in the Guide), the proprietor for some ungodly reason took to me and said I could have a free drink. Started with two Poppadoms, pickles and surprise, surprise they actually asked me if I would like pickles with my main course! wonders will never cease!! Very good and hot Chicken Vindaloo, Pullao Rice and Nan Bread - excellent meal, just right.' BP-D. Menu extracts: Noorani Kebab £2.90, minced chicken, coriander, onion and green chilli. Aliza Chicken £3.50, deep-fried chicken pieces in chick pea flour. Other members take note of Bill's persistence in getting his discount. Branch: Raj Bari, Sevenoaks, Kent and Alishan, Tonbridge, Kent.

Tenterden

BADSHA NEW ENTRANT

10 West Cross, Tenterden 01580 765 151

Owner, AH Shuab's restaurant seats 70 diners and serves an *'awful lot'* (he says) of Jalfrezi and Mossalla dishes. Has served stars like The Drifters. Wow! Takeaway: 10% discount. Stocks: Cobra. Price Check: Popadom 55p, CTM £6.45, Pullao Rice £1.85. Hours: 12 to 2.30 and 6 to 11.30.

Tunbridge Wells

MUNA'S RESTAURANT & BAR

70 High Street, T' Wells 01892 537113

Established in 1996. Seats 38. Modern design, black and chrome. Punjabi curries, à la carte and buffet is available every evening. À la Carte: Deluxe Grill, assortment of lamb and chicken tikka, kebab and prawns, served with potato salad and rice. Naan Toppers – warm nans topped with: Chicken Tikka Masala, Tandoori Prawn Masala, Lamb Boti. Buffet £15 – e-a-m-a-y-l with Poppadams with Chutney and Raitha, Vegetable Pakoras, Aubergine Masala, Fried Okra and Onion in Chickpea Batter, Indian Salad in lemon and mint Dressing, Hot Stuffed Red Pickled Chillies and that's just for starters! Buffet main courses include: Lamb Rhogan Ghost, Chicken Bhoona, Vegetable Balti, Saag Aloo, Tarka Dal with Rice and Bread, tremendous value. Hours: 12-2 / 6-11; Sun. closed.

TAGORE A-LIST

4 Neville Street, The Pantiles, Tunbridge Wells 01892 615100

Nur Monie's Tagore has moved fom Welling and the opulent decor of saris wall-hangings the shamiana (Moghul marquee) ceiling came too. Tagor's turns out fabulous north Indian curries. But its USP is specials from Pakhtoomn, which refers to the Pathan tribal people of Afghanistan and the rugged Pakistani passes, whose name for themselves is Phuktana or Pukhtun. Afghan food is pretty basic *(see page 66)*, especially at tribal level, involving kebab-skewer cooking and slow-cooking in pots, but Monie, a former economics graduate and Bombay-trained chef Rajendra Balmiki achieved two coveted Michelin stars in their Montparnasse, Paris Tangore, now closed, a feat never achieved by Indian restaurants in the UK. Head waiter Tapesh Majumber looks after front of houes. The Tagore offers a select menu. Starters include Kashmiri Lamb Tikka, Kebab Ke Karishma, a selection of kebabs (£17 for two, is popular). Main dishes are divided between six chicken dishes, five meat, six from the tandoor and three fish dishes. At £7, Patrani Mahi, pomfret coated in herbal chutney, leaf-wrapped and baked, is a rarity to be treasured. Murgh Chennai, is none other than Chicken Madras, but its is a cut above the formula version, Kadai Ghost Massala was wonderfully cooked with a rich sauce that you will remember and Koh-e-Avadh, is lamb knuckles simmered in the dum method. Raan E Buzkazi, leg of lamb from the NW Frontier. If you have room, there are some interesting desserts. Try Chocolate chip and nut Kulfi with rosewater syrup. It is all far from formula which makes is a must to try. ' *'On all occasions I have found their food to be a world apart from the traditional curry houses with the dishes being expertly cooked. Excellent value for money, service and explanation of the dishes is of a very high quality.'* PG. Takeaway 20%discount. Hours: 8-11pm. Branch: Kasturi, London EC1.

West Kingsdown

RAJDANI

17, London Rd, West Kingsdown 01474 853501

Proprietor Suna Meah runs it with other members of the family, including the chef. Good sized car parking; two ponds; a little decking-style bridge to cross over the ponds. Separate area for takeaway. Visited for dinner. Ate plain pops with chutney tray. Onion Bhajia, Chicken Aliza (chicken pakora), Tandoori Prawn, Chicken Chat in puri with plenty of crispy salad main course, huge tandoori king prawns in a cashew nut korma sauce, chicken with cashew nut sauce – delicious chicken tava – spicy but not hot. Plain Nan – light, fluffy – all breads that came out of the kitchen were really good. Red rose on leaving; We were introduced to a couple who dine here six days every week, and on the seventh, they visit other Indian restaurants. There's loyalty. Hours: 12 - 2.30 / 6 -11.30. <www.rajdhani.net>

West Wickham

BLUE GINGER

101 High Street, West Wickham 020 8777 4080

'Attractive, not as minimalist and basic as some new wave establishments. Staff, welcoming, knew what they were doing. Pops with good chutney in an unusual container. Aloo Bora, particularly good and flavoursome. Spicy Bindi, hot and crispy. We''ll be back.' G&CM. Takeaway: 10% discount. Banquet Night: Wednesday £9.95. Sunday lunch buffet £7.95.

Westerham

KINARA AT PITT'S COTTAGE

BEST PAKSITANI RESTAURANT

High Street (Limpsfield Road), Westerham 01959 562125

This restaurant changed hands in March 2005 since when we have had mostly praising reports and one, a bit disappointed.. *'We had been very excited by the prospect of having a Top 100 entry in our neck of the woods! We visited on a Sunday at lunchtime. They offer a buffet at £9.95 per person, however we asked to order off the main menu and they reluctantly agreed to this request. Service thereafter was efficient and friendly. The bill for three was £57.00 including a service charge of 10%. Overall we felt that the surroundings and service were certainly above average but found the food slightly disappointing.'* Alex e-mail. But Rachel loves it.*'Thought you might like to know of a new Indian restaurant opened in Westerham, it used to be called Pitts Cottage, but has been taken over by a guy from Dublin'* Kushi Mohammed – Ed) *'who currently runs a place called "Kinara", he has opened a Kinara in Westerham and I would thoroughly recommend it....the food is fantastic'.* RB. Menu Snapshot: Tandoori Trout £3.50; Aloo Tikki £3.25 - deep-fried mashed potato cakes with garlic and ginger; Keema Aloo £8.50 - minced lamb simmered with potato, tomato, onion, chilli, ginger; Lamb Lobia £9.95 - lamb fillet, green beans, ginger, garlic, cream; Paneer Nan £2.50 - stuffed with cheese. Takeaway: 10% discount. Stocks: Cobra. Price Check: Popadom £1.25 a basket, CTM £7.25, Pullao Rice £2.20. Hours: Lunch: Fri to Sun only, 12 to 3; Daily, 6 to 11.30. <www.kinara.co.uk>

TULSI

RETURNS TO TOP 100

20 London Road, Westerham 01959 563397

Tulsi (biological name *Ocimum Sanctum*), is the sacred basil plant of India, where it is grown as a symbol of good luck and good health. Owned by Deb, it has a small waiting area with tables and chairs, and an extended, slightly elevated, well-decorated eating area, with a polished wooden floor. Walls covered by framed posters of Bollywood film stars. Ambience is good with very friendly staff, well-dressed in national costume. Chef Anil K Hazra cooks wonderfully innovative Indian cuisine – just how many like it. *'This was our first visit on a busy Saturday night, but after a short wait we were seated. Service was excellent and the food delicious. This restaurant should still be in the top 100, removal for leaving an open credit card slip is harsh considering that this is standard in most restaurants.'* JB. OK Julie, I will. Thanks for your views. Hours: 12-2.30 (closed Sun. lunch)/6-11.30. Branch: Tamasha, Bromley.

LANCASHIRE

Area: North West
Population: 1,434,000
Adjacent Counties: Cumbs, Greater Man, W Yorks

Adlington

SHAPLA TAKEAWAY

178 Chorley Road, Adlington 01257 474630

'Shapla'schef and part-owner got Sharjus the reputation it had/has when he was the head chef back in the 1980s. Going there brings back the original Sharju experience that it seems to lack today. I travel at least twice a week to the Shapla by-passing several top restaurants on my 15 mile each way journey. Yours with good curry at heart'. AH.

SHARJU TOP 100

Church Street, Adlington 01257 481894

Mohammad Ali Shaju's 144-seater is easily found on the A59. Its resemblance to a residential bungalow ceases on entry. It is stylishly decorated with cream walls, ceiling and table linen, blue carpet, and 144 wicker chairs, in two dining rooms. Wooden fretwork screens give tables privacy. *'Modern, out of town restaurant, conservatory. Arrived at 6.45pm, as the large car park was filling up. A few moments wait before being ushered into conservatory, restaurant already full. Couldn't fault any of the dishes. Despite being busy, service was good, but indifferent. Not pressurised to leave, however it was all hands to the pump to get the table changed for the next sitting. We will return with our caravan, there is a site next door.'* T&MH. Takeaway: 20% discount. Hours: 12-2 / 5.30-11.30. (12am on Fri. & Sat.). Sunday 1-11.

Blackburn

SHAJAN

Longsight Road, Clayton-le-Dale, Mellor, Blackburn 01254 813640

Good curryhouse where you might get a discount if you show them this *Guide.*

Burnley

SHALAMAR

56 Church Street, Burnley 01282 434403

Ditto

Clitheroe

DIL RAJ

7 Parsons Lane, Clitheroe 01200 427224

Ditto

Fleetwood

AL MINAR

26 Larkholme Parade 01253 777787

Ditto

Haslingden

SUNAR GAW

16 Regent Street 01204 364915

Another one where you might get a discount if you show them this *Guide.*

Lancaster

BOMBAY

16 Jubilee House, China Street, Lancaster 01524 844550

And yet another one where you might get a discount if you show them this *Guide.*

Longridge

VICTORIA'S INDIA MOST WELCOME NEWCOMER

The Manse, Church St, Longridge 01772 785111

This is the story of entrepreneurship 'against the odds'. Tony and Carol Walters have done what so many say they wish to do: they have opened their 'dream' restaurant. The reality has been more of a nightmare, with the battle grounds consisting of acquisition of premises, planning permissions, builders, budgets, overspends, personnel, work permits and officialdom in general. But the couple believe in doing things correctly, and they achieved their opening in 2005. Early on they consulted Pat, whose advice was to obtain a top manager and top chefs – something easier said than done. But more of that later. Walters himself said 'some thought, that we were mad to open an Indian restaurant in Longridge. However, we concluded, that with the right head chef, a good location and superior local produce, that we would have the correct elements for a good restaurant. Victoria's India is a unique name for an Indian restaurant. The name evolved from the building's architecture. It is a beautiful 1865 Victorian villa that was built by the Rev Booth, then Longridge vicar. The church opposite and the school behind in Chapel St are from the same period and have the same, design elements. Being within a conservation area, the couple

wanted to keep the building substantially as it was. Now completely refurbished the building, is clean and modern, and I am pleased to report that original period features have indeed been restored and not replaced! Feel free to admire the tiled floor and the fire places. There are two dining areas, the larger is called the 'Albert' room and seats thirty diners, the smaller, the 'Victoria' room, seats twenty diners and is also available for private hire. A walled garden, which has an awning for those sunny and rainy days, seats a comfortable twelve diners. Long summer evenings can be enjoyed with cocktails or coffee and liqueurs (and perhaps a cigarette or two!). The owners engaged Didier Vincent as general manager, having worked in places as exalted as . P&O's Aurora and Oriana as well as the QE2. As for the food, the early decision was that whatever was on the menu, it would be cooked authentically, and not in curryhouse style. The kitchen is tiny (something celebrity chefs couldn't cope with) requiring good organisation. It is led by chef, Bishal Rasaily, who earned his spurs at Delhi's Maurya Sheraton under chef qereshi (of Dum Pukht fame) and London's celebrated Chutney Mary (see sw 10). He is assisted by Tandoori Chef Sanjeev Kashyap, who came to England via Delhi's 'Vishnu Garden' restaurant. Their specials include: Tandoori Fish Salad £5.50 - grilled salmon chunks and fresh green salad; Aloo Pakora £2.90 - potato wheels dipped in spiced gram flour batter, then golden-fried for crispness, garnished with coriander leaves; Chicken Malai Tikka £4/£9.90 - a creamy kebab of boneless chicken breast, blended with cream and cheese then grilled in tandoor; Sheek Gilafi £4/£9.90 - spiced ground lamb coated with diced bell peppers and onion, cooked on skewer in tandoor; Paneer Makhani - cottage cheese tossed in tomato, cream, cashew nut gravy and julienne of ginger, garnished with cream; Kadhai £8.50 - choice of chicken or lamb, stir-fried with finely chopped onion, ginger, garlic and green chilli, cooked in tomato juice, sauteed with bell pepper and finished with fenugreek leaves and kadhai masala; Royal Biriani £10.50 - Basmati rice steamed with tender curried lamb or chicken, enhanced with saffron, aromatic spices, garnished with almonds, sultanas and an omelette, served with vegetable curry sauce. Sunday Buffet Lunch: £6.95 adult, £3.95 for the younger curryholic. We have awarded Victoria's India the **MOST WELCOME NEWCOMER AWARD** against stiff competition from many London venues. Our reasoning is simple. Unlike so many London newcomers have almost unlimited budgets, resources and experts to achieve the job. The Walters did it on a shoestring, learning as they went, proving that it can be done. And what has been done for Indian cuisine is to bring London to Longridge, something that the whole of the north of England should take note of. Prices are within reach, and we hope Victoria's India becomes a serious destination for all devotees of Indian food. The website is unflashy and informative, and uniquely even lists it suppliers. I wish Victoria's India was my local. Lucky Longridge! Hours: 6 - 11.30 Tues-Fri; 6 - 11.30 .Sat, Last food orders: 10.30; 2 - 11.00. Sun/Bank Holiday (a la carte after 7). Mon closed. <www.victoriasindia.co.uk>

Lytham St Annes

BILASH BALTI — NEW ENTRANT

19 St Andrews Road St Annes 01253 780001

'I am writing this email so that you can maybe add my comments and experiences with regards to the Bilash Balti. I am a regular dinner at the Bilash and it is my favourite Indian restaurant. It was the first to introduce Balti dishes in the Fylde and every other restaurant seems to try and copy what they do. The food is excellent and the staff are very friendly and polite. Its a family-run restaurant with the owner , Mr Hoque and his sons running the place. I would give this restaurant 10 out of 10 - it's that good.' AC. Menu Snapshot: Fish Pakora £7.25, served with salad and Gobi Bhajee; Makhon Chicken £6.05, diced tandoori chicken, butter, tomato, cream; Kashmiri Korma King Prawn £7.65, with dried fruit; Kulcha Naan £1.70, stuffed with cheese and onion. Stocks: Cobra. Price Check: Popadom 40p, CTM £6.05, Pullao Rice £1.65. Hours: Sat to Thurs 12 to 2, / 6 to 12 Saturday 12.30.

MOGHUL

12 Orchard Road, St Annes 01253 712114

'I'm not usually prone to putting finger to keyboard but I feel I must share with you my recent experience at the above restaurant. My wife and I are, as you so well put it in your own words "curryholics" and on our annual pilgrimage to the west coast for rest and recuperation we enquired as to the whereabouts of a good curry restaurant, the hotelier pointed us in the direction of the town centre and to No 12 Orchards Road. On entering the establishment it was obvious from the outset that this was no ordinary place from the decor down to the service it oozed class. We were greeted by Mr Ali a most convivial host, within minutes of our unannounced arrival we were seated, drinks ordered and the menu brought to us. The list of dishes presented to us was mind-boggling and some of which I confess have never heard of before, I enquired into one dish – Achari Gosht (pickle-based lamb) which I wanted to try. Without any prompting and for no extra charge Mr Ali

asked his chef to prepare us a sample dish. It was exquisite. I shall not say what we finally ordered but just to say it was prepared and presented beautifully. Mr Chapman please pass this onto your loyal readers as a must go to venue you will not be disappointed.' GW.

Preston

SAGAR PREMIER

Clayton Brook Rd, Bamber Bridge, Preston
01772 620 200

'Chatting to regular customers, some of whom had driven over from Yorkshire!, their enthusiasm for Sagar quality continues to be very high. Interior still looks fresh and classy, a credit to the meticulous housekeeping and hygiene. Waiters know what their customers' favourite drinks are, so they are served by the time they walk through the door. Our meal of fresh Popadoms and pickles, Meat Samosas (on par with Depa Tandoori, London), Mixed Kebabs, best quality chicken breast and lamb in aromatic sauces, Dupiaza, Madras with piquant Pullao Rice and Sag Aloo were all generous portions and absolutely delicious. With several rounds of Cobra, the meal averaged £17 a head, very competitive. Sagar are unique in providing swift and efficient service, this makes for a very relaxing meal.' TE. Menu Snapshot: Machi Malai, fish curry, garlic, tomato, green chilli, crab meatballs, mustard and spices; South Indian Murghi, off the bone tandoori chicken, mincemeat, coriander leaves; Exotic Salmon, black pepper, cinnamon, spring onion and garlic; Tomato Rice; Garlic and Coriander Paratha. Takeaway: 10% discount. Hours: 12 to 2 and 6 to 11.30. Saturday and Sunday 1 to 11.30.

LEICESTERSHIRE

Area: East Midlands
Population: 912,000
Adjacent Counties: Derbs, Lincs, Northants, Notts, Rutland, Staffs, Warks

Leicester

Leicester is home to a good number of Gujaratis from India. In addition, many of its Asian community settled there in the 1970s when they became exiled from Africa, specifically Kenya and Uganda, where they had lived for generations, having been taken there as clerks and semi-skilled plantation labour by the British. Most contemporary Leicester Asians have little concept of the Indian subcontinent, few having ever visited it, but you would not know this from the quality of the food, particularly in the cheap and cheerful cafés, snack bars and sweet shops all over town. The first curry house, the Taj Mahal, opened in 1961 and is still there! I dined there that year, and when I asked for chilli pickle the anxious owner appeared and spent half an hour counselling me against eating hot food! (To no avail, I might add!) Now there are over 80 'Indian' restaurants on our database which, in a city of around 300,000 population, is a ratio of one 'Indian' restaurant per 3,750 people, making Leicester our second most densely curry-housed city in the UK (see Bradford, West Yorkshire). However, over a two week visit period, we found Leicester's restaurants, Indian and otherwise, to be virtually empty on weekday evenings. The City simply closes at around 6pm. What a terrible waste. We were also surprised to find that Leicester council do not allow pavement trading, so vital to the charisma of London's Asian communities. They say vegetables on the street is a health hazard! Get real Leicester, and get using your restaurants, before they close on you. Oh and yes, if you choose to have a go at me about this, your comments will be published here next time. We said all this last time and nothing has changed and no comment, but I'm still waiting!

Leicester, Belgrave Road

Paul Motley describes Leicester's 'Little India':

'Belgrave Road, just north of the city, is Leicester's golden curry mile. As well as containing a great selection of authentic, real Indian restaurants both vegetarian and non-vegetarian, Belgrave Road and the surrounding area offers an insight into Indian shopping for jewellry, fashion, cookware, food and spices plus much more all at bargain prices. Sundays seems to be a real family day out for the family unit of three generations together without attitude, something we seem to have lost these past years. Leicester has one of the highest percentages of Asian population in any town or city in the UK with a forecast that the majority of its population will be of ethnic origin by 2011. Leicester is quoted as an outstanding example of diversity and ethnic plurality and is internationally heralded as a model of community and cohesion. All this reflects in the

diversity of the food offered around the Belgrave/Melton Road Area of the city. You could be forgiven if you thought that you had miraculously been transported to somewhere in India and some may even feel a little intimidated by the fact the English faces are very few and far between, however the populous are very far from intimidating in fact by contrast the atmosphere is far far friendlier than the majority of town centres plus service in the many family run shops and business establishments really is second to none. By the way should each November, Leicester is renowned for attracting over 60,000 visitors for this important event, which is incidentally the highest number in the world outside of India.' PM.

BOBBY'S GUJARATI VEGETARIAN

154 Belgrave Road 0116 266 2448

Atul Lakhani (aka Bobby) owns a restaurant with two advantages – a license and very reasonably priced food, so it's ever-popular with a cafeteria-type atmosphere. Mostly Gujarati food, which is light and slightly sweet. You pay (credit cards taken) at the till. Hours: 11-10.30.

CURRY FEVER AWARD WINNER

139 Belgrave Road, 0116 266 2941

Established in 1978 by Anil Anand (head chef) and Sunil Anand (manager). They are related to the Brilliant and Madhu's Brilliant of Southall and Curry Craze of Wembley (*see* entries in Middlesex). The food is Punjabi, cooked just as they eat them at home. House specialities, which show the owners' Kenyan background, include: Jeera Chicken £13.90, one of this restaurants classic dishes, a must eat, fabulous whole chicken briskly fried with cumin seeds and powder; Pili Pili Chicken £13.90, whole chicken, hot and spicy sauce, another must eat; Mogo Shashlick £4.50, skewered cassava, onion, capsicum; Machusi Lamb £8.00, Kenyan style lamb, fenugreek sauce. Previously we gave it our **BEST IN THE MIDLANDS** Award. Though this time the award has moved elsewhere, it is an award which lasts for ever. *'Curry Fever – still the best in Leicester'* CM.. Takeaway: 10% discount. Service charge: 10%. Minimum Charge: £10.00. Stocks: Cobra. Price Check: Popadom 70p, CTM £7.80, Pullao Rice £2.50. Hours: 12 to 2, Tues to Sat; 6 to 11.20, Saturday to 12, Monday closed.

FRIENDS TANDOORI TOP 100

41 Belgrave Road, Leicester 0116 266 8809

Manjit Pabla's sophisticated and stylish restaurant serving superior (scrummy!) curries. Do book your table for the weekend, you will not be disappointed. Menu Snapshot: Lussani Kebab £4.75, chicken marinated in fresh garlic and roasted in the tandoor; Kali Mirch Ka Kabab £4.75, chicken rolled and marinated in cream and crushed peppercorns; Masaledar Champaan £5.50, tender lamb chops marinated in a ginger-masala base with yoghurt and grilled in the tandoor; Malai Kofta £6.25, mashed vegetables, deep-fried and cooking in a creamy sauce; Bhartha £6.25, roasted, smoked aubergines mashed and cooked with peas and fresh tomatoes. A traditional Punjabi dish with a smoky flavour; Daal Panch-Rattani £5.95, a combination of five lentils tempered with cumin, garlic, onions and tomatoes. Mrs Chapchal, take note: Gulaab Jamun £2.75, home-made, (yum yum!) served hot or cold with ice cream, lovely; Ras Malai £2.75, reduced milk shaped into discs and poached gently in full-fat milk, garnished with pistachios and saffron, wonderful. Don't forget to linger over the wine list, it really is an informative selection from all around the world including one of my favourites, Malbec from Argentina and at £12.95 a bottle extremely good value for money. Takeaway: 20% discount. Price Check: Popadom 40p, CTM £7.95, Pullao Rice £2.25. Hours: 12 to 2.30 /6 to 11.30, closed Sunday. <www.friendstandoori.co.uk>

SAYONARA THALI

49 Belgrave Road, Leicester 0116 266 5888

'This strictly Gujarati vegetarian restaurant is a must. It is not large (c 40 seats) nor is it plush but neither are the prices, it offers good vegetarian food at realistic prices in fact a Thali consisting of many different dishes, dhals, pickles plus bread and rice starts at a meagre £6.50 which if I remember correctly includes a sweet or savoury Lassi The other dishes on the menu give a choice of Southern Indian cuisine such as stuffed dosa , Idli both being served with Sambaar and traditional coconut chutney. Other choices include Northern vegetable both wet and dry dishes of exotic vegetables, lentils and legumes plus the Gujerati speciality Kudhi (a.k.a Kari) a yoghurt and gram flour based dish and not forgetting the Mumbai (Bombay) snack foods and a selection of breads from various regions. We found that the ground floor was completely packed, we apprehensively made our way upstairs. I say apprehensively because I have often found that a floor away from the main hubub and eye of the management is often out-of-sight-and-out-of-mind plus it can sometimes lack atmosphere. This was not the case, although at first we were

*alone two other groups followed us up within a matter of minutes and a member of staff was promptly available to offer us a menu and take our order when ready. There were four in our party and we decided to order a selection of which we could all take a quarter from each dish. Palak Paneer was delicately spiced and probably the best I have tasted, Navarattan (nine vegetables) Korma was aromatic, Baigan & Aloo Karai of which both vegetables being cooked until just al denté and presented in a rich spicy gravy, Sweetcorn Masala a simple vegetable but attractively cooked plus a humble traditional soupy Massoor Dhal plus pickles. We estimated just one portion of rice would be ample as we were ordering a mixture of chapattis and bhaturas, the latter being a deep fried semi leavened bread which I have very rarely encountered outside of this city and I must say this Northern Indian bread was far superior to those we were served in Southern India but then again I suppose that's quite logical. I never usually refer to cost when reviewing a restaurant, I strongly believe your palette should judge a meal not your purse. This occasion is an exception as I do think that the cost of just over £10 per person including a nominal amount of drink was exceedingly good value for money and a nice conclusion to an interesting day out and to my wife's amazement I didn't return home to Northampton this time with yet another cast-iron karai to add to my collection nor a stainless steel spice storage container (my wife is of the opinion that I think more of my Indian cooking utensils than I do of her. I do strongly protest as I love them both the same).'*PR. Hmmm, Paul, but do the pots love you? She must be wonderful.

SHARMILEE VEGETARIAN

71 Belgrave Road, Leicester 0116 261 0503

Opened way back in 1973 by Gosai brothers (manager, LK Goswami), this is a two-part venue. The sweet mart serves a rich assortments of Indian sweets, and such delightful items as Vegetable Samosas, Pakoras and Dahi Vadia, from 9.30am-9pm daily, except Mondays. The licensed restaurant is upmarket and vegetarian, decorated with marble pillars in shades of brown and dusky blue marble-effect walls, high-backed black chairs, white table linen. Tasty starters of Pani Puri, crispy puris served with spicy sauce, chickpeas and onion. Chanabateta, chickpeas and potatoes in a tamarind sauce garnished with onions. South Indian specialities: Masala Dosa, thin crispy pancake filled with potato and onion, Idli Sambhar, flat pulse balls, both served with Sambhar and coconut chutney. Takeaway 10% discount. Discount promised if you show them this *Guide.* Hours: 12-2.30/6-9.30, Sat. 12-9; closed Mon. except bank hols.

Elsewhere in Leicester

CURRY HOUSE — NEW ENTRANT

64 London Road, Leicester 0116 255 0688

Brick arches give this double fronted restaurant a clean and smart look. Originally opened in 1985 and taken over in 1997 by Mr Nisar Kolia, who is also the head chef. This is a family business, as Iqbal Kolia is front of house manager. Menu Snapshot: Karahi Wings £6.50, cooked in thick spicy sauce; Panir Tikka Sizzling £5.90, curd Indian cheese marinated in spices and cooked with peppers, onions, tomatoes in tandoor, served with salad; Navrattan Kurma £5.95, nine varieties of vegetables, served in a mild creamy sauce; Mattar Pilaw Rice £1.95, peas and rice. Stocks: Cobra and Kingfisher. Student Discount: 10%, lucky students. Price Check: Popadom 45p, CTM £6.50, Pullao Rice £1.60. Hours: 6 to 11.45, Saturday to 12, Sunday to 11.30. <www.the-curry-house.co.uk>

EK MAYA — NOMINATED BEST IN THE MIDLANDS

28 Dysart Way, Leicester 0116 262 1118

Kaycee Patel spent two years creating Ek Maya from a former warehouse to Leicester's biggest restaurant. It even boasts its own car park. Spread across two-floors, it has a 150-seats and room for 300 to stand. Downstairs is a 50-cover bar, while upstairs beyond the balcony there is a private dining area, complete with a lounge for 100 people. The adjoining Champagne room is the ideal chill area for private parties of up to 70. a There is even a retail area stocking a range of traditional artefacts, spices, books and crockery. The warm, earthy-hued colour scheme is very Mediterranean, while the rawness of the dark wood tables is reminiscent of Africa. Design inspiration from India dominates. There are the traditional gypsy paintings produced by special tribes in Rajasthan. Imprinted onto the hardwood tables in Sanskrit calligraphy is the charming old Indian adage, 'Daane daane pe likha hai, kaane wale ka naam", ('the diner's name is written on every morsel of food'). A huge cover on the ceiling has yantras and symmetrical tantric shapes painted in raw reds and browns, complementing the light/dark mix of the oak floor. Even the food

Ek Maya, Leicester

reflects the multicultural theme; Indian merges with the Mediterranean in dishes like Spicy Calamari Rings and Couscous with Tandoori Salad along with dishes and ingredients popular in Africa, such as Phaldari Plantain Kofta and Mogo Chips. A selection of traditional Indian food is also on offer, like the special Paneer Galoti Kebab, along with a special range of Ayurvedic dishes catering to different body types and taste combinations. As a restaurant clearly without conventions, there is no head chef. The four main chefs (one curry specialist, one desserts, one tandoori and one to oversee) are from five-star restaurants in India and their open-plan kitchen allows customers to see them in action. *Puja Vedi, ed Tandoori Magazine.* <www.ekmaya.com>

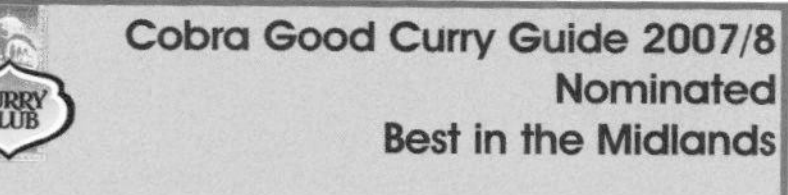

HALLI **NEW ENTRANT**

153 Granby Street, Leicester 01162 554 667

Owner Jaimon Thomas opened his ninety seater South Indian vegetarian restaurant in 2006. He hails from an Udipi village (Halli) in Karnataka. The wonderful thing about this style of food is that many of these small dishes are served complete with their own condiments, making every dish almost a course in it's own right. South Indian food is perfect for the diner who does not eat wheat; dishes are made from rice, which is, of course, the main staple of the region. On a visit to South India, you will see rice fields growing everywhere. Menu Snapshot: Idli £2.99, gently steamed rice and lentil cake, served with Sambar and chutney; Upma £2.99, semolina cooked with nuts, green chillies and ginger served with coconut chutney; Udding vade £3.25, golden fried lentil doughnuts, fluffy in the middle and crispy on the outside; Kajoo Pakoda £3.25, cashew nuts quick fried in a crunchy batter with aromatic spices; Gulla Podi £2.99, four pieces of aubergine puffs fried in a thin, seasoned batter; Masala Dosa £3.99, rice and lentil pancake filled with traditional fillings of seasoned potatoes, onion and peas, Masala Dosa is their most popular dish, Your Editors always order this delicacy – absolutely delicious!; Beetroot Sasami £4.45, Udipi Brahmin dish, beetroot cooked in yoghurt with green chilli, curry leaves and mustard seed; Jaggery Dosa £3.25, golden pancake smothered with warm cane sugar; Shavige Paysas £1.99, made from milk, vermicelli,

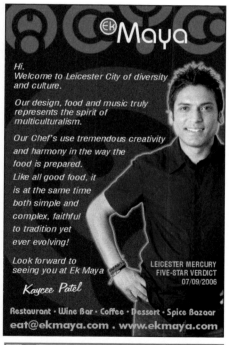

Halli, Leicester

sugar and cardamom pod. Takeaway: 20% discount. Stocks: Cobra. Hours: 12 to 2 and 6 to 11. <www.hallirestaurant.com>

KHYBER

116 Melton Road, Leicester 0116 266 4842

'The Khyber is a small and immaculately clean with a substantial following among the affluent end of the Leicester Asian business community. After so much of the plodding, ghee-flooded rubbish pedalled in too many restaurants around the country, the Khyber's food is a delight and an altogether more subtle experience than the food presented in the other establishments you list in the area that supply meat-based dishes. The chief chef is Ashok while the front of the house is supervised by Ashok's younger brother Dinesh. The food is simply outstanding and, many of the loyal clientele would agree, is rightly regarded among the cognoscenti as the best in the city. It is a little more expensive than its rivals, but genuine lovers of good food do not begrudge paying. So please, please honour them with a visit next time you are in town and I would absolutely, 100 per cent, guarantee that you will not be disappointed. In fact, I would go further. If you are struggling for company, I would be only too happy to join you and share an hour or two over some fine food. I have to say I am astonished that the restaurant I regard as the best in Leicestershire does not merit an entry in your publication. Best Wishes' JR. Shock horror, astonishment John, let's reinstate it, and I'll join you one day! So here's what we know: It is a cosy restaurant seating forty diners, remember to book for Friday and Saturday night! Opened in 1984 and still under the same ownership of Ashok Raval, who is also the head chef. His specials include: Lamb Chop Curry £7.50; Chicken Staff Curry £6.95, bet that's good!; Chilli King Prawns £12.60, mild, sweet and sour, fried in crispy batter and cooked with spring onions, fresh sliced garlic, black pepper, mild chillies and soy sauce; Special Naan £2.50, stuffed with vegetables, coconut and nuts. Stocks: Cobra. Price Check: Popadom 80p, CTM £6.95, Pullao Rice £2.50. Hours: 12 to 2 and 6.30 to 11.30. Sunday closed. <www.khybertandoorirestaurant.co.uk>

NAMASTE

65 Hinkley Road, Leicester 0116 254 1778

Partners, DK Dey (manager) and R Paul opened their fifty-four seater restaurant in 1994. Show a copy of this Guide to manager Mr Dey and you will receive a free starter. Very generous and regular customers will be treated to a complimentary drink after their meal. Chef Aziz says that his Mossalla and Pasanda dishes are most popular, however please try his Balti Special Menu, all served with choice of either Boiled Rice, Pullao Rice, Naan or Tandoori Roti. However, if you are celebrating, how about the Royal Kurzi Lamb for four persons £55.95, which includes all the business AND a complimentary bottle of wine. Takeaway: 10% discount. Discounts are available for students, nurses and OAP's, ID cards must be shown. Stocks Cobra and Kingfisher. Sunday Special Lunch: £5.95 per person. Price Check: Popadom 45p, CTM £7.95, Pullao Rice £1.75. Hours: 12 to 2, Thursday to Sunday only and 5.30 to 12, Saturday to 1. Sunday 12 to 12.

POPADOMS INDIAN

330 Welford Road, Leicester 0116 244 8888

Opened April 2005 by owner/manager Abdul Giash. House Specials include: Mixed Karahi £8.40, Tandoori Chicken, Chicken and Lamb Tikka, Sheek Kebab cooked in a sauce, served in a 'souk'; Genghis Said £5.70, barbecued chicken and spiced minced meat cooked with peppers, onions and tomatoes, served in spicy sauce; Aloo Gosht £5.50, (incidentally, one of Pat's choices) potatoes and lamb cooked in a medium or hot (hot for Pat) sauce; Cheese and Chilli Naan £1.95. Those who spend £20 or above on their takeaway are rewarded with a bottle of wine, red or white? Discounts for NUS: 10%. Sunday Buffet Lunch: £5.95 adults, £3.95 children. Delivery: 5 miles. Minimum Charge: £8. Stocks: Cobra. Price Check: Popadom 50p, CTM £5.90, Pullao Rice £1.60. Hours: 6 to 11.30. Sunday from 12.

RAITHA'S — NEW ENTRANT

23 Leicester Rd, Kibworth Harcourt, Leicester 0116 279 2323

During December 2004, Prakash Raithatha opened the cutely named Raitha's restaurant. Smart white building, with black timbers decorating the facade. The builders have been in and have built a very pretty raised terrace area, so you may sit outside, weather permitting – and nibble on your bhajia's. Specials include: Chicken Achari £7.45, spicy dish cooked with cumin and limes; Honey Chilli Chicken £4.95; Mussels £5.95; Sizzling Fish Platter £6.95 for one or £10.95 for two; Mushroom and Tomato Naan £2.45. Stocks: Cobra and Kingfisher. Takeaway: 10% discount. Price Check: Popadom 55p, CTM £5.45, Pullao Rice £1.95 Delivery: 6 miles. Hours: 6 to 11.30, Saturday to 12. <www.raithas.co.uk>

TAJ MAHAL

12 Highfield Street Leicester 0116 254 0328

Ali Ashraf, established his 100 seater restaurant way back in 1961, long before the Gujarati population arrived. To say it is an old hands and in safe hands is an understatement. It is Leicester's first and oldest and is does the traditional curryhouse formula, which when done well, makes a change from time to time. Anyway, it has a following now stretching over four generations and it was here that I was given the chilli-heat warning (see intro to Leicester above). Delivery: 3 miles, £15 minimum. Minimum Charge: £15.00. Price Check: Popadom 40p, CTM £7.35, Pullao Rice £2.30. Hours: 12 to 2 and 6 to 12, Saturday to 1.

THE ROYAL LEICESTER

Lockerbie Walk, Rushey Mead, Leicester

No phone because it's a pub and you can't book. 'It was Rob the accountant's stag night and rather than embark on the usual rowdy drunken night out with boys which per se ends with the groom being tied to the railings with his trousers flying from the nearest object, he had elected to go for an authentic Indian meal with his work colleagues which he perceived to be a safer option.' Has this got anything to do with a Restaurant Guide of high repute, Paul? Ed *'Five of us found our way to an Indian pub called The Royal Leicester, which serves good earthy authentic Indian food. From the outside it was a seventies building, the interior of which had escaped any attempt to drag it into the new millennium. Please regard this as an observation rather than a criticism because the place exuded character and warmth absent in modern, trendy wine-bar which seem to be the fashion at present. After choosing a Formica table we ordered drinks from the bar. The waiter politely enquired to our Gujarati colleagues whether the chilli heat should be toned down a little for his English friends, a considerate thought which was declined. We chose to have two large sizzling platters as appetisers and when I say large I mean large, these consisted of various meat and chicken kebabs without an E number in sight plus chilli-fried mogo chips, a chilli relish, a simple raita and a basic salad. All the chicken kebabs were moist well spiced and the seekh kebabs of a good texture and full of subtle flavour. The mogo made a good contrast to the meat selection and was something a little different than the norm. For mains we had King Prawn Masala, delicately spiced and cooked for just right. Methi Meat was full bodied with tender lamb chunks together the pungent green methi leaves, Chicken Masala which was delightful. The side dishes were also superb; Palak Paneer had generous chunks of soft paneer which had soaked up the flavour of the gravy and the spinach was not over pureed which is so often the case. The new kid on the block to me was a dish called Ondo, potatoes with split mung dhal in a well-balanced spicy gravy; the dish I was assured is of Gujarati origin. I definitely would return there again and will, the genuinely friendly and obliging staff plus the relaxed warm atmosphere of the place also enhanced the evening in general. Rob enjoyed his chosen stag night, his food and is now a happily married man.'* PM.

Lutterworth

EXOTIC SPICE — NEW ENTRANT

4 Church Street, Lutterworth 01455 203 000

Rafiqur Rahman opened his restaurant in 2002. Head Chef T Ali, serves Bangladeshi styled curries to a restaurant seating 60. Stocks: Cobra. Price Check: Popadom 50p, CTM £6.95, Pullao Rice £1.95. Hours: 6 to 12.

Market Harborough

RYHANS ESSENCE OF SPICE TAKEAWAY — NEW ENTRANT

30 Coventry Road 01858 419 039

Takeaway only, serving specialities including: Goan Prawns £4.95; Tumarion Mussels £4.25, cooked in garlic and tomato sauce; Chilli Squid £3.95, cooked with chilli and squid; Lamb Tikka Maldi

Tangar £7.95, onion, pepper, fried with tamarind and mango sauce. Owner A Hussan gets good reports: *'We must put pen to paper and congratulate you all at Ryhans on the excellent service and food you provide. We enjoy your smiling faces, when you bring us our much awaited fresh-tasting food. Keep the good work up.'* Mr&Mrs W. *'In little over six months, from a tiny shop front, Ryhans has managed to provide an excellent level of service and probably some of the best Indian food I have tasted. I recommend their Bombay Aloo.'* BC. *'Just a brief note to commend you on the excellent food you prepared for us last week, we all enjoyed it immensely.'* B&MW. *'Rhyans offers fresh, contemporary curries at fair prices and we look forward to enjoying many more curries in the years to come.'* J&BW. Loyalty Scheme: collect five stamps on your card and collect a free side and main dish! Delivery: 5 miles. Price Check: Popadom 50p, CTM £5.95, Pullao Rice £1.95. Hours: 5 to 11.

SHAGORIKA

16 St Marys Road 01858 464 644

Owning manager, Ala Uddin, opened his seventy seater in March 1980. Decorated in shades of pink with gold detail and Moghul arches. Menu Snapshot: Machali Aloo £4.25, flakes of Bengali fish wrapped in mashed potato and spices; Runner Bean and Mushroom Curry £6.25, Beef Al Amin £6.95, hot with cucumber and omelette; Tandoori Mixed Grill £8.75, lamb, chicken, prawn and king prawn grilled on charcoal in clay oven and served with salad and Naan; Onion and Garlic Naan £2.95. PM's opinion could describe 90% of the restaurants in this Guide.: *'The menu displayed some 200 heat-graded dishes. Effort was made somewhat to portray different regional foods such as Lamb Kovalam but its description bore no resemblance to any south Indian dish I know of. I decided to go for a very unadventurous Lamb Roghon Josh (in standard gravy with addition of fresh tomatoes to differentiate it from what would have been a lamb curry,) with Tarka Dhal (presentable), Bombay Potatoes (in ample gravy with no spice additions to perk them up) and Sag Paneer (individually cooked) with rice and chapattis (leaving a lot to be desired). Whilst there was nothing outstanding about any of the dishes, they were all exactly as expected – the type that seduced me years ago into my passion for spicy dishes. The restaurant did not promise a menu authentically cooked by Grandma Patel and served exactly what the sign said over the door. It did not need to compete with upmarket establishments because there are none in the town and for early on a Monday evening it was extremely well patronised.'* PM. Stocks: Kingfisher. Credit cards are accepted, but no cheques. Price Check: Popadom 60p, CTM £7.95, Pullao Rice £2.45. Hours: 12 to 2 and 6 to 11.30. Open all day on Bank Hols. <www.shagorika.com>

LINCOLNSHIRE

Area: East Midlands
Population: 988,000
Adjacent Counties: Cambs, Leics, Norfolk, Notts, E & S Yorks

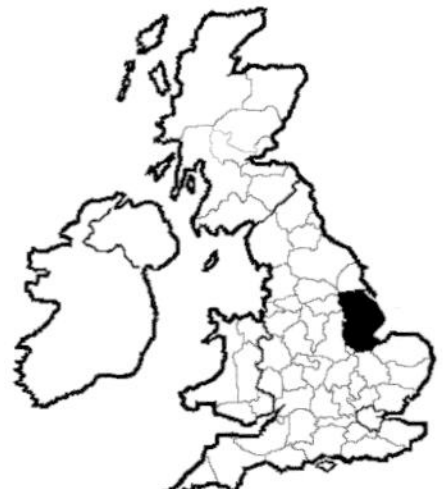

Boston

ROSE OF BENGAL

67 West Street, Boston 01205 363355

Good curryhouse where you might get a discount if you show them this *Guide.*

STAR OF INDIA

110 West Street, Boston 01205 360558

Ditto.

Bourne

SHALIMAR BALTI HOUSE

8 Abbey Road, Bourne 01778 393959

Ditto.

Grantham

BOMBAY BRASSERIE

11 London Road, Grantham 01476 576096

Ditto.

Grimsby

SPICE OF LIFE

8-12 Wellowgate, Grimsby 01472 357476

Ditto.

Lincoln

MACH BAR AND RESTAURANT
NEW ENTRANT

Weagby Road East North Greetwell
Lincoln 01522 754 488

It's located just outside the historic city of Lincoln. Says owner Mavinder Gosal *'As new restaurateurs, we wanted to give our first restaurant a personal touch, so we chose the first two letters of our names, Mav and Charlotte, to create MaCh'* Menu Snapshot: Breaded Khumbi. mushrooms stuffed with spiced vegetables, coated in golden breadcrumbs; Chicken Nambali Tandoori breast chicken, garnished with delicious mozzarella cheese., Salmon Pakora marinated, coated in a spicy batter & deep fried, served with a fresh crispy salad.Punjabi Jhinga, King prawns marinated in yoghurt, fresh coriander and mustard, cooked to perfection in the tandoor. Mixed Platter: chicken tikka, chicken wings, lamb chops and sheek kebabs.

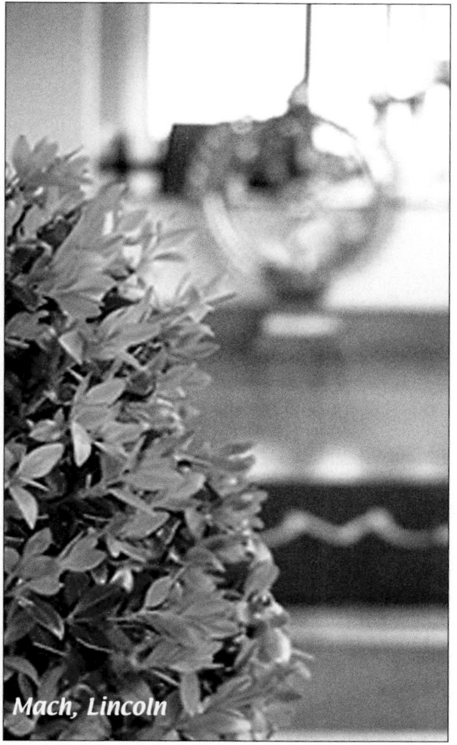
Mach, Lincoln

Mach, Lincoln

Ideal to share between 2. Mains include Shimla Pepper Chicken, cooked with sweet peppers in a spicy tomato based sauce; Goan Special, prepared with coconut milk and selection of spices to create a medium hot dish; Sajon Special. shredded tandoori chicken pot roasted with minced lamb, ginger, garlic & selected herbs & spices; Haash Tikka Sizzler. duck breast marinated and cooked in special spices, garnished with orange zest and Venison Special, served with a rich orange flavoured Grand Mariner based sauce. 24hr notice required for that one. All the favourites are also there. 6 - 11 <www.machrestaurant.co.uk>

MALABAR JUNCTION AT BARBICAN HOTEL

11 St Mary's Street, Lincoln 01522 522277

Delighted to see that south Indian restaurant is thriving in Lincoln. It came to our notice last time, and is still one of the few outside the London area. Though the majority of south Indians are vegetarians (for economic reasons more than choice) when you do get Kerelan meat and fish dishes, they are a refreshing change from the familiar dishes of north India. *(See page 75 for description of food).* *'The meal was delicious, including Vegetable Korma, Lemon Rice, Mushroom Rice, Coconut Rice.'* NT. Menu Extracts: Ghee Roast Masala £6, crispy pancake roasted in purified butter, filled with potato masala, served with sambar and chutney; Spinach Vada £3.50, fried doughnut made of split black gram batter, ginger, onions, green chilli, curry leaves, cumin soaked in seasoned and tempered yoghurt; Minced Lamb Cutlets £3.50, patties coated with breadcrumbs, served with tomato sauce and salad; Cashew Nut Pakora £2.50, cashewnuts dipped in spicy batter and fried; Lamb Chilli Fry £6.50, stir-fried lamb, mustard, red chilli, curry leaves, ginger, garlic, onion, tomato, garam masala and coriander leaves; Konju Kanava Masala £7, shrimps and squids cooked in thick gravy, flavoured with kokum. *'Yum yum!'* NT.

PASSAGE TO INDIA

435 High Street, Lincoln 01522 526166

Chef proprietor, Gulzar Hussain's restaurant seats seventy-five diners in two dining rooms. Menu Snapshot: all starters served with salad, yoghurt and mint sauce; Chicken Pakora £2.75; Lamb Delight £6.25, tikka with spicy sauce, garnished with crispy potatoes; Duck Biriani £8.00, served with vegetable curry; Chutney and Pickle Tray £2.50, that is a lot, hope they're good chutneys! Delivery: 5 miles, £10 minimum. Minimum Charge: £10. Set Lunch: £6.50, Set Dinner: £9.50. Price Check: Popadom 50p, CTM £5.25, Pullao Rice £1.80. Hours: 12 to 2 and 5 to 12.

PLANET MASALA NEW ENTRANT

Odeon Complex, Wigford Way, Brayford Wharf, Lincoln 01522 511 511

'A totally different style of Indian eatery. Dishes are under titles such as Wrap and Run; Flame Grill and Masala Handi. You just choose what style of food you wish to eat, this is what you can expect: Wrap 1, Shai Grill Seekh Kebab £3.25, wrapped in a soft chapatti with salad and spicy sauce served with spicy chips; Flame 3, Whole Flame Grill Mirchi Mirchi Chicken, marinated in achaar masala, red chillies, lemon flame grilled, served with two spicy chips or two Naan breads. Masala 6, Jhinga Kharai £6.95, prawns cooked in masala and tomatoes served with Naan bread and spicy Saffron Rice. Children's meals: Masala Chicken Burger £3.95, served with chips, soft drink and ice cream. 'Delicious Spicy Masala Chips, I am sure they cook them in paprika. Onion Bhajia was far too hot and I had to leave most of it, though I did feed it to the birds...' lucky birds! 'Mixed Vegetable Curry delicious with the Pullao Rice.' NT. So, Nigel liked it, more reports please.

RAJ NEW ENTRANT

7a St Marys Street, Lincoln 01522 536 109

'Stuffed Paratha, Paratha 80p, small, could have been bigger. Vegetable Samosas £1.50 also on the small side, but were very nice. Wonderful Coconut Rice 95p and Vegetable Bhajee £2.50. Competitive pricing and thankfully they remembered the Mango Chutney.' NT. Hooray for the chutney! and as for competitive pricing; they are very cheap. Menu Snapshot: Meat, Vegetable, Coconut and Dhal Samosas all £1.50 each!; Dhaka Potatoes £2.50, hot; Pullao, Plain, Egg Fried, Kheema and Naryal (coconut) rice all 95p a portion, great value. Price Check: Popadom 30p, CTM £3.50, Pullao Rice 95p.

Sleaford

AGRA AND BOLLYWOOD LOUNGE NEW ENTRANT

1 Pride Parkway, Enterprise Park, Sleaford 01529 414 162

This huge restaurant, seating 110, opened in 1988

and was taken over in 1994 by Enus Karim, who is incidentally the Head Chef. His special include: Agra Capsicum Noorani, whole green pepper barbecued and then stuffed with tender chicken cooked with 'chat masala', scrumptious!; Akbhari £8.45, filleted pieces of chicken or lamb cooked in the tandoor and mixed with richly spiced minced lamb, mustard seeds, capsicum and topped with fresh coriander; Mango Delight £8.45, barbecued strips of chicken breast, cooked in a creamy, mild, rich sauce topped with ripe mango. He also has plans to build a thirty bedroom hotel with conference centre and casino. His 'Bollywood Lounge' opened last November, where customers can enjoy a pre-dinner drink or relax with coffee and brandies after their meal. The lounge is also available for private parties ie: 'Elvis goes to Bollywood', fabulous!! Menu Snapshot: Chingri Nisha £3.85, Bengal Tiger Prawn coated with sweet almond and coconut powder wrapped in a crispy pastry; Bengali Roast £3.20, quarter of chicken roasted and smothered in a lightly spiced onion and tomato sauce; all Balti dishes are served with Naan bread for that essential sauce scooping; Kurzi Lamb £35.00, served with salad, Egg Fried Rice, enough for two! Delivery: 20 miles, £10 minimum. Takeaway: 10% discount. Price Check: Popadom 65p, CTM £6.40, Pullao Rice £2.25. Hours: 12 to 2 except Friday, and 5.30, Sunday 6 to 11.30. Branches: Agra 2, Ruskington, Lincs; Agra 3, Blyth, Notts and Choti, Lincoln.

INDIA GARDEN — NEW ENTRANT

19 Market Place, Sleaford — 01529 302 521

Menu Snapshot: Pili Pili Chicken £6.30, very hot with green chillies; Chicken or Lamb Deluxe £7.95, cooked with wine, almond, coconut, pistachio, fresh coriander and cream; Balti dishes all served with plain Naan Bread; Aloo Bagon £2.50, potato and aubergine; Chicken Pudina £5.15, medium with mint; Garlic Fried Rice £2.45; Butter Chapatti £1.10. Delivery: 3 miles, £10 minimum. Takeaway: 10% discount. Stocks: Cobra, Kingfisher, Budweiser and Becks. Birthday Special Deal: four or more must dine then birthday girl/boy dines free! Price Check: Popadom 55p, CTM £6.10, Pullao Rice £2.10. Hours: 12 to 2, except Friday, and 5.30 - 11.30, Friday / Saturday to 12.

Below: Celebrating curry at London's Banglatown Festival

Stamford

BOMBAY COTTAGE NEW ENTRANT

52 Scotgate Stamford 01780 480138

Established in 1994 by A Hussain and managed by H. Rahman. Menu Snapshot: Fish Chutneywali £3.10, tasty fish kebab with spicy fresh mint, coriander and green chilli chutney; Royal Quails £3.95, whole quails marinated in crushed spices, grilled over clay oven; generous Tandoori Mixed Grill £10.50, tandoori chicken, chicken tikka, sheek kebab, lamb chop, king prawn, salad, BUT, Naan Bread not included. Delivery: 5 miles, £15 minimum. Takeaway: 10% discount. Sunday Buffet: £9.90 per person. Price Check: popadom 50p, CTM £6.90, Pullao Rice £1.90. Hours: 12 to 2, Sunday to 3 and 6 to 11.30.

RAJ OF INDIA

2 All Saints Street, Stamford 01780 753556

Good curryhouse where you might get a discount if you show them this *Guide*.

STAMFORD BALTI HUT

16 All Saints Place, Stamford 01780 762 013

'Good central location, historic building. Tried Balti Achar Ghost (lamb) and Lamb Bhuna, good standard. Worth a visit.' JP

MANCHESTER
(Greater)

Area: North West
Population:Ranked 3rd
2,700,000
Adjacent Counties: Cheshire, Lancashire, Merseyside, Yorkshire

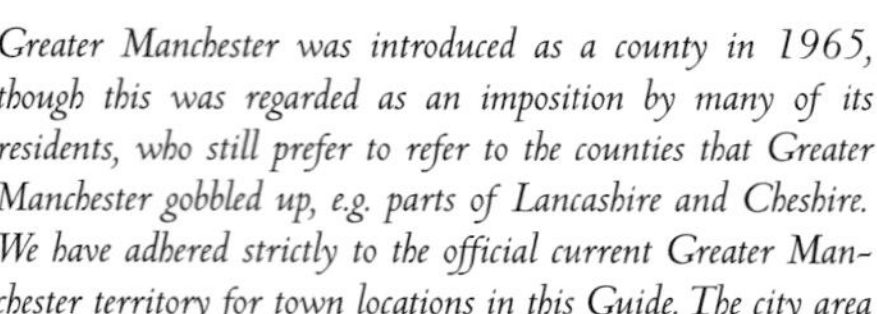

Greater Manchester was introduced as a county in 1965, though this was regarded as an imposition by many of its residents, who still prefer to refer to the counties that Greater Manchester gobbled up, e.g. parts of Lancashire and Cheshire. We have adhered strictly to the official current Greater Manchester territory for town locations in this Guide. The city area is shown in white (below), while the remainder of GM is shown in black

Altrincham
(inc Hale, Halebarns and Timperley)

BARINDA TOP 100

134 Ashley Road, Hale, Nr Altrincham
0161 926 9185

First opened in 1982, taken over by Javed Akhtar in 1998. Seats 70. Standard range of Curries, Tandoori, Karahi and Balti dishes. *'If you are a stranger to an area, you are never sure what a suburb of a major conurbation is like. When I saw 'Hale' in the Guide, I thought that sounds like 'Sale' and is likely to be the same!! What I soon appreciated is, to quote a colleague, that 'Hale is the poncey end of nicey – nicey Altrincham.' Having paid this area a visit, I can see what he means. It is a very designer conscious part of the Cheshire set– loads of restaurants and Mercs and Beamers to match.'* Well Mick, thanks a million. I'll forward the disgusted-of-Hales letters to you. that's Mick Wright of Bedfordshire. MW goes on *'Anyway, I found the Barinda without any difficulty– almost opposite the station on Ashley Road. I started with tandoori Chicken which has real melt in the mouth stuff, and then had bengan Murghi– I love Brinjals in the Asian cuisine, and this was a very good chicken and aubergine dish. I would say on my experience, albeit limited, it should at least be considered for the* **TOP 100'.** MW. OK Mick let's give it a whirl. Takeaway: 10% discount. Delivery: £12 min, 3-mile radi. Hours: 5.30-12.

DILLI NEW ENTRANT – TOP 100

60 Stamford New Rd, 0161 929 7484.

Dilli is the original name of modern India's Capital city, Delhi, India's gourmet capital. The Dilli restaurant delivers classic Indian Cuisine. It is also the first Ayurvedic restaurant in the north. Ayurveda, meaning life-knowledge uses traditional food ingredients which nourish specific parts of the body and counteract or prevent illness. Ayurvedic followers believe it relieve or prevent conditions like stress, heart disease, diabetes and asthma. It's a teaching that fries almonds to combat coughs, uses cinnamon to attack headaches, cloves to ease toothache, fennel to soothe sore throats, ginger for help with colds and arthritis, or garlic for blood pressure and rheumatism. Dilli is owned by chef-restaurateur

Dilli, Manchester

Kuldeep Singh, on-site chef is Raminder Pal Singh Malhotra,assisted by Ravi Bajaj, Uday Kumar Seth and Mohammed Naeem. Softly-lit, intimate venue, decorated in neutral tones featuring intricate wooden wall-hangings which have been hand carved by skilled carpenters in Delhi. Seats sixty downstairs and forty-five upstairs (which can be hired for private parties). Menu changes weekly, but specialities include: Murgh Handi Lazeez, chicken simmered in creamy yoghurt with garlic, cardamom, mace and saffron; Calamari Peri Peri, squid tossed with curry leaves, mustard seeds, peppercorns topped with seared King scallops. Lunch Menu: £7.95 two courses, £14.95 three courses. Service Charge: 12.5% discretionary. Hours: 12 to 11pm (10pm Sunday). Branches: Mela and Chowki, London W1 and WC1. <www.dilli.co.uk>

Ashton-under-Lyne

INDIAN OCEAN — BEST IN THE NORTH

83 Stamford Street East, Ashton 0161 343 3343

This is one of those remarkable establishments. It's a perfect curryhouse. It is the extraordinary level of care which we're talking about. It is owned by the charming Nahim Aslam. Seats 120. Large lounge with regular entertainments which attracts diners to stay and enjoy after dinner drinks with a cigar (there is a smoking menu). House specials: Chicken Chilli Masala – cooked with fresh green chillies. Chicken Chat Masala, chicken pieces with chick peas, garnished with roasted cashew nuts. Chicken Gorkali, red and green peppers, whole dried red chillies, tomatoes and Nepalese chilli sauce, spicy, served with Aloo Bhajia. Shahi Machlee, chunks of salmon, fresh coriander, ginger, garlic and mustard oil, with little green chilli and capsicum, medium spicy taste, served with Kulcha Nan and side salad. Buffet. *'We are regulars, where the welcome is always warm and friendly. First impressions are good as it is an attractive, clean and well presented restaurant. Good menu, appetising food, served pleasantly. Recommended.'* PR. *'Have had a few parties here and have really been looked after.'* JW. Hours: 5-1, Saturday -12, Sunday 1-1.

Bolton

ANAZ TAKEAWAY

138 St Helens Road, Bolton 01204 660114

You might get a discount if you show them this *Guide.*

GREEN BENGAL — NEW ENTRANT

158 Darwen Rd, Bromley Cross, Bolton 01204 304 777

Inspired by the graceful Bengal tiger, which lives in the forests, grassland swamps of Southern Asia, Zia Choudhury, opened the up-market eaterie in a blaze of publicity in 2006. This isn't Zia's first restaurant but this is the one he's most excited about.. Are you? Reports please.

HILAL TANDOORI

296 Chorley Old Road, 01204 842315

Good curryhouse where you might get a discount if you show them this *Guide.*

Dukinfield

CHUTNEY MASALA TAKEAWAY
NEW ENTRANT

1 The Square, Fir Tree Lane, Dukinfield
0161 303 0101

'Excellent takeaway with multi-award winning chefs (real ones, not the 'pay and display' variety). Open kitchen, comfy chairs, comprehensive menu, good selection of fish dishes. Shami Kebab £2.10, outstanding, succulent, tasty patties, well spiced, herb laced mince, nice bite, served with simple salad, garlic yoghurt sauce. Lamb Tikka Achari £4.70, really good, lots of tender , moist lamb tikka, perfectly spiced, completely free of gristle, fairly dry sauce, piquant character, very nice on taste buds. Chapatis £1.20, acceptable – a bit dry. A freshen-up towel and mint provided in your carrier bag.' RW. Delivery: 3 miles, £7.95 minimum. Menu Snapshot: Balti Peshwari Chicken Tikka £4.70, buttery sauce, almonds, raisins; King Prawn Bhangan £6.20, aubergines, tomatoes, green chillies, bay leaves, medium hot; Aloo Paratha £2.00. Price Check: Popadom 35p, CTM £4.50, Pullao Rice £1.20. Hours: 4.30 to 11.20, Friday and Saturday to 12.

HERB & SPICE

99 Foundry Street, Dukinfield
0161 343 5961

Good curryhouse where you might get a discount if you show them this *Guide.* <www.herbandspice>

SPICE OF BENGAL TAKEAWAY

145 King Street, Dukinfield 0161 330 1043

Formerly Imaams Royal Tandoori. *'Clean and bright takeaway. Revamped menu, usual culprits appear. All dishes were fresh, kept my eye on the microwave in the open kitchen, not used! Nargis Kebab £1.85, excellent, really a big ball of hot and juicy mince, richly spiced, still soft, thoroughly cooked egg in the middle, a real change. Only disappointment, no yoghurt sauce with the crisp salad. Balti Lamb Tikka Chat Masala £6.50, perfectly balanced, well accomplished sauce, thick with herbs and spices, slightly bitter edge to add piquancy, lovely tikka, tender and juicy. Garlic Naan £1.35, large soft, very enjoyable, but could have been better with more garlic. Tarka Dhal £1.65, well executed, great overall flavour, slight butterinesss from the garlic and caramelised onion. Will definitely be visiting again to try fish dishes.'* RW. Delivery. Price Check: Popadom 45p, CTM £4.60, Pullao Rice £1.35. Hours: 4 to 12, Friday and Saturday to 1.

Hyde

CLOVE
NEW ENTRANT

122 Market Street, Hyde 0161 367 8209

'Expensively and tastefully decorated in an achingly modern style. Only two shop fronts wide, appears amazingly spacious inside, with light painted walls, chromium fittings, lots of light wood and a laminated floor. Very comfortable waiting area. Friendly staff, bare tables and paper serviettes. Lamb Chops Tikka £3.60, impeccable quality, the depth of penetration indicating a suitable length of marinade, spicing was excellent, pleasantly hot, matching the tender, juicy flesh perfectly. They cried out to be picked up and gnawed and I was happy to oblige, very satisfying, served with crisp salad and delicious tangy yoghurt sauce. Machli Rocha with Peshwar Pullao Rice £12.50, great presentation, white square plate, large fish steak and potatoes, very subtle spicing, earthy taste of fish, no bones, sauce superb, rice packed with flakes of various nuts and fruit. Tarka Dhal £2.60, brilliant, great texture. Highly recommended.' RW. Takeaway: 20% discount. Price Check: Popadom 50p, CTM £6.90, Pullao Rice £1.80 Hours: 5.30 to 11, Friday and Saturday to 11.20. Sunday 2.30 to 10.30.

DAWAAT
NEW ENTRANT

32 Market Street, Hyde 0161 368 3374

Formally Taste of India. *'Spruced up inside in a simple style, welcoming. Seating for forty-eight diners on quality chairs, real tablecloths. Friendly and experienced staff. Reshmi Kebab £2.45, properly spiced tender minced kebab of a generous size with a soft omelette on top and served with crisp salad with a garlicky yoghurt sauce. Lamb Madras £4.75, hot and spicy, one-pot-sauce, flavoursome chunks of lamb. Pullao Rice £1.20, smashing fluffy rice. Tarka Dhal £1.95, smooth, thick, oozing garlic and caramelised onion, glorious Stuffed Paratha £1.90, aromatic bread, stuffed with plenty of vegetables, brushed with hot ghee.'* RW. Dawaat's Sunday lunch is a perfect for an early family dinner, choose a starter, main course with rice or chips and follow with an ice-cream for £6.95, children £3.95, great value, so see you there! Fully licensed. Delivery: 3 miles, £8 minimum, 5pm to 11pm. Price Check: Popadom 30p, CTM £4.75, Pullao Rice £1.30. Hours: 5 to 11, Friday and Saturday to 12. Sunday 4 to 11. CHEAP POPADOM

GARLIC NEW ENTRANT

43 Clarendon Place, Hyde 0161 368 4040

Latterly Bengal Lancer. *'Very smart, inviting single room for forty-four diners in designer style and comfort.A large window through to the kitchen reveals a spotless and vibrant working area. Friendly and efficient staff, real tablecloths with standard menu. Very well presented food, even the Chutney Daba was served with a flourish to accompany two hot Popadoms. Prawn Puri £2.20, smashing, managing the difficult task of being both flaky and soft. The prawn curry on top was a little lack lustre and didn't live up to the base. Lamb Tikka Biriani £6.20, utterly delicious, best I've had for many a year, perfect tasty rice with plenty of flawless meat. Tarka Dhal £2.00, great, positively pungent with garlic. A great all round experience.'* RW. Delivery: £8 minimum. Menu Snapshot: Kebab Snack £3.50, sheek kebab on naan with salad and mint sauce, great! Price Check: Popadom 30p, CTM £5.00, Pullao Rice £1.30. Hours: 5 to 11. CHEAP POPADOM!

SAFFRON TAKEAWAY NEW ENTRANT

30 Manchester Road, Hyde 0161 367 8600

'Open kitchen with smart, enthusiastic staff. Chicken Chat Puri £1.90, fantastic, small pieces of juicy chicken in a really sharp spicy sauce, deep-fried yet light and remarkably grease free puri. Podina Lamb £4.40 - excellent, really pungent dish, with loads of mint and ginger, fiery but tempered by the yoghurt. Great meat, fat and gristle free. Tarka Dhal £1.60, perfect, slightly thick. Garlic Naan £1.50, scrumptious, slightly crisp. Highly recommended.' RW. Delivery available. Menu Snapshot: Kebab Rolls from £3.00, Sheek Kebab on Naan; Chicken Tikka on Naan. Price Check: Popadom 30p, CTM £4.50, Pullao Rice £1.20. Hours: 5, Friday, Saturday and Sunday from 4 - 11.30, Friday and Saturday 12.

Leigh

INDIAN GOURMET NEW ENTRANT

239 Church La, Lowton, Leigh
01942 727262

'Smart modern restaurant, in shopping precinct. Tasteful light wood furniture , airy feel. Efficient staff, experienced. Real tablecloths with paper napkins. Reshmi Kebab £2.25, very well balance, spicy but not too hot, juicy, mouth watering served with really great very garlicky yoghurt sauce. Lamb Tikka Amlee £7, superb, delicately spiced, deliciously sour edge in the aftertaste, top quality meat, no fat, well marinated. Garlic Naan £1.60, excellent, light and fluffy, topped with generous spread of garlic. Very enjoyable.' RW. Menu Snapshot: Small Snacks all £3.20, Kebab or Tikka with salad and mint sauce wrapped in Naan bread, delicious lunch time food! Price Check: Popadom 45p, CTM £5.45, Pullao Rice £1.50. Hours: 5 - 11.

MANCHESTER CITY

(Manchester postcodes,
M1 to M46
Population: 433,000)

For the purpose of this Guide, we have included M postcodes (M1 to - M46) in all our Manchester City entries. There is no geographical logic to our putting postcodes into numerical order. They are frankly a jumble. But it is the system which exists, and to help narrow things down, we have divided the city into Central, East, South, West and North, using major roads as our arbitrary boundaries.

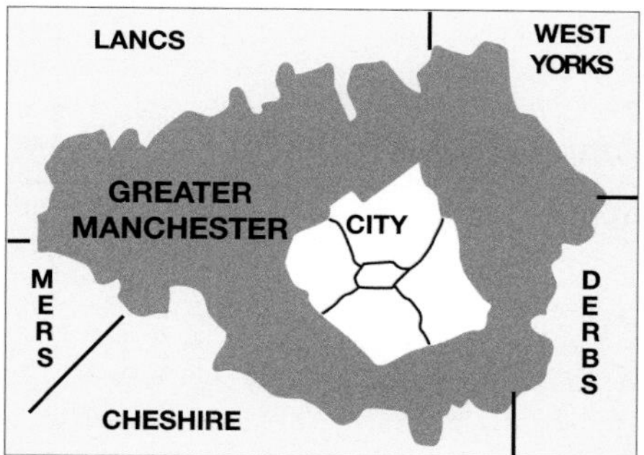

Manchester Central

M1 to M4

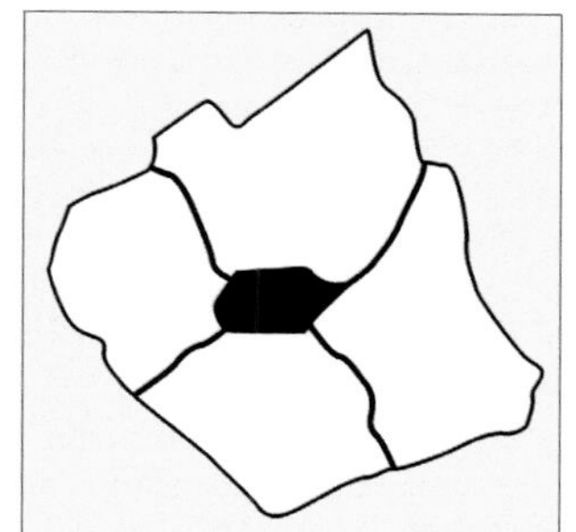

See map below for key to this map.

(restaurants listed in alphabetical order)

ASHOKA

105 Portland Street, M1 0161 228 7550

'The service can be a little slow, but the standard of food here is well worth the wait. Rashmi Kebab – god what taste, beautiful! £19.00 for one, but worth every penny.' MB. *'Lunch time and there's only one other sad git needing a fix. Reasonably well decorated, but could do with a touch up. Asked by waiter if I was having lunch, I said yes, he walked off, came back with two Popadoms and Chutneys. Raita - too salty and Onion Salad - devoid of anything but onion. Not impressed. Apparently, lunch £4.95 has no choices. Mystery Course Two - plate of salad arrived with good portion of Chicken Shashlik along with half a Nan. - excellent flavour, nicely spiced, very definite smoky flavour, tired salad, good Nan. Mystery Course Three - Chicken Jalfrezi - generous helping, good nicely spiced sauce, Vegetable Curry - good selection of vegetables but bland, Pullao Rice - generous portion, good flavour, light and fluffy.'* DB. Menu extracts: Chilli Chicken , green chillies, ginger, fresh coriander, capsicum and red chilli sauce. Rashmi Kebab, minced chicken, onion, green chillies, fresh mint, coriander, cooked over charcoal. Quail Makhani, butter, tomatoes, cream sauce. Hours: 12-2.30, Sunday closed and 6-11.30.

GAYLORD TOP 100

Amethyst House, Spring Gardens. M2
0161 832 6037

Owned by PK Chadha and R Kapoor, since '93. When it opened in the 1960s it was Manchester's first up-market Indian restaurant, and it pioneered the Tandoori oven in the city. The name is a play on the names of the original owners Gai and Lamba, who had opened one of Delhi's very first Indian restaurants called Kwality in 1948. By the 50's there were Kwalities all over India. But they were little more than caffs. Having made a fortune producing ice cream, the pair decided to go up market with their first Gaylord which opened in Delhi in 1958. Other branches soon followed in Bombay, London, San Francisco, Kowloon, Kobe Japan, and the Bahamas. The Gaylord seats 92 diners, and serves northern Indian cuisine. *'Reasonable menu selection, but what they offer is excellent. Good service in a very relaxing atmosphere.'* AKD. *'All four of us agreed that it was a wonderful curry with such different tastes. Started with Tandoori Fish, Onion Pakoras, Vegetable Samosas and Chicken Chat — very interesting salad, quite spicy — all good quality. Hot green chutney, harissa like substance was a favourite, to be used with caution. Superb Sag Chicken, best we have tasted! Excellent Chilli Chicken Tikka, char grilled flavour. Stunning Channa Kabuli, very hot, small pieces of raw chilli. Very impressed.'* KW. Sunday lunch buffet. Service: 10%. Takeaway 10% discount. Hours: 12-2.30/6-11.30. Sun. to 11.

KAILASH

34 Charlotte St, M1 0161 236 6624

Good curryhouse where you might get a discount if you show them this *Guide*.

SHIMLA PINKS

Dolefield, Crown Sq, M3 0161 831 7099

Seats 170 diners. Taken over in 2002 by Mrs GK Pannum. This restaurant is definitely not your average, it is sophisticated, modern restaurant, light, bright, green plants, minimalist, autumn coloured sofas, spot-lighting, stainless-steel bar with twinkling pin-spot lights. Chef Sudesh Singh produces food with a Pun jabi flavour. Popadoms are served with mint and yoghurt sauce, mango chutney and spiced onions, wow! Menu Snapshot: Spiced Potatoes and Garlic Mushrooms, £3.95, soft and fluffy spiced potato balls with sautéed mushrooms in garlic butter; Prawn and Mango Puri £3.95, light and crispy pancake style fried bread, embodied with, fresh Norwegian Prawns laced with a tangy mango mélange; Harrey Masaley Ka Gosht £8.95, cubes of tender lamb cooked in a medium spiced masala of spinach, coriander, mint, green chillies and bay leaves with

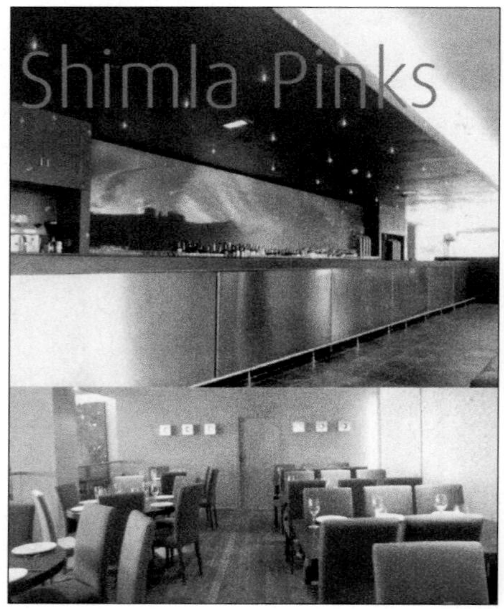

green cardamom, pepper and cloves; Tikhey Jinghey £12.95, jumbo king prawns marinated in a tomato, onion and capsicum masala, cooked in a heady sauce with pickling spices in mustard oil; Dried Fruit and Nut Naan £2.95, soft bread stuffed with cherries, sultanas, raisins and coconut. Takeaway: 20% discount. Stocks: Cobra. Service: 10%. Price Check: Popadom 75p, CTM £8.95, Pullao Rice £2.25. Hours: 5.30 to 11, Saturday to 11.30. Please note: It will relocate to a new site in the Spiningfield development after we go to print (current building to be demolished for re-development). <shimlapinksmanchester.com>

TASTE MASTERS — NEW ENTRANT

119 Oldham St, M1 — 0161 831 9600

'Gorgeous smells waft from the open kitchen. Basic menu. Chicken Pakora £1.50, nice, generously sized strips of chicken, tasty coating, freshly deep-fried, served with salad and heavily garlic yoghurt sauce. Lamb Karahi £4.00, scrumptious, rich sauce, pleasantly hot with plenty of quality lamb. Chapatis (two) £1.00, plain, soft and moist. Salty Lassi £1.00, very nice indeed! Great value for money.' RW. Delivery: 3 miles, £10 minimum. Menu Snapshot: Kebab Sandwiches, all served with Naan, salad and sauce: Lamb Kebab £2.80; Sheekh Kebab £3.00; Vegetable Kebab £2.20. Price Check: Popadom (two) 60p, CTM £5.00, Pullao Rice £1.00. Hours: 12 - 12, Friday and Saturday to 4am. <www.tastemaster.co.uk>

Manchester North

Consists of M7, M8, M9 M24 (Middleton), M25 & 45 (Whitefield) M25 (Prestwich), and M26 (Radcliffe)

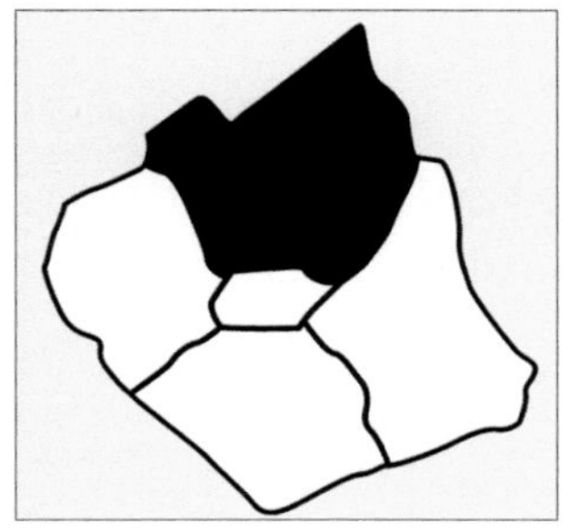

See page 289 for key to this map.

Manchester M8

CHAPATTI CORNER — NEW ENTRANT

152 Cheetham Hill Rd, M8 — 0161 834 0480

'Small cafe with very limited menu. Meat samosa, very good, although microwaved... I hate microwaved samosas and bhajia, yuk! ...the pastry turned soggy! Meat Curry packs a kick, tender, tasty sauce, nice fluffy rice.' DB.

LAZEEZA — NEW ENTRANT

142 Cheetham Hill Road, M8 — 0161 834 5656

'Predominantly takeaway kebab shop that serves curries as well. First quick lunch: Chicken Tikka Kebab, generous portion of chicken on large naan, loads of salad and sauce, all for £2.70 including free can of drink. Very filling and very good quality...' and how did it compare to your second visit *'... opted for Mixed Special, but order got lost in the translation and got Shish and Chicken Tikka Kebab, three very large kebabs on a very large naan with immense amount of salad. Took some time to polish off and couldn't eat for the rest of the day. At £3.90 excellent value.'* DB.

Manchester M25

Gorton (see also M45), Prestwich

GARDEN OF INDIA

411 Bury Old Rd, Prestwich M25 — 0161 773 7784

Good curryhouse where you might get a discount if you show them this *Guide.*

Manchester M26

Radcliffe

RADCLIFFE CHARCOAL TANDOORI

123 Blackburn Street, M26 — 0161 723 4870

Ditto

Manchester M45

Whitefield (see also M25)

LA IMRANS

Top of Elms Centre — 0161 796 0557

Ditto

Manchester East

Consists of M11 to M13, M18, M34, M35, M40, M43

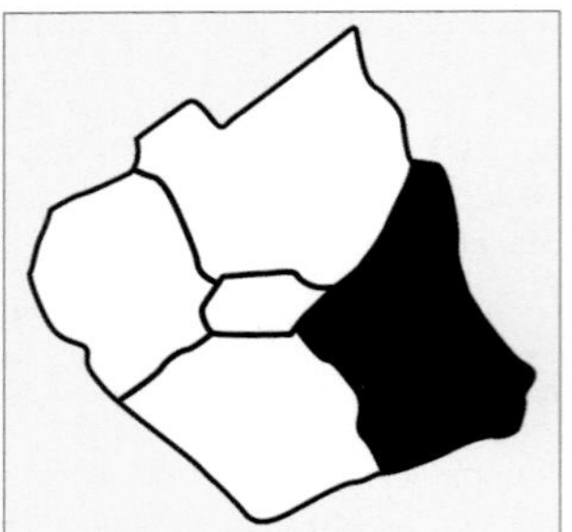

See page 289 for key to this map.

Manchester M34

Audenshaw, Denton

BARAKAT BALTI

699 Windmill Lane, Danebank, Denton, M34
0161 320 3232

Another good curryhouse where you might get a discount if you show them this *Guide.*

BLUE CROWN NEW ENTRANT

24 Ashton Road, Denton 0161 320 0005

'Bright and clean takeaway in the busy town centre. Comprehensive menu with plenty of house specials and also burgers, pizza, kebabs and fried chicken for those with a delicate constitution. Lovely starter, Meat samosas £1.50, obviously home-made, two tasty triangles of well spiced mince in filo case, served with chopped salad and a cool yoghurt sauce. Lamb Tikka South Indian garlic £5.50, nice, hot, spicy sauce surrounding well marinated chunks of tender white lamb (er, no, they sent chicken!), still enjoyable and the Pullao Rice was superb, really pungent and delicious.' RW. Menu Snapshot: Vegetable Mixed Starter £2.50, onion bhajia, vegetable samosa, mushroom dippers; Tandoori Lamb Chops £6.50 for six; Chicken and Cheese Kufta £5.50, boneless spring chicken marinated in yoghurt, herbs and spices cooked with meatballs and cheese. Takeaway: 10% discount, £15 minimum. No credit cards. Price Check: Popadom 30p, CTM £4.60, Pullao Rice £1.30. Delivery available. Hours: 4.30 - 12, Friday and Saturday to 1. CHEAP POPADOM!

Pearl, Audenshaw

PEARL NEW ENTRANT

119 Manchester Road, Audenshaw, M34
0161 301 5680

Naheem Akhtar, managing Director of The Pearl Restaurant Bar and Lounge is no stranger to the culinary world. His first venture, The Spice of Life, opened in 1997 and is now a successful takeaway and with The Pearl, Akhtar plans to expand his budding empire. Executive Chef, Ashok Kumar has developed a culturally cracking menu offering cuisine from an array of eastern countries including: India, Pakistan, Thailand, Sri Lanka and Nepal. Starting out in 1986 in New Delhi, Kumar has travelled extensively, including to Dubai and Mumbai creating menus and working with world-renowned chefs. He says: *'For me, being a chef is so much more than just cooking, it's a way of life.' And it's easy to appreciate his 'way of life'*, with dishes like Chicken Handi, Goan Machley and Jalparee Fish tempting diners. Situated by the Ashton canal, the 200 seater restaurant offers free car parking, disabled access, outside catering and takeaway option. An impressive outdoor area, elegant decor and chilled atmosphere makes it a great choice for private events.

Manchester South

Consists of M14 (Wilmslow Road, Rusholme) M15, M16, M19 to M23, M32, M33 and M90

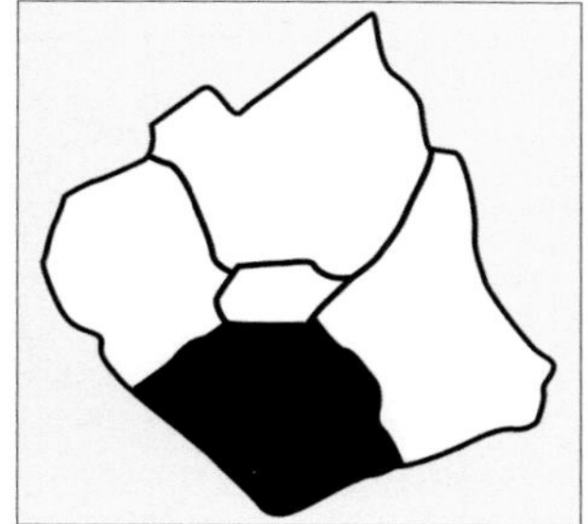

See page 289 for key to this map.

Manchester M14

Wilmslow Road, Rusholme

Wilmslow Road, extends for nearly 6 miles south from Manchester Centre. It passes through Rusholme, Manchester's main Asian area. To get there from the city centre it's best to walk – parking is normally a joke. Face south on the Oxford Road, with the BBC on your left, and go for about 800 metres, passing the Uni and then the Royal Infirmary. At the Moss Lane East junction, Rusholme and Little India starts. In the last five years the expansion has been amazing and is continuing unabated. From a drab and run-down look it now sports neon lighting to rival Las Vegas. Now, in the 600 metres from Moss Lane to Claremont Road, there are no less than 42 curry eateries – Indian snack and sweet shops, cafés and restaurants. As if that's not enough, there are numerous pubs, offices, chippies, Chinese, pizza joints, kebab houses and burger bars, Asian grocers and halal butchers. Some of the cheap and cheerful all-day cafés allow BYO (but always ask – it can offend some Muslims). Some are quite expensive licensed restaurants, the largest of which seats 400! A conservative estimate on curry consumption is 50,000 curries a week here. We believe this to be the curry record for a district. Any challenges? Go a further 900 metres along Wilmslow Road, and there are some 35 more curry eateries, making this a genuine Golden Mile. Almost any are worth trying. Most open all day.. Don't try reserving, you'll be lucky if they answer the phone. Just turn up, and if one is busy go to another. Our regular and prolific correspondent – DB *– tells us that, '...my overall experiences of Rusholme have been a little disappointing both culinary and service wise, considering there are so many curry houses vying for your custom.'*
Here are some of your favourites:

Rusholme

AL NAWAZ

74 Wilmslow Road — 0161 249 0044

'Nicely decorated, has been refurbished since my last visit, although the fish tank was still on the floor. Popadoms could have been crispier, with the usual chutneys. Lunchtime special confusing, you have to guess what meals are included in the deal. Meat Samosas, OK, with little salad and lemon. Chicken Jalfrezi with Pullao Rice, very large portion of quite tasty, rice, load of chicken, decent tasty sauce. Laboured service, but on the whole good value for money.' DB.

HANAAN — NEW ENTRANT

54, Wilmslow Road — 0161 256 4786

Good curryhouse.

LAL HAWELI

68 Wilmslow Road — 0161 248 970

Ditto.

ROYAL NAZ

18 IFCO, Wilmslow Rd — 0161 256 1060

Ditto.

SANAM SWEET HOUSE

145 Wilmslow Rd — 0161 224 8824

Despite AQ Akhtar's restaurant being huge (seating 160, plus a further 200-seat function room), it is so popular locally that it's often full, with queues waiting to be seated. *'The standard fare was very, very good . . . the Aloo Tikka was very tasty. A good first time visit.'* TOC. *'Quite nicely decorated, staff not overly friendly. Excellent Popadoms and chutney. Chicken Biriani, had flavour, fried onion garnish, tender chicken.'* DB. Hours: 12pm-12am. Branches: Abdul's, 121 318 Wilmslow Rd, and 298 Oxford Rd.

SANGAM — NEW ENTRANT

9 Wilmslow Rd — 0161 257 3922

Sagnam meaning 'meeting place' typifies the new-look Rusholme curryhouses. *Large spacious restaurant with warm welcome. Clean, nice decor and well lit. Standard menu nothing unusual. Waiter arrived with two Popadoms and Chutneys and took drink order. When I tried to order my food, he walked away. Manager came over and took my order (nice man, dreadful wig!) Chicken Tikka Biriani with Madras sauce. This arrived quickly, before I had finished my Popadoms. Very large portion of rice, delicate flavour, very acceptable and very dark red sauce. Tikka was sparse compared to the amount of rice, not an awful lot of flavour. Madras sauce quite tasty. Standard formula curry house.'* DB. David returned for a second visit. '*'Popadoms, crisp, fresh and large arrived with chutney tray of Mango and Onion, Cabbage (don't see the point), lime pickle and Raita. Chicken Tikka Dhansak with Pullao Rice arrived promptly. Good flavour (better than most of the Birianis I have eaten lately), fair bit of chicken, moist, charcoal flavour, sauce OK.'* DB. <www.sangams.co.uk> Branches: Sangam 3, 202 Wilmslow Rd, Heald Green, Cheadle, Cheshire, 0161 436 8809. Sangam 2, 762 Wilmslow Rd, Didsbury, M20 0161 446 1155.

SHERE KHAN

52 Wilmslow Road 0161 256 2624

Part of a chain of eight Shere Khans in the general north east area. They have created a big reputation and although we do get some blasters about service, they do seem to achieve satisfaction at reasonable prices, this branch in particular, because of its competitive location. See below M17 (Manch W) for more information. <sherekhan.com>

SHEZAN

119 Wilmslow Rd 0161 224 3116

Good curryhouse.

SPICY HUT

35 Wilmslow Rd 0161 248 6200

MS Mughal's simply decorated 60-seater serves traditional Pakistani curries and side dishes. *'A must whenever we visit Manchester. Always assured of a warm welcome and a good curry. Popadoms, pickles and generous portion of Indian salad provided as soon as you sit down 30p a head. BYO at this unlicensed venue. We often take a bottle of wine with us which is uncorked no charge without delay. Jugs of iced water provided without fuss, replenished automatically. Rice portions are so big, one between two is enough. Garlic Chicken, very good, large portions. Naan always good, light, fluffy, not too doughy. Meal for two £16 - what a bargain!'* EG. where you might get a discount if you show them this *Guide.* Delivery: 2 miles, £10 minimum. Hours: 5-2am; Sun. 3-1am.

TABAK

199 Wilmslow Rd 0161 248 7812

Mohammad Nawab's restaurant seats a MASSIVE 350 diners, on two floors. Pakistani curries and accompaniments on the menu cooked by chefs Raj Kumar and Abrahim Ali. *'A Bit scruffy, in need of redecoration. I was the only diner at first, but joined by some others later in my adventure. Sent the Popadoms back – stale. Chutney tray – poor, Raitha good. Excellent main meal, well flavoured rice, very good succulent chicken and a curry sauce near to perfect.'* DB. Hours: 12pm-1am.

ZAIKA NEW ENTRANT

2 Wilmslow Road, 0161 224 3335

On the golden mile. *'Bright, clean and attractive decor, with modern furniture. Standard menu. Asked for a bottle of Kingfisher, told they were out of stock, would Guinness do instead! Order the usual, two Popadoms with chutneys, Chicken Tikka Biriani, Madras sauce. Popadoms, excellent, warm and crisp, decent range of chutneys, on the menu at 70p, but did not appear on the menu. .Inexperienced waiter tried to remove them prior to the arrival of the main meal,, he should learn that I don't surrender them to anybody!...'* quite right!! *'Decent portion of Biriani, chicken tikka cut rather small, nice nutty flavour. Madras sauce very good, intriguing flavour. Overall a good meal, although the service did leave a little to be desired.'* DB.

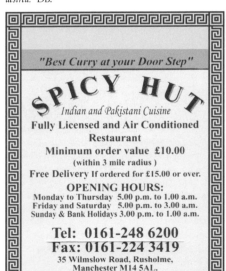

Manchester M19

Burnage, Kingsway, Levenshulme

NAWAAB

1008 Stockport Road, M19 0161 224 6969

Mahboob Hussain bills this as the biggest curry house – 350-seats on the ground floor plus 600 on the first floor. '

THIRD EYE

198 Mauldeth Rd, Burnage 0161 442 2900

Nepalese restaurant. Opened 1998. Seats 72. Cosy, traditional decor. Specials: Tangri, chicken drumstick stuffed with saffron minced lamb and nuts. Bhutan Chara, chicken with mushrooms and tomatoes. Kidney Masala, lamb kidney in spicy sauce. Discount possible if you show them this *Guide*. Takeaway: 10% disc. Del: £15 min, 3-miles. Hours: 5-12.

TONDORI ROYALE

682 Burnage Lane, Burnage 0161 432 0930

'Bob Hoque's 110-seater is very well-established (1980) and very well spoken of by the locals. 'It was packed! It is not difficult to work out why when you taste the cuisine. Atmosphere is electric and food well worth the 40-mile trip.' MB. It has a full house of familiar dishes. Fish dishes include Boal and Ayre. NW's favourite is Zhal Golda Chingri, king prawn cooked with chilli and ginger. *'Very good. Vegetable Pasanda had excellent flavour.'* RWI. *'A pleasant surprise tucked away in the Manchester suburbs. Try the Hopi for your starter – an interesting variation on the Chinese spring roll. Sizzling baltis with quality ingredients and accompanied by fluffy naans. Worth a go!'* PW. Discount possible if you show them this *Guide*. Delivery: £15 min, 3-miles. Hours: 6-1AM; Sat/Sun. 5-2.30am.

Manchester M28

Didsbury

THE ORIGINAL THIRD EYE

661 Wilmslow Rd, Didsbury 0161 446 2300

'I have visited at least 10 times over two years and it is still one . Run by the same family who started Katmandu on Burton Road and Third Eye on Mauldeth Road – the best chef is definitely in Didsbury. Small, seats forty and decorated in Didsbury chrome and glass style. Superb menu. Particularly recommended is the Aloo Chilli, Kidney kebab, Tarka Dal and they do a brilliant Garlic Nan with more garlic than Nan! . I love their Vindaloo with little pieces of chopped ginger garnish. Portions can appear small, but you will end your meal feeling nicely full rather than stuffed full.' . 'Staff polite and friendly.' KN. Menu extracts: Fish Tikka, cod marinated in spiced yoghurt and barbecued. Kidney Kebab5. Bari Masala, mince balls seasoned with herbs and cooked in a curry gravy. Bhutan Chara, chicken with mushrooms and tomatoes. Pommi Nan, stuffed with potatoes, cheese, herbs and spices. Hours: 12-2.30 (Weds to Sun) /6-12.

SANGAM 2

762 Wilmslow Rd, Didsbury 0161 445 1168

An Indian and Thai restaurant. situated above the House Shop. *'Modern restaurant,seating 140. Pale wood, chrome and a projection clock. Very smartly laid out with attentive uniformed staff. Standard menu with a good selection of specials. Lovely Seek Kebab £1.60, hot, spicy, great aroma, tender mince, really succulent, accompanied by a great salad and a cool yoghurt sauce. Impressive Lamb Rezala £6.80, a well concocted blend of spices making up a tasty sauce, juicy, tender, gristle free lamb, very nice indeed. Garlic Naan £1.60, good, thin, moist, slightly crisp base, a little sparse on the garlic, which was spread on the top. Tarka Dhal £3.40 poor, very hot and tangy, slightly undercooked, no trace of garlic. Overall good, recommended.'* RW. Indian Menu Snapshot: Lamb Chop Tikka £3.70, four pieces' Shahi Masala £6.80, cream, yoghurt, garlic, tomato, chillies and onions, hot; Roasti Lamb £6.80, pieces of lamb, on the bone, medium spiced, cooked home-style. Thai Menu Snapshot: Thod Man Pla £3.90, spicy Thai fish cakes with lime leaf and fresh pickle; Goong Tom Kha £4.30, prawn coconut cream and galangal soup; Gai Pad Krapow £7.50, fried chicken breast with basil leaf and chilli. Licensed. Price Check: Popadom (two) 80p, CTM £6.80, Pullao Rice £1.60. Hours: 3 to 12, Friday and Saturday to 1. Branches: Sangam, Rusholme and Cheshire.

Manchester M33

Ashton-upon-Mersey, Sale

SPICE CHEF

85 Washway, Sale, M33 0161 976 4577

Good curryhouse where you might get a discount if you show them this *Guide*.

Manchester West

Including M5, M6 (Salford) M17, M27 to M31, M41, M44.

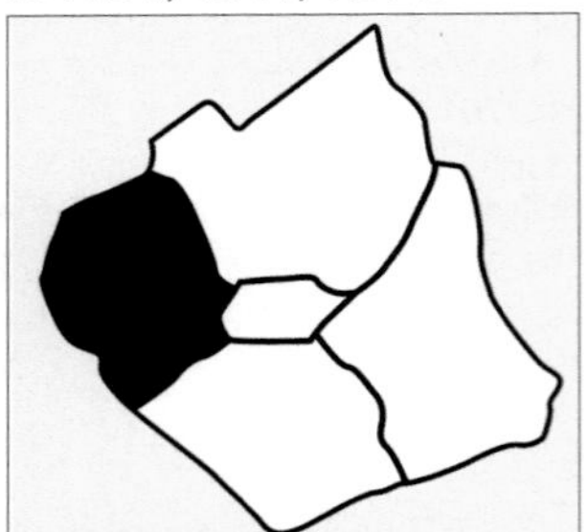

See page 289 for key to this map.

Manchester M17

SHERE KHAN EXPRESS

Orient Food Hall, Trafford Centre, M17
0161 749 9900

Opened on a prime corner location in the upper rotunda of the Trafford Centre. and must be one of the trendiest in the area. Seats a considerable 430. *'Lunchtime Buffet £7.99, Popadoms with mango chutney and onion,Onion Bhajia and Meat Samosas – very good, nicely spiced. Honey Chicken Wings - crispy, not much taste but I love them anyway. Chicken Tikka Masala – tasty but too sweet, Chilli Chicken Tikka Masala – seemed to be CTM with a few green chillies. Madras – nice chicken, sauce very tomatoey, Jalfrezi – quite bland. Acceptable Vegetable and Pullao Rice, Naan – not too thick, crisp around the edges. Un-named sweets on the buffet, had a fudge type things – OK, and two different types of custard thing that was delicious. Good value, if you don't, mind sacrificing quality for quantity.'* DB. Mon - Fri opens at 10am, Sat 9am, Sun 11am until 24:00. <sherekhan.com>

Manchester M30

Eccles, Irlam

PASSAGE TO INDIA

168 Monton Road, Monton, Eccles, M30
0161 787 7546

M Hassan Choudhury and H Uddin's serves 90 diners and you might get a discount if you show them this *Guide*.. Open 12pm-11.30pm. Branch: Gate of India, Swinton.

Elsewhere in Greater Manchester

Mossley

LAL QUILLA NEW ENTRANT

5 Manchester Road, Mossley 01457 839 777

Mr Mohammed Ali, opened his restaurant in 1998, it seats a substantial 100 diners and fish dishes are his specialty, Mas Mosalam £8.50, boneless fish, lightly marinated and garnished with herbs. However, Rogan Josh and Tikka are also very popular. Set meals are exceptionally good value for money, Menu A: Popadoms and Chutneys, Chicken Tikka, Onion Bhajia, Lamb Tikka Karahi, Methi Chicken, Mushroom Bhajee, Pullao Rice and Naan, £23 for two, £44 for four; Menu B: Popadoms and Chutneys, Onion Bhajia, Vegetable Samosa, Vegetable Roghan Josh, Vegetable Korma, Vegetable Bhajee, Vegetable Pullao Rice, £20 for two. Stocks: Cobra, Carling. Price Check: Popadom 60p, CTM £6.90, Pullao Rice 1.90. Hours: 5 to 10.30, Saturday to 11.30. Sunday 1 to 10.

Oldham

BRITISH RAJ

185 Lees Road, Oldham 0161 624 8696

Good Curryhouse where you might get a discount if you show them this *Guide*..

MILLON RESTAURANT

Westwood Business Centre, Featherstall Rd, South Oldham 0161 620 6445

Ditto.

Rochdale

LA TANDOOR TOP 100

A7, Bamford Precinct, Rochdale 01706 642037

Mrs S Habeeb's 68-seater is *'a superb restaurant, and be warned – book a table, as it gets very busy. We had Nargis Kebab and Vegetable Chaat for starters – a dream – and we followed with a main-course choice of Chicken Tikka Biriani and Chilli Chicken*

La Tandoor, Rochdale

La Tandoor, Rochdale

Balti, with a side dish of Malayee Kufta (vegetable balls in a coconut sauce with pineapple and peaches), Pullao Rice and Chupattis. It was all excellent, followed by ice cream, face towels, a free drink and after-meal sweets. 5. We'd eat there every day if we were locals!' RK. *'Now enlarged. Food still fab. Had forgotten this place until we read the Guide.'* RN. You might get a discount if you show them this *Guide.*, but probably not when they are very busy. Takeaway 20% off. Hours: 12.30-12.30 (1am on Sat.). Family banquets: Sunday £9, 12.30-6.

Stalybridge

BOWERFOLD SPICE — NEW ENTRANT

Mottram Rd, Stalybridge. 0161 303 9797

'Large and modern 120 plus seater restaurant, attached to Stalybridge Celtic's football ground. The only reason to visit the as football team being rubbish, unlike the splendid folk who play and support the magnificent Hyde United...' now, now, Ralph, we don't need football wars here!! *'...the single, large dining area of this establishment is nicely furnished with lots of light wood, magnolia walls and dichroic lighting...' what's dichroic? '...friendly, experienced staff plus real tablecloths. Tandoori Trout £3.50, great, whole trout in marinade allowed delicate, earthy flavour to come out, served with crisp salad and spicy yoghurt sauce. Lamb Panir £7.95, equally well executed, surprisingly fragrant and tangy concoction of curry with tasty Panir and good quality of lamb, scrumptious! Pullao Rice £1.80, delicate perfume; Tarka Dhal £2.95, good, ate well. A great meal in a splendid restaurant, very highly recommended.'* RW. Price Check: Pop 60p, CTM £7.20, Pullao Rice £1.80. Hours: 5 - 11, Friday and Saturday to 11.30. Sunday 3 - 10.30.

Stockport

(includes Chapel-en-Le-Firth, Heaviley Heaton Moor, Marple, Offerton, Romiley, Whaley Bridge)

KUSHOOM KOLY

6 Shaw Rd, Heaton Moor 0161 432 9841

Good Curryhouse where you might get a discount if you show them this *Guide.*. **6451**

Todmorden

ZAIKA CUISINE — NEW ENTRANT

759 Burnley Rd, Carnholme 01706 662 801

Owner, Zulf Ahmed describes his fifty seater restaurant as traditional and simple. Menu Snapshot: King Prawn Chat £2.95, served on puri bread; Zaika Mixed Masala £5.50, chicken and lamb tikka with almonds, coconut, mild and creamy; Nawabi £5.95, marinated and tandooried chicken or lamb, tomatoes, cucumbers and topped with omelette. Delivery: 3 miles, £10 minimum. Takeaway: 10% discount. Stocks: Cobra, Kingfisher and Bangla. Price Check: Popadom 50p, CTM £5.25, Pullao Rice £1.50. Hours: 5.30 - 11.30. Monday closed. <www.zaikacuisine.co.uk>

Wigan

SPICE LOUNGE — NEW ENTRANT

19 Bretherton Rd, off Wallgate
01942 494 909

Specials at this unlicensed. venue include: Spicy Bites, Chicken Tikka, Lamb Chops, Boti Kebab,

Panir Kebab all £2.60 and served with salad and dips; Spicy Snacks, Onion Bhajia, Vegetable,

Chicken or Meat Samosas all £2.50 and served Panir Kebab all £2.60 and served with salad and dips; Spicy Snacks, Onion Bhajia, Vegetable, Chicken or Meat Samosas all £2.50 and served with salad and dips; Spicy Wraps, Chicken Chat, Spicy Tuna, Chicken Tikka all £2.95 and served with salad and crispy Paratha; Spicy Birianis, chose from chicken, lamb or vegetable all £6.95 and served with Chana Aloo and Cucumber Raitha, delicious! All the regular curries are also on offer, but this restaurant has one of the best spins we've heard. It made the national press when local woman, Louise Thomas, got curry withdrawal symptoms during the late stages of pregnancy. For her fix she chose the The Taste Of Bengal, asking the staff which curry would start her labour and they said they had just the recipe. Within minutes of leaving the restaurant that night she went into labour and ave birth to Lucy. *'Since then'*, says owner Giash Uddin, *'pregnant women have flocked to the Standish eaterie to test the curry for themselves. It still works wonders and we get around three or four women a month coming in asking for the special dish.'* **BYO** no corkage charge, and they provide you with free glasses. Delivery: 3 miles, £15 minimum. Price Check: Popadom 50p, CTM £6.95, Pullao Rice £1.95. Hours: 11.30 - 3, Friday closed and 5.30 - 10. Branch: Taste of Bengal, 11, High Street, Standish, Wigan.
<www.thespicelounge.co.uk>

MERSEYSIDE

Area: North West
Population: 1,425,000
Adjacent Counties:
Cheshire, Lancs,
Greater Man

Liverpool

ASHA

79 Bold Street, Liverpool 0151 709 4734

GULSHAN TOP 100 AWARD WINNER

544 Aigburth Road, L19 0151 427 2273

In 1986 Mustafa and Salina Rahman found the perfect spot in Grassendale, Liverpool, for their new Indian restaurant. Mustafa proudly describes his wife as the backbone and founder of the business. Gulshan is a Persian girl's name meaning 'paradise or a mystic rose garden'. The Gulshan's bar/lounge area resembles a gentlemans' club with its Chesterfield sofas.The air-conditioned restaurant seats approximately 80, divided into two separate dining rooms (one non-smoking). It is decorated with a golden ceiling,s tained glass windows, chairs upholstered in red leather, through to the crisp linen on the tables, the bespoke china and cutlery. Features include cooking lessons by Mustafa and Salina. Notable starters include puri dishes with a choice of toppings: aubergine, lentils, mushrooms or buttered prawns, etc. Main Courses include the usual cast-list of Tandoori, Masala, Balti, Biriani and vegetarian dishes. Specials include: Murgi Mossaka, chicken barbecued tandoori style then prepared with keema (minced meat), tomatoes, cream and wine, topped with cheese; Kalla Chicken, chicken kebab cooked with banana and yogurt; Almond Maas Korma, boneless white fish cooked with ground almonds, yogurt, cream, coconut and rose herbs all three £6.95. Price Check: Popadom 60p, CTM £6.95, Tarka Dhal £3.50, Pullao Rice £1.95, Naan Bread £1.95. Hours: 5 -11, daily.
<www.gulshan-liverpool.com>

MAHARAJA SOUTH INDIAN
NEW ENTRANT

34 London Rd, City Centre 0151 709 2006

Treasure this one please Merseyside. It is a break-away from curryhouse fare, good though that may be. It specialises in South Indian Keralan cuisine. This style of food is quite different from 'curryhouse', but is really delicious. Hot is the norm in Kerala but they cool it for 'western tastes'! So if you want to up the chilli strength, tell them and the kitchen will be more than happy to oblige. Have the Rasam (hot and spicy soup, with floating slivers of garlic, curry leaves and a red chilli! – this is a DBAC benchmark, which if she doesn't get hiccups, it's not hot enough for her!), Masala Dosa, Sambar and Coconut Chutney are south Indian favourites. (see page 51 for definitions). Some diners have that choice for starters and go on to curries. I don't know how they do it. I'm too full for it. But the curries are worth trying. You can stay vegetarian if you like. All their vegetable curries are spot on. Contrary to popular belief, meat, chicken and fish dishes are the norm in south India. Try Lamb Cutlets: patties made of minced lamb and spices with bread crumbs and fried. Served with tomato sauce and salad. Malabar Chicken is cooked with coconut, curry leaves, garlic and mustard. Fish Mollee is a classic dish, so mild and gentle in its coconut base that even the Raj allowed it at table. And for pud Banana Leaf Cake: made of rice with a sweet filling of grated coconut, banana and jaggery wrapped in banana leaf and steam cooked. Hours: 12-3 /6-12.

SHERE KHAN NEW ENTRANT

17-19 Berry St, Liverpool 0151 709 6099

'The food is always of the highest quality, hot (temperature), the staff are friendly and the restaurant is kept immaculately clean. Don't let the one in the Manchester Trafford Centre put you off!' RW

UNI NEW ENTRANT

67 Renshaw St Liverpool 0151 709 6587

Originally opened way back in 1970, by Golam Kibria. Menu Snapshot: Cha-cha's £12.95, king prawns, spicy butter, coriander leaves, served with spiced potatoes and Pullao Rice; Choyu's Kazana £6.95, chicken, mild sauce, fresh cream, spicy vegetables in Rogan sauce, okra and spinach. Air-conditioned. Stocks: Cobra. Takeaway: 15% discount. Delivery: 3 miles, £15 radius. Price Check: Popadom 50p, CTM £6.95, Pullao Rice £1.50. Hours: 6 to 1, Friday and Saturday to 3. <www.unirestaurant.com>

Newton-le-Willows

TASTE OF INDIA

56 Market Street, Newton 01925 228458

Good curryhouse where you might get a discount if you show them this *Guide.*

Southport

THE KASTURI

40, Eastbank St, Southport 01704 533102

'Fairly large restaurant, nice 'seasidy' exterior decorated in typical style. Friendly, competent staff. Reshmi Kebab £2.55, outstanding, large, succulent, quality mince, well spiced, melt in the mouth, topped with a soft and fluffy omelette and accompanied by fresh, crisp salad and cool yoghurt sauce. Lamb Tikka Jaipuri £6.95, hots the spot, sharp, tangy and fat free lamb, well spiced. Tarka Dhal £2.45, OK. Garlic Naan £1.85, nice and light, well endowed with garlic, doughy in parts.' RW. Menu Snapshot: Tandoori Mixed Grill £6.50, includes Bhuna sauce, salad and a Naan Bread, hooray! Licensed. Price Check: Popadom 50p, CTM £4.95, Pullao Rice £1.45. Hours: 5.30 to 12, Friday and Saturday to 1.

Thingwall

RED CHILLI NEW ENTRANT

513 Pensby Road, Thingwall 0151 648 5949

Formerly Raj Balti, taken over in 2001 by G Miah, who is also the head chef. Seats sixty-five diners. Popular dishes include: Chilli Masala Korahi £7.50. Takeaway: 10% discount. Price Check: Popadom 50p, CTM £7.40, Pullao Rice £2.00. Hours: 5 to 11.30, Saturday to 12.

WIRRAL

The Wirral is neither a town nor a county and, until 1965, was part of Cheshire. Since then the northern part – a small, digit-like, curry-rich peninsula between the rivers Mersey and Dee – has been part of Merseyside. Ellesmere Port (q.v.) remains in south Wirral but is in Cheshire. Our choice of Merseyside Wirral curryhouse towns are in alphabetical order: See also Cheshire.

Bromborough,The Wirral

CURRY NIGHTS NEW ENTRANT

5 Coronation Dr, Bromborough
0151 343 9200

'Best curry I have ever had! Brilliant! Good service too.' HD. 'Ever present and ever reliable, can't beat it.' JN. 'Food is delicious, brilliant menu, staff are very friendly.' JO. Menu Snapshot: Balti dishes from £5.50, all served with Naan or rice; Amkey £9.50, tikka, young mango, kohli, tangy sauce, medium; Shosha £9.50, tikka, onion, green pepper, coriander leaves, cucumber, fairly hot; Garlic Mushroom £2.40. Delivery: 5 miles, £10 minimum. Takeaway: spend £10, two Popadoms free; spend £15, one Onion Bhajia free; spend £20, Vegetable Bhajee free. Price Check: CTM £5.50, Pullao Rice £1.60.

Moreton, The Wirral

EASTERN STYLE TANDOORI

11 Upton Rd, Moreton 0151 677 4863

Good curryhouse where you might get a discount if you show them this *Guide.*

SURMA TANDOORI

271 Hoylake Rd, Moreton 0151 677 1331

48-seater opened 1995 by Sharif Ali. Takeaway: 20% discount. *'Impressive upstairs restaurant. Well decorated and intimate. very smart staff, real tablecloths, plate warmers used throughout, good quality crockery. Chicken Chat £2.50, lovely light puri, delicate topping, tangy sauce with small pieces of tender tikka. Bhojelo Gosht £6.45, exquisite, wonderfully tender pieces of juicy and rich tasting lamb, plenty of onion and papaya. Garlic Naan £1.75, soft, plenty of garlic, slightly crispy crust. Matter Paneer £2.25, was glad I had this, rather sloppy side dish, adding contrast, cheese blended with lamb, excellent. Salad and pickle tray supplied with the meal. A great meal, recommended.'* RW. Pop 45p, CTM £6.45, Pullao Rice £1.75. Hours: 5.30 -11.30.

Wallasey, The Wirral

BANGLA VUJON — NEW ENTRANT

225 Wallasey Village 0151 637 1371

'Standard, formula restaurant. Well lit and pleasantly decorated and at the time of this visit, quite busy. Ordered Chicken Tikka Biriani, surprise, surprise, with a plain Madras sauce. Rang the order through and even though they were busy, it was ready when I arrived to collect it. Portions were not the largest I have ever seen but the quality was excellent. Good flavour running through the rice, good colour and charcoal flavour in the chicken. Madras sauce, superb. I have to hold my hands up and after dismissing this establishment as below par in the past, I may have to change my opinion if it continues to perform well.' DB. Perhaps another visit Dave?

BHAJI — NEW ENTRANT

135 Wallasey Village, Wallasey
0151 638 9444

'Well presented Chicken Tikka Biriani in a round tray, garnished with tomatoes, cucumber, lemon, but no omelette. At last a biriani was some flavour. Lots of excellent tikka, nut and sliced garlic (didn't go down well at work) and an excellent Madras sauce.' DB. Hours: Daily to 1030. Friday and Saturday to 11, Sunday to 10.30.

SHAPLA — NEW ENTRANT

59 King Street, Wallasey 0151 637 0888

'Opened in competition to the well-established Tandoori Mahal. I have driven past and it appears light and airy. My meal was a takeaway, Onion Bhajia, quite nicely spiced; Chicken Tikka Jalfrezi with Pullao Rice, nice tender chicken tikka but sauce not hot enough. Will try again, one stormy night in the winter.' DB. Delivery: 4 miles, £7 minimum.

TANDOORI MAHAL

24, King Street, Wallasey 0151 639 5948

This is one of Dave's favourites, and he tells of three visits: *'Sunday night after a full day drinking and eating at the Cricket Club's Cheese and Wine."* where do you put it? ..... *'Mixed Kebab, Onion Bhajia, Chicken Chat and Corn on the Cob (Jacs).'* ... haven't you converted her yet? *'... all excellent. Chicken Tikka in Vindaloo sauce, very tasty, but extremely hot.'* DB. *'Normal warm welcome on arrival, but a query was raised as to where we were on Bank Holiday, we had been missed... .BBQ at the cricket club and nobody could eat anymore. The food was everything that is expected. They will never win awards but they will never be short of custom.'* DB. *'After spending an enjoyable afternoon watching Man U being beaten in the cup final, we decided to go for a celebration curry. Popadoms up to standard, although I would like to see an more adventurous chutney tray...'* Agreed. *'...Onion Bhajia, three decent sized balls, moist in the middle and crisp on the outside. Jacs Lamb Tikka (yes, she's on to Indian food at last)' brilliant, you have converted her! and this has become her usual. I had Chef's Special, lamb, chicken and prawns in Madras sauce, topped with omelette and pineapple, very good. Deserves to be in the Guide for its longevity and consistency.'* DB. And it is.

West Kirby, The Wirral

ROYAL BENGAL

150 Banks Road, Kirby 0151 625 9718

Opened originally in 1971, taken over in 2000. Popular dishes include: Chicken Garlic Chilli. Sunday Buffet: £7.95. Stocks: Cobra. Price Check: Popadom 50p, CTM £7.25, Pullao Rice £1.75. <www.royalbengalwirral.co.uk>

MIDDLESEX

Area: All part of Greater London (west of London)
Population:1,200,000
Adjacent Counties: Berks, Bucks, Herts GL, Essex GL, London NW & W and Surrey GL

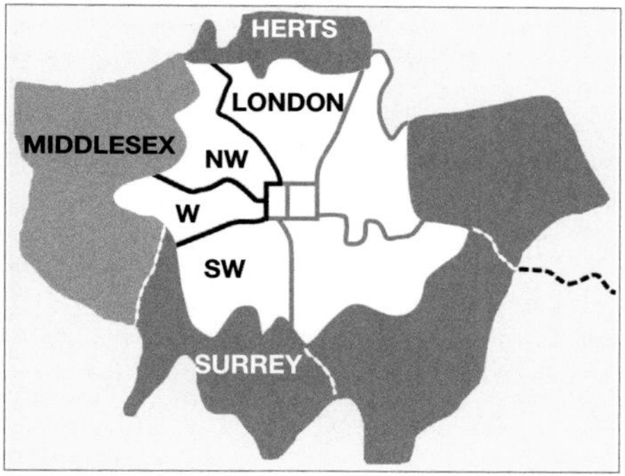

The county of Middlesex is very ancient. It once contained most of London, though this distinction became diminished when central London became autonomous during Victorian times. What was left of the county (located west and north of London) was completely 'abolished' when Greater London was formed in 1965, a move unpopular with Middlesex residents. Confusion exists because the Post Office still use Middlesex as a postal county. Postcodes add to the confusion. Enfield, for example, is EN1, EN2, EN3 in postal Middlesex but is in (Hertfordshire) GL county. Potters Bar EN6 is the same. Barnet is in postal Hertfordshire with EN4 and EN5 codes. It used to be in geographical Middlesex but is now a GL borough!

Ashford (Middlesex)

PEPPERS NEW ENTRANT

18 Woodthorpe Road 01784 420131

We have had several contented reports talking about this venue. The food is better than average and the menu contains all the favourite curries, suide dishes, rices, breads, chutneys and pickles. *'One day I had lunch at Zarin's Ashford Kent, and then on the same day popped in here for dinner. Both excellent. Way to go!'* RL.

TAMANNA'S

15a Station Road, Ashford 01784 420720

Good curryhouse where you might get a discount if you show them this *Guide*.

Brentford

PAPPADUMS TOP 100

GC1 and GC2, Ferry Quays, Ferry Lane, Brentford 020 8847 1123

Pappadums is sited on the banks of the River Thames is sited close to luxury apartments and overlooks Kew Gardens. Owner, Narinda and Satvir Sindhu pulled out all the stops creating this smart, modern looking 150-seater restaurant. It has a modernistic, double frontage, which looks out onto a large promenade area. Steps then lead you down to the Grand Union Canal and Thames. When weather permits, diners are welcome to eat outside, on wooden benches with chairs. Inspired by traditional Indian decor, the restaurant's weighty wooden doors have been shipped over from the subcontinent, but Pappadums remains a contemporary restaurant with a healthy take on many well-known dishes featured on the menu. and his restaurant menu features pan– Indian as well as occasional dishes from South East Asia. besides more substantial main courses, Pappadums also has a light lunch menu where spiced bites include Wraps, Kath Rolls and even Indianised paneer Spring Rolls. Chef Gupta from Oberoi hotels, and young personable Alston Wood from Sri Lankan are the team. Park in the underground car park (or you'll get a wheel clamp). *The menu at Pappadums is varied and includes dishes from other spicy countries, such as China and Thailand. Under the heading of 'Exotic Oriental Delicacies', you will encounter Nasi Goreng £15, 'lamb and chicken satay served with spicy fried rice, topped with fried egg and peanut sauce,' Honey Spiced Chicken £10, Thai Gaeng Pak 'stir-fried vegetables, tofu, scallions, mushrooms, hot and sour sauce.' I decided to stick to the Indian section and spied Machhli Ke Pakode, 'fried cod dish strips coated with mild spiced gram flour.' A generous portion was presented with a good salad and I enjoyed it very much. Pat had Kashmiri Lamb Seekh Kebab. Again a generous portion of tender, well pounded, spicy meat with salad. The chutney tray was left on the table for us to help ourselves. The menu highlights various dishes with a chilli logo, so we homed in on those choices. Chicken Chettinad, '...tempered with curry leaves, sun-baked red chillies and peppercorns,' (three chillies). I ordered Aloo Udaigiri 'potatoes braised with coriander, cumin and Bikaneri spiced chillies.' The Dal Makhani, 'slowly simmered black lentils' came in a small, highly polished brass bucket, complete with handle, filled to the brim and decorated with a swirl of fresh cream came to the table - quite delicious. A portion of Steamed Rice escorted everything.'* DBAC. **TOP 100.** Lunch and dinner, daily.

Eastcote

NAUROZ — NEW ENTRANT

219 Field End Road — 020 8868 0900

This restaurant means 'new' in the context of new year etc. But owner Raza Ali is an old hand; he specialises in creating new venues, then selling them. (Five Hot Chillies, Mirch Masala, SW16 & SW 17 and Karahi King, Wembley. All have good pedigrees making them popular venues for the locals who tell uds hoe much they enjoy it. *'Nauroz has recently opened. It's a family concern. All fresh food, including vegetables. This time they seem to have settled. Which is great for Eastcote. Authentic food, beautifully prepared, served in a spartan 'works canteen' kind of setting. Excellent quality and value.'* DT. *'Friends 21st birthday dinner. Open kitchen, which offers you the chance to see how the food is prepared... a little bit of theatre is always a good thing ...delicious food, value for money.'* LS. *Another* LS *visited and agreed. 'I stumbled upon this restaurant during a business trip. I travel a lot and consider myself some what of an expert!. The food I ate was delicious and great value for money, all freshly cooked that day. It was extremely busy and had a great atmosphere.'* LS.

Edgware

HAANDI

301Hale Lane, Edgware — 020 8905 4433

Sister brach to Haandi SW3 (see entry) and the same tasty Punjabi cooking with an African twist

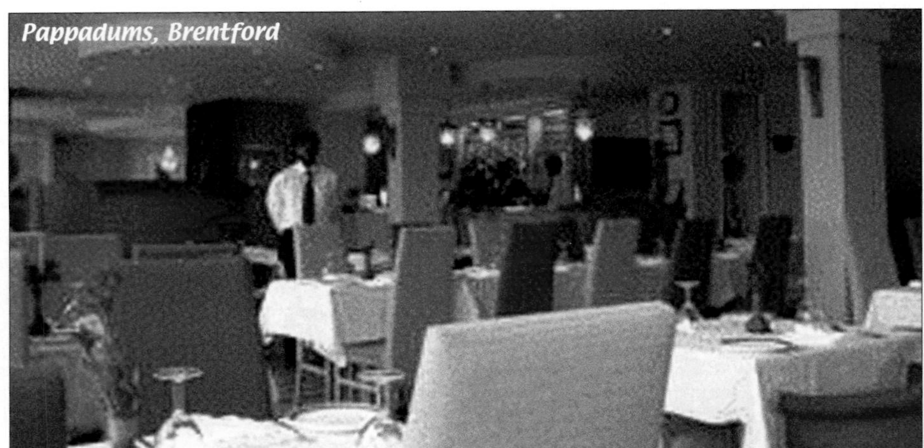
Pappadums, Brentford

at a much smaller price point. Everyone talks of the Kake di lamb on-the- bone, Asian style (and there are always plenty of local Asians in there.) is juicy aromatically flavour chunks of meat in a garam masala gravy. Also the sag Paneer was a fine rendition. Service charge: 12.5%. Hours: 12.30-3, Wed-Sun. 6-11 Sun-Thur; 6-11.30 Fri, Sat,

ZANZIBAR NEW ENTRANT

113 High Street, Edgware 020 8952 2986

Decent beer here and the pub grub is Punjabi/ Kenyan Asian. Full meals too. Packed with Asians and Bangra sounds. Hours: 12-3, Mon-Sat; 5.30-11, Mon-Thur; 6-11pm Fri, Sat; 12-10 Sun

Enfield

CHASE SIDE INDIAN NEW ENTRANT

135 Chase Side, Enfield 020 8367 9979

Commenced trading in 2002. Proprietor, Aktar Hussain has many restaurants to his credit. This particular restaurant has a modern feel, being decorated in cream with pale wooden floors. Menu Snapshot: Duck Tikka £6.75; Shahi Chicken Biriani £7.95, Pullao rice, sultanas, coconut and almonds, served with mixed vegetable curry; Village Style Begoon £6.25, fresh slices of okra, ginger, garlic, onion, tomato, pepper and cashew nuts, topped with fried discs of aubergine, fresh coriander leaves , saffron and onion. Stocks: Cobra. Takeaway: 10% discount. Sunday Buffet: £7.95. Delivery: 4 miles, £15 minimum. Takeaway Price Check: Popadom 50p, CTM £6.95, Pullao Rice £1.95. Hours: 12.30 - 5, Sunday only and 6 - 12. Branch: Tikka Cottage, Hot House and Bengal Spice in Hertford. <www.chaserestaurant.co.uk>

MEHEK

424 Hertford Road, Enfield 020 8443 1844

Bright (royal purple and gold), a cheerfully modern and stylish restaurant. Ashik Miah runs a popular restaurant serving Bangladeshi curries and accompaniments, Lamb Zacutti £6.95 being the most popular dish. Menu Snapshot: Paneer Puri Sag £3.25, cheese and spinach on fried bread; Tava Gosht Lahori £7.25, lean lamb, tossed on iron skillet, spices, herbs, crushed garlic and julienne of ginger, light sauce, fresh tomatoes, capsicum and coriander leaf; Delight £7.95, marinated spring chicken, almonds, raisins, pineapple, lychee, panir (cheese) and cream, mild; all Balti dishes (from £5.95) served with Naan; Garlic and Chilli or Tikka Naan £2.50. Stocks: Cobra, £4.25 a pint and Kingfisher. Sunday Buffet: £7.95. Minimum Charge: £25. Service: 10%. Delivery: 3 miles, £12 minimum. Price Check: Popadom 60p, CTM £7.25, Pullao Rice £1.75. Hours: 6- 11.30, Sat- 12. Branch: Bombay Spice, 201, Ordinance Road, Enfield. <www.mehekcuisine.co.uk

Hampton

MONAF'S

119 Station Road, Hampton 020 8979 6021

Named after its owner, Mr A Monaf, we hear good things about this restaurant, and its Sheesh Mahal sister. Monaf's is a well run, popular local. Sunday buffet. 10% takeaway discount. Hours: 12-2,30/5.30-12. Branch: Sheesh Mahal.

Harrow

BLUE GINGER NEW ENTRANT

383 Kenton Road, Harrow 020 8909 0100

This is the type of dive London Asians adore: It's brassy, charismatic, noisy (Bollywood movies on the flat screens), comfortable (sofas), modern (black granite), spacious, bright and airy. All the family is welcome. Dads and lads tank up in the well-stocked bar while the mums and babes in their high chairs drool over the kiddie's menu. It's club-like and fun. The menu is Punjabi with a bit of Chinese, and the prices sensible. Some tables on a outdoor patio. Hours: 12-3 Tue-Sun; 6-11 daily

CONNOISSEUR CUISINE OF INDIA TOP 100

37 High Street, Harrow-on-the-Hill
020 8423 0523

It's near the School, right up on the hill. Once you've found a parking place, admire the views overlooking London. Proprietor Sonny Walia and his team ensure you get a warm and professional welcome. Chef Ramesh Honatha trained at India's Sheraton Group. *'He's attractive and single – girls should try to book a table in the kitchen!'* DBAC. [Last time I go there with my wife, Ed.] *'Piaz Ke Pakode, gram flour coated crisp onion slices, sprinkled with chat masala, a large plate of crisply fried onion Bhajias as most know them arrived with a neat pot of coriander chutney – delicious. Pat loved his soft shelled crab, which came with a small salad of cubed tomato, onion and cucumber. Lachadar paratha was light and buttery. Aubergine, the smallest, plump baby aubergines, smothered in a spicy sauce. Chicken with pepper, lovely and spicy. Portions are generous.'* DBAC. Well worthy of joining our **TOP 100**. Hours: 12-2.30, except no lunch on Saturday and Sunday /6.30-10.30, Friday to 12, closed Monday.

HARROW TANDOORI

57 Station Rd, North Harrow 020 8861 1571

Curryhouse by name and curryhouse by menu, but cooked we suspect by Punjabis. Anyway you all say you find the food delicious. Hours: 12-2.30 /6.30-11.30, daily.

RAM'S NEW ENTRANT

203 Kenton Road, Harrow 020 8907 2022

You would imagine that every regional Indian cooking style now has a home in a restaurant somewhere in London. Yet here is another one – Surti a style of vegetarian cooking from Surat, Gujarat's main seaport city. Surat was where the English first landed in India in 1608, although this has no relevance here, except to say they must have eaten Kadhi (see below and glossary) which passed into language as 'curry'. My first chef-training was from Gujarati chef, Sat Gupta. He was from Baroda, but his wife was from Surat. The most memorable piece of advice she gave me was not to cook green vegetables in iron vessels or they will turn black. Let me set the scene: Gujarat has many vegetarians, and many superb restaurants in Wembley and Leicester. Gujarati cooking is mild and slightly sweet, using yoghurt and gramflour in many guises accompanied by fluffy rice, puffy puris, wondrously-cooked vegetables, sweet pickles and tempting puddings (see page 49 for details). Some Surti cooking differs in detail, especially with its use of green ingredients: green onion leaves (leela kanda) green garlic leaves, green moong lentils, fresh fenugreek and coriander leaves. The Surti Vaghar is a cooked mix of garam masala, red chilli, ginger and garlic. Favourite dishes include Lachko, a cake made from toovar dhal, turmeric, ghee and water served with sev and green chilli & onion chutney. Pattice, a potato rissole with a stuffing of coconut, chilli and sev. Gujarat, has a unique recipe, Patra a kind of Swiss Roll made from colcasia leaves on which is spread a spicy paste, rolled into cylinders, steamed sliced and fried. So the arrival of a Surti venue did give me a heightened sense of excitement. Ram's is a plain, white-walled café. The food is typically Gujarati sweet, though Surti chilli hot. Many typical vegetables were on the menu: such as beans, plantain, karela (bitter gourd), okra, purple yam (they turn out a good rissole version of this) and red and yellow, sweet potatoes (sakkarkan). Undhiyu is probably Surat's national dish. It contains all the above and typically has Muthias (deep-fried besan dough and fenugreek leaf). Dahi Kadhi (turmeric gold yoghurt and gram flour-based curry with ginger, curry leaves, mustard seeds and red chilli, appears with several vegetable options. A good rice dish is the ghee-laden Khichadi (rice and lentils) . Prices are more than reasonable, A la carte main courses from £3.50 The Thali meals offers a good choice of items, £4.99 lunch, £8.99 dinner. The ultimate choice is the £15 set meal of unlimited food and soft drinks. Service charge 10%. No smoking. Takeaway service. Hours: 12 - 3/6 - 11. Branches of Vijay NW6 and Satay, Uxbridge.

SAFARI NEW ENTRANT

14A Broadwalk, Pinner Road 020 8861 6766

Another pit-stop London Asians adore: thisone is a bit duanting from the outside (dark windows – like stretch-limos) but once inside it's all go (if a bit dark on the lighting side) with Asian families having a good time on food which is again above average Punjabi Kenyan (hence its name and decor). Hours: 6-12 Mon-Thur; 1-12 Fri-Sun.

SANGEETHA

196 Kenton Rd, Harrow 020 8907 9299

Harrow and surrounds is literally sprouting Indian venues, as its Asian population expands, and this venue is an example. It is part of a south Indian chain, and it is south Indian vegetarian (see page 75). The dosa are light and yet satisfyingly chewy, their stuffing redolent of curry leaves, green chilli, coconut and mustard seeds. Their sambar and rasam had the right degree of tempering, piquancy and flavour. *'If my wife doesn't get hiccoughs when she sips her rasam, it ain't hot enough ... on this occasion she did. The waiters told us to come back for their annual dosa and chutney festivals'.* PC. Service charge: and inexplicably weeny 2.5 per cent service. Hours: 11 - 10.30 daily.

Hayes

ASHA

60 Station Road, Hayes 020 8573 4717

Established in 1977. Fully licensed and air-conditioned. ' Takeaway: 10% discount, £10 min. Delivery: 5 miles, £10 minimum. Hours: 12-2.30/6-12.

THAMOULINEE SRI LANKAN RESTAURANT

128a Uxbridge Road, Hayes 020 8561 3723

We are often asked what makes a good restaurant, and by all our own yardsticks, Thamouline shouldn't! But, as any regular visit to the subcontinent will vouch, dirt and decor are not in the frame over there. It's service and good food which matter. *'Delighted to report that the food is still very good – they can still cook. With our usual bottle of red wine we nibbled Papadams, still the lightest we've ever tasted, with mango chutney, mint raita and a red-tinged coconut chutney. Then our usual Mixed Special starters: Vadai, Mutton Roll, Crab Claw and Prawn Kebab, with a green-tinged coconut chutney and tomato sambol all fresh, and enjoyed, still for just . I ordered my usual Kothu Rotti, chopped chapatti prepared with mutton, egg, onions and spices. It looks unpromising, but at it's a huge, filling portion – dry, spicy and a lovely change to wet curries. Pat's Thamoulinee Special Crab Curry, two crab shells, legs and claws, packed with meat, smothered in rich hot gravy, lived up to expectations . Special Fried Rice, was huge, with more coconut, tomato sambols and Achcharu (mixed pickle)'* DBAC. The meal cost here will not exceed £20 for two, plus £7 with a bottle of wine.

Hounslow

HORIZONS BAR — NEW ENTRANT

210 Hanworth Rd, Hounslow 020 8814 0044

With its sleek, polished and upmarket ambience, it's tough to tell that Horizons is the first culinary venture of co-owners, Bugsy Pankhania and Rakesh Patel. The pair are childhood friends, who together run Rockwood Estates Ltd, which brought Hounslow based premises - an old Army site - in 1998. In 2005 they began transforming

the old Drill Hall into a multi-purpose venue, which now comprises a 400 cover banqueting suite, a bar and what is now one of the area's most popular restaurants.Much of the credit goes to the head chef, Chandan Singh,, who with his 25 years experience has brought a taste of traditional north India to southwest London. With an impressive CV that includes working at five-stars like the Taj palace, Meridian and Delhi's Hyatt Regency, Singh has also cheffed in Germany, specialising in kebabs, curries an an exemplary mixed grill. Add too this, the swish interiors that include comfy black leather couches, plasma screens, polished porcelain flooring and top of the range computerised sound and lighting systems for the live bands. Hours: 12-2.30 /6.30-11.30 daily.

HOUNSLOW BRASSERIE

47 Spring Grove Rd 020 8570 5535

Open-plan restaurant owned and managed by Naveed Sheikh. Chef Ali cooks Pakistani. *'Meat Samosas, £1.50 are absolutely outstanding, the holy grail of samosas!'* TE. *'A very quiet Thursday evening, and there were no other diners until I left at 2030 hours. Samosas were fantastic, certainly the best I can recall. Chicken Tikka was very good with a smoky flavour and nice use of ginger as a garnish. Rice was fine. Three bored waiters gave okay service. Worth another visit if they stay in business.'* RH. Takeaway: 5% off. Hours: 12-3 (Fri. closed lunch)/6-12.

KARAHI MASTER LAHORE TANDOORI

795 London Road, Hounslow 020 8572 2205

Pakistani (Halal) 40-seater opposite Hounslow Bus Garage. Taken over by Mohammad Akmal. Specials include: Roast Lamb Leg £17.50, or, if celebrating with friends, Stuffed Whole Lamb £100 sounds great. Lunch-time specials for £5.95, please ask. **BYO** is allowed, 1 bottle per person. A free drink to Curry Club members from Mr Akmal – cheers! Delivery: £15 minimum (6 free Papadams), 4-mile radius. Hours: 12-12.

NEW HEATHROW TANDOORI

482 Great West Road 020 8572 1772

'Another business trip to London and find myself having dinner at the New Heathrow Tandoori. The door was opened by a Nepalese waiter, big smile and warm 'Good evening Sir'. Showed me to a table, brought menu and lager immediately. Managing owner, Meojanur Rahman popped over for a chat, he commented that since the superb facelift, custom had increased. It was busy that Wednesday evening. Meat Samosa £1.95, delicious, plenty of spicy lamb inside an incredibly light pastry, Mr Rahman used to be a pastry chef...' Ah! insider knowledge! *'...served with crisp salad and lemon. Chicken Tikka Bhuna £5.45, beautifully served in a white ceramic pot and comprised large thick slices of smoky breast meat in rich, piquant sauce. Mr Rahman says he adds more chilli when the weather is cold!'* Good for him. *'The breads, mango Kulfi and coffee were all delicious and served to consistently high standards. I appreciate that this restaurant continues to use hot plates on the tables...'* Agreed. *'...too many restaurant are dispensing with them. Highly recommended.'* TE. Menu Snapshot: Chicken Mahisuri £7.50, barbecued chicken, onion, peppers, tomatoes in a creamy sauce; Egg Potato Vegetable Curry £3.20/£4.75, medium sauce; Dhal Lalmirch £2.95/£4.50 lentils with fried red chilli, Chicken Tikka Naan £2.50. Delivery: 4 miles, £12 minimum. Sunday Buffet: £6.95, children half price. Takeaway: 10% discount, £10 minimum. Price Check: Popadom 50p, CTM £6.95, Pullao Rice £1.75. Hours: 12 to 2, Friday 11 to 1 and 5.30 to 11.30. <www.newheathrowtandoori.co.uk>

Ickenham

DARJEELING

89 High Road, Ickenham 01895 679300

Darjeeling is a popular local restaurant, serving the formal curry competently and successfully. From what we hear, there are many regulars, and the establishment has been going for many a year. Takeaway 5% discount. Deliveries, min order £30, 2 mile radius.Hours: 12-2.30/6-11.30.

Northolt

EMPRESS OF INDIA

40 Church Road, Northolt 020 8845 4361

Est. 1974, Ali, Zaman and EH Khan's 52-seater is a good curryhouse where you might get a discount if you show them this *Guide.*

Northwood

SHANTI

48 High Street, Northwood 01923 827856

Established in 1984, Mofiz Miah's 60-seater, t is a good curryhouse where you might get a discount if you show them this *Guide.*

Rayners Lane

PAPAYA

15, Village Way, Rayners La 020 8866 5582

It is Sri Lankan, though there are Indian curries on the menu too. The cooking is good and most Sri Lankan delights are to be found. *(see page 75)*. Service charge: 10% Hours: 12-12 Mon-Sat; 12-11 Sun. <www.papayauk.com>

Ruislip

RICE N SPICE TAKEAWAY

73 Station Approach, S Ruislip 020 8841 5498

Good venue where you might get a discount if you show them this *Guide.*

RARA NEW ENTRANT

528 Victoria Road S.Ruislip 020 8845 7094

Opened in 2004 by SP Tripathi and serves North Indian and Nepalese delights, Murg Besani Kebab £3.50, battered chicken, grilled in tandoor, being the most ordered dish. Simply and cleanly decorated in cream and dark green. *'Soon became popular with people in the area. Recommended starters are Tandoori Phool £3.50, spicy cauliflower and broccoli and Stuffed Potato £3.50, scooped out potato with fresh cheese and dry fruits; Kesari Jhinga £4.95, grilled king prawns in yoghurt and saffron. Main Courses: Crab Kofta Curry £9.95, with potato, cheese, delicate sauce; Karahi Chicken £5.95, sautéed chicken, cream and tomato sauce; and Chicken Tikka Makhani.'* David, it sounds like you have eaten your way through the menu! *'Sunday Buffet is a bargain at £6.95.'* DD. Agreed. Menu Snapshot: First round of Popadoms are complimentary, generous! Pepper Chicken Tikka £5.95; Sanfo Salmon Tikka £7.95, with fennel; Lamb Chops £6.95, marinated in yoghurt, garlic, ginger gravy; Kulcha £1.95, choice of potato, green peas, cheese. Delivery: 3 miles. Stocks: Cobra. Price Check: Popadom 50p, CTM £5.95, Pullao Rice £1.95. Hours: 12 to 3 and 5.30 to 11.

RUISLIP TANDOORI

115 High Street, Ruislip 01895 632859

This air-conditioned venue is an old friend of this *Guide.* It's a 52-seat Nepalese restaurant in black and white with flowering trees, Nepalese handicraft,

pictures and a beautiful golden Buddha, which is, we're told, 'the main attraction apart from the Nepalese food'. Owner KB Raichhetri might give you a discount if you show him this *Guide.* Takeaway: 10% off. Sunday buffet c£9. Delivery: £15 min, 2-miles. Hours: 12-2.30/6-12.

Southall

From a single acorn the former Maharaja, there is an satisfying number of sweet/snack centres, cafés and restaurants to be found on South Road and the Green, but mostly on the the Broadway, the main artery through Southall. Expansion westwards continues, where its unexpected bonus is a pleasing growth of Sri Lankan suppliers. These places cater primarily for their indigenous Asian population, a generally peaceful mix of Indian and Pakistani Sikh and Punjabi carnivores, enhanced by East African Asians and most recently, Somalis. If you are none of these, do not feel inhibited from entering. Everyone is treated equally and all are welcome. Some venues are licensed and modern, aiming at the younger Asians. Others are café-style and unlicensed. At all of them you'll find good, authentic cuisine in straightforward, functional eating-houses, at realistic prices. The food is served from early morning to late night, fast and fresh. One or two correspondents have bemoaned the use of the microwave to heat the food. We point out that a microwave is merely a heater, which has gained a poor reputation because it cannot heat pastry well (samosas for example). It is not to be despised, and does not demean the food it heats. Better that than unhygienically keeping the food warm in bainmaries for hours on end. Here we examine our (and our correspondents') favourite eating holes: Plans are afoot to call this mile-long Broadway, Punjabi Bazaar, giving it an identity such as Chinatown W1. Arches and gateways will welcome you in English and Punjabi, and there will be colourful urban folk art, decorations on shop frontages and lamp posts with art designs from Amritsar and Lahore.

BALTI & TANDOORI WORLD U

185- The Broadway, Southall 020 8867 9991

Not only does it do Balti dishes, aka Karahi by the Punjabis, and Tandoori items, it does a fascinating mix of dishes from Gujarat, Punjab, Kenyan Asia, and north and south India are all on offer. *'Service is very quick and informative. Though it is unlicensed, waiters kindly fetched beer and soft drinks from the adjoining off-license. Customers can try their hand at cooking their own dishes. All dishes were of a high standard and were more authentic Indian-style cooking than some other restaurants we've visited.'.* SF. Hours: 11.30-11.30.

BOMBAY

177 The Broadway, Southall 020 8560 4646

It is modern and trendy inside and out – all black and white paint and stained wood. There is a bar on which to prop yourself up on (if you can elbow the proprietor's friends out of the way who seem to treat the place like their local pub), a big TV for entertainment, many framed pictures of 'stars' and a party room which always seems to be full of beautifully sari-ed ladies having a roaring time with a booming disco and disappearing trays of steaming food being carried upstairs by some gormless youth. The menu is small but that's OK, with all you really need listed. The waiter noticed me gaping at the TV, turned over to Eastenders and put on the subtitles – how kind! Papadams are good with an excellent chutney tray – definitely hand-made, lovely. Curries are well above average but with one criticism, they are a little salty for my taste. Good value wine list. Enjoyable.

BRILLIANT AWARD WINNER A-LIST

72 Western Road, Southall 020 8574 1928

The Brilliant has long been on of the UK's most popular Indian restaurant and it has got even better with its new redec of which more later. Launched in 1975 as a one-unit thirty-six seater with a minimalist menu on the same site. Today the restaurant seats 250 in three units and is the country's first restaurant to hold civil marriages and has an upstairs banqueting suite, providing event catering and even karaoke nights. It is owned by Gulu Anand and Kewel Anand *(see page 57)*. A newly launched 'Healthy Option' a la carte menu, the brainchild of 22 year old Dipna, Gulu's daughter. Clienteles can now enjoy the renowned signature dishes such as Jeera Chicken £8/£16 and Masala Lamb £8, but new items which are cooked with olive oil and low fat yoghurt. Existing dishes have also been refined to suit a health-conscious palate. Long a pioneer in offering Vegetable Keema £8, soy mince with fresh peas, Brilliant's range of healthy options include: Tandoori Salmon, mildly spiced chunks of salmon with dill and no oil; Papri Chat £4.50, a crispy snack of chickpeas, tamarind chutney and low fat yoghurt; Methi Chicken £17.50 (for three), cooked with with olive oil and not an ounce of fat. Sides have also been given a makeover, Dhal Tarka £4.50, yellow lentils cooked with garlic and red chillies, though still retaining its flavour, eschews the traditional method of tempering which would usually leave a layer of fat on top of the dish. Bombay A greater choice of salads is on the menu while ghee (clarified butter) is now only utilised in moderation and even then merely to add flavour. Improvement has also been made in presentation with a keen eye to ensure that the dish focuses on the main ingredients and their natural colours. While Gulu and Kewel are still overseeing the runnings of the Brilliant, the mantle of carrying the restaurant's success into the future in gradually being passed to a new generation of the Anand family. Dipna, who has a passion and understanding of Indian food, is at the forefront of developing the restaurant's cuisine. Shankar, Dipna's 20 year old brother, is the establishment's General Manager. *See page 57 and 472.*
e:brilliantrestaurant@hotmail.com

Right: Brilliant's smart new decor showing its Kenyan roots

Brilliant Restaurant
Brilliant
Brilliant

CHHAPPAN BHOG NEW ENTRANT

1 The Broadway, Southall 020 8574 7607

An Asian sweet shop, (Mithai) which sells savoury items as well. Chhappan Bhog is an ancient Hindu description of a royal get-to-gather at which the attendees would enjoy Indian sweets such as Burfi (fudge) and Halva., The shop sells 56 sweetmeats and snacks. Branch 145 Ballards Lane, Finchley, N3. 020 8371 8677.

DELHI WALA NEW ENTRANT

11 King Street, Southall 020 8574 0873

This an exciting venue, the seemingly contradiction in terms, a vegetarian Punjabi. The state of Punjab is half in Pakistan half in north India. It is one of India's major culinary styles which began to evolve from early in the first millennium AD. It is perhaps the best known Indian food because the original curry restaurants in the developed world based their menus on Punjabi cuisine. Dairy farming is a major Punjabi industry and its prolific wheat crops, earn it the title 'the granary of India', and Parathas and Puris are staples. The food is very savoury and fenugreek leaf (methi) and mustard leaf (rai) are virtually staples. One might be forgiven for believing that all Punjabis eat meat. In fact about 40% of the Punjabi population are vegetarian, so robust curries like Punjabi Keema, Methi Aloo, Aloo Ghobi Methi and Sag Paneer and Mattar Valor – Pea and Bean Curry are typical.

GIFTO'S LAHORE KARAHI AND TANDOORI BYO

162 The Broadway, Southall 020 8813 8669

'Went by train after parking problems at Madhu's (but it was a Sunday). Good decision, because local road restrictions last until 8.30 pm. The Lahori leg of lamb pre-ordered was running late. The cunning ploy to get us to order starters worked, but the leg was so special when it did arrive, nothing was sent back. How they get the flavour so deep into the meat I know not, but the dressing and marinade were excellent. Did not come off the bone as well as the Sarkhel's shank or chicken but tasty right through. Pretty upmarket after its revamp, though still soft drinks only. So cost for 4, blow out meal was £52 ,of which the leg was £20 (plus the Cobra from from the "cousin's" shop next door). Must now go on a fruit diet for a few days I fear.' C & MC. **BYO.** Open all day. Branch Gifto Express, 147, The Broadway Southall. 020 8843 0101

GLASSY JUNCTION

97 South Road, Southall 020 8574 1626

Drive north over Southall railway station bridge, observing the tiny (and excellent) kebab house on its brow on the left and ahead you can't miss the amazing vista of Glassy Junction. It's a pub, whose exterior is clad with gigantic Hindu figures. Being a pub, it serves booze just like any other pub. Its clientèle is largely young trendy Asians, the like of which abound in Southall. Bangra and Hindi movie music blares out. Add the chattering, and the noise is more deafening than a migrating flight of starlings. As to the food, there's a splendid selection of tandoori and curry items. *'If you intend to visit any of Southall's unlicensed venues, you can always have "a pre-visit" to the Glassy, though after that I find it as well to have water! Pakora's at the Glassy were as good as ever, though the place seems to have changed hands. It was getting a vigorous clean while we were there.'* C&MC.

KARAHI TANDOORI KABAB CENTRE

161 The Broadway, Southall 020 8574 3571

Owner AF Choudhury and Manager Dalawar delightedly tell that their venue, known locally as TKC, was an original of the genre, founded in 1965, early days in Southall's currinary development, and that there have been numerous copiers, not least the ones dead opposite. And what is the genre? Firstly, it is and was uncompromisingly Asian in food style and service, though, all are welcome, of course. In 1965, few whites visited it, now things have changed, and they are as taken for granted as the Asian clientèle. The venue is open-all-hours, and the price is right – inexpensive, and designed to attract regular local custom several times a week at breakfast, lunch tea or dinner. Next, standard shop full-length windows ensure that when walking past, you are immediately attracted to the display cabinets containing all sorts of tempting snacks such as Pakora, Bhel Poori, Gol Goppas, Jeera Pani (cumin water), Tikki, Samosa, Indian sweets, etc. Alongside, and equally on show are the chefs, under head chef Farooq, and they soon learn to show off, much as do Tepiyakki chefs in the Japanese equivalent. Their freshly cooked Tandooris, Kebabs and breads, Punjabi Karahis and curries are cooked to order, and are quite delicious. Inside is a clean and tidy, no frills café-style restaurant, seating 66, with formica tables, and waiter-service. Head chef Farooq's menu says 'please specify your taste of chillies when ordering. His Appetisers include: Reshmi Spring Lamb Boti, tender succulent pieces of lamb marinated in double cream roasted in the tandoor £3.50. Paneer Tikka, chunks of vegetarian cheese marinated with spices and baked in tandoor £3. Main courses: Nehari, shank of lamb served in a spicy sauce £4. Zeera Chicken, made with butter and cummin seeds £5. Sarson Ka Saag, mustard and spinach leaf £3.50. House Specialities: Chargha, fully roasted and tenderly spiced, free-range chicken, a recipe from the inner Punjab £6.50. Chappal Kebab, beaten mince steaks cooked and served on a sizzler, a speciality from the North-West Frontier Province £4. Try the Kulfi Faluda, a Pakistani version of the Knickerbocker Glory £1.80. Pinad Da Buffet £6.99. All food is prepared with Halal meat. Alcohol is strictly prohibited. It gets very busy with all age groups, from the pensioners, mums and babes in the day to the young trendy ebullient fun-loving Asians at night and weekends. Hours: 9am-12am. Branch: Tandoori Express on Jalebi Junction, 93 The Broadway, Southall.

MADHU'S BEST IN UK AWARD WINNER

39 South Road, Southall 020 8574 1897

Opened 1980. Punjabi cuisine with Kenyan twist. *In those days it was a friendly, busy cafe-style restaurant It is as different now as it could be, except that it remains busy and extremely friendly. In our previous Guide (2004) we made it the UK's number one restaurant. We know that when we make a restaurant no one, all the celebrity critics beat a path to the door. We are flattered, but this being Southall, we waited for them to pooh-pooh our decision, but to a man and woman, they all agreed. But more importantly you our public agree too. Loads of you have visited and written in. But before we quote a few of your views, I must describe one of our own visits. A friend of ours is a top international sales person in a blue-chip computer systems company. We promised to take him and his wife to the UK's number one Indian restaurant. He had not heard of Madhu's before, and as we got closer, you could sense a slight anx in him. We managed to park outside (very rare) and the anx was visible. But once inside, the décor, setting, table lay-up, and service, not to mention the food and drink, literally blew him away. "Incredible ... We get a lot of foreign visitors come to our offices. Often they ask to be taken for a curry. Up till now, no one had been able to guarantee a prestigious local. Now we can", he confided later. Here are some more comments: 'Not much more that I need to say about this excellent establishment except that food quality, service and ambience were as excellent as would be expected for a restaurant aiming to keep it's place right there at the top. My notes aren't copious but suffice to say, my visitor from the USA and I were suitably impressed with the magical Buzi Bafu and the other dishes that we ordered. Overall opinion – outstanding, will continue to recommend to lovers of authentic Indian food and will continue to come back as often as I can!'* SO. *'We moved to the curry desert of Devon from Berkshire and regularly ate at Madhu's Brilliant, a great exponent of the skills of cooking great Indian food.'* AF. *'We were delighted to be told by Annan that the Iceland car park can now be used again for Madhu's,a visit to savour-can you get him to disclose the Jeera chicken recipe please? '* C & MC. Menu Snapshot: Masala Fish £10, fillet of Tillapia (fresh water fish from Kenya's Lake Victoria) cooked with masala sauce, flavoured with roasted cumin seed; Makni Chicken £10, chicken pieces simmered in a mild gravy, enriched with butter and cream, aromatically spiced with cardamom and cinnamon; Methi Chicken £10, chicken pieces simmered with fresh and fry fenugreek in a traditional savoury Punjabi sauce; Karela Aloo £7, combination of bitter gourd and potatoes, flavoured with pomegranate; Dall Makhni £6, black urid lentils, stirred over a slow fire for many hours, flavoured with green cardamom (one of DBAC's favourites); Hara Bhara Kebab £6 for six pieces, finger sized kebabs made from cottage cheese, green peas and fenugreek, flavoured with coriander (another one of my favourites); Aloo Papri Chat £5 for two, crunchy combination of fried wheat crisps (papri), boiled potato cubes, chickpeas, chopped onion in a fresh mint and tangy tamarind sauce, garnished with fresh coriander, served cold (delicious and again, one of my favourites); Mogo Jeera Fried £5 for two, fresh cassava pan-fried with roasted cumin and ground black pepper, or deep-fried and seasoned with spices (do try these fried, really good); Boondi Raitha £3.50, yoghurt flavoured with cumin, ground black pepper and tiny crisp gram flour puff balls. House Special, Boozi Bafu, on the bone £18/£36, spring lamb chops, gently simmered in onion and tomato sauce, with freshly ground spices. Stocks: Cobra. Price Check: Popadom 50p, CTM £10, Pullao Rice £3.50. Hours: 12.30 to 2.45 and 6 to 11.30, Tuesday closed. <www.madhusonline.com> *See pages 29, 40 & 74.*

MOJ MASTI NEW ENTRANT

37 Featherstone Rd, Southall 020 8893 6502

Serving authentic Karachi Pakistani food and opened by Natasha Shaikh with husband Anees in

2005. Moj Masti seats 130 people in four modern-imaged rooms managed by Ali Ikram – the Kat-a-Kat food bar, Ju Ju`s jungle with water features, low lighting and greenery, an Oriental-style dining zone (upstairs) inspired by Pakistan`s northern border with China with has some influence on the country`s cooking culture (fried rice and chilli chicken on its menu). The fourth room is available for hire and has a dance floor. Moj Masti opens 8am for buffet breakfast (with such light dishes as lassi. halwa, chana, puri and aloo curries). As with all Southall restaurants, kids are welcomed. Children will enjoy Lollipop Chicken with chips and salad. Head chef Asif Ali's starters include Udaan Lajawab £3.50, chicken wings BBQd in special sauce..Specials include Goan Fish £7.20, coley or kingfish grilled or steamed with Goan spices; Nihari Lamb £5.90, Haleem, £5.90, lentils, wheat and lamb puree; Lahori Fried Fish and Chicken Peer Bhai. The most remarkable dish is Kat-a-Kat (see Tak-a-tan on page 51) a Karachi speciality dish, rarely-found in the UK, named after the clattering noise the chef's special tools make as he simultaneously chops and cooks the ingredients on a tawa (flat pan). This is Pakistani's version of Tepinyaki in that it is performed in front of its customers. Before that at Moj Masti diners select their own meat, namely chicken (murgh), minced lamb (keema) brains (magaaz), liver (kalegi) , kidneys (gurda) or lamb testes (kapooray) and vegetables. Then they watch as it is cooked in front of them. All Kat-a-Kat dishes cost £6. This is one dish you must try. No alcohol served but BYO welcomed with no corkage charge. Delivery 3 mile radius, but no Takeaway. Price Check: Popadom 60p, CTM £5.50, Tarka Dhal £3.50, Pullao Rice £2.50, Naan Bread £75p. Hours: 8am to midday, main menu midday to midnight . <www.mojmasti.co.uk>

NARGIS KAPURI PAN

NEW ENTRANT

25 The Green, Southall 020 8574 5041

All you get here is Pan or Paan, pronounced 'parn', which is best defined as a collection of edible ingredients, ranging from very bitter to very sweet folded, samosa-fashion in the paan leaf. We believe Nargis is the only paan shop in the UK, but in the subcontinent, Paan is a massive industry, involving an army of 'paan wallahs', traders, who prepare 'paan masalas' or mixtures, dispensing their wares in smart restaurants, at home door-to-door, or at street kiosks. Paan (Betel) leaf eaten in one mouthful, as a digestive after a meal. The darkish green, heart-shaped leaf is bitter, the mouth-feel coarse and the taste acquired. The ingredients include certain aromatic spices, for example aniseed, green cardamom, cloves and fennel,cucumber, marrow, watermelon and pumpkin seeds. To counter the bitter tastes, sugar crystals or sugar balls are used. The exact choice of ingredients is left to the customer. For a small price you can experience a major taste aspect of real India in Southall. And the Indophile can buy tablas and sitars at Bina Musicals, a few doors down the street.

OMI'S

TOP 100

1 Beaconsfield Road, 020 8574 1831

Established way back in 1976, by Mukesh Kharbanda and partners. Congratulations are in order, thirty years is quite an achievement! Mykesh himself cooks north Indian and Kenyan Asian curries at Omi's. The shop front stands slightly back from the pavement, making room for parking for 6-8 vehicles. A short menu above the counter describes what is on offer, along with the Specials of the Day. The most popular dishes are Karahi Chicken, Ginger Chicken and Palak Chana. Since we were taken here years ago by Indian journalist KN Malik (*'I want to show you Indian food at its best'*), we can safely say this is the Indians' Indian restaurant. We love his food and adore Mykesh's idiosyncrasies. It has the usual plastic tables and chairs, making for a clean and tidy restaurant, but it's the freshly-cooked food you go for. Licensed. Delivery: small charge. Remains in our **TOP 100.** Stocks: Cobra. Price Check: Popadom 50p, CTM £5, Pullao Rice £2.25. Hours: 11 - 10.30, Saturday to 11, Sunday to 9.30.

PALM PALACE

80 South Road, Southall 020 8574 9209

Sri Lankan/south Indian, a scarce resource in the UK, and still unique in Southall, although several High Street shops sell Sri Lankan ingredients. The redec has now bedded itself in (expensive chairs, granite tables, smart wood floor etc, and black-shirted waiters, still as friendly as ever, their service, though a tad slow is always with a flourish). It is marginally busier than before, but I said it before and I'll say it again: Southall's Asians are a conservative lot – but the if-it-ain't-Punjabi-it-ain't-edible view is slowly changing. Even Sanjay from Madhu's is a convert to Palm Palace. And, as we say every time, so it should. My bench mark crab curry from an early ownership has never matched, but it's still an exciting dish, especially fired up to incendiary level for those of us who cannot do without chilli. There's nothing like picking and sucking out crab meat from legs and shell and dousing it in rich Sri Lankan gravy. Messy shirt-sprinkling stuff, yes, but a slow, pleasurable experience, which is a contender for my desert island luxury. Hours: 12-3 daily; 6-11 Mon-Thur; 6-11.30 Fri-Sun

PUNJABI KARAHI

175 The Broadway, Southall 020 8574 1112

Once you get towards the Hayes end of Southall's Broadway you are spoilt for choice of Karahi Kebab houses. Me, I think I'd better move house and live there, then I could rotate round them each day. The menu and concept, prices and hours is identical to the others on the block and is just as worthy of your visit.

NEW ASIAN TANDOORI CENTRE
TOP 100

114 The Green, Southall 020 8574 25791

There is nothing new about this venue. It began trading in 1959. Indeed it is still known as The Roxy, although its English transport caff namesake closed over four decades ago. In its place came an Asian version of the same – one of those long-standing restaurants which serve the local community morning, noon and night. Founders Mr Sagoo and Mr Thakhar strategically set up two such venues, located at either end of Southall. have finally retired and sold their 157 The Broadway venue to the next door halal butcher, who has renamed it The Kashmir. Well, I say nothing new, but they have had a smart redec. When you enter the Roxy, there may be a queue, even outside the door, but it won't take long before it's your turn. Long glass counters display tempting Indian sweets and savoury snacks (Bhajias, Kebabs, Samosas, Aloo Tikki, Dahi Vasa, etc.), curries (Murgh Masala, on the bone, Bombay Potato, Sag Paneer, Sag Gosht and more, all cold but will be reheated in the microwave on request), Channa Dal, Rice (Plain, Pullao and Biryani) and breads. *'Pick up a tray and tell the chap behind the counter what you want and whether you are eating in or taking out. Portions are generous and I have to restrain myself from over-ordering. When you have paid (cash or cheques only), take your tray to the other room and seat yourself.'* DBAC. *'The absolute curry experience, should be compulsory for all members to visit! Sample the vast range of dishes on offer, all authentic and served up in a no-nonsense style. We ate vast quantities of food, including Pakoras, Dal (black bean), Chicken and Meat Curries, Rotis and rice. Service with a smile, staff friendly. Highly recommended, must be very high in the* **TOP 100.'** DB. They also serve a wonderful chutney, sticks of carrot, slices of onion, embalmed in a tamarind and yoghurt sauce, delicious, I can't get enough of it. You can **BYO** (but please ask) though they do sell Cobra, which all makes for a great meal out. Fresh fruit juice and Lassi are available. They don't take credit cards, hardly surprising as your meal will be under a tenner. New hours since last time. Now you can get an early Punjabi breakfast: try Mango Lhassi (as good as any smoothie) with a lentil dish eg (Kabli Chana) and bhatura, large deep-fried bread like a large puri, on which you sprinkle sugar, all washed down with Indian tea. Hours: 8-11 (12pm on Fri.-Sun.). It remains high in our **TOP 100.**

SHAHANSHAH VEGETARIAN

60 North Road, Southall 020 8574 1493

Gill Baljinder (manager) and Johl Sarbjit, have since 1984 specialised in cooking from north and south India at their vegetarian restaurant, which seats 30 diners. Samosas and other snacks are the most popular items ordered. Indian sweets are made on the premises, so you can be sure they are fresh. Set dinner £5. Sunday lunch £4.Branch: Shahanshah Vegetarian, 17 South Road, Southall.

TANDOORI EXPRESS ON JALEBI JUNCTION

93 The Broadway, Southall 020 8571 6782

Owner Abdul Chaudhury, manager Mr Shauket, and head chef Rassaq's bright and colourful venue appeals to the local young and trendy population. It is often full of chattering, bright young Asians babbling on in animated Southall cockney accents. A richly painted and decorated rickshaw can be seen outside on the wide pavement which enhances the environment. Also a cook makes Jalebis, those crispy, deep-fried squiggles, immersed in syrup, right there on the pavement. You can't get fresher than that, and if you've not seen it done, here's the only place in Britain we know of that does it on view. Great Pakistani curries and fresh breads are a big pull, along with snacks such as Samosas, Pakoras, etc. There is also a vast sweet counter to pile on the pounds (weight that is, not the bill). Starters include: Club Sandwich, finest chicken and lamb BBQ fillings £3. Shami Kebab, mince meat and lentil burger 50p. Dahi Bhalla, lentil flour doughnuts soaked in yoghurt £1.50. House specials: Masaladaar Raan, whole leg of lamb roasted in the tandoor with all the natural juices and flavours sealed within, a Moghul dish from Lakhshmi Chauk, Lahore, £15. Alcohol is strictly prohibited. Hours: 9am-11pm. Branch: 161 The Broadway, Southall.

Sudbury

FIVE HOT CHILLIS NEW ENTRANT

875 Harrow Road, Sudbury 020 8908 5900

Once a venue is entered in this *Guide* it can become busier than before. Sometimes this leads to a decline in service, care, cooking and everything except till. But this is unlikey here. And since we have been asked frequently to mention Five Chillies, here it is. Cooking is Punjab. The venue is a cheap and cheerful caff. The clientele is largely Asian, and the atmosphere is intensely friendly. Meat and Chicken on-the-bone, as it should be. Dishes which burst with flavour, and individualism. Price probably around a tenner, and they take credit cards. It is unlicensed. You can **BYO** with corkage no charge. Hours: 11 - 11, daily.

Teddington

BENGAL BRASSERIE

162 Stanley Rd, Teddington 020 8977 7332

Good curryhouse where you might get a discount if you show them this *Guide*.

Twickenham

THE NAZ NEW ENTRANT

20 Church Street, Twickenham 020 8744 9181

First opened in 1990, Neswar Ali and his son Mohammed Shayed's Naz is open for business once again now updated following a nine week revamp from top to bottom. It retains the classic and traditional atmosphere inspired by Neswar, while Mohammed's input offers a contemporary mix with his modern ideas. Located in the heart of Twickenham, an area presenting plenty of eating-out options, The Naz has always been a popular spot, especially on rugby days, as they are a stone-throw from Twickenham Stadium. and now boasts a new kitchen, rich interiors, 86 covers and an added extension. With a collective experience of 38 years between them, the father and son duo own and run the joint.

The Naz, Twickenham

PALLAVI SOUTH INDIAN NEW ENTRANT

Unit 3 Cross Deep Court, Heath Rd, Twickenham 020 8892 2345

This Kerelan first floor restaurant is a branch of the Radha Krishna Bhavan. The menu is the same

(*see* SW17). It specialises in Kerelan food, but also does a full listing of curry favourites (chicken, meat et al). Our advice is to ignore the latter and enjoy the thing they do best. Service charge: 10%. Hours: 12-3 daily; 6-11 Sun-Thur -12, Fri, Sat. <www.mcdosa.com>

SAGAR — NEW ENTRANT

27 York St, Twickenham — 020 8744 3868

This is another south Indian restaurant but with a difference. It specialises in Udupi vegetarian cuisine. This one is a branch of the Sagar, Hammersmith, W6. The background and menu details are the same. Hours: 12-2.45, Mon-Fri; 12-11.30, Sat; -10.45, Sun.

TANGAWIZI — NEW ENTRANT

406 Richmond Rd Richmond Bridge
E. Twickenham — 020 8891 3737

Mr and Mrs Meghji opened Tangawizi in 2004I, its name giving no clue as to its cuisine. In fact Tangwizi is Swahili for 'ginger', (the couple are Kenyan Asians. The USP is that the chef worked with Vineet Bhatia (*see* SW3) so now we have it; the cuisine is fusion Indian. Menu Snapshot: Nutty Samosa £6.95, a tasty blend of spinach, potato and pine nuts filled into cocktail sized pastries; Rosemary Kebab £6.95, spiced tender minced lamb; Roasted Pepper £6.95, potatoes, peas, nuts and cheese served in a roasted pepper; Fish Amritsari £7.50, cubes of tilapia delicately spiced and coated in a light batter; Chowk Ki Tikki £4.50, pan fried spiced potato cakes served with fresh mint and tamarind chutney, Lassoni Dhingri £4.95, button mushrooms mixed with chopped garlic, green chillies and coriander coated in a crispy batter, served with tomato chutney; Tangawizi Aaron Platter £8.95 each (minimum 2

Tangawizi, Twickenham

people), lamb chops, chicken tikka, seekh kebab, tiger prawns, paneer tikka and chowki ki tikka. Stocks: Cobra £4.95 a pint, Kingfisher. Delivery: 3 miles, £15 minimum. Price Check: Popadoms complimentary, CTM £8.25, Pullao Rice £2.75. Hours: 6.30 to 11, Sunday closed.

Uxbridge

SATYA — NEW ENTRANT

33 Rockingham Rd, Uxbridge — 01895 274 250

Satya. meaning a feast, is located in two colourfully decorated, bright and airy rooms with c shiny floorboards. The south Indian cast list is present and correct. Doas, Rasam, Sambar and the rest (see page 75), and we like the fish repertoire, kingfish, pomfret and prawns, laced together with cardamom, curry leaf, turmeric, garlic ginger and coconut. And Udipi temple dish caught our eye.: Mathanga Erissery, gourd curry with lobia (black eye beans). Not as cheap as many in the genre. c£25 per head for food plus wine. The weekday lunch buffet at £6.50 is good value. Hours: 12-3, 6-11. Branches Ram's and Vijay, NW6.

Wembley

For Asian produce, cafés, restaurants and atmosphere Wembley is in our view as good as Southall. Unlike Southall, its large Gujarati/East African population gives Wembley food a different (predominantly vegetarian) taste from Southall. B ut we do observe that the Gujaratis are spreading further afield (to places like Harrow for example) and as with Southall, their places are being taken by south Indian, Sri Lankan and Somalis. *There are still many good sweet/snack shops/cafés and restaurants crammed with Indian goodies, but now there is more choice. Here are your favourites:*

ASIAN KARAHI

272 Ealing Road, Wembley 020 8903 7524

Small venue (25 seats) which exudes careful service and thoughtful cooking. The usual range of Karahi style cooking is available all week, but at the weekend, they offer some really authentic stuff, not for the faint-hearted: Niharhi – marinated leg piece (shank) of lamb served with a spicy gravy, Paya – lamb trotters with thick gravy, Brain curry, Haleem – an almost gruel-like mash of crushed wheat and lamb and Haandi dishes all of very high quality. Spicing is done to taste.

CHETNA'S BHEL PURI TOP 100

420 High Road, Wembley 020 8903 5989

A large, very popular vegetarian licensed restaurant with vegan dishes. *'You often have to queue here. We waited on the pavement until they called out our number, but it is well worth it. They do deluxe Masala Dosas, and a great Vegetarian Thali main course. Their Bhel Puri is gorgeous, with its crispy, crunchy textures, and its tart, hot and savoury tastes, and there is a variant called Aloo Papdi Chaat'.* JM. Alongside dishes from Gujarat and south India, they serve pizzas , reflecting the craze, not only amongst Wembley Asians, but continuing to sweep Delhi and Bombay! Hours: 12-3/6-10.30.

CHOWPATTY NEW ENTRANT

234 Ealing Road, Wembley 020 8795 0077

A decade ago, Chowpatty beach, at the northern end of Bombay's celebrated Marina Parade was famous for its wheeled stalls selling the world's most exquisite Bhel Puri and Chaat. Then the 'clean-up' authorities stepped in and banished the traders and renamed Bombay Mumbai. All that is left is the memory, recalled at this vegetarian venue in the form of huge vivid murals. The Bhel *(see page 72)* and Chaat here also brings back those memories, and is as good as it gets. The owners themselves tell us they are not from Mumbai, but come from northern Gujarat, ie in the desert area which borders Rajasthan, where the cuisine is called Kutchi. So you can order Kadhi, Gujarat's national soup-like dish of turmeric, gram flour and yoghurt, or BajraRoti, Rajasthan's millet bread, or Kutchi specialities the like of Baingan Oro (aka Baigan Burtha, the smoky grilled, mashed aubergine dish). Other Gujarati breads (not usually encountered in the UK) include Missi Roti maize flour bread with red chilli and Methi Thepla a wheatbread with fresh fenugreek leaf. Vegetable Kebabs are masterly, as are the Pakoras. On offer are Thalis £4-£9 are great as is the satisfying set buffet (11-4 Sun) at just £4.50. 'Chinese' items too, but there is enough original choice on the menu to leave that for another time. Service charge: 10%. Delivery 5 miles over £12). Hours: 11-3, 5.30-10, Mon-Fri; 11-11.30, Sat; -10, Sun.

DADIMA NEW ENTRANT

228 Ealing Road, Wembley 020 8902 1072

Another exciting restaurant in that here is yet another speciality Gujarati restaurant. Here the owners tell us they're from Ahmedabad (Mahatma Gandhi's birth place. Dadima (granny in Gujarati) certainly is family run, and I wouldn't be surprised if Granny herself was there in charge of the kitchen. She would most certainly be the matriarch and what she says goes. I myself received my first chef training from Gujarati, Sat Gupta. Prior to that I was cooking loosely Punjabi flavours. I found the sweetness and mildness of Gujarati food *(see page 70)* quite a shock, and a big change for my palate used as it was to chilli and savoury tastes. But India is far more complex than that. Bearing in mind that a person's tolerance to chilli is a personal matter, for those who that do like it 'hot', will find the food of Ahmedabad, and of Dadima, quite robust and spiky. *'We cook it with lal masala (mixture of rd spices') including chilli and coriander.* Try Gran's Thali for a filling selection of Dadima-style cooking. Vegetable curries, rice, dhal, yoghurt, pickles and puris from £3. Hours: 12-3/5-10, Mon, Wed-Fri; 12-10 Sat, Sun

GANA NEW ENTRANT

24 Ealing Road, Wembley 020 8903 7004

Authentic Sri Lankan food *(see page 73)* including an array of rice-based dishes, and the celebrated Kotthu Roti (strips of chulatti interspersed usually with a spicy minced meat (keema) curry. Here it is more akin the Brum's Tropical Balti, in that the kitchen sink goes in: *'very special sir , said the waiter.– lamb, beef, chicken fish and prawns. And it was too. Never met that combination before or since, but it was quite nice'* heg. The don't take credit cards. Set lunch £4.50 House wine £7 Hours: 10 -11, daily.

KARAHI KING

213 East Lane, Wembley 020 8904 2760

Fabulous food, Kenyan Asian curries, kebabs and Tandoor items being showily prepared by the on-view chefs in their open kitchen. Try Mogo Bhajia a pakora of sweet potato complete with a super imli (tamarind) chutney, or the fabulous tandoori (including the breads) and note the love-it-or hate-it taste of Kala Namak (black salt). If you do get past the starters, try the curries for meat-eaters and vegetarians. Methi Murgh divine. No credit cards. No corkage, so **BYO.** Hours: 12-12 daily.

KARAHI RAJA

195 East Lane, Wembley 020 8904 5553

Established in 1993 by Mushtaq Ahmed. Restaurant seats 150 in two rooms. Pakistani curries are cooked by B Hussain. House specials include: Haandi Chicken – chicken on the bone cooked with herbs, tomatoes and spicy thick sauce. Paya – lamb trotters Lahori style. Vegetarian dishes: Karahi Egg, scrambled egg, tomatoes, coriander and green chillies. Unlicensed and **BYO** allowed, no corkage charge. Hours: 12-12 daily.

MARU'S BHAJIA HOUSE

230 Ealing Rd, Alperton 020 8903 6771

At Ealing end of this gourmet paradise road, is Maru's opened by yes, Maru in 1984, and it was one of the road's first, and as they say the first is often the best. It provides family unique style vegetarian curries and accompaniments from East Africa. Their Bhajias are the real thing, and they are even spelt correctly, rather than the formula Bhaji. Try their Potato Bhajias, besan-batter-coated, deep-fried and served with tamarind (imli) chutney as a real treat to die for. Strictly No alcohol allowed. Hours: 12-9.30pm..

MARUTI BHEL PURI

238a Ealing Rd, Wembley 020 8903 6743

A vegetarian restaurant serving inexpensive melt-in-the-mouth delights, such as Dosas with Sambar and, of course, the namesake Bhel Puri. Try their Karahi Corn-on-the-Cob. *'All fantastic stuff for the lucky residents of Wembley. I wish I lived nearer.'* DC. *'After eating our fill of Papadoms, we started the proceedings with Jeera Chicken. Good value in terms of standard of cooking. When there is a concert or football match at the Stadium, a set dinner buffet is provided. Dishes were full of spices and excellent. Service was very friendly.'* AN. Hours: 12-10; closed Tues.

POOJA COTTAGE

305 Harrow Rd, Wembley 0208902 4039

Est '85 by T Moniz, as Wembley Cottage, this 45-seater is Nepalese. Baban in the kitchen cooks up unusual delights which include Mariz (pepper) Chicken £5.95, Nepalese Chicken Bhutuwa, highly spiced £6.25. Chicken Chowla,cooked in tandoor, mixed with ginger/garlic £5.95. *'Not terribly impressed with the food.'* RM. *'Very impressed with the food. Recommended to me by so many of my colleagues.'* CT. Hours: 12-2.30/6-11.30.

SAKONI

119 Ealing Rd, Alperton 020 8903 9601

Alcohol is not allowed at vegetarian Sakoni, which to some (including Asians we know) is a shame, but which seems not to deter from its popularity as its longer hours (breakfast!) and expansion proves, although the Upton Park branch has now closed. (see branches below). This founder branch is now enormous, with its conservatory extension serving that Asian of Asian delights, Paan (*see page* 95) It's family-run by Gujaratis Kenyans who know about the food and tradition. But they offer variety to their regular Asian customers (of whom there are many) – dishes such as Chinese vegetarian noodles and Bombay Sandwich, white sliced bread with spicy spreading, a kind of relic of the Raj, the like of which you still, amazingly find in Indian public schools and army messes. Such things make a change, but I for one prefer Sakoni's authentic Indian items (Dosai, Vadai, Uthappam et al, in a pleasant and informal atmosphere. *'Service good and quick. Generous portions. Chutneys are freshly prepared and not removed from the table every few minutes, which makes a change from most other Indian restaurants. Recommended.'* RM. Hours: 9am-11 / 12-10 daily.. Branches: 116 Station Rd, Edgware; 6 Dominion Parade, Station Rd, Harrow; 180 Upper Tooting Road, SW17.

SARAVANAA BHAVAN NEW ENTRANT

531 High Rd, Wembley 020 8795 3777

Saravanaa Bhavan is a rival to the Woodlands chain of south Indian vegetarian cafés that dominate south India and elsewhere. They are no-nonsense, no-alcohol, no-haute-décor caffs which serve substantially good food at no-nonsense prices. Unlike its Tamil Nadu and Kerelan sister branches, this one serves Punjabi and Chinese dishes. Hours 11-10, daily.Branch: Manor Park, E12.

WEMBLEY TANDOORI

133a Wembley Rd, Wembley
020 8902 2243

First opened in 1984, taken over by Mr D Chhetry in 1999 and given a Nepalese menu. Specials include: Momo, Simi Soup, Nepalese Chicken Bhutuwa, Nepalese Vegetable, Aloo Tama. Delivery: £16 minimum, 2-mile radius. Hours: 12-2.30/6-11.30; Sat. 6-12.

WOODLANDS TOP 100

402a High Street, Wembley 020 8902 9869

South Indian vegetarian food, expertly done. See reports in the branches Hours: 12 -2.45/6-10.45. UK Branches: London SW1 and W1, W4.

NORFOLK

Area: East
Population: 818,000
Adjacent Counties: Cambs, Suffolk

Downham

DOWNHAM TANDOORI

56 High Street 01366 386 110

40 seater curryhouse opened 1996 by Abdul Ali Manchurian. Chicken £7.75, sweet and sour, medium hot sauce, to a local following, who are very lucky and sometimes get a 20% discount. Takeaway: 10% discount. Price Check: Popadom 55p, CTM £7.75, Pullao Rice £1.75. Hours: 12 - 2.30/6 - 11.30.

Great Yarmouth

BOMBAY NITE

25a King Street 01493 331383

Good curryhouse where you might get a discount if you show them this *Guide.*

King's Lynn

INDIA GATE

41 St James Street 01553 776489

Ditto

Norwich

JEWEL OF INDIA NEW ENTRANT

41 Magdalen Street, Norwich 01603 666601

'First visit was on opening night, very fresh and clean interior if a little sparse. Small waiting area but seated immediately. Very attentive waiters and extensive menu, including fish and duck dishes. Chicken Dhansak the way it is meant to be, hot sweet and sour £4.75, deliciously different Hash Tikka, marinated duck £7.95, salads, popadums and pickles all very fresh. Portion sizes and meat content very good, food service a little slow (opening night) but arrived very hot with a delicious fluffy garlic naan £1.60. A very pleasant dining experience'. JB. *'Our third visit. Appetisers include more unusual duck and mushroom dishes. Main course of Bengal Naga £11.95, the biggest prawns I have ever seen, delicately marinated in hot chilli and beautifully cooked — a complete meal in itself served with fresh salad and tandoori onions. Raj Hash, marinated duck £8.95, again spiced beautifully to compliment the strong duck meat. Naan bread very soft and springy, popadums fresh as was salad and accompaniments, rice cooked to perfection. There is also a large selection of vegetarian dishes, including veg options of the main dishes and plenty of side dish choices. Usual selection of coffees, alcoholic drinks and desserts. Vegetable Dhansak £3.95, most beautiful version of this dish I have ever tasted - ingredients included chick peas, mixed beans and fresh potatoes and vegetables. This is a vast improvement to the many other restaurants that think they can get away with serving vegetarians second rate ingredients, namely cheap frozen mixed veg - for this alone this restaurant gets my vote!'* JB.

Sheringham

LABONE

40 Cromer Road 01263 821 120

'Opposite the main car park, which also serves the railway station, which is incidentally a steam line. It was a Sunday night at around 8.15pm, and were pleased to find ourselves in an extremely attractive and restaurant. Decided on Popadoms and pickles to start, got one plain and one spicy with four different pickles. Murgh Jalfrezi £6.25, quite hot, for my main and Chicken Rogan Josh £4.10, a bit bland, couldn't taste it after numbing my tongue with mine, for Monica, which we ate with Mushroom Rice, excellent, plenty of

mushrooms and Naan £1.50, probably a bit on the small side, compared to what we get in West Yorkshire. Very good service and we paid just £24 which we thought reasonable.' T&MH. Banquet Night: Tuesday, £12.95 per person, including four starters, three main courses, three side dishes, pullao rice, Naan, sweet and coffee. Sunday Buffet, £7.50 adult, £6 children. Air-conditioned. Hours: 12 - 2.30 A/6 - 11.30. Branches: Prince of Bengal and Rojone Takeaway, Mundesley Rd, N Walsham. Norfolk. <www.laboneindiancuisine.co.uk>

Thetford

SAFFRON INDIAN CUISINE

17 St Giles Lane, Thetford 01842 762000

Good curryhouse where you might get a discount if you show them this *Guide.*

NORTHAMPTONSHIRE

Area:
Central East Midlands
Population: 646,800
Adjacent Counties:
Beds, Cambs,
Leics, Oxon

Brackley

PRINCE CALCUTTA

36 Market Place, Brackley 01280 703265

Good curryhouse where you might get a discount if you show them this *Guide.*

Irthlingborough

EASTERN SPICE NEW ENTRANT

56 High Street 01933 650 044

Established in 1972 and taken over in 2004 by Foyzur Rahman and managed by Majibur Ali. Large restaurant, seating 100 diners and serving Bangladeshi curries. Delivery: 5 miles, £16.95 minimum. Sunday Buffet Lunch: £8.95. Stocks: Cobra, £2.95 a bottle. Price Check: Popadom 50p, CTM £6.95, Pullao Rice £1.85. Hours: 6 -11.30. <www.easternspiceindiancuisine.co.uk>

Kettering

MONSOON BAR & INDIAN

Ebenezer Place, Kettering 01536 417421

Curryhouse est 1998 by P Sadrani in a colourfully painted Tudor style restaurant, seating 90. Takeaway: 20% discount. Delivery: 4-mile radius. Hours: 5.30-12. You might get a discount if you show them this *Guide.*

THE RAJ

46 Rockingham Road 01536 513 606

A large a/c restaurant owned by Goyas Miah, seating 110 curryholics in two contemporary dining rooms. Creamy walls, wooden floors and chairs with blue seating. In the bar area, the wood and blue theme continue on bar stools and tub chairs. 'Having booked a table, only to find they had a party on and we would be 'lost in the crowd', I suggested we try the Red Rose.' DL. And you did, see next entry! Menu Snapshot: Mussels £4.25, marinated in chilli and coriander sauce with a hint of garlic; Lamb pepper £2.95, marinated lamb cubes barbecued with green pepper; Swordfish Maach £10.95, delicately spiced and simmered in medium hot sauce; Amer Murgh £9.95, barbecued chicken, cooked with mango pulp and medium spices; Dhokkar Dolna £4.25, potato and lentil curry. Four-course business lunch Monday to Friday £4.95 per person. Stocks: Cobra £2.95 a pint and Kingfisher. Delivery: 3 miles, £10 min. Sunday Buffet: £5.95. Price Check: Popadom 50p, CTM £8.95, Pullao Rice £1.95. Hours: 12 - 2 / 15.30 - 12, Sunday 12 - 12. You might get a discount if you show them this *Guide.* <www.therajrestaurant.net>

Kingsthorpe

BOMBAY PALACE

9 Welford Road 01604 713899

'On the spur of the moment decision to visit this old friend, proved to be an excellent decision. Whilst staff and decor hadn't changed at all, the menu had undergone a massive revamp. New dishes include: Chicken Puri £3.75; Garlic Mushroom on Puri £3.25; Chicken Pakora £2.95; Vegetable Pakora £2.60; Venison dishes from £5.65. 'Spicy Popadoms, very good with OK Chutneys; Vegetable Pakora, lovely, really nice; Reshmi Kebab £2.75, superb, cooked perfectly; Chicken Tikka Biriani £7.75, OK with very good

Chapatti; Meat Thali £9.95, very generous portions, beautifully cooked, I couldn't finish it all with lovely, fresh and light Naan Bread £1.10. First class service. Will not leave it so long to return!'' DL.. Fully air conditioned. Delivery: £10 minimum, 5 miles. Price Check: Popadom 35p, CTM £5.75, Pullao Rice £1.50. You might get a discount if you show them this *Guide.* Hours: 5.30 - 11.30, Fri Sat - 12.

Northampton

FAR COTTON TANDOORI

111 St Leonards Rd, Far Cotton, Northampton 01604 706282

Good curryhouse where you might get a discount if you show them this *Guide.*

INDIAN PARADISE

39, Barrack Road 01604 622228

'Arrived, having not booked but soon found a table and offered drinks and Popadoms whilst selecting from the menu. Nice decor with excellent chairs.' I have seen the chairs and they are very attractive, upholstered in either blue or red with very high backs. 'Gosht Xacuti £8.95; Khumb Mutter £6.45 (with chicken tikka), Keema Naan £1.45, Chapatti 65p, Tarka Dall £1.95, all beautifully presented and cooked to perfection. Service was a little too attentive at times, asked how our meals were at least half a dozen times, but put this down to being recently opened. Bring your own alcohol, hooray!' DL. Specials: Masala Roasty Duck £9.95, strips of tender duck breast marinated and cooked in a rich spicy tomato, onion and herb sauce; Hot Peri £8.45, chicken and meat cooked together with diced potato in a tangy sauce prepared with special fiery chilli sauce; Dhingri Palak £6.45, chopped spinach leaves and button mushrooms lightly fried in a strong cumin and ginger sauce. Takeaway: 10% discount, £10 minimum. Delivery: £8 min, 5 miles. Price Check: Popadom 40p, CTM £5.10, Pullao Rice £1.50. Hours: 12 - 2/5.30 - 11. <www.indian-paradise.co.uk>

MAHARAJAH

146 Wellingborough Road 01604 637 049

'Located on ''Curry Street' the most competitive area for Indian restaurants in Northants. A new frontage and interior decor have resulted in a terrific re-vamp. Recovering from a very tedious cricket AGM, we were immediately shown a table. Popadoms and drinks offered straight away whilst we selected from the extensive menu. Shami Kebabs, very good; Tandoori Mix, lamb, chicken etc, very hot and tasty; Lamb Parsee, very hot in flavour and beautifully cooked; Chicken Koria, excellent and a chicken special dish (name escapes me!)...' that's NO good. '...fantastic. Tarka Dhal, tremendous; Mushroom Bombay Aloo and Keema Naan, all superbly cooked. Manager introduced himself and offered complimentary pints of Kingfisher!' how very generous! '£48 for three.' DL.

MEMSAHIB

357 Wellingborough Rd 01604 630214

'The Memsahib opened in 2001 and was the first restaurant in Northampton to be owned and managed by Indians oppose to Bangladeshis, specialising in Punjabi food. It is housed in the old Mansfield shoe factory and is spacious, light and airy with minimalist decor. It is divided into a very plush lounge area, boasting very comfy cream leather sofas where you can relax pre and post meal and the restaurant itself which is incidentally non-smoking although smoking is permitted in the lounge area. All the staff are smartly unpretentiously presented in smart pressed shirts and neckties, which excludes the ladies who wear smart blouses. It is also very quirky to hear the Asian owners speak in a very broad Scottish accent sounding like a very educated Billy Connelly. I went on Sunday afternoon for a three course buffet with the added bonus of Live Jazz. I have never been impressed with the e-a-m-a-y-l buffets as they tend be very unimaginative. However, the Mem Saab however surpassed itself on every course. The starters consisted of a salmon and red snapper dish, seekh and shaslik kebabs, onion bhajis, garlic tossed mushrooms, vegetable pakoras, chilled shrimps and popadoms, these were also accompanied with fresh homemade pickles and chutneys such as tamarind, apple, piquant onions, mango chutney plus fresh green coriander and mint chutney. The main course offered a mildly spiced garlic chicken, a rich lamb dish in a clinging spicy gravy which boasted very large cubes of good quality lamb, a mixed aubergine and potato dish, ma-ki -dhal which is very much a Punjabi speciality consisting of whole black urid dhal in a spicy buttery gravy and Kudi with gram flour dumplings which is a another Northern India speciality with a yoghurt and gram flour gravy lightly spiced with turmeric, a dish which I would never have dared to order as the description never has appealed to me but I'm really glad I did try it. Naan bread was also supplied and on my request chapattis were supplied at no extra charge (some of the best I have ever eaten). The sweet trolley had a vast array of fresh seasonal fruits plus Rasgullah. The afternoon was a very enjoyable experience and the unobtrusive background entertainment added to the pleasure. The final bill for two of us was approximately £36 which also included 4 drinks in total, this sum perhaps a little over the average but the restaurant is far better than average and goes from strength to strength. Incidentally The Mem Saab have now opened a sophisticated champagne & cocktail bar in the adjoining building which is called Corkers, reports are good but far from

a cheap nights drinking by all accounts but probably a small price to pay for a select environment and clientele.' PM. *'PS: Of an evening try the Lamb Nibari,served in thin gravy with aromatic spices in particular cardamom and ground cloves garnished with thin julienne slices of fresh ginger.'* Branches: Glasgow, Nottingham and Leicester.

RAJPUT BALTI

224a Wellingborough Rd 01604 637336

Shahab Uddin. Seats 50, serves Bangladeshi formula curries, cooked by chef Shofor Ali. Good curryhouse where you might get a discount if you show them this *Guide.* Hours: 12-2.30/6-12.

RIVER SPICE TANDOORI NEW ENTRANT

Garden Village The Causeway, Great Billing Northampton 01604 411700

'In the grounds of a garden centre on the outskirts of Northampton in a former nightclub premises but the advantage of its location is that it doesn't attract the twenty pints and hottest curry brigade but has strong appeal to those who enjoy a well-presented, superbly cooked more authentic Indian meal in a very friendly and relaxed atmosphere where courtesy and service is second to none. After several visits, I went to try out the skills of the new Indian chef, who according to the Indian owner has the ability to cook authentic Indian regional food. The menu offers tried and tested favourites, unusual house specialities, plus some blackboard specials, which included a Kenyan-Asian dish of Piri Piri chicken, a special ginger chicken plus many authentic vegetable dishes. We made our choice and waited in anticipation in the bar. The meal arrived and we were not disappointed: the lamb dishes were cooked to perfection boasting a thick gravy, minimum oil and no over spicing; the chicken dish, a new introduction, was a dry dish cooked with fresh green chillies and honey, which I suspect is not authentic, but good all the same, whilst the two new vegetable dishes we tried consisted of very spicy paneer, which had been lightly fried and had taken on the flavours of the rich tomato gravy and an aubergine dish which was cooked in yoghurt-based gravy. All in all a very pleasurable dining experience pushing the culinary boundaries further towards the East than the West. I long to see one hundred percent authentic Indian dishes but this venue produces a compromise which attracts many ethnic diners on a regular basis.' PM.

STAR OF INDIA

5 Abingdon Av, Northampton 01604 630664

You might get a discount if you show them this *Guide.*

THE VOUJON NEW ENTRANT

Alexander Terrace, Harborough Road Kingsthorpe, 01604 718882

Anwar Ali's latest Voujon is: *'Situated on a corner, the is of contemporary design with large windows with modern wooden venation blinds. The interior is modern minimalist with the warmth of light spicy colours very carefully co-ordinated and complimented by the custom-painted Indian pictures. No expense had been spared with wood, marble and terracotta carpeting defining the slightly different levels and areas. We were warmly greeted and showed to our table which was neatly set with starched linen colour co-ordinated napkins and cloth. We were promptly served drinks and offered the menu. Between the three of us we ordered lamb tawa, a mixed chicken & lamb roghon, vegetable rice, side dishes of the very English bombay potatoes plus breads to each diners personal taste. The dishes arrived twenty minutes later, very politely and efficiently served and after some five minutes or so the waiter courteously enquired if everything was to our liking. Whilst none of the dishes were badly cooked and the portions were very acceptable, with the breads light and fluffy, I can only say there was nothing at all remarkable about the dishes; they did not fulfil the promise of the imaginative descriptions on the menu. Mind you, a very recent holiday to India might have made me over critical and I did enjoy my earlier visit to their Wellingborough branch. Also, I have only heard praise since it opened, and I imagine it will thrive and prosper plus gain immense popularity as have the established sister restaurants. However after all the good effort and money going into the well thought-out design it has missed a golden opportunity to offer more creative and authentic Indian food in keeping with the forward thinking image which it has tried so hard to portray.'* PM. Branches: Wellingborough & Long Buckby.

CHUTNEYS NEW ENTRANT

86 High Street, Rushden 01933 411 994

'A round of Popadoms and chutneys set us up nicely before the starters. Shamee Kebab - finely minced and ground steak fried with herbs and spices, and Chicken Tikka - lived up to the billing on the menu. Impressed with house special, Tandoori King Prawn Massalla - tasty, not too hot and cooked to perfection. Tawa Chicken - cooked with paprika, onion, tomato and herbs with a touch of garlic and shredded ginger. Shabzi Chaatwalla - crispy stir-fried vegetables in a sweet and sour sauce, mixed with chat masala, paprika and red chilli served with Pullao Rice - enjoyed. We shared a Cheese and Onion Naan, which made a refreshing change from my usual Peshwari. Each dish tasted as good as they sounded and portions were more than enough.' SW.

NORTHUMBERLAND

Area: North East
Population: 311,000
Adjacent Counties:
Borders, Cumbria,
Durham, Tyne &
Wear

Bedlington

FRONTIER KARAHI HOUSE

46 Front St, West Bedlington 01670 820222

You might get a discount if you show them this *Guide.* Hours: 5.30-1; closed Mon.

Berwick-upon-Tweed

MAGNA BEST IN THE NORTH

39 Bridge Street, Berwick 01289 302736

Jahangir Khan owns this 80-seater family business. It has been in our *Guide* since we started it in 1984. *'And no wonder.'* says CC member Michael Fabricant, MP. Free car park 100 yards away. The building is impressive, made pretty by flower boxes. Inside is cosy, with inviting green sofas in the bar and the Magna's certificates, many of them ours, line the walls. *'A pretty restaurant with smartly dressed black-tie waiters.'* MF. Its menu is unpretentious, standard formula food beloved by all curryholics,. It is also very well cooked. Specials include: Murghi Mossalla, Ash de Bash and Chandee Dishes, very mild with fresh cream and mango from £8.50. Shim Dishes, cooked

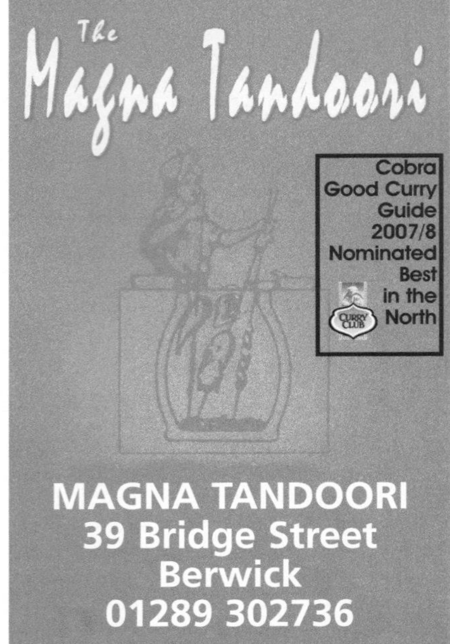

with green beans from £8.50.. *Once again I felt I had to put pen to paper. I feel my local, The Magna, still comes out on top for taste, quality, service, cleanliness, value and very polite friendly staff. I personally find this restaurant one of the most stress free environments I can think of and my wife and I often have a drink or two after our meal and just relax. I'm glad to see it remains in the Guide's estimation.'* BA. *'My husband and I have been coming to this restaurant for many years. We never book a table, we just turn up. Always greeted pleasantly and politely and given excellent service while we are there. Although we have very hearty appetites, we invariably take a 'doggy bag' home. We feel fortunate to have the Magna here.'* SS. *'Having spent the day visiting the many attractions, it is always important to have a good meal, in pleasant*

Magna, Berwick

surroundings with good quality service and value for money - all is provided at the Magna. Staff always courteous, taking your coat and carrying drinks through to the table. Especially appreciated.' KR. Menu Snapshot: Shami Kebab £3.25 - spicy mince fried like a burger; Chana Chat on Puri £3.75 - curried chickpeas on fried bread; Ash De Bash £11.95 - tender duck strips roasted in charcoal oven and then cooked with bamboo shoots and spices; Chicken Biriani £7.95 - served with vegetable curry; Pineapple Curry £3.75; breast of chicken 50p extra. Delivery. Takeaway: 20% discount. Price Check: Popadom 50p, CTM £7.95, Pullao Rice £2.00. When we told Jehangir Khan that he was nominated this Guide's **BEST IN THE NORTH** Award, he was over the moon about it. We are over the moon with it too. Takeaway: 20% discount. Hours: 12-2 except Sun/5.30-12 daily.

Corbridge

CORBRIDGE TANDOORI

8 Market Square, Corbridge 01434 633676

'SM Shahjahan's small restaurant est. '89 'is hidden above a shop was restaurant is above a bookshop, parking is difficult in this small village. Turn left as you enter the building and climb the stairs, if you turn right you walk into your reflection in a full length mirror! No preamble, we were shown directly to our table, with a widow overlooking the square and church. Tastefully decorated, with a few cobwebs on the very high ceiling. Brusque service, our order was taken without comment. Mixed Kebab £3.60, two pieces each of lamb and chicken, a Sheek Kebab with salad and Raitha, far far better value than other restaurant. Bhuna Prawn Puri £3.20, enjoyed. Chicken Tikka Rogan £6.90 and Chicken Karai £7.00 - very very good. Takeaway's doing a steady trade.' T&MH. Hours: 12-2.30/6-11.30.

THE VALLEY BEST IN THE NORTH

The Old Station House, Corbridge 01434 633434

Corbridge station building in the beautiful Tyne valley, was built in 1835 for Stephenson's railway. It is no longer used as a station although it is on the important Newcastle-to-Carlisle railway line. Trains stop at Corbridge station throughout each day, but passengers do not use the old building any more. That is until Daraz (Syed Nadir Aziz) turned it into a stylish, up-market Indian restaurant in 1991. Seats 80, car parking for 20 directly outside. A feature of which is a unique service, for parties of 10 to 80 from £28.50 a head, including return travel. Uniformed restaurant staff welcome you at Newcastle Central Station and escort you by train to The Valley. En route, choose four courses from the à la carte menu. The order is rung through on a mobile. Your starter is awaiting your arrival. *'It beats ordering a taxi.'* GM. Of course, individuals can make their own way here and back by scheduled train – but beware a fairly early last train. Or, there is parking for 12 cars. Why not book your takeaway by phone en-route, collect, pay and eat it, without leaving the train? As for the restaurant, there is a reception room and 80 seats in four connecting rooms (one of which opens onto the eastbound platform). Decor is lush and Indian. And the food? Chef Pervez Ahmed's menu contains all the CC (currinarily correct) favourites plus some good specials. *'Arriving at this impressive building at about 7.30pm, we enquired if we could have a table for 8.15pm. We were assured there was no problem, so, gave us a chance to walk back along station road for a pint of decent, real ale at Dyvels. We arrived back on cue to study the menu in the bar, complete with a photograph of Daraz, the owner and Pat Chapman. Were shown to a window table, we watched a train pull into the station, just outside the restaurant.'* entertainment as well! *'Very impressive menu, had quite a problem deciding on main dishes. Disappointed with Mixed Starter £8.95 for two – just one each sheek kebabs, lamb tikka and chicken wings with sizzling onions – are we spoilt in West Yorkshire? Monica ate Luari Mangsho £8.25 and I, Special Bhuna Gosht £8.95 – I must say these were very good, but looked similar. Pullao Rice also very good and Naan tasty with portions just about right. A memorable meal for its situation.'* T&MH. Menu Snapshot: Dahi Baigon £4.25 - grilled aubergine, stuffed with vegetables, topped with spice yoghurt; Chingri Varkee £4.50 - grilled pepper stuffed with spicy prawns; Salmon Bhaja £11.50 - fried with fresh herbs, garlic, ginger and raw onion; Duck Masallam £10.95 - breast marinated in herbs, cooked and served in a spicy, creamy sauce with coconut; Beef Adrok £9.95 - topside cooked with fresh herbs and lot of fresh ginger. Chef's Choice: seven course surprise (the only surprise being that the chef chooses your meal) dinner - £59.95 for two and £110 for four - sounds wonderful! Takeaway: 20% discount. Price Check: Popadom 75p, CTM £8.50, Pullao Rice £3.00. We are delighted that the Valley is nominated **BEST IN THE NORTH.** Hours: 6-10; closed Sun. Branch: Valley Junction 397, The Old Station, Archibold Terrace, Jesmond, Newcastle. and Valley Connection 301, Hexham *(see alongside)*. <www.valleyrestaurants.co.uk>

Hexham

DIWAN-E-AM

4- Country Mills, Priestpopple, Hexham 01434 606575

Diwan-e-am was the Moghul palace meeting room. And Mr Choudury's 86 seat venue, est in 1983. is aptly named. *'Pleasant decor and environment, friendly and helpful staff. Menu extensive, but no curry house inventions such as vindaloo here. Starters include the excellent Diwan Khata Mita Soup (garlic and lentils) and Mathu Vortha (grapefruit with chilli and coriander). Main course selection includes a wide range of duck and fish dishes. More expensive than the 'usual' curry house, but good value given the high standard of the meals.'* CF. House-style cuisine (staff curry) on demand for regular customers. You might get a discount if you show them this *Guide*. Takeaway: 20% discount. Hours: 5.30-11pm; Sun. 6.30-10.30pm.

VALLEY CONNECTION 301 NEW ENTRANT

Market Place, Hexham 01434 601234

Prime location in the centre of the market place, next to Hexham Abbey. Very smart inside. For Menu details see The Valley alongside.

Morpeth

TANDOORI MAHAL

17 Bridge Street, Morpeth 01670 512420

Suroth Miah opened its doors in 1980. The interior is sleek, with white walls and a deep red carpet, which is also reflected in the very smart wooden chairs upholstery and the large lamb shades that hang from the ceiling. Crisp, white table linen and yellow roses decorate each table. Original art work hangs, sparingly, on the walls. It all makes for a very upmarket and calming dining experience. Food is served on large white oval platters, which shows off the vibrant colours of the food beautifully. Specials include: Murgh Tikka Paneer £3.95 - marinated pieces of chicken tikka, fried with cheese, onions and green peppers; Tali Machi £4.95 - fish fillets marinated in spicy batter and pan fried, tempered with brown onions; Murgh Masala £8.50 - spring chicken off the bone cooked with minced lamb, onions, spices, herbs, nuts and sultanas; Tawa Murgh £7.95 - tangy moong dal and boneless chicken cooked with freshly prepared spices on a tawa griddle. General Bilimoria Chenin Blanc / Shiraz Pinotage £11.50. Price Check: Popadom 65p, CTM £6.95, Pullao Rice £2.20. You might get a discount if you show owner Suroth Miah this *Guide*.Hours: 12 - 2.30/6 - 12, Sunday - 11.30. <www.tandoor-mahal.co.uk>

NOTTINGHAMSHIRE

Area: East Midlands
Population: 1,045,000
Adjacent Counties:
Derbs, Leics,
Lincs, Yorks

Nottingham

(includes Basford, Beeston, Mapperley, Radford, Sherwood, and West Bridgford.)

4500 MILES FROM DELHI

41 Mount Street 0115 947 5111

The name says it all - it's literally 4550 Miles from Delhi. Danny Punia owns this 4000 sq m former public house, which has been transformed internally and externally to include a ten metre high glazed atrium in which the bar is located. A halved motorised-rickshaw (tuk-tuk) gives a new meaning to wall-hanging. Suspended cylindrical stainless steel lights over the bar, a bronze staircase and solid oak and recycled slate flooring on which sit 130 Italian made chairs with bronze inlay work in the dining area overlooking an open kitchen. Chef Mahaneshwar Pal, previously with Delhi's Taj

Palace Hotel has developed a North Indian menu that also includes a choice of set meals priced at c£18 per person. Popular dishes include Tikkas, and Seekhs, Aloo Tikkis and a selection of simmered curries cooked by the Dum Pukht pot method. *(see p50)*. Punia hopes to open further branches, naming each after its distance from Delhi and has plans to open a 4320 Miles from Delhi in London, and 4480 Miles from Delhi in Sheffield. An open 'theatre' kitchen enables you to watch the chefs from Delhi as they work. 'Can you mention that restaurant is closed on a Sunday, we made a trip there last weekend only to be disappointed.' jb. It is now open on Sundays, but always ring first.Hours: 12 - 2.30 / 6 - 10.30. <www.milesfromdelhi.com> Branch: Shimla Pinks, London Road, Leicester

BEESTON TANDOORI

150 High Rd, Beeston 0115 922 3330

Good curryhouse where you might get a discount if you show them this *Guide*.

BOMBAY BICYCLE SHOP TAKEAWAY

511 Alfreton Rd, Basford 0115 978 6309

Ditto takeaway. Hours: 5.30-12.

THE INDIAN COTTAGE

5-7 Bentnick Road (off Alfreton Road), Radford, Nottingham W 0115 942 4922

Pretty black beams, white frontage and inviting curtained windows at Naj Aziz's 40-seater in 2 areas (smoking and non-smoking). Very stylish restaurant, un-Indian, unfussy, light and bright, Wedgwood blue ceiling and magnolia walls. Walls are decorated with hanging carpets and back-lit fretwork, tiled floor, large palms in white pots. We hear that the food is family-style. Hours: 6-10.30 Tues.–Sat. Closed 16-30 Aug, a week at Christmas.

KASHMIR

60 Maid Marian Way 0115 947 6542

Good **BYO.**curryhouse where you might get a discount if you show them this *Guide*.

LAGUNA

43 Mount Street 0115 941 1632

Another good curryhouse where you might get a discount if you show them this *Guide*.

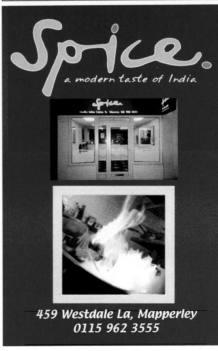

SAAGAR TOP 100

473 Mansfield Rd, Sherwood 0115 962 2014

Mohammed Khizer leads the kitchen brigade at his Victorian-style 98-seater on two floors est 1984. *'We found it to be good in all departments, and to me cleanliness comes before everything else. It was all spotless, and most inviting'.* RCF. *'Have visited this restaurant regularly since 1988. Wonderful Lamb Tandoori and Prawn Puri. My favourite 'Indian Restaurant.'* HW. Menu Snapshot: Kashmiri Chicken Tikka £4.90 - topped with Kashmiri sauce; Chicken Anguri £9.95 - mild and fruity, cooked with pineapple, banana, prunes, grape juice and fresh cream; Nizami Masala Chicken £9.95 - cooked with nuts, coconut, yoghurt and sesame seeds; Butter Chuppati £1.00, Spinach and Yoghurt Bhajee £4.50. Takeaway: 10% discount. We have had poor reports about several of our previous Nottingham favourites, and of course, Chand has shut to allow a property development to take place, so it is a pleasure to retain Saagar in our **TOP 100.** Front of house is managed by Imtiaz Ahmed, leaving Mr Khizer to do his thing in the kitchen, assisted by Amjaid Parvaiz. ' Discounts for *Guide* readers at lunch times. Hours: 12-2.15 /5.30-12 daily.

SPICE TAKEAWAY NEW ENTRANT

459 Westdale La, Mapperley 0115 962 3555

Farooq Younis owns opened his takeaway in 2000 and he's proud of it. All the favourite dishes are here at good prices – Pakistani style curries and accompaniments, and yes, CTM rushes out of the door! Delivery: 3 miles £10 minimum. Price Check: Popadom 40p, CTM £5.90, Pullao Rice £1.60. Hours: 5 - 11.30, Saturday - 12. Sunday 4.30 - 11.

Southwell

SANAM BALTI HOUSE

15-17 King Street, Southwell 01636 813618

Early Victorian listed building, established in as the Taj Mahal in 1990, and taken over by Khalid Mahmood in 1994. The 50-seater boasts a splendid spiral staircase. Rooms are open plan with ornate Moghul style arches to doorways. Beautiful jade colour, lighting subdued crystal reflecting the traditional Indian art. All tables are covered in fine contrasting linen, sparkling silverware and fresh flowers. Centre of attention has to be a 26-cubic-feet fish tank, which is set within an existing chimney and can be viewed from both rooms. Chef-owner, Khalid Mahmood or *'Chef Saab'* originates from Pakistan's Kashmir. *'Tastefully decorated. All food was hot, excellent Pullao Rice and Peshwari Nan.'* LW. Specials include: Makhani Tandoori Chicken, Marinated Tandoori Chicken with Makhani Sauce (green peppers, onions, tomatoes, methi, garlic sauce). you might get a discount if you show them this *Guide.* Hours: 5.30-11.30

Stapleford

MOUSHUMI

124 Derby Rd, Stapleford 0115 939 4929

Good curryhouse where you might get a discount if you show them this *Guide.*

OXFORDSHIRE

Area: South Central
Population: 622,000
Adjacent Counties: Bucks, Berks, Glos, Middx, Northants, Warks, Wilts

Banbury

SHEESH MAHAL

43 Oxford Road, Banbury 01295 266489

Mohammed Khalid is owner and manager and you might get a discount if you show him this *Guide.*

Bicester

BICESTER TANDOORI

15 Market Square, Bicester 01869 245170

Mrs Dilwara Begum may also give you a discount if you show her this *Guide* at her 40-seater. Delivery: £15.95 minimum, 3-mile radius. Hours: 5.30-11.30 (12am on Sat.).

Chinnor

CHINNOR INDIAN

59 Lower Road, Chinnor 01844 354843

Saidur Rahman may give you a discount if you show him this *Guide*. Hours: 5.30-11.30 (12am on Sat).

Chipping Norton

ANARKALI

6 West St, Chipping Norton 01608 642785

Proprietor A Uddin may give you a discount if you show him this *Guide*. Hours 12-2.30/6-11.30.

Didcot

SUNKOSHI TANDOORI

226a Broadway, Didcot 01235 812796

Nepalese: Menu Extracts: Shak Shuka, minced lamb, fresh cream, topped with egg, mild. Prawn Chatpat, green chillies, green peppers, onions, ginger, hot. Hours: 12-2.30/6-11, Fri/Sat to 11.30

Faringdon

AZAD TANDOORI & BALTI

14 Coxwell Street, Faringdon 01367 244977

Rabia Khanom Ali may give you a discount if you show him this *Guide*. Hours: 5-11.30. Sun. 12-11.30.

Henley-on-Thames

GAZAL

53 Reading Road, Henley 01491 574659

They may give you a discount if you show them this *Guide*. Hours: 12-2/6-11.

Oxford

AZIZ

NOMINATED BEST BANGLADESHI

228 Cowley Road, Oxford 01865 794945

Azizur (Aziz) Rahman is an extremely personable

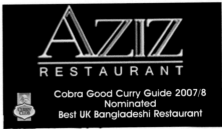

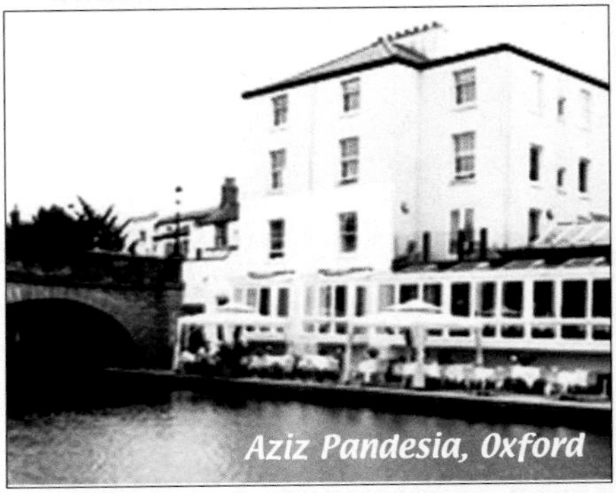

Aziz Pandesia, Oxford

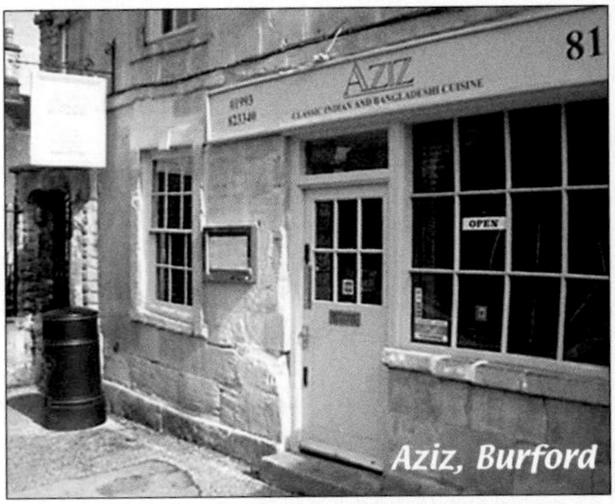

Aziz, Burford

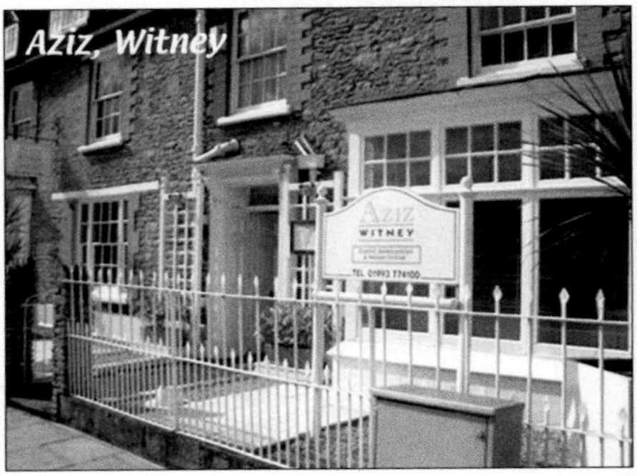

Aziz, Witney

man, and a successful restaurateur. From a start-up in 1990, he now has four Aziz restaurants in Oxon. His smart 90-seater Cowley Road Aziz has always stood out for sophistication in decor, service and accurately cooking real Bangladeshi food, distinctively, and not in the manner of so many Bangladeshi-owned curryhouses. Because the menu is using Bengali words, dishes may seem unfamiliar, but it is an encyclopedia of Bangladeshi food, and many of the old favourites are there too. Starters include familiar items such as Tandoori Murgh, Boti, Samosa Pyazee (Onion Bhaji) and Sheek Kebabs at from £4.15. Less usual are Maach Bora £4.75, is fish cake) Galda Chingri Aar Puri, £5.75 is sweet & sour king prawn with puri bread and Chott Pottie £4.15, chickpeas, egg and potatoes spiced with coriander. Mains include Hush Bhuna £9.50, duck with onion and tomatoes, Razalla £8.75 lamb or chicken with yoghurt, cream, butter and chilli, Ada Gosht £7.95, tikka lamb, dryish with ginger, and onion, Murgh Kaliya £8.50, chicken with black pepper in a creamy sauce. Bangladesh being big fish on curries, there is a good selection from £8.75: Bhuna Aiyr £8.75. with onion and tomatoes, Sak Buaal £8.75 with spinach. Galda Chineri Kodu £10.95 is large king prawns with pumpkin. Vegetable dishes (from £6.25) include the delightfully named Dimm Dall, egg and lentil curry, Sarso Baigun, aubergine fried with mustard seed , Sobzi Korma £6mild and creamy , Sobzi Patia, sweet and sour vegetable - hot and Sobzi Razalla, mixed vegetables with butter, cream & chillies. *This restaurant oozes class from the moment you step through the door. Truly deserving of it's status near the top of the Top 100. The ambience, service and food are all top quality. All the dishes that we tried were beautifully served, expertly cooked and well crafted, with a number of dishes (including a good range of vegetarian dishes) that I have not seen before. I remember a chickpea dish that I had as being particularly good (must take more notes next time!). Overall opinion: Excellent, will continue to happily recommended this restaurant and will definitely return.'* SO. *'Emphasis on subtlety. A splendid meal.'* WC. *'Impressive reports confirmed. Mid-week the place was packed. Decor is upmarket and smart, the food well prepared and served in generous quantities. This is where the middle class, the academics and well-off students of Oxford eat and entertain. Service was slow but the place was very busy. Parking can be a problem.'* PAW. Takeaway: 15% discount. Sunday buffet 12-4.30, £9.50 per person, children £4.75. Hours: 12-2.15 (not Fri)/6-11.30 daily; Sun. 12-4.30. Nominated **BEST BANGLADESHI**. Same details at Aziz Burford, 79 High Street, Burford, Oxon, 01993 823340 and Aziz Witney 79 High Street, Witney, Oxon, 01993 774100. Whilst Aziz Pandesia, Restaurant and Bar serves Indian, Bangladeshi and Thai cuisine at I Folly Bridge, Oxford 01865 247775.

KASHMIR HALAL

64 Cowley Road, Oxford 01865 250165

Said Meah opened his 50-seater in 1970 and he may give you a discount if you show him this *Guide*.

SHIMLA PINKS

16 Turl Street, Oxford 01865 243783

Formerly the Taj Mahal which was established in 1937 on the first floor above Whites, making it Britain's third ever Indian restaurant. They may give you a discount if you show them this *Guide*.

RUTLAND

Britain's smallest county
Area: East Midlands
Population: 36,500
Adjacent Counties:
Cambs, Leics, Lincs

Leicestershire's bureaucratic loss is Rutland's gain. Back again after decades of non-existence, it was restored to county status by popular demand in 1997, making it once again Britain's smallest county — it is geographically smaller than the city of Birmingham.

Oakham

RUTLAND BALTI HOUSE

18 Mill Street, Oakham 01572 757232

Opened in 1984, under the name Oakham Tandoori, it was taken over in 1996 by Abdul Khalique. His restaurant seats forty diners and serves Bangladeshi style curries and accompaniments. Stocks: Cobra at 31.90 for a small bottle and £3.30 for a large bottle. Sunday Lunch Buffet: £5.90. Hours: 1 - 3, Sunday only and 5.30 - 12, Saturday to 12.30.

SHROPSHIRE

Area: North west (Welsh Border)
Population: 450,000
Adjacent Counties: Cheshire, Clwyd, Hereford, Powys, Staffs, Worcs

Bishops Castle

GANGES NEW ENTRANT

12 Market Sq, Bishops Castle 01588 638543

'Small restaurant in a picture perfect rural market town - whose idyll is crowned with two working breweries.' Real ale - fabulous. 'Interior is functional and inviting, good decor and stylish furnishings complete with crisp white linen. Lovely starter - Rashmi Kebab £2.50 - pair on tender, well spiced patties, topped with a moist, tasty omelette and fresh crispy salad. A pleasant yoghurt and mint sauce rounded the dish off. Roshuni Lamb £5.70 - enjoyable, hot, rich and dry sauce, thick with herbs and garlic. Good Garlic Naan £1.80 - if a little doughy, plenty of garlic. Tarka Dhal £2.15 - fairly well balanced, rather lumpy lentils.' RW. Menu Snapshot: Stuffed Green Pepper £2.90 - chicken, prawn or vegetable; Tandoori Mixed Grill £6.95 - Spring Chicken, Lamb, King Prawn, Minced Kebab, served with salad and Tandoori Naan; Banana Naan £1.80; Banana or Pineapple in Spice £2.15 each. Popadom 50p, CTM £5.70, Pullao Rice £1.70. Hours: 12-2.30, Saturday & Sunday only and 6- 12.

Church Stretton

JAIPUR

6 Sandford Av, Church Stretton 01694 724667

'Parking really easy in this sleepy little town. Efficient rather than friendly service. Rectangular restaurant, nicely decorated, usual Indian prints hang on amber coloured walls. Pint of Kingfisher £3.50 and £2 for a half, Tetley's was more reasonable £2.50 a pint. Shared Mixed Kebab £3.95 - two pieces each of Lamb and Chicken Tikka, and a rubbery Sheek Kebab on the usual salad. On asking for the Raitha, go a blank look, then "Oh! you mean the mint sauce." This came in a gravy boat. Monica's Chicken Capsila contained large strips of chicken breast with chunks of capsicum, nicely spiced medium to hot. My Jaipur Special Jalfrezi - pretty good, although not sure if any king prawns were present, chicken and lamb well cooked, tender, adequate portion. Prices reasonable, mint chocolates arrived after the meal. Will eat there again.' T&MH. Menu Snapshot: Jaipur Grill Special £8.95 - Chicken and Lamb Tikka, King Prawn, Tandoori Chicken served on a sizzling pot with medium spicy spinach and Keema sauce; Bengal Fish Masala £9.95,fillets of ayr; Shim Bhajee £2.95, french beans; Meetah Pullao Rice £1.95,fruit cocktail rice. Fully licensed. Takeaway: 10% discount. Price Check: Popadom 50p, CTM £6.95, Pullao Rice £1.90. Hours: 5.30 --11.30, Friday and Saturday 6.30 - 12.

Newport

SHIMLA

22 St Mary's St, Newport 01952 825322

Good curryhouse where you might get a discount if you show them this *Guide*.

Shifnal

SHIFNAL BALTI NEW ENTRANT

20 Broadway Shifnal 01952 460142

Owner manager, Faz Ali opened his 90-seater, **BYO** restaurant in 1995. Menu Snapshot: Bangladeshi Fish Fries £3.85; Bombay Duck (1 piece) £1; Machli Diya Bhojan £8.95 - fresh water Bangladeshi fish, garlic, coriander, lemon juice, green chilli - mild, medium or hot!; Chicken Tikka Coriander £8.80, served with salad; Apna Pachando £9.50, whole trout, fresh coriander, garlic, green chilli, lemon, turmeric, cumin, cinnamon and cardamom; Garlic and Mushroom or Peshwari and Coriander Naan £3.15; Chutneys and Pickles are FREE. 'Celebration' meals include lobster from £45 and whole leg of lamb from £48.95 - wonderful for a special occasion, like a big birthday. Price Check: Popadom 55p, CTM £7.65, Pullao Rice £1.95. Hours: 5.30 - 11.30, Sat to 12.30.. <www.faz.ali@blueyonder.co.uk>

Shrewsbury

CLAY OVEN TAKEAWAY NEW ENTRANT

131 Hereford Rd, Meole Brace, Shrewsbury 01743 343222

Martin Kabir opened his takeaway in 2004. Clean

and bright exterior, painted red and white. Chicken Tikka Masala and Chicken Korma are the most popular dishes cooked by chef Kamal. Menu Snapshot: Garlic Mushrooms £1.95; Special Clay Oven Biriani £5.95 - tender diced lamb, spring chicken, prawn, prepared with basmati rice, topped with egg omelette; Garlic Special Lamb £5.10 - marinated lamb cooked with garlic, peppers and coriander, Tandoori King Prawn Mosala £7.50 - cooked in clay oven, then a delicate cream sauce; Coriander Fried Rice £1.80; Chilli Naan £1.40. Price Check: Popadom 50p, CTM £5.10, Pullao Rice £1.40. Hours: 5pm to 10.30. Branch: Shalimar, 23, Abbey Foregate, Shrewsbury.

SHERAZ

79 Wyle Cop, Shrewsbury 01743 242321

Originally opened way back in 1959 - was it an Indian restaurant then?, but taken over in 1990 by its current owner, N Begum. Seats seventy five diners on two floors. Menu Snapshot: Tandoori Salmon £3.60; Scallop Bunju £5.95 - cooked with tomato, onion, garnished with fresh green pepper; Butter Chicken £5.95 - very mild, cooked in tandoori with cream and butter; Keema Pullao Rice £2.00; Chilli Naan £1.70. Glad to see that the European menu has been reduced to just Roast Chicken, Steak and Scampi, all served with chips and peas, prices from £4.95. Stocks: Cobra and Bangla, £3.20 a pint. House wine is a very reasonable £7.50 per bottle. Delivery: 3 miles, £12 minimum. Takeaway: 15% discount. Price Check: Popadom 65p, CTM £6.70, Pullao Rice £2.30. Hours: 5.30 - 12, Saturday to 1.

SOMERSET

Area: South West
Population: 878,000
Adjacent Counties: Bristol, Devon, Dorset, Glos, Wilts

Bath

BENGAL BRASSERIE

32 Milson St, Bath 01225 447906

Managing proprietor, Mukhtar Ali opened his forty seater restaurant in 1987, which is still going strong with Chef Moqozull Ali by his side, serving CTM to his regular customers. Mukhtar had said he will give *Guide* readers a percentage off their bill on his quietest night, which is Sunday - so eat out on Sunday to take him up on his offer! Menu Snapshot: Bengal Platter £12.50 - quarter Tandoori Chicken, Chicken and Lamb Tikka, Sheek Kebab, Tandoori Chop, Pullao Rice, Naan and salad - what a feast! Service Charge: 10%. Stocks: Cobra and Bangla. House wine is a very reasonable £8.50 a bottle. Takeaway: 10% discount. Price Check: Popadom 45p, CTM £7.25, Pullao Rice £1.50. Hours: 12 to 2.30 and 6 to 11.30, Friday and Saturday to 12. <www.bengalbrasseriebath.co.uk>

THE EASTERN EYE BEST IN THE WEST

8a Quiet Street, Bath 01225 422323

140-seater, owned by Suhan Choudhury, pink and blue with most impressive Georgian interior, in one large room with three domes. *'Average high-street curry house it is not! It's a spectacular, huge and most impressive first-floor restaurant. Soft lighting, pink and blue colours, restful atmosphere. Tablecloths and cutlery are of good quality, even the hot towels are so thick they could almost have been squares of carpet! Stuffed pepper, whole green stuffed with spicy diced chicken, barbecued, nicely blackened, delicately spiced, interesting but filling starter. Onion Bhajia, two round bhajias, the best we have tasted for a long while, light, crispy and spicy. Prawn Puree – excellent, large succulent prawns, tangy sauce. Good, fresh and varied salad garnishes. Chicken Tikka Masala – most ordinary, standard offering. Chicken Mon Pasanda, excellent, different, mild, yoghurt based sauce, very herby. Lamb Jalfrezi, large tender chunks of lamb, thick dark sauce, hotness hits you after first couple of mouthfuls. Vegetable Bhajee,good variety of diced vegetables, nicely spiced and enjoyable. Peshwari Nan and Pullao Rice were both good, nan not sickly and rice contained smattering of diced vegetables to make it interesting. Prices slightly above average, but for decor and type of restaurant, very reasonable. Service efficient and friendly. 10% Guide reader discount. An excellent meal in an elegant restaurant.'* MW. *'Incredibly wide menu Quality Excellent Quantity Copious Decor Out of this world Service Prompt and polite Comfort Excellent Comments We went for the non vegetarian set meal which came to £38 for the two of us. It included: Kebab; Chicken Jalfrezi; Sultan Puri Pullau;*

Mixed Vegetables; Naan; Popadoms; Chutney; Sweet; Coffee. Also bottle of Bangla (£3.95) Mineral water £1.70. The kebabs were mightily impressive and highly spiced. Mark 9/10.' G&MP.Service charge: 10%. Specials include: Mon Pasanda – slightly hot, enlivened with herbs and yoghurt, Shah Jahani – chicken breast, slightly spiced, shallow fried in ghee, blended with homemade cheese and cream, Sultan Puri Pilau – from Uttar Pradesh, spiced rice with lamb and cashew nuts, served with a gravy. Bangladeshi food nights, seafood buffet. Service 10%. Minimum charge: £10. Takeaway: 10% discount. Hours: 12-2.30/6-11.30. **AWARDED BEST IN THE WEST.** *See page* 53.

JAFLONG RESTAURANT

78 Lower Bristol Rd, Bath 01225 330144

Rashel Rahim 's Jaflong began in 1994 with the opening of the 'Balti House' as restaurant and takeaway business. In 2002 it was refurbished as Jaflong, a famous tourist attraction situated in Bangladesh. With its new modern contemporary design and trained staff, it specialises range of Bengali and Indian dishes. Chicken Tikka Masala £7.50 Bombay Aloo (Hot Potato) / Vegetable Bhajee £3 Basmati Pilaw Rice £2.25 Naan £2. Hours: 12-2.30/6-11.30. <www.jaflong-bath.co.uk>

JAMUNA

9 High St. Bath 01225 464631

Ahmed Choudury's Jamuna seats sixty-four diners.Menu Snapshot: Tandoori Platter £12.50 - tandoori chicken, chicken tikka, sheek kebab, lamb tikka, Naan and Pullao Rice - what a feast!; Sultan Puri Pulao £12.95 - spiced rice with lamb and cashew nuts, served with lamb curry; Vegetarian Platter £9.25 - potato and cauliflower curry, mushroom bhajia, lentils, yoghurt, bread and rice; Garlic Naan £2.30. *'Entry to this restaurant is up some unprepossessing stairs to the first floor dining area. However, once there it is smart, with chandeliers and decorated in soft pinks and greens. It seats about 60 plus, with tables for 2, 4 and 6 people, and the dining room commands a good view over the nearby gardens and River Avon. We arrived at 8.30, to find it remarkably empty (only one other table was taken). We were shown to a table for two, but asked if we could have a table for four to give a little more room. This request was refused, as according to the manager 'it will be crowded tonight'. So rather disgruntled at having to sit at a small table in a virtually empty restaurant, we studied the menu. The menu offers the usual dishes, with perhaps one or two less common items (for example Xacutti), but basically it is a standard list. The Onion Bhaji starters were very good indeed. Two large, crispy bhajias, which were loosely assembled making them crisp throughout and pleasantly light and crumbly. The Chicken Tikka starter was less remarkable, having a few pieces of only very lightly tandooried lumps of chicken, which because of the paucity of the marinade meant they were not particularly flavoursome. My main dish of Lamb Pathia was quite good, although again nothing outstanding. Cooked in a rich, dark sauce it was certainly hot and pleasantly spiced, but the lamb was rather chewy, and with a very 'lamby' (perhaps 'muttony' might be a better adjective) flavour. The Chicken Tikka Bhuna was quite tasty, but both myself and my wife – who does not like hot curries – considered it mild rather than 'medium' as described on the menu. Once more though, it was no more than OK, which at over £8 for seven small pieces of chicken made not particularly good value. Mixed Vegetable Bhaji was a good mix of vegetables, nicely spiced and cooked, while the Peshwari Naan (plenty of coconut paste, but nothing else) and rice were average. The service was quick and efficient, and the prices (perhaps predictable in Bath) were above average, plus they add 10% for service (although to their credit they do not leave an empty space for a further tip). However, bearing in mind that the portions were just about adequate and the meal, while OK, was nothing more than a reasonable standard high street formula curry, meant that it did not live up to the image the interior presents, nor represents good value for money. It's not one I would return to, and nowhere near as good as the Eastern Eye that I used last time I was in Bath. Oh, and the table incident. Well, they did fill up as the evening progressed, although I noted that there were still several tables for four still empty when we left. We could have had one after all!* MW. Takeaway: 10% discount. Stocks: Cobra and Kingfisher, £3 a pint. House wine: £11.95 a bottle. Service Charge: 10%. Price Check: Popadom 70p, CTM £8.60, Pullao Rice £2.70. Hours: 12 to 2.30 and 6 to 11.30, Saturday to 12.30. Branch: Rajdoot and group. <www.jammunabath.co.uk>

PRIA NEW ENTRANT

4a Argyle Street, Bath 01225 462323

Owner by Ahmed Choudury's Rajpoot group, and managed by Pria, it seats 40 and serves Bangladeshi styled curries. Chefs Specials: Balti Tandoori Special £6.25 - tandoori mix in spicy sauce; Lamb or Chicken Jontiapuri £6.25 - very hot - all served with Rice or Naan. House Specials: Katloma Naan £6.25 - stuffed with lamb and served with spiced potatoes and rice; Green Masala £5.35 - chicken or lamb, green herb sauce, chilli, lime and garlic.

Takeaway: 10% discount. Stocks; Cobra and Kingfisher. Price Check: Popadom 50p, CTM £7.50, Pullao Rice £1.60. Hours: 6 - 1.30, Fri & Sat to 2. <www.priarestaurant.co.uk>

YAK YETI YAK — NEW ENTRANT

12 Argyle Street, Bath 01225 442299

Opened in early 2004 and is a family run business offering Nepalese food. Access from Argyle Street is down numerous of flights of stairs. You are met with the pleasant smell of incense and a friendly waiter. The restaurant is agreeably simple, having plain tables covered in an easy-wipe tablecloth, painted rough stone walls and a nice, unaffected atmosphere. The only pointer to something different is a small area where you can sit on cushions rather than chairs, if you are supple enough. Apart from this area, it seats about 30, unless there is another room I couldn't see. We had: Starters: Momo (eight small dumplings, steamed dumplings with spiced pork) , slightly heavy but quite tasty; Melekhu Macha (spiced deep-fried salmon chunks) (half a dozen sizeable salmon bunks), delicious crisply fried, delicately spiced and very moorish and served with homemade chutneys — a hemp seed chutney with the Momo and a different one with the salmon. Mains: Kukhurako Bhutuwa (pieces of spiced chicken stir-fried with tomato, onion, garlic and ginger), Khursani Kukura (marinated chicken stir-fried with green chilli, tomato and spring onions), spicy!; Aloo Tamar (fermented bamboo shoots stir-fried with potato and black-eyed beans), Bakula Banda (broad beans and white cabbage stir-fried with spices), Maaska Dhal (spiced split black lentils with herbs), a bit too smooth and 'buttery' in flavour for me; Chamsur Sag (spinach and watercress stir-fried with spices and herbs) and Hario Simi Ra Aloo (green beans and new potatoes cooked with spices). It proved a good selection, and all were delicious, different and very fresh-tasting. The service unhurried yet attentive and very friendly. Despite the slightly naff name it was a splendid little restaurant and we all thought it an excellent meal — pleasant, delicately spiced different food in homely unpretentious but comfortable surroundings. I'd go back any day, despite the limited menu.' MW.

SPICE CLUB — NEW ENTRANT

10a Eastover, Bridgwater 01278 433 334

Mohammed A Miah opened his restaurant in 2005, it seats sixty-two diners and serves Bangladeshi styled curries. Quite easy to find, situated in the heart of Bridgwater in Eastover, two doors away from Woolworths, opposite Bridgwater community centre and there is parking nearby! Menu Snapshot: Mogo Masala £3.25 - deep-fried cassava tossed in peppers with garlic and ginger; Kashni Bora £3.95 - chicken tikka wrapped in special spiced potatoes with breadcrumbs coating; Dhom Aloo £2.25 - roasted potatoes with spice rounded with breadcrumbs and deep-fried; Palok Panir Pakoras £2.95 - crispy round balls made with spinach, white cabbage and cheese all sounds delicious! Banquet Night: Thursdays, Popadom with chutney, starter, main course with rice or bread and to finish, Vanilla Ice Cream and coffee all for £9.95. Takeaway: 10% disc, £12 min. Price Check: Pop 60p, CTM £6.25, Pullao Rice £2.25. Hours: 12 - 2/6 - 12. <www.spiceclub.cjb.net>

Clevedon

MOGHULS TANDOORI

33 Old Church Rd, Clevedon 01275 873695

Good curryhouse where you might get a discount if you show them this *Guide.*

INDIA COTTAGE — NEW ENTRANT

Shaftesbury Rd, Henstridge 01963 362963

'This fine curryhouse amid beautiful rural countryside, has been open since 2003. It is run by partners with many years in the Indian restaurant business in London and they obviously know what they are doing, as any visit here will make immediately and abundantly obvious. The restaurant is beautifully adapted from for business premises (a dentists, I think) and comfortably accommodates 58 diners. There's a good range of starters including so novelties -- Nargis Kebab (Egg in mincemeat, barbecue and served with omelette); Fried Salmon or Cottage Kebab (minced kebab, rolled in dough and grilled). A very good range of standard Tandoori dishes and some delicious Masala dishes including King Prawn Masala, Butter Chicken and Chicken/Lamb Pasanda. Chef's Favourites offer some real delights and I very strongly recommend Chicken/Lamb Tikka Marchia, which is cooked in a brilliant red spicy sauce with green chillies. This has the "Wow!" factor. The usual standards are here, all beautifully delivered. Try their Sagwala on Dhansak, go on... Main courses are about £5/6and the servings are generous. A very welcome item in the menu is a list of Value Set Meals. Go for the Raja (for two and you get Tikka Wrap and Onion Bhaji for starters; followed by Chicken Balti, Chicken Tikka Masala, Sag Paneer, Bombay Aloo -- with Pullau Rice, Keema Naan and Popadoms. All for £25! They tell me there are pretty busy. We were there on a midweek evening and the house was three quarters full. You will get a warm welcome. The service is immensely obliging and pretty quick. (Disabled access is OK over a shallow step.) Plenty of Parking. The India House is on the A357 on the Blandford to Wincanton road. It's easily reached from Sherborne and Wincanton and it is well worth looking up. Yours to the last spoonful, Devout in the Way of the Curry.' BG.

Midsomer Norton

SHAPLA

43 High St, Midsomer Norton 01761 410479

Good curryhouse where you might get a discount if you show them this *Guide.*

Minehead

ALCOMBE TANDOORI NEW ENTRANT

67 Alcombe Rd, Alcombe 01643 706 591

'Always enjoy visiting this excellent establishment including two visits during a week-long family break down in Dunster. Greeted by friendly, welcoming staff, despite our late arrival - 11.30pm having attended a bat-walk evening at the castle. The food was once again excellent and the staff lively, friendly and attentive. When you see the food list below it is because of the two visits, not because we were greedy (honest!). Fortunately, we didn't find Batwing Bhaji on the menu!' Starters Fish Potato Chola, which was delicious, lightly spiced fish with great textures; Chicken Momo - chicken cooked with an complimentary blend of spring onions, spices and green pepper; Prawn/King Prawn Puri which were excellent versions of this perennial favourite; Mixed Kebab - a selection of chicken tikka, lamb tikka and sheek kebab, which were perfectly spiced and cooked – all very good indeed. Main Delhi-ite Sea Bass - perfectly cooked and spiced sea bass on a bed of spicy chick peas and potato- fantastic! Chicken Kata Masala - a most enjoyable blend of diced chicken, in a thick spicy sauce; Sunset Salmon - a salmon fillet fried with onions, peppers and tomatoes in a very complimentary sauce with yoghurt and coriander (the menu states 'defies description' and I can't argue with that and for all the right reasons). Devil's Tamarind was another stunning original with lamb that has been marinated in tamarind, cooked in the tandoori and then pan fried with spices – tangy and delicious, superb! Lamb Tikka (excellent) and Shabji Bhuna - medium spiced mixed vegetables; Chicken Korma also very good. Overall opinion – excellent, wouldn't hesitate to recommend and will definitely visit again when in the area. It's also a great treat to discover an Indian restaurant that offers not just one but two excellent fish dishes.' so. Menu Snapshot: Mussels £4.60 - Bengali style, garlic, salt, methi leaves, cream, butter and white wine - sounds fabulous!; Chingrijhool £11.95 - two succulent whole king prawns in medium thick sauce, served with Pullao Rice; Murg or Gosht Ka Achar £7.95 - leg of spring lamb, braised golden brown, sliced onion, ginger, garlic and unground garam masala, thick sauce. Takeaway: 10% discount, £10 minimum. Price Check: Popadom 60p, CTM £6.95, Pullao Rice £2.20. Hours: 12 - 2/5.30 - 11.30.

Wellington

TASTE OF INDIA

2 North Street, Wellington 01823 667051

Good curryhouse where you might get a discount if you show them this *Guide.*

Weston-super-Mare

AVON TANDOORI

16 Waterloo St, Weston 01934 622622

Ditto.

CURRY GARDEN

69 Orchard Street, Weston 01934 624660

Ditto.

STAFFORDSHIRE

Area: Northwest Midlands
Population: 1,070,000
Adjacent Counties:
Cheshire, Derbs,
Shrops,
W Mids, Worcs

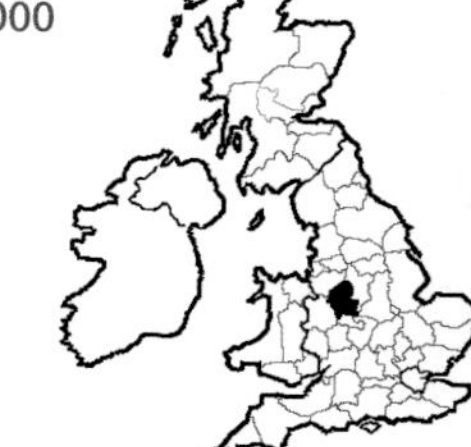

Cannock

JASMINE

125 Hednesford Road, Heath Hayes,
Cannock 01543 279620

Good **BYO** curryhouse where you might get a discount if you show them this *Guide.*

SANAM BALTI HOUSE

NEW ENTRANT

193 Cannock Rd Chadsmoor 01543 513565

A huge restaurant seating 160 diners in three rooms on two floors - wow! - the waiters must be fit! Waheed Nazir took over the Sanam in July 2000. His restaurant doesn't have a alcohol license - so bring your own drinks, beer, wine or spirits. Head chef, Mohammed Zabair's, Mixed Grill at £8.95 is very popular and includes: Chicken Tikka, Sheek Kebab, King Prawns, Tandoori Chicken, Curry Sauce and Naan - WHAT A FEAST! Parking is located just across the road, fifty places, so no problem there. Menu Snapshot: Lamb Chops £2.95 - marinated spring lamb chops, skewered and chargrilled; Fish Masala £3.25 - marinated haddock, deep-fried; Balti Chilli Masala £6.95 - finely chopped onions, capsicum, tomatoes, hot green chilli sauce; Aloo, Mushroom, Peshwari or Vegetable Paratha £1.75; Mushroom Fried, Egg Fried, Garlic or Peas Pullao £2.65, Pickle Tray £2.50. Delivery: 10 miles. Price Check: Popadom 75p, CTM £7.95, Pullao Rice £2.25. Hours: 5.30 - 12.30, Friday and Saturday to 2. <www.sanam-balti.8m.com>

Hednesford

BENGAL BRASSERIE

44 Market St, Hednesford 01543 424769

Good curryhouse where you might get a discount if you show them this *Guide.*

Kingsley Holt

THORNBURY HALL RASOI

TOP 100

Lockwood Rd, Kingsley Holt 01538 750831

This unusual restaurant is approximately 10 miles east of Hanley (off the A52) in a renovated Grade II listed building, once a manor house. Since 1994 it has been owned and managed by Mr and Mrs Siddique, who have brought style and Pakistani food to this beautiful location. It has three public areas, including a conference room. Rasoi appropriately means 'kitchen'. The main restaurant leads from the bar and is decorated in gold and terracotta, ceramic floor, open fire for winter

Thornbury Hall Rasoi

evenings. The Shalimar room, named after gardens in Pakistan, is decorated in green and gold, large windows and doors leading to garden. Dance floor, sparkling globe and sound system. Lahore dining room, large, elegant, richly decorated Georgian plaster ceiling, swagged curtains and a brass teapot, it nearly reached the ceiling! Many of the old favourites are on the menu. Starters include familiar items such as Tandoori Murgh, Boti, Samosa Pyazee (Onion Bhaji) and Sheek Kebabs at from £4.15. Less usual are Breaded brollies, deep fried mushrooms £3 or Chaat-e-phal, seasonal fresh fruit, potatoes, chickpeas mixed with spices, £2.50..Mains include Karhai Dhasi Salan, chicken or lamb pieces cooked with potatoes. £6.95; Thornbury khatta-mettha chicken or lamb fried with pepper, sweet and sour., £6.95; Karhai Lahori Chaska, chicken or lamb in a special sauce masala, unique and hot, £6.90; Karhai Jinga Rassadar, Prawns cooked with special spices, coriander and coconut, £9.90. Pulao Arasta Dehlvi, basmati rice cooked in a very special 'stock' with golden onions, £2.50; Nan-e-Babria wholewheat bread, filled with mincemeat ,£2.50. *'The in-laws live close by. The main hall is very grand, but not always open. Other areas are elegant and comfortable. Service good, including some staff from the village in*

Pakistani dress. Excellent flavours and quality. Sensible portions.' DrHM. *'Fantastic restaurant. Magnificent settings in a listed building. Karahi Murgh Jalfrezi, the best my husband has ever tasted.'* MR&MRS C. Sunday Lunch buffet is a real family occasion, Booking is advisable. £ 9.99, kids £ 5.50, under 5s free. We're pleased to retain it in our **TOP 100.** Hours: 12-2.30/6-11 (11.30 on Fri. & Sat.). <www.thornburyhall.co.uk>

Leek

BOLAKA SPICE — TOP 100

41 Stockwell Street, Leek 01538 373734

When we published the last *Guide*, proprietor, Abdul Choudhury, celebrated his rise to the **TOP 100** by holding a glittering social evening. He invited civic dignitaries from across the district, who all enjoyed a specially prepared four-course menu consisting of Popadoms, assorted starters and an authentic Bangladeshi main course, accompanied by rice and breads. Mr Choudhury said, *'We are absolutely delighted, we aimed to reach the TOP 100 and we have achieved it!'* He also donated 20% of his takings to the Leek branch of the British Red Cross. *'Primarily a formula curryhouse, but two features make it stand out – the Haandis menu and a small specials board. Keema Motor is an outstanding and rich mix of lamb, chick peas and spices. At Christmas, a divine Turkey Tikka Masala with vegetables. Aubergines in a Sweet Sauce is Wow! Service polite and efficient.'* PK. *'Friendly and cosy, good welcome. Tables clean and ready with candles and flowers. Quality unbelievably good every time.'* ja. *'Have dined here many times, food always very fresh and tasty.'* rm. *'A friend gave me a hint that this place had a good reputation. Pickles and Popadoms offered as an appetiser were fresh and moorish. Starter, Chingri Begun and Mint Lamb Balti both impressed with flavours. Impeccable service.'* AEH. *'The best we have been too. Very friendly staff, clean tables, relaxing atmosphere and the best food – absolutely fabulous. Our favourite.'* ss. You might get a discount if you show Abdul this *Guide*. Abdul, please celebrate again being retained in our **TOP 100.**

PABNA

16 Ashbourne Road, Leek 01538 381156

'Pleasant clean decor and highly attentive staff. Well spiced Chicken Tikka for starter. Excellent Chicken Tikka Masala and delicately flavoured Pullao Rice. Cobra served alongside a reasonably extensive and interesting wine list. I have visited on three previous occasions with my father and look forward to the next visit!' NG. So, Nick, did your father pay the bill? Menu Snapshot: Gilafi Sheek Kebab £2.80 - spicy; Melon with Cointreau £2.55 - not curry at all, but sounds delicious, very pallet cleansing!; Tandoori Duck £6.95; Butter Chicken £5.35 - tikka in creamy sauce; Amere Chicken £8.75 - mango, wine, cream and almonds served with Pullao Rice; Naga Fall £6.35 - yes, it's the famous Bangladeshi chilli - very hot!!!; Zeera Aloo £2.10; Banana in Ghee £2.10. Price Check: Popadom 35p, CTM £5.55, Pullao Rice £1.40. Good curryhouse where you might get a discount if you show them this *Guide*.Hours: 5 to 12.

Lichfield

EASTERN EYE — TOP 100

19b Bird Street, Lichfield 01543 254399

Abdul Salam's venue represents a Swat valley house, right up in Pakistan's northern mountain ranges (just a nan nudge from Baltistan). It is famous for its forests and ornate wooden carved furniture, showing Buddhist influences going back 2,000 years. The beams, pillars and window are from Swat. The bar front is from neighbouring Afghanistan, the chairs are Rajasthani and the table tops are from 150-year-old elm. *'Count the rings,'* enthuses Mr Salam. The toilets are a 'must-see' on your list. The theme is Agra's Red Fort – probably India's best example of a Moghul residence. The food is well spoken of. Specials include Murgh with Apricot, marinated chicken with apricot yoghurt sauce, cream and fresh coriander. Rajasthani Paro Breast – pigeon. Michael Fabricant, MP, MCC (member of the *Curry Club*) continues regularly to take his seat at the Eye as a loyal local, rating it highly, as do so many other reports we get, e.g. *'From entering you know it'll be good. Decor reminded me of Putney's fine Ma Goa's (London sw). In a mild mood, had Murgh Special with apricot which was delicious. My friend loved his Eastern Eye Mixed Massala (king prawn, lamb and chicken).'* rl. *'Still my favourite. Mr Salam still very much in charge, evolving the menu and new dishes. Cooking excellent – far superior to average curry fare. Chicken and Banana, Chilli Chicken, Special tandoori Masala (inc chicken, lamb, king prawns) are all excellent. Amazingly light Naans. Wine list still consists of an armful of bottles placed on your table to take your pick from – a tradition I hope will remain and includes good examples from Spain and Australia. Deserves to be in the* **TOP 100.***'* PJ. *'The food was unusual and beautifully presented on huge oval china plates. Will definitely try it again if we're ever in the area.'* K&ST. Discounts for CC Members on Sundays. Hours: 12-2.30 (Sat. only)/5-12.

LAL BAGU

9 Bird Street, Lichfield 01543 262967

Good curryhouse where you might get a discount if you show them this *Guide.*

Newcastle-under-Lyme

BILASH

22 Highland Keele Road 01782 614549

Good curryhouse where you might get a discount if you show them this *Guide.*

BOMBAY CLUB — NEW ENTRANT

325 Hartshill Road, Hartshill 01782 719191

A thoroughly modern restaurant, minimalist chic, wooden floors, plain walls. Is Executive Chef: MZ Salim still working here? He was 'chef de parti' at the Oberoi in India, so we can expect great curries. Lets have a look at the menu.... Tikke Murgh Malai £3.95 - diced chicken breast marinated in cottage cheese and cream, char grilled in the clay oven; one of my favourites Tangri Kabab £3.75 - drumsticks char grilled with cream and cashew nuts paste - lovely;Lahsuni Jhinga £6.95 - char grilled king prawns in medium spiced brushed with garlic paste; Paneer Pakora £3.50 - cottage cheese dipped in butter and deep fried - a starter not for the calorie conscious! Aud E Chengazi £9.95 - roasted lamb slices cooked in a rich medium sauce with mint and coriander; Nilgiri Korma £7.95 - cubes of mutton sautéed with brown onion paste and green masala, served mild or hot!; Makai Khumb £7.95 - mushroom and corn cooked in a masala sauce - well, all looks good! *'Most of the curry houses I have visited serve curries which are surrounded by a pool of oil but not this one. I have yet to find a place like it. The chef cooks the most delicious curries I have ever tasted. I have tried many times to get the recipes for two of my favourites but, not being adept at making curries I have ben unable to recreate it. Recommend Jhinga Mumtaz and Chicken Makhni together with rice made from nuts and honey whose name escapes me and if by any chance you are able to create them I would be grateful if you pass the recipe on to me.'* MM.

KAVI — NEW ENTRANT

Clayton Lodge Hotel, Clayton Road, Newcastle 01782 613093

The attractive 50 room Clayton Lodge Hotel has (from £45.00 per night) has received a multi million pound refurbishment involving its ballroom and meeting area endowing it with beautiful marble floors and crystal chandeliers. Located about 2.0 miles from Stoke centre (2 minutes from J15 /M6) it has a major attraction for readers of this Guide – its Indian restaurant Kavi. White and black marble, blonde wood, a modern look and splashes of colour, and a plasma screen with Bollywood movies vies for attention with the open-plan kitchen. This is the preserve of chef Avinash Kumar, ex Baylis, Slough, Berks (see entry) and Claridges Delhi. Starters include: Mussels & Scallops £6.95, flavoured with coconut; Shakar Kandi Chaat £5.25, sweet potato chaat topped with pomegranate seeds; Mix Vegetable Potli £3.25, assorted vegetable spring rolls; Ajwaini Macchi £7.25, tandoori grilled haddock scented with carom seeds. Main Courses include: Venison Chop Masala £10.95, chops simmered in

Kavi, Newcastle-under-Lyme

red wine and served with a masala sauce; Murg Kafrial £8.95, chicken breast charcoal grilled and stuffed with minced chicken served with a green Goan sauce; Quail Hara Masala £9.95, Whole fresh quail simmered in a mint and coriander chutney. Veg dishes include Palak ke Kofte £7.95, spinach dumplings stuffed with prunes and served with a korma sauce. Desserts include: Gajar ka Halwa £4.25, carrot pudding wrapped in a French crepe; Rasmalai £3.75, milk pudding dumplings dipped in sweetened reduced milk. Open from 6pm, seven days a week. Branch Kavi's, Wolverhampton <www.claytonlodge.co.uk>

Rugeley

BILASH

7 Horsefair, Rugeley 01889 584234

Good curryhouse where you might get a discount if you show them this *Guide*.

Stoke-on-Trent

(including Burslem and Hanley)

ASHA TAKEAWAY

42 Broad St, Hanley, Stoke 01782 213339

Good curryhouse where you might get a discount if you show them this *Guide*.

MONZIL

44 Broad St Hanley Stoke 01782 280150

Ditto.

Uttoxeter

KOHI NOOR

11 Queen Street, Uttoxeter 01889 562153

Good **BYO** curryhouse where you might get a discount if you show them this *Guide*.

SUFFOLK

Area: East
Population: 685,000
Adjacent Counties: Cambs, Essex, Norfolk

Brandon

BRANDON TANDOORI

17 London Road, Brandon 01842 815874

Good curryhouse where you might get a discount if you show them this *Guide*.

Bury-St-Edmonds

MUMTAZ INDIAN

9 Risbygate Street, Bury 01284 752988

Ditto.

Felixstowe

BOMBAY NITE

285 High Street, Walton 01394 272131

Ditto.

Ipswich

GULSHAN TAKEAWAY NEW ENTRANT

9 Stoke Street, Ipswich 01473 692929

Originally opened in 1996, taken over in 2003 by Mohibur Rahman. Menu Snapshot: Vegetable Chat £2.40; Butter Lamb £6.75 - lightly spiced, butter, fresh cream and almond; Balti dishes from Jalfrezi to Tikka Masala, all £7.95 regardless of whether you choose chicken, lamb or prawn, served with Pullao Rice or Naan - good deal!; Mushroom or Onion Fried Rice all £2.25; Stuffed, Peshwari, Keema, Garlic with Coriander or Onion Naan all £1.95. Delivery: 6 miles, £12 minimum. Credit card accepted. Price Check: Popadom 60p, CTM £6.50, Pullao Rice £1.95. Hours: 5 - 12, including Boxing Day. <www.gulshantakeaway.co.uk>

PASSAGE TO INDIA NEW ENTRANT

27 Fore Street, Ipswich 01473 286220

Opened in 1991 and owned by R Uddin. Nassir Uddin runs the kitchen, is this is brother? Restaurant seats 140 diners in three rooms and Nassir cooks Bangladeshi styled curries for his regulars. Beware, the starters menu goes on for an age - no less than forty-four dishes - must be a record. So, tell me (unmarked, brown envelopes only please!) how many Popadoms with chutneys will you munch your way through before you have come to your decision? Menu Snapshot: Naga Dishes from £7.35, very hot dish prepared with special chilli, originating from Bangladesh. No, not originating but unique to Bangladesh, so, there, now you know!; Indian Omelette with chips £8.95 Brinjal Pakora £2.95, one of my favourites!; Sardine Puri £3.05, one of Pat's (along with the legendary Naga! - waiters think he's mad!!); Dim (egg) Biriani £6.95, served with Basmati Rice - I wonder if they are soft or hard boiled, whole or sliced, or perhaps a lightly fried egg (as in Malaysian cuisine) gently laid on the top of the rice, served with Curry Gravy and salad - good meal!; Pizza Paratha with Egg £2.95 - sounds colourful! Takeaway: 10% discount. Delivery: 3 miles, £30 minimum. Price Check: Popadom 70p, CTM £7.65, Pullao Rice £1.95. Hours: 12 - 2.30/ 5.30 - 12. <www.apassagetoindiaipswich.com>

TAJ MAHAL

40 Norwich Road, Ipswich 01473 257712

'*Good quality formula curries. Never going to set the world alight, but enjoyable Prawn puree followed by Lamb Karai. Good service and fair prices make this an oasis in Ipswich.*' You might get 10% a discount if you show them this *Guide*.

Lowestoft

AHMED

150 Bridge Rd, Oulton Broad 01502 501725

Boshor Ali's cute little restaurant has just 28 seats. '*Brilliant.*' says PJ. Hours: 12-2.30pm/6-11.30pm. Branch: Jorna Indian Takeaway, 29-33 Wherstead Road, Ipswich.you might get a discount if you show them this *Guide*.

ROYAL BENGAL

69 High Street, Lowestoft 01502 567070

Good curryhouse where you might get a discount if you show them this *Guide.*

SEETA

176 High Street, Lowestoft 01502 574132

Ditto.

Newmarket

ARIF INDIAN NEW ENTRANT

30 Old Station Rd, Newmarket 01638 665888

Looks like a *contemporary restaurant from the outside but very much in the old mould inside – not quite flock wallpaper. Meat dupiage £4.90, Chicken curry £4.50, Chicken biriani £7.35, Tarka dhal £2.90, Paratha £1.90. An excellent, well served meal. Obviously popular as quite busy on an early Thursday evening. Recommended when in Newmarket'* JP.

SURREY

Area: Home Counties (south of London)
Population: 1,068,000
Adjacent Counties: Berks, Hants, Kent, London, Sussex

Parts of Surrey were absorbed by Greater London in 1965. We note affected towns/boroughs.

Addlestone

SONALI

198, Station Rd, Addlestone 01932 830424

Mr and Mrs Shima Rob took over this takeaway in June 2006. Saturday night is their busiest night and CTM is the most popular dish. Regular customers are given a bottle of Cobra if they spend £18 or over. Menu Snapshot: Sonali Kebab Roll £3.50 - Sheek Kebab in Naan, salad and mint sauce; Nipa's Garlic Kebab Golap £6.25 - marinated minced chicken, fried leeks, extra garlic, cooked in the tandoor served with salad and mint sauce - fairly hot; Special Tikka Masala £5.95 - chicken, mild, sweet, fruity sauce with almonds, sultanas, cashew nuts, cream, coconut powder, lychees and butter; Chicken Chat £3.95 - chat masala, chicken, cucumber, a sweet and sour dish served on a puri; Moolie Bhajee £2.50 - white radish, slightly hot; Quorn Rice £2.15; Peshwari, Garlic, Onion or Chilli Naan all £1.60. Takeaway: 10% discount. Delivery: £10 minimum, 5 miles. Credit cards accepted. Price Check: Popadom 60p, CTM £5.5, Pullao Rice £1.75. Hours: 5 to 11 (however, if you wish to dine at lunchtime, please book in advance.

Ashtead

MOGHUL DYNASTY

1 Craddock Parade, Ashtead 01372 274810

Good curryhouse where you might get a discount if you show them this *Guide.*

Byfleet

RED ROSE OF BYFLEET

148 High Road, Byfleet 01932 355559

Ditto.

Camberley

DIWAN EE KHAS

413 London Rd Camberley 01276 23500

Good curryhouse where you might get a discount if you show them this *Guide.*

RAJPUR

57d Mytchett Road, Mytchett, Camberley 01252 542063

Good curryhouse where you might get a 10% discount if you show them this *Guide.*

SUNDARBAN NEW ENTRANT

Lakeside Complex, Wharf Rd Frimley Green 01252 838868

Real Indian food on an 80-seater boat, with al fresco tables at a venue with an hotel, disco, cabaret

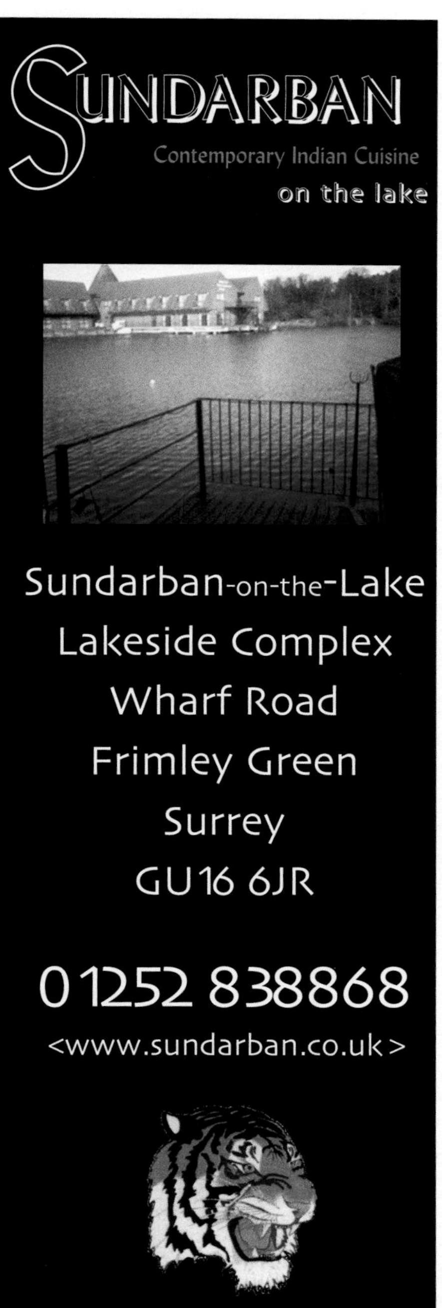

club (where the World Darts Championships are televised from) and fitness centre with pool on the Lakeside Complex site! Sounds like the Editor is on something; but no, it's all true. So you can check in, swim, have a beauty treatment, fill up on the best Indian food outside London, watch a cabaret show, have a work-out in the disco, go to bed on-site, have a work out in the gym before a hearty English breakfast and check out! The picture in the ad, alongside shows the view from the boat looking at the hotel. We do not have further pictures to show you because it opens after we go to print. For that reason, we are unable to bring you the menu, but we have had a sneak preview and it looks really promising. This new venture is owned by Lodue Miah, who runs the Madhuban in Liss, Hants with exceptional skill. *(See entry).* But although Lodue is Bangladeshi, he has opted to move forward from the curryhouse formula. He has engaged highly-trained (Indian hotels) Indian chefs and managers. Reports please.

Carshalton (Greater London)

ROSE HILL TANDOORI

320 Wrythe Lane, Rose Hill 020 8644 9793

Good curryhouse where you might get a discount if you show them this *Guide.*

Chipstead

CHIPSTEAD TANDOORI

32 Chipstead Station Parade 01737 551219

Seats fifty diners in two rooms. Menu Snapshot: Assorted Starters £4.05 - Tikka, Kebab and Onion Bhajia; Tandoori Lamb Chops £6.50; Lamb Xacutti £6.95 - tender lamb, roasted fennel, cloves, garlic and ginger; Manchurian Chicken £6.45 - hot, sweet and sour, with green chillies; Duck Mo Mo £7.95 - tender duck, medium spiced; Vegetable Malaya £3.60 - with pineapple; Lemon Rice £2.45 - with coconut and honey. Sunday Buffet: £7.95 adult, £5.95 children. Banquet Night: every Tuesday, £9.95 each. Takeaway: 20% discount, £10 minimum - cash only, or, 10% discount, £10 minimum - cheque and credit cards. Delivery: £12 minimum. Price Check: Popadom 55p, CTM £6.50, Pullao Rice £1.95. Hours: 12 - 2 and 5.30 - 11, Friday and Saturday to 11.30. Monday closed.

Cobham

SPICY CHIMNEY

40 Portsmouth Rd, Cobham 01932 863666

Good curryhouse where you might get a discount if you show them this *Guide.*

Cranleigh

CURRY INN

214 High Street, Cranleigh 01483 273992

You might get a 10% discount if you show them this *Guide.*

CARDAMOM NEW ENTRANT

Freeland House, High Street 01483 277 145

'On a cold, snowy Tuesday evening the restaurant was almost full so it already has a good following. Very attractive appearance, nearly all white inside and out, fairly plain and modern. Glassware and cutlery particularly attractive and of really good quality. Different dishes are served on different shaped plates with a mound of rice already on the plate where appropriate. Generally efficient and pleasant service. All food was excellent, though Brinjal Bhaji £2.90 chunks too large and needed a bit more cooking with a more generous hand with the spice. Served nicely and in generous portions. I was really disappointed that the Indian desserts had been discontinued, it really is time English diners became a bit more adventurous and not just opt for an ice cream. Luckily, Gulab Jaman £2.50 was the only one left, very good.' HC. Agreed re: Indian desserts, however, I think the problem lies in the fact that we all eat too much for our first and second course and just can't face a dessert. I am definitely a pudding person, and would order a Ras Malai or alternative if available, but never an ice cream! Menu Snapshot: Achari Gosth £9.95, lamb, citrus fruit, sour yoghurt, served with Pullao Rice; Badami Korma £6.95, chicken tikka, yoghurt sauce, garnished with green pepper and fried onion; Duck Mosalla £10.95, yoghurt marinated sauce, mild spices, baby potatoes, served with Pullao Rice. Takeaway: 10% discount. Price Check: Popadom 60p, CTM £7.25, Pullao Rice £2.05. <www.cardamonindian.co.uk>

Croydon (Greater London)

(Includes Addington Hamsey Green, Selsdon and Shirley)

BANANA LEAF

27 Lower Addiscombe Road, Croydon 020 8688 0297

Opened in 1988 by Rajkumar Rengaraj, who will greet you on your visit, as he is also the manager. Nearest Tramlink/Rail Station East Croydon and Bus Route 289 and 410. Chicken Chettinadu £6.60 - tender chicken cooked in a rich, dark sauce of cinnamon, cardamom and onions, is chef T Sundaram's most ordered dish and is also one of my personal favourites, when I eat South Indian food. Seats seventy in two dining rooms. Menu Snapshot: of course the menu lists all the usual North Indian favourites, but lets forget those and go straight to the South Indian dishes: Masala Vadai £2.25 - chana dhal, doughnut shaped savoury snack, spiced with black peppercorns, stuffed with ginger and fennel seeds, served with fresh coconut chutney; Curd Vadai - stuffed with coriander and tomato; Bonda £2.75 - spicy potato balls dipped in gram flour batter and deep-fried; Masala Dosai £3.20 - a crispy pancake, made from urad flour and rice flour with fenugreek, stuffed with spiced potato and onion served with sambar and fresh coconut chutney; Utthapam £4.30 - pizza-style pancake topped with mixed vegetables; Rava Masala £4.90 - made with semolina, spiced potato, onion, curry leaves, ginger, cashew nuts and sultanas; Malabar Fish Curry £6.75 - two pieces of Indian ocean Kingfisher in a sauce made from fresh coconut milk and a mixture of spices; Fried King Prawns £8.95 - marinated in ginger, garlic, fennel seeds and curry leaves, mixed with fresh coconut and potato, served with yoghurt mint dip, Tamarind Rice £2.60. Stocks: Cobra and Kingfisher, £3.30 a pint. Price Check: Popadom 50p, CTM £6.00, Pullao Rice £2.10. Hours: 12 to 2.30 and 6 to 11.30, Sunday to 11. <www.azzz.co.uk/bananaleaf>

THE DEANS

241 London Rd, Croydon 020 8665 9192

The Deans opened in 1993 and is named after its chef-owner Salam Ud Din and manager Zaka Ud Din. It is a massive, fully-licensed restaurant seating over 150 diners in two dining rooms, decorated in white with the 'sparkly' mosaic mirror Indian arches to be found in the Moghul palaces. It has a small but typically authentic Pakistani

Punjabi menu, serving tandoori items and well-spiced curries. RE tells us of four visits: 1: *'A large busy restaurant favoured by Asians. Also does a very brisk takeaway. Apart from the papadoms (they are grilled which I don't like), the food is excellent. Lamb Nihari was "special"— very tender, quite hot with a distinctive ginger flavour. Lovely dish.'* 2. *'Happy to go back as I was in the area. Seekh Kebabs freshly cooked and spicy, Chicken Tikka fresh and moist. Service is efficient and friendly.'* 3. *'Third time is supposed to be lucky – not this time. Seekh Kebabs and Chicken Tikka were fine, but the Dhall Gosht, so good last time, was awful – undercooked meat in a pale, tasteless sauce. A chap on the next table was complaining that his curry was far too salty. A shame. I will (eventually) go back, but not for some time.'* 4, *'After a culinary disaster last time, I decided to give Deans on more try – Glad I did. Seekh Kebabs were great, in a hot iron plate with fried onions. Haandi Dhall Gosht – very good, hot, spicy, full of flavour and very tender meat. Service good and friendly, busy with families.'* RE. Specials: Handi dishes, chicken, Methi Gosht £5. Handi Aloo Chana, Dhal-stuffed Karela (bitter gourd). **BYO** no corkage. Delivery: £10 min, 3-miles. Hours: 12-2.30/6-11.30 (10.30 Sun.). '

KERELA BHAVAN

16 London Rd, W. Croydon 0181 668 6216

South Indian Restaurant right next to West Croydon Railway Station. *'The usual Indian background music was playing as we entered this pleasant restaurant. There are about 50 seats, set in alcoves, which gave a more intimate feel and was very nice. The waiter was very friendly and attentive. It was about half full. Ray headed for the toilet as he always does – two reasons: Firstly to wash his hands as he eats with his fingers; and secondly to include in his reports to you. He thinks the toilets often reflect the standard of hygiene throughout the establishment. These were fine— everything worked and there was plenty of soap etc. Poppadums came. They were nice and crispy and dry. Even I like poppadums. For a starter Ray had Parippu Vada, which were two spicy fried lentil cakes. I tried a bit and said it tasted like a dry spicy bun. Ray said I was a Philistine, smothered his with onions, lime pickle and raitha and said I did not know what I was missing. For his main course, Ray had Kerala Meat Chilli. This consisted of quite hot cubes of very lean and tender lamb, which had been marinated in a sweet & sour marinade, then cooked with green chillis and capsicums. It was a dry dish, but very spicy. Ray enjoyed it and said he would recommend it. He also had a Kerela Veesu Paratha, a sort of bread in strands. This was most unusual but a good accompaniment to the chilli meat. He also had a dall, which was very runny & bland. The bill was £22.90 and there was an added 10% service charge.*

PANAHAR

316 Limpsfield Road, Hamsey Green, Croydon 020 8651 9663

Good curryhouse where you might get a discount if you show them this *Guide.*

PLANET SPICE A-LIST

88 Selsdon Park, Addington, Croydon 020 8651 3300

Opened in 1999 by the very talented Emdad Rahman of Babur SE23 fame. This fantastic restaurant is well decorated in a modern and

Emdad's Happy chefs

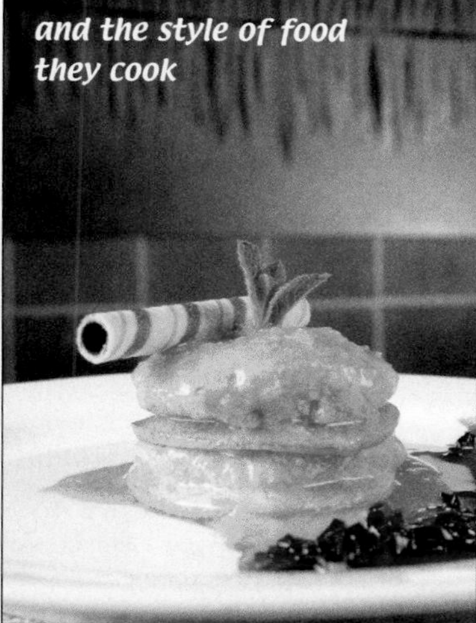
and the style of food they cook

colourful style. Raj Pandy is the head chef and he delights his regulars with Masala Roast Lamb Shank, braised with spices and ground sesame seeds, then marinated in strained yoghurt and finally pot roasted to melt in the mouth - scrumptious! Menu Snapshot: Begun Dolma, baby aubergine stuffed with mildly spiced, creamy red pumpkin; Murgh Pattice, potato cakes stuffed with mince chicken, topped with dried peas curry; Gilawat Ke kebab, melt in the mouth mince lamb stuffed with lentils and raisins, flavoured with mace, cardamom and saffron; Betki Balchao, strips of battered betki fish stir fried with a hot and sour Goan sauce; Hariyali Murgh, boneless breast of chicken cooked in a smooth, hot green sauce of mint, spinach, coriander and green chilli; Madras Snapper, tomato based hot fish curry tempered with curry leaves, mustard seeds and coconut; Crispy Fried Potatoes, thinly sliced potatoes, dusted with gram flour and fried mango powder, then deep-fried; Porial, green beans and aubergines combined with cashew nuts, onion seeds, coriander and garam masala; Subze Tandoori, red pumpkin, green peppers, onion, okra, tomatoes and carrots all marinated in traditional spices and yoghurt, Lime Rice with Cashew Nuts. Service: 10%. Sunday Buffet: £9.95. Delivery: 3 miles, £10 minimum. Price Check: Popadom £1 for a whole basket!, CTM £7.50, Pullao Rice £1.95. Branch: Babur, 119, Brockley Rise, Forest Hill. SE23 <www.planet-spice.com>

RUPEES TAKEAWAY

184 Wickham Road, Shirley, Croydon
020 8655 1866

Seats 32. Est 1963. and is Croydon's oldest (?). Mr Islam has been serving three generations of customers and you might get a discount if you show them this *Guide.* Hours: 12-3/6 to late.

Dorking

RED CHILLI — NEW ENTRANT

A24 Horsham Road, Mid Holmwood, Dorking 01306 644816

Wasimul Choudhury opened hid 100-seater in 2005 in a smart and bright building with parking outside and a big red chilli hanging beside the entrance door. *'It will have to rely on passing trade or build up a really good reputation. Fairly quiet on a Tuesday evening. Decor, really attractive and modern, sparkly lights in ceiling, not obviously Indian. Water feature in entrance. Lovely quality china and cutlery, waiters all in blue shirts and ties. Menu large but very conventional, shame, had hoped for a more adventurous choice. Service poor, friendly, just unprofessional. Wine opened incorrectly, plates handed across the table to the diner. But the food was excellent and attractively presented in plain white dishes. Everyone was really pleased with everything, King Prawn Butterfly - really special. Overall a very pleasant evening.'* HC. Menu Snapshot: Paneer Pakora £2.85; Bhatak Raja Naga Shahi £6.95 - duck with the famous naga chilli; Dhal Makhni £4.95 - black urid dhal, ginger, garlic, cream, butter; Fish Makhmali Kebab £7.95. Price Check: Popadom 55p, CTM £5.95, Pullao Rice £1.95. Hours: 12 - 2.30 / 5.30 - 11, Friday and Saturday to 11.30. <www.redchillidorking.com>

East Molesey

GOLDEN CURRY

19 Hampton Court Parade, East Molesey
020 8979 4358

Good curryhouse where you might get a discount if you show them this *Guide.*

PALACE INDIAN CUISINE

20 Bridge Rd, East Molesey 020 8979 1531

E Eshad's 60-seater is yards from Hampton Court Palace. DD. Chef's special: Murag Tikka Rajella, yoghurt based, spicy cooked with massala sauce and fresh garden mint. Hours: 12-2.30/6-11.30.

SHAHEE MAHAL — NEW ENTRANT

101 Walton Rd, East Molesey 020 8979 0011

'I notice *your website does not list the above restaurant. It's owned by a chap named Shiraz - not sure of spelling - but he has been running this place since 1974 and I can assure you it really is first class-we had our wedding reception there. fe.*

Epsom

LE RAJ — TOP 100

211 Firtree Rd, Epsom Downs 01737 371371

Owner chef Enam Ali's 110 seater Le Raj is in outer Epsom (it's on the A240/A2022) in a line of shop fronts. *'A very different Asian restaurant— more like a*

Mediterranean Bistro than any Indian I have been in before. The presentation and style of the food is equally radical– as to whether it was chic will probably be a matter of individual taste. The place was deserted, and we were the only two customers. Our opinions on the food were frankly divided. My Kashmiri colleague thought it was well presented, but the food was tasteless. I thought it was absolutely not what you expect in your formula curry house, but I liked it, once I realised that it was aiming for a more sort of European / Asian fusion type of food than just a curry based fare. The decor of the place reflects this– all warm apricot walls and sun bleached yellows elsewhere. So what did we have: Kaathi Kebabs as a starter– minced meat roasted on a skewer in the kebab, my colleague Chingri Modu– KP's cooked with honey, fresh lime and tamarind sauce. The kebab was not as spicy as I expected, never the less it was tasty and I enjoyed it. For main course I had murg– e– mutazan, which was pieces of chicken cooked with cardamom and yoghurt, and gosht– e– jalali, which was described as 'spectacular dish of lamb, cooked with very strong spices' and had a two chillies sign against it. My friend for this was not justified, and that the dish was just about medium heat. I did try some, and I had to agree that it was not really as 'two chillies' as I would thought. However, it was very tender and tasty, even though it was not a 'fire eater!' We also had a Brinjal Bhajee and lime pickles, both of which were excellent, and a similar standard Akbori (chilli and mint) nan. I think if we ever crossed their threshold again, my colleague would request a more liberal hand with the chilli and methi etc. Although it was to my mind, and taste buds, not at all the norm for a curry house, I thought it was excellent, once I had got over the culture shock of going in a curry house that was not really one at all?? I celebrate diversity, so 'vive la difference' as far as Le Raj is concerned.' MW. .Min charge: £15. Hours: 12-2.30/5.30-11.

Esher

PANAHAR TANDOORI

124, High Street, Esher 01737 000000

'Easily the best curryhouse in the area, no mistake. Friendly service, atmosphere fine but always crowded, booking almost essential, not surprisingly.' D&DP

SHERPA KITCHEN NEW ENTRANT

132 High Street, Esher 01372 470777

A branch of our Award-Winning Gurkha Kichen, Oxted. *(See page 347).*

Ewell

SRI KRISHNA INN NEW ENTRANT

332 Kingston Road, Ewell 020 8393 0445

Formerly Bombay, managing owner, M Krishna

Das took over this restaurant in 2001. It seats seventy diners and served Southern Indian cuisine and Masala Dosa is their most popular dish. Delivery: 3 miles, £20 minimum. Set lunch and dinner £24 for two. Minimum charge: £15. Licensed: stocks Cobra and Kingfisher, £2.90 a pint. House wine: £10.50. Price Check: Popadom 50p, CTM £4.95, Pullao Rice £2.20. Hours: 12 - 3/6 TO 11.

Farnham

DARJEELING

25 South Street, Farnham 01252 714322

MA Rahman and S Islam's 46-seater is stylishly decorated, with mahogany wood panelling everywhere, brass plates decorate the walls and there is a large brass peacock in the window. *'Very unexceptional in appearance and all the same as previous visits - consistent. Menu, prices, decor and general style are the same as hundreds of Indian restaurants all over the country, but the service is efficient and food well above average. Friendly and efficient with very modest prices. Extensive menu with a few Chef's Specials - the only restaurant, I know, to offer Broccoli Bhaji. Most enjoyable with a car park right opposite and they serve a very good Gulab Jamun - a plus.'* HC.You might get a discount if you show them this *Guide.*

Fetcham

FETCHAM TANDOORI

248 Cobham Road, Fetcham 01372 374927

'We have consistently good reports from local friends. After a evening lecture a quick visit seemed a good idea. A lighter style decoration and attractive furniture made a much better impression, since our last visit, on entering. Made very welcome and drinks arrived promptly (the wine list is very poor). Extensive menu, nothing unusual. Popadoms, unfortunately rather thick and stodgy.' The popadoms that I like the best are made by a company called Liljat and are wrapped in cellophane with a picture of a small boys face and a hideous pink bunny rabbit! These popadoms are really lovely, light and crisp. I think this is because they are incredibly thin. Anyway, the boxed ones you get in every supermarket, are quite horrid, far too thick and heavy. DBAC. *'Relished good, with exceptionally delicious mango chutney.' Onion Bhajia - flat disc style, very good. Chicken Makhone - excellent, lovely thick, almondy sauce with very good Mushroom Rice. Excellent and generous Fish (boal) Masala, I was encouraged to have the fish as, 'it only has one bone in the middle'. According to one waiter, they find that diners are very wary of ordering fish because of the bones and even the chicken now has to be off the bone. Sag Bhajee - one of the best I have had. Brinjal Bhajee also excellent. We were really pleased, all the food was well above average. Service, friendly, attentive and efficient with a very pleasant atmosphere - we shall return very soon.'* HC.

Guildford

CINNAMONS

4 Chapel Street, Guildford 01483 300626

'Decor very open, light and modern, could be any cuisine. Menu very appealling. Good, friendly service, all young men dressed in identical blue shirts and trendy ties. Food outstandingly good, attractively served in white china dishes and in sensible rather than generous portions. Only grumble, delivery of food unacceptably slow. They did apologise and offered free liqueurs. Espresso coffee served with good quality chocolates. No Indian desserts. Definitely wish to return.' HC. Takeaway: 20% discount. Hours: 12-2.30/6-11.30.

BOMBAY SPICE

17 Park Street Guildford 01483 454272

'A very cold evening, we had the table moved away from the window, but it wasn't much better, the restaurant was inadequately heated. The wine ordered by Danny came unopened and was offered for inspection. At last, I thought, we have found a restaurant where they know how to serve wine - no such luck. The glasses filled too full, I was asked if I would like to taste it! The food was very good, all dishes were above average and the portions were generous. Mushroom Rice - particularly good. King Prawn Mahli - mild in a coconut sauce. Manager very professional, willing waiters just inept. Definitely will return.' D&HC. Hours: 12-2.30/5.30-11.30.

Hampton Wick

ORCHID NEW ENTRANT

5 High St, Hampton Wick 020 8977 9111

'We are fans of yours, have many of your books and cook curries regularly. We have visited some of your recommended restaurants also. We thought you should know about the above restaurant which has been opened in 2006. We are regular visitors. We think the food is some of the best we have ever tasted, and the service superb. Well worth a visit.' S&NB.

RESHMI NEW ENTRANT

90 Molesey Rd, Hersham 01932 219291

'My mum, who was born and brought up in India loves it! Very, very smart restaurant with welcoming staff. Excellent food and service. Good loos. Don't go late on a Friday lunch - they go to prayers. £20 a head.' A&UK.

Horley

FORT RAJ BALTI

74 Victoria Road, Horley 01293 822909

Good curryhouse where you might get a discount if you show them this *Guide.*

NEW CURRY BENGAL NEW ENTRANT

25 Station Road, Horley 01293 784255

Chef owner, Muhib Miah's modern restaurant seats fifty diners and he serves Bangladeshi styles curries to his regulars, who particularly enjoy the way cooks Chicken Tikka Masala. Muhin took over the restaurant, which was called Bengal Curry, in July 2006. Menu Snapshot: Duck kebab £4.25; Cashew Nut Aloo Moti £2.50; Tandoori Mixed Grill £8.50, served with a Naan; Lamb Shank Xacuti £7.50, medium; King Prawn Biriani £7.95, served with Vegetable Curry; Crispy Fried Potato £2.50, Garlic and Onion Naan £1.90. Delivery: 5 miles, £10 minimum. Sunday Buffet: £9.95 per person. Licensed: stocks Cobra, £3.00 a pint, house wine £8.95 a bottle. Price Check: Popadom 50p, CTM £7.95, Pullao Rice £1.95. Hours: 12 - 2/6- 12. Branch: Lingfield Tandoori, 9, High Street, Lingfield, Surrey. <www.currybengal.co.uk>

FORT RAJ

74 Victoria Road, Horley 01293 822909

J*'Needed a fix near Gatwick Airport). What a nice place! Started with a Duck Tikka which was fairly unusual and caught my eye. The portion size was not great but it was just the job for a started. The six pieces of spicy duck come with a generous side salad and a small tub of dipping sauce which had a subtle orange flavour (I would have personally preferred a hot chilli sauce but that was just me!). For a main course I chose the Chicken Xacuti which was similar to the recipe in your restaurant cook book. The portion was man sized and nicely presented. The food itself was great and with just a slightly bigger Tandoori Roti, the bowl and plate would have been clean. After finishing everything I asked for the bill and when it arrived it came along with a complimentary brandy! Total cost £18.45. £7.00 of this was my lager bill so the total food cost was £11.45. Well worth a visit! As by the way is its near neighbour The Curry Inn (less than 100 yards away) but that is another story. Cheers'* DC, ATT.

Kingston-upon-Thames (Greater London)

MONTYS TANDOORI

53 Fife Road, Kingston 020 8546 1724

70-seater Nepalese restaurant, owned by Kishor Shrestha. South Indian face-masks decorate the white walls and hang from cream drapes. Hand-painted silk pictures of Indian scenes cover the walls, the floor is tiled. Specials: See Ealing, W5 for details *'Service is excellent, unobtrusive, polite and no mistakes. Food is plentiful and piping hot.'* ST. Takeaway: 10% off. Hours: 12-2.30/6-12.

SRI KRISHNA INN NEW ENTRANT

332 Kingston Rd, Kingston 020 8393 0445

This is a south Indian (Kerelan) restaurant, and it is these items you should plump for, rather than the curryhouse favourites. No one does better vegetarian food than Kerela. The bench mark is the dosa, sambar lentils and rasam soup. *'I tried these for the first time since returning from Cochin. Lovely'.* RC. *'Lentils, gourds and light spicing means inexpensive ingredients and the cost here is minimal. Two of us filled up for £28 inc Cobra'*RL. Set thali (Sun) £8.95. House wine £8. Hours: NOON-3, 6-11 Mon-Thur, Sun; NOON-3pm, 6-11.30 Fri, Sat. Branch: Sree Krishna Inn 332 Kingston Road, Ewell, Surrey 020 8393 0445

Leatherhead

LAL AKASH NEW ENTRANT

31 High St, Leatherhead 01372 377000

'Were very impressed, modern decor and smartly dressed waiters. Onion Bhajia - four small spheres, very light and crisp. Butter Chicken Tikka - very rich and good, but spicier than most Butter Chickens. King Prawn Malakhasi - Chef's Special - rather like a Korma but richer. Very good Mushroom Rice with generous amount of chopped button mushrooms. Brinjal Bhajee - large, well cooked and spiced chunks. Gobi Bhajee - excellent. All portions about right. The restaurant was nearly full all the time, although service was professional and efficient it would have been even better if there had been just a few smiles.' HC. *'All the dishes we had were wonderful,*

three starters, all served with generous garnishes of salad. Three main course which were very good, again generous portions and side dishes which kept up the standard. Super Naan, really puffed up and charred, far too many are served up in an anaemic state. Mushroom Rice – particularly good, light and fluffy, exactly the right texture.' HC..

Mitcham

CHAK 89 — **NEW ENTRANT**

Bond Road, Mitcham — 020 8646 2177

Opened in 2005 by Fukhera Khalid. Seats a huge 140 diners and serves Punjabi food: Tawa Chicken dishes, Garlic and Chilli Fish and Grilled Talapia being house specials. Fukhera also has an adjoining banqueting room. Weddings and parties can be catered for in this elegant room, up to 600 people. Licensed: stocks Cobra, £2.50 a pint, house wine £10 a bottle. Price Check: Popadom free, CTM £6.00, Pullao Rice £2.00. Hours: 6 - 12, Friday and Saturday to 1. Monday closed.

Morden (Greater London)

INDIAN VILLAGE

10 Morden Ct Pde, London Rd — 020 8640 8556

Good curryhouse where you might get a discount if you show them this *Guide*.

BLUE JUNCTION

2 Crown Parade, Morden — 020 8540 2583

Opened summer 2005, as primarily a contemporary bar. Its outdoor seating enhances its popularity as a stop for after-work drinks and weekend parties. At lunchtimes there is a mixture of European and Indian dishes eg. Lamb Kofte Burger £4.95, served with a yoghurt sauce, salads and sandwiches. Gourmet Wrap £3.95, Roti,or Naan with Spicy Lamb, Chicken or Paneer & Pea fillings served with lime pickle & yoghurt. Or there is the Balti Bowl:£4.95. In the evenings they serve a classical Indian menu. An old friend of this Guide and now restaurant critic on The Guardian, Humayun Hussain has even commented on the *'excellent vegetable dishes'* and he likes the chef: *There's much to like about Chef Sebastian Fernandes menu'.* HH. Here are some of the evening dishes: Lollipop Chicken £3.50, a starter of chicken drumsticks dipped in lightly spiced gramflour batter and fried. Lamb

Dum Biriani £8.95, lamb sautéed in Indian herbs & spices, cooked with basmati rice and mint leaves. Raarha Chicken £7.95, a Punjabi delicacy made with chicken, minced lamb, ginger, garlic & fresh chillies. Paneer Tikka Shashlik £8.50, cubes of paneer marinated in a yoghurt-based masala, with peppers, onions & tomatoes. Kerelan King Prawn Moilee £9.95, A Kerelan-style dish from the west coast of India. Sautéed king prawns with curry leaves, mustard & Indian spices cooked in traditionally spiced coconut milk. Price Check: Popadoms £1.95, Naan £1.95, CTM £7.50, Tarka Dhal £3.95. Hours: 11 - 11 M to Th, -2AM Fri. 2PM-2AM Sat; 4-11 Suns. <www.bluejunction.co.uk>

Motspur Park (Greater London)

MOTSPUR TANDOORI

365 West Rd, Motspur Park 020 8949 4595

Good curryhouse where you might get a discount if you show them this *Guide.*

New Malden (Greater London)

CHARLIE'S INDIAN CUISINE

276 Burlington Rd, New Malden 020 8949 7476

Ditto.

Newdigate (nr Dorking)

ALI RAJ

Parkgate Road, Newdigate 01306 631 664

Established 1994. Fully licensed. IT is on a country road near Gatwick. We occasionally turn up at the Ali Raj on the way back from a week in Spain. We tell them of our curry-desert holiday. Typically, the waiters haven't been to Spain, so we tell them to go for a week on a cheap charter flight and consider opening a restaurant! On our last visit, it was very late, probably nearing midnight and as we approached the bar lights were still on. We stopped right outside the door (probably on yellow lines - but hey! only curb crawling curryholics are likely to be driving about at this time of night! Was the chef still there? We were in luck! We had already decided on the plane over a G & T, that if they were still open and would accept a takeaway order, we would not be fussy and just order simple dishes, like curry and rice, no Tikka, Tandoori or Naan - far too complicated. So, Chicken Dhansak £6.25 including Pullao Rice and King Prawn Jalfrezi £8.00 was ordered. While we stood at the bar, eagerly waiting for the brown paper bag containing our feast to emerge from the kitchen, the waiters cleared tables and polished glasses. We told them we had been to Majorca and dropped heavy hints that perhaps they should go to Majorca as the British holiday maker was in need of a good curry house (there are some bad ones, in Magaluf and Palma Nova, however, on our last trip we found a lovely Indian restaurant in Palma, called Basmati, it is near the Oliver fruit and vegetable market). After a short wait our takeaway appeared and off we went. I must keep a plastic fork and spoon with napkins in the glove compartment of the car for our next visit! During the summer the owner grows tomatoes in the back garden. Large plants line the perimeter, heavy with ripening fruit. I don't think you can eat in the garden which is a shame as it has a very sunny aspect. Sunday Buffet: 12 - 2.30, adults £7.95, children £4.95. Minimum Charge: £10.00. Menu Snapshot: Chicken Chat £2.95, in a light tangy sauce; Ranghani £6.50, chicken with honey and ginger; Sundorbon £6.85, chicken, prawns, sweet and sour; Bengal Fish Korai £7.10; Sag Paneer £2.50; Mushroom Rice £2.60. Price Check: Popadom 40p, CTM £6.20, Pullao Rice £1.80. Hours: 12 - 2.30/6 - 12.

Oxted

GURKHA KITCHEN AWARD WINNER AND A-LIST

111 Station Rd, East Oxted 01883 722621

Oxted town is divided by the railway, like Woking, which is very irritating. We drove up and down Station Road West twice before we realised about the other Station Road, not so easily reached by car, on the other side of the tracks. We arrived at 8pm and our coats were taken immediately by the waiter, who sat us in the reception/waiting area. The floor is boarded, which makes it slightly noisy, but the whole look is very elegant. Beautiful hand-forged black steel chairs, the seat and back were wickered, the seat then covered in a small patterned carpet with a fringe on two sides. White linen tablecloths and napkins, large, fragile wine glasses, drinking receptacles for the connoisseur, their slender stems making a lovely bottle of Argentinian Norton red wine the more enjoyable. I asked our waiter if a lot get broken. 'Yes,' he said proudly, 'and I break the most.' At the back of the restaurant an area is decorated with a small roof as in a Nepalese village, fishing net and basket hanging from the wall. The food is accurate cooked Nepalese. But it isn't earthy village food. It's slightly evolved and modern, yet indisputably Nepalese. *'Yes, it's spot on. Extremely interesting menu with not one dish that appears on a standard high street curry house menu. We had first class starters: Bhutuwa (excellent melt-in-the-mouth chicken livers stir fried in a delicately spiced light sauce served in a small wafer basket), Vegetable Khaja (filo pastry wrapped up like spring roll, but not so thick with vegetable filling and mint and mustard dressing. They were cut in half, diagonally, a small green salad with the dressing decorating the centre of the plate, the Khaja in four corners. Extremely mild, but tasty. Main dishes (Mooli Chicken, Piro Lamb and Hariyo Machha – monkfish wrapped in spinach prepared in a mild, dry fruit sauce) were all superb, with the flavouring of each being totally different and distinct from the others. Portions not large, but sufficient. Prices marginally higher than average.'* MW. *'Nepalese cuisine served here in sophisticated modern surroundings. A mystery into the unknown as nothing whatsoever on the menu was familiar. However, fortified by large bottles of Kathmandu beer, we chose dishes that sounded good. All were, nicely spiced and tasty. Only the breads were disappointing but perhaps they were meant to be like that – who knows! Well worth a visit, helpful, friendly waiters. Only £60 for three – worth every penny!'* CS. *'Friends 40th birthday celebration. Large party of over 20 adults, plus 10 children. Sunday evening buffet. Food excellent as was ambience and service. Looked after our noisy group often and extremely well.'* SO. Palungo Sag, steamed spinach sautéed with fenugreek seeds; the spinach was fresh. Gurkha Aloo, diced delicately, prepared in turmeric and cumin seeds, mild potato cubes fried a little brown on the sides. Rashilo Bhat, rice cooked with bay leaf, cardamom, garnished with brown onion £1.95, light, fluffy and flavoursome. Joano Patre, bread with carom seed £2, just like a Nan really, quartered, very good. Golbeda Ko Achar, fresh tomato pickle, spicy, a good accompaniment to all dishes. Everything was delivered in separate white china dishes, the plates hot. An **A-LIST** restaurant. Sunday buffet 1-10pm. Hours: 12-2.30/6-11 (11.30 on Fri. & Sat.).

Redhill

EXOTICA TANDOORI

18 Cromwell Road, Redhill 01737 778624

Good curryhouse where you might get a discount if you show them this *Guide*.

Reigate

VILLAGE BRASSERIE

10 West Street, Reigate 01737 245695

Good curryhouse where you might get a discount if you show them this *Guide*.

Richmond-upon-Thames (Greater London)

ORIGIN ASIA TOP 100

100 Kew Road, Richmond 0208 9480509

'*What a gem this is. Situated on two levels inside, the lower level extends past the kitchen, which is semi open-plan to the restaurant, allowing you to see the chefs practising their art in front of your eyes as you pass. There is also a very pleasant alfresco dining area at the front on the restaurant. The quality of the food was superb with a number of innovative and authentic tasting dishes on offer. The Bater Khada Masala (marinated quails pot roasted in onion and tomato masala with crushed dried mango) was truly outstanding, as were the Lehsooni Whitebait (whitebait marinated in crushed garlic and caraway and then gram flour batter fried), Bhutta Kebab (kebab of fresh baby corn wrapped in a spiced mash of corn and potatoes) and the Gilafi Seekh Kebabs (char grilled minced lamb kebabs wrapped in fresh aromatic vegetables) for starters. For main courses, the Lamb Shank Xacuti (cooked in a hot and spicy Xacuti masala) was sensational along with the Tawaki Bathak (duck breast pot roasted with coconut, cumin, mint and coriander) to name but a few. The service was excellent as well, with the staff coping admirably with our group of 12 raucous friends enjoying a stag night together. In fact we enjoyed it so much that two of us slipped in the day afterwards for a 'light' lunch! Obviously our behaviour couldn't have been too bad the night before, as we were not banished on sight! Overall opinion – truly excellent and innovative. I would not hesitate to recommend this establishment or to return here. In fact if they have managed to maintain this quality of food and service I would not be at all surprised to see them nudging their way into the Top 100!* s.o.

Staines

ANCIENT RAJ

157 High Street, Staines 01784 457099

Good curryhouse where you might get a discount if you show them this *Guide*.

Surbiton (Greater London)

AGRA TANDOORI

142 Ewell Road, Surbiton 020 8399 8854

Ditto.

AJANTA

114 Ewell Road, Surbiton 020 8399 1262

Ditto.

JORAJ

163 Ewell Road, Surbiton 020 8390 0251

Ditto.

Tolworth (Greater London)

JAIPUR

90 The Broadway, Tolworth 020 8399 3619

The external decor makes this venue unmissable. Its huge pink stone pillars make it stand out, a fact not unnoticed by the local council, who in the early days spent a considerable amount of time, and presumably money, trying to force owner S.U. Ali to remove them. Fortunately bureaucracy lost, and the pillars remain; indeed, they continue inside, giving a very Indian feel to the interior. India's Jaipur is the pink city, where every building is made from pink sandstone. Naturally the Jaipur's theme is pink too, with *'an amazing sugar-pink decor, with friezes of dancing ladies seemingly sculpted out of the wall.'* DD. *'Thoroughly enjoyable.'* DRC. *'One of my regular haunts.'* PD. You might get a discount if you show them this *Guide.*

Virginia Water

VICEROY OF INDIA

4 Station Approach 01344 843157

'We moved ***to the curry desert of Devon from Berkshire and regularly ate at the Viceroy-of India in Virginia Water, a great exponent of the skills of cooking great Indian food'*** AF You might get a discount if you show them this *Guide.*

Warlingham

INDIA DINING NEW ENTRANT

6 The Green, Warlingham 01883 625 905

Decorated in a modern style, white linen, cream walls, deep brown chairs, Asad Khan opened his restaurant in 2003. Chef Rajeev Kumar has created an exciting menu. Menu Snapshot: Grilled Sea Bream Fillet £5.95, with pomegranate extract; Soft shell crab £8.95, with spicy hand picked white crab meat; Tandoori Chops £10.95, red deer with crushed fennel and cumin seed; Chicken Cakes £4.95, pan-fried with basil and ginger; Spiced Lentil Fritters £4.50, served with crispy spinach and sweet tamarind; Fresh Grilled Wild Prawns £24.95, with stir fry of vegetables and masala mash potato; Lamb Shank £10.95, braised in coriander, onion and Greek yoghurt, served with steamed rice; Hyderbadi style Biriani £8.95, with a seasonal vegetable with mixed vegetable raitha; Garlic flavoured spinach £3.50; Bread Selection £3.50 , mini plain naan, mini garlic naan and mini paratha. Licensed: stocks Cobra, £2.75 a pint, house wine £9.95, however, for those who enjoy a good glass of wine, please have a look at the extensive wine list - you won't be disappointed. Sunday Lunch: two courses £9.95, from 12.30 to 3. Early Dining: two courses and coffee £10.95, from Sunday to Thursday, 5.30 to 7. Delivery: 4 miles, £15 minimum. Service Charge: 10% of parties of six or more. Price Check: Popadom 50p, CTM £6.50, Pullao Rice £2.50. Hours: 12 - 2.30/ 5.30 - 11. <www.indiadining.co.uk

Walton-on-Thames

ORIENTAL CURRY CENTRE

13 Church Street, Walton 01932 222317

Good curryhouse where you might get a discount if you show them this *Guide.*

Weybridge

GOLDEN CURRY

132 Oatlands Dr, Weybridge 01932 846931

Good curryhouse where you might get a discount if you show owner Enayeth Khan this *Guide.*

THE HUSSAIN

47 Church St, Weybridge 01932 844720

Ditto if you show owner M Suleman this *Guide.*

Whyteleafe

CURRY GARDEN

242 Godstone Road 01883 627237

Ditto if you show owner Akhlaqur Rahman or Moynoor Rashid this *Guide.*

Woking

JAIPUR TOP 100

49 Chertsey Road, Woking 01483 772626

Jaipur is the pink city of India. This elegant 60-seater, established in 1993, is owned by Nizam Ali and his two delightful sisters, Reggi and Sophi, all of whom I met in their gorgeous Sylhet home, during a monsoon storm a few years ago. Menu Snapshot: King Prawn Butterfly £3.95, fried on breadcrumbs, Raj Badak Shaslik £4.95, duck with capsicum, onion, ground cumin, Panir Shaslik £3.95 - curd cheese, capsicum and onions in tangy sauce; Lal Masley Tava £8.95, red salmon with tomato, onions and aromatic spices, served sizzling; Lamb Nepali £5.95, hot, fiery dish of red chilli, potato and yoghurt; Chutney Tray £2.00 – includes mango chutney, coconut chutney, lime pickle, mint sauce, tamarind sauce and onion salad.Takeaway: 10% discount. Delivery: £12 minimum. Price Check: Popadom 50p, CTM £5.95, Pullao Rice £2.50. Hours: 12 - 2.30/6 - 11.30. <www.jaipurrestaurant.co.uk>

KHYBER PASS

18 The Broadway, Woking 01483 764710

Good curryhouse where you might get a discount if you show manager Jafar Abdul Wahab this *Guide.*

LOTUS OF BENGAL

45 Goldsworth Rd, Woking 01483 766226

Good curryhouse where you might get a discount if you show owner Mostaque Rahman this *Guide.*

Worcester Park

MUNAL — NEW ENTRANT

76 Central Rd, Worcester Park 020 8330 3511

Amrit Thapa owns this seventy-four seater, Nepalese restaurant has done so since 1998. Lets see what chef Mahesh Rana can and does cook up for us: Momo £3.05, meat dumplings lightly spiced Nepalese style, served with salad; Fried Squid £3.15, marinated in herbs and deep-fried; Bhuteko Prawns £3.15, fried prawns, highly spiced. Minimum Charge: £12. Licensed: stocks Cobra, £2.70 a pint, house wine £9.95 a bottle. Delivery: 3 miles. Takeaway: 10% discount, minimum £10. Price Check: Popadom 50p, CTM £5.90, Pullao Rice £2.20. Hours: 12 - 2.30 / 6 - 11.30, Friday and Saturday to 12. <<www.munalrestaurant.co.uk>

SUSSEX

Area: South
Population: 1,512,000
Adjacent Counties:
Hants, Kent, Surrey

This county has been divided into East and West Sussex since the 12th century, and obtained separate county councils in 1888. For the purposes of this Guide we combine the two.

Barnham

PASSAGE TO INDIA

15 The Square, Barnham 01243 555064

In a small village, Mr Muhammed Yousuf Islam's 58-seater is a well established curry house enjoyed by its locals.Hours: 12-2.30/6-11.30. (12 -Fri/Sat.).

Bexhill-on-Sea

SHIPLU

109 London Road, Bexhill 01424 219159

Good curryhouse where you might get a discount if you show owner Abdul Kalam Azad this *Guide.*

Brighton

400 restaurants in this town and most including the Indians are overpriced for tourists. Here are the best of a poor bunch (see also Hove)

BALTI HUT

2 Coombe Terrace, Brighton 01273 681280

30-seater, est. '97 by Dost Mohammed, serving formula curries and Balti specials from c£5. *'Informative menu, with plenty of unusual delights. I used my naan to mop up every last trace of my Tandoori Nowab, excellently cooked and very delicious. Forget location prejudice.'* N&D. Service 10%. Hours: 6-11.30pm (12am on Sat.)

BAYLEAF

104 Western Road, Brighton 01273 773804

Established in 1998. Seats 87. *'Bingo, an oasis in the wilderness of mostly mediocre formula curry houses in Brighton.*

Bills itself as an Indian Brasserie and it's certainly different from yer average eaterie. Light airy room with tiled floor, polished wood tables and a cool blend of jazz and blues background music. Not a Balti, Pakora or Vindaloo in sight – about 12 starters and 12 mains, of mostly unusual dishes. The price for mains (about £6.90 per dish) was inclusive of side dishes of Dhal and Vegetable of the Day, so it was pretty good value. Food was uniformly excellent. Chicken Chaat gets a special recommendation – a really good interpretation of what is rapidly becoming in some places a very hackneyed (and oily- ugh!) dish.' SM. *'An unusual and refreshing different menu, although for the unadventurous some standard curries are available. I had Chicken Chaat followed by a Bayleaf Khasi – fresh lamb pieces with onion and red chillies, which came with Dhal and a Vegetable Curry. Good quantities and the quality of food was excellent. Offered a drink on the house.'* MK. Specials include: Chicken Nilgiri (with spinach and mint).. Takeaway: 15% discount. Delivery: £10 min, 3-miles. Hours: 12-3/5.30-11.30; Sat. 12-12.

DELI INDIA NEW ENTRANT

81 Trafalgar Street, Brighton 01273 699985

An Indian delicatessen and teashop providing Indian meals and snacks, teas and drinks. Owned by Jamie Keen and Farida Pathan, a cook since the age of 13, rustles up a regularly changing menu to eat in or take away which will always include at least two meat curries such as Chicken Kalya, and Minced lamb curry, both £4.95 and two vegetarian curries, eg: Gujarati vegetables and Kidney bean and pepper, £4.40 and at least one dhal all served with either basmati rice or two chapattis in the price. Also available are savoury snacks, dips and soups and Indian sweets such as halwa, gulab jamon and naan khataay (Indian shortbread). Deli items include a wide range of spices, chutneys and oils. Recipes and advice are available. *'I've eaten here several times and have thoroughly enjoyed the experience each time. Not only is there a wide and varied choice of delicious food but there is also an outstanding range of teas'* (99 varieties) *'the like of which I have never seen anywhere else. I have found the portions to be a good size and the prices very reasonable. Furthermore having the chance to purchase teas and ingredients for my own home makes each trip very enjoyable. I definitely recommend this to anybody with a fondness for good wholesome curry.'* PL. *'The vegetable thali lunch including 2 x veg curry, dhal, rice, veg samosa, two bhajis, two dips, chapatti: was excellent, really good value for money at £6.00 and a great way to taste different dishes. It all tasted fresh, healthy and home-cooked. It's great to have good quality Indian food in such nice, bright surroundings and also be able to buy ingredients in the shop or buy some food to takeaway. I'm a big fan of Indian food and definitely recommend Deli India.'* JP. <www.deliindia.com>

GOA SPICE OF LIFE NEW ENTRANT

5, Richmond Pde, Brighton 01273 818149

'Menu Unusual – my first Goan Restaurant with some most unusual choices Quality Starters outstanding, main courses good Quantity Adequate; Decor most peculiar 1970s retro with yellow and green wooden panelled walls Service very friendly but excruciatingly slow at a time when they weren't even busy. Background music rather intrusive. Tables reasonably spaced out. Starters: Popadoms and chutney – not the freshest. Meat samosa – huge portions stuffed with very spicy meat which was very dry and course but tasted wonderful; Chicken Tikka, well marinated with an intense taste. Main Course: Chicken Xacuti – Chicken not marinated, in a spicy coconut sauce; Chicken Vindaloo, fruity chilli flavour to the sauce which was ultra hot but rather lacking in variety. Side dish: Aloo Achar. Accompaniment: Pullau Rice, Naan. Bill: £24.89 plus £2.50 tip. Total: £27.39. Mark 7/10' G&MP.

MEMORIES OF INDIA

9 First Floor, Brighton Marina 01273 600088

'An unusual place to find an excellent Indian restaurant. A large well decorated emporium has plenty of good ambience. The staff and helpful friendly and attentive. We only had main courses, the Chana, Chicken Bhuna, and CTM were all good. The Chicken Dhansak was exceptional. Side dishes of Bombay potato and pakoras were also up to standard. If there is any slight criticism then it is that the prices were slightly high, but in view of the location, décor and quality it is a minor point.' AG. Hours; 12 - 12.

Brighton Marina

Memories, Brighton

POLASH

19 York Place, Brighton 01273 626221

Formula 60-seater, owned and managed by Nosir Ullah who might give you a a discount if you show him this *Guide*.. Licensed but **BYO**, no corkage. Takeaway: 10% off. Del: £10 min. Hours: 12-2/6-12.

Burgess Hill

SHAPLA

226 London Rd, Burgess Hill 01444 232493

No airs and graces at this restaurant, but boy did the curry hit the spot. It was marvellous. Chicken Tikka Massala and Karai Chicken were exceptional.' N&D

Chichester

MASALA GATE NEW ENTRANT

8 St Pancras, Chichester 01243 776008

'An immediate warm welcome received from the proprietor, Murad and upon entering into conversation about his menu which is definitely different, it transpired that he has been trained under Marco Pierre White in London, and we could see this influence with the stunning presentation of the the starters... vive la difference! One member of staff, unusual for an Indian restaurant, a young lady, not English but Slovakian, with her charming accent, was the very model of a professional hostess, immediately seeing to customers with drinks and Popadoms. To finish our meal, most unusual, a choice of Homemade Desserts, including Cardamom Creme Brulee and Cinnamon Panacotta with sweet chilli strawberries - has to be tried to be appreciated.' CVF.

MEMORIES OF INDIA

Old Bridge Rd (A259), Bosham Roundabout, Chichester 01243 572234

Abdul Jalil's formula curryhouse is nicely decorated, peach walls, tablecloths and napkins, and blue carpet. Separate bar, highly polished floor, cane chairs and tables, green plants. *'Had a takeaway and despite the decor which made us think it would be expensive we found it to be very reasonable. My only complaint, Sag Paneer was made with cheddar. Helpful staff, despite being busy.'* SW. Specials: Lamb Podina, with garlic, fresh mint and coriander; Ayre Jalfrey, Bengali fish cooked with chillies, garlic, peppers in a hot spicy sauce. Takeaway: 15% off. Min charge: £13.50. Hours: 12-2.30/6-12.

SHAPLA TANDOORI

Eastgate Square, Chichester 01243 775978

'On second floor above old swimming pool. Very functional feel with bright pink emulsion painted walls. Usual menu with handful of unusual dishes – King Prawns in Mustard Sauce. Food well spiced, good chunks of garlic, chilli and excellent Nan bread. Service was a bit "dump it all on the table and run". Still worth including.' CC. *'Visited here twice before, being the closest to the Festival Theatre. Typical curryhouse fayre but done passably well. I enjoyed their Chicken Dhansak (quite hot) and yes the Nan bread is excellent. Good value for money too.'* DC.

Crawley

BLUE INDIA NEW TO OUR TOP 100

47 High Street Crawley 01293 446655

We ate here before a flight from Gatwick. The portions were so big, (and delicious) we had the overs packed up and took them on the flight with us to be enjoyed next day on the terrace accompanied by a bottle of Rioja – lovely!Extracts from Kirti Rewart's menu: Appetisers: Crab Malabar cooked with spices in white wine and mango, topped with cheese, £5.95; Salmon Shah, flavoured with mustard, dill, coriander and fresh lime, £4.95. Magic Mushrooms coated in lightly spiced mince lamb and bread crumbs, fried until golden brown., £3.95; Shingara (Vegetable Samosa) £3.25; Bollywood Shank: lamb cooked in a rich tomato and coriander sauce, cooked with spicy mince lamb, £12.50; Chicken Kama-Sutra. Lovers beware this is an aphrodisiac. *('didn't work the time we had it!')* RCF. Half a spring chicken cooked with wine; Chettinad, a dish comprising 18 different spices. A choice of chicken or lamb - in a hot sauce of ginger, garlic and coconut, a delicacy of the Chettinad homes in Madras; Shatkari (a regional dish of Sylhet - Bangladesh), cooked in calamansi juice, lemon leaf and naga chilli ...a crisp, hot and slightly tangy flavour Akhni biriani, cooked with Himilayan basmati rice in a sealed pot, flavoured with cardamom, cinnamon, cloves and rose water served with a medium bhuna sauce. Wide choice of choice of vegetable dishes and breads. Desserts: Some Inidan desserts on the menu but we liked the Menage a Trois: a mix of white and black chocolate mousse topped with dark chocolate. *'Restaurant is bright and spacious and is aimed*

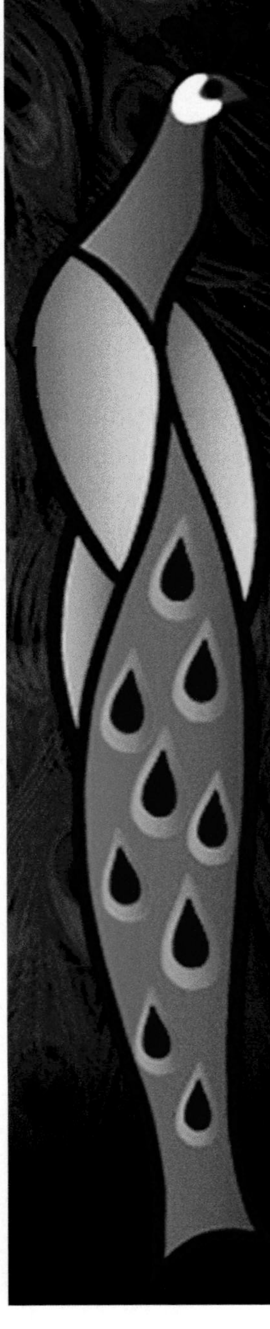

Blue Mango, Crawley, and their delightful peacock

more up-market than average. Menu includes a good choice of Chef's Specialities as well as the standard range of curries. We started with a large tray of small triangular plain and spicy Popadoms £1 including mint sauce, chutney and tomato relish. Bottles of Kingfisher were £3 each and a glass of house white wine at £4, seemed expensive...' We agree! *'Achari Jolpa Chicken - with peppers, tomatoes, coriander, Indian achar (pickle) and olives. My companions, Duck Xacutti - in masala with roasted aniseed, javantri (nutmeg), fenugreek, red Goan chillies, coconut and cinnamon; Macher Jhol Bengali - fish curry in a hot sauce, (a little too hot for my friend). We shared a Sag Aloo, Bhindi Bhaji, Pullao Rice and a tray of various small Naan breads. We still felt hungry, so finished with Carrot Cake and Indian Summer - mixed fruit, both served with ice cream. We all thought the food excellent and very tasty. Service was friendly and efficient.'* MPK. And so do we and we have pleasure in elevating Blue Mango into our **TOP 100** category. Hours: 12 - 2.30 / 6 - 11 daily <www.blueindia.co.uk> Branch Haywards Heath.

TAJ MAHAL — NEW ENTRANT

2 High Street, Crawley — 01293 529755

Crawley's oldest Indian eatery, it opened in 1969. But owner Belayat Hussain, who owns two other restaurants, doesn't stand still. In 2004 he invested £600,000 on a major refurbishment which transformed the quaint local eatery into a modern and bright environment where diners can enjoy the same quality of food that has remained consistent for over 35-years. The 150-seater is divided over two levels, the lower of which has warm golden yellow walls, wine red high back chairs and sleek hardwood flooring that gives a polished, clean-cut finish. It also coordinates with the wood partition and banister that lead up to the upper level of the restaurant, which is more traditional with deep red carpeting and fitted cushioned seats. There is a miniature waterfall, which is enclosed in two fibreglass sheets and a couple of bubble tanks behind the slick granite bar. The large glass entrance windows let in a bright, fresh and natural ambience. Managed by Rajpal Singh with the kitchens under Head Chef, Gurudath Panapil, who trained at New Delhi's Taj Hotel. His specialty is Mangalorean cuisine, from the southern state of Karnataka, but at Taj Mahal he cooks up treats from across the country. Traditional Mangalorean dishes like Kori Gassi are served up alongside more popular options like Saag Gosht and Chicken Shaslik. *Puja Vedi, ed Tandoori Magazine..* <www.tajmahalcrawley.co.uk>

ZARI

214, Ifield Dr, Ifield, Crawley 01293 553009

'The Zari is wonderfully different – up market, classy, clean, subtle light, dimmer switches, high back light wood chairs. Generous portions – two Rice and Sag Aloo £2.30 for three people. Although not advertised I often order a portion of masala sauce for my veggie daughter. Takeaway for four £39.95.' BW. Starters include : Machli Papeta na Pattice, flakes of fish, mashed potato, herbs and spices. Murgh Tikka Mariali,spicy green chicken tikka. Main course: Zari Jhalak Machli,crunchy pomfret on bed of crispy fried onions and aubergine salad, served with tangy sauce. Hours: 12-2.30/6-11.30.

Eastbourne

INDIAN PARADISE

166 Seaside, Eastbourne 01323 735408

Good curryhouse where you might get a discount if you show owner A Khalique this *Guide*.

Hailsham

RAJDUTT NEW ENTRANT

46 High Street, Hailsham 01323 842847

Originally opened in 1978 then taken over in 1990. Abdul Ali heads the management team, serving seventy in two rooms. Head Chef, Abdul Malik's 'Specials' are very popular and include: Chicken Silsila - chunks of chicken breast in fresh herbs and spices. Takeaway: 10% discount. Licensed: stocks Cobra £3.90 a pint bottle, house wine £9.95 a bottle. Menu Snapshot: Fish Tikka £4.95, marinated salmon barbecued; Kurzi Lamb £69.95, whole roasted leg of lamb with accompaniments; Sag Panir £2.65; Cucumber Raitha £1.65. Air conditioned. Hours: 12 - 2/6 - 11, Friday and Saturday to 11.30.

Hastings

SPICE OF INDIA

177a Queens Rd, Hastings 01424 439493

Good curryhouse where you might get a discount if you show them this *Guide*.

Haywards Heath

BLUE INDIA NEW TO OUR TOP 100

18 The Broadway 01444 410020

The menu, and all details are the same as its Crawley Branch , see alongside. We are pleased to elevate this branch to our **TOP 100.** Hours: 12 - 2.30 / 6 - 11 daily. <www.blueindia.co.uk> Branch Crawley.

CURRY INN

58 Commercial Square 01444 415142

Opened in 1987 by Abru Miah, His restaurant seats 58 diners in one dining room. *'We went for the Times £5 lunch. Bill for four of us came to £ 57 with tip, but draft Kingfisher was £3.90 per pint so that helped explain the difference. Portions were generous for the price, esp. chicken tikka starters. Very good average for the area.'* C & MC.. Delivery: 5 miles, £20 minimum. Licensed: stocks Cobra and Kingfisher £3.80 a pint bottle, house wine £9.40 a bottle. Price Check: Popadom 60p, CTM £6.40, Pullao Rice £1.90. Hours: 12 - 2.30/ 6 - 11.30, Fri / Sat to 12. Branch: Curry Inn, Station Approach, Heathfield: 01435 863 227. You might get a discount if you show Mr Miah this *Guide.*

Heathfield

MR INDIA

28 High Street, Heathfield 01435 866 114

Manager Shah F Athar, wrote to Pat, telling him that Mr India took great pride in the way they presented their style of Indian cuisine and would like his customers to comment. So reports please!

Hove

ASHOKA

95 Church Road, Hove 01273 734193

Good curryhouse where you might get a discount if you show them this *Guide.*

CURRY MAHAL NEW ENTRANT

169 Portland Road Hove 01273 779125

The Curry Mahal seats a staggering 100 diners in three air-conditioned dining rooms. Opened originally in 1971 and taken over in 1999 by Shykul Malique. His restaurant served Bangladeshi styled curries and accompaniments.Menu Snapshot: Chatga Prawns £13.95, king prawns, marinated in a mixture of spices and cooked in a clay oven, curried in medium hot sauce with onions, green peppers, tomatoes and coriander; Komlapuriya Chicken or Lamb £10.95, flavoured with Grande Marnier and mandarins; Lamb Satkora £11.95, cooked with tender slices of lamb, satkora, tomatoes, onions, garlic and garnished with fresh green chillies and coriander, fairly hot. Licensed: stocks Cobra, £4.15 pint bottle, house wine £9.95 a bottle. Takeaway: 10% discount. Delivery: £15 minimum. Price Check: Popadom 50p, CTM £8.95, Pullao Rice £2.15. Hours: 12 - 2.30, Friday closed and 5.30 - 11.30.

GANGES

93 Church Road, Hove 01273 728292

Good curryhouse where you might get a discount if you show them this *Guide.*

IKARIM'S TANDOORI

15 Blatchington Road, Hove 01273 739780

Ditto.

KASHMIR

71 Old Shoreham Rd, Hove 01273 739677

The Kashmir has been owned by Subab Miah since 1979, so it's not surprising that he has built up a steady trade with many regular customers, who look forward to his 'sale inducements' which include FREE Onion Bhajia or Vegetable Samosa, when you spend £10 or more on a takeaway – even better, a FREE Bombay Potato or Mixed Vegetable Curry, when you spend £15 or more on a takeaway or delivery - wow! But it doesn't end there - Special Offers (Sunday to Thursday) buy two Vegetarian Specials (all £3.00 each) and get a third free! Show Subab this *Guide* and you might get a further discount. .Del: 3 miles, £10 min. Price Check: Popadom 50p, CTM £5.20, Pullao Rice £2.10. Hours: 7 - 12.

Lewes

SHANAZ

83 High Street, Lewes 01273 488038

Good curryhouse where you might get a discount if you show them this *Guide.*

Newhaven

LAST VICEROY

4 Bridge Street, Newhaven 01273 513308

AS Ahmed's fifty-seater opened way back in 1986. Since our last *Guide* he has morphed his venue from the Last Viceroy to Viceroy, presumably in the interest of progress. Well you would be forgiven if you thought his menu was stuck in that era. But more morphing, and hey presto, there are two menus, one with Korma to Madras for the diehards, and the other with more useful dishes such as: Goat Cheese Samosa £4.50, pastry parcels stuffed with spinach and delicately spiced goat's cheese; Jalapeno Delight £4.95, whole jalapenos stuffed with cream and cheese, fried with coated breadcrumbs; Chicken Lazeez £7.95, fillets of chicken breast in a silky smooth almond and tamarind honey sauce; Mahi Monk Fish £8.95, chunks of monk, prepared in a rich lentil sauce; Lamb Shank £8.95, garnished with curry leaves, coconut milk, mustard and black cumin seeds; Shan e Pumpkin £3.95, cubes of pumpkin spiced with fresh curry leaves. You might get a discount if you show them Mr Ahmed this *Guide.*. Delivery: £15 minimum in Newhaven area, £20 minimum, 5 miles for other areas. Price Check: Popadom 75p, CTM £7.50, Pullao Rice £2.20. Hours: 5.30-11.30.. <www.viceroynewhaven.co.uk>

Nutbourne

TAMARIND AND MOONLIGHT EXPRESS **NEW TO OUR TOP100**

Main Road, Nutbourne 01243 573149

Set in this small village, in a freestanding building which could once nave been a pub, whose distinction is a brown and cream Pullman railway carriage standing forlornly at the back of the yard. They plan to refurbish it or buy a new one, and hey presto we will have the Orient Express in Nutborne. Think what stylish occasions could take place on board. Ample parking puts one in the mood to enjoy the food. Inside ambience is welcoming as are the staff. There is a wide range of choices on the menu, and cooking is as distinctive as the Pullman. We asked last time, should it be in our **TOP100 CATEGORY.** You said yes, and so be it. *'Our takeaway order was good, and we were very impressed with our subsequent dining-in. Extensive menu. My wife had Patrani Machli (salmon fillets with mild spices baked in foil), and she said it was among the best fish dishes she has ever had. I had the Goa Machli Curry also made with salmon and also excellent. Tarka Dhal and boiled rice were OK.'* RH

Peacehaven

INDIAN & NEPALESE SPICE & FLAVOUR **NEW ENTRANT**

314 South Coast Rd, Peacehaven 01273 585808

Faizur and Ayesha Choudhury own this restaurant, which they opened in 2002. Bright and airy restaurant decorated in citrus colours with a wooden floor and polished wood tables. Menu Snapshot: Chicken Bahar £5.95, with sliced mango; Lamb Korai £5.95, with green peppers, tomatoes, medium dry thick sauce; Dall Samba £2.95, sour and hot lentils; Cheese/Peshwari or Garlic Naan all £2.25. Nepali Dishes: Prawn and Duck Salad £3.25; Napali Beef £6.50, with garlic, peppers and tomatoes; Roast Chow Chow £6.50, noodles stir-fried with roast tikka chicken and lamb, medium hot or spicy; King Prawn tawa £7.50, shallow fried King prawns (in shell) with spices served with salad. Minimum Charge: £10. Licensed: stocks Cobra and Kingfisher, £1.95 a small bottle, house wine £7.95 a bottle. Price Check: Popadom 60p, CTM £5.95, Pullao Rice £2.25. Hours: 5 - 11.

Rye

SIMPLY SPICE **NEW ENTRANT**

5 High Street Rye 01797 224222

Originally called Tiger Coast. Head Chef: N Islam, holds regular 'Elvis' theme nights - better book for that one! His Simply Spice Tiger Grill at £12.95 and Modhu Murgh are his most popular dishes. Stocks Cobra, £3.95 a pint bottle, House Wine £11.95 a bottle. Delivery: 5 miles, £20 minimum. Price Check: Popadom 50p, CTM £6.95, Pullao Rice £2.10. Hours: 5.30 - 11.30. <www.rye-tourism.co.uk/simplyspice>

Seaford

BENGAL PALACE

30 Church Street 01323 899077

Established in 1987 by Eleas Hussain, who is also in charge of the kitchens, and he is also offering a

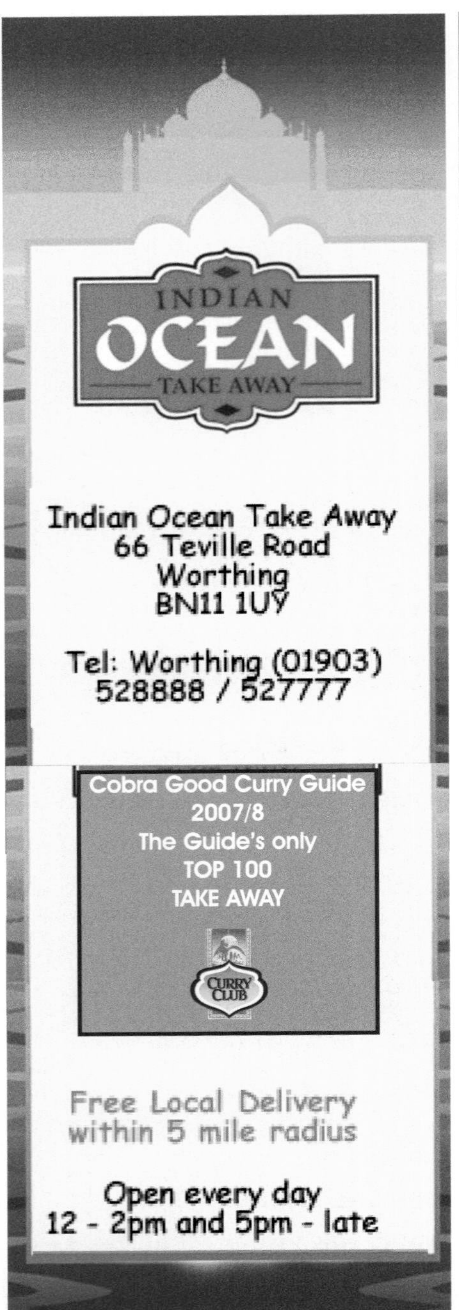

very generous discount to clients, who show their copy of this *Guide:* you will get 5% off your bill! Price Check: Popadom 75p, CTM £8.95, Pullao Rice £2.35. Hours: 12 - 2.30/5.30 - 11.30.

Uckfield

RAJDUTT — NEW ENTRANT

Eastbourne Road, Uckfield 01825 890 234

Owner, Amol Sil's restaurant seats seventy diners in three rooms and they have their own car park. Menu Snapshot: Amere Chicken £6.95 - mild sauce with mango, fresh cream and almonds; Lamb Nashille £7.95 - fillets of lamb in green chilli, ginger, spicy hot sauce; Tandoori Chef Specials £8.95 - chicken and lamb, skewered with tomatoes, capsicum and onion cooked in a brandy sauce; Murgh Noorani £7.95 - breast of chicken, stuffed with minced prawn in light herbs, finished in sweet, sour and hot sauce, served sizzling; Akbari Murgh £7.95 - tender chicken medallions smothered with pineapple, almonds, raisins, finished in a delicately ginger sauce. Interesting fish specialities: all £7.50 - Kalamari Vojon - squid in delicately spiced, fairly hot sauce with thinly sliced capsicum, onions, crushed chillies and crushed mustard seeds; Roop Chanda Biran - pomphret fried with light spices and covered with deep-fried onions and potatoes; Boal Dopiaza - fried chunks of boal with onions, in medium sauce. Takeaway: 10% discount. Licensed: stocks Cobra, Kingfisher, £3.90 a bottle, House Wine £7.95 a bottle. Price Check: Popadom 55p, CTM £6.75, Pullao Rice £1.75. Hours: 12 - 2/6 - 11, Saturday 5.30 - 11.30. Branch: Maloncho, Staplehurst, Kent; Malonco, Peacehaven, East Sussex and Raj, Calpe and Jeava, Spain.

Worthing

INDIAN OCEAN TAKEAWAY — NEW TO OUR TOP 100

66 Teville Road, Worthing 01903 528888

Located near Worthing main railway station. Established in 1998 by Yusuf Khan, who has clearly built up a loyal following, by giving them just what they want! These are just some of their comments: *'Indian Ocean was recommended by a friend. Food is very tasty and always cooked to perfection. Service is extremely polite and friendly.'* D. *'Not only is it across the road from where*

I live, the proprietor, his family and staff are always very polite and friendly. Very nice food, very tasty and plenty of it.' SB. *'Tasty, well priced food and goof polite service.'* JN. *'Delivery service is very quick.'* BF. *'The best Prawn Bhuna - £4.95.'* HE. Menu Snapshot: Mixed Starters £3.45 for two - Onion Bhajia, Lamb Tikka and Chicken Tikka, served with salad and mint yoghurt sauce; Chicken and Mushroom Curry £5.45; Keema and Peas Bhuna £5.45; Prawn and Mushroom Korma £5.45; Keema, Peshwari, Garlic, Panir, Spicy (chilli, garlic, coriander) and Kulcha (vegetable) Naan all £1.75. Desserts also available, from Chocolate Mousse to Raspberry Parfait - all £2.95 - just the way to finish off a spicy meal! Credit card accepted and over the phone, so no fiddling change with the delivery driver at the door. Delivery: 5 miles, £8 minimum. Price Check: Popadom 45p, CTM £5.95, Pullao Rice £1.75. Hours: 12 - 2/5 to late! <www.indianoceantakeaway.co.uk>

KUMARI NEW ENTRANT

171 Findon Road, Findon Valley,Worthing 01903 877376

'A polite "moan"(mild of course unlike my taste in curry!). "Observation" would be a better word. Disappointed as a Sussex resident to see Worthing not well represented in the 2004 Guide. No doubt the Guide would have to be twice the size if you put in every report, but in terms of good/ordinary/bad, I did write to you about Kumari (our preferred local), a good authentic Nepalese. Small family run, attention to detail, freshly cooked, (over) large helpings decent spices. Opened the shop next door as a Nepalese "gift shop"! Hard to see it doing too well on the outskirts of Worthing, but you cannot knock the effort. Aways worth a visit-cost £90 (with the freebie). Has raised over £2000 for the local St Barnabas hospice by dint of extra buffet night on last Tuesday of each month-always cooked fresh, not food sitting in tureens for hours on end. Out for a takeaway tonight. Cannot remember when I last had 3 curries in one week, life is on the up. Signing off for a "round the world in 74 days" trip, so will be suffering from curry deprivation on our return I fear.' C&MC.

SHAFIQUE'S

42 Goring Road, Worthing 01903 504035

Shafique Uddin opened in forty-eight seater restaurant , bearing his name in 1986. Thali's are good value: Tandoori Thali £12.30 - Chicken Tikka, Sheek Kebab, Tandoori Nibbles, Tandoori King Prawn, Vegetable Curry, salad and Naan; Vegetable Thali £9.50 - Bhindi Bhajee, Mushroom Bhajee, Aubergine Bhajee, Tarka Dhal, Pullao Rice, Raitha and Naan. You might get a discount if you show Mr Uddin this *Guide.*. Delivery: 5 miles. Sunday Lunch: buffet £7.95. Licensed: stocks Cobra, £3.95 a bottle, House Wine £8.95 a bottle. Price Check: Popadom 50p, CTM £8.25, Pullao Rice £1.95. Hours: 12 - 2.30/5.30 - 11, Friday and Saturday to 12. <www.shafiques.com>

TASTE OF BENGAL TAKEAWAY

203 Heene Road, Worthing 01903 238400

Managing owner, AM Kalam, opened his takeaway in 1984. Chef, Faruk Kalam, cooks up all your favourite Bangladeshi styled curries and accompaniments. Delivery: 5 miles, £10 minimum. Price Check: Popadom 40p, CTM £4.75, Pullao Rice £1.60. Hours: 5.30 - 11. You might get a discount if you show Mr Kalam this *Guide.*

TAJDAR NEW ENTRANT

Horsham Road Findon Village Worthing 01903 872225

Worthing knows the proprietor of this eighty seater restaurant, but not here. Abdul Monnan, owned Worthing's former TOP 100 restaurant - Mahaan. He sold up in July 2005 and decided on a new restaurant - Tajdar. Chef's Specialities: Chicken Chilli Masala - spicy hot dish, fried in a mixture of chillies, capsicum, coriander and tomatoes, served with Pullao Rice; Salmon Chutney - small flakes of red wild salmon, cooked in ghee with garlic, red chilli, coriander and served with boiled rice; Lamb Rezala - slightly hot and sweet, cooked in a tangy sauce, served with Pullao Rice - all £10.45. Chauffeur Service: a pick-up and drop-off service, for customers within 5 miles of the restaurant and are in a party of four or six, the cost for this is £5 each way - sounds like a good deal! And if you don't feel like the traditional stuffed and roasted turkey with all the trimmings, but do feel like a curry, then you are in luck, 'cos Abdul opens for lunch on Christmas Day. Stocks: Cobra, £2.90 a bottle, house wine £9.45 a bottle. Delivery: 5 miles, £10 minimum. Takeaway: 10% discount. Price Check: Popadom 45p, CTM £7.45, Pullao Rice £2.25. Hours: 12 - 2/5 - 11.30. Branch: Millan, 274, Upper Shoreham Road, Shoreham , West Sussex <www.tajdar.com>

TYNE & WEAR

the county of egg Naans

Area: North East
Population: 1,100,000
Adjacent Counties: Durham, Northumberland

Gateshead

(includes Bensham, Bill Quay, Low Fell and Shipcote)

BILL QUAY TAKEAWAY

78 Station Road, Bill Quay 0191 495 0270

You might get a discount if you show Syed Amir Ali. this *Guide.*

CURRY GARDEN TAKEAWAY

53 Coatsworth Rd, Bensham 0191 478 3614

Ditto at Abdul Malik Choudhury's takeaway.

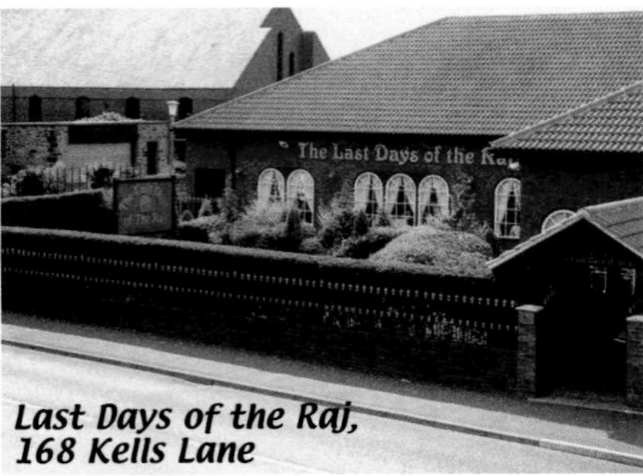

Last Days of the Raj, 168 Kells Lane

Last Days of the Raj, 168 Kells Lane

THE LAST DAYS OF THE RAJ

218 Durham Road, Shipcote, Gateshead 0191 477 2888

Ditto at this takeaway-only.

LAST DAYS OF THE MOGUL RAJ

565 Durham Road, Low Fell, Gateshead 0191 487 6282

Run by Ali and Ali. Formula curry house. Special: Raj Lamb and Cabbage. Hours: 12-2 (Sun. closed)/6-12am.

THE LAST DAYS OF THE RAJ

NOMINATED BEST IN THE NORTH

168 Kells Lane, Low Fell, Gateshead 0191 482 6494

Athair Khan's up-market 100-seater has stylish decor – pure 30's Art Deco, complete with grand piano. Live music Thursdays. Crisp linen tablecloths laid on beautifully presented tables, brass light-fittings, ceiling-fans, trellis-climbing plants, and fresh flowers. Luxurious surroundings,

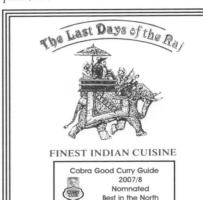

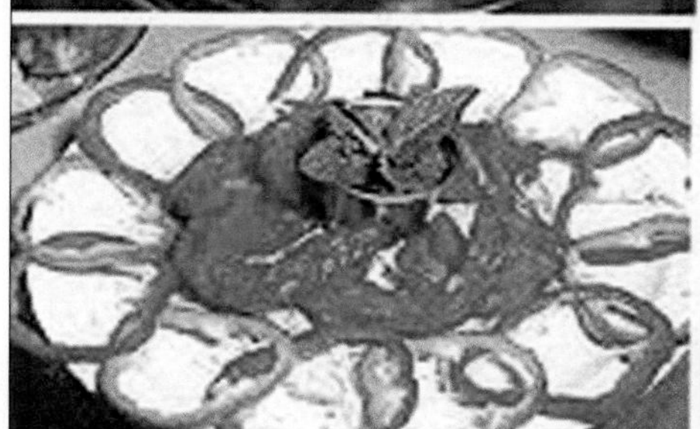

The Days of the Raj,

with friendly and efficient waiters. The bar is spacious and well stocked. This restaurant must have one of the biggest and most comprehensive menus in the country; it is quite a delight. You will find all the regular formula curries with some regional and authentic dishes including recipes from the British Raj, Country Captain, a dry dish cooked with chicken breast, onion, ghee, chillies, ginger, garlic, turmeric and salt. Raj Lamb and Cabbage is cooked with yoghurt, poppy seeds, lemon juice, green coriander, garlic, onion, fresh coconut, green chillies, ground coriander, ginger, cinnamon and cumin with ghee.. You will also find on the menu a few dishes with an oriental flavour, such as Dim Sum, Oriental King Prawn Rolls and Butterfly Breaded Prawn, and there is a Pizza or two – quite fabulous, definitely a **TOP 100** restaurant. Hours: 12-2 (closed Sun.)/6-11. Branch: Last Days of the Raj, Durham Road, Low Fell, Gateshead. <www.thelastdaysoftheraj.co.uk>

THE DAYS OF THE RAJ NEW ENTRANT

Harewood House, 49, Great North Road, Gosforth 0191 284 9555

'Situated above a golf shop. On entering, we were greeted by a maitre d' and shown to the waiting / bar area just beside the piano "very posh". Very smart and very clean. We started with Popadoms and

The Days of the Raj,

the pickle tray, which we soon finished. As we waited with anticipation for our main courses, the pianist entertained us with a mixture of old and new classics. Fifty-five minutes later, our main courses arrived.' Good job you had the pianist! *'King Prawn Sri Lanka £7.55 - good, with just the right amount of coconut. Duck Bhuna £5.95 - Ok, but would have benefited from some better pieces of meat. Butter Chicken £5.25 - got the thumbs up. However, Chicken Patia £3.70 - quite bland. Naans and Rice, all good, as were the mixed sweets and betel nuts that were served with the bill. Service was a little chaotic. Overall, did enjoy the meal, which was reasonably priced.'* DMCK. Price Check: Popadom 55p, CTM £6.25, Pullao Rice £1.85. Hours: 12 - 2, except Sunday and Bank Hols and 6 - 11 daily. <www.thedaysoftheraj.co.uk>

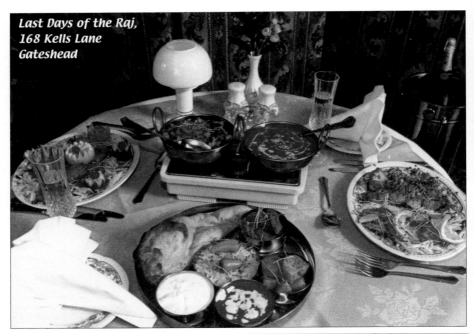

Last Days of the Raj, 168 Kells Lane Gateshead

Newcastle-upon-Tyne

(Includes Denton Burn, Forth Banks and West Jesmond)

BINDI CAFE NEW ENTRANT

261 Whickham View, Denton Burn 0191 274 5505

*'It is, as it says, a cafe-style curry house with ceramic tiled floor and wrought iron chairs and tables. Knowing the area, I wondered about leaving the car but when we found a parking right out side and what our co-diners were driving - it put my mind at ease. Greeted at the door by a well dressed waiter. Starter with Fried Paneer - looked a little lonesome on the plate by itself, but tasted great. Chutney Mary...' is that your wife? 'had King Prawn Bhajia £3.50 - got the thumbs up. My main course was delicious - Chilli Chingri Masala £6.95, while Chutney Mary opted for King Prawn Uree, which she enjoyed, especially the fresh green beans. We shared Pullao Rice and Egg Naan - of a good standard. Staff very pleasant and attentive and facilities very clean - li*lac toilet seats - cool! All very reasonably priced.' DMCK. Delivery: £8 minimum. Stocks: Cobra £3.25 a 700ml bottle and Kingfisher £1.75 a 330ml bottle. Price Check: Popadom 40p, CTM £4.25, Pullao Rice £1.65. Hours: 5.30 - 12. <www.bindicafe.co.uk>

LATIF NEW ENTRANT

1 Clayton St West, Newcastle 0191 230 3780

'Latif is the third name for this elegant restaurant in the last 10 years. Mr Syed Latif offers an extensive menu with all the usual dishes. A great restaurant for every occasion with friendly and helpful staff.' DMCK.. Menu Snapshot: Nawabi Baro Chingri £4.75 - king prawn with herbs and spices, rolled in breadcrumbs, deep-fried in ghee, served with salad and mint sauce; Chicken and Egg Pullao Rice £2.95; Beef Rasoon £7.50 - medium sauce, extra garlic and fresh coriander, Raitha £1.25 - potato, onion, cucumber or mint. Takeaway: 30% discount. Price Check: Pop 60p, CTM £6.95, Pullao £1.95. Hours: 12 - 2.30, except Fri and 6 - 12 daily.

RAJ — NEW ENTRANT

31 Pudding Chare, Newcastle 0191 232 1450

'Having just watched Newcastle United get trounced 5 - 0 by Chelsea, we left the pub full of doom and gloom. Looking for something to cheer us up on a dull Sunday evening - we headed for the Raj. A cosy little restaurant with a friendly atmosphere and pleasant decor - it is surrounded by four Italian restaurants. A standard menu with all the regulars. Ask for the special offer menu, between Sunday to Friday, priced at £6.95. You start with a Popadom and Pickle Tray, then a choice of six starters, then a choice of ten main courses dishes, followed by ice cream or a cup of coffee. Definitely more entertaining that the football match!'' DMCK. Price Check: Pop 75p, CTM £6.25, Pullao Rice £2.10.

SACHINS

NOMINATED BEST IN THE NORTH

Old Hawthorn Inn, Forth Banks,
Central Newcastle 0191 261 9035

Originally opened in 1984, taken over in 2000 by Kulmeet Arora. This is an Indian restaurant, serving Punjabi curries. *'We have been open for over two decades, and I think we are known as Newcastle's best kept secret.'* says Kulmeet, though Sachins have been in our **TOP 100** for several editions, and now you are in our **A-LIST.** He continues: *'we are the only Punjabi restaurants in the city, run by Punjabis with a passion for Indian food.'* And superb Punab it food it is too. *(See page 73).* Chef, V Joseph's Chooza Lucknowi £20.95 (for two) - a full baby chicken cooked in spices, stuffed with minced chicken and served with a mild mince chicken sauce - is his House Special, however, Jalfrezi and Makhani does fly out of the door! Menu Snapshot: Machhi Tandoori £7.50 - pieces of monk fish marinated and barbecued in the tandoor; Aloo Tikka £4.50 - potatoes mixed with peas, spices and deep-fried in small pieces served with tamarind sauce; Paneer Pakora £4.50 - pieces of curd cheese deep-fried in gram flour batter; Lal Goshat £7.50 - Punjabi hot dish, diced lamb marinated in yoghurt, red chillies and spices, cooked on a very slow heat; Bhein Aloo £4.25 - lotus roots and saute potatoes, steam cooked in an oil based masala and served with sauce; Malai Kofta £4.25 - fresh grated vegetable marrow cooked with gram flour batter and deep-fried, served in a cream, tomato and onion sauce; Daal Makhani £4.25 - mixed split black shiny and

Sachins, Newcastle

yellow beans cooked in butter and fresh cream. Licensed: stocks Cobra, £3.95 a bottle, house wine £3.50 a glass. Price Check: Popadom 75p, CTM £8.50, Pullao Rice £1.95. Hours: 11.30 - 1.30, Sunday closed and 6 - 11.15. <www.sachins.co.uk> *See page 90.*

SHIKARA

52 St Andrew's Street, Central Newcastle 0191 233 0005

Good curryhouse where you might get a discount if you show owner Bodrul Haque this *Guide.*

SPICE BOLLYWOOD NEW ENTRANT

The Studio, Yellow Quadrant, Metro Centre 0191 460 9449

Ravi Dhuggas' Punjabi restaurant in the centre. provides a welcome menu change to the many curry house formulae venues. We hear of great savoury tastes at affordable prices. More reports please.

SPICE CUBE NEW ENTRANT

Gate, Complex, Newgate Street, Newcastle Centre 0191 222 1181

Located on the top floor of The Gate leisure complex, is Jalf Ali's Indian bar, cafe & restaurant. This Punjabi is no curryhouse! It has a glassy, stainless-steel modern look with hard floors, and Punjabi Zee Music pounding out on on a large wall-mounted plasma screen in the lounge area. The service is professional and discreet, and the cuisine is by Oberoi Hotel-trained Dinesh Rawat. Fast food includes wraps, masala burgers, naanwiches and kebabs. *'A la carte includes starters such as Tandoori Citrus Prawns, Lamb Tikka and Shish Kebabs. Mains includes the usual selection of goshts and murghs, tikkas, tandooris, subs and accs and we were drawn to Kashmiri Kofta Curry and Spice Cube's piece de resistance Vindaloo Beef. All is cooked to a high standard with reasonable prices'.* LC.. Hours: 12.00-14.30/17.30-23.30 and Sat/Sun 12.00-23.30. <www.thespicecube.co.uk>

THE SPICERY NEW ENTRANT

Denton Bank, Denton Rd, N'cstle 0191 274 9464

Bangladeshi restaurateur Martin Rohman, whose chain of restaurants the largest in the North East, entirely revamped Denton Bank's previously neglected Sporting Arms pub in 2006, pulling it away from its former notorious reputation. It holds 100 covers in the main dining area and 20 in the bar. The contemporary minimalist and elegant decor is defined by its dark wooden floors, aubergine walls and discreet lighting establishing an intimate and stylish ambience. Trained and brought over from Bangladesh, Spicery's head chef Moklis Rahman creates the regular menu with tandoori and fish specialties including Machli Tomato and Murgh Handi Lazeez. Branch: Cinnamon, North Rd, Durham. *Puja Vedi, ed Tandoori. Magazine*

THALI

44 Dean St, Central Newcastle 0191 230 2244

A Bangladeshi curry restaurant, seating fifty-two diners. Syed Ahmed says he is in charge of *'supervision'.* Tikka Masala and Jalfrezi is very popular with customers. Menu Snapshot: Dahi Baigon £3.50 - grilled aubergine stuffed with mixed vegetable and fresh yoghurt; Baja Mach £4.50 - lightly spiced fish, pan-fried and served with spicy onion sauce; Murgh Badami £7.90 - breast of spring chicken cooked in a creamy sauce with ground cashew nuts and almonds; Raitha £1.50 - cultured yoghurt in herbs with cucumber or bananas; Egg Pullao £3.10 - fresh egg, herbs and spices cooked with basmati rice. Licensed: stocks Cobra, £2.90 a bottle, house wine £10.90 a bottle. Note: starters are only available when ordered with a main course - why? sometimes we just want a huge plate of mixed starters with salad and chutneys - makes a good and filling early or late dinner. Price Check: Popadom 60p, CTM £8.20, Pullao Rice £2.90. You might get a discount if you show owner Syed Ahmed this *Guide.* Hours: 12 - 2.30/6 - 12.

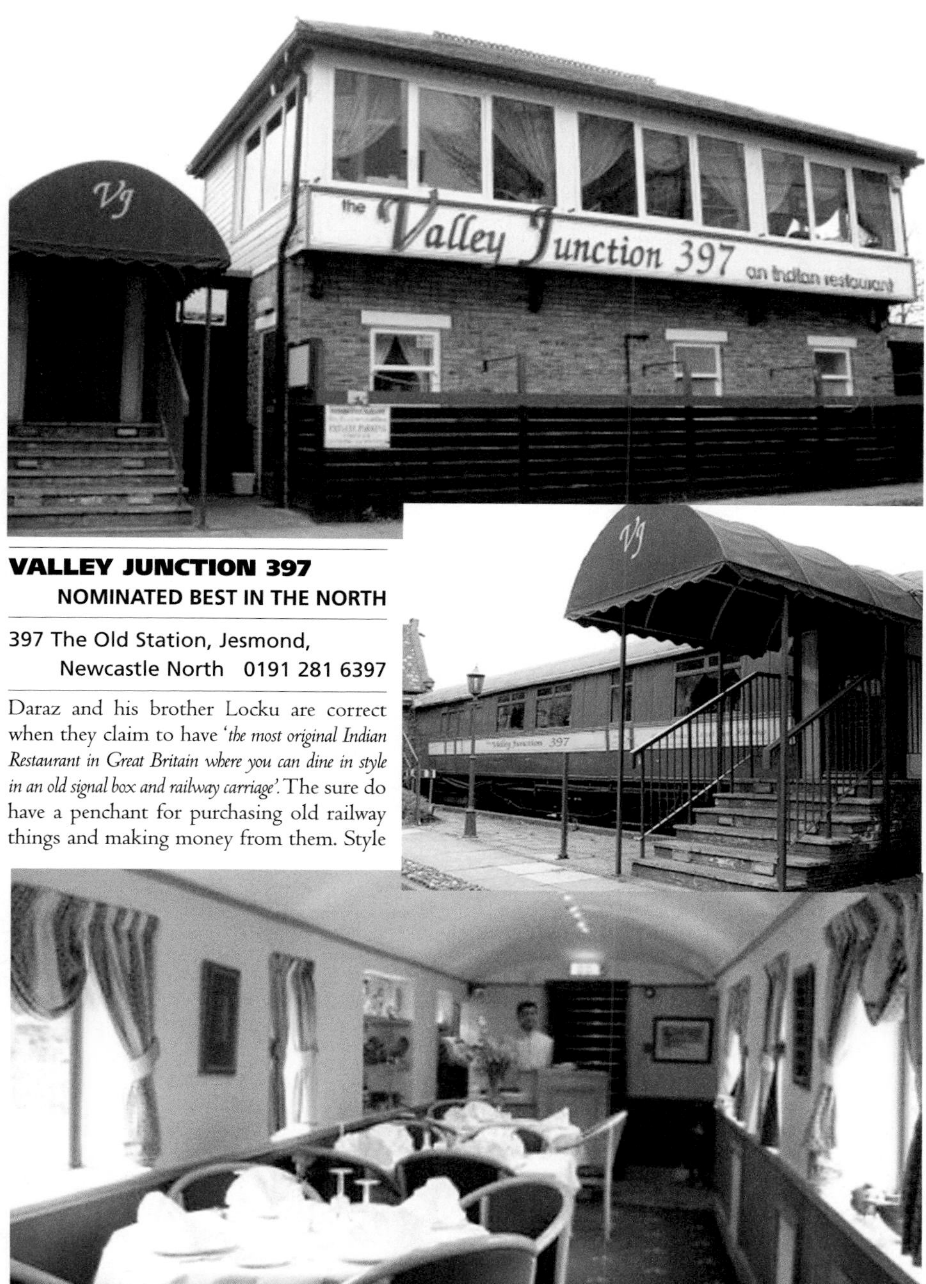

VALLEY JUNCTION 397

NOMINATED BEST IN THE NORTH

397 The Old Station, Jesmond, Newcastle North 0191 281 6397

Daraz and his brother Locku are correct when they claim to have '*the most original Indian Restaurant in Great Britain where you can dine in style in an old signal box and railway carriage*'. The sure do have a penchant for purchasing old railway things and making money from them. Style is the word, First they spend a great deal to achieve it. This venture was formerly the 'Carriage Pub'. The carriage in question was built for the Great Northern Railway at Doncaster in 1912. Numbered 397, it was a saloon for *'wealthy families to hire for their journeys'*. Says Daraz: *We bought it in the third month of 97. The was numbered 397,and the coincidence couldn't be ignored, hence the name 'The Valley Junction 397'.* Now incorporated into the restaurant, it is decked out in greens and golds, and still earns its keep for the well-heeled. Like its sister restaurant, it has quickly earned a reputation for good food, indeed the menus are identical. Says RL: *'A delightful dining experience. (For those not familiar with the area, it is next to Jesmond Metro station, down a subway. Our table was in the old railway carriage – a tight squeeze, so a lot of 'scuse me's.) Chringri Moslai delicious, Chicken Kebab great too. One minor quibble would be the phone ringing, and the waiters calling through to the bar.'* RL.Chingri Varkee, grilled green pepper stuffed with spicy prawns. Tandoori Dhakna, chicken wings marinated in fresh herbs and spices, served with minty yoghurt sauce. Murgh e Khazana, breast of chicken cooked mainly with mild spices and honey, in a creamy sauce. Mangsho Pesta Ke Shadi, top side of beef cooked with a blend of mild spices and pistachio nuts.. Branch: The Valley, The Old Station House, Station Road, Corbridge, Northumberland. and Valley Connection, 301, Market Place, Hexham, Northumberland.

VUJON — AWARD WINNER, A-LIST

29 Queen St, Central Newcastle 0191 221 0601

Stylish restaurant, seating 90 on two floors, with a party room for 40., established in 1990 on Newcastle's quayside, by the elegant Mr Matab Miah. Like its owner, Vujon exudes class, care and style. From the uniform to the decor, it's all just perfect. *'The waiters seem to smile all the time.'* RL. *'Comfortable, well-lit and very clean. No standard curries, but starter and main courses proved interesting and a good choice.'* KDF. *'Most luxurious surroundings in Newcastle. Excellent tandoori starter.'* T&KM The food is somewhat stylised and can disappoint those expecting the regular curryhouse experience. But stick with it and be open minded. For those with an inexhaustible appetite, try the Vhandaris Surprise, a ten course banquet. *'We had it and enjoyed it, but we dieted for a day per course – 10 days!'.* HEG. It was our previous **BEST IN THE NORTH EAST AWARD.** Remains in our **A-LIST**. Hours: 11.30-2.30 (except Sunday)/6.30-11.30.

South Shields

PASSAGE TO INDIA — NEW ENTRANT

4 Burrow St, South Shields 0191 427 5202

Fully licensed. *'This is a good place for a curry. I shall not comment about individual dishes on this occasion, but only a simple statement that the food is nice, the decor is clean, simple and appealing, and the staff are very friendly and obliging. The meals are reasonably priced.'* DRK. Menu Snapshot: Lamb Chop £2.60; Kashmiri Chicken £5.50 - medium curry with bananas, nuts and sultanas; Singapore Chicken £4.50 - fairly hot with bindi (okra); Peas, Lemon or Pineapple Pullao all £1.70; Coconut, Chilli, Mushroom or Cheese Naan all £1.40; Pickle Tray 45p per person - must be the cheapest pickle tray in the country! Takeaway: 10% discount. Price Check: Popadom 40, CTM £5.30, Pullao Rice £1.40. Hours: 12 - 2/6 - 12, Friday and Saturday to 1.

SAFFRON BALTI HOUSE

86 Ocean Rd, South Shields 0191 456 6098

Good curryhouse where you might get a discount if you show owner Abdul Kadir this *Guide.*

STAR OF INDIA

194 Ocean Rd, South Shields 0191 456 2210

The first curryhouse in South Shields, it opened in 1960, and was taken over by M Faruque in 1972. Seats 60, light gold and white wall coverings, burgundy seats, alcove seating on both sides of restaurant. You might get a discount if you show Mr Faruque this *Guide.*

Sunderland

CAF BLUE COBRA — NEW ENTRANT

15 Green Tce, Sunderland 0191 567 2022

'Bright and inviting Indian restaurant in the centre of Sunderland. The food was very good with a number of interesting vegetarian and seafood dishes on the menu, but I relied on my benchmarking dishes of King Prawn Puri and Lamb Korai, both of which were very good. I visited with a large group of people from a course that I was on and everybody was impressed. The service was very good and the staff friendly and efficient. Overall opinion – very good. Would recommend and visit again.' SO Hours: 12– 2; 6-11.30. No lunch Saturday.

CHESTER TAKEAWAY

NEW ENTRANT

69 Chester Rd High Barnes 0191 510 8835

Head Chef, Syed Moynul Islam is also the owner and his most popular takeaway dish is (yes - you guessed it!) Chicken Tikka Masala (£5.70). Credit card accepted. Price Check: Popadom 50p, CTM Pullao Rice £1.70. Hours: 5 - 12, Saturday to 1.

NAZ

NEW ENTRANT

4 St Thomas Street, 0191 510 2060

Seats 150 curryholics in two dining rooms. Ahmed Bashir is the owner and head chef, and he has some interesting dishes on the menu. Menu Snapshot: Aloo Pakora £2.45 - chunks of potato and onion, marinated in gram flour, spices and fresh coriander, then fried; Bhuna Channay on Puri £2.45 - spiced chickpeas served with puri (fried crispy bread); Murgh Monchorie £6.95 - spring chicken, tomato ketchup and purée, ginger, garlic and green chillies; Nargis E Kofta £5.95 - lamb minced meat balls, herbs, spices, cooked in gravy, garnished with coriander; Jhinga E Kabir Biryani £9.95 - basmati rice, herbs, spices, prawns, flavoured with saffron, garnished with egg and tomato, king prawns, served with vegetable curry; Gulab Jamon £1.90 - sweet, mild balls, deep-fried and dipped in a thick sugar syrup, served hot or cold. Stocks: Cobra, £2.25 a large bottle, £1.45 a small bottle. Delivery: 7 miles, £8 minimum. Sunday lunch buffet: £6.95 a person. Price Check: Popadom 60p, CTM £5.95, Pullao Rice £1.75. Hours: 12 - 11.45.

Whickham

JAMDANI

3 The Square, Front Street, Whickham
0191 496 0820

Good curryhouse where you might get a discount if you show Mr A Miah this *Guide.* Hours: 12-2/6-11.30.

MOTI JHEEL TAKEAWAY

9 Front Street, Whickham 0191 488 0851

Another good curryhouse where you might get a discount if you show owner Mr MM Rahman this *Guide.* Hours: 12-2/6-11.30

Whitley Bay

HIMALAYA

33 Esplanade, Whitley Bay 0191 251 3629

Good curryhouse where you might get a discount if you show owner Abdul Goffar this *Guide.* Hours: 12-2.30/5.30-12.

KISMET

177 Whitley Rd, Whitley Bay 0191 297 2028

'The best Indian restaurant we have been to.' KW. Takeaway: 10% discount. Hours: 12-2 (Fri. closed)/6-12. Good curryhouse where you might get a discount if you show owner Shohid Ahmed this *Guide.*

SHAHENSHAH

187 Whitley Rd, Whitley Bay 0191 297 0503

'Food first-class. Chicken Tikka terrific, full of flavour.' MB. *'My local for a year.'* SN. *'We found the restaurant busy in a quiet and efficient way. Cobra the perfect accompaniment.'* PP. You might get a discount if you show owner Abu Taher this *Guide.* Hours: 12-2.30/6-12.

TAKDIR

11 East Parade, Whitley Bay 0191 253 0236

Good curryhouse where you might get a discount if you show them this *Guide. Owner* Majibur Rahman. Hours: 5.30-12am. Branches: Akash, 3 Tangier Street, Whitehaven, Cumbria; Al Mamun Takeaway, 5 John Street, Cullercoats T&W.

Winlaton

BALTI HOUSE

18a The Garth, Front Street, Winlaton
0191 414 2223

Established in 1996. Seats 42. Specials include: King Prawn Peli Peli, King A 34-seater. Owner F.I. Khan continues to promises a takeaway discount of 20% if you show them this *Guide.* You can't get fairer than that! Hours: 6-12. Branch: Balti House, Newcastle.

WARWICKSHIRE

Area: Midlands
Population: 526,000
Adjacent Counties:
Derbys, Shrops,
Staffs, W Mids,
Worcs

In Warwickshire - Tandoori Mixed Grill is referred to as 'De-Lux' (sic)

Coleshill *B46*

BALTI COTTAGE NEW ENTRANT

107 High St, Coleshill, B46 01675 464122

Changed name from Golden Tandoori in 2006. A 42-seater owned by Abdul Mannan and managed by Enam Uddin who might give you a discount if you show them this *Guide.* It is unlicensed and they welcome **BYO.** All the curryhouse favourites are there and: *'We love it! Excellent greeting, clean upmarket and modeersn. Lovely smiling faces, wonderful food.'* AD. *'4th visit in 2 months. Looking forward to our next'.* SS. Hours: 5.30 - 12. <www.balticottage.com>

balti
cottage
Bangladeshi & Indian
High Class Balti & Tandoori Restaurant
BRING YOUR OWN DRINKS
TAKEAWAY SERVICE
10% DISCOUNT
OPENING HOURS
OPEN 7 DAYS A WEEK
INCLUDING BANK HOLIDAYS
5.30PM TILL MIDNIGHT
107 High Street, Coleshill,
Birmingham. B46 3BP
Tel: 01675 - 464 122 / 464 945
www.balti-cottage.com

POLASH BALTI CUISINE

85 High St, Coleshill, B46 01675 462868

A chapatti throw from the NEC, and just inside the Warwickshire/W Mids border, is Coleshill. And much, it seems to the delight of the locals, is this 32 seater cosy curry house, opened in 1997 and run since 98 by Adbul Mannan, it is decorated in cream, blue velvet chairs and carpet, with engraved glass screens dividing the seating. Parking for 30 to rear of restaurant. Chef Taj Ullah cooks up the curries. Special: Bengal Fish Masala, Bangladeshi fish on the bone, cooked with herbs, coriander, served with rice. *'What an experience! Such attention, such luxury, such choice and such cooking! Our congratulations and thanks to the Polash'.* HFC. Takeaway: 10% discount. Delivery: £15 min, 3-mile radius. Hours: 5.30-12.

Henley in Arden *B95*

PICKLES NEW ENTRANT

Liveridge Hill, Henley, B95 01564 784411

Azizur Rahman opened in 2004. It is rather a large establishment, seating 90 diners (but on special nights, he can accommodate 120). Decorated in a contemporary style with wooden floors. The tables are laid simply with crisp white linen, square white china and unfussy dark leather chairs. The overall look is very stylish and upmarket. However, the prices are very reasonable for such a lovely restaurant and the menu choice very interesting. Menu Snapshot.Shredded tandoori chicken parcels with carrot and red chard salad £4.25; Trio of samosas served with cucumber salad and garlic and chilli dip £4.45; Tandoori duck and noodle stir-fry served with spring salad £4.95; Chittagong crab salad served with garlic croutes and mango dressing £5.95; Grilled courgettes filled with dall naga £8.95, served with tomato petal salad; Lamb cutlets marinated with cumin £10.95, served with roasted root vegetables and roshuni tarkari sauce; Pan fried black bream £11.95, served with spiced aubergines and malabar sauce; Shredded confit of duck flavoured with tandoori spices £12.95, served with spinach rice and orange jalfreze sauce; Spiced spring vegetable parcels £8.95, served with

Pickles, Henley

Pickles, Henley

Pickles, Henley

coriander couscous and peach dressing; Carrot Pullao £2.50; Mushroom Naan £2.50. Delivery: 3 miles, £15 min. You might get a discount if you show them this *Guide* Price Check: Popadom 90p, CTM £8.95, Pullao Rice £2.25. Hours: 12 - 11. <www.picklesfusion.com>

Kenilworth

THE COCONUT LAGOON A-LIST AWARD WINNER

149 Warwick Rd, Kenilworth 01926 851156

Opened in 1999 within the Peacock Hotel, Kenilworth. It is an astonishingly good restaurant, as good as any in London and big surprise for the provinces, where genuinely "Indian" establishments are so few. Since our last Guide, more Coconut Lagoons have been opened, see branches. Decorated in the vibrant spicy colours of southern India. Seats 60. *'Bright, clean, very pleasant surroundings. Very knowledgeable staff gave clear explanation of food, origin, preparation etc. So good we went back the next night!'* AD. *'Our first visit, recommended by friends. Warm, courteous welcome. Excellent guidance to menu, food beautifully presented.'* JK. *'Reminded us of holidays in India.'* Menu Snapshot.

Masalai Paniyaram, spongy and savoury crumpets served with tomato chutney. Karaikudi Cutlet, minced lamb cutlets with almonds and sultanas on a spicy sauce. Paneer Roti, pan fried crispy soft cheese with onions and tomatoes in a light and fluffy roti. Shakoothi, Goan style chicken roasted with mild chilli, tamarind, mustard seeds and fenugreek in a thick sauce, served with mango rice and aviyal. Goanese Vindaloo, cooked with garlic, red wine and flavoured with cider vinegar and dried chillies, served with tamarind rice and lentils with snakegourd. Konkani Porial, crisp mangetout parcels of minced pork cooked in sherry and lightly steamed - mild and flavoursome. Accompanied with mango rice and stir-fried vegetables. Andra Shank, an absolute favourite of Pat and myself shank of lamb slow cooked in a delicate kuruma bringing out its full range of flavours, served with lemon rice and aviyal. Malabar Omelette, strips of Malabar coast omelette in a thick curry with lemon rice - a complete meal! Aviyal, poached aubergines, french beans, carrots, potatoes and green banana in a thick coconut sauce. *'Starters innovative, main courses small but well presented, excellent quality.'* GS. *'Food very tasty and South Indian dishes.'* NR. *'Food delicious, very different. Quite expensive.'* BP. *'Delightful decor. Wonderful Ghee Thosai £4.25, conical rice flour pancake, home-made chutneys. Unusual vegetable dishes - lentils and snake gourd. A pearl in the Stratford oyster.'* PO. *'Fresh and original food, served well. The best in the area, having been here for three weeks on business, I have visited most.'* CE. *'Different from any other we have visited, from internal decor to the ambience one experiences and most importantly the cuisine. Choice and quality of food that really is a world of difference. Well done!'* JEC. *'An elegant setting, exceptional food. A joy to the tastebuds.'* B&RF. *'Comfortable with discreet background music.'* IL. We can verify all of the above as we have visited several times and have stayed the night, which is a must - lovely colonial suite with everything you could possible want - recommended. *'Booked a table in the Malabar Room but were offered both menus and ordered from the Coconut Lagoon menu - better choice. Good ambience. Don't like the credit card slip being left open, when a service charge as been added to the bill. Tasty chutneys served with Popadoms.'* G&MP. Feast dinner c £25, four courses. £2.50 pint lager, £9.95 bottle house wine. *BYO* allowed - corkage £7.50. Takeaway: 10% discount. Branches: London EC1, Stratford-on-Avon and Birmingham. (*See page* 80 *and Raffles below*). <www.coconutlagoon.com>

INDIAN EGDE — NEW ENTRANT

50 Warwick Rd, Kenilworth 01926 850100

Mutashir Miah – call me Matt – has owned this restaurant since 2005. He has two partners, Shelim Adbul, manager and Kobir Ali, head chef. Their restaurant seats sixty-four diners in two dining rooms. Note: no minimum charge, but one main dish must be order by every diner. Stocks: Cobra, £2.80 a bottle. House wine £10.95 a bottle. Price Check: Popadom 75p, CTM £7.95, Pullao Rice £2.25. Hours: 5.30 - 12, Saturday to 12.30.

RAFFLES — TOP 100 BEST UK RESTAURANT GROUP AWARD

57 Warwick Rd, Kenilworth 01926 864300

Under the same ownership as Coconut Lagoon. *'As the name suggests, really a Malaysian restaurant, menu is made up of Malaysian Malay, Malaysian Indian and Malaysian Chinese. Very different range of dishes from each cultures, from starters to main courses. Style of restaurant redolent of old Empire and evokes a real feeling of being in Raffles Hotel in Singapore. Lighting and atmosphere good. Make the best Gin Slings I have ever tasted - including Singapore.'* [That, Clynt, wouldn't be difficult. The Singapore Slings at Raffles, Singapore are very poor indeed, however, I am pleased to say that the cocktails served here are fantastic. *'Caution: take great care if you go beyond three. Food is truly out of this world. Menu changes with new dishes being introduced every few months or so, but favourites have been retained. Claypot and Pandri Perratal are simply a must. Absolutely delighted.'* CRS. *'Have always found the food well prepared, clearly freshly cooked and with subtle spicing.'* KN. *'Our favourite restaurant. Unusual and imaginative menu, food superb, beautifully cooked and presented. Service impeccable. Toilet immaculate.'* IS. *'My first visit was a surprise 60th birthday - fantastic. The food, ambience, the courteous was we were all greeted and looked after. Delighted.'* VAB. *'Group of 60, pre-arranged banquet Malaysian menu. Greeted with a Singapore Sling , good start to evening, food served on platters, more than ample. Everyone has an enjoyable evening. Highly recommended.'* RD. *'First class.'* VB. *'Have been many times, also to sister restaurants Coconut Lagoon. Always a pleasant experience, although, a non-smoking area would be appreciated!'* TN. *'Superb Colonial decor, fine crystal glasses and crisp well laundered linen. Ikan Goreng - delicious, Udang Bakar Kerinc - sensational, Hianese Chicken - unforgettable - I could go on!! Exceptionally consistent - can't wait to return!'* BW. *'Murtuabale - savoury Indian bread layered with minced beef, lightly toasted in a griddle - a light and crisp texture. Mysore Anda - slow cooked lamb served with Roti and Malaysian Coleslaw. Pandri Perratal - pan fried spicy pork in a uniquely blended rich sauce served with yoghurt rice, beetroot, a bundle of long green beans, coleslaw and Appatam – an exquisite dish given the contrasting spicy pork together with cool yoghurt rice. A superb experience, but at a price!'* Three course dinner c£24, Four course dinner c£26. Hours: 12-2.30 and 6.30-12.30. Branches called Georgetown at London SE1, Stratford-on-Avon, Leeds and Nottingham, *(See above and p 78)*.<www.rafflesmalaysian.com>

Leamington Spa

BALTI VHUJON TAKEAWAY

NEW ENTRANT

50a Queen Street, Cubbington, Leamington Spa 01926 423 828

MJ Hussain is the proprietor of this Bangladeshi takeaway and he has provided ten large whicker chairs (with cushions), so you can sit back and wait for your takeaway in comfort. Snapshot Menu: Tikka Roll £3.95, chicken tikka wrapped in a Naan, served with salad and mint sauce (great lunchtime meal, so much better than a supermarket sandwich - The Ed); Akbori Murghi Keema £6.20, chicken tikka cooked with lamb mince meat and boiled egg, medium spiced; Chicken Tikka Capsila £5.50, with fried green pepper, green chilli, onion, dry and spicy dish; Raita £1.20, cucumber or plain. Takeaway: 10% discount, £10 minimum. Delivery: 3 miles, £10 minimum. Credit cards accepted. Price Check: Popadom 45p, CTM £5.60, Pullao Rice £1.80. Hours: 5.30 - 11, Friday and Saturday to 11.30. Sunday closed.

Balti Vhujon, Leamington

BOMBAY TANDOORI

38 Regent St, Leamington 01926 420521

Established 1980, and managed by MK Ahmed. Seats fifty-eight curryholics. Delivery: 3 miles, £9.95 minimum. Minimum Charge: £9.95. Takeaway: 20% discount, 10% on Saturday. Menu Snapshot: Fish Kufta £3.95, spicy fish balls; Prawn or Chicken Fried Rice £3.95; Tandoori Mixed Grill £10.95, served with salad and Naan; Lassi Sweet or Salty £1.50. Licensed: stocks Cobra, £2.95 a bottle, house wine £7.75 a bottle. You might get a discount if you show Mr Ahmed this *Guide*. Price Check: Popadom 50p, CTM £6.95, Pullao Rice £1.95. Hours: 6 - 1, Fri & Sat to 2.

Nuneaton

RAJDHANI

1 Cambourne Drive, Horeston Grange, Nuneaton 01203 352254

Good curryhouse where you might get a discount if you show them this *Guide*.

Rugby

TITASH INTERNATIONAL BALTI

65 Church Street, Rugby 01788 574433

Their motto, 'Smell, Hear, See, Touch, Taste.' *'First visit to this impressive establishment. Furnished in a contemporary style. The food did not disappoint with a large and tasty Garlic Naan to accompany the Vegetable Rogan Josh. Equally generous from a portion perspective was the delicately flavoured Chicken Tikka Masala. Bottled Cobra and Kingfisher was cool and the service attentive but not pushy. Not the cheapest meal we have experienced but it certainly represented good value for money.'* N&JG. Menu Snapshot: Popadom 80p - thin wafer of pea flour (well, actually, no! - popadoms are made from a white lentil - dall moth); Fish Tikka £4.90 starter / £9.70 main, cod pieces, delicately spiced and grilled in a charcoal clay oven; Chicken 65 £11.20, pieces of chicken cooked in Chef's ingredients – hot! (sounds interesting!); Spicy Dal £2.70, spiced channa dal, cooked with onions; Assorted Pickles and Chutneys 55p. Takeaway: 20% discount. Delivery: 5 miles, £20 minimum. Hours: 5.30 - 12.

Stratford-upon-Avon

COCONUT LAGOON AWARD WINNER

21 Sheep Street, Stratford 01789 293546

This is the second-to-open branch of Coconut Lagooon, Kenilworth, where you will find menu and other details. The restaurant is on two floors, with an interesting balcony overlooking the ground floor.

LALBAGH BALTI

3 Greenhill Street, Stratford 01789 293563

Fully licensed and air-conditioned, this Bangladeshi restaurant was established in 1985 by Joynal Abedin. It seats forty-five diners in one large room and is decorated in a traditional style with yellow ochre and terracotta. Menu Snapshot: Keema Hari Mirch £7.25, minced lamb cooked with chickpeas, green chillies, herbs and spices; Chicken Baburchi Wala £7.95, boneless Tandoori Chicken cooked in a yoghurty masala sauce, wedges of boiled egg, minced lamb, almonds and fresh cream; Murgh Kebab Masoor £7.50, chicken with pink lentils, chilli pickle, ginger, garlic, cumin and fresh coriander; Prawn and Mushroom Pullao Rice £2.95. Mini Charge: £10 per person. Takeaway offers for regular customers – 20% discount on orders under £25 – free bottle of wine on orders over £25. You might get a discount if you show Mr Abedin this *Guide*. Price Check: Popadom 40p, CTM £7.25, Pullao Rice £1.95. Hours: 5.30 - 12, Saturday to 2. Branch: Bengal Brasserie, 5, Worcester Road, Great Malvern. 01684 575 744.

GEORGETOWN AWARD WINNER

23 Sheep Street, Stratford 01789 204445

Malaysian restaurant and a branch of Raffles, Kenilworth Warks, where you'll find menu details.

THESPIAN'S

26 Sheep St, Stratford 01789 267187

Fully licensed and air-conditioned. Menu Snapshot: Aam Chicken £3.50, cooked in spicy hot mango sauce; Grilled Quail £4.95, marinated in honey, tamarind and chilli, then roasted; Shami Kebab £3.50, minced lamb spiced with fresh garlic, coriander, chick peas and fried; Chicken Naga £7.50, hot and spicy, marinated chicken with Bangladeshi chilli (Pat's favourite, however, he prefers lamb!). *'Provided me with a very enjoyable curry at sensible prices. Portions very generous and very pleasant management!'* CC. Mrs Chapchal - have a look at the 'fishy' meals - great choice: Roshni Delight £7.25 , mildly spiced Tiger Prawns, cooked with egg yolk, cinnamon, cardamom and garnished with cheese; Saffron Fish £10.95, salmon soaked in egg yolk, pepper and garlic. Shallow fried in olive oil, served with salad and Saffron Rice; Meen Kakri £8.95, Silver hake in a spicy sauce, turmeric, chillies, coriander, onions and garlic; Lobster Beruda £11.95, medium spiced with aubergine, served with Pullao Rice; Boal Bhuna £8.95, Boal from the rivers of Bengal cooked with green chillies; Kamal E £9.50, lightly spiced halibut fillets in medium sauce. Delivery: 3 miles, £15 minimum. Takeaway: 10% discount. Price Check: Popadom 50p, CTM £7.50, Pullao Rice £1.95. Hours: 5.30 - 12. <www.thespiansindianrestaurant.co.uk>

USHA INDIAN CUISINE

28 Meer Street, Stratford 01789 297348

Opened way back in 1966, then it was called the Kashmir. Nazrul Islam took the restaurant over in 1995 and renamed it Usha. Menu Snapshot: Tandoori Mixed Grill with Naan £10.95; Lemon Chicken £7.95, with onions, tomatoes and fresh lemon; Achar Lamb,£7.95, lamb with onions, tomatoes, and pickle; Murgh Akbari £7.95, very mild and creamy, almonds, sultanas, coconut, fresh eggs. Takeaway: 15% discount. Cobra, £3 a bottle, glass house wine £1.90. Price Check: Popadom 50p, CTM £7.95, Pullao Rice £1.90. Hours: 5.30 - 12, Saturday to 12.30.

Thespian's, Stratford

Warwick

WARWICK SPICE NEW ENTRANT

24 Smith Street, Warwick 01926 491736

Proprietor, Hussain, took over this 60-seater in 2000, when it was called Veranda. Menu Snapshot: Chat £2.95, chicken or potato spiced in tamarind sauce; Belpuri Chana £2.95, chickpeas, tomatoes, aubergine, lentils and egg; Tandoori De-Lux (sic) £7.95, Chicken Tikka, Tandoori Chicken, Lamb Tikka, and Sheek Kebab, served with Naan; Naga Chilli from £4.80, a spicy hot dish, cooked with authentic Naga chilli, and presented in a thick, deep, warming sauce (Pat would definitely order this dish), Hussain's (managing owner) Special Salad £2.95, chopped tomatoes, cucumber, onions, capsicum, and coriander leaf (with or without chillies), Cheese and Garlic/Cheese and Tomato/Cheese and Onion Naan all £2.70.Cobra and Kingfisher £2.50 a bottle, house wine £8.95 a bottle. Delivery: 3 miles, £15 minimum. Takeaway: 10% discount. Price Check: Popadom 50p, CTM £6.25, Pullao Rice £1.90. Hours: 5.30 - 11.30, Saturday to 12. <www.warwickspice.co.uk>

WEST MIDLANDS

Area: Midlands
Population: 2,600,000
Adjacent Counties:
Staffs,
Warks, Worcs

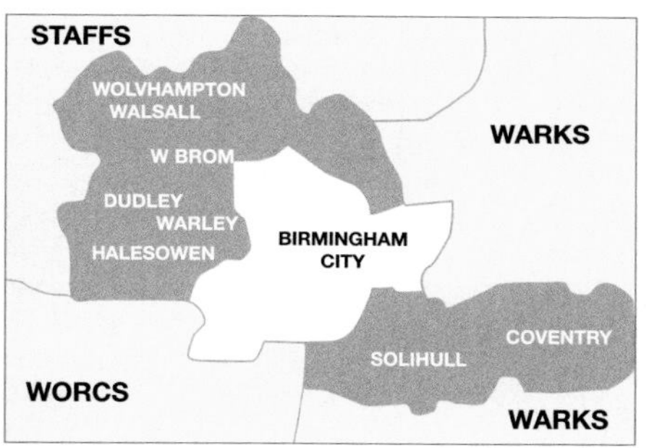

West Midlands was introduced as a county in 1965 and contains the conurbations from the Black Country at its west, through to Coventry in the east. At its hub is Birmingham city.

Birmingham City

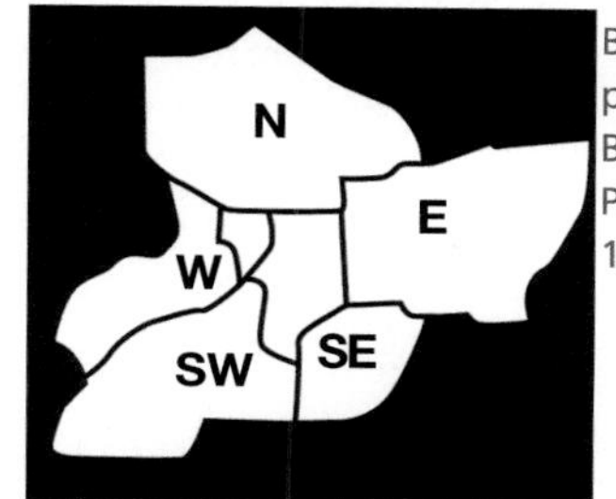

Birmingham postcodes, B1 to B46
Population – 1,018,000

Unquestionably Britain's number two city, Brum has come vibrantly alive with investment in its infrastructure. For the purposes of this Directory, we divide the city into geographical areas, in which are grouped postcode zones B1 to B48 although, as ever, there is no sequential logic to postcode numbering. They are frankly a jumble. But it is the system which exists, and to help narrow things down, we have divided the city, using major roads as our arbitrary boundaries. We start with Birmingham Central, then go south to the adjacent Balti Zone, next North of the city, then East, South East, South West, and West. Further B postcodes, b62 (Halesowen) to B93 (Solihull) follow, listed alphabetically by their suburb name.

Birmingham Central

Postcodes B1 to B5

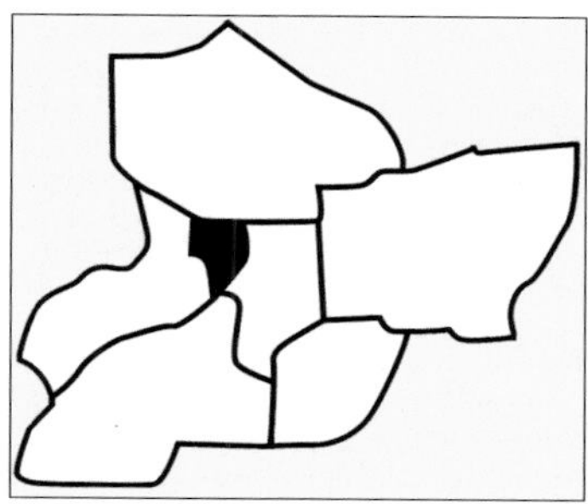

(restaurants listed in alphabetical order)

ALOKA

6 Bristol Street, Digbeth, B5 0121 622 2011

The Darjeeling, Steelhouse Lane, was Brum's first curry house. It opened c 1946, and has long-gone. The Shah Bag was next on Bristol Street, and had opened by 1957. I know because I always came here by Midland Red bus once a week on my day off, from as 'far afield 'as Coventry, where I lived and worked. Hard to believe now but Coventry had none then I don't know when the Shah Bag became the Aloka, but it is now. During the 1960s, the spread of the curry house was as prolific as the city's building. Now it's Birmingham 320, Coventry 50. So here's to the Aloka, a pioneer indeed!

BARAJEE

265, Broad St, 1st Floor, B1 0121 643 6700

Owned by successful restaurateur Moula Miah, of Rajnagar International Restaurant Group, (see Solihul, West Midlands) Barajee overlooks Brum's exciting canal system. Dishes on the menu include monkfish cooked in olive oil, garlic and bay leaves and simmered in spiced tomato sauce. Chefs: Abdul Rouf and Abdul Khalique have also developed set menus where prices start at c£16 per head for a veg meal and c£20f or a meaty version.. Lunch & dinner daily. <www.restaurantbarajee.com>

BLUE MANGO NEW ENTRANT

5, Regency Wharf, Broad Street, Gas St Basin, Birmingham, B1 0121 633 4422

Kal Dhaliwal returns to Birmingham's Broad Street after Shimla Pinks. The 120 seater Blue Mango Brasserie & Bar has chefs, under Nitin Bhatnager, from different regions of India. Closed on Sundays. *'Another central Birmingham place, very modern decor*

Blue Mango, Birmingham

Blue Mango, window view

with lots of crazy enormous flower arrangements on the tables. Only visit if you are very hungry - the enormous Onion Bhajia starter is a meal in itself. They should make a separate dish out of the delectable chickpea curry with accompanies the Samosas - excellent food.' JQ. Upstairs is the 170 seater Jimmy Spice's Buffetworks where you can mix and match Indian, Thai, Chinese and Italian food. <www.bluemangorestaurants.co.uk> Branch: Jimmy Spice, B'ham, B1.s

COCONUT LAGOON AWARD.WINNER

12 Bennetts Hill, B'ham, B2 0121 643 3045

This is the fourth Coconut Lagooon branch to-open. *'Starters Special Bread £3.25 Leera Vadan £1.25 Main Course Fennel Flavoured Lamb £11.25 Hyderabad Dulcha £9.75 Side Dish Lemon Rice £2.25 Dessert Kulfi £3.75 Indian Bread and Butter Pudding £4.75. Mark 9/10'.* G&MP. See Kenilworth Warks, for more details and p 80..

ITIHAAS BEST IN THE MIDLANDS AND BEST IN UK AWARDS

18 Fleet Street B'ham B3 0121 212 3383

Raj Rana is the driving force behind Itihaas. His previous background was jewellry and property management. At 28 in 2005, and with no catering experience he opened a restaurant. But he didn't want just another Birmingham curry house, of which there are hundreds. He wanted to bring to Birmingham the type of upmarket Indian establishment till then only seen in London. Birmingham until then had nothing like it before. Raj says *'Itihaas is a pure labour of love for me and is simply one man's interpretation of royal cuisine and royal service, yet still having a relaxed and informal atmosphere.'* His property background led him to a 5,500 sq ft site on the corner of Fleet Street and Newhall Street, rather aptly in the Jewellry Quarter and the edge of Brum's Business Sector, and he bought its 125 year

lease. '*What I got was, a concrete shell.*' It was below seven storeys of luxury apartments, requiring a massive odour filtration system which pumps smells to the roof, where they are cleansed. Next Raj set about furnishing and decorating it with literally no expense spared. It cost Raj some £2m to achieved this goal, but you need more than money. Very early on he recruited Satpal Gill (Saif) to take charge of the culinary side. Until then Saif had been a senior chef at Madhu's Southall Middlesex, the Top UK restaurant in our last Guide. Itihaas is a unique name in the trade; it means history, and apart from

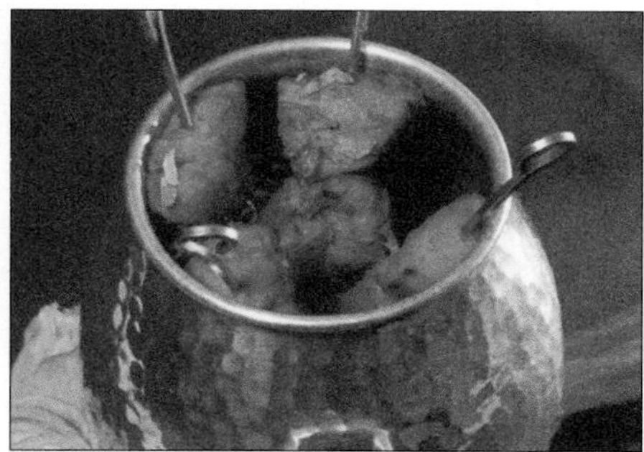

its own recent history, the menu, which is one of the best we've seen, carries a fascinating history of India, and more of that later. Next Raj employed a manger: Ajay Bhatia, who glides around supervising front of house. On arrival, pretty hostesses wearing traditional silk saris will receive you and will seat you in one of their three dining rooms. The 'Colonial Dining Room,' seats seventy diners, has plate glass windows which are shuttered in traditional colonial style, with dark polished wood. The windows overlook the canal, and a terrace, which can be accessed through double doors. At the time of our visit the canal was in possession of the odd supermarket trolley, a bicycle etc, you know the stuff. Brum council have made some vague promise re spending tax payers money to restore the canal by cleaning out the rubbish. And I bet the tax Itihaas is paying will more than pay for it, so once cleaned and kept clean, it will be a great spot to enjoy a cocktail and canapé party or for a more formal seated occasion and enjoy a clean waterway. Inside, the luxurious look is completed with white table linen, sparkling crystal, and chandeliers. Perhaps you could say it is decorated a little like a Gentleman's club, it's definitely very smooth. Downstairs the 'Maharajah Dining Room' which seats sixty, is decorated with

Indian artifacts, paintings and carved stone elephants. The third dining room, the 'Tiffin Room' is accessed from the Maharajah Room, through two large, 300 year old Indian wooden doors, or so the publicity material says. Knowing India's propensity for manufacturing antiques, take the hundred off and I'll believe it! The 'Tiffin Room' seats an exclusive twelve, and to add to the experience, the room possesses it's own bar and you will be assigned your very own butler, wow! Under Saif is head chef, Sheraton Delhi Hotel trained, Amardeep Saka, heads the, twenty-strong, kitchen brigade. The food is Punjabi with a Kenyan Asian twist, with a little fusion and a soupcon of

Chinese. Menu Snapshot: Mirchi Murgh £7.95, tender baby chicken, tossed in fresh ginger and garlic, pan fried with fresh chilli, dressed with coriander and tomato juliennes; Chingari Jingah £9.95, king prawns, with chillies, roasted garlic and lemon; Chotte Kofta £8.95, lamb balls spiced with cardamom and clove, with tangy sauce; Nana-sa - Dosa £6.95, crispy pancake, filled with spiced potato and vegetables, served with coconut chutney and lentil soup, yum yum!!; Maari Aloo £6.95, dry roasted potato wedges, ground black pepper, drizzled with tangy soy sauce; Pilli Pilli Bhogah £5.95, assorted fresh vegetables lightly fried in spiced crispy batter; Masala Champay £9.50, juicy lamb chops barbecued in the clay oven drizzled in a chutney made from paprika and lemon, I've eaten these, VERY good! ; Padhina Keema £9.50, minced lamb, tossed with ginger, garlic, cumin, coriander and mint leaves, Pat really likes Punjabi-style Keema; Paneer ka Tukrah £8.95, homemade cheese, marinated in garam masala, yoghurt, ginger, chilli and coriander leaf; Koila Murgh £12.95, whole chicken marinated in yoghurt and herb paste, seared over hot charcoal; Bhangan Aur Tamatar ka Bhartah £6.95, smoked aubergine with sun dried tomatoes, peas, red onions and thick masala sauce; Hara Bara Kofta £7.25, pan fried mixed vegetable dumplings, think dry tangy sauce, garnished with ginger and chilli; Pyaz aur Lassan ka Kulcha £2.50, garlic and onion stuffed bread, one of Pat's favourites; Gosht Basmati £10.95, spring lamb, cooked on the bone, basmati rice, saffron and herbs, we both fight over this one!; Bhundi Raita £2.50, deep-fried gram flour pearls , homemade yoghurt, roasted cumin and coriander. Now to the puddings!!, Garam Gazarh Hallwa Naraam Kulfi £3.25, hot carrot cake with almonds and pistachio, served with kulfi, I know this is good, 'cos I've tried it. Coconut Kheer £3.75, Punjabi rice pudding, grated coconut, cardamom; Mithai Chawal aur Hallwa £3.75, sweet basmati rice, raisins, cashew, almond, a semolina cake, lovely! We are absolutely delighted to award this restaurant the **BEST IN THE MIDLANDS** and the **BEST UK RESTAURANT.** Our reasoning is that this is a courageous venture. But more importantly, for the first time it has brought London-style Indian culinary sophistication to Birmingham, and about time too. And we have to say that it has

Saif, left and Raj proudly showing their two Itihaas Cobra Good Curry Guide Awards.

caused some grumpiness from two rival Brummie restaurants, who feel they are better than Itihaas. Are they? You tell us. Our unique **TOP** restaurant award has only been given to five restaurants since we started giving this Award in 1991. Itihaas is the sixth. *(see page 29)*. Hours: 12 - 3, Monday to Friday only and 6 - 11.30 daily, Sunday to 10.30. <www.itihass.co.uk>

JIMMY SPICE'S — NEW ENTRANT

5a, Regency Wharf, Broad Street, B1
0121 643 2111

Over the past 15 years, Amrik Singh Uppal and Kuldip Singh have been involved with such *Guide* entrants as Killermont Polo Club, Poppadum Express, Shimla Pinks, Blue Mango, 4550 Miles from Delhi and Pickle Johns, not to mention the pan-Asian Yellow River Cafe chain. Now under the trading name East & West Restaurants Group, their new ambition is to establish a UK chain of venues. Jimmy Spice's Buffetworks opened in 2004 in an old glassworks in the prestigious Regency Wharf development and seats 180. The concept is novel; offer authentic cuisine from

India, Thailand, China and Italy all served as a eat as much as you like! buffet. Simply choose from the dishes on display and the chefs will immediately cook in a theatre style display in front of you. Uppal and Singh have a strong management team who arguably believe the food served at most UK establishments has *"lost its authenticity and has been Anglo-sized" (sic their website).* They cite the lack of skilled ethnic chefs in the UK as one of the causes of the problem. To run the culinary activities, they hired Gopal Singh, who had been with India's Hyatt, Oberoi and Taj hotels. Prices: Sun to Weds: £12.95 pp / Thurs to Sat: £14.95 pp. Child Buffet: £6.95. Lunch Buffet: £5.95, pp.. Child: £2.99. Lunch: 12-2.30 /5.-11 / Sunday to 10. Branch: 64 Station Rd, Solihull, B91. <www.jimmyspices.co.uk>

LASAN NOMINATED BEST IN MIDLANDS

3 Dakota Bldgs, James Street, St Pauls Square, 0121 212 3664

Established in 2002 by Jabbar Khan with Aktar Islam managing. Ninety diners seated in three beautifully decorated rooms - blonde wooden floor, creamy walls, wooden table, white leather chairs, large bronze statues, spot lighting. Tables are laid simply with modern cutlery and white napkins. Head chef Mukesh Sharma presents his dishes on white plates. Here are some of them: Starters: Aloo Brie Tikki. Potato balls flavoured with ginger and cashew nuts, stuffed with brie. Served with tamarind sauce.,£3.95; Goan Lemon Sole Kafrial Yoghurt and mint marinated fillet of

Lasan's Sag Paneer

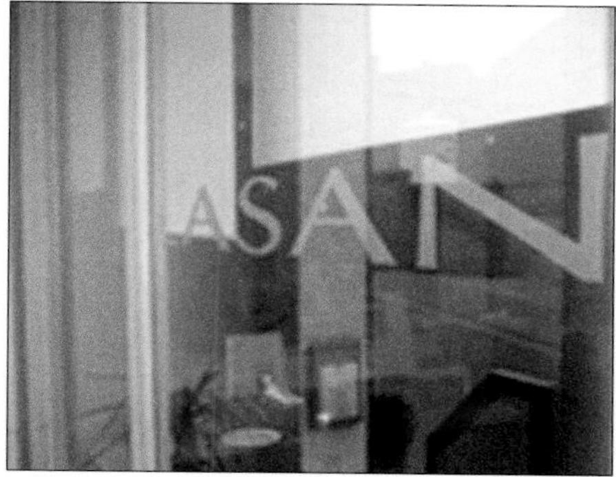

lemon sole, tandoori roasted, served with tomato cucumber salad and mint coriander dressing, £6.50; Gulafi Seekh Kebab Minced lamb flavoured with nutmeg and cloves coated with chopped, chillies, peppers and onions. Cooked in tandoor, served with fresh mint sauce, £5.25; Mans Ke Shooley Smoked lamb fillet marinated with hung yoghurt and mustard oil cooked in the tandoor, served with salad and mint coriander sauce., £5.95. Mains: Seabass Moiley A south Indian style preparation of Seabass cooked in coconut milk tempered with mustard seeds and whole red chillies, served with pilau rice, £12.95; Lagan Ki Bathak Seared breast of duck served with onion and tomato curry flavoured with roasted coconut, poppy and melon seeds. Accompanied with pilau rice, £14.95; Taar Korma, £11.75 Braised tender lamb cooked in delicious onion and cashew nut sauce.,£11.75; Lal Mans Pitika £12.95 A delicacy of Rajput, cardamon and clove smoked tender lamb chops, cooked in spicy curry. Served with masala mash, £12.95; Murgh Jugal Bandhi Poached chicken breast stuffed with sauté spinach simmered in fried onion and tomato mussalam curry, £9.95. Service Charge: 10%. House Wine £12.95. We understand Lasan will relocate during 2007. Hours: 12 - 2.30 / 6 - 11. Sunday 12 - 9. <www.lasan.co.uk>

MAHARAJAH AWARD WINNER

23 Hurst St, Birmingham B5 0121 622 2641

N Bhatt's Maharajah is a small place (62 seats on two floors) and booking is recommended. The food is Indian, cooked by Gurmaj Kumar and Jaskarn Dhillon. The menu looks a little ordinary, but the food is still always spot on. Ask about the Special Dish of the Day. I recall this restaurant serving Biriani topped with edible silver leaf (vark) when it first opened in 1971. It was the first time I'd seen it used in Britain, though traditionalists in India would not contemplate the dish without it. It was a Moghul fetish, of course, the emperor permitting a gold leaf garnish only on the food for himself and the chosen member of the harem (the dish of the day!), while his wives had to make do with silver leaf. They believed it to be an aphrodisiac. It is not for me to comment on the validity of this claim and neither can the Maharajah's diners – they no longer serve it, sadly. Service is mature and careful, and the place is often full to bursting. Waiting bookers are deftly dispatched to the downstairs bar. Such competence is rare and welcome. We continue to receive plentiful reports on the Maharajah. *'Having spent many years enjoying some of the better Indian restaurants in London I do not share your enthusiasm for all types of curry.' [really? Ed!!!] 'but very much favour Nepalese and North Indian cooking. But on moving to Shropshire in 1987 can think of few worthwhile restaurants to visit other than the Maharajah. I have visited this well established restaurant a few times mainly Xmas office outings. I visited with colleagues in February and more recently in August. The menu is short and I nearly always have Chicken Dhansak. My father calls it the 'Prince of Curries'. If you get a good hot sweet sour one with pineapple or lemon then I can see why. The Maharajah's is good but not the best, no pineapple or lemon juice! However the service is good, friendly and efficient and the food is consistent if not inspiring.* RAC. Elevated to our **A-LIST. HOURS**: 12-2/6-1; closed Sun. & bank hols.

MILAN INDIAN CUISINE

93 Newhall St, B'ham B3 0121 236 0671

Dhirendra Patel's 120-seater, established in 1989, is decorated in pastel shades, giving it a light and airy feel. The bar area is typically Indian with beaten copper drinks tables and large coffee pots. Chef Balbir Malhi's menu features all the usual curry house favourites from Korma to Jalfrezi but there is also an extensive vegetarian section. Paneer Tikka £2.50, spicy paneer cooked in the tandoor. Stuffed peppers filled with coconut, potatoes and coriander. Reshmi Mattar Paneer, homemade cheese with herbs, spices, peas, cashews and corn. You might get a discount if you show Mr Patel this *Guide*. Hours: 12-2/6-12.; Sat. 6-12; Sun. closed. Branches: 129 Stoney Lane, B11, 238 Soho Rd, Handsworth B21, and 296 Abel Street, Milpitas, nr San José, California, US.

MOKHAM'S OF DIGBETH

140 Digbeth High Street, Birmingham B5
0121 643 7375

Of Naz Khan's venue AM says *'Mokham's pride themselves on their cooking so you may have to wait as all the food is freshly prepared. Tandoori Sheeksh Kebab is certainly one of the best I have ever tasted. Balti Exotica is meat, chicken, prawns, mushroom and pasta, without doubt unique in my experience. A very substantial dish, served up in the traditional black bowl, it was beautifully spiced and the pasta blended superbly but when combined with my Nan bread it left me feeling like Pavarotti.'* And RW says: *'Small but smart genuine Balti house in the city centre. Very friendly, family run. Extensive menu. Fresh papadoms, light and well cooked chat, tender Lamb Tikka cuts in a mild to medium sauce. Light and fluffy naans buttered and pleasantly sweet.'* AM. Unlicensed, **BYO** welcome and you might get a discount if you show Mr Patel this *Guide*. Hours: 12-2.30/6 - late.

PRÂNA NOMINATED BEST IN MIDLANDS

121 Suffolk Street, B'ham 0121 616 2211

Restaurateur Tarrun Arora worked with Hyatt and Taj Group of Hotels in India, USA and Europe and has co-ordinated events for 1000 people. His love of international travel was the creative spark for Prâna Restaurant and Lounge. He chose Birmingham as it is one of the most vibrant and culturally exciting cities in the UK, with a flourishing restaurant scene. It is lavishly gorgeous (see page 48) and the sort of place to go for that big evening out, though I suspect they have attracted a hardcore of clientele, who will be making it there weekly local. There really is no need to go anywhere else. Prana possesses a striking black and orange colour themed restaurant, bar, lounge and nightclub that wouldn't look out of place in London, which is about time! - we, who don't live in London, do have taste, you know! To introduce you to the Prâna experience a theatrical, sweeping staircase, takes you to the dining room. A specially designed carpet, makes dining in the orange velvet semi-circled booths, which can seat six, wrapped around black wooden tables, which are lit in the middle with glass, (very discreet and effective), very sophisticated. The floor is dark wood, on which square black tables for couples stand with upholstered, black and orange patterned spoon backed chairs - lovely. Black napkins, silver cutlery, white china and sparkling balloon or flute glasses makes for a very upmarket experience.

Don't ignore the cocktail list; you certainly can't ignore the bar; it's on the right hand side at the bottom of the staircase. The bar is brightly lit, and on glass shelves stand lots and lots of bottles and I am pleased to report that there are 'z' bar stools for the 'bar-flies'. Ladies rave about the cocktails, or is it the barman? However, good things don't come cheap (the cocktails, that is), so expect high prices! An extensive wine menu has been compiled and designed to compliment the food. Exec Chef Parvinder Multani is Oberoi-trained and ex Cafe Lazeez, London (sw6), has taken over the reigns in the kitchen and offers Indian food - great! Menu Snapshot: Bhalla Papri Chaat @3.95 - combination of lentil dumpings, savoury biscuits and chickpea salad, topped with fruity tamarind sauce and sweet yoghurt; Almond Pears £3.95 - crumb-fried pear shaped potato croquettes spiked with slivers of almonds served with a combination of sauce; Paneer Sandwich Pakora £4.95 - crispy fried Indian cheese filled with the tangy mint served on salad leaves, with sweet mango chutney; Saffron Chicken Tikka £5.45 - succulent morsels of chicken breast marinated with saffron, cream and cheese, glazed golden in the tandoor and served with small salad; Chargrilled Swordfish £5.95 - dill and carom seeds marinated swordfish cubes chargrilled, served with salad leaves; Lamb Seekh Gilafi £5.95 - spiced minced lamb, skewered with crunchy peppers, onion and glazed; Chicken Dum Malai Korma £7.95 - slow simmered, chicken breast, in rich sauce of almonds and cream infused with saffron and spices; Raan Sikandari £17.95 for two - whole leg on lamb, slow braised in rich onion and yoghurt sauce, served with salad, red onions and tomatoes; Saffron Scallops £13.95 - seared scallops flamed with pernod, cooked in saffron infused cream, served with steamed rice and tender asparagus spears; Duck Breast £12.95 - pan roasted Barbary duck served on a bed of orange, apricot and raisin pilaf, with wild rocket, apple and cider chutney; Aloo Udaigiri £6.95 - new potatoes stir-fried with cumin, curry leaves and spices; Bhindi do Pyaza £6.95 - crispy Okra tossed with spices and onions, Naan £1.95; Garlic Naan £2.75. Indian Puddings! - Gulab jamun £3.95 - fried dumpling of cottage cheese, reduced milk, soaked in rose flavoured syrup, Gajar Ka Halwa £4.25 - finely grated carrot, slowly heated with cardamom, almonds, pistachio, served with vanilla ice cream - MY FAVOURITE!! Service Charge: 10%. Day or night, Prâna is available for: Daytime Brasserie; Private Dining ;Meeting Room ; Event Holding; The Retreat (Mithai Room); Outdoor Catering. Email your reservation to: <www.pranarestaurant.co.uk> *(see page 48/9)*

SHAH'S — NEW ENTRANT

55 Station Street, B'ham B5 0121 643 5723

Jamshied Ali Shah's (hence the name of the restaurant) restaurant seats sixty-two diners. It is situated in the city centre, off Hill Street, behind New Street Station, next to The Old Rep. Head Chef: Fazal Said's most ordered dish is King Prawn Goa £10.50, with fresh green chilli, garlic and coconut cream sauce, garnished with coriander leaf and ginger - sounds delicious! I am pleased to report, that the Tandoori Mixed Grill Special £8.95, includes a Naan and is served with salad. Menu Snapshot: Nargis Kebab £3.60, spiced minced lamb stuffed with boiled egg, dressed with omelette; Paneer Tikka £3.95, spice marinated cheese cooked in clay oven; Banglar Prew £8.95, King prawn, delicate cuts of lamb and chicken tikka pieces marinated in seven ground spices, cooked in a creamy sauce; Sadhu Machh £11.50, monk fish marinated and cooked in the clay oven with kebab style pepper and tomato, served with Bombay Aloo and Pullao Rice. Delivery: 3 miles, £25 minimum. Licensed: stocks Cobra £2.75 a bottle, House Wine £2.80 a glass. Delivery: £15 minimum. Price Check: Popadom 70p, CTM £6.60, Pullao Rice £2.35. Hours: 5.45 - 1, Saturday to 2.30. <www.shahsrestaurant.co.uk>

SHIMLA PINKS

214 Broad St, B'ham B5 0121 633 0366

Moe Kohli bought it from Kal Dhaliwal's Oriental Group and has already sold it to former general manager Kamile Ahmed. Just west of Central TV, this fully licensed and upmarket. *'Desperately cold and tempted to go to the nearer Chinese from the concert hall, but we remembered how much we enjoyed Shimla Pinks several years ago. No reservation was needed for a Friday evening. A large restaurant with acres of empty tables, which remained empty while we were there. It is still excellent, very stylish restaurant with an attractive modern decor, quality china and cutlery with shaped handles so the knives are placed upright on the table. The menu is large and attractive and really needs a long period to read thoroughly. The wine list is good, much better than most Indian restaurants. Serving staff are in all black and were very helpful and efficient. Popadoms, very thin and crisp with superb relishes. Chicken Besaali, a more tangy butter chicken; Malabari Sole Curry - really excellent; Onion Bhajia, very different, large strips of floured onion in a sort of untidy heap presented on a garnished long platter...'* I make my Bhajia's just the same - it means that they cook much more quickly, thus absorbing less oil, which can't be a bad thing! DBAC *'Saag - very good, in a creamed style. The menu has seabass and monkfish, not the usual Indian fishes. Food beautifully presented on large white plates sprinkled with parsley. Everything, the food and service, was excellent. Food was not expensive, especially considering the quality and presentation, but the drinks are quite highly marked — the young couple at the next table were horrified at the price of the beer.'* HC. *'Pricey (meals for 2 with a bottle of wine was £102) but the food was of good quality. Murgh Sagwala (chicken cooked with fenugreek and spinach) was tasty as was the Lamb Rogan josh and the Connoisseurs Mixed Thali for starter was excellent (especially the salmon). Side dishes of Bhindi bhaji and Methi Aloo were competent. Mind you, I do hate having a service charge of 10% automatically added. Overall, nice ambience but I'm not sure the cost was justified.'* RN. Branches: Shimla Pinks Manchester M3. Oxford, Johnstone Strathclyde, and London EC. Hours: 12-2.30, weekdays/6-11 every day.

ZAFRONI — **NEW ENTRANT**

55 Newhall Street, B'ham 0121 212 2511

Midland's restaurateur, Rafique Chowdhury has opened a new 100 seater restaurant Zafroni. His popular Rafique's won Best Restaurant Overall Restaurant in the 2002 taste of Staffordshire awards. Good reports received.

Birmingham Balti Zone

Consists of B10 to B13

(restaurants listed in alphabetical order within postcode)

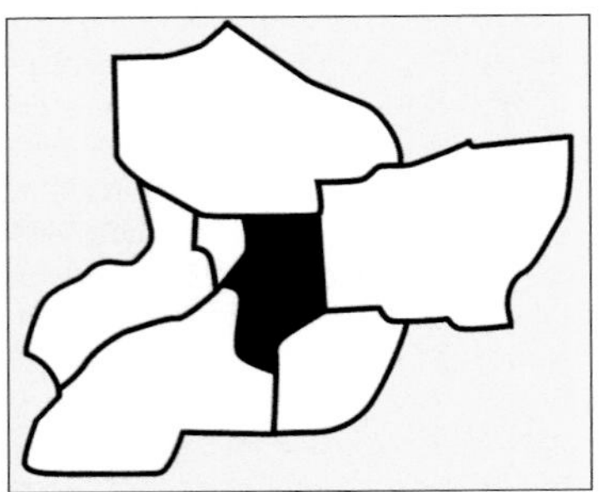

See page 374 for key to this map.

The Balti Zone starts about 2 miles south east of the city (follow the a34), and is thickly spread around the suburbs of Small Heath, Sparkhill, Sparkbrook and Moseley (b10 to b13). The population is largely north Pakistani, mostly from Kashmir's Mirpur, adjacent to which is the district of Baltistan, high up in the Pakistani mountains. You'll find recipes and more about this subject in my newly republished 'Balti Bible'. Those who doubt the existence of Baltistan should visit k2 Baltihouse, upon whose walls is the biggest map of the region that I've seen, and it is from there that Balti originated. But for those who prefer to say it did so in a bucket in Birmingham, you are certain to get the nation's best Baltis here. There have been innumerable changes here over the last two years. Too many venues has led to empty houses, even at the weekend, and subsequent closures. One result is the e-a-m-a-y-l buffets, which, whilst value for money, never, in our view compare in quality to individually cooked baltis. Here are the views of the lucky scribes who live there, and those who visit:

Birmingham B11

Sparkbrook, Sparkhill

ADIL 1 — **AWARD WINNER**

148 Stoney Lane, Sparkbrook 0121 449 0335

'Do you know what happened to Adil's in Sparkbrook ? Closed according to our son. Now there was a cafe style balti to die for.'. c&mc.C & M C. No idea what 'closed' is about. Maybe it wa a redec. As far as we know they are open, thriving and still to die for. Established 1977. The menu reads: *'We have a bring-you-own alcoholic drinks policy at Adils. There is an off-license right next door.'* I wonder if they own it? Menu Snapshot: Green Chilli Bhajia £1.00; Chicken and Mushroom Balti £5.10, I know that this is a very popular choice; Balti Lamb Aloo £5.10, another popular choice; Tandoori Naan 90p; Tandoori Table Naan £4.00 - many can share this elephants ear of a bread! other wise you can choose one of the following from £1.50, Peshwari (nuts and fruit), Garlic, Keema, Kulcha (vegetable stuffed), Dhaniya (coriander), Mushroom, Paneer (cheese) and Ginger; Kulfi £1.50, Mango, Malai (cream) or Pistachio flavour; Gulab Jaman 90p - I love these, especially slightly warmed!; Barfi 70p, chocolate (yum! yum!), pistachio, almond or cherry flavour. *'Menu Incredibly wide Quality Variable Quantity Fine Decor Conventional Balti House Service Good Comfort Uncomfortably cramped Comments Starters: 22 x popadoms; Green chillies bhaji £1; Tandoori chicken £2.30; Mixed grill £5.50; Sheek kebab £2.20 x 6; Onion bhaji £1.50; Pakora £1.20 x 2 Katlama £1.50; Chicken pakora £2.50 x 2; Tandoori Fish £2.20; Chicken tikka £2.90; Lamb tikka £2.90; Prawn puri £2.90. Main course: Tropical Balti —*

Baltis from the originator, Adils. Note the Elephant Naan.

not enough meat; Balti Lamb Desi with peas and aloo – magnificent; Balti Chicken Jalfrezi x 2; Muchi Special; Balti Chicken Spinach and Mushroom; Balti Chicken Tikka Mince with Prawn; Balti Chicken Tikka Spinach; Balti Chicken Mushroom Jalfrezi; Tandoori Mixed Grill; Balti Chicken Tikka Mushroom. Accompaniments: Table Naan £4 x 2 Mark 7/10. Wildly differing standards here: the Tandoori Mixed Grill was awful, the Tropical Balti little better but the Balti Lamb Desi and the Balti Chicken Tikka Mince with Prawn were both superb. Bill £142.15 for 11.' G&MP. Fully air-conditioned. Delivery: 2 miles (£1 per extra mile), £15 minimum. **BYO.** Price Check: Popadom 50p, Balti CTM £5.35, Pullao Rice £1.50. Hours: 11.30 - 2.30 / 4.30 - 12. Saturday and Sunday 12 - 12. <www.adilbalti.co.uk>

DESI KHANA — ANP

706 Stratford Rd, Sparkhill, B11 0121 778 4450

'This *is my favourite. Decidedly Asian – European customers are rare – strict Muslim. Glass top tables and a shortish menu, but the food is great food. Sheeh Kebab freshly cooked on sizzling platter, excellent. Peshwari Gosht in a balti, had quality lamb pieces in a thick, tasty sauce. The price for one person was high by comparison with most others in the area, but the food is good.'* RE.

MILAN SWEET CENTRE — V

191 Stoney La, Sparkbrook 0121 449 1617

A branch of the Milan restaurant in 93 Newhall Street, Birmingham B3 (see entry above). This is a takeaway venue for Indian sweets, and savoury snacks. The selection is huge and satisfying, at prices too cheap to ignore. Sister t/a branch at 238 Soho Road, Handsworth, B21

ROYAL NAIM — AWARD WINNER

417 Stratford Rd, Sparkhill 0121 766 7849

The Nazir brothers' restaurant is huge – 180 seats on two floors, yet it doesn't feel oversized. It's open all hours, of course it's **BYO**, no corkage charge and the food prices are very reasonable. You can fill yourself for £6, and blow up for £16. You are made welcome and are served with prompt efficiency throughout. The portions are still huge, and more importantly, the food is as tasty as you can get in any style of 'Indo-Pak' restaurant. Order from the menu located under the glass table top. The selection is huge, with every Balti combination you can think of and some more. Then leave it to Chef Shaffique and his crew to get cooking, while your taste buds tingle. But before your choice arrives, get nibbling on a papadom, if for nothing else, to taste the lurid red delicious chutney that accompanies it. Unless your stomach is horse-sized, don't order more than one Balti, and don't eat too much before it arrives – it's a huge portion. Order rice if you must, but doing it the Pakistani way, with no cutlery, and huge naan breads to tear and scoop with is hugely satisfying. And then it arrives, served the Balti way, in 10" steel karahis (Balti pans) the food cooked in the pan, made black with thousands of hours of cooking. It's more than filling and great fun. The Naim also produce deep frozen Baltis for retail outlets and local schools. *'No wonder Birmingham's education standards are starting to rise!'* AM. *'The atmosphere was building before we found the actual restaurant because of the community in which it is situated and the numerous other Balti restaurants surrounding it. The basic nature emphasised*

the excellent food. Owner very attentive and helpful. Returned a month later. Once you get the Balti in front of you and taste it you don't want it to end.' SR. *'Visited on a busy Saturday night. Standard of service, choice, quality of food and value for money is very high. Party of eight, four adults, four children, plenty of choice for all. Our large Naan £3 covered the table. Washed down with a jug of Lassi. Ras Malai for pudding is hard to beat. My children insisted I make a detour two days later on our return from Kendal to Suffolk to revisit the Royal Naim.'* DB. You might get a discount if you show Mr Nazir this *Guide.* Delivery: £10 min, 3-miles. Hours: 12-1am; Sat. 12pm-3am.

TY'S JAZZ & SPICE

132 Stratford Rd, Sparkhill 0121 773 1632

Authentic Kashmiri cuisine here *'and excellent too'* AN. The clue's in the name. This place hums, literally with its emphasis on live jazz on certain days. Established in 1999. Seats 80 in chic, modern decor. *'Very impressive decor, high ceilings, drape curtains, chandelier. Mixed Grill, Lamb Tikka, Chicken Tikka, Tandoori Fish, Sheesh Kebab, wonderful mixture of flavours. Very large quantities, top-quality ingredients. Service slow with starters but these were obviously freshly cooked, so understandable.'* GG&MP. Private park for up to 30 cars with CCTV.

Birmingham B12

Balsall Heath, Sparkbrook, Sparkhill

AL-FRASH

186 Ladypool Rd, Sparkbrook 0121 753 3120

'Menu Extensive with some unusual choices Quality Outstanding Quantity Copious Decor Pale painted walls Service Polite, prompt and interested Comfort Comfortable chairs. Tables quite well separated Comments Starters: Popadoms x 7; Tandoori Chicken £3.50 superb marinade, very tasty, huge portion; Bhuna on Puri Meat £3.50 very good, big portion; Nargis Kebab £3.50 beautiful; Bhuna on Puri Chicken £3.50 very flavoursome. Main Course: Lamb Marricha £7.50 spicy and delicious; Jeera Chicken £7.50; Chicken Tikka Pepsila £7.95; Tandoori Mixed Grill £8.95 the best! Side Dishes: Cauliflower Bhaji £3.25. Accompaniments: Pullau rice £2.10 x 2; Chilli Naan £2.20. Drinks: Cobra 6 x £2.90; Bitter Lemon 1 x £1.20. Bill: £77 plus £5 tip. Mark: 8/10.' G&MP. ***'Al Frash has had a very extensive facelift and the entire restaurant looked very professional and attractive. We hadn't been too impressed by the buffet style of recent times and this does seem to have vanished.'*** R&NT. **BYO**

ALI BABA

250 Ladypool Rd, Sparkbrook 0121 449 4929

We like Mr Aslam's logo:a chap holding a sizzling Balti, sitting on a flying carpet (beats cars for home delivery?) *'Clean comfortable.* **BYO** *(no charge). Very good Sheek Kebab 70p, freshly cooked and spicy. Nice Roti. Lamb Bhuna, prepared with extra chilli, very accommodating.'* RE. You might get a discount if you show Mr Aslam this *Guide.*

DAWAT

Ladypool Road, Birmingham, B12.

'This was my usual birthday treat, a day in Brum, a curry ***in the evening and the Good Food Show on Sunday (nice to see you both at the Blue Dragon stand).'*** And you too Richard & Nicki. All over now that Blue Dragon have been bought out by food giant ABF. No more shows, at any rate for us at the moment! Sad cos we met so many Curry Club members that way! Anyway back to the Dawat: ***'We decided very early on that we would return to the Dawat since we had such a great time last year. The staff had changed and so, it seemed, had the chef. The clientele were not the usual crowd but more of a middle class crowd. The service was good – very friendly – but the food was (sadly) very mediocre. My wife had her usual chicken biriani whilst I plumbed for the chicken dhansak. Oh, I started with tandoori fish (hake) and this was very good. However, the***

main courses were very non-descript and both looked, and tasted, exactly the same. The medium naan, however, was very good and large! We probably will not go back, nor recommend friends to go there. The meal for 2cost £ 23.00. R&NT.

IMRAN'S BALTI HUT

264 Ladypool Rd, Sparkbrook 0121 449 1370

'Baltis, superb. Family Nan, unbelievable – 3 feet by 2 feet. BYO from "offy" next door. Excellent value for money.' RS. *'Claims to have been around at the time of the first-ever splitting of Balti bread in Brum. Spacious and includes in-view cooking for those who like to see a Sheeksh Kebab being cooked live. My main course Balti Chicken and Mushroom had an impressively spicy kick. Unusually you can also get a family Chapatti also Quail Balti (a dish which has now achieved almost protected status).'* AM. *'Lamb Jalfrezi, meat tough and lacked depth of flavour. Chicken Korma – too hot for a Korma and for my wife.'* RE. **BYO** Hours: 12pm-12am.

KING'S PARADISE

321 Stratford Road, Sparkhill 0121 753 2212

Owned by Mahboob Hussain. *'Balti Tandoori Butter Chicken, very smooth-tasting, in bright red sauce with some onion in there. Peshwari Naan, large, tasty with just a hint of syrup.'* GG&MP. Mushroom Naan sounds great! **BYO.** Private car parking. You might get a discount if you show Mr Hussain this *Guide*. Hours: 12-2.30/5.30-12.

KUSHI

58 Moseley Road, B12 0121 449 7678

Messrs Mohammed and Haydur's 62-seat *'Kushi appears to have picked up just about every cup apart from the Jules Rimet. However, never mind the awards, try the food. Kushi's Kebab is one of the best of its kind as are the sizzling Shashliks. Wide choice of main courses including Kushi's new and highly valued range of "saffron" dishes. Good selection of Nans from Keema to Kulcha'.* AM. *'All nine of us agreed that this was a magnificent Balti house.'* GG&MP. You might get a discount if you show them this *Guide*. Delivery: £10 minimum. Hours: 5.30pm-1am (2am on Sat.); **BYO** Sun. 6pm-12am.

LAHORE KARAHI

357 Ladypool Rd, B12 0121 449 9007

This one is probably the best of the buffet bunch. RE is a frequent customer, and here is an amalgam of his views. *'A large self-service, always bustling busy restaurant, with space for 300 diners. Small car park at the rear, but otherwise can be difficult. Many Moslem and Seikh customers. E-a-m-a-y-l – amazing variety of food for c£7. Sheekh kebabs good and tasty, roti not too thick, lamb dall superb, mixed dall nice consistency, spinach lamb, on the bone really tender meat.and delicious. Keema Peas – delightful. Great food and great value. The trouble with buffet style restaurants as good as Lahore is knowing when to stop eating. Having said that I then went for seconds! Highly recommended.'* RE. *'Everything qualifying for the top melt-in-the-mouth award. Highly recommended.'* MJB. **BYO**

LAHORE KEBAB & PAN HOUSE

187 Ladypool Road, B12 0121 440 3264

'You can't go much more down market than this. Predominantly a takeaway offering just seekh kebabs, fish massala, samosas, pakoras, tikkas etc. In other words no main courses. However, what they do serve is freshly cooked and very good. Worth going for a cheap snack.' RE.

ROYAL AL FAISAL

136 Stoney Lane, Balsall Heath, B12
0121 449 5695

Spelt Faisal, or Faisel, the other venerable Balti, contemporary with Adil's (1982) from whom it is a few doors away, is Mohammed Ajaib's smartly decorated restaurant in shades of green. Seats 150 diners, tables of four. This early leader is now following the buffet trend and is, we hear, as busy as ever. *'Celebrating a momentous victory for Northampton's Saints, away at Gloucester. On recommendation, pulled off M42 to visit Royal Al Faisal. 6.30pm – very busy. Now a Balti Buffet Restaurant. One price of £5.95 – all you can eat. Faced with a huge array of dishes. Starters: Tandoori Chicken, Onion Bhajia, Mushroom Bhajia, Sheek Kebabs with Popadoms and Chutneys plentiful. Main courses: wide range of Baltis, vegetarian and meat, Tarka Dal Balti – first class. Excellent value for money. Convenient shops nearby to purchase your own drinks.'* DL. *'Food is good but I think the Lahore Karahi Buffet has the edge. Twice in one week is OK in the name of serious research! Must return again soon.'* RE. **BYO.** Hours: 11.30am-12am

SEVEN SPICE

53 Moseley Road, B12 0121 440 4408

Cooking is from the Punjab, so expect spicy but not necessarily hot curries. Menu Extracts: Popadoms a mere 25p – is this the cheapest? Samosas also a bargain at 55p,either meat or veg. Min charge: £7. Credit cards accepted. **BYO**. Secure car park at rear. Takeaway: 10% discount.

SHANDOR

353 Ladypool Rd, B12 0121 449 5139

'Very similar to Lahore Karahi Buffet next door, but on a smaller scale. Not so much choice, but what there was was excellent.' re. *'Visited as result of write-up in Guide. Ethos has changed – to a buffet style – pay one price and e-a-m-a-y-l . Many other local*

restaurants have also changed to this style. A pleasant experience, none-the-less. My wife enjoyed it because she could try a bit of everything.' MR&MRS T. *'Incidentally it is licensed and £4.50 for a bottle of Sparkbrook's finest Liebfraumilch must make every hour a happy one.'* AM. Private car parking. Hours: 12 to late.

SHEREEN KADAH U BYO

543 Moseley Road, Balsall Heath, B12
0121 440 4641

'Busy and cheerful. Large open barbecue by the window where the kebabs etc are freshly cooked to order. Sheeh Kebabs were excellent, balti meat superb. Unfortunately, my wife's Chicken Kurma was awful – too spicy and the sauce had curdled. To be fair they took it off the bill. Very good value.' RE. On subsequent visits RE reports: *'Food was excellent, service was brisk and friendly, the clientele was largely Asian. Back to a good standard after my disappointing visit.'* RE. *'In the display cabinet is a selection of Kebabs on an array of sharp skewers which look like a Zulu armoury after an attack on Rourke's Drift.'* AM. **BYO.** Children welcome before 11.30pm, [that's way past their bed time!] Menu Extracts: Popadom 30p [wow] Family Nan £2.60. Chana Fried Rice £1.40, Tropical Biriani £8, Ras Malai £1, Barfu 45p, Jalebi 45p. Hours: 11am-12am.

Birmingham B13

Moseley

DEOLALI BAR RESTAURANT NEW ENTRANT

23a St Mary's Row, B13 0121 442 2222

Better known for its Pakistani Balti houses, Moseley, is now unexpectedly home to a new Indian fine-dining experience, Deolali. Even its name is unexpected. Deolali is a town 100 miles north-east of Bombay. In the 19th century the British Raj army had a transit camp there. Soldiers who had finished their tours of duty were posted there to await their return home on troop ships. But these only left India between November and March, and at worst a soldier might have to wait for eight months in the raging Indian summer, with literally nothing to do. Sheer boredom caused some to behave eccentrically, and the word 'doolally' entered the dictionary meaning "mad" or "eccentric". Co-owner Tariq Zaman smiles if you know this (so tell him!), but he is serious about his restaurant and has dug deep into his bank of ideas and his pocket to ensure the restaurant stands out from the crowd. Taking his extensive restaurateur knowledge, Tariq knew he wanted a design concept completely unconventional that wouldn't necessarily depict a standard Indian restaurant. he building was an old coach-house for the next door pub that dates back to the 18th century, where he fashioned a minimalist interior, which he describes as a barn conversion because of its high ceilings and solid oak beams. Split across three levels, the first floor leads into the entrance and stepping up to the second level is the 50-cover bar and a private dining area that seats around 15 people, with views of the 130-cover restaurant. The dark brown leather seats and oak flooring and tables are each placed to complement the beams, which are the highlight of the interiors. Head Chef Salim Sukha picked up his trade at Goa's fabulous seven-star Leela Beech Hotel and Delhi's luxury Hyatt, before joining Tariq at Spice Avenue and The Spice Exchange (Guide entrants) which Tariq owned. Sukha takes a modern approach to traditional cooking. The menu, which is brimming with fresh dishes includes such specials as Goan Green Masala Salmon and Deolali Monkfish as well as sweet desserts like Lemon Mousse served with Mango Sorbet and Gulab Jamun with Honey and Ginger Ice Cream. *Puja Vedi, Ed Tandoori Magazine..*

K2

107 Alcester Road, B13 0121 449 3883

N Pasha and M Niam's 58-seater is named after the highest mountain in Pakistan, shown on the biggest map of Baltistan (to prove it exists to the doubters) on one wall. Peppered Chicken £3.10, is Chino-Tibetan (a Baltistan influence) with its sweet and sour chicken prepared with a mixture of black and green pepper, ginger, soya sauce, sugar and lime.

SPICE AVENUE

562-4 Moseley Road, B13 0121 442 4936

In a corner-site on the fringe of the Zone, it's a smart licensed restaurant with rear car park *'which is handy. Attentive and friendly staff. Food OK. A bit overpriced [compared with the rest of the Zone].'* RE. *'The Balti Ginger Chicken is a straightforward but excellent combination. However, the lamb Shahan is an excellent exotic alternative with tender lamb cutlets stuffed with garlic mushrooms. Accompanying onion kulcha will make your eyes and mouth water.'* AM. *'Menu Conventional Quality Outstanding Quantity Adequate Decor Pale walls Service Superb Comfort Acceptable Comments Starters Popadoms x 12*

Prawn Puree £3.95Tandoori Mixed Grill £4.95 x 5 Main Course Balti Mix £7.95 x 3 Balti Chicken Tikka £6.25 x 2 Hara Gosht £6.95 Nans Keema Naan £2.25 x 2 Peshwari Naan £1.95 x 2 Garlic Naan £1.75 Plain Naan £1.25 Mark 9/10 Extremely impressive meal all round.' G&MP.

SWEET CHILLIES CUISINE

NOMINATED BEST IN MIDLANDS

836 Yardleywood Rd, B13 0121 443 2737

Iqbal Hussain's impressive building, houses this stylish restaurant. A very grand porch welcomes you, complete with colonial palms and a red carpet! Inside, a modern, contemporary feel, including wooden floors, deep brown leather high back chairs or booths (they look really comfortable!), white linen and spot ceiling lights - lovely. Menu Snapshot: Bombay Duck 80p, dry roasted fish; Sweet Chillies Spice Wings £2.90, marinated in sweet, hot and tangy paste, stuffed with ground herbs, barbecued in the clay oven, served with fried onions, peppers, tomatoes and coriander leaves; Baigan Maza Dhai £3.50, aubergine deep-fried and filled with spiced minced chicken and vegetables, garnished with home-made, low fat Raitha; Shobzi Celery £2.80, chopped and fried celery in butter sauce, cook with citrus flavour vegetable and topped with poppy seeds; Pigeon Musaka £6.95, layers of pigeon breast, stuffed with spicy mushrooms, served with a spicy game sauce and Paratha; Lamb Shank Tara £7.95, lamb shank braised, medium hot, served with spicy mint and curry sauce, served with herb noodles; Deewana Naga Gosht / Murgh £6.95, marinated lamb or chicken, cooked with Sylheti chilli and onions, in a very hot and spicy sauce; Shahi Chocolate Korma £6.95, chicken, lamb or vegetable braised in a chocolate gravy, enriched with cream, almonds and coconut, Neramisha £2.75 - red kidney beans, Bengali runner beans, medium gravy with onion, capsicum and coriander; Chillie (sic) Chips £1.95, steak cut chips cooked in chillies; Bengal Spice Naan £2.40 – garlic and coriander filled unleavened bread with cheese topping, chillies can be added. There are many more lovely sounding dishes, so please visit and tell us what you think! Delivery: 2 miles, £12 minimum. Takeaway: 15% discount. Minimum Charge: £10. Licensed: stocks Cobra £2.75 a bottle, house wine £9.95 a bottle. Price Check: Popadom 50p, CTM £6.95, Pullao Rice £1.75. Hours: Lunch by pre-booking only and 5.30 - 11.30, Saturday to 12, Sunday to 11. Branch: Sylhet Spice, Kings Heath, Birmingham; Shahi Palace, Foleshill, Coventry; Bengal Delight, Holbrooks, Coventry. <www.sweetchillies.com>

Birmingham North

Consists of B6, B7, B19 to B24, B35, B42 to B44

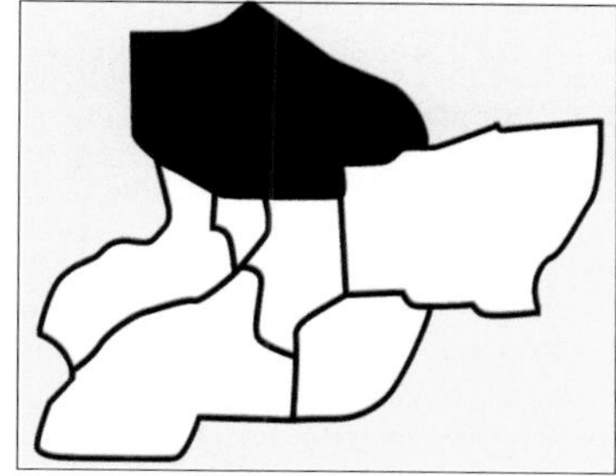

See page 374 for key to this map.

Birmingham B21

Handsworth

MILAN SWEET CENTRE

238 Soho Rd, Handsworth, B21 0121 551 5239

A branch of the Milan restaurant in 93 Newhall Street, Birmingham B3 (see entry). This is a takeaway venue for Indian sweets, and savoury snacks. The selection is huge and satisfying, at prices too cheap to ignore. Sister t/a branch at 191 Stoney Lane, Sparkbrook, B11.

Birmingham B23

Erdington

NOORAANI BALTI HOUSE

248 Slade Rd, B23 0121 373 5227

Proprietor, M Jahangir, opened his forty seater Balti House in 1994 and Chicken Balti at £4.50, a plate full (or should that be a Balti full,) just rushes out of the door. The modern kitchen is open, so diners can see the chefs cooking and all meat and poultry is Halal. Menu Snapshot: Chicken or Lamb Balti with a choice of mushroom, spinach, okra, channa, aubergine, aloo, vegetable, kidney beans or egg - all £4.50; Prawn Balti with a choice from the above - all £4.95; King Prawn Balti with a choice from the above - all £5.50. Traditionally eaten with Naan 85p, or Family Naan £2.75, that's big enough to share! However, there is a large selection of stuffed Naans, choose from keema (minced meat), garlic, vegetable, cheese, peshwari (fruit and nuts), coriander - all £1.60. Delivery: 3 miles, £7 minimum, telephone your order through and pay by credit card. You might get a discount if you show Mr Ahmed this *Guide.* Price Check: Popadom 40p, CTM £5.75, Pullao Rice £1.75. Students Discount: 10% on all takeaway. Hours: 5 - 2.

SAMRAT TANDOORI

710 Chester Road, B23 0121 384 5900

Established 1983 by Iqbal Raza Chowdhury. Seats forty eight diners. Licensed: stocks Cobra and Kingfisher, £3 a bottle, house wine £7.95 a bottle. Delivery: 6 miles, £10 minimum. You might get a discount if you show Mr Raza this *Guide.* Price Check: Popadom 50p, CTM £6.15, Pullao Rice £1.75. Hours: 5 - 1, Saturday to 2.

STOCKLAND BALTI TAKEAWAY

332 Marsh La, Erdington, B23 0121 377 8789

Owned and managed by Mrs Amina Begum since '93 serving competent takeaway curries to her regular crowd. **BYO.** She might give you a discount if you show her this *Guide.* Delivery: £10. Hours: 5-12am (1am on Fri. & Sat.).

Birmingham East

Consists of B8, B9, B25, B26, B33, B34, B36, B37, and B40 (NEC)

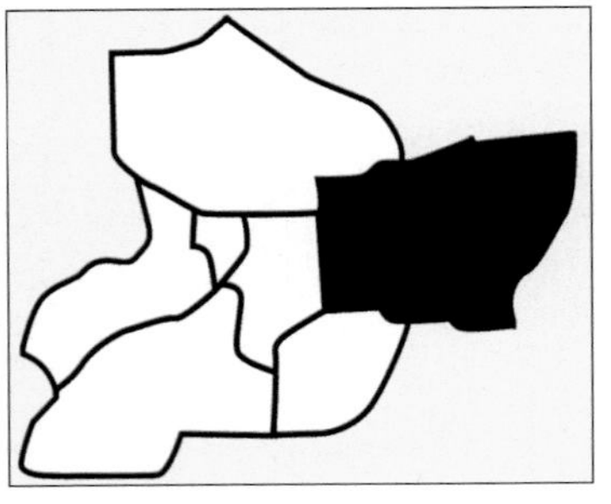

See page 374 for key to this map.

Birmingham B9

Small Heath

IIB NE GHANI

264 Green Lane, B9 0121 772 8138

First opened in 1981, taken over by Nazrul Hussain in 1998. with Bilal Miah (manager) Chef Abdul Ahad's open kitchen allows customers to see their formula curries cooking. **BYO.** Takeaway: 10% discount. You might get a discount if you show Mr Hussain this *Guide.* Delivery: £8 min 3-miles. Hours: 4.30pm-12am; Sat. 4.30pm-1pm.

Birmingham B25

Yardley

YEW TREE COTTAGE

43 Stoney La, Yardley, B25 0121 786 1814

Established 1979 by Jamal Chowdhury. The unassuming exterior hides a huge restaurant, seating 180 diners on two floors. Inside it is nicely decorated with wooden flooring, large green plants, white linen and comfortable upholstered chairs - all very bright and tidy. Restaurant Theme Nights: Sunday: Buffet - £6.95 children/£4.95 children – booking advisable; Monday: Gourmet Dinner £9.95 adult/£6.95 children – four courses from the a la carte menu; Tuesday: Balti Night - £6.50, choice of any Balti with a Naan; Wednesday: Chef's Choice £7.95, tasty treats the from the head chef, starter and main course; Thursday: Ladies Night £8.95: Bhajia, choice from a la carte menu and a glass of wine - sounds great! Menu Snapshot: Could be the biggest menu I have ever seen, there are an incredible 223 dishes to choose from - Tikka Sandwich £3.50, Tikka in a Naan with salad dressing; Mix Grill Sandwich £4.50, Chicken and Lamb Tikka, Sheek Kebab in Naan; South Indian Garlic Chilli Murgh £7.25, barbecued chicken, fresh garlic, chilli sauce, fresh coriander, crispy green chillies - hot; North Bengali Fruity Murch £7.25, creamy, mild, fruity dish with barbecued chicken pieces; Masala Kulcha £1.50, leavened bread stuffed with capsicum, onions, spices then cooked in the char coal oven. Delivery: 3 miles, £15 minimum. Takeaway: 10% discount, £10 minimum. Cobra and Kingfisher, £2.90 a bottle, house wine £8.95 a bottle. You might get a discount if you show Mr Chowdhury this *Guide.* Price Check: Popadom 50p, CTM £7.25, Pullao Rice £1.70. Hours: 5 - 12.30, Saturday to 1.30; Sunday 6 - 12.30.

Birmingham B26

Sheldon

SHABAR TANDOORI

4 Arden Oak Road, B26 0121 742 0636

Good curryhouse where you might get a discount if you show them this *Guide.*

TITASH INTERNATIONAL

2278 Coventry Road, B26 0121 722 2080

Away from home? Have to endure the dreaded catering, dispensed expensively and with a straight face at the neighbouring NEC, railway station, airport, and hotels of varying pretensions? Want to know of an alternative close to hand? That's what this *Guide* is for. Titash is a good curryhouse.

VARSHA NEW ENTRANT

2250 Coventry Road, B26 0121 743 6572

'*This is a must, when ever in the NEC arena area - contemporary decor, friendly staff with long memories). Achari and Handi dishes are our favourites here and have not been bettered elsewhere. Street parking is adjoining.*' JP.

Birmingham South East

Consists of B27 and B28

(Beyond this is Knowle and Solihull – see entries)

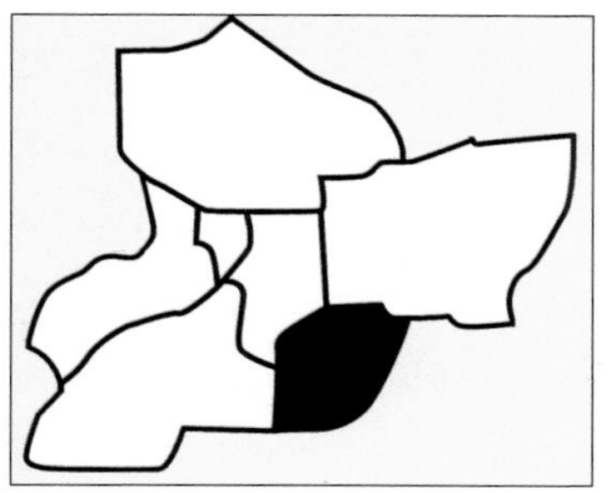

See page 374 for key to this map.

Birmingham B27

Acocks Green

DEVDOOT

1st Floor, 37 Westley Rd, B27 0121 706 4842

Good curryhouse where you might get a discount if you show them this *Guide.*

MOGHUL

1184 Warwick Road, B27 0121 707 6777

Ditto.

Birmingham B28

Hall Green

MIZAN

1347 Stratford Road, Hall Green, B28 0121 777 3185

Formerly J Jays, KA Rahman's curry house seats 66. Takeaway: 10% off. Minimum charge: £5. Special: Saag Kamal Kakri, spinach and lotus roots. You might get a discount if you show Mr Rahman this *Guide.* Hours: 12-2pm/5.30-12 (12.30 on Fri. & Sat.).

Birmingham South West

Consists of B14, B29 to B31, B45, B47, B48, B60

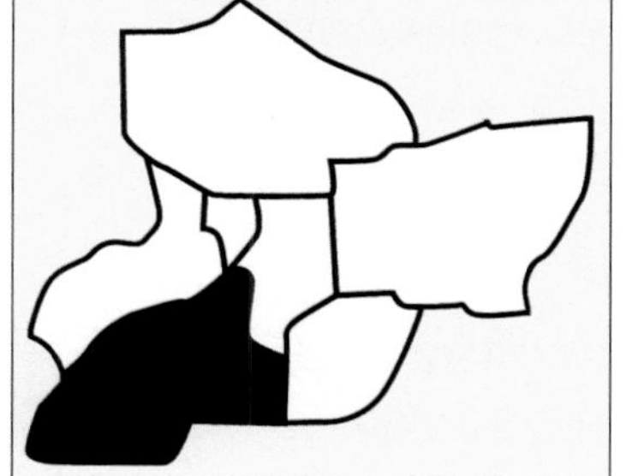

See page 374 for key to this map.

Birmingham B14

Hollywood, Kings Heath, Selly Oak

KINGS BALTI

13 York Rd, King's Heath, B14 0121 443 1114

Est 1994 by Salim Miah. Seats 62 diners. Most Popular Dish: Balti Chicken Dan Gali, tikka, cashew nuts, sultanas, almonds, pistachio, garnished with fresh banana. I do hope I have got this right, but Jalim is only licensed to sell Beer, not spirits or wine, so, please **BYO** (no corkage charged). Menu Snapshot: Katia Kebab £2.60, Sheek Kebab rolled up a Chapatti; Panir Tikka

£2.25, cubes of marinated cheese, dipped in gram flour, fried; Tandoori Mixed Grill £8.95, Chicken and Lamb Tikka, Sheek Kebab,King Prawn, rice, curry sauce and Plain Naan - wow! what a feast! Balti Chana Batata £4.50, chickpeas, diced potato, onions, herbs, spices, garnished with coriander - medium hot; Keema, Peshwari, Onion, Garlic, Vegetable or Cheese Naan all £1.45. Takeaway: 10% discount, £5.50 minimum. Price Check: Popadom free, CTM £5.75, Pullao Rice £1.95 Hours: 5 - 11.

MILLENNIUM BALTI — NEW ENTRANT

796 Alcester Road South, Kings Heath, Birmingham B14 — 0121 430 6155

Seats forty-four diners. Unlicensed, so **BYO!** The three course meal for £7.50 is very popular. Takeaway: 10% discount. Delivery: 3 miles, £8 minimum. Price Check: Popadom 50p, CTM £5.50, Pullao Rice £1.60. Hours: 5.30 - 12.30.

Birmingham B29

Selly Oak

DILSHAD INTERNATIONAL

618 Bristol Rd, Selly Oak, B29 — 0121 472 5016

Established in 1978. Seats 80. Specials include: Achar Gosth , Champa Koli Bahar 5, Fish Bengal.. Takeaway: 10% discount. Hours: 5.30pm to late.

Birmingham B30

Cotteridge, Stirchley

RAJPOOT

1831Pershore Road, Cotteridge, B30
0121 458 5604

Watir Ali's 94-seater is *'A glitzy little place with friendly service. All the family use it regularly.'* JAD.You might get a discount if you show Mr Ali this *Guide.* Hours: 6pm-2am.

YASSER TANDOORI

1268 Pershore Road, Stirchley, B30
0121 433 3023

Established in 1987 and still under the same management (A Hussain and Sarwar Khan). Yasser seats 80. Unlicensed **BYO**. Menu Snapshot: Balti Chef's Special Tropical £6.40 - prawn, chicken, lamb and mushroom; Balti Prawn or Fish £5.80; all dishes can be made hot or mild for 20p - what a cheek! twenty pence for the tip of a teaspoon of chilli powder!! Naan £1.20; Medium Naan £3.20; Family Naan £4.60. Minimum Charge: £5.00. Takeaway: free Popadom, mint sauce, £10 min. Delivery: 3 miles, £10 min. You might get a discount if you show them this *Guide.* Parking for 12 cars. Price Check: Popadom 45p, CTM £5.95, Pullao Rice £1.70. Hours: 4.30 - 12, Sat to 1.

Birmingham West

Consists of B15 to B18 & B32

(Beyond this is Halesowen, Smethwick, Warley and West Bromwich – see entries)

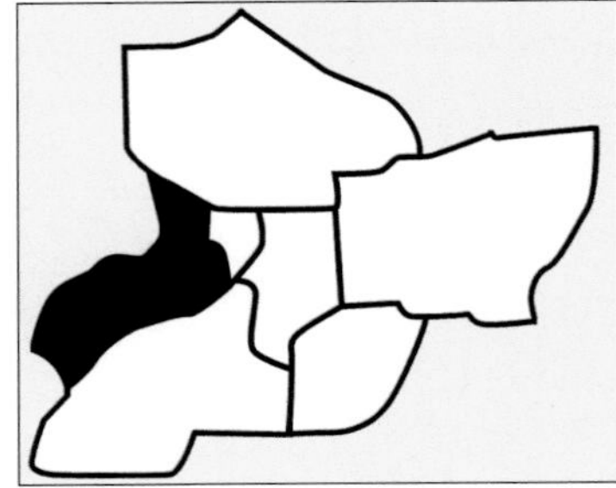

See page 374 for key to this map.

Birmingham B16

Edgbaston

J JAYS

2 Edgbaston Shopping Centre, Five Ways, B16
0121 455 6871

Good curryhouse where you might get a discount if you show them this *Guide.*

Birmingham B32

Quinton

SOHO INDIA

417 Hagley Rd West, B32 — 0121 421 3242

Good curryhouse where you might get a 10% discount if you show them this *Guide.*

Tabla drums and sitar players

Remainder of West Midlands

Coventry

CAFÉ TAMARINDS

376 Kenilworth Road, Balsall Common, Coventry 01676 533 308

'Contemporary decor and car parking, friendly staff. Rajastani Lamb - excellent, Onion Naan - excellent, Channa Bhuna - excellent. Special offers on Sunday and Monday evenings.' JP.

DESI DISH NEW ENTRANT

Far Gosford Street, Coventry

'Menu Extensive and unusual Quality Quantity Decor Service Comfort Comments Popadoms 80p x 3 Peshwari Naan £2.50 Metha Maaz £9.95 Chicken Korma £8.50 Aloo Murgh Masala £8.50 Side Dish Aloo Chole £4.50 Accompaniment Pullau Rice £1.95 Peshwari Naan £2.50 Onion Kulcha Naan £2.50. Lager x2 Coke x2 Jug of Lassi £5. Mark. 8/10'. G&MP.

THE MINT NEW ENTRANT

13, The Butts, Earlsdon, Coventry 024 76226111

'Menu: very extensive with many unusual choices Quality: Excellent Quantity: Copious and how! Decor: pale pastel painted walls in one long room in ultra modern style Service: Faultless Comfort: Deep leather chairs, beautiful wooden tables widely spaced with no infringement on others Starters:: Popadoms 4 x spicy, 2 x plain. Paneer Tikka £3.75; beautifully marinated cheese; Reshmi Kebab £4.50, good; Tetul Mix £4.50; extremely generous portions, beautifully presented; Chicken Tikka Chat £3.50 very good with generous portion. Main course: Chicken Pasala, wonderful marinade in beautifully creamy sauce £6.95; Tandoori special mix, very nice but lamb a bit chewy £8.95; Lamb Afghan Chana, lamb slightly chewy but otherwise excellent £6.95; Chicken Ghurka Masala very nicely spiced with a kick to it £7.95. Accompaniments: Pullau rice £1.95 x 2; Cauliflower Bhaji £2.95; Bombay Potato £2.95. Mark 8/10 Bill £71.25 plus £7.75 tip. We have visited several times since it opened in 2006. It has an excellent innovation as far Coventry Curry Houses are concerned in as much as you are able to byo and a very welcoming ambience to boot. All in all a most welcome addition to the ranks'. G&MP. *'Menu Very wide Quality Variable Quantity Copious Decor Pure white throughout Service Excellent Comfort Long narrow room with tables of 4 with leather chairs Comments Starters: Nargis Kebab £3.50 excellent; Mixed Vegetable Pakora £2.50; Chicken Tikka Chatt £3.50 well prepared and excellent taste; Stuffed Pepper Chicken £3.95 Lovely. Main course: Northern Indian Garlic Chilli Chicken £6.95 underspiced, chicken undermarinated. Chasni Tikka Chicken £6.95 very tender juicy and well marinaded; Chicken Balti £5.95 not impressed at all. Was bland,*

lacking in flavour and not marinaded enough; Chicken Korma £5.50. Accompaniments: Peshwari Naan £1.95, Pullau Rice £1.95 x 2; Onion Naan £1.95. Mark 8/10 Bill £50.50 plus £4.50 tip. Starters were superb but a couple of the main courses could have been better.' G&MP.

MONSOON TOP 100

20 Far Gosford St, Coventry 024 7622 9651

'Menu conventional; Quality top class; Quantity copious; Beige-yellow pale wallpaper with prints of Asian women; Service: ultra quick; Comfort: Acceptable – reasonable space between tables Comments My concerns over the Monsoon having lost its elevated status as a result of the previous owner leaving were well and truly allayed following this visit. It maintained its outstanding standards in every respect with this meal. You simply can't beat it in terms of Balti House Cuisine. Starter - Tandoori Chicken £2.25, superb. Marinated wonderfully, huge portion, delicious taste. Main – Balti Keema Tikka £4.95. Nasi Goreng £2.25. Popadoms 50p x 2. Pint Cobra £2.60. Total Bill £13.05. Mark 9/10.' G&MP. *'Menu Limited Quality Good Quantity Very Good Decor Pale painted walls Service Excellent Comfort Fairly small restaurant, tables quite close together. Approx 28 covers Comments Starters Popadoms x4 Chicken Pakora £2.95 Superb Tandoori Chicken £2.95. Well marinated, but small quantity. Main Course Lamb Pathia £4.75 Lamb Ceylon £4.75 Accompaniments Garlic Naan £1.75 Keema Rice £2.30 Bombay Aloo £2.50. Total Bill £32. Mark 9/10.'* G&MP. And on another occasion: *'Starters Masala Fish x2 £2.95 wonderful Chicken Pakora £2.25 very very good very spicy Sag Puree£2.95 excellent very light. Main Course Chicken Tikka Dhansak £5.25 outstanding Chicken Balti with Mushroom and Spinach £5.45 absolutely stunning 10/10. Balti Mince with mixed vegetables very good; Vegetable Biryani too hot for me but made with fresh vegetables. Accompaniments: Nasi Goreng £2.25 Pilau Rice £1.65 Peshwari Nan £2.25 Papadums x 4 free!+ drinks Bill: £46.85 + £3.15 tip Total £50 Overall mark 9.2/10. The verdict: back on the form that made it well worthy of a place in the top 100. Please make sure it stays there.'* G&MP. Certainly will Graham.

THE OCEAN NEW ENTRANT

46 Jubilee Crescent Radford, Coventry

'Most dishes conventional but some unusual choices. Quality: Very good. Quantity: More than adequate. Décor: Old-fashioned with painted stone walls. Service: Very polite, prompt and pleasant. Comfort: 56 covers – not too cramped but no segregation of smokers a downside. Comments: Starters Stuffed Pepper with meat £2.40 very nice, spicy but not too heavy. Tandoori Chicken £2.30. Well marinated and tasty. Main Course Chicken Pasanda £5.65 Pleasantly sweet, copious sauce; Balti Chicken Tikka Chilli Massalla £6.25, well spiced with good quality chicken. Accompaniments Bengal Fried Rice £2.10 Very spicy with fresh green chillies. Peshwari Nan £1.65 Nice and sweet but no syrup and few sultanas. Side dish Mattar Paneer unusually sweet. Bill: £26.60 with £2.60 tip. Overall mark 8/10. The verdict: certainly worth another visit especially as they gave us a 15% discount card as we left!' G&MP.

ROJONI NEW ENTRANT

477 Beake Avenue Coventry

Menu Fairly wide with some unusual special dishes. Quality Very Good. Quantity: Copious. Décor: Strikingly colourful. Vibrant. Service: Exemplary. Comfort: Excellent. Starters: Papadoms x6 Dhal Soup £2.50 Very comforting with slices of garlic and lemon. Tandoori Chicken £2.85 Absolutely gorgeous- marinade spot on. Chicken Chat £2.95 Very spicy. King Prawn Puri Not very special. Main Course Tandoori Mixed Grill £8.50 Very good. Lamb Mirch Masala £5.95 Sauce excellent but lamb chewy £5.95. Chicken Jhallosi £6.95 x2 Very well done ^ chicken very spicy. Accompaniments Peshwari Nan £1.85 Pilau Rice £1.85x2 Side Dishes Cauliflower Bhajee £2.95 Mattar Paneer £2.95 Total cost £80.20 + £8 tip Overall mark 8.7/10 We were very impressed!

SHAHI PALACE

367 Foleshill Road, Coventry 024 7668 8719

Good curryhouse where you might get a discount if you show them this *Guide.*

SHAPLA

171 Daventry Road, Cheylesmore, Coventry 02476 506306

Established in 1984, when it was called Cheylesmore Balti. Arab Ali took over the restaurant in 2003 and changed its name. Seats sixty diners and Chicken Tikka Masala and Chicken Jalfrezi are the most ordered dishes. Menu Snapshot: Sizzling Fish Biran £7.50, spicy fried fish served with fried onions; Chicken Chashney £7.50, with honey and cream; Chicken or Lamb Biriani £7.95, served with curried vegetables; Bangla Naan £2.25, green chilli, coriander and onion. Licensed: stocks Cobra, £2.70 a bottle, house wine £2.25 a glass. Minimum Charge: £5.00. Takeaway: 25% discount. Price Check: Popadom 75p, CTM £7.50, Pullao Rice £2.30. Hours: 5 - 11.30, Friday and Saturday to 12.45.

SHIMLA SPICE NEW ENTRANT

1 Copthall House, Coventry

'Menu, wide if conventional Quality Mine superb, Melinda's poor; Quantity More than adequate; Decor Brightly painted walls; Service Excellent; Ambience spot on; Comfort Round tables with 4 seats- a little close together. Comments Starter Fish Biriani £ 4.25 Delicious and beautifully spiced. Popadoms £1.50 x2. Main Course Lamb Pathia £6.50 Wonderfully sour. Beautiful lamb, very tasty. Vegetarian Thali £12.75 Very disappointing. Dall hard, something burnt in it. Vegetable Curry and Bombay Potato almost identical. Accompaniments Peshwari Naan £2.40, very doughy.. Total Bill £37 + £2 tip. Mark 7/10. G&MP.

SONARGAON

153 Daventry Rd, Coventry 024 7650 4670

You might get a discount if you show them this *Guide. Good'* GG&MP.

TURMERIC GOLD

166 Medieval Spon St, Coventry 024 7622 6603

Opposite Bonds at Skydome. Jay Alam's restaurant seats ninety diners in six rooms, on two floors (the waiters must be fit!). The exterior of the building has been painted royal blue, and is alive with a

georgeous forest of flowers. For real twosome pampering you can dine in one of the luscious booths (illustrated above). Menu Snapshot: Crab Spring Rolls £5.25, beansprouts, carrot, celery, crab meat, wrapped in a roll, served with spicy sauce; Goa Tiger Prawns £5.75, grilled tiger prawns, spinach, with coconut and cream sauce; Rawlpindi Curry Puff £5.25, highly spiced lamb, dried red chillies, sweet vinegar sauce, puffed bread, served with chat masala dressed, crispy salad; Emperors Chicken Chilli £11.25, stir-fried with fresh green chillies, carrots, mushroom, capsicum, pineapple, and coriander leaf, served sizzling. *'Menu :Extremely extensive Quality: Good Quantity: Adequate Decor: Garish with pictures of bare breasted ladies on the wall Service: Faultless Comfort: Fine Comments Starters:: 4 x spicy popadoms; 2 x plain popadoms; Chicken Pathia £4.25; Rawalpindi Curry Puff £5.25; Sheek Kebab £5.25; Paneer Shashlick £3.75; Main Course: Lamb Mustard Chilli Bhuna £8.95; Chicken Ginger £8.95; Achari Chicken £8.95; Tandoori Platter £12.95!! Accompaniments: Peshwari Naan £2.65; Lemon rice £3.25; Pullau rice £2.95; Side Dish: Cauliflower Bhaji £3.45 – flavour beautiful but texture mushy; Drinks: glass of red wine £3.70 x 2 Stella Artois £3.30 x3 Bill; £100 (including £6.70 tip) – the most we have ever spent as a group of 4. Mark 8/10 Excellent meal spoilt by the excessive cost* G&MP. Cobra

£3.30 a bottle, house wine £10.25 a bottle. Takeaway: 15% discount. Price Check: Popadom 70p, CTM £7.75, Pullao Rice £2.95. Hours: 12 - 2 / 5.30 - 11.15, Saturday to 12.15. <www.turmericgold.co.uk>

Dudley

BALTI 4 U TAKEAWAY

63 Halesowen Road, Netherton, Dudley
01384 240230

Afruz Ali opened his takeaway in 2000, Azom Ali is his head chef. Madras and Tikka Masala are his most ordered dishes. Menu SnapshoYou might get a discount if you show them this Guide.Nargis Kebab £2.85, spiced minced, shaped and stuffed with boiled egg, fried in butter and topped with omelette; Stuffed Peppers £2.85, stuffed with spicy chicken, meat, vegetable; Tandoori Chicken Keema and Peas £5.25; Sag Dall Bhajee £2.50, spinach, lentils, garlic and ginger; Prawn Pullao Rice £2.75; Keema, Peshwari, Onion, Mushroom, Coriander, Stuffed, Garlic or Cheese Naan, all £1.95 each. You might get a discount if you show them this Guide. Delivery: 4 miles. Price Check: Popadom 50p, CTM £5.50, Pullao Rice £1.75. Hours: 5 - 12.30, Sat to 1.20.

Halesowen *B62, B63 & B65*

AMEENA

192 Hagley Road, Hasbury, Halesowen, B63
0121 550 4317

Hiron Miah's 78-seater (est. 1974) *'I've only tried this restaurant once. The food was good standard, and while I was waiting regulars were warmly welcomed.'* NR. *'Have visited twice recently, on first occasion the food was exceptionally good – in particular the Chicken Tikka Buna and the fresh naan bread. Second visit was not so good, but still of a standard that I would choose to call again if in this area.'* RJP. *'Slightly downmarket feel to the place but not the food! Prawn Bhuna is delicious with the sauce adding a tasty extra. Chicken Jalfrezi with thin strips of ginger laid on top lattice work fashion. Enjoyed the Sag Aloo. Cobra a pleasant fix. Waiters cheerful and attentive. In the guide and deserves it.'* MS. You might get a discount if you show Mr Miahthis *Guide.* Delivery: 3 miles, £10 minimum, 5.30-10. Hours: 5.30-12. (Fri. & Sat. to 1am).

RED PEPPERS

8 Hagley St, Halesowen B63 0121 550 8588

Head chef, Mr Islam is also the proprietor and opened his restaurant in 1989. His Jalfrezi and Madras curries are very popular with the locals. Menu Snapshot: Tandoori Fish £3.75; Chicken Makhani £5.95, mildly spiced, spring chicken, fragrant spiced, ground almond, butter and cream; Chana Paneer £2.25, chick peas and cheese, mild spices; Masala Kulcha £1.80, leavened bread stuffed with mildly spiced vegetables. Delivery: 3.5 miles, £10 min. Takeaway: 10% discount. Price Check: Popadom 55p, CTM £5.95, Pullao Rice £1.80. Hours: 5.30 - 12, Fri & Sat to 1.

Knowle

BILASH

1608 High Street, Knowle, B93 01564 773030

Mashud Uddin and Nowab Ali's Bangladeshi curry house seats 64, party room 40. Set in black and white surroundings, dating back to the 16th century. Special: Jeera Chicken Dilkush, spring chicken, coconut, jeera, tomato and mixed spices. *'Very good quality.'* J&MCL. Takeaway: 10% off. You might get a discount if you show them this *Guide.* Hours: 5.30-12am. Branches: Bilash, 82-90 Priory Road, Kenilworth. Bejoy Takeaway, 763 Old Lode Lane, Solihull, West Midlands.

KNOWLE INDIAN BRASSERIE

1690 High Street, Knowle, B93 01564 776453

Est 1995, Hossain Miah's a/c Bangladeshi curry house seats 45. *'Menu Extremely extensive and very cheaply priced considering location Quality Excellent Quantity Huge Decor Beige Service Extremely variable, problems in kitchen transmitted to restaurant Comfort Acceptable Comments Starters: 4 x spicy popadoms, 2 x popadoms; platter for 2 £7.50 very tasty; Reshmi Kebab £2.95 not exceptional; Sheek Kebab £2.50 very spicy. Main course: Lamb Jalfrezi £5.80; Tandoori deluxe £7.50; Garlic Korai Chicken £7.50; Chicken Tikka Sylheti £5.65. Accompaniments: Peshwari Naan £1.90; Pullau rice £1.80 x 2; Peas Pullau Rice £2.05. Side dishes: Chana Masala £2.55 – excellent; Cauliflower Bhaji £2.55 unimpressive. Mark 8/10. Bill £67.35 plus £5 tip.'* G&MP. You might get a discount if you show Mr Miah this *Guide.* Takeaway: 10% discount. Delivery: £12 min 3-miles. Hours: 5.30-11.30; Sun. 5.30-10.30.

Lye

PEPPER AND SPICE

204 - 205 High Street, Lye 01384 893933

At Sabber Iqbal's 40-seater you can get these intriguing specials: Pepper Chicken, capsicum stuffed with tandoori chicken. Fish chat, fish in a sweet and sour sauce. Balti Chicken and Mushroom, Naan. You might get a discount if you show Mr Sabber this *Guide.* **BYO.** Delivery: £7 minimum. Hours: 6-12am.

Oldbury *B69*

SAFFRON NEW ENTRANT

909 Wolverhampton Rd, Oldbury 0121 552 1752

'Saffron is situated just off the M6, on the way back north from the NEC, and as everyone who has visited the NEC, knows, that the food is awful and expensive, so, no excuse, off to the Saffron for a lovely meal! 'As a lunch diner I was surprised that there were other diners as this restaurant is a fair way outside a town centre. A modern, well lit and nicely decorated establishment. The service was prompt and unfussy, although I gave up trying to get a plain Madras sauce with Biriani...' Oh dear! *'Ordered Popadoms, crisp and light, Chutneys, onion, mango and yoghurt, very acceptable. Murgh Biriani, seemed like a small portion when it arrived with the rice plated and moulded, but when attacked it was surprisingly a lot of food.'* I've been there, thought, "what a mean little portion," and then when I have finished my meal, it looked like I hadn't even started! *'Garnished with fried onions and coriander (no omelette), the rice had a good flavour, in fact was very spicy, chicken well cooked and tender. Vegetable curry sauce containing peas, green beans, tinned carrots and a hint of cauliflower was quite mild but very tasty. Overall, I would love to try this restaurant in the evening as I feel it has great potential.' I object to a 10% service charge and then having the credit card bill left open.'* DB. Naughty naughty in fact, Very Naughty, naughty! Menu Snapshot: Saffron Machli £4.50, seabass marinated with saffron and shallow fried; Chowk Ki Tikka £2.75, potato patties, rich filling of asafoetida, fresh peas, black cardamom, pepper, ginger, garlic and coriander, golden fried; Machli Tikka Ajwani £9.95, cubes of Hake dipped in sugar cane vinegar, steeped in cream cheese marinade, spiked with ajwain and lemon; Murgh Khali Mirch £6.50, demi-dry and light chicken with roasted ground black pepper; Pindi Channa £2.50/£4.95, chick peas, spicy melange of pomegranate seeds, cumin, ajwain, rock salt, tempered with ghee; Dal Tadkawali £2.50/£4.95, whole urid and moong dal simmered with tomato, onion, tempered with whole red chillies, cumin and garlic; Enda Chawal £2.35, rice with eggs. Takeaway 10% discount. Price Check: Popadom 50p, CTM £6.50, Pullao Rice £1.95. Hours: 12 - 2.30, Mon to Fri and 5.30 - 11.30.

Smethwick *B66*

HAWELI NEW ENTRANT

509 Hagley Rd, Bearwood, Smethwick B66 0121 434 4869

Opened in 1993 by Mohammed Ashraf, who is also the manager and will be there to greet you when you visit. And, yes, Chicken Tikka Masala is the most popular dish. Delivery: 1 mile. Cobra, £2.50 a bottle, £7.50 for a bottle of house wine. Price Check: Popadom 40p, CTM £5.50, Pullao Rice £1.75. Hours: 6 - 12, Sat to 1.

Solihull

B90 to B93

JIMMY SPICE'S NEW ENTRANT

64 Station Rd, Solihull, B91 0121 709 2111

In 2006 the second branch in in the former Wates Wine Lodge, turning it into a 300-seat restaurant with a 100 -seat bar called NYC. *'Solihull's funky interior design is home to impeccable customer service led by Managers Chander S Ahuja and Harshit Vyas. Chefs specialising in each kind of cuisine served have been recruited to ensure that the food served is authentic to their regions, while Head Chef, Indra Mani runs the kitchen operations and ensures that chefs maintain the quality that made the restaurant group famous. Mani has had extensive experience at some of India's five-stars, including New Delhi's Grand Hyatt. The sleek wine room on the second level has a capacity of 150 and serves a collection of fine wines and Champagnes along with teas and the usual round of cocktails'. Puja Vedi, Ed Tandoori Magazine..* After we go to print, they plan to open their third Jimmy Spices, a 400-seater with a 150 seat bar called NYC in Sutton Coldfield. Plans are afoot to open in six major cities in the with sites they tell us are already confirmed in London, Leeds & Manchester. Lunch Buffet: £5.95. Child: £2.99 (Under 10 years). Dinner buffet: Sunday to Wednesday: £12.95;

Thursday to Saturday: £14.95. Child: £6.95 (Under 10). What do you think of this concept? Hours: 12.00 - 2.30 / 5.00 -11.00; Sun to 10.00. Branch and more comment: Broad Street, Birmingham, B1. <www.jimmyspices.co.uk>

THE LLOYDS

7 Station Rd, Knowle, Solihull 01546 477 5777

Air-conditioned. Seats 140 diners. Proprietor Nanu Miah opened his restaurant in February 2003. It is quite amazing that Naga Chicken is his most popular dish, and with its extremely hot chilli, I can only think that his regular customers are what the American call 'Chile Heads.' Menu Snapshot: Boal Biran (cat fish) £3.95, fried with a touch of butter, herbs and garlic; Tandoori Mixed Grill from 5.95, served with mint sauce and fresh salad; Shobji Bihari Tawah £4.95, bindi, cauliflower, green beans, courgette, peas, sweetcorn, sprouts, medium spiced, dry curry; Cheese and Garlic Naan £2.25. Licensed but BYO allowed. House Wine £9.75. Credit cards not accepted. Takeaway: 10% discount. Delivery: £11.50 min. min Charge: £10. You might get a discount if you show them this Guide. Price Check: Popadom 50p, CTM £6.50, Pullao Rice £2. Hours: 5.30 - 11. ul <www.thelloydsindian.com

RAJNAGAR INTERNATIONAL

NOMINATED BEST IN THE MIDLANDS

256 Lyndon Rd, Olton, Solihull, B92 0121 742 8140

Dr Moula Miah is the owner, and a nicer man you will not find. He has taken the Bangladeshi curryhouse formula to its heights at his three venues (see branches). It is a useful 10 Minutes from the NEC and airport. Modern décor, clean lines, greeat unfussy food and care from the Doc himself and his staff. *'It really is exceptionally good.' mm. 'Interior decor, pale pink and cream walls, cream carpet — optimistic re spillages!, stylish tables and chairs with monogrammed linen exudes quality and class. Attentive service, swiftly delivered Popadoms, chunky pickles and cold lager. I chose Meat Samosas (spring roll style), Chicken Tikka Dupiaza, Pullao Rice and Nan – ALL SUPERB!'* TE. It is probably the best in the area, and we are happy to promote Rajnagar to our **A-LIST.** Hours: 5 till late. Branches: Shaades of Raj, 52, Station Road, Solihull, Barajee, Braod Street, B'hm. <www.rajnagar.com>

Stonnall

MANGO TREE

NEW ENTRANT
NEW TO OUR TOP 100

Chester Road, Stonnall, WS9 01922 457344

Mango Tree Indian Restaurant & Bar is a newcomer (2003) enthusiastically run by Rajinder Ram, aka Raj, (whom your editor met when working on Carlton Food Network TV) with his wife Sangeeta and in-laws Anita and George Kattapuram. former Veeraswamy Head Chef is South Indian Marriappan Sethurajapillai aka Murray, whose speciality is seafood. (note the lobster dishes). Curry chef is ex Taj Gateway, Bangalore chef Tikhan Khan is the curry expert, with Gnana Prakasam on Tandoors and South Indian cuisine also from Taj. You'll find the range of north Indian favourites plus Biryanis, Idli Sambhar and Masala Dosa, but perversely on from Sundays to Thursdays! *'If you are ever in the West Midlands try the Mango Tree on the Chester Rd, Stonnall near Sutton Coldfield. This is Southern Indian food unlike most Indian restaurants which as you know are Bangladeshi. Fish is a speciality, so too the Sunday Lunch. This a lovely restaurant not the normal curry house, and should be in the guide'* BP. <www.mangotree.biz>

Stourbridge

NEEL AKASH BALTI AND TANDOORI

2F High Street, Wollaston, Stourbridge
01384 375919

Chef Mujibur Rahman's 60-seater. You might get a discount if you show them this *Guide.* Takeaway: 10% off. Delivery: £8 min, 3-miles. Hours: 5-12.

Mango Tree, Stonnall

Murray sets the world alight at Mango Tree

Sutton Coldfield *B72 to B76*

ASIAN GRILL

91 Park Rd, Sutton C'fld, B73 0121 354 7491

Formula curryhouse opened way back in 1968. If you, or any other business for that matter, have survived that long, you must be good. Hours: 5.30pm-12am (1am on Fri. & Sat.).

RICKSHAW TAKEAWAY

NEW ENTRANT

1 Stockland Court, 121, Chester Rd, Streetly, Sutton Coldfield, B74 0121 580 9400

Established by Mr Rahman in 1996. Brightly decorated in a deep pink, almost aubergine colour. The service counter is natural wood, and customers can rest on bar chairs, which sit around the room, while waiting for their takeaways. Former Walsall football manager, Paul Marson, patronises the venue. Chef's Recs: all £5.50: Korai Chicken , garnished with coriander and tomatoes; Lamb Pasanda, rich and creamy dish with almond flakes; Chicken Tikka Chilli Bhuna, fairly spicy and dry with green chillies. Price Check: Popadom 50p, CTM £5.50, Pullao Rice £1.60. Delivery: 5 miles, £10 min. Hours: 5 - 11, Sunday to 10.30.

Walsall

EAST END

9 Hawes Close, Walsall 01922 614800

Muhibur Rahman is proud of his veteran 1967 curry house and he might give you a discount if you show him this *Guide*. . Special is Green Chilli Chicken Tikka Masala. Hours: 5.30-12am.

GOLDEN MOMENTS

3 Ablewell Street, Walsall 01992 640363

Established in 1993. Seats 100. *'Having eaten Indian food for 25 years this establishment must rate as the one of the best. Staff, service, surroundings and food are excellent.'* BD. Specials: Betatawada, mashed potatoes with herbs and spices, battered and deep-fried. White Chicken Tikka, delicately spiced, wonderfully tender. Dhaba Gosht, small cubes of lamb, Tandoor-cooked, in a thick sauce. Takeaway: 15% discount. Hours: 6-12am.

KING BALTI

89 Ablewell Street, Walsall 01922 620376

Good **BYO** curryhouse where you might get a discount if you show Dudu Miah. this *Guide*. 6-1am.

SAFFRON

42 Bradford St, Walsall 01922 627899

Fully licensed 105-seater, smart restaurant in two rooms, opened in 1963. *'Superb genuine Balti house within easy (post meal) wobbling distance of the railway station. Excellent starter, Nargis Kebab, spicy Scotch egg style, crisp salad, yoghurt sauce. Mixed Balti, lovely medium thick sauce with a well balanced and mouth watering blend of spices, sizable chunks of lamb and chicken, plus some small but juicy prawns, medium hot. Lovely light Chappatis* £1.10 *a little on the dear side. Good service, real tablecloths.'* RW. E-a-m-a-y-l buffet : c£8 on Weds. & Thurs eves & Sun. lunch. Menu Extracts: Chicken Tikka £5.25, with orange or lemon sauce; Spice and Garlic Fish Fry £2.50; Salmon Samosas £2.25; Cheese Layered Crispy Paratha £1.90; Liver Puri £2.65 Prawn and Coconut Puri £2.75. *'All delicious!'* RL. You might get a discount if you show Mr Ahmed this *Guide*.. Delivery: £8 min. Hours: 5.30-12.30, Friday and Saturday - 1.30. Sunday 12.30-12.30.

Warley *B65 to B68*

AL MOUGHAL

622 Bearwood Rd, Warley, B66 0121 420 3987

Pakistani-style at this 100-seater managed by Mumtaz. *'Reasonably clean, down-market but cheap and cheerful. Chicken Karahi Tikka Massala Special and three Chapatis, waiter advised only two – spot on. Food competent and tasty. Tremendous value. If this place was a wine it would be a Blue Nun.'* PAW. [Yuk! Let's settle for a 'Brown Nan' and the old ones are the best ones! -Ed] **BYO.** You might get a discount if you show Mumtaz this *Guide*. Hours: 6-12am.

Wolverhampton

inc: Albrighton, Compton, & Wednesfield

KAV

NEW ENTRANT

Park Hall Hotel, Park Drive, Goldthorn Park, Wolverhampton 01902 331121

Park Hall Hotel is a privately owned hotel, (a

Park Hall Hotel

member of the Best Western Group) . It is set in five acres of grounds and is an 18th century listed building, once the ancestral home of the Dudley family, then a school. In 1947 Grigg and Brettell Brewery bought the building and Park Hall has continued to run as a hotel since that date. It has plenty of rooms and a huge car park, but its real gem is its restaurant. Enter the foyer and the bar and as you come to Kavi Indian note the waterfall and glass floored pool complete with large goldfish. The restaurant itself is on two levels., the upper running along the whole area, looks down onto the main room. A plasma screen playing Bolywood movies is sert amongst Indian decor. Menu snapshot: Starters, include Tikkas and Tandoori items with such ingredients as Tiger Prawns, Rabbit, Salmon and Paneer. Prices average £6.50. Main courses include also offers a good mix, 17 dishes, which include Guinea Fowl, Lamb Shank and Duck; Amritsari Talli Machi £9.95,pan seared fillets of fresh seabass on a bed of sautéed red cabbage with mild pasanda sauce; Jhinga Kali Mirch (£9.95), Jumbo prawns in masala sauce. Price check: Pilau Basmati Rice £2.75, Peshwari Naan £2.50). <www.parkhallhotel.co.uk>

NEEL AKASH NEW ENTRANT

31 School St, Wolverhampton 01902 716 975

Simply decorated in soft yellow and pale blue, with wooden chairs and white plastic tables, giving an informal cafe style at Mr Ahmed's pit-stop. Menu Snapshot: (with takeaway prices) Tandoori Fish £3.95; Lamb Tikka £5.50, served with salad; Methi Gusta £5.50, beef, onion, coriander leaves; Karahi Chinghri and Murgh £6.95, king prawns cooked with chicken, fresh coriander, green pepper, garam masala, cinnamon, served in sizzling iron karahi; Cucumber Raitha 90p; Kulcha Naan £1.50, stuffed with vegetables. Delivery: 3 miles, £10 min. Takeaway 10% discount. Price Check: Popadom 50p, CTM £6.25, Pullao Rice £1.95. <www.nellakash.co.uk> Branch: Basmati, 230, Birmingham Road, B43.

WILTSHIRE

Area: South West England
Population: 627,000
Adjacent Counties: Berks, Dorset, Hants. Oxon

Calne

SPICE OF BENGAL NEW ENTRANT

Wood Street, Calne 01249 811833

'Slightly out of the town centre and doesn't look very impressive from the outside. Two or three tables were occupied, when we arrived. A fairly big restaurant, steady stream of diners and takeaways while we ate. Impressive decor, not sumptuous or posh, just very smart and cosy. Prompt service, efficient, slightly friendly, which is the way I prefer it.' Yes, some waiting staff can be just too familiar. 'I've mentioned frequently before the extortionate price of draught beer in Indian restaurants, so didn't begrudge £2.70 for two halves of Kingfisher. Sheek Kebab £2.90, came on a bed of shredded cabbage, a bit of tomato, cucumber and sweet Raitha, excellent, slightly hot, very moist. A slight delay before our mains were served (four couples came in), Chicken Tikka Patiala £6.90 (served with mint chutney) and Chicken Korai £6.95, perfection. Broad strips of tender chicken tikka, not the usual chunks, with creamy sauce and garnished with strips of boiled egg. Monica's Korai, cooked very well with chunks of onion and capsicum. We shared Mushroom Rice £2.20, chopped mushroom a bit chewy, but enjoyed and a Naan £1.55. Also, Aloo Gobi as a side dish, his was awful. A very satisfactory £25.30 with linen napkins and microwaved hand towels. All in all, very impressive.' T&MH. Takeaway 10% discount. £10 min. Price Check: Popadom 50p, CTM £6.70, Pullao Rice £1.90. Hours: 12 - 2/5.30 - 11.30, Fri & Sat to 12.

Chippenham

AKASH TANDOORI & BALTI

19 The Bridge, Chippenham 01249 653358

Established in 1979 by Nurul Huda Islam, an old friend of this *Guide*, having been in since our first edition and who might give you a discount if you show him this *Guide*. His cheerfully decorated restaurant, in lemon with royal blue, seats forty-six diners in three rooms. Lamb Shang £12.50, lamb on the bone in a medium sauce is Chef Nazrul's most popular dish. Menu Snapshot: Duck Tikka £4.50 and Tandoori Chops £4.30, both served with salad; Shahjani Chicken £7.10, with garlic and minced lamb; Chicken Choti Poti £6.80, with eggs and chick peas; Tandoori Fish Masala £1.90, with Bangladeshi fresh water fish. Tandoori starters and main courses are only available in the evenings, unless pre-ordered for lunch (that's because the tandoor takes hours to heat up.). Price Check: Popadom 60p, CTM £6.90, Pullao Rice £2.20. Hours: 12 - 2/6 - 12, Fri & Sat to 12.30.

ASHOKA

62 Market Place, Chippenham 01249 461234

Swapan Roy will welcome you when you dine at his Ashoka and he might even give you a discount if you show him this *Guide*. . Menu Snapshot: Chicken Chat or Aloo Chat £3.25 / £2.95, fresh coriander, green chillies, tamarind and chat masala; Kakra Bhuna £7.95, crab meat cooked with fresh herbs, onions, garlic and tomato sauce; King Prawn Malaikari £12.95, large prawns spiced and cooked in coconut milk with a mild and creamy sauce; Chana Aloo £2.65, spiced chickpeas and potato. Prices: Pop 65p, CTM £6.95, Pullao Rice £1.95.

TAJ MAHAL

51 Causeway, Chippenham 01249 653243

Good curryhouse where you might get a discount if you show them this *Guide*.

GOA BALTI HOUSE NEW ENTRANT

Devizes Road, Everleigh 01264 850850

Founded by *'the brilliant and charming'* RG Hasan, on the site of a garage and filing station. So let's get filled! *'A long time family favourite of ours and great for a family get-together. Hasan (the boss) had decorated the restaurant with a big 'happy birthday' sign. Delightful ambience, spacious, obviously well appointed, but somehow homely too, in this very quiet little Wiltshire village. The premises used to be a garage, so has inherited splendid, copious parking. Enterprising menu with old high street favourites are well represented which would satisfy the most hardened old 'blimp.' Recommended starters Chicken Liver on Puri; Stuffed Mushroom; Prawn Patia; Chicken Stick Masala and the Mixed Kebab is a prize winner. Main courses we have sampled and found delightful are Chicken Shashlick; Karahi Gosht; Kashmiri Chicken; Cucupaka, Tandoori baked chicken with minced meat in metal pot; Goa Special, tandoori baked chicken laced with almonds, sultanas, cashew nut etc in a spicy yoghurt sauce and their fabulous Chilli Chicken Masala. There is also a fine list of vegetable Balti dishes and they have a very good hand in Parsee dishes, sweet, sour and pretty hot, very much my thing at the moment...' Chicken Dhansak is one of my favourites! '* RG. Takeaway 15% discount.

Ludgershall

MUGHAL

33 Andover Road, 01264 790463

Mrs Bushra Rahman might give you a discount if you show her this *Guide. at her* 44-seater. 12-2.30/6-12

Marlborough

THE PALM NEW ENTRANT & TOP 100

Knowle Farm, Froxfield, Marlborough 01672-871818

'Wiltshire can now boast a grand, new Indian restaurant; and I mean grand, too. The Palm at Froxfield, on the A4 between Hungerford and Marlborough, opened in 2006. It is a very welcome addition to the curry landscape. 't's the place place to take the kids when you visit them at Marlborough College.' Lucky kids Professor! Bob. 'The Palm, to put no finer point on it, is really classy. It was initiated by Hasan, the founding force behind the brilliant Goa restaurant, Everleigh. With help and encouragement from friends and colleagues at the equally renowned Gandhi, Winchester, Hasan has opened really spacious and well appointed premises at a former run down steak house. The Palm looks splendid as you pull in and you'll notice the very large parking area at the rear. The entrance is wide and has splendid access and is easily negotiated by wheelchair. Seating accommodation is designed comfortably to accommodate groups of diners and there's room for about 140 guests. The menu is is not curryhouse, rather it is real home-style Indian cooking. Menu Snapshot: Palms Machli (sea bass marinated in lemon and garlic, with tamarind and pineapple sauce); Jhinga Butterfly (deep fried king prawns with lemon, butter, bread crumbs and mustard). There's an enticing range of Kebabs that includes a particularly fine mince lamb Seekh Kanjara and all the usual

Tandoori and Tandoori Masala dishes. Mains: listed under 'Authentic Indian Dishes' you will find several utter gems, including Karahj Gosht/Murgh (a Punjabi country dish of braised lamb/chicken with a sauce that includes ginger, onion, tomatoes, red chillies and fresh coriander) and Fish Ameritoshori (salmon fried in chunks with cashew nuts and tomato). The Dhansak is highly recommended and among Chef's Specials you will find a beautifully warm and creamy Kashmiri Chicken; magnificent Green Fish (Halibut) Curry; Garlic Chicken; Lamb/Chicken Jhalfrezi and a superb stir fried Chicken Peshwari beautifully seasoned with cumin seeds. The Vegetable side dishes are delicate and well varied and you must try Aloo Baigan – potato and aubergine curry. Have no fears – for the traditionalists there is a fine selection chicken/lamb old friends – Dupiaza, Rogon Josh, Madras (and be warned, this is fiery) and Bhuna. But my advice is go up country and explore new territory. As for prices, well, considering the comforts of the place, the cheerful service and the exciting bill of fare a main dish for more or less £10 plus the odds and ends is very well worth it indeed. There is a very good take away service, too. An added point in their favour is the disabled toilet. Now these should be obligatory and are required under the recent legislation. They should be taken for granted but we all know, they ain't. Al in all, The Palm has the lot.' RG. For you Bob, I am making it a **TOP 100.**

Melksham

MELKSHAM TANDOORI

26 Church Street, Melksham 01225 705242

Mr Mahammed Mayna's attractive Cotswold stone building is adjacent to a car park. Its bar/reception are in a long narrow room with 50 seats beyond and a further attractions is that she might give you a discount if you show her this *Guide.* .

Salisbury

ANOKAA NEW ENTRANT & TOP 100

60 Fisherton St, Salisbury 01722 424142

Set in the heart of Salisbury, Anokaa is smart and popular. The decor is captures all the colours of India and the chic table settings enhance the venue's understated elegance. The waiters in traditional outfits will warmly welcome you in a true Indian styles; their service is efficient and subtle. Owner Solman Farsi works closely with his Indian chefs to deliver dishes which, although traditional have been *'lightened up to suit modern palates'.* 'Lightening' may include inexplicable adjectives. For example appetizers include 'hand-picked' Crab Cake '(hand-picked – what else; feet?)' , fused ('fused')? with ginger, basil and fennel seeds, £5.75 Orrisa Style Chilli Fried baby squid, with cumin, yoghurt and cucumber, or Multani Jinga - wild (wild? not tame?) King prawns 'cured' in a special marinade of yoghurt, £6.50. Main course dishes are equally interesting including vegetarian dishes. *'It really deserves to be in the Guide. There is an a la carte menu and the food is presented beautifully. I had Bhaarotiya (chicken breast stuffed with spinach and served on korma sauce with saffron rice). My husband had 'Old Delhi-style chicken curry (in aromatic spices with fresh cream and tomato with saffron rice). We also had Tarka Dall. Both were so delicious that we had to swap plates half-way through. The decor is modern and tasteful. Background music is modern and pleasant. The service is friendly. We were the last customers of the night and we didn't feel under pressure to rush our meal so they could close. We paid just under £30 including a glass of wine and a beer, which was very good value. Shame I live in Surrey, otherwise I would be a frequent customer.'* SK *This exciting new restaurant has been beautifully decorated and furnished in a modern design that serves dishes that are out of the ordinary an are extremely tasty. The dishes are a little more expensive than others in the city, which is only to be expected in a restaurant of this calibre of service, decor and cuisine. On weekdays they also serve an excellent help yourself lunch at a very reasonable charge with a variety of starters, main dishes and a sweet. I have also had several of their takeaways in the evening and have found the food to be of an excellent quality and ben made to feel equally welcome as when I have eaten in the restaurant. Commended.'* RC & DY.. Menu Snapshot: Shandesh £4.25, shredded chicken mixed with parsley and caraway seeds, coated into bread balls, lightly fried and served with tamarind sauce; Kakor £4.95, crab and cod cake with fennel and onion seed; Kafna £3.55, mussels on shell, cooked in white wine and parsley sauce; Shakoni Baigon £3.55, aubergine sandwich with spinach and cheese, coated in batter served with date chutney; Pakora's £3.10, crisp nuggets of spinach,

Anokaa, Salisbury

potatoes, onion and crushed coriander seed, deep-fried and served with sweet chilli sauce; Bombay Style Squid £4.95, with green chillies and ginger, very hot!; Nariket Duck £13.95, glazed Gressingham duck breast in coconut and cinnamon, medium spiced and served with Lemon Rice; Tandoori Seared Lamb Rack £11.95, in a mint and onion sauce, served with Masala Mashed Potato; Roasted Aubergine £3.10, stir fried with coriander, onion and tomato; Indian Runner Beans £3.10, in spices and spinach; Herbed Brown Rice £3.10; Apricot Lapta £2.20, apricot and yoghurt dip. I agree with you, Reverend, the dishes on the menu are out of the ordinary and they sound delicious! Price Check: Popadom 60p, CTM £8.10, Pullao Rice £2.50. Pre and post theatre menu has a two course meal with wine for £15pp available from 5.30- 7 and 9-10.30. Lunch buffet or Thursday: enjoy the table magician. Despite the adjectives, we happily put this new entrant into our **TOP100**. Hours: 12 - 2/5.30 - 10.30. <www.anokka.com>

ASIA

90 Fisherton St, Salisbury 01722 327628

'It was packed on both visits, a good sign. Mainly formula but always flavoursome and enjoyable. Pleased we went.' SO.

Swindon

BHAJI'S TAKEAWAY

76 Thames Avenue, Swindon 01793 533799

Opened in 1997 by Iqbal Ahmed. Chef Uddin, has created Meal-For-One £12, Popadom, Onion Bhajia, Mint Sauce and Salad, Chicken Bhuna, Bombay potato, Pullao Rice and Naan; Meal-For-Two £19, Chicken Tikka, Onion Bhajia, Mint Sauce and Salad, Chicken Tikka Masala, Lamb Bhuna, Bombay Potato, Pullao Rice, and Naan. You might get a discount if you show them this Guide. Delivery: 4 miles, £12 min. Price Check: Popadom 70p, CTM £5.95, Pullao Rice £1.80. Hours: 5 - 11.30, Fri & Sat to 12.

BIPLOB

12 Wood Street, Swindon 01793 490265

Rokib Alo and Fozlur Rahman's 60-seater has a separate lounge/bar area seating 20. Well explained menu. House specials include Tandoori Duck Tikka , and Tandoori Duck Bonani (cooked with cream, cashews and brandy) and Fish Buzon – Bangladeshi river fish and Begun Bahar – chicken in a herby gravy.. Minimum charge £10. You might get a discount if you show them this *Guide.* Hours: 12-2.30/6-12am. Branches: Raja Takeaway, Cheltenham, Rajdoot, 35 Castle St Cirencester, Glos.

CURRY GARDEN

90 Victoria Road, Swindon 01793 521114

R Khan's large restaurant was established as far back as 1969. It seats 80, and judging from reports, these are often filled, so it's popular. Chef specials: Tandoori King Prawn Jalfrezi, with green chillies. *'Good'* G&MP. Show Mr Khan this *Guide* and you'll will get a 10% discount. Takeaway: 15% less. Hours: 12-2pm/5.30-12. Sundays & bank holidays 12-12.

GULSHAN

122 Victoria Rd, Old Town 01793 522558

Owned and managed by Abdul Kahhar who might give you a discount if you show him this *Guide.* . Seats 80 on two floors connected by a spiral staircase. *'Very smart decor, pleasant attentive waiters. Extensive menu, mainly Bangladeshi. Muglai Paneer, cheese, mixed fruit, almond, sultanas, fresh cream in mild sauce served with Onion Bhajias and beer, cost c£10 A nice idea was the revolving sweet tray with the bill.'* DS. Sunday all-day buffet c£8. Takeaway: 15% discount. Hours: 12-2.30/6-12am;. Sat. 6-1am.

LALBAGH

171 Rodbourne Rd, Swindon 01793 535511

Proprietor: Abdul Kahhar opened his restaurant in 1997 and it seats fifty-four diners. Sunday Lunch: buffet £8.50. You might get a discount if you show them this Guide. Delivery: 4 miles, £15 min. Price Check: Popadom 60p, CTM £6.90, Pullao Rice £2.00. Hours: 12 - 2/6 - 11.30. <www.lalbagh.net

PICKLE JOHNS

25, Wood Street, Swindon 01793 509921

Atul Sarpal's Pickle Johns Pub & Restaurant (named after Indian gentlemen from the early part of the twentieth century, who was sent to this fair land to be educated in some of England's finest public schools (Eton, Harrow, Winchester). On their return to India they had adopted English manners.... and the English in turn perceived them as jovial and eccentric characters. In India, they were named "PickleJohns". Most of the dishes are Indian cuisine but some are English and fusion. Hours: 12-2/6-11:30. Branches Popadom Express, Basingstoke and Southampton Hants.

RAFU'S TANDOORI TOP 100

29-30 High Street, Highworth, Swindon 01793 765320

Opened in 1982 by Mr Rafu as the Biplob; renamed to prevent confusion. It remains popular. *'Very good'* G&MP. *'Menu large and varied choice. Complete satisfaction. Best Jalfrezi in the West. Good service, pleasant atmosphere, superb location. Everything nice except the prantha (too greasy).'* ZI. *'Menu had wide variety and choice. Quantity more than adequate. Service very courteous and polite. Atmosphere very convivial. Very good quality meal and good value.'* KS *'We visit weekly. Extensive and varied menu. Generous quantities. High quality. Outstanding service. Excellent Bangra. Hasina Chicken – best in Europe!'* IG&JN. *'The wine list is very good for an Indian restaurant. Whenever we go to Rafu's we know we are going to have a top-class meal, with friendly people, in pleasant surroundings.'* JS. Hours: 12-3pm/6pm-12am. Hours: 5pm to late. Remains in our **TOP 100.**

SPICY AROMA

144 Cricklade Rd, Gorse Hill, 01793 488700

Established in 1996, Abdul Rouf Ali's Aroma now seats 64 in two dining rooms decorated with 'mahogany effect with cream background, with a classic wooden effect bar'. Specials: Scampi Chilli Masala, thick onion, ginger and garlic sauce. You might get a discount if you show Mr Ahmed this *Guide.* Minimum charge: £6.95. Sunday lunch buffet: £7.95. Takeaway: 10% discount. Delivery: £12 min 5-miles. Hours: 5-12.30am; Sat. 5-1.30am.

Warminster

AGRA

32 East Street, Warminster 01985 212713

Air conditioned and licensed . Kamal Uddin's restaurant Shofique Miah (manager) seats fifty two diners in two rooms. He took over the restaurant (which was originally established in 1977) in 2005. Kamal is also head chef and his Tapeli (fish), Roshni and Pistachio Korma dishes are his favourites. min Charge: £5.00 per person. Price Check: Popadom 60p, CTM £8.50, Pullao Rice £2.50. Hours: 12 - 2 and 6 - 11. Sunday 12.30 to 10.30. Branch: K2, Heathrow

Wootton Bassett

MEMORIES OF INDIA

21 High St, Wootton Bassett 01793 852365

Situated opposite the Aptly named curriers ' Arms! *'OK'* G&MP. *'Bhajia and Samosa freshly made, nicely presented and delicious! Fragrant, fluffy Pullao Rice. Lots of meat in Keema Nan. Massive portion of Chicken Biryani. Chicken Tikka Bhuna, lots of well-marinated breast meat.'* TE. *'This little gem deserves a mention. Extraordinary food, quality and service at a low price.'* AE. Delivery: free on orders over £10. Hours: 12-2.30/6-12am (1am on Fri. & Sat.).

WORCESTERSHIRE

Area: Midlands
Population: 552,000
Adjacent Counties: Glos, Hereford, Shrops, Warks, W Mids

Bewdley

THE RAJAH OF BEWDLEY

8 Load Street, Bewdley 01299 400368

Anwar Uddin's 34-seater is in a grade 2 listed cottage with soft lighting and exposed beams. *'Food excellent, the people extremely friendly, offering a high standard of customer service.'* SH. *'Good'* G&MP.Special: Tandoori

Lobster. You might get a discount if you show Mr Uddin this *Guide*. Takeaway: 10% off. Minimum charge: £4.95. Hours: 5-11.30pm.

Evesham

MAHEEN'S — NEW ENTRANT

68 Bridge Street, Evesham 01386 49704

'Evesham's one way system has a plethora of no entry signs, so couldn't get to park very near. Has an excellent outlook, over-viewing the River Avon. Maheen's occupies the bottom storey of a large building, on first impressions, the entrance was not favourable, however once inside we were greeted by a Sanjeev Bhaskar lookalike, Mukit Miah. The restaurant is modern and minimal, in fact it looks more like a wine bar. The tables had black tablecloths with white trim, artificial black lillies were also black, I liked it. Service was prompt, only draught Carlsberg and Tetley bitter. Starters were predictable, but prices were as cheap as we've seen for a long time. My spiced Popadom arrived with burnt edges and Monika's plain looked like it came from a packet. Any misgivings were quashed when our mains arrived, delicious Lamb Zeera £5.95, in a rich tomato sauce. Chicken Chilli Bahaar £5.95, tender slices of chicken in a bright red sauce with a couple of sliced chillies which despite these was not too hot. A large plate of Mushroom Pullao £2.25 and a Naan £1.50 was more than enough. I really meant it when I said to the waiter that we really enjoyed it.' T&MH. I am sure he knew you did! Prices: Pop 40p, CTM £5.95, Pullao Rice £1.75. Hours: 6 - 11.30, Fri & Sat to 12.30.

RILYS OF EVESHAM — NEW ENTRANT

2-3 Waterside, Evesham 01384 45289

As in many restaurants up and down the country, Rilys is no exception, Chicken Tikka Masala literally runs out of the door. If you are feeling more adventurous, then do try Head Chef Hoque's Buffet Nights, where you can eat lots of different dishes which he prepares on Monday and Tuesday nights, from 7pm to 10pm, adult £8.50, children £5.50. Menu Snapshot: Tuna Bora £2.95, seasoned and shallow fried, served sizzling with salad; Avocado Fol Fruit £2.95, roasted and filled with mildly spiced fruit; Green Chilli Bhajia £2.25, whole jalapeno's coated in spicy batter, fried in vegetable oil, apparently one of chef's favourite. He is not alone, as Pat's would order these tasty morsels if dining at Rilys. Rangeela Khana Balti £7.25, chicken and lamb tikka, fresh spinach, simmered in a medium hot sauce with fresh ginger; Black Eye Beans and Mushroom Balti £4.95; Plain Naan £1.50/£2.95/£6.95. Takeaway 10% discount. Delivery: 3 miles, £15 min. Stocks: Cobra and other brands of Indian beer, £2.95 a pint, house wine, a very reasonable, £8.95 a bottle. Price Check: Popadom 50p, CTM £6.25, Pullao Rice £1.75. Hours: 5.30 - 12, Sunday to 11. <www.rilys.co.uk> Branch: Hotel Montville.

Rilys of Evesham

Great Malvern

BENGAL BRASSERIE

5-7 Worcester Road 01684 575744

Masum Choudhury took over the establishment in 2000 (when it was a Chinese) and called it Bengal Brasserie. Menu Snapshot: Tandoori Mixed Special £8.95, tandoori chicken, chicken and lamb tikka, sheek kebab, tandoori king prawn, served with Nan, vegetable curry sauce, green salad and mint sauce, wow! what a meal; Chashi Chicken £6.95, marinated and grilled in tandoor with onion, green pepper, cooked in yoghurty sauce, medium; Murgh Kebab Masoor £6.25, chicken with pink lentils, chilli pickle, ginger, garlic, cumin and fresh coriander leaves; Prawn and Mushroom Pullao Rice £2.95; Cheese and Garlic Naan £1.95, Persian Biryani served with fried banana and omelette. Delivery: £15 min. min Charge: £10. Cobra £3.00 a pint, house wine is good value at £8.50 a bottle. Price Check: Popadom 40p, CTM £8.25, Pullao Rice £1.95. Hours: 5 - 12.

Kidderminster

EURASIA TAKEAWAY

Unit 1, 19, Stourbridge Rd 01562 825861

Syed Hussain might give you a discount if you show him this *Guide*. Specials include: Jamuna (a hot dish cooked with chicken, meat, prawn spices, herbs and green chilli, garnished with an egg). Delivery: £10 min, 4-mile radius. Hours: 5-12.

NEW SHER E PUNJAB

48 George St, Kidderminster 01562 740061

Puran Singh who might give you a discount if you show him this *Guide for his* great Punjabi flavours (est 1971). Evenings only .

Redditch

BALTI SPICE TAKEAWAY

65 Popular Road, Batchley, Redditch
01527 596802

Good curryhouse where you might get a discount if you show them this *Guide.* Hours: 5-12; Sat. 5-1am.

HOTEL MONTVILLE AND INDIAN FUSION NEW ENTRANT

101 Mount Pleasant, Southcrest,
Redditch 01527 544411

This small hotel with restaurant opened in 2005 by Mukid Rahman. All rooms are nicely appointed and have their own ensuite facilities. The fusion restaurant seats 86 diners in two rooms and is decorated stylishly in natural tones and polished wood., spot lights and the odd green plant make for a very relaxed upmarket atmosphere. Seafood is their speciality, have a look at these lovely dishes: Roopashi £3.95, Bengal Chandu dish marinated with a touch of butter, garlic, onions, cooked in the clay oven; Machli Chaat £3.95, mackerel cooked in garlic, tomatoes and capsicum; Spice Lemon Prawn £6.95, a whole lobster grilled in a sweet and sour sauce; Lime and Ginger Seabass £8.95, pan fried served on a bed of sautéed spinach and red pepper, accompanied by cumin new potatoes, drizzled with vine cherry tomato and fish broth, very fusion! For those are are not keen on anything from the sea (that's me!) Chicken Dakhna £2.95, marinated chicken nibblets cooked hot and spicy in the clay oven; Afghan Chi Chat £3.95, chick peas and chicken cooked with spice then wrapped in a soft flat and thin bread, perfect lunch time food! Other treats include: Duck Naga £7.95, the famous Bangladeshi chilli; Amli Liaon £7.95, Tandoori lamb pieces spiced with bay leaves, garam masala and baby tomatoes; Cheese Naan £1.95. Cobra £2.95 a pint and house wine £8.95. You might get a discount if you show them this Guide. Min Charge: £10. Price Check: Popadom 50p, CTM £6.95, Pullao Rice £1.50. Hours: 6 - 11. Branch: Rilys of Evesham and Waterside, Evesham, both in Worcs.

Tenbury Wells

SHAMRAJ BALTI HOUSE

28 Cross Street, 01584 819612

Owned by Mr Rahman, seats 60, party room 14, formula curries. You might get a discount if you show him this *Guide.* Takeaway: 15% off. Hours: 12-2.30 (Sat. & Sun.)/5-12am.

Upton-on-Severn

PUNDITS

9 Old Street, Upton 01684 591119

'We booked the previous night, a good job, the place was very popular, despite being the most expensive in the area. A memorable place because the maitré greeted my wife with a kiss on the cheek and shook my hand even though it was our first visit. Enjoyed my Morche Roshun (garlic and chilli) Chicken Tikka, billed as hot, however, I may have been suffering from mouth numbness caused by my Chicken Vindaloo in Ilfracombe a few days previously. Good service.' T&MH. Menu Extracts: Chomothkar Talk Murgh Roti medium spiced, lemon chicken tikka on thin chapati bread; Podina Roshun (mint and garlic), mint sauce, whole roasted garlic cloves, roasted tomatoes and coriander with vegetables, chicken, lamb or prawns.

Worcester

BOMBAY PALACE

38 The Tything, Worcester 01905 613969

Abdul Rob tells us his 40-seater has 7 parking spaces at the back. Specials include: Kebabi Kofta, Chi Tik Pudina, Chicken Tikka Dhareswari and Tam Shami Moss. *'luckily wee booked early and went to an already heaving restaurant after Worcester's annual civil war enactment, performed we're told by bank managers and porcelain factory workers'* HEG. You might get a discount if you show Mr Rob this *Guide.* Takeaway: 10% off. Delivery: £10 min. Hours: 6-12am; Sat. 6-1am .

MONSOON TOP 100

35 Foregate Rd Worcester 01905 726333

White painted angled pillars and wooden stained concertina doors make this 120 seater restaurant stand out on Foregate Road. Established in 1999 by Rahman (manager), Choudhury and Choudhury. Reception has been painted in a creamy colour with comfortable sofa's upholstered in paprika. The restaurant has a light and airy feel, with bleached wooden flooring, paprika and cinnamon painted walls, original art hangs sparingly on the walls with matching chairs in paprika, cinnamon, turmeric and indigo. Natural wooden tables are economically laid with crisp white linen napkins and generous wine glasses. Specials: Tangri Kebab, drumstick marinated in cashew nuts, spices and served with tamarind chutney. Achar Wali Machi, salmon steak pickled in spices, served cold with salad. Parsi Jinga, tiger prawns in mint, turmeric, garlic and tamarind juice. Lamb Shikampuri, mince lamb balls stuffed with coriander, ginger, onion, raisins in curry gravy. Daal Panchmela, a mix of five varieties of lentils. Stays on our **TOP 100.** Takeaway: 10% discount. Hours: 6-12, Friday and Saturday to 1. Branch: Cheltenham Tandoori, 2 Great Norwood Street Cheltenham, Gloucs. Tel: 01242 227772.

PASHA NEW ENTRANT

56 St Johns, Worcester 01905 426327

Manager, N Haque's restaurant, seats 68 diners. Opened in 1987 as Pasha Indian Cuisine and has remained under the same management. Menu Snapshot: Nargi's Kofta £2.50, spicy minced lamb deep-fried in butter, served with a light omelette and fresh salad; Mushroom Delight £2.50, stuffed with spicy vegetables and deep-fried; Methi Gosht £5.95, with fenugreek, medium hot; Chicken Hasina £5.50, mildly spiced, dried fruit and nuts with fresh cream; Garlic Potato £2.75, rich sauce; Mushroom Pullao Rice £2.75, selection of Chutneys 45p. Sunday Buffet: £6.95 adult, £4.50 under 12's, 12.30 - 2. Cobra £3.10 a pint. House wine is a good value £7.95 a bottle. You might get a discount if you show them this Guide. Price Check: Popadom 50p, CTM £6.75, Pullao Rice £1.95. Delivery: £1 charge. Hours: 12 - 2/5.30 - 12. <www.pasha-online.co.uk>

SPICE CUISINE TOP 100

39 Bromyard Rd,.Worcester 01905 429786

Hidden away behind Birmingham Midshires Building Society, just over the river bridge from Worcester Town, it has been owned by the same family for years, Muslims from Pakistan. *'Plain, simple and clean decor. Friendly and efficient service. Staff Curry - lamb on the bone in a thick, tasty, spicy sauce, cooked for hours with a thin rolled and crispy Nan.* **BYO** *welcome, they will chill and open. Manager - Iffty Shah (cousin of Masteen who manages the Kashmir in Birmingham).'* RE. *And extracts from some of Ray's other visits: 'Toilets always clean with hot water, soap and dryer...' 'Chicken Korma for Mrs E., which chef Ashar cooks just right for her and best of all, a large portion of staff curry with sauce to die for...' 'Brilliant as ever, freshly made Kebabs, spicy...' 'Father's Chicken Madras was entirely to his liking, chunks of tender chicken...' 'quality never varies...' 'Chicken on the bone and Aloo for me - excellent as usual...' 'My brother is also a curryholic - two portions of Sheek Kebab - excellent. Lamb on the bone for two - very tasty with side dish of thick dhal...' 'Keema with Peas and Aloo plus Pullao Rice - a change for me - was superb, fairly dry but spicy, minced lamb in a Balti with potato chunks. Apparently Keema is not a popular dish - much under-rated in my view.' ... 'Lamb Chops, on the bone, which was the staff curry for the night. About six chops which had been cooking for hours so that the meat was falling off, served with a rich, quite hot sauce - superb. Roti to go with it, what else would you want for a Sunday dinner?' 'Washer-upper has been promoted to Tandoori Chef and made a very good start with Seekh Kebabs.. Unlicensed: BYO - they will chill and open it for you. Small card park with narrow entrance at the rear. Toilets always have hot water, soap and dryer. Non-smoking section.'* RE. Takeaway: 10% discount. Delivery: 3 miles, £10 min. Small car park at rear. Hours: 5.30 -11.30.

SPICES TAKEAWAY NEW ENTRANT

9 Barbourne Rd, Worcester 01905 729101

Hidden away behind Birmingham Midshires Building Society, just over the river bridge from Worcester Town, it has been owned by the same family for years (1988, the Haques from Pakistan. by MM. is running a special offer, a very nice special offer, if you collect your takeaway and it must cost more than £20, he will give you a free Balti Bombay! House Specials: Deshi £5.45 - hot and spicy, Sylheti Chicken £7.45, thick sauce, served with Basmati Rice and Handi Bengal £5.45, with aubergine, tomatoes. However, Chicken Korma and Tikka Masala are also very popular. Menu Snapshot: Aloo Roshaun Mushroom £2.25, mild spiced potatoes, garlic and mushrooms, fried with spices; Bangladeshi Roll £2.75, spring rolls stuffed with chicken and vegetables; Jhinga Malai £8.95, king prawns, roasted in tandoor with mild spices, fresh cream, butter; Chana Sag £2.10; Chicken Fried Rice £2.45; Garlic and Mushroom Naan £1.70. Price Check: Popadom 40p, CTM £5.25, Pullao Rice £1.70. You might get a discount if you show them this *Guide.* Delivery: 3 miles, £1 delivery. Hours: 5.30 - 12, Sat to 1, Tuesday closed. Branch: Shunarga, 44, High Street, Pershore, Worcestershire.

SPICEY BITE TANDOORI

NEW ENTRANT

79 Wyld's Lane, Worcester, 01905 353235

Mamun Rashid's Menu snapshot: Chicken Sador, chicken and minced lamb cooked in medium spices. Joy Bangla, famous medium-hot Bangladeshi dish with pieces of chicken tikka cooked in spices and flavoured with fenugreek leaves. Kori Bahgla Kebab, charcoal-roasted Kebabs cooked in a medium-hot Bangla style for the exotic taste of Bangladesh, all £5.45. Lamb Muktaaj £5.10, cooked with fresh ginger and herbs in a spicy sauce. Price Check: Popadom 40p, CTM £5.25, Tarka Dhal £2.00, Pullao Rice £1.45, Naan Bread £1.40. Free delivery on orders above £8. Hours: 5.30 - 12. <www.spiceybite.co.uk>

NORTH YORKSHIRE

Area: North
Population: 1,042,000
Adjacent Counties:
Cumbria, Durham,
Lancs, E & W Yorks

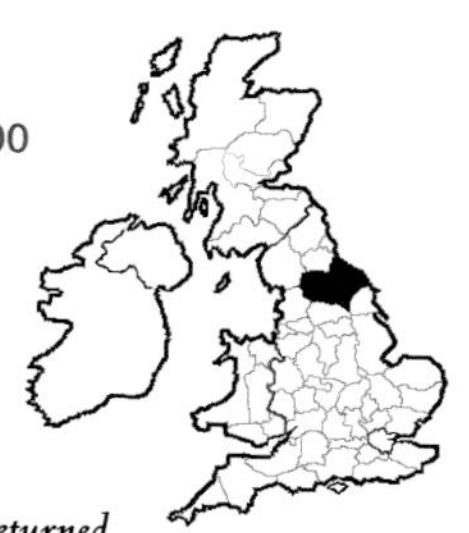

1997 *county changes returned 'Cleveland' south of the Tees, to North Yorks. At the same time, the changes created a 'new' Yorkshire county by transferring territory and towns from 'North Humbs' into East Yorkshire. This restored Yorkshire as Britain's biggest county. Because the area is so large, we deal with these four counties in their current administrative formats and in compass order,* N, E, S, W.

Beadlam

HELMSLEY SPICE CLUB

NEW ENTRANT

Main Road, Beadlam (Hemsley) 01439 772400

The Spice Club in Beadlam was once the White Horse Inn, now completely re-furbished it is the latest in the Jinnah group.s. It is situated on the busy A170, midway between Helmsley and Kirbymoorside, off road parking is available in their private car park. It's a modern and contemporary restaurant with 65 covers plus a separate bar where customers are welcome to have a drink whilst waiting for a take-away or just to enjoy the ambience. Menu details: see Harrogate and York below. Hours: 5.30 - 11.00. <jinnah-restaurants.com>

Bedale

TASTE OF INDIA

32 Market Place Bedale 01677 423373

Bedale is an old Yorkshire market town with a large cobbled square, p*lenty of free parking* surrounded by interesting shops, old inns takeaways and the Taste of India. Est 1989, the smallish restaurant has undergone extensive refurbishment. *'A group of us decided to try it last Wednesday evening and had a mixed, but enjoyable overall, experience. Popadoms with pickles, Mixed Kebab, Meat Samosas £2.10, Onion Bhajia £2.00, Chicken Tikka Curries, Rice, Saag Aloo £2.45 and Naan £1.50 were all fresh, superb quality, nicely spiced an thoroughly delicious. The portions were generous and with drinks and coffee, the bill came to £15 per head, which proved excellent value for money. The service (from a sullen lad with a silly haircut) was second rate and only repeated prompting ensured that our needs were met.'* TE.. Tony, I can hear myself saying 'the youth of today' just like my parents! Takeaway 10% discount. Price Check: Popadom 50p, CTM £6.50, Pullao Rice £1.70. Hours: 6-11.30, Fri & Sat to 12.

Harrogate

JINNAH — NEW ENTRANT

34 Cheltenham Parade 01423 563333

Est 2003 and seats 110 in a converted stone chapel, which was part of a Wesleyan school and is now a listed building. *'The interior is pleasantly different, being cavernous with its high ceilings and two large hanging lights. Seating is either in the main well or along the slightly raised area around the edge. Decorated in terracotta and green colours with brown and beige chairs, and green imitation marble easy-wipe table tops, wall lights, plates and cutlery (yes, even the knives and forks) with the name of the restaurant. Smartly dressed waiters impart the look of quality. It was Sat night and packed. The menu was almost too clever by half with too many dishes described as 'amazing.' Onion Bhajias £2.25, were two large flat patties like hamburgers in shape (they could have been put in a bun and called bhajia burger) and were OK, pleasantly spiced, edges nicely crisp but the middle was stodgy. They came with a small salad garnish and spicy pink Raitha. Pepper Garlic and Chilli Chicken £6.50, good, thick, tomatoey sauce, pleasant underlying spicy hotness, which percolated through with eating rather and an immediate assault on the tongue. Chicken Tikka £2.25, disappointing, unusual slices rather than chunks, it looked as if it had been fried. Had little of the usual spicy marinade or taste associated with the tandoor. Vegetable Bhajia £2.50, good, excellent selection, okra, aubergine, courgette, peppers, cauliflower. Peshwari Naan £1.95, good, light and well filled. The service was friendly and efficient.'* MW. Price Check: Popadom 35p, CTM £6.50, Pullao Rice £1.75. Hours: 5.30 - 11; Sat to 12; Sun 12- 11. Branches Beadlam and York. <www.jinnah-restaurants.com>

RAJ RANI TAKEAWAY

235 Skipton Road, Harrogate 01423 529295

Ahad Miah, the proprietor of this takeaway only, is offering *Guide* readers 15% discount on collected takeaways over £15 on Mondays and Tuesdays.

Malton

RAJ TANDOORI

21 Church St, Norton, Malton 01653 697337

Opened in 1992 by S Islam, who also manages his restaurant. Menu Snapshot: Naan Kebab £2.60, spicy minced meat in bread; Chicken, Vegetable or Paneer Pakora £2.10; Raj Special Biriani £7, chicken and meat cooked together with saffron rice, almonds, sultanas and served with vegetable curry; Chicken Thali £750, Korma, Bhuna, Dhansak and a plain curry dish; Mushroom, Vegetable or Egg Pullao £1.80, Pickle Tray £1. Delivery service: please ring for details. Takeaway 10% discount. Cobra £1.90 a pint, house wine £7.50 a bottle. You might get a discount if you show Mr Islam this *Guide.* Price Check: Popadom 40p, CTM £6.50, Pullao Rice £1.50. Hours: 5.30 - 12.

Middlesborough

CLEVELAND TANDOORI

289 Linthorpe Rd 01642 242777

32-seater opened in 1991, taken over in 1996by

owner-chef Abid Hussain who might give you a discount if you show him this *Guide*. He serves some Pakistani gems: Shalgum Gosht is meat with turnip and Lahori Gosht, meat with okra. There is a range of Haandi dishes. For the yet-to-be-converted-to curry, try Abid's Anglo Indian Coronation Chicken, created in 1953 by London's Cordon Bleu school in honour of QEII's Coronation: diced chicken cooked with apricots in a creamy sauce. E-a-m-a-y-l Sunday, Monday, Tuesday. Hours: 6-12am (2.30am on Fri./Sat.).

Northallerton

AROMA — NEW ENTRANT

1 Zetland St, Northallerton 01609 774239

Chef Nitamul Hoque's Menu Snapshot: Mas (fish) Tikka £3.95; Jorda Aloo £7.30, lamb and potatoes, sweet and sour, garnished with sliced of fried potato; Tropical Twist £5.95, mild dish, coconut milk, strawberries, mangos, bananas and pineapple, served with sweet Raitha; Gosth Pata £5.75, lamb medium sauce, topped with roast onions and garnished with fresh cream; Keema Peas Pullao £1.90, Fruit Rice (sounds nice!) £1.90, Mint Sauce 40p. Takeaway: 10%. Hours: 6 - 11.30, Fri & Sat to 12.

LION OF ASIA — NEW ENTRANT

88a High St, Northallerton 01609 772767

Fully licensed. 'Down a narrow dark alley, up some iron stairs, through a metal door and a 'greasy spoon' type interior, not the most attractive location, but the curries are good.' TE. Well, it's the food that really counts! Menu Snapshot: Special for One £11, Popadoms, Sheek Kebab with Mint Sauce, CTM, Special Fried Rice and Chupatti or Popadoms, Chicken Tikka with Mint sauce, Lamb Tikka Masala, Mushroom Fried Rice and Naan, good value set meals! Price Check: Popadom 40p, CTM £5.50, Pullao Rice £1.80. Hours: 6 - 12, Fri & Sat to 1. Monday closed.

SPICE OF INDIA

1a Friarage St, Northallerton 01609 777600

'Continues to live up to its reputation for food cuisine, cheerful service and value for money.' TE. The rice and bread are very good value and all Chef Specials are all served with Pullao Rice. Menu Snapshot: Duck Tikka £3.15; Rass Lamb £5.95, marinated lamb, tandooried, cooked with pineapple, lychee, garnished with cucumber and tomato, served with Pullao Rice; Trout Biriani £9.95, spicy sauce served with Pullao Rice; Keema, Vegetable, Mushroom, Egg, Peas, Fried, Lemon, Channa, Coconut or Moglai (vegetable and egg) Pullao, all £1.90; Peshwari, Keema, Garlic, Coriander, Chilli, Egg, Vegetable and Cheese Naan, all £1.60.

Ripon

BALTI HOUSE — NEW ENTRANT

16 Kirkgate, Ripon 01765 602597

'Located near the architecturally impressive Ripon Cathedral, so they get a good share of the tourist trade. 15% more expensive than Moti Raj! Menu quite varied, distinguishing between Haandi and Balti styles of cooking and refers to Balti originating from Baltistan.' Good, quite right too! *'I hadn't heard of that so checked it out on the internet and indeed there is such a place west of Kashmir.'* TE. Tony, I am shocked! You, who are a curry aficionado and have never heard of Baltistan! DBAC. *(See page 66)*. Delivery: 3 miles, £10 min. Takeaway 10% discount . Min order: £7 per person. Credit cards not accepted. Starter and side dishes can not be ordered without a main course. A ludicrous rule especially seeing as they have a minimum order, and you can tell 'em that from me! Price Check: Popadom 40p, CTM £, Boiled Rice £1.95. Hours: 5.30 - 10.20, Fri & Sat to 11.30.

MOTI RAJ

18 High Skellgate, Ripon 01765 690348

'A busy road with many buses passing, the owner was washing the windows when we arrived (using an old ghee bucket for the water!). We sat at the bar and were given ice-cold Cobras and the menus, containing a 'priced matrix' format of meat/fish against the variety of curry sauces, so simple and logical, other restaurants take note. Recently refurbished in soft pastel shades with double layer of linen on the tables. Toilet had been re-tiled and were immaculate. Warm Popadoms, fresh pickles, seven delicious curries, four blends of rices, three different breads and a lovely Sag Aloo £1.70, were delivered, set on proper hot plates and demolished by us all, wash down with even more Cobra, nothing was left! Following coffee, the bill worked out at £22 each which is very reasonable for a good city centre restaurant. A mature favourite of locals and visitors to Ripon. It offers excellent service, high quality cuisine and good value for money, highly recommended.' TE. You might get a discount if you show them this *Guide*. Delivery: 3 miles, £8

min. Price Check: Popadom 40p, CTM £5.00, Pullao Rice £1.40. Hours: 5.30 - 12.

Settle

SETTLE TANDOORI

9 Commercial Courtyard, Duke St, Settle 01729 823393

50-seater est 1998 by Abdul Rob who might give you a discount if you show him this *Guide.* 5.30-11.30.

Skipton

AAGRAH AWARD WINNER

Devonshire Pl, Keighley Rd 01756 790807

'Compact restaurant that oozes quality, from the sturdy menu to the stylish decoration. Forty to fifty diners can be comfortably accommodated on lavishly decorated wooden chairs at tables with thick cotton tablecloths. Nicely appointed interior with a pleasing colour scheme and well finished decorative ceilings mouldings and sparkling chandeliers. Very efficient and knowledgeable staff. Pakistani / Kashmiri cuisine from a comprehensive menu with several specials. Complimentary Popadom and Chutney Tray. Exquisite starter, Bihair Kebab £2.80, several thin strips of top notch lamb, marinated in garlic, onion and spices then briskly fried to give a pungent aroma and an absolutely mouth watering taste, flavoursome and succulent meal perfectly balanced with a complex and challenging spicy accompaniment. A fresh salad with the emphasis on onion, complimented perfectly with a squeeze of lemon and cool mint sauce dripped over the top. The main course was even better, Jinghra Achar £9.95, top quality king prawns with a pronounced yet delicate flavour with a fleshy, not rubbery, mouth-feel. These were served in an incredibly complex sauce with a stunning aroma, a really rich taste that had a bite. Served with a brilliant Peshwari Naan £2.20, a leavened bread spread with a sticky coconut jam, light and tasty, generously topped on the outside with coconut, almonds, onion, sultanas and more pistachio nuts, delicious. A top class meal that I will remember for a long time.' RW. Well, Ralph, I am so glad that you enjoyed your meal. Question: has anyone tried the Whole Stuffed Lamb £199.95, whole lamb marinated in vinegar, yoghurt, garam masala, bay leaves, ginger and garlic, stuffed with rice, boiled eggs, new potatoes, mushrooms, and then oven baked, served with side dishes, rice and salad, sounds absolutely wonderful! If you have, do let me know what it was like. The menu says it feeds fifteen people, what a banquet! Hours: 6 - 12, Sunday to 11. *See page 19. Menu details and list of branches see Shipley. W. Yorks.*

Tadcaster

AAGRAH AWARD WINNER

York Road, Steeton 01937 530888

120-seater, which opened in 1996, is the sixth of the very popular Aagrahs. It's on the A64 near York, with easy parking. Details in Skipton above.

Thirsk

RAJ OF INDIA NEW ENTRANT

42 Long Street, Thirsk 01845 526917

'A lovely market square and the famous horse racing course and the Raj,a mature restaurant with its sister, 'Tandoori Night' in York. I am working at the North Yorkshire Police headquarters and the office recommended the Raj. Offers a wide selection of Balti dishes with deliciously spiced sauces, served on proper hot plates, swiftly by smart, cheerful waiters who are focused on attentive customer service. Very busy with locals, business people, tourists and race-goers. I especially liked the smart, elderly (70's) gent with a military bearing who marched in and said to the waiter, "I'll have a large Beef Madras and a litre of house red!" TE. Free Pickle Tray with every takeaway. Menu Snapshot: Aloo Chat £2.10; Raj Special Biriani £6, Tandoori meat, chicken and prawn with saffron rice cooked together in almond and sultanas, served with Vegetable Curry; Sirloin Steak Masala £6.50, best English steak marinated and served with mushrooms and Pullao Rice; Kulcha Nan £1.70, stuffed with onion and cheese. Price Check: Popadom 40p, CTM £4.95, Pullao Rice £1.60. Hours: 12 - 2.30, Sunday only; 6 - 11.30, Fri & Sat to 12.

York

AKASH

10 North Street, York 01904 633550

38-seater owned by JU Ahmed who might give you a discount if you show him this *Guide.* Hours: 5-12.

BENGAL BRASSIERE

York Business Park, Ings Lane, Nether Poppleton, York 01904 788808

Owner, Dobir Malik opened his lovely restaurant in 1999. It is a new, brick built, building with clean lines, and inside, decorated brightly with cream

Representing the next generation of curryholics, this young man is a regular at York's Bengal Brasserie.

Bengal Brasserie, York

walls, fuschia upholstery, wrought iron light fittings and seats 100 diners. The menu is not your ordinary curry house, with Bengal Special Chicken Patil £8.95 being the most ordered dish! Menu Snapshot: Morich Bahar £3.95, fried whole green pepper filled with aloo, chana, begun herbs and spices; Murgh E Dilruba £3.95, fillet of chicken breast wrapped in cheese; Liver Tikka £3.95, chicken livers marinated and served with green salad; Paneer Pakora £2.95, cubes of cottage cheese, battered and deep-fried; Duck Tikka Masala £8.95; Korma Murgh Tikka £6.95, mild and creamy chicken tikka with coconut and almonds; Chicken Tikka Chom Chom £7.95, barbecued chicken, potato, chickpeas in medium sauce, garnished with coriander and spring onion; Chilli Begun £5.95, aubergine, spicy sauce, green chilli and capsicum, Chilli and Coriander Naan £2. Fully licensed and air conditioned. Cobra, £2.70 a pint, house wine £9.95 a bottle. Price Check: Pop 45p, CTM £7.15, Pullao Rice £2. Hours: 5.30 - 11.30. <www.bengal-brasserie.com>

JINNAH AT FLAXTON NEW ENTRANT

Malton Road, Flaxton, York 01904 468202

Large and imposing purpose built restaurant on the A64 mid way between York and Malton. Seats 150 people in two lounges, two bars and an extensive dining area. *'Cleverly constructed so that the interior is split into cosy areas around a central pavilion affair. Bespoke Manned by a uniformed staff who glide around in a manner probably not seen since Lyons dispensed with the Nippies.'* Blimey Ralph, that's showing your age. – we're talking the 1940's (and for those who haven't a clue what us wrinklies are on about, educate yourselves on the web!) *'Pleasant starter, Chatt Patta Chicken £3.25, a dish I last tasted in Brick Lane. Plenty of thin slices of breast meat, marinated in an incredibly rich and sticky sauce with a delicious bite. Slices of onion and red pepper added bite, superb. Main course kept up the high standard, Hasina Lamb £9.95, top quality meat without a trace of fat or gristle, mouthwatering sauce, piquant blend of herbs and spices fused in sweated down spinach. Fantastic pungent aroma, with star anise and cardamom and chillies added zing. Good Chappatis £1.50 for two. Real tablecloths and hand folded napkins. Beaming manager, knew most customers by name. Very enjoyable.'* RW. *'Our Guide has proved a great source of information and during 2006, we have particularly enjoyed our visits to the Jinnah, Flaxton.'* N&G.

Menu Snapshot. Punjabi Masala Fish £4.25; Pathan Balti £6.95, lamb cooked with fresh spinach, ginger and capsicum; Salmon Masala £10.95, stir-fried with spring onion, green chilli, bullet chilli, garlic, ginger, ground black pepper, tomatoes and coriander leaves; Spinach Paneer £5.95; Hot and Spicy Nan £2.25. Gift Vouchers available. Privilege Card: 10% discount. Sunday Buffet.12 - 10 and Buffet Dinner: Monday and Wednesday, 5.30 - 10, adults £9.95, Children £5.95. Hours: 5.30 - 11 Mon to Fri ;12 - 11. Sat & Sun.Branches: Beadlham, Harrogate and elsewhere in York. <jinnah-restaurants.com>

VICEROY OF INDIA — TOP 100

26 Monkgate, York — 01904 622370

Part of the Jinnah group (see above).*'A most enjoyable and varied buffet served all day Sunday at a reasonable price of £9 (less for children, including - slightly surprisingly our 14 year old son). The rest of the menu calls for a return trip when we are in the area '.* SH. 5.30 - 11, Mon to Fri; - 12 Sat; 12 - 11 Sun. Branches: York Spice Club, 1 Monkgate, York; Jinnah Takeaway, 18 The Village, Haxby, York. 01904 750082, open 4.30 - 12 daily.

EAST YORKSHIRE

Area: North
Population: 580,000
Adjacent Counties: Lincs, N S & W Yorks

1997 *county changes created this 'new' Yorkshire county by transferring territory and towns here from 'North Humbs'.*

Beverley

NASEEB

9- Wednesday Market — 01482 861110

44-seater est 1988 by Abdul Muzir, Very pretty restaurant, Indian painting, white walls, arches, ceiling fans, blue tablecloths and napkins, velvet chairs and curtains. You might get a discount if you show Mr Muzir this *Guide.* Hours: 6-11.30.

AKASH — NEW ENTRANT

63a Toll Gavel, Beverley — 01482 882090

'Fifty seater, very popular restaurant, situated upstairs in a pedestrianised centre of this busy market town. Very experienced and efficient staff. Large open room, simply decorated and nicely furnished. Reshmi Kebab £2.60, two, very juice and succulent, with a perfectly cooked omelette on top, small, crisp salad and thick yoghurt sauce. Meat Thali £15, half portions of prawn, lamb, chicken and vegetable curries, all distinctly different and tasty, all complimented each other. Also provided a Nan bread, very light, fluffy, enjoyable and Tandoori Chicken, very well marinated, nicely charred at the edges and salad. Overall an excellent meal.' RW. Credit and debit cards accepted. Delivery: 2 miles. Menu Snapshot. Aubergine Bhaji and Puri £2.20; Tandoori Mixed Korahi £6.95, chicken and lamb tikka, sheek kebab, tandoori chicken and king prawn, medium hot sauce; Special Nan £1.75, stuffed with cheese, garlic and coriander leaves. Price Check: Pop 30p, CHEAP CTM £5.10, Pullao Rice £1.30. Hours: 5.30 - 11.30, Fri & Sat to 12.

KHANS OF BEVERLEY

Wylies Road, Beverley — 01482 868 300

Wylies Road is off Beverley's North Bar Without. Rafiq Siddique is rightly proud of his pretty venue. The hexagonal exterior, and the Valentine's pink dining room, overall seating 50 in delicate

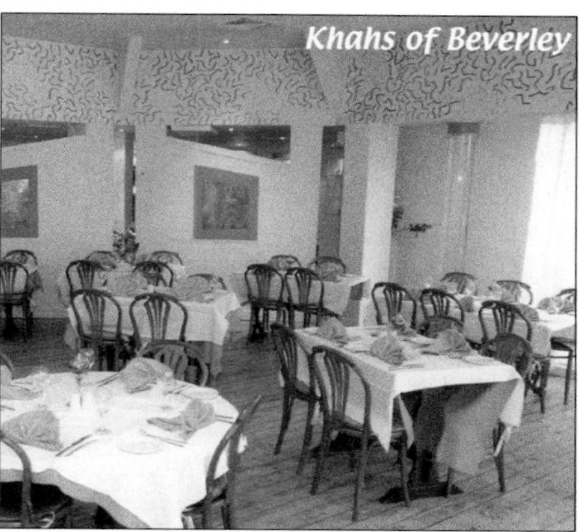
Khahs of Beverley

Bentwoods chairs and wood floor. Rafique's cousins run the excellent Thornbury Rasoi, Kingsley, Staffs. The food at Khans is under the care of Mohammed Shabir, and it provides all the favourites. *'We frequent Khans. Food produced is excellent and service is second to none.'* BU. Mr Siddique might give you a discount if you show him this *Guide*.

Brough

ASHAM BALTI NEW ENTRANT

108a Main Road, Newport 01430 449289

Mr Shamsul Islam has owned the Asham since 2005, he is also the head chef. *'I still fondly remember my first experience of Bangladeshi cuisine, Sher E Bangla, Hammersmith. I was a young telecommunications engineer and had been posted to work at the BBC in west London around the time of the Bangladesh war. Bangladeshi restaurant were opening up all over London and I had never tasted anything like the delicious meals that were on offer at prices even I could afford. Many years later, I am the MD of a telecoms company back in my home area of east Yorkshire. Wonderful place but lacked a really good curry restaurant. The opening of Asham Balti has put that right. All the usual curry favourite are on offer, but for the polite and helpful staff, nothing is too much trouble. Specialities include Bangladeshi fish garnished with Aloo Methi and unusual kinds of chillies, which I have never experience before.' RS. Are you talking about the legendary 'Naga.' 'Yet again had a wonderful meal. Have used this venue from the day it opened as a takeaway, some sixteen years ago. Staff warm and friendly and service excellent. Have recommended it to people from as far as Cypress.'* MR&MRS JG. Specials: Roshoon Eh Mirchi Murgh £5.95, chicken in hot thick sauce, garlic, green chillies, peppers, onion and tomatoes and coriander leaves; Maachli Biriani £8.95, two whole trout, shallow fried with onions, served with fried long grain Patna rice, garnished with tomato, cucumber, onion, lemon, coriander leaves and green chillies. You might get a discount if you show them this Guide. Delivery: 7 miles, £2 min. Takeaway: 10% discount. Cobra £2.25 a pint, house wine £8.50 a bottle. Price Check: Popadom 40p, CTM £, Pullao Rice £1.75. Hours: 5 - 11.30.

Hessle

LIGHT OF INDIA

27 The Weir, Hessle 01482 649521

Saiful Islam Tarafdar's Light is under the shadow of the fabulous bridge, and does 'fabulous takeaways only' KY. Special: Indian Burger, pitta bread with spicy kebab and salad £1.90. Curry Sauce and Chips £1.90! [Phew!] You might get a discount if you show Mr Tarafdar this *Guide*. Hours: 5-12 (12.30 on Sat.).

Hull

TANDOORI MAHAL

589 Anlaby Road, Hull 01482 505653

Abu Maksud and Mizanur Tarafder's 64-seat restaurant is a favourite of RKC. *'Have been regular customers for years. We have always received first class service and excellent food.'* PT. You might get a discount if you show Mr Ahmed this *Guide*. Hours: 6-12.

Yarm

RAJ BARI NEW ENTRANT

49 High Street, Yarm 01642 888004

'After some brilliant walking on the North Yorkshire Moors, I (we) were ready for a curry! We found two Indian restaurants on the high street, one quite posh, the Raj Bari, which opened in 30 minutes, this meant a swift pint in the pub. A modern and comfortable restaurant with traditional Indian nick-naks. Swift and efficient service, not particularly friendly. Usual starters of House Special Mixed Starter £3.95 for me and Sheek Kebab £2.95 for Monika. Both good but had to ask for Raitha.' That really annoys me, traditionally, Tandoori starters are always served with salad and Raitha! *'I ate Chicken Jalfrezi £5.95 and Monica Chicken Tikka Rogan £6.95, we shared Nan bread and Mushroom Pullao. I was a little disappointed, but Monica thought the dishes rather good, must have been having an off day. Prices reasonable.'* T&MH. Tony, you said you had spent the day walking on the moors, perhaps you were just too tired to enjoy your meal. min charge: £8.95. Credit cards accepted. Sunday night buffet. Takeaway 10% discount. Price Check: Popadom 40p, CTM £6.95, Pullao Rice £1.60. Hours: 12 - 2, Friday closed and 5 - 11, Fri & Sat to 11.30.

SOUTH YORKSHIRE

Area: North
Population: 1,280,000
Adjacent Counties:
Derbys, Lincs, Notts,
E & W Yorks

Barnsley

CURRY MAHAL

28 Barnsey Road, Dodworth, Barnsley 01226 201188

Air conditioned. Opened in 1999 by MG Uddin and partners, seats sixty four diners and Chicken Korma rushes out of the door! Menu Snapshot: Aloo Chop £2.30, mashed potatoes, fried with spices; Hari-Lal Chicken or Lamb £6, sliced tikka stir-fried with onions, green peppers, and mushrooms; Sylhet Biriani £6.80, sliced chicken tikka, boiled ice, chick peas, nuts, sultanas, garnished with cucumber, coconut, served with curry sauce; Chilli Nan £2. Cobra £2.30 a pint, house wine £1.90 a glass. Price Check: Popadom 70p, CTM £6.80, Pullao Rice £2.20. Hours: 6 to late. <www.currymahal.com>

JALSA

7 Pitt Street, Barnsley 01226 779114

Emdadur Rahman established his Jalsa in 1992. It is a comfortable, smart, 50-seater with a delightful reception area and bar. And Mr R might give you a discount if you show him this *Guide.* Hours: 6-12.

K2 TAKEAWAY

5 Royal Street, Barnsley 01226 299230

Kashmiri Balti takeaway-only establishment. *'Excellent.'* TH. Owner/manager/chef Ditta might give you a discount if you show him this *Guide.* Hours: 6pm-3am (4am on Sat., 12.30am on Sun.

Doncaster

AAGRAH AWARD WINNER

Great North Road, Woodlands, Doncaster 01302 728888

Opened in 1995, the fifth of the very popular (so booking advisable) Aagrahs. This 90-seater is a franchise run by cousin Liaquat Ali. *'I would put it at no. 1 in Doncaster, and there's a lot of competition.'* JF. (*See Shipley, W. Yorks for detailed comment.*) Specials include: Achar, Hyderabady and Masala dishes. Takeaway: 10% discount. Hours: 6-11.30; Fri. & Sat. 6-12; Sun. 6-11. *See page 19. Menu details and list of branches see Shipley. W. Yorks.*

INDUS

24 Silver Street, Doncaster 01302 810800

Long-established (1968) 175-seater, old friend of this Guide where you might get a discount if you it to owner Karim Din, or manager M Ilyas. Modern, upmarket Anglo/Indian decor. *'A sophisticated restaurant.'* DC. *'Is and always has been our favourite in Yorkshire.'* WHH. Takeaway: 10% discount. Delivery: £20. Sun. buffet £12. Hours: 12-2/6.30-11.30.

TAJ COTTAGE NEW ENTRANT

9 North Gate, Tickhill, Doncaster 01302 745745

MK Zaman 's Cottage opened in 2002, licensed and seats 90 diners in three rooms. A typically

English building, white washed with black beams, lovely. Dining rooms decorated very simply without much hint of being an Indian restaurant, very calming. Menu Snapshot: Chicken Pakora £3.50; Kolijee Puri £3.50, spicy chicken liver served with flaky pastry; Chicken Achanak £7.50, sliced tikka, medium spiced, garnished with garlic, green chillies and fried potatoes; Macher Tarkari £9.50, fresh fish, thick, medium sauce. Cobra £2.90 a pint, house wine £10.50 a bottle. You might get a discount if you show them this Guide. Price Check: Popadom 60p, CTM £7.50, Pullao Rice £2.20. Hours: 6 - 11.30.

TAJ MAHAL

32 Hallgate, Doncaster 01302 341218

Proprietor, Raja Munir Akhtar, opened his restaurant in 1989. Cobra £2.30 a pint, house wine £9.95 a bottle. min charge: £10.15 per head. You might get a discount if you show them this Guide. Price Check: Popadom 50p, CTM £7.50, Pullao Rice £2.20. Hours: 5.30 - 12, Sat to 1. Branch: Peterborough, Cambs

Pontefract

VICEROY NEW ENTRANT

Front Street, Pontefract 01977 700076

Owned since 1991 by head chef, Akram Lohn. His restaurant seats eighty-four and Chilli Chicken is the most popular dish. Delivery: 3 miles, £7 min. Cobra £2.65 a pint, house wine £7.70 a bottle. You might get a discount if you show them this Guide. Price Check: Popadom 30p, CTM £5.25, Pullao Rice £1.60. Hours: 5 - 1.

Rotherham

THE HIMALIA TAKE AWAY
NEW ENTRANT

129 Ferham Rd, Rotherham. 01709 512321

'This establishment is not in the best location in Rotherham, (where is ?)'[thanks Andy, no readers left in S.Yorks now!] *'and most non-locals will drive past it without knowing it exists. It looks ordinary but the food always has been very good. It's been there since 1995 and is family run. This week I had a kursi murgh (4.20), Peshwari Naan (1.40) and pullau Rice (1.10).This was as usual, on the large side, good quality and on time after order. I usually have their Palak Ghost (3.20) which I find excellent, full of flavour and with that 'strong' earthy taste I like in sag dishes. The take away has an open plan kitchen and everything is on view as you wait for your food. I can honestly say that I have never had a bad meal from this place.'* AM. Delivery free over £6 four miles. Hours: 6 - 12, Sun to Thurs; - 1 Fri & Sat.

MUGHAL CURRY CENTRE

1 Bellows Rd, Rawmarsh 01709 527084

Good curryhouse where you might get a discount if you show them this *Guide.*

Sheffield

ALMAS INDIAN BRASSERIE
NEW ENTRANT

34- High Street, Dore, Sheffield
0114 262 0883

Opened in July 1996 and managed by Bodrul Islam. Locals love the Methi Murgh and Methi Gosht Masala, both £6.50. Menu Snapshot: Spicy Chicken Livers £3.90, fried with onions; Keema Aloo £2.90, shallow fried patties made of minced lamb and potatoes; Char Masala Kofteh £6.90, meat balls in spicy gravy. Price Check: Popadom 45p, CTM £6.90, Pullao Rice £1.70. Hours: 6 - 11.

ASHOKA A-LIST

307 Ecclesall Rd, Sheffield 0114 268 3029

Established in 1967 by Mrs M Ahmed, this 38-seater is managed by Kamal Ahmed. *'The best Indian restaurant we have been to, including many in the London area and Birmingham. We went back to it every night of the week [while attending a scientific meeting in Sheffield]. We cannot praise its delicate and distinct flavours too highly, and the friendly, efficient service. '* J&AF. Yours is one of many contented reports, so we are happy that this well-established and well run venue stays in the elite **TOP 100.** Most ordered dish Bhel Puri, (*see page 75*), Liver Puri – chicken livers, stir-fried in masala, served on bread. *'One of the finest Indian restaurant in South Yorkshire. Diners are assured of excellent service, an amenable atmosphere and outstanding service. Comprehensive and high quality wine list. Book early to avoid disappointment.'* D&CS. *'Just wanted to send you a glowing report. Not only was the vegetarian curry superb, but the waiters were friendly'* KH. Takeaway: 10% off. Hours: 6 (Sun. 7)-11.30.<www.theashokarestaurant.com> *See page 93.*

BALTI KING NEW ENTRANT

216 Fulwood Rd, Broomhill 0114 266 6655

Opened in 1994 by Hanif Hussain. Seats a huge 120 diners in two rooms and the menu choice is even bigger! Regulars love it..... *'I have visited regularly for over eleven years and have always had the most excellent service and lovely food.' jb. 'Over the past thirty years I have been a curry enthusiast. Consistently received a very warm welcome at the Balti King, which I am pleased to say is extended to all customers and have enjoyed an excellent meal from the comprehensive and imaginative menu, at a very fair price in a pleasant and convivial atmosphere.'* JF. *'You will have to go a long way to better the dining experience at Balti King, Fulwood Road. Have become regular visitors, well worth a journey.'* J&PP. Menu Snapshot: Mixed Grill, £4.50 for two / £9 for four, includes chicken, lamb and fish tikka, seekh kebab and lamb chop or the Vegetable Sizzler, £3.50 for two / £7 for four, includes onion, potato and mushroom bhajia, samosa and pakora. Min charge: £10. Cobra £2.70 a pint, house wine £9 a bottle. Price Check: Popadom 35p, CTM £6.20, Pullao Rice £1.50. Hours: 12 - 5/6 - 3. Branch: in Leeds. You might get a discount if you show them this *Guide.* In fact you had better get a good discount.! They have used several my own Balti Cookbook photos on their menu without permission (You can see one on page 85). Flattering? Yes, but it doesn't pay my bills and is a breach of copyright.

BENGAL SPICE

457 Manchester Rd, Sheffield 0114 288 8666

Good curryhouse where you might get a discount if you show them this *Guide.*

BILASH TAKEAWAY

347 Sharrow Vale Rd, Sheffield 0114 266 1746

Opened in 1986, making the Bilash an old trusty friend of Sheffield! Abdul Jahir is the proprietor and with manager Ibrahim. *'We have been eating takeaways from the Bilash for over ten years and every time we eat one, we ring the chef to compliment him, never been disappointed. Delicious food, always fresh and well prepared.'* ANON. Menu Snapshot: Macon Chicken £4.50, Tandoori chicken, of the bone, spices, fresh cream and plenty of garlic; Lamb Katmandu £4.50, garlic, ginger and fried chillies; Chicken Malaya £5.95, banana, pineapple, sultanas and cream, mild. Students get a 10% discount. Price Check: Popadom 40p, CTM £4.15, Pullao Rice £1.20. Hours: 5.30 - 12, Sat to 1. <www.bilashtandoori.co.uk>

DILSHAD

96 The Dale, Sheffield 0114 255 5008

Good curryhouse where you might get a discount if you show them this *Guide.* Hours: 6-12; Sat.-12.30.

ELINAS

282 Sharrow Rd, Sheffield 0114 267 9846

Ditto. Hours: 5.30-11.30; Sat. 5.30-12.

EVEREST TANDOORI

59 Chesterfield Rd, Sheffield 0114 258 2975

Ditto. Hours: 6-1am; Thurs -2am; Fri. & Sat. -3am.

JAFLONG

182 Northfield d, Crookes 0114 266 1802

Ditto. Hours: 6-12am (1am on Fri. & Sat.).

NIRMAL'S

189 Glossop Rd, Sheffield 0114 272 4054

Nirmal's is an iconic entrant in this *Guide* and has been there since we began in 1984. It is renowned for the Gupta's home-cooked Indian food. We have always rated it in the Top 100. The place is quite small and the walls are lined with photos and memorabilia of a long career. We have had fewer and fewer reports recently. We did get this one from one of our experienced reporters: *'The comments in the last Guide sum it all up. It is one of those restaurants that you would travel a long way to visit'.* SO. HEN we had this report which we keep anon but is from a totally reliable source: *'The place was empty, but it was Sunday night. The room is a bit dark but there were balloons up from a previous part, which made it friendly. Much expectation because of this place's reputation. Pops and a good array of chutneys on the table were lovely. The menu was the first surprise. It was curryhouse pure and simple. Where were Nirmal's own dishes? The waiter was pleasant and we ordered some benchmark dishes (Dhansak, Sag Gosht, Aloo Gobi, Pullao Rice and a Paratha). The food arrived fairly soon. It didn't look attractive. All dishes were the same brown colour., Then the first mouthfuls: raw spices, all dishes tasting similarly flavourless, the sauce from one pot, greasy and uninviting. We took a few more mouthfuls then asked for it to be packed to take away. We paid the bill, and as we left we noted an Indian woman and man (the Guptas?) who were sitting (not dining) in the other room (bar area) throughout, but had never come to see if we were OK. They seemed jovial enough when we left, simply saying "goodnight, Come again." Not likely! Just down the road a bit was a skip. The takeaway was deposited in it, something we've NEVER done before, and we went off hungry and bitterly disappointed.'* ANON.

SAFFRON CLUB NEW TO OUR TOP 100

The Old Baths, Glossop Rd 0114 2766150

Naz Islam's Saffron occupies part of Sheffield's historic Glossop Road Baths, a building dating back to 1871. In keeping with the building's historic pedigree, Naz has kept his interior classic, but with a contemporary edge. The 68-seat restaurant is divided into four distinct quarters with a mixture of carpet and hardwood flooring and wallpaper and paintwork that lends an element of sophistication to each section. The cuisine is also split into classic and contemporary style dishes. While the classic menu retains a strong degree of traditionalism, the contemporary dishes give diners the chance to try something a little different. With over 15 years experience, Executive Chef, Faruk Khan has specialised in Mughal cooking Menu Snapshot: Halka Squid Masala £4.20, squid flame fried in light spices; Aloo Palak Tikki £2.90, pan-fried potato cakes with a spinach and cheese filling; Parsee Murgh £3.50, minced chicken with garlic and ginger, deep-fried; Aanari Jhinga £9.90, king prawns cooked with ground pomegranate in a slightly tangy sauce; Maachi Biran £9.90, medium spiced fish, pan-fried and served on a bed of garlic spinach accompanied with curry sauce; Hariyali Murgh £7.50, chicken cooked with mint, coriander, fresh and pickled chillies in a spicy sauce; Lamb Hyderabadi Biriani £8.50, saffron rice served with cucumber and tomato raita and curry sauce. The wine list, it is a cut above the average with many interesting choices. Cobra £2.90 a pint, house wine £10 a bottle. Takeaway 15% discount. Price Check: Popadom 60p, CTM £6.90, Pullao Rice £2.30. Welcome to our **TOP 100.** Hours: 12 - 2/6 - 11.

THE SPICE VALLEY NEW ENTRANT

570 Manchester Road, Stocksbridge, Sheffield 0114 283 1292

'I have just won a copy of your book in a competition, and here goes my first input for you.' Thanks, Andy, first of many I hope! Ed *'Had a meal tonight at reasonable and clean with a fair menu, including a few I have not heard of before including Chicken Geera (sic) (cooked with ginger). Channa puree for starters was very nice, whilst the Geera was plentiful and very tasty. the Peshwara Naan was huge. The highlight? This had to be the Mango Lassi, (£3.95) for a large jug. this is actually hand-made in the place and not out of a bottle. My friends had a Jalfrezi and a CTM between them with no complaints. The staff were very friendly. All in all, a good effort ... .though could have played Indian music on the tape rather than the canned stuff they had on.'* AM. .Hours: Sun - Thur 6 - midnight and Fri/Sat 6 - 1am)

WEST YORKSHIRE

Area: North
Population: 2,125,000
Adjacent Counties: Derbyshire, G Man, Lancs, N & S Yorks

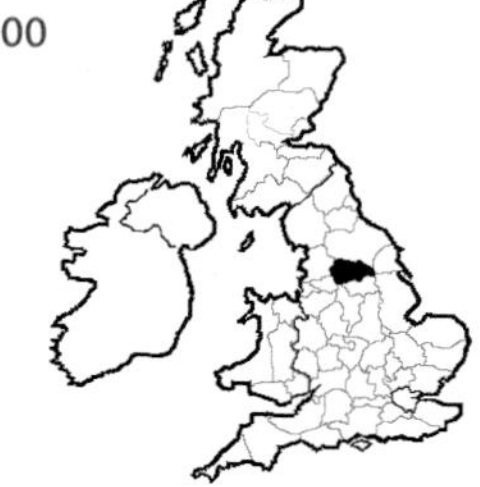

Batley

BOMBAY PALACE

3 St James Street, Batley 01924 444440

Location: off the A652 Bradford Road from Dewsbury, easily accessed from M1 junction 40. Balti 74-seater in an old converted bakery, with many features still apparent, such as the dough mixers. Opened in 1992 by G. Maniyar and Shahid Akudi. Brick walls display Moghal paintings, open fire. *'Upstairs with a light industrial theme, very pleasant surroundings which includes a separate family room. Popadoms are complimentary after giving your order. Food excellent, every dish has its own flavour. As the level of hotness tends to be gauged higher than most restaurants, this will suit the fire eaters. Portions are generous, one rice is enough for two. Staff extremely friendly and efficient.'* PVI. *'My wife and I have been regulars since it opened. Our current favourites are Seekh Kebabs – beautifully spicy, not too hot, fresh and tasty. Nargis Kebabs – full of flavour with a velvety texture. For special occasions there are banquet menus, which again represent excellent value for money.'* TN. Specials include: Shikari dish, Achari dish, and Palace Raan, whole leg of lamb, marinated for 24 hours in herbs, yoghurt, almonds and cashews, cut into slices, plenty for 4, £65. **BYO.** You might get a discount if you show Mr them this *Guide.* Delivery: £10 minimum, 3-mile radius, £6 minimum, 2-mile radius. Hours: 6-12.

SPICE GARDEN

2 Market Pl, Birstall, Batley 01924 471690

Specials at Abrar Hussain's Pakistani 74-seater include the Grand-Slam – it's four different meats, vegetables, prawns, massive portion – so now you know! Takeaway: 10% off. Delivery: £7, 3-miles. **BYO**. You might get a discount if you show Mr Hussain this *Guide*. Hours: 5-12.

Bradford

(inc: Baildon, Chapel Green, Great Horton, Idle, Manningham and Thornbury)

Bradford has a high pedigree curry background, with its very well-established, largely-Pakistani population. This means Halal meat and few veg at the many unlicensed cheap n' cheerful spit n' sawdust caffs. Since many are strict Moslems, not all welcome BYO. In such establishments, please check with the staff that you may BYO, and even if 'yes', always drink discretely and in moderation. The restaurants, sweet shops and cafés are much more widely spread around than, say, Southall. Curryholics must locate them, for their excellent, uncompromising ethnic food at real value-for-money prices.

ASHA

31 Cheapside, Bradford 01274 729358

Good curryhouse where you might get a discount if you show them this *Guide*.

BOMBAY BRASSERIE

1 Simes St, off Westgate 01274 737564

Established in 1983. Taken over in 1998 by Ali Shan. The building was once a Presbyterian church and makes a fantastic venue, seating 150. *'Great atmosphere, and food, indeed a memorable occasion, and something quite out of the Bradford norm.'* AN. Hours: 5.30-11.30pm; Fri. & Sat. 5.30-12.30; Sun. 12.30-11. *'Scores 8/10'* DB.

INTERNATIONAL TANDOORI

40 Manville Terrace, off Morley Street, Central Bradford 01274 721449

'The food, while not being particularly sophisticated, is excellent.' MB.

KARACHI

15- Neal Street,Bradford 01274 732015

Claims to be the UK's first curryhouse. It wasn't. It's not even the first in Bradford. The Kashmir, (see next entry) opened in 1958. The Sweet Centre, Lumb Lane in 1964, and the Kashmir, third in 1965. Still, it's a long time in curry circles. *'Limited menu but others dishes can be asked for, provided no long preparation is required. Proudly home-run with friendly and unflappable staff. Cheap, cheerful and excellent food. To round off a cracking meal I had a homemade Pistachio Kulfi, frozen solidly, but melting into a sweet and spicy mush.'* RW. *'Food is good quality, service is friendly. Decor reminded us of a school canteen, and the Guide is correct – the toilets are dreadful. Goes without saying that in Bradford it came with three chapatis. However, this was its undoing, as they were too thick meaning that you left feeling bloated.'* HR.

KASHMIR

27 Morley St, Bradford 01274 726513

The restaurant holds about 200 on two floors, downstairs – formica tables, upstairs – carpeted, tablecloths. *'A very popular restaurant with its local clientele.'* AT. *'Seekh Kebabs 60p very good flavour, Meat Roghan Josh £ 3.90 – not as spicy as other dishes but still good. Good service, pleasant staff.'* L&CH. Hours: 11am to 3am. Branch: Kashmir, 858 Leeds Road, Bradford Centre. 01274 664357 (near the hospital).

KEBABEESH NEW ENTRANT

165 Newline, Greengates 01274 617 188

Proprietor, Tayub Amjad's play-on-word restaurant (kebab-ish – get it?) serves Pakistani-style curries with interesting wines (check out the list, Red Bell Black Shiraz from Australia and Cutler Creek Zinfindel from California are both reasonably priced.) A modern, open plan and strikingly stylish restaurant seats seventy-five diners. Creamy walls, earthy coloured, large slate tiles cover the floor and absolutely lovely, hand-made wrought iron chairs surround marble topped tables. Cubed glass walls, green plants and ceiling spot lighting add to the calming look. 'We all had a fabulous night on Sat, but it was the food that made it!' ls. Menu Snapshot: Jalapenos £2.95, green peppers, filled with creamy sauce and coated in crispy breadcrumbs; Fish and Spinach £6.95, chunks of Haddock, spinach leaves, fenugreek, rich sauce;

Kebabeesh, Bradford

Chicken Manchurian £6.95, chicken off the bone, deep-fried in spicy batter, served with sweet and sour Punjabi sauce; Lamb Peshwari £6.95, tender lamb, cooked in a delicious rich sauce, using whole and nectar of almond, garnished with fresh green coriander and medium spices; Spicy and Potato Nan £1.95. Delivery: 5 miles, £5 min. Price Check: Popadom 40p, CTM £5.95, Pullao £1.25. Hours: 5 - 12, Sat to 1.

MUMTAZ PAAN HOUSE

386 Great Horton Road, Great Horton, Bradford SW 01274 571861/4

'Still as good as before, fifteen previous visits. Karahi dishes superb, various strengths offered! Breads top rate as are the pickles.' HW. *'They serve only the real thing! Hard to check your bill due to payment method (the waiter leaves a copy of your order at the table inside a folder which you take to the cash desk, where codes are entered into the till, and you are uncertain whether service charge has been added). Despite that, food was superb, and I shall return.'* PS. *'IOne of the finest curry houses in the country.'* AF.

PAZEEKAH BYO

1362 Leeds Road, Thornbury, Bradford E 01274 664943

Ex bus driver Mazhar-ul-Haq's tells us he likes to change the decor and the menu regularly, *'because that's what customers want to see.'* Successful Pakistani restaurant, seats a considerable 130 diners. Chef/manager is son Mohammed Jamil. Hours: 4-12.30 (1.30am on Sat.). They also own an 18,000 sq ft Asian Superstore, selling Asian food, and utensils at 91 Edderthorpe St, off Leeds Road, Bradford.

RAWAL

3 Wilton Street, off Morley Street, Central Bradford 01274 720030

Owner-Chef Abdul P Butt cooks Pakistani curries in his open kitchen, Mobin Iqbal manages the 50-seater and promises a 10% discount to *Guide* readers. Special: Grand Slam, mixture of meat, chicken, keema and fresh vegetables, served with Pullao Rice £5.70. Zam-Zam Special, meat, chicken, king prawns, and chick peas, served with Pullao Rice £5.70. Rawal claims *'Once tried never forgotten'.* DC says it is indeed true: *'Great price, great food'.* Takeaway: 10% off for students, 3 chappatis or boiled rice with each order. **BYO.** Hours: 5 - 2 (3am on Fri. & Sat.); closed Mon.

SHABAB — NEW ENTRANT

1099 Thornton Rd, Bradford 01274 815760

'A fairly modern detached building, nicely decorated with lots of Indian artifacts. Glass covered tables, low Indian style chairs with nice carpet. A table for two was no problem and were asked to sit in the takeaway area, menus were set out. After 5 minutes no one asked if we wanted a drink, so I asked a passing waiter, profuse apologies were offered. Cobra, only £2.50 a pint Prices had been slashed, my Vegetable Platter £1.75 (not £2.50), Seekh Kebab £1.45 (not £2.20). Fantastic, really, really tasty, Murgh Mushroom Balti for me and Gosht Jalfrezi for Mon, Zeera Aloo (one of my favourites, Tony, DBAC) Mushroom Pullao and a huge Nan. Complimentary Popadoms at the start, but no sweetened fennel or aniseed. £23.95 for two including tip. Thoroughly recommended.' T&MH. Delivery service. Price Check: Popadom complimentary, CTM £5.90, Pullao Rice £1.50. Branch: Shabab, 2 Eastgate, Leeds, 0113 246 8988 <www.shabab.co.uk>

SHAH JEHAN

30 Little Horton La, Central Bradford 01274 390777

Aka Ormar's Shajehan or just Omar's, after their owner/chef Omar Gulzar Khan. His three branches have identical menus. The Horton Lane branch seats 150 and is spread over three rooms. It is stylish and luxuriously decorated, with lovely leather sofas to relax on, while waiting for a takeaway, and pretty red chairs for your table. Goods comments on all three branches, usually: *'An extremely smart and well laid out restaurant with friendly service throughout. We had the whole leg of lamb ordered 24 hours in advance. Superb. Highly recommended.'* CT. *'Very, very, very good.'* LH. Hours: 12-2.30/5.30-12am. Branches: 6 North Gate, Baildon, Bradford N; 726 Manchester Road, Chapel Green, Bradford S.

SHIRAZ BYO

133 Oak Lane, Manningham, Bradford N
01274 490176

Mohammed Gulbahar and manager Mohammed Aslam might give you a discount if you show them this *Guide.* Mohammed Afzal cooks competent Kashmiri curries and Baltis. Hours: 4pm-2am.

SHISH MAHAL

6 St Thomas Road 01274 723999

Mohammed Taj's 54-seater *'is next door to one of the best pubs in Britain, The New Beehive – tremendous real ale with genuine character. The food at this* **BYO** *restaurant is nothing short of marvellous. Flavour literally explodes in the mouth. Friendly and informal service.'* SL. You might get a discount if you show him this *Guide.* Hours: 4PM - 3am.

SWEET CENTRE TOP 100

106 Lumb Lane, Bradford 01274 731735

Opened in 1964, and was Bradford's second curry venue. At the counter you order savouries and sweets by the pound. I know because way back, I purchased 120 samosas here for a *Curry Club* function, and we all found the measuring process a wee bit complex. Eventually they settled for 15p each and the sams were worth the sum! The sit down's fun too: *'Unlicensed all-hours cafe, cutlery on request. Asian clientele. Food cheap.'* DC. *'Excellent. The service is good and the food very tasty.'* SL. Asian Breakfasts are available. Hours: 7.30am - 10pm. The massive 280-seater restaurant alongside at 110-114 Lumb Lane shares the phone, the kitchens and the same wonderful food and service. Hours: 12pm -1am. Can't think why we haven't elevated it to our **TOP 100** before

TASTE OF BENGAL

79 Bradford Rd, Idle, Bradford N 01274 618308

Originally opened in 1980 as Passage to India, renamed in 1995 to Taste of Bengal. Now owned by Mrs Abdus Subhanand managed by Abdul Qayum, it's a small restaurant – thirty seats only, so you better book for those all important Fri & Sat nights. Menu Snapshot: Spicy Chicken Wings £1.95; Fish pakora £2.25; Murgh Jaflong £5.45, chicken with chilli and lime; Gosht Niralee £5.95, lamb with mild, creamy sauce, almond and onion. Delivery: 3 miles, £10 min. Takeaway 10% discount. Min charge: £5.95. Credit cards not accepted. You might get a discount if you show them this Guide. Price Check: Popadom 30p, CTM £6.95, Pullao Rice £1.20. Cobra £2.20 a pint, house wine £6.95 a bottle. Hours: 6 - 12, Sat to 12.30. <www.taste-of-bengal.co.uk>

Dewsbury

ZAM ZAM TAKEAWAY

5 North Road, Ravensthorp, Dewsbury
01924 469677

First opened in 1980, taken over by Perwaiz Khan in 1994. Main dishes are served with either three Chapatis, Rice or Chips. You might get a discount if you show Mr Khan this *Guide.* Hours: 6-12.30; Sat. 6-2.30; Sun. 6-1.

Garforth

AAGRAH AWARD WINNER

Aberford Road, Garforth 0113 287 6606

Nephew Wasim Aslam manages this 175-seater, opened in 1993, and the fourth of the very popular Aagrahs, refurbished 2006. Car parking for 90. Hours: 6-11.30; Fri. & Sat. 5.30-11.30. *See page 19. Menu details and list of branches see Shipley. W. Yorks.*

Guiseley

SAFFRON NEW ENTRANT

Guiseley Retail Park, Otley Road, Guiseley.
01943 877222

'On the *way back from the Test Match at Headingley we called in and they were just laying the buffet out. Popadoms and chutneys, there wasn't a choice of starters but we were served with Seekh Kebaba and Tandoori Chicken Tikka. Both were beautifully spiced. There was a selection of five chicken and lamb dishes together with Palak Paneer and Bombay Aloo. A large naan and pullau rice were brought to the table as we were invited to help ourselves. They were all well seasoned and spiced. We could have had any one of them as a main meal and been more than happy.. Besides the high quality of the ingredients and the way the starters and main courses had been cooked, the care and attention was carried forward to the desserts. They were not the ubiquitous jelly, fruit salad etc. but jellabies, ras mali, gulam jelab and more. All freshly made. All this is served in a well appointed dining room by attentive and knowledgeable staff. At under £10 a head you get a top class Indian meal for the price of an average, bog standard take-away. The a la carte menu looks outstanding with novel slants on traditional dishes at a veery reasonable price. We would recommend this to anyone who enjoyed the food of the Sub-Continent. For those who don't know if they will enjoy it; the staff will ensure they do. Just ask.*

Halifax

CROWN TANDOORI

31 Crown Street, Halifax 01422 349270

Good curryhouse where you might get a discount if you show them this *Guide.* Hours: 6-1; Sat. 6-3.

Huddersfield

AAGRAH AWARD WINNER

250 Wakefield Road, Denby Dale, Huddersfield 01484 866266

'Occupies a former pub on the main road through Denby Dale, a town more famous for its pies! The layout makes for a surprisingly intimate restaurant, yet being spread across two floors gives a lot of covers. Well executed decoration, in keeping with the former role of the building, think smart pub with a sub-continental theme. Brilliant starter, Makrani Jingra £4.50, really piquant batter that allows the taste of the large and top quality king prawns to shine through and was perfectly complimented by the dipping sauce. The salad was up to scratch as well. Lamb Hyderabadi £7.70, absolutely top notch gristle and fat free lamb in a really rich and thick sauce that was bursting with a whole host of tastes that almost overwhelmed the palate.' So, you enjoyed it then! *'Garlic Nan £1.95, nice, just a hint to doughiness. Tarka Dal £2.60, a tad light on the garlic. Highly enjoyable and equally recommended.'* RW. Price Check: Popadom 50p, CTM £7.70, Pullao Rice £1.70. Hours: 6 - 11.30, Sunday to 10.30. *See page 19.* *Menu details and list of branches see Shipley. W. Yorks.*

SERENA

12 St Peters St, Huddersfield 01484 451991

Ihsan Elahi's *'modern and chic'* Pakistani formula curry house, established in 1993, seats 62, the party room, 40. Chef Khalid Hussain's specials include Balti and Karahi dishes, and Hawahan Muragh, chicken with pineapple, cream. *'Good quality, well prepared dishes. Value for money, service excellent.'* JT. You might get a discount if you show Mr Elahi this *Guide.* Service 10%. Takeaway: 15% discount. Hours: 6-11.30.

Ilkley

EXOTIC TANDOORI

10 Church Street, Ilkley 01943 607241

Shah Marshal Alom's traditionally decorated 50-seater has golden arches and hanging plants. Special: Boul Mas, Bangladeshi fish . You might get a discount if you show Shah this *Guide.* 5.30-12.

SABERA

9 Wells Road, Ilkley 01943 607104

This old friend of the *Guide* first opened in 1974. Taken over by Abdus Sattar in 1998, it is, we hear: *'A clean restaurant with pine panelling and 48 seats. I enjoyed my Kalajee Gurda Dil and will return to try some of their other dishes.'* DM. You might get a 10 % discount if you show Abdus this *Guide.* Delivery: £10 minimum, 2-mile radius. Hours: 5.30-12.

Keighley

SHIMLA SPICE

14 South Street, Keighley 01535 602040

Opened its doors in 1998 under the directions of Mohammed Ayub and his two brothers, who had their 70-seater built from scratch on a useful corner site. Interior is decorated beautifully, ornate plasterwork on ceiling and walls, colonial fans, large chandelier, 'Tiffany' lamps and cane furniture.. Seats seventy-five diners and unlicensed, however, you can **BYO**. Menu Snapshot: Mixed Paneer £7.30, chicken. lamb, prawn, mushroom and king prawns in a cheese and coriander sauce; Tandoori Bemisaal £7.60, off the bone tandoori chicken, minced meat, served with Pullao Rice and salad. Credit cards accepted. Del: 5 miles, £8 min.

Takeaway 10% discount. Price Check: Popadom 35p, CTM £6.95, Pullao Rice £1.80. Hours: 6 - 12, Sat to 1. Branch: 69, Otley Road, Shipley.

Knottingley

JEWEL IN THE CROWN

110 Weeland Road, 01977 607233

Pakistani curries at Manager Adnan Miraf's 40-seater. *'Excellent food at reasonable prices. Service friendly and efficient. Recommend the Punjabi (Tandoori) Mixed Grill.'* IB. You might get a discount if you show Mr Miraf this *Guide.* Hours: 6-12.

Leeds

(includes Headingley, Horsforth, Kirkstall, Oakwood, Morley and Stanningley)

AKBARS NEW TO OUR TOP 100

15 Eastage, Leeds 0113 245 6566

n 1988, Shabir Hussain, 18, decided he wanted to open his own restaurant. In 1995 the dream was realised with the opening of a small restaurant,

Akbars, Leeds menu cover

seating 28, on Leeds Road, Bradford. Recently it has expanded considerably. See branches below. Akbar's specialises in sizzling pan-cooked baltis from Baltistan, an extreme mountainous region of north Pakistan. Menu offerings: Allam Khan's Lahori Style Dishes, Original baltis, Special baltis, Handi of the day, traditional Desi-Apna Style, accompaniments and Desserts. *'After a business meeting our leader invited five of us to Akbars for dinner. Centrally situated on Eastgate (near the famous Playhouse) we were swiftly met at the door by a smiling waiter and seated with a Cobra beer. Akbars is a large Victorian building, converted to be an 'theme' restaurant with lots of black marble and the upstairs bar fronted by an Egyptian Tutenkhamun display. The ceiling was filled with a myriad of star lights (or was that the effect of the drink?) The overall effect was an exotic ambience that set the scene for a relaxing meal. We noted that for a wet Tuesday night, Akbars was very busy with locals and business clients. Warm, crisp Popadoms and a tangy selection of pickles were washed down with more Cobra and some nice Rioja followed by starters of Sheek Kebab £1.95, Chicken Tikka £2.65, Chicken Samosa £1.95 and Prawn and Chicken Puri £2.45, all were tasty, well cooked and presented with a crisp side salad. Around us it was amusing to observe the waiters carrying tall stands with hooks carrying various Nan breads the size of bath mats! Of course, we had to have two of these 'Family Nan,' £3.50. Despite their size, had a lovely, light texture (Akbars must have a giant tandoor to cook these). Pullao Rice, Sag Aloo and Dhal (not Sophie) were also ordered. Main course comprised of Chicken Tikka Bhuna £5.45, Chicken Tikka and Keema Balti £5.65, Chicken and Chilli Balti £5.45 and a Lamb and Spinach Balti £5.45, these were all beautifully spiced and served in large pots, with a min of oil. All portions were over generous, so were could not manage a sweet, despite the excellent choices.' I see on the menu, Gajar Halwa (carrot cake), which I love! An upmarket restaurant with excellent cuisine, efficient service, providing a highly enjoyable experience.'* TE.

We are happy to elevate Akbar's to our **TOP 100** status. If Shabir can handle his rapid expansion, it could join our **A-LIST** next time. Branches; 1276 Leeds Road, Bradford, 01274 773311; 6-8 George Hudson Street, York 01904 679888; 73-83 Liverpool Road, Deansgate, Manchester, 0161 834 8444; Sheffield: 300-seater opening 2007 near the Meadowhall Shopping Centre. <www.akbars.co.uk>

AKBAR'S THE GRAND NEW ENTRANT & NEW TO OUR TOP 100

Minerva Hse, 16, Greek St, Leeds 0113 242 5426

Branch of Akbar's (see above). Akbar the Grand was the epithet given to the greatest Moghul emperor. A wonderful restaurant, leather chairs,

Akbar the Grand, Leeds

glass tables, pin spot lighting. *'Certainly lives up to its name with highly modern decor across a spacious split-level restaurant with ceiling, wall and floor lighting creating a luxurious ambience. On entering we were swiftly greeted and shown to our table by a smartly dressed waiter who placed fresh linen napkins on our laps and took our drinks order. Ice-cold Cobra, crisp Popadoms and delicious sauces were followed by curries, King Prawn, Chicken and Tikka Dupiaza and a fragrant Pullao Rice, served in large ceramic bowls. The massive 'Family Garlic Nan' arrived hanging on a tall pedestal, we tore into it and found it had a beautifully light texture. Definitely recommended.'* TE. Price Check: Popadom 65p, CTM £8.95, Pullao Rice £2.65. <www.akbars.co.uk>

AZRAM'S SHEESH MAHAL

348 Kirkstall Rd, Leeds NW 0113 230 4161

First opened in 1987, taken over by head chef Azram Chaudhry. Seats 76 with a further room for 38. Up the road from YTV studios, Azram's as the locals know it, set on its prominent corner site. Pakistani Specials include: Kofta Special, Balti Murgh, Murgh Punchabi Masala; Chicken Laziz £5.90, with garlic, lemon, tomatoes and black pepper; Gosht Palak Paneer £6.50, Indian cheese, lamb and spinach; Keema Chana £6.20, minced lamb with chickpeas. Cobra, £2.50 a pint, house wine £9.99 a bottle. You might get a discount if you show them this *Guide*. *'Highly recommend the food, service and ambience. All dishes reasonably priced. Azram is a first rate host, well liked by clients. Welcomes children and family groups.'* EP. Price Check: Popadom 30p, CTM £5.70, Pullao Rice £1.80. Hours: 5-12am (open for lunches from Nov. to end Jan.). Branch: Sheesh Mahal, 48, Harrowgate Road, Chapel Allerton, Leeds. <www.sheeshmahal.co.uk>

Azram's
Sheesh
Mahal Restaurant
346 - 348 Kirkstall Rd,
Leeds, West Yorkshire
0113 230 4161 or 0113 230 7799
Open 7 days: 5.00pm till midnight
Azram's SHEESH MAHAL

CHIRAAG BALTI

30 Chapel Hill, Morley, Leeds S 0113 253 5720

40-seater, owned since 1997 by T. Hussain who might give you a discount if you show him this *Guide*. *'Excellent Seekh Kebabs £1.60, Very tasty Balti Lamb Rogan Josh £4.95. Service good, staff very pleasant.'* L&CH. Hours: 6-12 (Fri. & Sat. to 1am); closed Tues.

DARBAR TOP 100

16 Kirkgate, Leeds Centre 0113 246 0381

A turbaned doorman welcomes you at *'a very ordinary street-level door, but upstairs the decor is a revelation.'* HJC. It's exotic, with traditional Moghul paintings and an antique Hawali (palace) door, specially brought from India. *'Has a very impressive interior. Room is large and the decor promotes the Indian Palace feeling – spacious yet warm and elegant'.* AG *'Excellent restaurant, especially at lunchtime, self service buffet. Probably deserves* **TOP 100,** *although I am always slightly suspicious of Indians with grandiose decor.'* RC [You'd be suspicious of India then, Robert! -Ed]. *'Very good*

Georgetown, Leeds

service and cooking. And, the decor is marvellous.' SL. *'Overall this restaurant is superb.* HJC. Special: Murgh Lahori, bone-off spring chicken, tangy spices, green coriander, cream, yoghurt, tomatoes and ginger. Daal Mash, white lentils cooked in butter with ginger, garlic and fried onion. Strawberry Lassi (large jug). Minimum charge: £18 evenings. Lunch e-a-m-a-y-l c£6. Hours: 11.30-2.30/6-11.30 Sun. closed.

GEORGETOWN — AWARD WINNER

Dysons Clock Building, 24, Briggate, Leeds
0870 755 7753

Another new Georgetown restaurant has opened in Leeds in the historic Dyson's Clock Building attached to the Leeds Marriott Hotel, Colonial Malaysian Restaurant, It is a very elegant restaurant indeed,with all the original shop fittings, perfectly restored. You can eat curries from Malaysia, Indian and China. I have eaten here and it is all fabulous. Singapore Slings are the BEST! For full menu details and prices see Kenilworth Warwickshire.. *See also pages 78 & 80.*

HANSA'S GUJARATI VEGETARIAN

AWARD WINNER – BEST VEGETARIAN

72 North Street, Leeds 0113 244 4408

This is a rarity, even in the London area: a Gujarati vegetarian restaurant, but here in Leeds it is a northern treasure owned by Mr Kishor and Mrs Hansa Dabhi. Your editor received this charming e-mail recently: *' Hope you can still remember us, now that you are an International Celebrity.'* (!!! Ed) *'Anyway please note herewith the latest accolade collected by Hansa as Curry Chef of the Year in the hope that maybe you'll find time to visit us one of these days.'* from Kishor and Hans. Certainly will, Ed. The press release said: *'Leeds Guide Magazine voted Hansa Curry Chef of the Year 2004, making her the only woman so accoladed.. Amongst the judges were Yorkshire TV's Calender girl Gaynor Barnes, Radio Aire's DJ Rossie and actor Jeremy Child Hansa's pure Indian vegetarian food proves once again that a good curry need not always be a meat curry. Hansa's restaurant has been*

A Hansa Thali

serving her brand of Indian vegetarian home-cooking with influences from her East African and Gujarati background since 1987, making it 'Leeds' best kept secret!' But it is not this Guide's best kept secret. We awarded Hansa's **UK BEST VEGETARIAN** in 1992. *(See page 29)* which keeps them in our **A-LIST.** To see what is on offer on the Gujarati menu see page 73. Hansa does all these things perfectly plus many other delights as well, such as Bhel Puri and Dosa. For those new to it try the Thalis: 2 shaks (curries) rotli or puri, plain or pilau rice, daal or kadhi, farsan, shrikhand or mango pulp, papad and a glass of lassi- sweet or salty. £ 9.25; or 2 shaks, rotli, plain rice, daal, papad and a glass of lassi. £ 7.95 Only *'I particularly enjoyed the crunchy, spicy flavour of the Shrikhand.'* DM. *'As a non-veg I went with an open mind. Food was fine but portions small.'* DB. *'Exquisite Lassi, portions small.'* DO'R. Sunday Buffet Lunch, 12 - 2pm, £7.25 Adults, £3.50 Kids. Early Bird Menus: Two for One from 5 - 6 weekdays. Hours: 5 - 10 Monday - Friday / 6 - 11, Saturday/ Closed. <www.hansasrestaurant.com>

KASHMIR

162a Woodhouse La Leeds 0113 245 3058

Unlicensed, **BYO** 72-seater restaurant, managed by T Mahmood who might give you a discount if you show him this *Guide*. . Price check: Papadam 20p, CHEAP!!! CTM £4.60, Pullao Rice 95p. Hours: 12pm-3am.

NAWAAB KHAN NEW ENTRANT

496 Roundhay Road, Oakwood, Leeds
0113 240 9911

Previously called Jinnah. Seats 110 diners, in three years. Proprietors: JE Humphrey and M Sajid. A clean and tidy restaurant decorated in cream and red. *'Menu is exhaustive with hundreds of varied speciality dishes such as Nosheri Lamb, Achari Chicken and Nihari lamb which I find myself ordering time and time again. Dishes are all simply superb in terms of their taste, variety of flavour and quality ingredients.'* t&c. *'Our family party meal was at the Nawab Khan restaurant and it was excellent, we intend to become regulars at this venue.'* R. Menu Snapshot: Prawn Pakora £3.25, with onions, herbs, spices, coated with gram flour and deep-fried; Sindi Machli £3.50, haddock marinated in spices, dipped in egg yolk and bread-crumbs, deep-fried; Nosheri Chicken £7.95, boneless chicken marinated, garlic and ginger sauce, pot roasted, fresh tomatoes, cumin seeds, bayleaf, cardamom, garnished with coriander leaves and grated ginger. Dall Bhuna £5.50, lentils cooked in mild sauce; Herbal Nan £2.50, filled with coriander leaf, onion, cumin seed, mint leaves. You might get a discount if you show them this *Guide*.

Nawaab Khan, Leeds

Nawaab Khan, Leeds

Takeaway 10% discount. Kingfisher £2.50 a pint, house wine £9.95 a bottle. Price Check: Popadom 50p, CTM £6.70, Pullao Rice £1.95. Hours: 6 - 11.30, Sunday 12 - 11.

NAWAAB NEW ENTRANT

1 Wellesley Hotel, Wellington Street, Leeds 0113 244 2979

'After a business meeting on a cold winter evening in Leeds, our team visited Nawab, centrally situated on Wellington Street (near the Railway Station), we were swiftly met at the door by a smiling waiter and seated with a Cobra beer. Part of the ground floor of a large Victorian hotel, converted into a modern 'brasserie' theme. Nawab was very busy with local office workers. Warm, crisp Popadoms and a tangy selection of pickles were washed down with more Cobra's followed by Chicken Tikka Dupiaza £5.95, King Prawn Madras and Chicken Madras £5.95 with fragrant Pullao Rice and Nan Bread £1.50. Nawab is an up-market restaurant with excellent cuisine, efficient service and provides a highly enjoyed experience with good value for money.' TE. Price Check: Popadom 40p, CTM £6.95, Pullao Rice £1.95. Branches: Nawaab, 32, Manor Row, Bradford and Nawaab, 35, Westgate, Huddersfield. <www.nawaab.net>

POLASH TOP 100

103 Town St, Stanningley 0113 256 0989

M Arif's huge 150-seater spacious restaurant in former Conservative Club is popular. *'I had a family party and asked the Polash to cater for me. The resultant banquet was beyond praise.'* EF. *'Our daughter, then 14, says that the Polash Chicken Korma was her favourite, even though she has tried others in many other Indian restaurants.'* BT. *'We were impressed. Food tasty. Service a little stretched at busy times.'* IEF-E. *'How much we enjoy our visits. Excellent food, courteous staff.'* MG. *'Always welcoming and courteous, high standard, always consistent, always start with Chicken Tikka followed by King Prawn Khass.'* JS. *'Combination of service and freshly cooked food, makes the Polash our favourite.'* MH-R. *'Very smart inside. Good mix of standard and unusual dishes – Chana Aloo Puri was superb. Friendly attentive service..'* M&SR. *'Excellent restaurant. Best starters we have tasted anywhere.'* MM. *'Standard of food and service is superb. Choice is tremendous, carefully prepared, garnished and served with a smile. Reasonably priced – half the cost of the Aagrah!'* MR&MRS DH. *'We tell all our friends of the Polash.'* MC. *'Tandoori Mixed Grill, an enormous plate full of Tandoori Chicken, Chicken and Lamb Tikka, Lamb Chops, Seekh Kebab, Liver and fresh salad with a Vegetable Curry (does anyone actually finish that lot?) Very popular facility.'* RW. *'Speciality curries are our firm favourites: Nargisi Kofti (inc Mushroom Rice), Murgh Keema Aloo (inc Lemon Rice) and Garlic Chicken Balti (inc Pullao Rice) – truly excellent.'* DF. *'Proprietors are always on hand to oversee, spotless kitchen.'* pjs. *'Well presented, tasty, freshly prepared and served food. Meat is lean – important to us.'* DA. *'Good car park. Deceptively large restaurant, we had pre-booked. Seething on a Saturday night, much activity from waiters, slowish service. Vegetarian Platter, excellent value, very nicely presented and very tasty. Chilli Chicken Mushroom was not what I expected – chicken, grilled, Pullao Rice, Mushroom Curry, salad and mild Korma sauce – no room for anything else.'* T&MH. Menu Extracts: Smoked Chicken Raan £2.95; Prawn Pakora £2.95; Lamb Chops £2.80; Chicken Achar £7.95, served with Lemon Rice; Lamb Kaju £7.95, cashew nuts, served with Garlic Nan. Hours: 5.30-11.30 (Mon. & Sun. to 11).

TARIQ'S

12 St Michaels Road, Headingley, Leeds 0113 275 1881

Owned and managed by Bobby Sharma, who might give you a discount if you show him this *Guide*. this Balti House seats 64. Special offer meal deal, Thursday and Sunday before 10pm. Dining in – free papadams and chutneys – nice touch. *'Windies were playing England and it was stopped by rain. After waiting till early evening in hope, there was a stampede down to Tarriq's just round from the cricket ground. Got there first, luckily – they were queuing within minutes. Superb meal made up for a wet day.'* IB. Price check: Papadam 20p, CTM £4.90, Pullao Rice £1.20. Lager £2 bottle, house wine £6.50. Hours: 5.30-2.30am (3am on Sat., 12.30am on Sun..

Pontefract

ROTI

North Baileygate, Pontefract 01977 703915

Arshad Mahmood's 110-seater (party room 40) is bright and airy with tented ceiling, beams, cream-with-green napkins, marble table tops, wicker furniture. Abdul Aziz's kitchen on view behind glass. Pakistani food. *'Excellent quality, bordering on the expensive.'* KH though this might be eased if get a discount by showing Arshad this *Guide*. Hours: 5-12.

VICEROY

6 Front Street, Pontefract 01977 700007

First opened in 1990, taken over in 1994 by Chef Akram Hussain Lohn . He cooks Pakistani food at his 60-seater, managed by Susan Ruckledge who might give you a discount if you show her this *Guide*. Takeaway: 30% discount. Delivery: £6 minimum. Hours: 5-1am.

Pudsey

AAGRAH AWARD WINNER

483 Bradford Road, Pudsey 01274 668818

Located midway between Bradford and Leeds, the second Aagrah is Head Office, as well as a 72-seater managed by Arshad Mahmood opened in 1986. Car parking for 25. Specials include: Achar, Hyderabady and Masala dishes. Takeaway: 10% discount. Hours: 6-11.30; Fri. & Sat. 6-12; Sun. 12.30-11.30. See below.

Shipley

AAGRAH AWARD WINNER

27 Westgate, Shipley 01274 594660

At the time of writing, there are nine Aagrahs, all in Yorkshire, and all **TOP 100**s in this guide. It was here in 1977, refurbished in 1999, that this 50-seater was opened by Mohammed Sabir. The notion to expand came from son Mohammed Aslam (then a London bus driver) assisted later by brother Zafar Iqbal, who now runs this one. It is notable for its Kashmiri-style decor with attractive block-print table linen and those fabulous hand-made, hand-painted colourful lacquered chairs with the cute tinkly bells, especially commissioned in Pakistan (£60 each). Gradually Aslam encouraged his extended family to join the enterprise as managers, staff and cooks. With increasing impetus the other branches have been brought on-stream, as stylish and up-market restaurants. We hear contentedly from many regulars who visit twice or more a week, and visitors from afar. Their average age is over 25 (no after-pub teenage louts here). Their average spend of £20 gives the chain a turnover of *c.*£4 m. The food is Pakistani, which self-taught cook Aslam has insisted that all family members also learn, training in both the kitchens and out front to NVQ level. This way the service and food in all the Aagrah restaurants is of equal standard. There is ample choice in the identical menus and here is a Snapshot: Starters include Yahknee, spicy chicken soup, and Panir Pakora, Indian curd cheese fritter; Chicken Liver Tikka £2.60, marinated and cooked over charcoal, served with salad; Makrani Jhinga £3.90, tail prawns marinated with lime juice and green chillies, dipped in paste and deep-fried, served with sauce and salad; Paneer Kebab £2.60, crushed cheese, mixed with spices, coriander leaves, green chillies, mint leaves and deep-fried, served with salad; Lamb Chop Piaz £6.95, spring lamb chops marinated and cooked over charcoal, briskly stir-fried with onions, capsicum, green chillies, mushroom, tomato and coriander leaves, served on a sizzler with Hyderbadi sauce; Vegetable Ginger £5.95, cauliflower, courgette, aubergine, carrot, peas, turnip, and capsicum with a substantial amount of ginger,, garlic, tomatoes, coriander leaves, aniseed, green chillies and black cardamom. Main courses include many meat, chicken and fish dishes. Aslam's current *pièces de résistance* are Murgh Hyderabady, spring chicken, tangy spices, coriander, cream, yoghurt, tomatoes, ginger; Balti Liver, with garlic, ginger, chillies, tomatoes and coriander. Balti Bhindi Aloo Paneer, curd cheese, bhindi and potato, onions, ginger, garlic, coriander. Family Nan, Cheese and Onion Nan. Takeaway: rice and 3 chapattis free. Takeaway 10% discount. Price Check: Popadom 50p, CTM £7.50, Pullao Rice £1.70. Hours: 6-12. Fri./Sat -1am.

Branches: N. Yorks: York Rd, Steenton, Tadcaster, Nr Yorks, 01937 530888; Devonshire Pl, Keighley Rd, N. Yorks, 01756 790807; Great North Rd, Woodlands, Doncaster, S.Yorks, 01302 728888; 4, Aberford Rd, Garforth, W. Yorks, 0113 287 6606; 250, Wakefield Rd, Denby Dale, Huddersfield, W. Yorks, 01484 866 266; St Peters Square, Quarry Hill, Leeds, W. Yorks, 01132 455667; 83, Bradford Rd, Pudsey, W. Yorks, 01274 668818; 27, Westgate, Shipley, W. Yorks, 01274 583338; Barnsley Rd, Sandal, Wakefield, W. Yorks, 01924 242222. *See page 19.*

Wakefield

AAGRAH AWARD WINNER

108 Barnsley Road, Sandal, Wakefield 01974 242222

The seventh of nine Aagrahs, a 100-seater, opened in 1986. Parking for 40 cars. (See above for details.) Also able to offer accommodation – so don't drink and drive, just stay over at the Sandal Court Hotel. Takeaway: 10% discount. Hours: 6-11.30; Fri. & Sat. 5.30-11.30; Sun. 6-11. *See page 19.*

THE ISLES AND ISLANDS

When he failed to capture the British Isles, Napoleon dismissed us as a nation of shopkeepers. Were he around today, he might observe that we are now a nation of curry house keepers. Some isles, including Lundy, the Isles of Scilly, Uist, Mull, etc., have no curry houses but, for neatness, we group those that do together. For those who delight in collecting useless information, Lerwick, capital of the Shetland Isles, contains the nation's most northerly curry house (and still probably that of the whole globe). It is 600 miles from London and 800 miles from our most southerly curry house in St Helier, capital of Jersey.

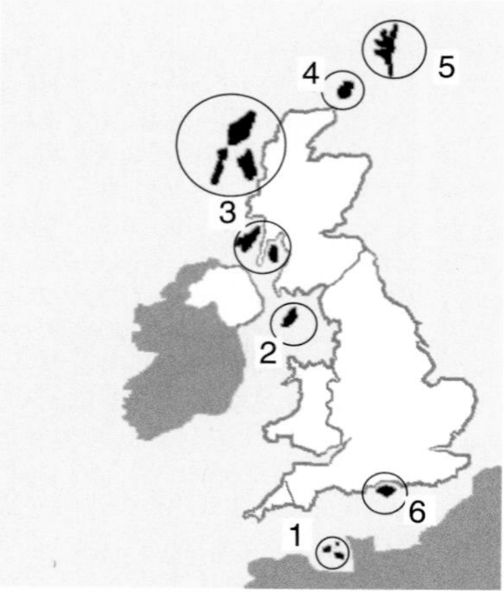

CHANNEL ISLANDS

1 on the map

Area: off the French Normandy coast.

ALDERNEY

NELLIE GRAYS INDIAN CUISINE

Victoria Street, Alderney 01481 823333

Established 1996, owned by Matin Miah (formerly the head chef of Jersey's Bombay Brasserie), and managed by Ashraf Makadur. Seats 50 in two dining rooms. Two parking spaces at rear of building. Jalfrezi most popular, chef's special Tarkari. Service: 10%. Hours: 6-11; Sun. 12-2.

GUERNSEY

Population: 66,000

L'Eree

TASTE OF INDIA

Sunset Cottage, St Peter, L'Eree 01481 264516

Owned and managed by Tony Fernandes, who is from Goa, since 1989. Pink stone wall design with maroon seating for 60 diners. Chef Paltu Bhattachajee holds court in the kitchen serving specialities such as Sardines on Puri, Tandoori Lobster and Bhuna – market price and subject to availability. Takeaway: 10% discount. Set lunch: c£12 and £26 (for two). Hours: 6-11pm; closed Mon. Branch: Taste of India, St Peter Port.

St Peter Port

SPICE INDIAN CUISINE

North Plantation, St Peter Port 01481 722422

Changed ownership to Matin Miah and name on the 1st March 2004. Credit cards accepted. Cobra, £3.95 pint, house wine £9.95 bottle. Price Check: Popadom 50p, CTM £8.50, Pullao Rice £2.00. Hours: 12 - 2/6 - 12.

TAJ MAHAL

N. Esplanade, St Peter Port 01481 724008

Mujibul Hussain's 60-seater is located in the heart of St Peter Port opposite the main public car park. *'Charming and attentive staff. Interesting menu – imaginative main courses and unusual vegetable side-dishes (Uri Besi, mangetout and butter beans; Balar Aloo, mashed potatoes with garlic; Baygoon (aubergine, spinach and chickpeas) which was sampled by non-veggies with some envy! Delicious Chicken Sholay arrived flamed in brandy. All food was fragrantly spicy with subtle differences between each dish.'* cc. Hours: 12-2/6-11.30 (12am on Sat.).

TASTE OF INDIA

2, Mill Street, St Peter Port 01481 723730

Established in 1990. Seats 50. Owned and managed by Tony Fernandes. Decorated in maroon. Specials: Bamboo Shoot Masala – a dry curry. Takeaway: 10%. Hours: 6-11pm; closed Mon. Branch: Taste of India, L'Eree.

JERSEY

Population: 75,000

St Aubin

SHAPLA

Victoria Road, St Aubin 01534 746495

'Hasna Kebabs, lamb marinated in yoghurt, tandooried with onions, peppers and tomatoes, really tasty. Chicken Jalfrezi, aroma terrific. Simply perfect Lamb Rogan Gosht. Polite and helpful waiter.' MB. Hours: 12-2/6-12am.

St Brelade

BENGAL BRASSERIE

11 La Pulente, St Brelade 01534 490279

'Favourite dish is the Chef's Balti – like no other – chicken, lamb, prawns, egg, kidney beans, mange tout, you name it. Portions more than adequate. Service best on the island, staff very friendly. Al fresco in the summer. Only 30 yards from St Ouens beach. Best place to see the sunset.' GL. Hours: 12-2/6-11.30.

St Helier

NEW RAJ

8 Burlington Parade, St Saviours Road, St Helier 01534 874131

Owned and managed by Kass Malik since 1984. Seats 60 in two dining rooms. *'Onion Bhaji was good, Chicken Chat not so good, being insipid and needing some salt. Chicken Dhansak was well spiced, my wife's CTM was rated the best she has had for some time..'* MW. Hours: 12-2/6-12.

SHEZAN

53 Kensington Pl, St Helier 01534 22960

A small restaurant seating 40. *'Meal very good. A bit expensive, but worth it.'* SC. *'Owner, Shani Gill, is always the gentleman. His endeavours to satisfy all his customers have made him many friends.'* GDM.

TAJ MAHAL CENTRAL

La Motte Street, St Helier 01534 20147

'Classy and luxurious restaurant. You are surrounded by running water and tropical fish. Had best ever Tarka Dal.' TM.

ISLE OF MAN

2 on the map alongside

Area: Off the English N W. coast.

Population: 76,000

Douglas

SAAGAR TANDOORI

1 South View, Queens Prom 01624 674939

Mr and Mrs Chowdhury and Mr Jaigirdar's might give you a discount if you show them this Guide at their 60-seater: *'the best I've been to.'* RR. *'One time we tried the special Kachee Biriani – 12 hours' notice required to prepare it. It's partially cooked Basmati rice layered over meat marinated in spices, yoghurt and herbs then cooked in the oven – perfumed with saffron. £25 for two. Delicious. Next time we brought friends and tried Kurzi Lamb – 24 hours' notice is required for this extravaganza (c£50 for four). We've yet to try £75 whole leg of lamb marinated in fresh ground spices with lamb mince meat cooked in the oven. Starters, sides, rice & breads for four included.'* AN. Hours: 12-2/6-12am.

Ramsey

SPICE OF LIFE

8 Peel Street, Ramsey 01624 816534

We enjoyed the food, and would have done had it been in Manchester' GB. *'Bizarre note on the door, We do not serve drunks.'* DMcC.

SCOTTISH ISLES THE WESTERN ISLES

3 on the map alongside

Area: The Outer Hebrides or Western Isles comprise an island chain off the Scottish

Population: 26,000.

Isle of Bute

INDIAN PAVILION

7 Argyle St, Rothesay, Bute 01700 504988

Est. 1993 by Bobby Mahey, 30-seater. Dave Mahey cooks north and south Indian and Goan food. Delivery charge 95p. Hours: 5pm-12.30am.

Isle of Lewis

STORNOWAY BALTI HOUSE

24 South Beech, Stornoway 01851 706116

46-seater previously Áli's Takeaway, now owned by Mohammed Ahmed - Moe to his friends. Takeaway: 10% discount. Hours: 12-2/5-11.30;. Sat. & Sun. 5-11.30.

Isle of Skye

SPICE HUT INDIAN

Bayfield Road, Portree 01478 612681

Formerly the Ghandi. *'Difficult to find – at the rear of the big car and coach park near the Tourist Information Centre. A bizarre experience. We turned up at 1pm to find "Closed" on the door. However, we tried the door anyway and it opened. Two bored looking Asian teenagers were folding napkins, and one lethargically showed us to a table in the otherwise totally deserted restaurant. He took our order with his now customary lack of charm, and we prepared for the worst. However, the food arrived very promptly and was actually delicious. Vegetable Rowghon was fragrant and packed with fresh tomatoes. Garlic Chicken Tikka was equally good. It is an enormous shame that a clearly excellent chef is having his hard work marred by a front of house crew displaying such shameless amateurism.'* CC. *'Good.'* G&MP.

ORKNEY ISLANDS

4 on the map on page 428

Area: 70 small islands 16 km north of mainland Scotland.
Population: 19,500

Kirkwall

MUMTAZ

7 Bridge Street, Kirkwall 01856 873537

'Comfortable and modern restaurant. All food very tasty. Service good and efficient.' PAWW. Hours: 12-12am.

DIL SE — NEW ENTRANT

7 Bridge Street, Kirkwall 01856 875242

Opened by Anwar Hussain in June 2005. His restaurant is simply and nicely decorated with traditional embroidered wall hangings and seats a considerably seventy diners. *'I find that it's the side dishes I enjoy the most, I could live off dhal and I love Sag Aloo. My mouth still waters when I think of it.'* DF. Menu Snapshot: Bombay Roll £3.50 - sheek kebab rolled in a deep-fried Indian pancake with fresh onions, served with our mint dip and salad; Tandoori Mixed Grill £12.95 - tandoori chicken, chicken and lamb tikka, sheek kebab, tandoori king prawn and nan - horray for the nan and king prawn!; Lamb Tikka Achari £7.95 - with a tangy mango twist; Colli Bhaji £2.75 - spiced cauliflower florets; Coconut Rice £2.30. Cobra, £2.50 a bottle, house wine £3.75 a glass. Credit cards accepted. Price Check: Popadom 60p, CTM £7.95, Pullao Rice £2.10. Hours: 4 - 11.<dilserestaurant.co.uk>

SHETLAND ISLANDS

5 on the map on page 428

North of Orkney and the northern-most part of the UK are 100 Shetland islands, of which the main one is known as Mainland.
Population: 22,000

Lerwick

RABA INDIAN

26 Commercial Rd, Lerwick 01595 695554

'Well-cooked Indian cuisine at reasonable prices. Samosas, Bhajia and Chicken Tikka Masala were all delicious.' AIE. Hours: 12-2/4.30pm-12am. Sunday buffet: 1pm -11pm. Adults £9.50/Kids £6 (à la carte also available).

ISLE OF WIGHT

6 on the map on page 428

Area: Off S.E. English coast, county status.
Population: 133,000

Cowes

COWES TANDOORI

40 High Street, Cowes 01983 296710

At Ashid Ali's 64-seater. DB *'loves the Podina Gusht and Garlic Chicken'* and L&CH found *'Tasty Sheek Kebabs'*. You might get a discount if you show Mr Ali this *Guide*. Hours: 12-2/6-12am.

Newport

NABAB PALACE

84 Upper St, James St, Newport 01983 523276

Jila Miah's 54-seater serves *'good, competent curries and accompaniments at reasonable island prices, eased by his offer to give a 10% discount to readers of this Guide..'* L&CH. *'Decor clean and comfortable, service efficient. Starters: King Prawn – fresh and well cooked. Chana Puri – well spiced. Vegetable Dhansak was good. Tarka Dal very good. Garlic Nan – plenty of fresh garlic..'* AG. Hours: 12-2/6pm-12.

NORTHERN IRELAND

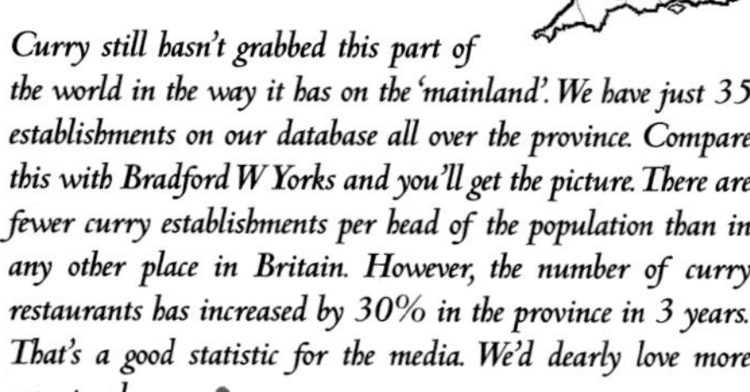

Shares a land border with the Republic of Ireland (Eire).
Population: 1.6million

Curry still hasn't grabbed this part of the world in the way it has on the 'mainland'. We have just 35 establishments on our database all over the province. Compare this with Bradford W Yorks and you'll get the picture. There are fewer curry establishments per head of the population than in any other place in Britain. However, the number of curry restaurants has increased by 30% in the province in 3 years. That's a good statistic for the media. We'd dearly love more reports, please.

Belfast

ARCHANA

53 Dublin Road, Belfast 02890 323713

'I'm sure you'll not remember me; I gave you initial training in Macs.' [course I remember you Ann]. *'I don't like hot spicy food but I do like tasty food and when I asked the waiter for help, he took a lot of time and trouble to recommend a dish which turned out to be delightful and suited my taste perfectly. My partner had their mixed grill and said it was the best he's every tasted – so with compliments flying I thought you ought to know, just in case they're not in you guide! We love good food and always go back to restaurants that please us - this will definitely be one of them. Great web site by the way.'* AO. *'Visited last weekend around 7pm. Quite the most expensive (over £9 for a Dhansak without rice, for example) and poorly cooked food I have eaten in many years of eating curry. All our meals had barely cooked onion in them and my Sag Aloo had the consistency of a child's meal. Other diners sending back their rice as cold. Service surly, almost aggressive. Your sign on the door, needs taking down.'* GT. Who's right?. Reports please.

SONALI

701c Lisburn Road, Belfast 02890 666833

Formerly Ghandi. *'The food took a fairly long time to arrive, but this proved to be more of a case of care being taken with every dish than sloppy service. One immediately noticeable feature of the entire meal was the restrained use of ghee for which the chef is be commended. Each dish was fresh and light with its own distinctive taste well brought out. The top of my list of Belfast curry houses.'* DMcD.

JHAMA

133 Lisburn Road, Belfast 02890 381299

110-seater. *'We found the Tandoori Crayfish superb and different £11.95.'* CD. Hours: 12-2/5.30-11.30. Branch: Tamarind, Carrickfergus; Bithika Takeaway, Belfast.

MOGHUL

62 Botanic Avenue, Belfast 02890 326677

Established 1984 and taken over in 1998 by H Sirpal. Formerly Maharaja. Seats 80 diners. Specials: Tikka Special £7.95 – marinated chicken, mild sauce with mangoes and banana. Pakora Curry £5.95 – fairly hot, with yoghurt, gramflour and Punjabi spices. Paneer Makhani £6.95 – chef's own paneer, mild buttery sauce. Kebabs (delivery only): Donner, Sheesh, Chicken Tikka etc available from £3 and Chicken Burger with salad . Delivery: £1 charge. Hours: 12-2/5-12

EIRE

Republic of Ireland

Shares a land border with Northern Ireland.
Population: 3.5million

Dublin

JAIPUR — NEW ENTRANT — TOP 100

41 South Gt Georges St, Dublin 01 677 0999

'Chic and modern, fifty seater in the south of the city. Friendly and helpful staff, a mixture of Indians, Irish and Chinese. Nicely decorated and inviting. complimentary Popadoms a 'traffic light' array of Chutneys. Modern interpretation of dishes. Jaipur

Jugalbandi €12 - enjoyable selection of Aloo Tikka, Tandoori King Prawn, Tandoori Salmon, Lamb Tikka and Tandoori Chicken Wing, all served with five concentrated and intensely flavoured, different sauces. Excellent Nalli Ghost 20 euro - really well cooked, tender lamb leg of the very best quality, lovely rich taste served with a thin sauce that did compliment the flavour of the meat. Very nice Nan €3 - coriander blending well with the lamb. Fair Tarka Dal €4.50 - bit thin. Good restaurant.' RW. Real Indian chefs ... real Indian food. Welcome to our **TOP 100.** Branches: Jaipur, 21, Castle Street, Dalkey: 01 285 0552; Jaipur, 5, St James's Terrace, Malahide: 01 845 5455 : <www.jaipur.ie

SHALIMAR NEW ENTRANT TOP 100

17 South Great Georges Street, Dublin 2 01 671 0738

'A rarity - an Indian restaurant run by Indians! Upmarket decor, de rigeur for this art of super-cosmopolitan Dublin, with light and airy main room, subdued colours and Bauhaus simplicity in the furniture. Some sixty-four guests are attended to by knowledgeable and discreet staff. Limited menu choice, but authentic dishes and modern interpretations, all very nouvelle cuisine. Complimentary Popadoms. Tandoori Masal €8.99- exquisite, thin medallions of best tender, perfectly cooked beef, interspersed with layers of tomato and red pepper, with three loops of different sauces - outstanding. Raan E Sikandari €18.95 - had a lot to live up to and succeeded brilliantly, a stunning bottom thigh joint of lamb, the meat partially cut away, but left enough to pick up and gnaw at, well marinated and cooked to absolute perfection, with a really hot and spicy marinade. Splendid Nan, light and fluffy, lovely perfume from the coriander leaves. Tarka Dal €6.95 - without doubt the best I have ever had... perfect blend of garlic, onion and lentils.' rw. Welcome to our **TOP 100.** Credit cards accepted. Price Check: Popadom €95, CTM €10.09, Pullao €2.50. Hours: 12 - 2.30/5 - 11.30, - 12 Fri / Sat.

Galway

EASTERN TANDOOR NEW ENTRANT

2 Spanish Parade, Galway 0191 564819

'Eight Popadoms with pickles - sweet mango, chilli and Lime all Pataks. Prawn Pui €6.30 - mild but tasty. Eastern Delight €10.90 - plenty for two and good mix. Beef Balti €13.50 euro - very mild as was the Madras! Chicken Jalfrezi €13.40 - bland. Bhindi €6.50 euro - fresh and good, Pullao Rice enough for six! Nan good, Chapatti €1.50 too thick for me. Excellent decor and service.' NC. Takeaway: 20% discount.

SCOTLAND

Population: 5 million

In 1965, much to the Scots' disgust, the age-old mainland Scottish shires and counties were amalgamated into nine large counties (or regions). In 1996 new changes resulted in only three staying totally unchanged (D&G, Fife and Highland). Two others have the same boundaries but new names: Borders became Scottish Borders, while Central once again became Stirling. Tayside is no more, being split into two (Angus and Perth & Kinross). Part of Grampian has been retained, with its western part returning to Moray. Northern Strathclyde has become Argyll & Bute, while the rest of Strathclyde, and the whole of Lothian have been split into sixteen Unitary Authorities, administering the larger cities and surrounds. For the time being, and until Scotland itself takes all these changes for granted, we retain in this Guide, the nine former counties (listing their ancient shires and/or new names within them, as relevant). Scotland's population of just over 5 million (less than that of central London) occupies a land mass nearly half that of England, though most of her curry houses are in and around the large cities. We'd adore a huge postbag of Scottish reports for our next Guide please.

DUMFRIES & GALLOWAY

Contains Kirkcudbrightshire (centre) and Dumfriesshire (east), referred to as Galloway. and Wigtownshire (west).

Area: Southwest Scotland
Population: 148,000
Adjacent Counties: Cumbria, Scottish Borders, Strathclyde

Dumfries

JEWEL IN THE CROWN

48 St Michael Street, Dumfries
01387 264183

Good curryhouse where you might get a discount if you show them this *Guide.* Hours: 12-2.30/6-11.

FIFE

Area: East Scotland
Population: 355,000
Adjacent Counties:
Lothian, Tayside

Cupar

ARMAAN OF CUPAR NEW ENTRANT

102-104 Bonny Gate, Cupar 01334 650600

Habib Chowdhury opened in 2005with 80 seats which on Fri & Sat nights are busy. On other days you might get a discount if you show Mr Chowdhury this *Guide*. Specials: Chicken and Lamb Parsi £7.95. Del: 4 miles, £2.50. Cobra £2.50 600ml, house wine a £6.95 bottle. Prices: Pop 75p, CTM £7.95, Pullao Rice £2. Hours: 12 - 2/5 - 11.

PASSAGE TO INDIA

76a Crossgate, Cupar 01334 650677

Zahid Raja's 50-seater serves North Indian curries and accompaniments. Delivery: 8 miles, £1 charge. Cobra, £2.50 a bottle, house wine £8.50 a bottle. Price Check: Popadom 70p, CTM £7.60, Pullao Rice £1.90. Hours: 4.30 - 10.30, Fri & Sat - 11

Glenrothes

NURJAHAN

Coslane, Woodside Road 01592 630649

Manirul Islam's 110-seater is decorated to a very high standard. Roomy carver-chairs at all tables. *'Truly magnificent meal. Spotless. More than generous quantities. The best quality we have ever tasted. A superior restaurant in every aspect.'* MAJF. Waiters very polite and helpful. You might get a discount if you show them this *Guide*. Hours: 12-2/5-11. (Fri. & Sat. to 12am); Sun. 4-11.

St Andrews

BALAKA BANGLADESHI AWARD WINNER A-LIST

3 Alexander Pl, Market St 01334 474825

Even before you enter Abdur Rouf's up-market and sophisticated 52-seater, note the frontage floral display. He has won awards for it. The unique feature is the huge kitchen garden at the rear, in which Mr Rouf grows all his own herbs and many vegetables. More foliage inside with palms dividing

A warm Scottish welcome at the Balaka

Rows of fresh corainder growing in Balaka's garden

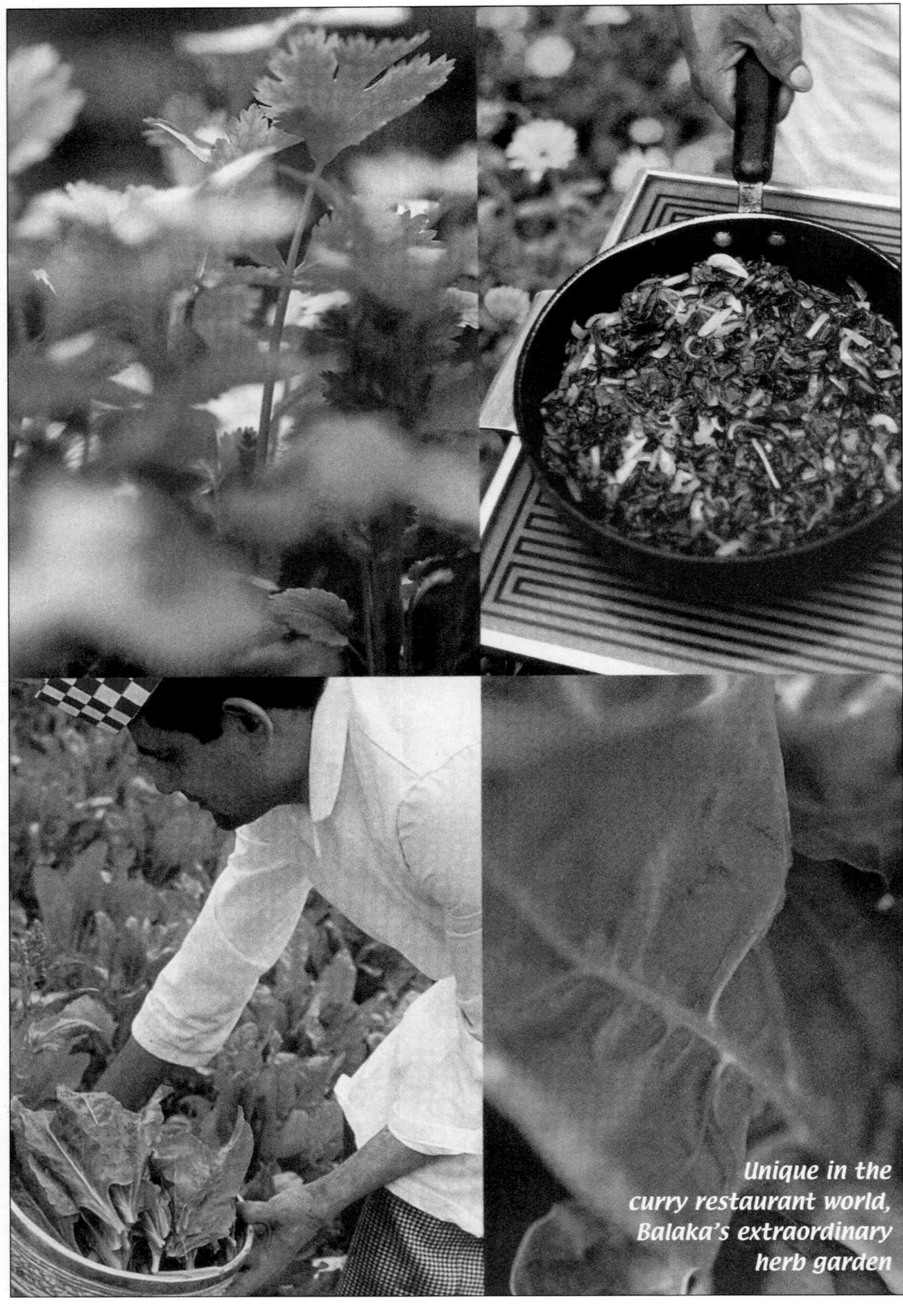

Unique in the curry restaurant world, Balaka's extraordinary herb garden

tables and hand stitched Bangladeshi tapestries on the walls. Balaka's unusual name means a 'swan'. Unusual dishes on the menu include Mas Bangla – salmon marinated in lime, turmeric and chilli, fried in mustard oil, garlic, onion, tomato and aubergine. I had the privilege of being trained to cook this dish by chef Abdul Monem which I reproduced at a lecture at St Andrews University for the Chemical Soc and all of Mr Rouf's friends. I hope they enjoyed it as much as I did. We then moved on to the restaurant for a fabulous meal. Amazingly the restaurant has no tandoor, which is detectable in the flavours of the breads and tikkas. But that aside, Mr Rouf's team continues to provide outstanding food in superb surroundings. We have lots of contented customer reports. All show a friendly, caring patron, and here's proof: *'Is still excellent.'* M. *'We dined here with a large party of friends from the Netherlands and around the world. The evening was a tremendous success – wonderful food and service.'* TGM. *'Nice decor, good service. Good portion of wonderful Afghani Gosht.* ANON. *'Not bad curries.'* T&KM. It seems to me it's always busy, and if you are really lucky you might just see Sean Connery on the nearby golf course. Please book your table. Credit cards accepted. Cobra, £4.90 a pint, house wine £11.95 a bottle. Delivery: 20 miles, £2 charge.. Comfortably in our **A-LIST**. Hours: 12 - 3 and 5 - 12.30. Sunday lunch closed. *See page 27.*<www.balaka.co.uk>

GRAMPIAN

Contains Aberdeenshire, Banff, Kincardine and Morayshire, all formerly known as Grampian.

Area: North East Scotland
Population: 537,000
of which Aberdeen
212,000
Adjacent Counties:
Highland, Tayside

Aberdeen

CINNAMON **NEW ENTRANT**

476 Union Street, Aberdeen 01224 633 328

Opened in 2005 by Khalia Miah. His restaurant is stylishly decorated inside and out. A fairly small

Cinnamon, Aberdeen

frontage, but never the less, impressive. Two gun metal grey planters, planted with cacti are situated either side of the entrance door. Inside, beige brick walls, round mirrors with the restaurants logo engraved, wooden black slatted screens provide privacy for diners and a striking paprika red, metal stair case, takes customers upstairs to the gallery dining area. Menu Snapshot: Malai Tikka £4.95 - rich creamy yoghurt sauce with a hint of cardamom and white pepper; Pani Poori £4.45 - puffed crispy wheat biscuits, filled with spiced chicken, peas and potatoes; Ginger and Cinnamon Tiger Prawns £6.95; Saffron Stuffed Red Pepper in Cottage Cheese £11.50 - coloured pepper sauce diced cottage cheese and coloured pepper cooked with tomatoes and onion, tempered with mustard, curry leaves, cinnamon and clove; Okra Pachandi £7.10 - fried okra, mixed yoghurt, ground

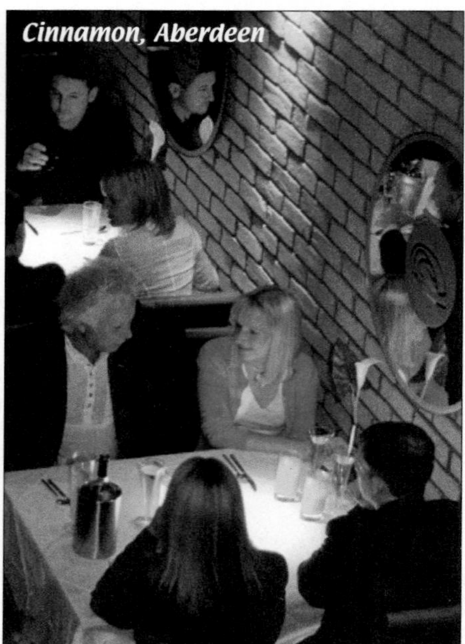
Cinnamon, Aberdeen

coconut, cumin seeds in coconut milk sauce; Tamarind and Dried Red Chilli Rice £3.05; Date and Almond Naan £3.45; Pomegranate and Coconut Chutney £1.40. Licensed: stocks Cobra. Hours: 12 - 12. Branch: Cumin, 25, Victoria Terrace, Kemnay, Aberdeenshire.

Elgin

QISMAT

202 High Street, Elgin 01343 541461

Established in 1987 by Liaquat Ali. Seats 100 diners in a modern and brightly decorated restaurant with wooden polished floor, palms, coloured seat pads and air-conditioning. Delivery: £10 minimum, within Elgin only. Hours: 12-2pm/5-11.30pm; Sun: eve only. Branch: Qismat, Millburn Rd, Inverness.

Ellon

NOSHEEN

5 Bridge Street, Ellon 01358 724309

Established in 1989. Owned by Khalid Ahmed. Restaurant decorated rather lavishly in crimson ceiling and chairs, cream walls, green tablecloths and brass light fittings. Seats 92. Banquet A: £14.50 – Papadams and Spiced Onion, Pakora, Bhoona or Korma, Patia, Pullao Rice and Nan – for two. You might get a discount if you show Mr Ahmed this *Guide.* Takeaway: 10% discount. Delivery: £12 minimum in Ellon, £18 minimum outside Ellon. Hours: 5-11.30. (Sat. to 12am).

Inverurie

BANANA TANDOORI

56 Market Place, Inverurie 01467 624860

A well-established restaurant, owned since it was opened in 1987 by Syed Mujibul Hoque who might give you a discount if you show him this *Guide.* *'Waiters efficient and friendly. Buffet night is worth a visit.'* AMCW. Open 12-2.30/5.30-11.30.

HIGHLAND

Contains Caithness, Inverness, Nairn, Ross & Cromarty and Sutherland and small parts of Argyll and Moray.

Area: North Scotland
Population: 212,000
Adjacent Counties: Grampian,Strathclyde, Tayside

Inverness

QISMET TANDOORI

1b, Millburn Rd, Inverness 01463 716020

Established in 1998 by Liaquat Ali; your host is pictured on the takeaway menu and he might give you a discount if you show him this *Guide.* Seats 100 and is brightly decorated with polished wooden floor and chairs, white tablecloths, palm trees and spot lighting. Specials: Chicken Tikka Sonali, with finely chopped ginger, green chillies and onion, medium hot. Mazedar, lamb tikka with Worcester sauce, lemon juice, cream and cheese. Takeaway: 10% discount. Hours: 12-2/5-11.30.

Nairn

AL RAJ

25 Harbour Street, Nairn 01667 455370

Mobarok Ali's 70-seater has helpful waiters who might give you a discount if you show them this *Guide*.. Hours: 12-2/5-11.30.

LOTHIAN

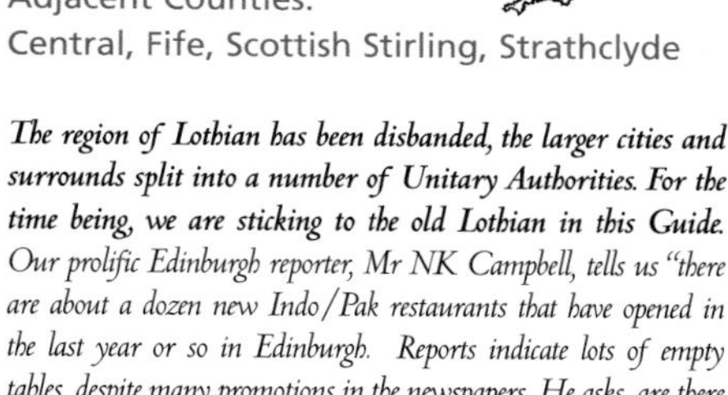

Area: Mid Eastern Scotland
Population: 774,000 of which Edinburgh is 454,000
Adjacent Counties: Central, Fife, Scottish Stirling, Strathclyde

The region of Lothian has been disbanded, the larger cities and surrounds split into a number of Unitary Authorities. For the time being, we are sticking to the old Lothian in this Guide. *Our prolific Edinburgh reporter, Mr NK Campbell, tells us "there are about a dozen new Indo/Pak restaurants that have opened in the last year or so in Edinburgh. Reports indicate lots of empty tables, despite many promotions in the newspapers. He asks, are there too many new openings?" What are your views? Are there too many curry houses in the whole UK?*

Edinburgh

Includes Blackhall, Dalry, Greenhill, Roseburn, Stockbridge and Viewforth

(Leith is entered separately)

FAR PAVILION — TOP 100

1 Craigleith Rd, Stockbridge, Edinburgh W 0131 332 3362

Est. 1987, this 125 seat restaurant has menus from Chef Abdul Aziz and an award-winning wine list. *The Scotsman's* Gillian Glover says *'the walls bore dimpled panels of buttoned velvet. Even the staff were upholstered.'* Remains in our **TOP 100**. The *Guide-readers* discount eases the bill as does the e-a-m-a-y-l Tuesday 6.30-10, £11.95 and lunchtime buffet. Takeaway: 10% off. Hours: 12-2 (weekdays)/5.30-12am; closed Sun. except Dec.

IGNITE — NEW ENTRANT

272 Morrison Street 0131 228 5666

Owner: Mr Khan Good reports received.

KEBAB MAHAL

7 Nicholson Square 0131 667 5214

'Very good place, probably the 2nd oldest in Edinburgh. Have eaten in and had takeaway.' NKC. *'Recommended. Not upmarket or designer, but the food is extremely good and consistent and also quite cheap.'* DR DD. Hours: 12-12, Fri / Sat to 2am!

KHUKURI

W Maitland Street 0131 228 2085

Nepalese specials, eg: Bhenda Momo, steamed spicy minced lamb, Bara, thick lentil pancake, garlic, ginger, spices, both served with Nepali dip. Trisuli Poleko Machha, marinated baby fish, cooked in tandoor, served with green salad. Kukhura Hariyali, spicy yoghurt sauce, mint, coriander, green chillies. Solukhumbu Bhenda, from East Nepal, long slices of lamb stuffed with mint, in spicy sauce of onions, garlic, ginger, tomato. Aloo Tama Bodi, potato, bamboo shoots, black-eye beans. Hours: 12-2, Sunday closed and 5.30-1.30, Fri/Sat to 12, Sun to 11.

KHUSHI'S BYO

16 Drummond Street 0131 556 8996

Established 1947 therefore the first in the city. *'Good and as busy as ever.'* NKC. *'Nice short menu, good helpings, very good meat, perfectly marinated. Fair service, nice Italian waiter. Clean, light-painted decor, very clean toilets. Good comfort on padded benches and formica tables. Excellent big starters. No alcohol, but most people brought big jugs (2-3 pints) of beer from the pub next door. Madras was now a Vindaloo; Bhuna and Korma could have been Madras.'*NC. **BYO** Hours: 12-3/5-9. (Fri / Sat 9.30) Closed Sundays except during Festival. Branch: Khushi's of West Lothian, Mid Calder.

LANCERS BRASSERIE — TOP 100

5 Hamilton Place 0131 332 3444

70-seater opened in 1985 by Wali Udin JP, managed by Alok Saha. Head chef is Badrul Hussain. Beautifully decorated, stylish restaurant for business and special occasions. Pink suede on the walls, tiled floor, highly polished tables. Dinner for One c£20 - Assorted Kebabs - lamb, chicken, fish and vegetable kebabs; Chicken Tikka Masala - mild sauce; Lamb Passanda - with almond sauce; Sag Panir - spinach and cheese; Sabzi Pullao - vegetable rice; Naan and coffee. Menu Snapshot: Murghi Chatt £4.95 - small pieces of chicken cooked with tomatoes, and cucumber in hot and spicy sauce; Panir Cutlet £3.55 - shallow fried cheese cutlet; Ghee Bhat £2.45 - buttered basmati rice with fried onion; all stuffed Naan £2.75. Hours: 12-2.30/5-11.30.

OLOROSO — NEW ENTRANT

33 Castle Street, Edinburgh

NKC. ate here with his family and had a, 'super duper meal.' More reports needed, please. Menu Snapshot: Tandoori Quail with Potato Chat £6.50; Today's Curry £8 - with Rice and Popadoms; Aloo Muttar £5.50 - Pentland potatoes with peas in a light tomato curry sauce served with Puri (flat bread); Punjabi Salmon £6.50 - served with the warm Turmeric Rice; Bread Pakora £4.50 - homemade bread stuffed with, cheese, onions and spices, served with mint dip.

SHAMIANA

TOP 100 — PREVIOUS AWARD WINNER

14 Brougham St, Edinburgh 0131 228 2265

First opened in 1977, taken over in 1992 by co-owner brothers Nadim (manager) and Mohammed (head chef) Butt. Seats 37. Specialises in Pakistani Kashmiri cuisine. *'I have been a regular customer of your excellent restaurant for around seven years and have been consistently impressed by the quality of your food. I also appreciate the professional manner in which your restaurant is run, and that last orders are taken at 10pm, thus restricting clientele to genuine curry enthusiasts.'* TN. *'The food at Shamiana is excellent and the standard during the last ten years has been first class'* A& AM. *'Another excellent meal. My business colleagues look forward to further frequent visits now that our office headquarters are located around the corner'* TAS. *'Very good menu, set meal £12.95 a head. Strangely small quantities but excellent, top notch, melt in the mouth lamb. Very good Keema and Peshwari Nans. All food hot to the table.'* NKC. *'We hadn't booked, it was midweek, it was packed, we got the penultimate table. Popadoms crispy, good chutney tray, but naughty, naughty – don't put tomato ketchup in the cachumber ever again! Samosa, was shaped like a spring roll, but tasted very good. Main course portions good. Pat ordered his beloved Methi Chaman Gosht, with spinach, fenugreek, fresh oriental herbs and hot spices , and pronounced it authentic and delicious. I had the Pakistani equivalent of CTM – Kashmiri Chasni Tikka, spicy, and equally good. Rice and breads enormous.'* DBAC. Great to see Kulfi Pista, Gulab Jaman and Garjar Halwa on the dessert menu. Hours: 6-10.

SINGAPORA

69 N Castle St, Edinburgh 0131 538 7878

Malaysian-Singaporean 65-seater owned and managed by chef C Pang. Decor is *'dominant decorative wood and high ceiling reminiscent of colonial-style romance, the waitresses in national dress.'* AG. Satay: Chicken, Beef, King Prawn or Tofu, marinated, skewered and char-grilled, served with a delicious peanut sauce (five sticks). The Malay Kari – chicken, beef, or vegetables in a coconut base, and Redang Beef, the national dish curry. You might get a discount if you show them this *Guide.* Takeaway: 10% off. Delivery. Hours: 12-2.30/6-10.30. Sun. closed winter.

SURUCHI

14a Nicolson Street 0131 556 6583

Unique at Herman Rodrigues' 70-seater is his careful selection of his own beautiful photographs of India which hang on the walls. Suruchi means, in most Indian languages, good taste, an apt name when considering the decor has been imported from India, and is clean and smart. Jaipur blue/turquoise tiles adorn the walls. Table linen is vegetable-dyed pink and tableware is beaten coppered brass. It serves real home-style Indian food. Well-situated for a pre-theatre (which is opposite) curry dinner. Regional Indian food festivals held monthly. *'Very tasty, I can highly recommend it.'* SK. Menu Extracts: Dalvada, crispy lentil and curry leaf fritter, Simla Chaat, chickpeas, potatoes, cucumber, coriander and banana topped with tangy sauces; Nirvana, chicken, lemon grass, mustard seed, curry leaf, lemon and creamed coconut; Venison Maharaja, cubes of Scottish venison marinated with spices and baked in tandoor; Neeps and Tatties, ginger, cummin; Coriander Paratha. One of our correspondents has sent a menu, 'the translation of it's Indian dishes into Scots Language is hilarious, I can translate if you have trouble?' Lets see how we go: Chana Masala , *a rare trait fur yer taste buds. Sappie chick peas cookit wi spices in a rich tomatay an ingan sauce,* Tandoori Gobi, *moothfaes o caller cauliflooer, steepit in a tandoor sauce o ginger, garlic, yoghurt an spices,* Dakshni Murgh (medium), *a curry wi teeth. Chucken cookit wi black pepper an aniseed in a reamy coconut base,* Aloo Palak, *tatties tossed wi spinach;* Vegetable Pullao, *rice steered wi s mister-maxter o vegetables;* Paneer Nan , *stappit (filled) wi caller (fresh) cheese.* Many thanks Stewart for the menu. Food festivals held regularly ie: Goan. Menu Extracts: Mussels, shallow fried with onions, ginger, vinegar, chillies; Mince Cutlets, mince, potato cutlets with fresh coriander; Aloo Tikki, potato dumplings, cashew nuts, coconut, spices; Chicken Shakuti, nutmeg, black pepper, coconut, spices; Lamb Chops, marinated with vinegar, chilli, black pepper, baked in tandoor; Smoked Aubergines, smooth curry, mashed aubergines, fennel seeds, two course £9.95. Takeaway: 33% discount. Hours: 5.30-10.30.

TIPPOO SAHIB

129a Rose St, Edinburgh 0131 226 2862

A Pakistani 60-seater restaurant opened in 1982 as the Shanaz by the Parvez family and renamed in 1996 *'Chicken Mancharry, tandoor-cooked, with freshly grated chilli, garlic and ginger, Chicken Nentara, cooked with onions and methi, and Massalidar Gosht, meat cooked with pickles, and Karella Gosht meat with bitter gourd. 'First class quality food, staff and atmosphere. Reasonable prices.'* RC. You might get a discount if you show them this *Guide.* Hours: 12-2/5-12; Sat. 12-11.30; Sun. 5-11.30.

VERANDAH BEST IN SCOTLAND

17 Dalry Rd, Edinburgh 0131 337 5828

At our Awards ceremony, the Award for **BEST IN SCOTLAND** was ungraciously received by another Scottish restaurant in another city. We graciously therefore transfer the Award to this highly deserving and highly appreciative restaurant. It's a tiny 4-seater, and the first opened (in 1981) by Wali Tasar Uddin, MBE, JP. It is now run by his nephew, Foysol Choudhury, who describes it as *'reassuringly low-key'* serving northern Indian and Bangladeshi cuisine. It's a pretty, relaxing restaurant with cane chairs and bamboo-slatted wall blinds, a clever and effective illusion.. DBAC says: I first ate there, well, let me see, a very long time ago, the decorations were unfussy, in fact simple but never-the-less effective and the food served in generous portions. We continue to get many appreciative reports: *'First class restaurant by any standards. The welcome and the ambience of this establishment is all that once could wish for, when sitting down to dine. The welcome is friendly, the staff attentive and the food is flavoursome and well prepared. We have been before and do recommended it. We are fortunate in having restaurant so this calibre in Edinburgh.'* ANON. *'The staff were very polite and welcoming with an excellent neat table. The candle was a beautiful touch. Been before but only for a takeaway, even better sitting in. Would definitely return. Thank you staff, you were all fabby!'* LH. *'coming here for two years, and always recommend it.'* FC. *'We have been coming here for twenty five years, you may think us biased.*

However, although visiting once a year, we have never had a poor meal. The extremely high standard of food, delicate flavours of creamy Lamb Pasanda £6.25 and Chicken Tikka Masala £6.25, are a bench mark, which other restaurants can only hope to approach. Even after a years absence, the warm family welcome sets the mood for an excellent experience. Portions generous, menu extensive and meals very reasonably priced.' ckl. *'I visit quite often, always friendly, excellent food, prices reasonable. Everything is clean, including the toilets. There is no background music, which is very good, as I am hard of hearing. Friends and colleagues always impressed.'* ADK. *'Second to none.'* PS. You have to visit their website to see the array of stars who have visited here; to name just two: Clint Eastwood and

Shorof, Foysol, Clint, Misbah and Babul

Cliff Richard. Weekday Lunch Menu: £5.95 per person Menu Snapshot: Mach Kebab £2.95 - fish cooked with garlic, ginger and coriander leaf; Amer Murgh £5.95 - chicken cooked with mango pulp, cream and mild spices; Palok Gagor Cashew Nut £3.95 - fresh spinach, carrots, nuts, medium hot. Delivery: £15. Hours: 12-2.15/5-12am.

ZEST

15 North St Andrew Street 0131 5556 5028

Pretty cafe– style restaurant, polished wooden floors, glass shelves, tubular steel chairs and pastel colours. Seats 55 diners. Delivery: 2 miles, £15 minimum.Hours: 5.30 - 11.30.Specials: Kashi Garam Masala. Licensed: £4.75 for a pint bottle of Cobra, £9.95 for a bottle house wine. Branch: Eastern Spices and Bombay Feast.

Leith

BRITANNIA SPICE AWARD WINNER

150 Commercial Street, Britannia Way, Leigh 0131 555 2255

Once it was known that the ex Royal Yacht Britannia was to be retired in derelict Leith docks, Wali Tasar Uddin decided to open a restaurant to assist the regeneration of the area, now called Ocean Terminal. He chose the former Glenmorangie Whisky warehouse at the dock entrance. He hired Arshad Alam to design the venue to reflect the *'gracious lady of the seas'*, which had taken up residence within sight of the new premises. It opened in 1999. This gorgeous nautically-themed restaurant, seating 130 diners, (served by frequent buses from the city centre) has blue chairs, polished wooden tables and floors, brass railings and blinds that look like sails and is is perfect stop-off after you have visited the the Yacht or the other people-magnet, the Scottish Executive building. The menu is divided by countries - Bangladeshi, Thai, Nepalese, North Indian and Europe - mix and match, if you like! Menu Snapshot: Tom Kha Gai £3.95 - (Thai) chicken in a rich coconut soup, flavoured with fresh galangal, lemon grass, kaffir lime leaves and mushrooms; Maccher Bhorta £3.95 - (Bangladesh) baked fish, minced with onions, green chillies, mushrooms and fresh coriander leaves, tempered with mushroom seeds; Shatkora Gosht £9.95 - (Bangladesh) tender pieces of lamb cooked in a medium hot sauce with rinds of a the Shatkora citric fruit, lemon leaves and Bengali chillies; Special Chicken £11.95 - (Bangladesh) diced king prawns, wrapped in thin filleted chicken and cooked in a rich and mild sauce; Pad Ho Ra Pa Kub Nua £10.95 - (Thai) thinly sliced pieces of beef, stir-fried with a selection of traditional Thai spices and basil - hot; Chicken Panaeng £8.95 - (Thai) medium to hot, with lime leaves, red pepper, coconut milk and red chilli paste; Himalayan Momo £9.95 - (Nepal) minced meat

Wali Uddin and the crew with his much deserved Best in Scotland Award. Wali has done more for the Scottish curry industry than anyone.

Britannia Spice, Leith

mixed with spices, enclosed in pastry and traditionally steamed; Mixed Tandoori £15.95 - (Northern India) lamb and chicken tikka, sheek kebab, tandoori chicken, king prawn served with salad, Naan and mild sauce; Palok Gajor Cashew Nut £6.95 - spinach, carrot, cashew nuts, medium hot. '*What a great restaurant, lovely surroundings, great courteous service and the food is just up with the very best. We had Chicken Tikka Chasni Masala bit more spicy than your average CTM and Methi Murgh. The Aloo Jeera was simply divine, the Okra tasty, if a bit oily.* **TOP 100** *stuff no doubt, elegant.*' T&KM. '*Very, very tiny helpings - beautifully plated. Very, very expensive.*' NKC. '*Whilst on business, my colleague and I found ourselves staying at the Holiday Inn Express (adjacent to the restaurant). We walked past the restaurant at 7pm - it was empty, deciding on a beer first. Returned at 8.30pm - it was packed, despite this we got a table! Excellent starters of Assorted Kebabs. Main courses: Northern Indian Garlic Chicken with hot sauce, Harrey Masaley Ka Gosht, cubes lamb in green masala or coriander, mint, green chilli, curry leaves and spices, a superb, best ever tarka Dal. Very impressive, worthy of its guide entry. Will visit again!*' DL. For the totally unadventurous there is a small choice of English dishes – steak, roast chicken etc. Price Check: Popadom 75p, CTM £8.55, Pullao Rice £2.95. Takeaway: 15% discount. Delivery: £50 minimum, 5-mile radius. Hours: 12-2, Sunday closed / 5-11.45. *See page 11.* <britanniaspice.co.uk>

GULNAR'S PASSAGE TO INDIA

TOP 100

46 Queen Charlotte St, Leith 0131 554 7520

Mohammad Ridha Saleh's 82-seater Passage, serves north Indian and Kashmiri food. '*Many are the nights I've spent there feeling like a desert king, being fed the most amazing food under the drapes that give the establishment the air of a Bedouin tent. One Arabic dish at Gulnar's especially emphasises this feeling: Helahil, chicken cooked with sweetcorn, onion, fresh coriander and chilli, served on a bed of rice with salad, a superb dish with a wonderful mix of flavours. Try Halabcha, spiced and roasted aubergine cooked in the tandoor with chicken, yoghurt, tomatoes, onions, garlic, chilli and coriander, a hot dish that tantalises the tastebuds; Aloobora — spicy potato balls filled with minced lamb. Potahari Sangam — minced lamb fried with fresh herbs and spices, garnished with coconut, wrapped in a puri. Rooflifter, lamb and chicken marinated, tandoor-cooked and prepared with mint, nuts and spices. An incredible edible experience.*' GR. '*Recommended by several people, but to be honest we thought it sounded a bit too good to be true. We soon realised that all that accolade was not exaggerated. We went for the atmosphere mainly, but were very thrilled with the variety and quality of the exotic food. A great cheer to a marvellous place which had given us one of the best nights out in the UK for a long, long time.*' FA. Hours: 12-2/5.30-12. (1am on Sat.).

STRATHCLYDE

Contains the former counties of: Argyle, Ayrshire, Dunbartonshire, Lanarkshire and Renfrewshire.

Area: Central west Scotland
Population: 2,255,000
of which Glasgow
578.000
Adjacent Counties:
Borders,
D & G, Central,
Highland, Lothian

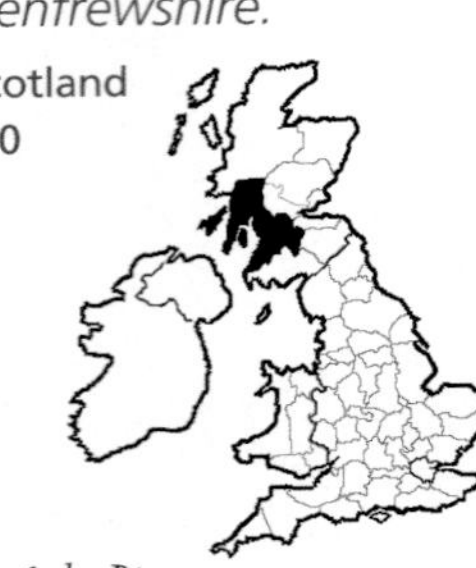

Strathclyde (meaning "valley of the River Clyde") is an historic subdivision of Scotland, and was one of the regional council areas of Scotland from 1975 to 1996.Note: For this edition we are continuing to use the old region of Strathclyde here, but we point out that Northern Strathclyde has become Argyll & Bute, while the rest of Strathclyde is divided into a number of Unitary Authorities, administering the larger cities and surrounds.

Coatbridge

ASHOKA SHAK COATBRIDGE

Showcase Leisure Park, Baillieston, G69

Opened 2002 as a fast food outlet. Thali lunch at £7.95 Mon-Sat. Hours: Daily 12 - 11. *See Glasgow.*

PUNJAB EXPRESS

22 West Canal Street, Coatbridge
01236 422522

Opened in 1993 by the Dhanda brothers, Kally and Tari. The Punjab Express is part of the former Coatbridge Central Station House. Built in 1899, the building still has many of the period features. The station was closed by Lord Beeching in 1963 and the restaurant is situated in what used to be the station master's accommodation. Downstairs, in the former ticket office, is the Pullman Lounge.

GLASGOW

Includes Battlefield, Finnieston, Hillhead, Muirend, Nitshill, Pollockshields, Scotstoun, Townhead

Glaswegians are at pains to tell us that Glasgow curries are 'the real thing, the best anywhere' ... 'everywhere else is a pale imitation, especially the pakoras', writes one person frequently. The reason is a largely Pakistani population, and this means gutsy, spicy Kashmiri/Punjab-style curries, as are found in Southall and Bradford, which are quite removed from the Bangladeshi curry house formula. Put another way, Glasgow's curries are the authentic thing, once tasted, never forgotten. The argument about whether Glasgow or Edinburgh is best for curry or the curry capital is fatuous. Glasgow has come a very long way since its tenement-block, 6pm pub-closing, Mars-bar-loutishness reputation. Modern Glasgow is breathtaking. Its Indian restaurant scene is as good as it gets. Here are your favourites:

ALISHAN — NEW ENTRANT

250 Battlefield Road, Battlefield, Glasgow
0141 632 5294

Proprietor, M Ayub Quereshi, has owned this restaurant since 1987. He can seat forty-eight curryholics in his dining room. Menu Snapshot: Chef's Platter £9.50, chicken, lamb, vegetable, mushroom, fish pakora; chicken chat; chicken and lamb tikka; shiekh kebab; spiced onions and popadoms - what a feast! to share with friends! Cobra, £2.50 a bottle, house wine £2.20 a glass. Price Check: Popadom 60p, CTM £7.70, Pullao Rice £1.60.Takeaway: 10% discount. Delivery: 5 miles, £10 minimum. Hours: 5 - 12.

AMBALA SWEET CENTRE

178 Maxwell Rd, Pollockshields, Glasgow S
0141 429 5620

This is a franchise operated by Mrs S Ahmad. (See Ambala, Drummond St, London, NW1.) As well as the counter takeaway sweets and snacks, chef Akmal cooks a small range of curries for the 26-seat restaurant. *'Lamb Bhoona is amazing!'* DF. Alcohol not allowed. No credit cards. Hours: 10am-10pm.

THE ASHOKA

108 Elderslie St, Glasgow 0141 221 1761

Balbur Singh Sumal opened Glasgow's first Ashoka in 1968. He went on to found a big group (see next entry) but this one is no longer part of the group. It was taken over in 1995 by the Purewal brothers and in 2002 by Cyrus. Reports please.

THE ASHOKA GROUP

There have been Ashoka restaurants in Glasgow since 1968. Balbur Singh Sumal grew the number to six during the 1980s (including the original at

Elderslie Street, noted above). The remainder, became part of Charan Gill's Harlequin Group. Mr Gills old the group to Sanjay Majhu who claims it is Europe's largest chain of Indian restaurants, (turnover £12m). It is in rapid expansion mode especially focusing on cheap food and fast food. Yet despite that service and food is at a very high standard, high enough for us to give one of their restaurants the **BEST IN SCOTLAND AWARD**. The group's portfolio at the time of writing is 17 restaurants. They operate a central reservations, take-away and freephone delivery 'hotline': 0800 195 3195. There's also a cookbook (one recipe of which requires you to use lychees to make their Lamb Rogan Josh!!!). while at <www.ashokaspiceshop.com> spices can be bought. Head office, 23 Crow Rd, G11, 0141 342 5200 <www.harlequinrestaurants.com> We list the Glasgow restaurants here:

ASHOKA ASHTON LANE

19 Ashton La, Hillhead, G12 0800 195 3195

(behind Hillhead Underground Station). Absorbing Indian market scene mural. Thali Lunch £4.95 or 2-course Lunch Menu £6.95, Mon-Sat 12- 5. Pre-Theatre Menu £11.95 served 5pm6:30. Hours: Mon-Thurs: 12 -12. Fri-Sat: to 1am Sun: -12.

ASHOKA AT THE MILL

BEST IN SCOTLAND

500 Corselet Rd, G53 0800 195 3195

Ashoka at the Mill is described as the group's 'jewel-in-the crown'. It is indeed located in a 'medieval' farmhouse /old mill. The location is off the M77 at J3 – go west half a mile along the A726, turn left and follow the signs, and suddenly you've left industrial Glasgy behind and combines an historic setting with a classy contemporary twist in its vast interior. The Grand Buffet is the

The Mill's winning team

centrepiece. Family Room with a *'cyber-jungle mural and more gadgets and gizmos than the S.S. Enterprise'* will keep the kids quiet. The food, according to IMcT: *'is not all Indian, but it's all at the Ashoka standard worth travelling for.'* Specials include Goanese fish and prawns, Kala Mirch Masala, sliced chicken breast in a peppery, tangy herbal sauce. Buffets Mon - Thurs from 5: £11.95; Friday 12-6.30:,£10.95; from 6.30, £14.95; Sat 5-6.30: £10.95; from 6.30, £14.95 Sunday 5 - 6.30: £10.95; from 6.30:, £12.95. Weekend Lunch Special (Sat / Sun) 50% off all a la carte curries. Hours: Mon-Thurs: 5-11; Fri:12-12; Sat: 4 -12; Sun: 4-11. Seema and Rajesh Saraf manage the place and were presented with the best in Scotland category of the renowned Cobra Good Curry Awards. [albeit after a rather ungracious start]. Said Rajesh: *'I am particularly proud to receive this award against stiff competition as it is chosen by Pat Chapman's Curry Club, Britain's first and foremost authority on Asian food, based on his own mystery shopper reports and customer feed back. So thank you to all our regular diners at the Mill!'*. Hours: Mon-Thurs: 5- 11; Fri:12-12; Sat: 4-12; Sun: to 11.

ASHOKA BEARSDEN

9 Kirk Road, Bearsden, G61 0800 195 3195

Opened in 1997. Has undergone a makeover under new franchise owner Imtiaz Aslam. The most obvious change is to the restaurant's decor, with the former dark burgundy and mustard replaced with rich creams and deep browns. And a range of colonial artifacts and traditional Indian antiques and bric-a-brac - from sitars and tablas to swords and even bullets - now adorn the walls, with subtle traditional Indian lighting giving the restaurant a warm and intimate ambiance. Party room: Harlequin Suite. Kids free Sun when accompanied by an adult. Pre-Theatre Menu £8.95 served 5-6:30. Hours: Sun-Thurs: 5-11. Fri & Sat: 5-12.

ASHOKA REGENT BRASSERIE

Closed, undergoing refurbishment until end 2007.

ASHOKA SHAK NEW ENTRANT

Phoenix Leisure Park, Linwood 0800 195 3195

In 2001, the first Ashoka Shak rose from the ashes of the former 'Harry Ramsden's' at the Phoenix Leisure Park Linwood, close to Glasgow Airport. New design. Thali menu – the ultimate fast Indian dining experience Thali lunch at £4.95 available Mon-Sat. Hours: Daily 12 - 11.

ASHOKA SOUTHSIDE

268 Clarkston Rd, Glasgow 0800 195 3195

Raj and colonial décor with period pictures, photographs, artifacts and memorabilia adorning the walls. Pre-Theatre Menu £8.95, daily from 5-6:30. Hours Sun-Thurs: 5-11.30; Fri/Sat: 5-12.

ASHOKA WEST END

1284 Argyle Street, G3 0800 195 3195

Opened 1982 near Kelvingrove Art Gallery and Museum on the corner of the longest street and shortest road in the city. Pre Theatre Menu £8.95: 5-7. 25 seats upstairs, 35 downstairs Kids eat free on Sundays when accompanied by an adult. Hours Sun-Thurs: 4-12.30; Fri & Sat: 5-1am.

Ashoka, West end

CAFÉ INDIA

171 North St, Charing Cross 0141 248 4074

North street can be found at Charing Cross and runs parallel to the M8 motorway and is accessed from St Vincent Street or Kent Road. It sits across the road from the Mitchell Library. Described (by its owner Abdul Sattar) as *'Britain's first-ever designer buffet restaurant'*. It certainly has changed since it opened in 1979, its seating by 1999 having reached a monumental 560 seats. The ground floor is open-plan and bright. The seats are expensive high-backed pale wood with pink or blue upholstery, depending which zone you are in, and there are some alcove tables. The area called the galleries in the lower floor is moody, with darker reds and wrought iron. There is provision for self-service via a smart counter. Both floors have eye-catching artwork and light fittings. Young clientèle love it and their set meals, which are a speciality, and the Friday/Saturday e-a-m-a-y-ls (at £12.50). Sattar it seems is proud of the fact that he served 1160 diners in a single day. Takeaway: 10%. Hours: 12-12; Sun. 3-12. <www.cafeindia-glasgow.com>

CHAPATI I

2017 Dumbarton Road 0141 576 0118

Chain of 11 takeaways, est. 1983 by Iqbal S Gill each of which has its own personnel, but are overseen by Deepa Gill (service) and Harnak Singh (chef). Curries, Kebabs and Pizza. Prices are not cheap for takeaway: Onion Bhajia £2.25, Mango Chutney 70p, Potato and Cauliflower Curry £3.50. Most ordered dishes: Karahi Chicken and Chicken Jullander. Hours: Sun.-Thurs. 4-12.30; Fri. / Sat. 4pm-1.30am. Branches: (All Glasgow area) Chapati 2, 1576 Dumbarton Rd, 0141 954 3154; Chapati 3, 339 Dumbarton Rd, Partick, 0141 337 1059; Chapati 4, 20 Byres Rd, 0141 334 4089; Chapati 5, 354 Paisley Rd W, 0141 427 6925; Chapati 6, 468 Dumbarton Rd, Dalmuir, 0141 952 9210; Chapati 7, 182 Paisley Rd W, Renfrew, 0141 885 2313; Chapati 8, 5 Lennox Dr, Faifley, 01389 879914; Chapati 9, 3 Greenock Rd, Bishopton, 01505 862 222; Chapati 10 39 Main St, Busby, 0141 644 1971; Sajjan, 2372 Dumbarton Rd, Yoker, 0141 951 1839. Neelim, 1590 Dumbarton Rd, Glasgow, 0141 959 6265.

KAMA SUTRA NEW ENTRANT

331 Sauchiehall Street 0800 195 3195

In 1996, it opened (opposite the Dental Hospital)

to widespread curiosity, with the locals speculating as to what might be about to happen behind the stylish frontage. The venue's PR machine added to the mystery: *'the legend come alive over a candlelit cornucopia of exotic eastern cuisine. Be it a romantic dinner a deux, or a fun night out with friends, you can indulge in the food of love, every which way you want. Private affair? The salubrious suite downstairs provides the perfect backdrop for special celebrations by night.'* Phew! Don't need any aphrodisiacs here then.! the sizzling addition to the The sultry and sassy design innovation caused a sensation, and the sniggering soon stopped. The minimalist elements of wood, iron, slate and stone are guaranteed to appeal to your most basic instincts. During daytime the venue is frequented by the suits: Lunchtime 'Quickie' Buffet £5.95 Mon-Sat: 12pm till 3.30pm). Buffet: Monday and Tuesday Evenings £10.95 6.30-9.30. Pre-Theatre Menu (£7.95) 3.30-6.30 daily and Sunday 5-6.30. Private room available for parties of up to 80. Hours: Mon-Thur: 12-12; Fri-Sat: 12 -12.30am; Sun: 5- 12.

KOH I NOOR — TOP 100

235 North St, Charing Cross — 0141 204 1444

Glasgow's earliest Indo-Pak opened in 1961, and boasts to be the originator of the famous e-a-m-a-y-l buffet nights (Mon.-Fri. 7-9pm). Authentic Indian and Pakistani design with authentic Asian decor, with hanging rugs, arches etc. *'Fabulous decor.'* DBAC. Northern Indian formula curries. Its 150 seating is now small in comparison with other Glasgow venues, but is still big considering the national average of 50, and it's still very busy. *'Not only was the service friendly and helpful but the food arrived very promptly, considering the number of people there. The Chicken Dansak was excellent and the naan breads terrific'.* RA. *'Excellent. Samosas so filling, had to leave most of my main course!'* SF. *'Starters very impressive, quantities large. Garlic Nan not for the faint-hearted: beautiful. Chicken Tikka Chasini and Chicken Nentara memorable.'* HB. *'Absolutely superb. In a class of its own.'* BS. We have a difference of opinion here. *'Average, not Top 100, food not good enough.'* T&KM. *'Visited on three consecutive nights, although had to pay a hefty £26 for Popadoms, starter, main course rice and Nan. Still think it currently the best Indian I've tried. Lamb Lyallipour - eyewatering hot, so succulent and tasty. Garlic Chilli Lamb - superb. Quick service, highly efficient, polite. My girlfriend Birgit - not a spice freak like me requested a mild curry. The waiter sensed that something was wrong, whisked here Okra Korma away and brought back a different one, declaring this would be palatable and indeed it was.'* DP. Hours: 12-12. (Fri. & Sat. to 1am).

MASALA JAK'S — NEW ENTRANT

The Quay, Springfield Quay — 0800 195 3195

'Back in the Great American Gold Rush of 1849,' says the venue's spin, *'thousands of prospectors headed to the USA to panhandle for gold. Many found fortunes, thousands died, a few found fame, but perhaps the most famous of all was Jagir Singh, known as 'Masala Jak', who left the Punjab for the USA. Jak found no gold, but did find fortune when he introduced the cowboys of the Wild West to the delights of Indian Cuisine. His fame travelled across America, a legend was born. Old tales tell that the words 'Masala Jak' derived from Mister Jagir Singh, maybe true...maybe not'.* Decidedly not! But the food at the Quay is good.Hours: 12 - 11. *(See Ashoka group)*

MOTHER INDIA — NEW TO OUR TOP 100

28 Westminster Terrace — 0141 221 1663

A well-known Glasgow landmark, Mother India opened its doors for business in 1992, and is run by Monir Mohammed. *'The jewel of Glasgow. Small unpretentious restaurant, Top 100 no doubt about it!'* t&km.*'I've been an avid user of your Curry Guide since 1995 an have travelled the length and breath of the UK always with a copy under my arm! I have eaten curry in most cities and cook my own when at home. I was amazed that Mother India was not in the TOP 100. I've eaten in every TOP 100 in Edinburgh and Glasgow and in Edinburgh, the best in my opinion is Shamiana and in Glasgow, Mother India. The service, atmosphere and quality of food are second to none in the city. Really fresh ingredients with excellent use of spices cooked to perfection. Cumin Chicken and Courgette - excellent. Lamb Saag - melt in your mouth staff. Some times, I am tempted away to Ashoka or one of the other TOP 100 Restaurants but always return to Mother India for a better fix! They even do a, Sunday to Thursday, 'eat as much as you can,' menu for £12.50 - fantastic value. Make it a top 100!'* JT.OK,OK. Mother India has a very relaxed

atmosphere and although the restaurant is licensed you can **BYO** (wine & beer, no spirits). Snapshot:: Spiced haddock; chicken with spinach leaf; kheer (rice pudding). Lunch £6.95; Pre-theatre £7.95 (Fri & Sat £8.95); Dinner £12.95 - £16.95. Seats: 120. Hours: 12-2, 5.30-11.

MISTER SINGH'S INDIA — TOP 100

149 Elderslie Street — 0141 204 0186

Satty Singh owns this 90-seater restaurant, as its eponymous title suggests, and like other Glasgow restaurants, as part of the Harlequin Group *(see Ashoka above)* it benefits from group marketing and purchasing muscle. Decor combines ethnic and traditional Scottish with stark white walls and dramatic bursts of cobalt blue creating a magical Mediterranean milieu, and hand-carved wooden balustrades and mirrors. Manager Jamil Ahmed, and the waiters wear kilts and the girls wear salwars; Younis Ahraf (who wears chef's whites, by the way) does curried Haggis! And we hear that there's a French influence at work in the kitchens too. '*Without question the best I have visited! Vast menu. Fantastic food, good portions. Booking essential, even mid-week. Brandy-drinkers beware. They have a 200-year-bottle of Napoleon's brandy at £35 a shot!*' GD. '*For me, it is a 'must' when I am travelling to Glasgow! The food is so good and tasty, particularly the Chilli Garlic Chicken.*' RA. '*We must have been the second couple to enter the restaurant but within 30 minutes the whole place was packed and we took this to be a very good sign indeed. We were impressed by the amount of food on the plate. When the main course arrived I can only say it was the best curry I have ever tasted and that includes my own, spicy hot but very tasty. One of the finest curries in the country*'. GC. Executive Lunch (Mon-Fri: 12-5pm) £6.95 Pre-Theatre (Daily from 5-6.30pm) £8.25 Weekend Brunch (Sat: 12-5pm, Sun 2.30-5pm) £6.95 (one child under 12 eats free for every adult dining a la carte) Football Hospitality Packages: £14.95 Delicious 5-course lunch plus free taxi to the big match available for all the home games (advance booking essential). Function Suite: Private areas available for corporate dining or celebrations Opening Hours; Mon-Thurs: 12-11.30; Fri-Sat: till 12; Sun: 2.30-11.30.

MURPHY'S PAKORA BAR — TOP 100

1287 Argyle S, Glasgow — 0141 334 1550

Like Mr Singh's above, now part of the Harlequin Group, it still retains its owner Teresa Doherty, herself, with a good eye for sound bites: '*It was love at first bite! As we sank our baby teeth into our first chunk of pakora, there were loud karahis of more mum!*'[groan] '*The word Pakora, to a Scot, slips off the tongue as easily as haggis, neeps and tatties. It's one of those snacks that can be eaten at any time of day or night ... one bite is never enough. At Murphy's the chef's a Scot (R. McGregor) which is why there's Haggis Pakora. Beam me up, Scotty.*' CW. And there are 30 others including Chilli. Or there are Pizzas – traditional or with an Indian twist. Of course, it is a licensed bar, selling, well Murphy's of course! Takeway: 10% off. Hours: 12pm-12am (1am on Fri./Sat.).

RAWALPINDI — NEW ENTRANT

321 Sauchehall Street, — 0141 832 4180

'*This restaurant is one my friends and I go to regularly. Good prices and quality, unlike others nearby that are overpriced. Decor perhaps a bit tired though, good. Regular is unspectacular fare. Pakora, from £2.50 - excellent, Mixed Vegetable Curry £5.45 - from buffet was good value. Lamb Curry £5.75 - was quite gristly. Service was if anything a bit over eager - the fact that I was still eating, should have been a clue that I was not finished yet! However, as the restaurant was quiet, they were possibly, just over staffed. Reservations about the lamb curry were probably due to the festive season and normally no problems. A slightly disappointing visit to a dependable restaurant, but I'm sure I'll be back. Would recommend it a a good basic Indian.*' JK. Menu Snapshot: Chicken Chat £2.95 - drumsticks marinated in spicy yoghurt and lemon juice just barbecued in the clay oven and cooked in a tangy sauce served with salad; Onion Bhajia £2.75 - original or rings (rings sound good! I wonder if they are like the fried onions rings, the ones you get in a Pub - hope so!) served with sauce and salad; Egyptian Kebab £9.45 - chicken, tomato and mushrooms, on skewer with full garnish; King Prawn Lalpari £10.50 - with red wine and green chillies. Takeaway: 10% discount. Hours 5 - 11; Fri & Sat - 1; Sunday,1 - 12.30.

SPICE OF LIFE NEW ENTRANT

1293 Argyle Street 0800 195 3195

Near Byres Road and the city centre, behind Hillhead Underground Station, it attracts the suits in the daytime, and the young crowd at night.The setting is modern, with contemporary murals and an imaginative spectrum of lights which subtly change as darkness falls. Take a pre-dinner aperitif in the cocktail bar before ascending to the balcony where the booths and tables for two await. Kids free very Sunday when accompanied by an adult. 2 course lunch £5.95, Thurs/Fri. Pre-Theatre Menu £8.95 served daily from 5-7. Hours Sun-Wed: 5-12. Thurs/Fri: 12-2/5-12 (See Ashoka earlier)

VILLAGE CURRY

129 Nelson St, Glasgow 0141 429 4610

'Superb. Religious place, no alcohol, no BYO, must be Halal as 90% of customers of Asian appearance. Very good middle range menu, not short or too long. Good quantities, very good prompt service. Good comfort, amazing decor. We were taken upstairs to an excellent restaurant, all fitted out in dark, polished tables and chairs, nice stone coloured walls, huge red/yellow/gold paisley ceiling drapes to give a huge tent effect. Being a Friday night, we booked. Hive of industry - eating!' NKC.

WEE CURRY SHOP

7 Buccleuch St, Glasgow 0141 353 0777

Everything about this eatery is small, including the menu – smaller than a paperback book. *'Really good. Very wee indeed. Seats approximately 20 with one chef and one waiter. Vegetable side dishes seem to have low priority. My pal has been eating here for years.'* GG. The menu has also probably the smallest selection we have ever seen. However, as the saying goes, better to cook one dish well than ten badly. There are only four starters to choose from: Vegetable or Chicken Pakoras, Aubergine Fritters and Mutter Paneer Puri. There are a few more mains to choose: six Chicken dishes, prices from c£6 to £8; one Lamb, a Karahi dish; four Vegetables eg: Aloo Sag, Black Eye Beans and Broccoli and one Dal. To accompany your curries, there is Basmati Rice , Garlic Potatoes, Chappati 60p, Paratha and Raitha £1.20. We agree: you don't need anything more!

ZEERA

181 Kirchintilloch Rd, Bishopbriggs, 0141 772 9393

Toni Ghani and his father (both share the same name) have been designing and building Indian restaurants for well over a decade and have recently taken up ownership of Zeera. Distinctive, with its expansive windows that look into a tasteful furniture – South African black marble floor tiles, black walls, and comfy leather chairs in the dining area.

Helensburgh

CAFE LAHORE

33 West Clyde Street 01436 674971

'Light, clean and simple decor. Helpful, cheerful and friendly service. Very varied menu, one of the biggest I've seen. I opted for the buffet, came with enormous starter of Mixed Pakora, eight main dishes, two rices and bread. Nan disappointing, hard as leather. However, if you order fresh, you are in for a treat – small is the size of a moderate coffee table! Quite fantastic Lassi and Chai. Excellent Lal Toofan. Recommended.' RT. Menu Extracts: Fish or Paneer Pakora, Garlic Okra, Chicken lyallpuri, green chilli and coriander; Hasina, tender lamb, marinated, onions, capsicums, tomato, baked in tandoor, sauce, served on sizzler; Mix Hot Rice, fried rice, chicken, lamb, prawns, fresh green chillies, served on hot sizzler. Buffet Nights: 6-11, £9.95, children under 12 half price. Takeaway: 10% discount. Delivery: £15 minimum. Hours: 12-2.30/5-12, Fri/Sat to 12.

SCOTTISH BORDERS

Formerly called Borders Contains four burghs Peeblesshire, Roxburghshire, Selkirkshire and Berwickshire.

Area: Southeast Scotland
Population: 110,000
Adjacent Counties:
D & G, Lothian,
Northumberland, Strathclyde

Jamuna
Tandoori
Finest Indian Cuisine
(fully licensed)
10% Discount for Takeaway
Meals ordered by telephone
(delivery service available)
opening hours:
Monday - Sunday
12 - 2pm 5pm - 11.30pm
9-10 Market Place, Eyemouth, TD14 5HE
Tel: 018907 51007

Eyemouth

JAMUNA NEW ENTRANT

36 Market Street, Galashiels 01890 75007

Good curryhouse where you might get a discount if you show them this *Guide.*

Galashiels

SWAGAT

36 Market Street, Galashiels 01896 750100

Ditto. *'Well lit, comfortable little place. Service is good. Very tasty Jalfry.'* GMcG. Hours: 12-2/5-11.

Hawick

SHUGONDA BALTI HOUSE

4 Station Building, Dove Mount Place
01450 373313

Ditto at BM Talukder's 50-seater Bangladeshi curry house. Hours: 12-2/6-11.30.

STIRLING

Formerly called Central

Includes most of the former county of Stirlingshire (except Falkirk) and the south-western portion of the former county of Perthshire.

Area:
Mid Scotland
Population: 88,000
Adjacent Counties:
Lothian, Strathclyde,
Tayside

Drymen

DRYMEN TANDOORI

5-7 Stirling Road, Drymen 01360 660099

65-seater, est 1994 by Sohail Wahid who might give you a discount if you show him this *Guide. 'Does quite a tasty little number of average curries, a tad on the expensive side and carry out staff at least are a little unfriendly and disinterested.'* T&KM. Takeaway: 10% discount. Delivery: £10 minimum, 5-mile radius. Hours: 12pm-12am.

TAYSIDE

(Inc Angus, Kinross and Perthshire)

Area: East Scotland
Population: 395,000 of which Dundee 141,000
Adjacent Counties:
Central, Fife,
Grampian, Highland,
Strathclyde

Dundee

ASHOKA EXPRESS NEW ENTRANT

3, Wellgate Centre, Dundee

Harlequin Leisure Group, *(see page 442)* has entered the fast food market with the combined name of Ashoka Express./Italy Express which the Group hope to roll out all over the UK. The Centre's food

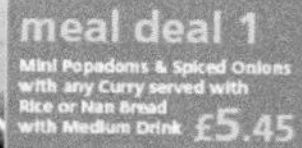

court, already comprises a number of well-established food operators.The dual entrance into the food court - from both the rear and the front of the Wellgate - means that it is always very busy. It offers a range of curries and 'meal deals'. Hours: Mon-Wed, Fri, Sat: 10 - 6. Thurs: till 8 Sun: 10 - 5. Branch: Ashoka Shak, Camperdown Leisure Park, Dundee, Fast food but with sit-in area. *See page 442.*

DIL SE **AWARD WINNER**

99 Perth Road, Dundee 01382 221501

Abdour Rouf's 150-seat Dil Se restaurant (pron dill see and means, 'from the heart.') was presented with the Dundee Civic Trust Award for its outstanding contribution to the improvement of the city when it opened in 2003. Billed as the largest Bangladeshi restaurant in Scotland it specialises in Bangladeshi, Indian and Thai cuisine Clients dress up to eat here, as the modern and stylish air of this restaurant requires it. The fresh, organic ingredients, herbs and vegetables, are grown in the garden behind its sister establishment, The Balaka, St Andrews. Locally produced salmon is also a speciality, served marinated in chilli, coriander and cumin - delicious and healthy! *'Its sister restaurant, the Balaka in St Andrews, Fife has been thrilling curryholics, myself included, and winning prestigious Curry Club awards for 21 years. Decor is modern and minimalist and the toilets are like a fake leopard skin coat - absolutely spotless. The Dil Se menu is a carbon copy of The Balaka's and every last morsel of food is cooked to order.'Please be patient,' says the blurb on the front page. 'Good food is like art and like at it takes time.' We kicked off with chilli pickle - careful, friends, this red hot stuff will seriously blow your tights off - and a pile of popadoms that were so fresh I'm surprised they didn't try to slip the haun. Then came the real starters - Chicken Tikka and a Shami Kebab. Simple Chicken Tikka is always a smart option if you want to judge any Indian - or, in this case, Bangladeshi restaurant. The Tikka at Dil Se was perfect. Every mouthful burst with flavour - particularly when smeared thickly with the awesome chilli pickle - and I loved the tasty little burnt bits. From the list of fifteen or so chef specials, I tried the Mas Bangla, salmon fillet, marinated in lime juice, turmeric, green chilli and several other spices then fried in mustard oil with garlic, onion, tomato and aubergine. Believe it or not, it tasted even better than it sounds, and special doesn't even begin to describe it. I said it before and I'll say it again, why can't more curry houses start using salmon? It always works well'.* Tam Cowan, Dundee Record. This is an outstanding, caring restaurant, and following the tradition of its sister, the Balaka in St Andrews, Fife, we took great pleasure in giving it our **BEST IN SCOTLAND AWARD 2004/5 AWARD.** Delivery: 20 miles, £2 minimum Hours: Sun.-Thurs. 5pm-1am; Fri. & Sat. 12am-1am. Open Christmas Day. Branch: Balaka, St Andrews. *See page 27.*

Dil Se, Dundee

Perth

MANZIL

13 York Place, Perth 01738 446222

You might get a discount if you show Rana Ali them this *Guide.* at his 85-seat curry house. Hours: 12-2/5-11.30. Branch: Tandoori Knights, Princess Street, Perth (takeaway only).

TANDOORI NIGHTS

12, Princes Street, Perth 01738 441277

Ditto at this 38-seater est 1998. Specialities: Chicken Nashedar c£7 – barbecued chicken or lamb in a spiced cream based sauce with cashew nuts and flavoured with brandy. Menu also has Turkish kebabs, Italian Pizzas and European Dishes. Takeaway: 10% discount. Delivery: free in Perth. Hours: 5-12am. (Sat. to 1am).

WALES

Population: 2.9 million

For Wales as with England, the Guide runs alphabetically in county and town order. In 1996 a large number of Unitary Authorities replaced the six Welsh counties (regions) which had themselves replaced the age-old shires and smaller counties in 1965. To provide a convenient geographical division of Wales in this Guide, we retain the six former counties (listing their shires within them). With a population of under 3 million, (nearly matched by Greater Manchester alone) and only 270 curry restaurants in the whole of Wales, (there are more in London sw) we cannot say Cymru is big on the nation's favourite food. And we would very much welcome a plethora of Welsh reports for next time.

CLWYD

Contains Denbighshire, Flintshire and Wrexham and (recently) Conway.

Area: North Wales
Population: 421,000
Adjacent Counties: Cheshire, Gwynedd, Powys, Shrops

Deeside

BENGAL DYNASTY AWARD WINNER

106 Chester Road East, Shotton, Deeside 01244 830455

Monchab Ali bought a former guest house in1991 and converted it into a stylish, spacious restaurant. In 2001, the restaurant re-opened after having had a complete face-lift at a cost of over £200,000. A stunning new entrance, bigger windows, change of interior colour, new floor. It is air-conditioned, purpose-built, airy and elegant, luxury and a fabulous Demonstration Kitchen allows diners to see the technical wizardry of the Corporate Chef Partha Mitra and his brigade preparing and cooking their food. The smartly-furnished restaurant managed by Rico is fully-licensed, and seats 92 customers in modern comfort and the roomy lounge bar, 40. It has disabled access. Chef Mitra's north Indian and Bangladeshi include such specials as Kashmir Rezala, Chicken

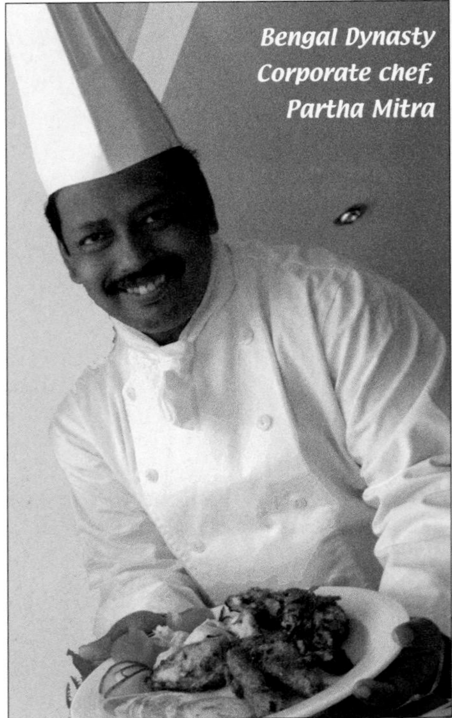

Bengal Dynasty Corporate chef, Partha Mitra

Bondhu, Satkora (citrus) Gosth and Bengal Fish Curry, . *'Truly exceptional place. The food was just the business. This restaurant is well worthy of its Best in North Wales rating.'* MW. *'Immense size of restaurant – huge. Politely greeted and guided to bar. Can see why this restaurant features so highly in the Guide.'* MW. *'Outstanding.'* WAJ. The Dynasty's Bangladeshi food festival was raved over by locals, as were the cookery demos, sometimes from Monchab himself. Takeaway: 15% discount. Delivery: £12 minimum, 5-miles. Hours: 12-2.30/5.30-11.30; Sun. 12.30-11. Branch: Bengal Dynasty Northwich Cheshire and Llandudno Gwynedd. <www.bengaldynasty.com>

PLAZA AMANTOLA

Welsh Rd, Sealand, Deeside 01244 811383

Opened in 1997. A pretty restaurant decorated in reds and greens with soft, comfortable sofas to relax on while taking coffee and liqueurs after a satisfying spicy meal. Seats 300 diners in two rooms. *'Incredibly impressive looking restaurant. A large and imposing free-standing building by the main North Wales Coast Road (A55) and right opposite RAF Sealand. Large car park complete with fountain and elephant statues leads to an elegantly decorated interior that must be capable of seating at least 200 in its many rooms and alcoves. Diners wait in a plush seating area near bar. Very friendly and knowledgeable staff, some of whom are noticeably local! Extensive menu, though the special dishes have made up names, which I found detracted from the cuisine. Very nice Chicken Chat £3.20 - very light and remarkably grease free Puri with pleasant and delicate taste of its own. Topped with lovely combination of small pieces of tender chicken in a mouth watering sauce topped with a generous sprinkle of Chat Masala. Lamb Rogan Josh £6.50 - just as good, excellent pieces of lamb, free of fat and gristle, served in a tasty, tangy sauce rich in herbs and spices. This was served with a light and fluffy, mould of al-dente Pullao Rice £1.85 - well perfumed and lump free. A smashing meal.'* RW.. *'Arrived at lunchtime to find one other couple happily ensconced in the restaurant. Sat in the bar and ordered from the special menu while the waiter got my Kingfisher. Didn't bother with Popadoms, but ordered Meat Samosa - touch on the small side, accompanied by a good portion of crisp fresh salad, nicely spiced, overall quite impressed. Chicken Jalfrezi - nicely presented, had a good amount of chicken, plenty of sauce if a little heavy on the peppers and onions and very heavy on the green chillies...'* (Pat would love it!) *'...chicken was nice and moist with good flavour, sauce had a nice kick with a good after taste. Pullao Rice plated by waiter, had a slightly aniseed flavour. Overall an excellent lunch.'* DB. Price Check: Popadom 40p, CTM £5.50, Pullao Rice £1.85. Takeaway: 10% discount. Delivery: 5-mile radius, minimum charge £15. Hours: 12-2/5.30-12. Saturday and Sunday 12 - 12

Flint

VERANDA

11-15 Chester Street, Flint 01352 732504

Chef owner, Adbul was previously at Balti Nights, Connahs Quay. *'The food has improved, the menu is different, lots of fish and shellfish ie: fresh mussels plus ostrich meat - very tasty, and the staff friendly and welcoming. Place buzzing and if you get a table at the back, you can catch a glimpse of the cooking in the kitchen. They also make a chicken Tikka flambée, where they pour Sambuca onto the sizzling platter and flames shoot two feet in the air.'* DV-W. Menu Snapshot: Ostrich Tikka £4 - served with salad; Mussels £9.50 - fresh mussels steamed with a lively broth of chillies and curry leaves; King Prawn Gratin £11.50 - barbecued with butter sauce, topped with cheese; Family Naan £3.50. Credit cards accepted. Delivery: £10 minimum order. Price Check: Popadom 70p, CTM £5.75, Pullao Rice £2.00. Hours: 12 - 2.30/ 5 - 11. Sunday Buffet 12 - 7.

RAJ BALTI

70 Chester St, Flint 01352 733633

'Chicken Phal is consistently good, as hot as a phal should be. Good portions, excellent takeaway and home delivery service, although the eating area is rather small. **BYO.**' SA&AP.

Llangollen

SPICE LOUNGE

36 Regent Street, Llangollen 01978 861877

'Service was polite, smart and efficient. Popadoms and pickles excellent. Started with Chicken Chat, excellent, succulent. Sheek Kebab and Aloo Puri , good. Main courses: Chilli Masala (inc PR), very red, very hot, superb flavour. Lamb Dhansak, good. Very tender Lamb Pasanda, but sauce was colour of CTM? House Special Balti, very filling, well worth the extra pence. Fresh, hot Pullao Rice and excellent, stinking of garlic, Garlic Nan £1.40. Hot towels and complimentary brandies served. Overall a great meal.' MPW. Hours: 12-2, Sat / Sun only and 6-12.

Wrexham

CHIRK TANDOORI

1 Station Av, Chirk, Wrexham 01691 772499

'Appears smart and and well ordered, staff exceptionally polite,

helpful and efficient. Meal for four was truly outstanding in every aspect. I ordered Prawn Phall (not on the menu) which was one of the best I have ever tasted — hugely prawned and no evidence of the dreaded Campbells Tomato Soup syndrome! My three shipmates were equally impressed with their choices.' DC. Hours: 6- 11.30.

JAMUNA

18 Yorke Street, Wrexham 01978 261142

'Service excellent, hot food, tasty good portions, although my husband would like more sauce with Jalfrezi. Plenty of chicken in Dhansak and Balti, well presented. Reasonably priced house wine.' dv-w. Takeaway: 10% discount, minimum £13. 20% discount, minimum £17. Menu Extracts: Murghi Masala £11.20, half spring chicken, creamy sauce of minced meat; Chana Special £6.95, tomatoes, green peppers, onion, chick peas, bhuna sauce; Service: 10%.

DYFED

Contains Cardigan, Carmarthenshire & Pembrokeshire.

Area: West Wales
Population: 356,000
Adjacent Counties:
Glam, Powys, Gwynedd

Carmarthen

TAJ BALTI

119 Priory St, Carmarthen 01267 221995

Opened in 1995 by Lias Miah who might give you a discount if you show him this *Guide.*. *'My husband and I always enjoy their fare. Elegant decor, service excellent and friendly, with superb food. Muted traditional music, intimacy of individual booths, a special atmosphere. Tandoori Mixed Grill declared the best ever.'* JF. Hours: 6-12.

Llanelli

BENGAL LANCER

43 Murray Street, Llanelli 01554 749199

78-seater opened by Ahmed Ali in 1986 who might give you a discount if you show him this *Guide.* . Muzaffar heads the cooking brigade. Hours: 12-2.30/6-12. Branch: Anarkali , Swansea.

VERANDAH

20 Market Street, Llanelli 01554 759561

Opened in 1985 by Mr A Khalique who might give you a discount if you show him this *Guide.* . Restaurant seats 64 diners and has bright turmeric walls, indigo carpet and shelving with chilli-red and orange chairs and sofas. Special: Charga Mossalla (half spring-chicken, with tomatoes, green peppers & red wine). Hours: 6-12. (Sat 12.30).

Tenby

BAY OF BENGAL

1 Crackenwell Street Tenby 01834 843331

'Tenby is a lovely place and has some excellent restaurants. Very good meal at The Bay of Bengal. Beautifully furnished, restaurant looks out to the sea, food matched the view. Chicken and Chickpea for Linda and King Prawn Bhuna for me - so many prawns!' MG.

GLAMORGAN

Contains West, Mid & South Glamorgan.

Area: South Wales
Population: 1,346,000
Adjacent Counties:
Dyfed, Gwent, Powys

In 1996, the counties of West, Mid and South Glamorganshire were disbanded in favour of 11 Unitary Authorities to administrate the 11 large towns (incl Newport) in the area. For Guide convenience we have retained the former Glamorgan geography. For Newport see Gwent.

Barry

MODERN BALTI

290 Holton Road, Barry 01446 746787

Established in 1982 by A Akbar, who is also the manager and will welcome you on your visit. Menu Snapshot: Chicken Nugget Tikka £2.40 - the kids will love that one! Balti Tandoori Grill £3.55' chicken and lamb tikka, sheek and balti kebab, served with salad and mint sauce. I would call that a mini mixed grill! Pakora Masala £3.90, spicy potato, vegetables and flour in a thick spicy sauce; Lamb Kalia £5.60 - with green chillies, garlic potatoes, coriander leaves, hot spicy sauce. Licensed: stocks Cobra, £1.95 a bottle and house wine £6.95 a bottle. You might get a discount if you show Mr Akbar this Guide. Price Check: Popadom 45p, CTM £4.70, Pullao Rice £1.55. Hours: 5.30 - 12.30, Fri & Sat - 1.30.

SHAHI NOOR

87 High Street, Barry 01446 735706

Maybur Rahman's restaurant is one of Barry's most popular curry houses. It serves all the favourite Bangladeshi and Indian dishes: Starters , Tandoori, Balti and Curries, Specials, and Accompaniments. Nothing is overlooked. We hear of careful service and cooking, and a well-respected venue by its many regulars. Hours: 12-2.30/6-12.

Bridgend

CAFÉ BANGLA

53 Nolton Street, Bridgend 01656 750070

This fifty-five seater restaurant was opened by M Uddin. His most popular dish is Jhinga Caldeen £8.10, king prawns cooked with garlic, ginger, lime juice, cream, coconut and mixed spicy chillies - sounds wonderful! Other House Specials to tempt

Café Bangla, Bridgend

you include: Goa Lamb Vindaloo £6.95, marinated lamb cooked with fresh green chillies, paprika, tomato purée, fenugreek and coriander; Komola Chicken £6.50, spiced chicken in a rich orange sauce with fresh cream; Murghi Masala £7.45, shredded tandoori chicken, minced lamb in a medium hot sauce. Sunday Buffet: £7.50 adult, £4.50 children. Takeaway: 10% discount. Licensed: lager £2.60 a pint, house wine £7.95 a bottle. You might get a discount if you show Mr Uddin this Guide. Hours: 5.30 to 11, Fri & Sat - 11.30. Sunday 1 to 10. <www.cafe-bangla.com>

Caerphilly

CASTLE GATE NEW ENTRANT

5 Castle View Shopping Centre, Nantgarw Hill, Nantgarw, Caerphilly 029 2088 1106

Koysar Hussain' venue is part of the Empire Group Restaurant, see next entry. Hours: 12-2 except Friday / 6 - 12. <www.empiregroup.info>

Cardiff

BALTI EMPIRE

157-159 Albany Rd, Roath 029 2048 5757

Owner Mujib Mohammed created the Empire Group, a group of six South Wales-based Asian restaurants formed with an aim to *"raise the standard of Asian cuisine"* in South Wales. They now Official Restaurants of Cardiff County Council Festival, and are currently holders of a number of regional awards, including the South Wales Echo Indian Restaurant of the Year. They We have also set up an annual Asian Food & Culture Festival. All six off the curryhouse menu with all your favourites. Members: Castle Gate Caerphilly (above), Bay Leaf, Jinuk and Mujib's Cardiff and Indian Empire, Caldicot, Gwent. Hours: 12 - 2 except Friday / 6 - 12. <www.empiregroup.info>

BAY LEAF

29 High St,Llandaff, Cardiff 029 2056 7400

Mohammed Saiam established it in 2000 in the historic settings near the Cathedral. Quality Indian food at a competitive price, in a pleasant atmosphere. Hours: 12 - 2 except Friday / 6 - 12. <www.empiregroup.info>

Café Naz, Cardiff

CAFÉ NAZ AWARD WINNER

8 Mermaid Quay, Cardiff 029 2049 6555

Cafe Naz maintains a classic Indian identity with ultra modern fittings. Customers are welcomed in the bar and seating area complete with a crescent of fashionable, soft minimalist seats facing a chic wooden bar.The service is polite without being stuffy, a standard which is maintained throughout the evening. Cafe Naz's family ownership and management have created a warm, caring environment, a rarity in restaurants of this high calibre. The food is simply divine, and at its currently deflated prices, is a treat not to be missed. Views of Cardiff bay and St. David's hotel are enhanced in the summer when meals are served on the balcony. Entertainment includes a vast (yet amazingly unobtrusive) screen silently playing the best of Bollywood and occasionally traditional Indian dancers. The on-view kitchen is behind glass and you can watch the cooks at work. The menu contains 30 starters 32 main courses and a extensive wine and beer list. The non veg platter is a feast for two, with two types of chicken (tikka and tandoori), lamb seek kabab, pakodi each given in ample portions. Set Lunches: c£8 or c£6. Delivery £12, 2 miles. Hours: Mon to Thurs 2 - 3/ 6 - 12 Sat & Sun: 12 -12. Branches, London E1. Cambridge. *See page 40.*

JINUK NEW ENTRANT

185 Cowbridge Rd East, Canton, Cardiff 029 2038 7778

Shahin Ahmed's venue is part of the Empire Group Restaurant, see Balti Empire, previous page. Quality Indian food at a competitive price, in a pleasant atmosphere. Hours: 12 - 2 except Friday / 6 - 12. <www.empiregroup.info>

JUBORAJ NOMINATED BEST IN WALES

10 Mill La, Hayes, Cardiff 029 2037 7668

Cardiff's Juboraj Group, consisting of five quality restaurants, three in Cardiff, one in Newport and the other in Swansea were awarded Best Business to the Community Award at the Welsh Awards 2003 held at St David's Hall, Menu snapshot: Starters include Bhajees, Samosas, Pakoras, kebabs and Tandoori items. Main courses: Karahi Duck - tender pieces of duck barbecued and tossed in medium spices with onions, tomatoes and green peppers; Chicken Shashlick, cooked in the clay oven with green peppers, onions and tomatoes, served with a mild sauce; Machli Biran, salmon steak delicately spiced & gently fried Sag Paneer, spicy spinach and cottage cheese; Paneer Chilli Massala, with fresh green chillies and Special Fried Rice, with eggs, peas, onions, almond and spices. Desserts include Sticky Toffee Pud, Apple and Blackberry Crumble. This branch is *'Fairly large, comfortable restaurant, good reputation, very popular. Visited by Tom Jones'* [wow!] *'In my opinion, one of Cardiff's best. Another visit, and the food once again was excellent.'* JB. *'Food excellent, service not.'* G&MP. *'Celebrating Liverpool FC's nail biting penalty shoot out victory in the Worthington Cup, we took the Guide's advice and headed for this restaurant. Service initially prompt, but as the fans from both sides descended, things got a little hectic at times!. Popadoms and Kebabs (Shami and Sheek) both excellent. Main courses, Chicken Madras, Chicken Sagwalla accompanied by Pullao Rice, Nan and Tarka Dal, excellent! Food a little more expensive, guess that was a result of its town centre location! Will visit again – hopefully after the FA cup final!'* DL.Hours: 12-2/6-12am. Branches 11 Heol Y Deri, Cardiff 029 2062 8894, also 84 Commercial St, Newport 01633 262646 and 20 Wind St, Swansea. 01792 649944. *See page 50.* <juborajgroup.com>

JUBORAJ LAKESIDE

Lake Road West Lakeside 029 2045 5123

Love the chairs in this restaurant, made from cane with wicker and upholstered in a richly coloured paisley styled material and a scrolled back, really nice. *See above and page 50.* Hours: 6-11.

SPICE MERCHANT

The Big Windsor, Stuart Street, Cardiff Bay 029 2049 8984

Mike Ahmed spent £450,000 to give the Windsor Hotel, an historic docklands pub, a new identity.

Spice Merchant, is a modern ground and first floor 180 seater . The first floor lounge and restaurant seats up to 130. Ahmed is also actively involved in promoting the Indian Food festival – a yearly event, held in Aberystwyth. He says: *'Spice Merchant does not add any preservatives or additives to our food to enhance flavours and only use the finest ingredients. Customers are invited to see our kitchens and meet our chefs, who have been brought in from first class hotels in India to ensure authenticity.'*

Kenfig Hill

MUKTA MAHAL

104 Pisgah Street Kenfig Hill 01656 746000

'Once a Bingo Hall. Spacious layout with large water fountain. It is possible to have a Thai / Indian mixed meal - the only problem - what to choose! Quality of food very good indeed with excellent service, even on busy nights. Worth a detour off the M4 at junction 36. Highly recommended.' KN. Thai Specials: Tord Mun Pla, deep-fried spicy fish cakes with cucumber, salad, delicate sweet and sour peanut; Yum Woonsen, spicy glass noodle salad with prawns and chicken; Gaeng Mad Sa Man Gai, spicy Muslim chicken curry, sweet potatoes, coconut milk, peanuts; Pla Rad Prik, crispy fish fillet topped with a hot chilli and garlic sauce. Indian Specials: Chicken Pakora; Chicken Makhani, barbecued chicken tossed in butter, yoghurt, fresh cream, tomatoes and spices, Lamb Tikka Mahal, green chillies, garlic, coriander; Keema Rice. Takeaway: 10% discount. Hours: 12-2.30/5.30-12, Friday and Saturday to 12.30. Sunday 12-12.

Swansea

ANARKALI

80 St Helen's Road, Swansea 01792 650549

Fully licensed and air-conditioned 60-seater established by A Rahman way back in 1978. Such long-standing gives it an assurance, experience and confidence with a long list of regulars. Menu Extracts: Crab Malabar, made from flaked fresh crab, sauteed with spices.Mahasha, cabbage leaves stuffed with lamb mince, rice and selected green herbs, sweet and sour flavour. Goan Lamb Vindaloo, marinated lamb with hot chilli, fresh green chilli, paprika, tomato puree, fenugreek and coriander. Sunday Buffet: c£9 eat as much as you like. Hours: 5.30-12, Saturday to 2, Sunday 12-12.

BONOPHOL BANGLADESHI

TOP 100

93 Sterry Road, Gowerton 01792 875253

Owned by the delightful Mohammed Al Imran since 1990, its name change from Gowerton Tandoori in 1996 to Bonophol gives it a unique and pretty name, meaning 'forest flower'. The exterior is elegantly picked out in attractive tones of green and gilt, and this theme continues inside, with with chandelier, modern Bangladeshi art and forty cane chairs. For those who like to know these things, the logo on the menu is a map of Bangladesh, in the national flag colours. What you get at this 40-seater fully licensed restaurant is *'fine Bangladeshi Cuisine, with all my favourites, done conscientiously and very well.'* EG. *'Managed by a well-known pleasant and cheerful person known to all as Abdul – he has been around for years. Quality of food is very good, service also good'.* CMJ. *'Excellent impression, very clean, glass of Sherry for every customer on the house. Reasonable prices, very big portions.'* JM. *'Small, well furnished and pleasant atmosphere. Laid back service with basic menu. Excellent Chicken Jalfrezi and Mushroom Rice, fair portion.'* IB. Takes part in regular Bangladeshi food festivals with other Swansea restaurants. Menu Extracts: Murg Nawabi, barbecued chicken, blended with fresh herbs and spices, garnished with chopped spiced egg. Sunday Buffet: 12-5, c£7 adult, c£5 children Takeaway: 10% discount. Delivery: £10 minimum, 4-mile radius. Hours: 5.30-11.55 (Fri & Sat. to 12.25am); Sun. 12pm-11.55.

KARMA 3

3 Victoria Road Swansea 01792 477848

Opposite Swansea Leisure Centre, Karma's frontage is very striking, decorated with blue mosaic, so you can't miss it. Furniture, wood and wrought iron, was specially imported. The restaurant is deceiving in size, in fact it is quite big, with dining rooms upstairs and down. Licensed. Sunday Banquet, served between 12-10: adult £7, child £4.50. Monday to Saturday two course lunch a bargain at £4.95. Hours: 12-2/6-11

LAL QUILA

480 Mumbles Rd, Mumbles, Swansea
01792 363520

Formerly Ocean View. And because we are now in full colour we take the liberty of showing you tah view. (overleaf) *'Completely refurbished, now has very*

Gorgeous Mumbles

Swansea Bay, Mumbles top left

attractive decor, waiters wear smart uniforms. Probably Swansea's most upmarket restaurant. Everything is spotless with quick and friendly service. I particularly like the Chicken Methi with lots of fresh fenugreek. Food generally good.' JD. *'Very stylish, airy atmosphere with wonderful views over Swansea Bay. Over-formal, but efficient service and excellent, unusual menu – ostrich and monkfish. Fair portion of Mangalorian Fish Curry and excellent Aloo Paratha. Quality and nice for a change.'* IB.

MIAH'S — NEW ENTRANT

St Paul's Church, St Helens Road, Swansea 01792 466244

Abdu Miah opened it in 2001, and it's the venus Swansea talks about. They call it unique because it's in a former church. It's not the first curryhouse in a church, but done well it does lead interesting venue, and yes, it the décor is done well here. The bar is now the high altar, picked out with gothic arches in its front panels. Over it is a funky modern chandelier. Tables line the blonde wood floor. Your eye is drawn to the sweeping staircase, which shows off the huge stained-glass gothic window, and up to the fabulous vaulted roof. The stairs sweep left and right and take you to the balcony. But you can't eat the décor. We have desisted entering Miah's before because you tell us of uncaring service, excess red colouring and cold food. But of late we have had more cheering reports, and we'd like more please. The menu offers all the .Bangladeshi curryhouse favourites, and there is a section called the 'connoisseur's menu' with a selection of chef's specials. Prices a bit higher than average. Lunch and dinner daily. <www.miahs.net>

MOGHUL BRASSERIE — TOP 100

81 St Helen's Rd, Swansea 01792 475131

60-seater, opened in 1989 by Shazan Uddin, who is also the chef, managed by Ashik Rahman. Bangladeshi and Balti cuisine. *'Have been regulars for several years. Consistency is the key word for Mr Uddin. Efficient service in very pleasant surroundings. Excellent Chicken Tikka Karahi, Sali Boti and my favourite Pathia (prawn and chicken). Mr Uddin recently exhibited a wonderful Cockle Masala, at a Culinary Festival. Superb!'* A&AP. *'We have never come across anywhere that comes even close to the wonderful cuisine served at the Moghul.'* E&ME. *'Scores: 6/10.* DB. *'Varied menu, beautiful decor and excellent attentive service. Fair portion of Chicken Sali and Mushroom Rice. Everything about this restaurant was top notch. Fully deserves TOP 100 Award. Excellent.'* ib. Menu Extract: Shankar Thai £9, Pullao Rice, Bombay Aloo, Bhindi Masala, Niramish, Baigon Samosa. Sunday Buffet: c£9. Set Dinner: c£20 for two. Takeaway: 10% off. Remains in our **TOP 100.** Hours: 12-2.30/5-12 (2am Fri. / Sat.). Sun 12-12.

NAWAB

12 Christina Street, Swansea 01792 470770

Opened in 1976. Mr Miah (manager) House wine £7.50 a bottle.Price Check: Popadom 50p, CTM £5.50, Pullao Rice £1.80. Delivery: 2 miles, £10.

GWENT

Monmouthshire

Area: Southwest Wales
Population: 454,000
Adjacent Counties: Glamorgan, Gloucs, Herefordshire and Powys

In the 1996 reorganisation, Monmouthshire was restored for some purposes and Gwent for others, including for this Guide.. Newport became an independent Unitary Authority, and we retain it here.

Abergavenny

SHAHI BALTI

5 Mill Street Abergavenny 01873 792011

'Having gone to visit friends, they chose the venue and booked a table – good job too – very popular with locals and those from out of town. Had a drink in the tiny bar, whilst table was readied. Chose a rather unimaginative Chicken and Potato Balti, pleasantly surprised, tasty indeed, good value at £6.50. Suggested a vegetable Thali for friend, who is unused to eating spicy food. Very impressed, a very appetising selection with ample portions. One other thing to note - Nan's, tasty, substantial.' MD. Hours: 6-11.30

INDIAN EMPIRE NEW ENTRANT

Park Wall Crick, Caldicot 01291 431144

Kazad Uddin's venue is a member of the Empire Group, see page 453. *'Situated 3 miles from the Welsh border town of Chepstow and 12 miles from the city of Newport on the A48., it is well positioned with ample parking. Inside is pristine with background music creating a very relaxed atmosphere, seating in the air-condition restaurant is for around 180 people. The friendly waiters and excellent customer service makes sure that your visit to the restaurant is memorable and you defiantly return again. I made two visits to the restaurant to meet the Manager Tufayer Ahmed and the Chef Abdul Boshor along with the staff in the busy kitchen and the second visit was to see the food preparation. The Kitchen was clean and tidy and there was always someone with a mop ready to clean up any spillages. All the cooking instruments were cleaned once finished with. Chef showed me how they prepare their bases and rice for the day, which were Masala, Korma, Curry and Pillau Rice. From experience on my two visits the bases were cooked with fresh ingredients and the meals were also cooked to a high standard with fresh spices and nice presentation for the customer. Chef said, "if customers spend good money the customer deserves good food." The kitchen staff were very synchronised with everyone knowing their part to play in the kitchen from prep work to the customers final dish on the table. The report rounds off with a tasting of the food. My wife and I ordered Chicken Tikka Masala twice (one was madras hot), a Keema Naan, a plain Naan, Keema fried rice, pillar rice and chips. The food was all I expected it to be hot, fresh and spicy. I highly recommend this restaurant. Once a month the restaurant has a buffet night so you can taste all the different food from the Indian and east Asia sub continent.'* MJ. Hours: 12-2 except Fri / 6 - 11.30. <www.indianempire.co.uk>

Crumlin

RAJDOOT

17 Main Street Crumlin 01495 243032

'Feeling hungry on the way home from Newport one night. Have tried it a few times since, even though it is quite away from my home, about 10 miles. I particularly like the Roghan Gosht, which was rich and creamy with a good portion. The Rajpoot Thali was excellent with a very good fruit salad. £21 for two.' PH. Hours: 5.30-12, Friday and Saturday to 12.30.

Monmouth

MISBAH TANDOORI

BEST IN WALES

9 Priory Street, Monmouth NP25 3BR
01600 714940

D Miah opened his 80-seater restaurant in 1990. It is situated in the historic Market town of Monmouth. The restaurant itself is situated by the Monnow, it is also in the immediate vicinity of Monmouth castle and the ancient Market square. The restaurant is in an ideal position for visitors, being located conveniently close to the main A40 dual carriageway. Birmingham is less then I hour, M4 (Newport) 20 minute, Bristol 40 minute, Cardiff 35 minute way. This comfortable venue exudes customer care. Mr Miah's Misbah attracts celebs, and he's delighted to tell you about them (ask him – each one has a tale). Chef A Rahman heads the chef brigade. Menu Snapshot: Bengal Fish Mossala (freshwater fish from Bangladesh cooked in tomato and onion, Zahan Special, medium, aubergines, spinach, potato, chickpea, mixed vegetables; Jamdani all mild, chicken cooked with cheese, cream c£7.95; Spicy Wing Masala £4.95; Baigan Aloo Masala £5.95 - aubergine and potato; Shahi Rice £3.95, almond, sultanas, peas, onion and spices; Special Nan £2.25, stuffed with vegetables, egg, cheese and spices. *'As good as all the reports I have read: clean, friendly, basic menu, good service.*

Misbah, Monmouth

Strangely quiet for a Friday night though. Excellent Chicken Jalfrezi and Pullao Rice. Excellent.' IB. *'Warm, personal welcome. Intimate friendly service. Appealingly presented tables. All senses catered for. Wonderful food, succulent meat, stupendous prawns – all flavours beautifully blended, a richly textured Tarka Dal. Fluffy and exotically flavoured Rice and above all FRESH Mango! Gastronomic excellent.'* GL & DT. *'Have visited for takeaways and sit-down meals for over five years. Consistently, exceptionally high standard. Feels like home.'* jt. *'Popadoms and chutneys arrived immediately. Exciting menu with authentic dishes. Clean toilets.'* s&dt. *'Food superb and promptly served.'* HE. *'The quality of the food is a good mix between the comfort blanket of the traditional and the innovative and new.'* ar. *'Delicious, wonderful food, lots of lovely vegetarian dishes.'* j&ha. Super stuff. Misbah has been in our *Guide* since it opened. It has achieved **TOP 100** status last time and now it has achieved the ultimate: **BEST IN WALES.** Restaurants like this are what this *Guide* is all about. Minimum charge: £10.00. Set dinner: £11.95 per person. Takeaway: 10% off. Price Check: Popadom 50p, CTM £7.95, Pullao Rice £1.95. Hours: 12 - 2.30, Fri & Sat - 2/ Weekdays 6 - 11, Fri & Sat 5.30 - 11.30. <www.misbahtandoori.co.uk> *See page 67.*

Misbah, Monmouth

Newport

BALTI NITE — NEW ENTRANT

8 Gladstone St, Crosskeys 01495 271 234

Chef, Abdul Kahim's restaurant est 1995, seats, 40. Specials include: Chicken Kohlpuri £6, hot and spicy with turmeric, cumin, coriander and green chillies; Nilgiri Mirch £6, sautéed lamb with coconut, ginger, mint and coriander leaves and Ayre Mossala £7, Bangladeshi freshwater (boal) oven baked in sauce with coriander leaves, green peppers, green chillies, spinach, ginger and mustard, Cobra £5 a pint, house wine £8 a bottle. Del: 3 miles, £20 mini. Price Check: Popadom 40p, CTM £7, Pullao Rice £2. Hours: 5.30 - 12.

JUBORAJ

84 Commercial Street, Risca 01633 262646

Good decor, classy, almost temple - ish, very clean and inviting. Welcoming, friendly staff, attentive. Good and pricey menu... got to pay for that refurbishment. *'...Very tasty, fresh Mixed Starter – onion bhajia, meat samosas and chicken pakora, small portion. Lamb and Prawn Madras with Pullao Rice and Aloo Gobi, very good portions with generous sauce, not at all oily, flavoursome. Delicious Chicken Tikka Masala. Special Fried Rice a bit disappointing, seemed very similar to Pullao Rice. All in all very good.'* PAH. Menu Extracts: Juboraj King Prawn, cooked in shell; Coriander Chicken, fillets, ground coriander; Kohlapuri, hot and spicy chicken, turmeric, cumin, coriander, green chillies. Hours: 12-2/6-12. *See pages 454 and 50.* <juborajgroup.com>

THE KOH I NOOR

164 Chepstow Road, Maindee, Newport 01633 258028

Mrs L Khanan's venerable 60-seater was established in 1978, and has appeared in most of our *Guides*. We've said before that nothing on the menu changes. Chef Tahir Ullah's curries are listed under such categories as mild, fruity, fairly hot, very hot, hottest and most-favourite. In other words this is one of the early curryhouses with its clutch of once-a-week regulars. Nothing wrong with that, especially since you might get a discount if you show them this *Guide*. Hours: 12-2.30/6-1am. Sun. 6-12.

GWYNEDD

Contains: Caernarfonshire and Merionethshire and for the purposes of this Guide, Anglesey.

Area: North Wales
Population: 240,000
Adjacent Counties: Clwyd, Dyfed, Powys

Abersoch

EAST MEETS WEST

The High Street Abersoch 01758 713541

'Very new and modern establishment in heart of quaint North Wales village. Open, light and airy interior, subtly decorated. Run by young and friendly staff, service efficient and cheerful. Excellent Reshmi Kebab, single large succulent, well spiced kebab, topped with large, well cooked omelette. Nice, crisp salad, but yoghurt sauce would not have gone amiss. Superb Lamb Balti Rogan Josh, tangy, beautifully balanced sauce, plenty of tomatoes, well cooked onions and peppers. Stuffed with good cuts of tender lamb, though gristle and tough lumps were present. They take the translation of Balti literally, my curry was served in a copper plated stainless steel bucket! Very well cooked Chapati for two, soft, moist but not doughy or salty. Very enjoyable, highly recommended. Up to Top 100 standard.' RW. Menu Extracts: Bengal King Prawns, hot with green chillies, bay leaves, cinnamon; Agni, Chicken or Lamb Tikka cooked with onions, green peppers, cooked in brandy and set alight; Egg Nan; Keema Paratha . Hours: 6 to late.

Dolgellau

LEMON GRASS

Finsbury Square, Dolgellau

This is a story about a restaurant which still insist on imposing ridiculous rules. There are many which do it. I have written on this topic for Tandoori Magazine, the brand-leader industry magazine, but I don't expect such owners to read the piece, let alone open their minds to commercial applications (ie making more money). Here is Steve's sobering report: *'There is a gap in the 2004 Guide between Porthmadog and Aberystwyth, so as I was staying in the middle of the gap, I went looking. There are curry houses listed in the phone book in Tywyn, Barmouth and Dolgellau. The one in Tywyn looked a bit run down, and of the two in Barmouth, the Indian Clipper looked the more promising. However, having placed my takeaway order, the waitress came back and informed me that only full vegetable dishes (and not side dishes) were available. That's their choice but not mine.' Their prices were already higher than average, and there's nothing like feeling a little bit ripped off to suppress my appetite, so I decided to try elsewhere. So, no report....' What is their problem! what is wrong with side dishes! don't they want your business? 'The other in Barmouth looked a bit scruffy, so with petrol running low and the only petrol station still open in Dolgellau, my options were closing quickly. So to The Lemon Grass - double shop width but not very deep. Food arrived in fifteen minutes with a free Popadom, plastic containers didn't leak at all, despite the winding roads back home. Food was unexpectedly good, Balti Chicken Dopiaza was as good as I've had, and the two vegetable dishes were distinctly different. Mixed Vegetable Curry was particularly nice and reminded me of the one at the Malabar, London, W8 but slightly firmer texture. I'll definitely be going there again....'* ST.

Llanberis

SPICE OF LLANBERIS NEW ENTRANT

32 High Street, Llanberis 01286 871983

In Abdul Jalil 2005 took over the Balti Raj and renamed it. There are sixty seats and chef Suruk Miah cooks up Bangladeshi styled curries, including Shere e Bangla £6.50 - medium dry spiced chicken and lamb tikka with spring onions, green peppers, herbs, garlic and mushrooms served with vegetable curry sauce; Sylheti Chicken £6.50 - marinated, sliced chicken, lightly spiced, medium hot sauce, boiled eggs, green peppers - recommended with Pullao Rice; Jomuna Issa £6.50 - prawns, medium sauce, garlic, ginger, coriander leaves. Cobra, £2.90 a bottle, house wine £8.50 a bottle. You might get a discount if you show Mr Jalil this *Guide*. Price Check: Popadom 50p, CTM £6.95, Pullao Rice £1.80. Hours: 5 - 11. Branch: Polash Balti, 28, Penlawst, Pwllheli.

Llandrindod Wells

CHAMELEE SPICE NEW ENTRANT

Emporium Bldg, 2 Temple St 01597 823844

Opened in 1995 by Abdul Khalique. Korma and Tikka Masala are his most popular dishes. Menu Snapshot: Nargis Kebab £2.85 - boiled egg covered with a thin layer of minced lamb cooked in a clay oven and garnished with a delicate sauce; Spiced Potato and Garlic Mushrooms £2.75 - soft, fluffy spiced potato balls served with salted mushrooms in garlic butter; Tandoori Mixed Grill £9.10 - lamb and chicken tikka, tandoori chicken, sheek kebab, king prawn and nan; Salmon Spice £6.95 - salmon steak, lightly spiced, garnished with coriander and spring onion, Peshwari, Onion, Coriander, Vegetable or Garlic Nan all £1.60 each. Price Check: Popadom 50p, CTM £7.95, Pullao Rice £1.85. Cobra, £3.75 a bottle, house wine £7.95 a bottle. Hours: 5.30 - 11.30, Fri & Sat - 1.

Llandudno

BENGAL DYNASTY AWARD WINNER

1 North Parade, Llandudno 01492 878445

Manikur Ahmed opened his 86-seat Bengal Dynasty the day before Bangladesh Independence Day, in 1988. Llandudno is a really fabulous seaside town with gorgeous Georgian buildings running in an arch along the waterfront. Lewis Carroll wrote *Alice in Wonderland* in this seaside resort. The Bengal Dynasty is situated upstairs in three dining rooms in one of these fine buildings. Popular dishes include: Jalfrezi, Masala, and Korai Specials:: Chicken Bondhuk; Lamb Satkora Bangladeshi citrus fruit; and Macher Tarkari, a Bangladeshi fish dish. All Tandoori dishes are served with green salad and mint yoghurt. *'I was about to settle for fish & chips when I saw it, upstairs above a shoe shop. I had Lamb Tikka to start and then Chicken Bhuna, which was excellent.'* AG *'King Prawn Butterfly followed by my usual main courses. A very accomplished meal. Keema Nan was the highlight together with a homemade Kulfi. Gets my vote.'* JL. *'Service was welcoming, prompt and polite. Pops and chuts fresh and crisp. Main meals were large, everything was hot and well presented. An enjoyable experience, but not outstanding.'* SR. *'Menu was wide and varied. Papadoms and chutneys excellent. Raita exceptional. All meals were served piping hot with hot plates and the portions were satisfying. Waiters were very accommodating in making changes to dishes for our individual tastes. Smart, clean and tasteful surroundings. Highly recommended.'* NC. Takeaway: 15% discount. Cobra, £2.90 a bottle, house wine £8.95 a bottle. You might get a discount if you show Mr Ahmed this Guide. Price Check: Popadom 60p, CTM £7.75, Pullao Rice £1.70. Hours: 12-2.30. (4.30 on Sun.)/6-11.30. Branches: Bengal Dynasty, Deeside, Clwyd and Northwich, Cheshire.

Bengal Dynasty, Llandudno

Porthmadog

PASSAGE TO INDIA

26 Lombard Street 01766 512 144

'We have been visiting for nearly twenty years and have seldom had a bad meal. The restaurant is relatively small and gets very busy at weekends and throughout the summer. It is advisable to book, unless

the visit is scheduled for a winter weekday evening. Your patience and pre-planning will invariably be rewarded by good food and unhurried service. The portions are very generous and the Vegetable Roghan Josh £4.50, is always particularly good. There is something on the menu to satisfy even the most confirmed and critical curry lover.' N&JG. Menu Snapshot: Chicken or Lamb Naga £6.95, cooked with garlic, onion, and the extremely hot Naga Morich chilli. Price Check: Popadom 50p, CTM £6.85, Pullao Rice £1.85. Hours: 6 - 11.

POWYS

Contains Montgomeryshire, Radnorshire and Brecknockshire

Area: Central East Wales
Population: 130,000
Adjacent Counties: Clwyd, Dyfed, Glamorgan, Gwent, Gwynedd, Herefordshire, Shropshire

Llansantffraid

TANDOORI PLAICE

Waterloo Hse, Llansantffraid 01691 828152

Takeaway only est 1994 by Shoakoth Ali. Black ash coffee table with red chairs for waiting customers. Menu Extracts: Keema Chana Masala, minced lamb, chick peas, masala sauce; Pista Nan, pistachio nuts; Green Lamb Masala, lamb pieces with peas, green herbs, touch of cream, butter. Credit cards not accepted. Hours: 5-11.30, Fri/ Sat to 12.

Newtown

SHILAM

49 Broad Street Newtown 01686 625333

I have been recommended to visit this restaurant and it certainly did not disappoint. Clean, fairly modern surroundings. Service very friendly and prompt. Good all round menu. Superbly presented, very good food, garnished platters rather than the traditional oval stainless dish. Tandoori Trout starter exceptional and Vindaloo had lots of bite. Loads of green chillies in very hot Jalfrezi. Most impressed.' KN. Menu Extracts: Bangol Maslee £6.75, spicy trout. Chicken Green Masala £5.75, tandoori chicken, freshly ground chilli, coriander, onion, green pepper, garlic, ginger, spinach, lime, pickle flavoured sauce, served with salad. Delivery service. Hours: 5.30 -12, Fri/Sat to 2.

PREEM NEW ENTRANT

Pool Road, Newtown 01686 625534

Mehoraz owns this eighty seater. Head chef: Shamim Uddin. cooks Bangladeshi style curries. Menu Snapshot: Stuffed Pepper £2.95, chicken or lamb or vegetable; Tandoori Duck £7.95; Tandoori Cocktail £9.95, chicken and lamb tikka, king prawn, sheek kebab, tandoori chicken served with plain nan - lovely!; Chicken or Lamb Delight £12.95, with cointreau, cream and almonds. Cobra £2.35 a bottle, house wine £8.50 a bottle. Minimum charge: £10. Delivery: 3 miles, £15 minimum. Price Check: Popadom 50p, CTM £6.95, Pullao Rice 31.90. Hours: 5 - 12.

Cinnamon, Aberdeen, p 436

SPECIAL FEATURE

We are doing something unique here by publishing our first ever Indian restaurant review of an Indian restaurant. But this is no ordinary restaurant. It is arguably:

The World's Best Tandoor Restaurant

BUKHARA

Hotel Maurya Sheraton, New Delhi
110 021, India Tel: +91 11 2301 0101

The Indian Tobacco Group (ITC) took a decision to open a hotel chain in the mid 1970s. They chose to call it the Welcom Group, which has caused computer spell-checks to go into hyper-drive ever since, but Welcom it is spelt and welcoming it certainly is. To obtain experience staff, the well-healed ITC poached personnel, reinforced by opening a chef and management training school. As for their property portfolio, they rented or purchased a number of heritage palaces in prestige locations, at the time languishing into disrepair, and refurbished them and linking with Sheraton they invested in new builds. Delhi's magnificent Maurya Sheraton hotel was the first of the latter. Opening in 1978, it proclaimed new standards of luxury, previously unseen in India's capital city. Restaurants are a major part of a hotel's success, and Maurya was endowed with an Indian, a Chinese and an all-day café/coffee shop. The new group's gourmet chairman was the main instigator. He wanted a restaurant whose sole function was to serve tandoori cuisine, something then, as now, little known in India. He had come across Tandoori cooking (ironically rumour has it, in London's upmarket Gaylord W1, although he would also have met it at Delhi's Motijeel (see London WC2). After much deliberation, the ITC directorate elected to humour their new chairman by opening a small tandoori restaurant in the hotel gardens. If it failed, so what?

They located it alongside the main hotel, in view of the pool and gardens. The room could be demolished without a trace if needs be. They called it Bukhara, named after the famous historic Silk-Road town of that name in Uzbekistan. When it opened it had just 50 seats and it was more than doubled shortly after. to 130-covers,. Decor is attractive but not exceptional. It is unmistakably rural and rugged, with stone-clad walls, deep crimson flagstone, beaded screens, rough hewn furniture with copper pots and urns suspended from the ceiling. Seating is on uncomfortable low wooden stools, facing thick oak tables completing the rugged look. There is no cutlery, and everyone wears a gingham bib which doubles as your napkin. Even the menu comes on a block of wood. Nothing, apart from annual tidy-ups, has changed since the Bukhara opened. It is astounding that while other restaurants constantly update their menus to follow trends and tastes, the Bukhara menu, established by the late Master Chef Madan Lal Jaiswal and Todar Mal has not changed by even one item.

So what made it so popular that within one year you had to book months in advance, and still do so? Firstly, the atmosphere is electric. The service is as good as it gets. It was the first restaurant to put its several tandoori ovens and chefs on view behind glass, and although now widely copied, one just knows this was the original of its genre. The open kitchen is inviting and guests have always been welcome to watch and even photograph the busy chefs as they prepare food off the tandoor. It was something the chefs had to become accustomed to. The food at the Bukhara describes

itself as northwest frontier cuisine, consisting of delicate marinades, low fat succulent tandoori fare, tikkas and kebabs, wispy breads, lyrical dhal and choice vegetables, all so ordinary looking in print on the menu ... all done so exquisitely. The main signature dishes are Whole Leg of Spring Lamb, marinated in a mixture of malt vinegar, cinnamon and black cumin braised in the marinade, skewered then finished in the tandoor and Murgh Malai Kebab, a creamy kebab of boneless chicken blended with cream cheese, lemon juice and green coriander, grilled in the moderate tandoor, and their trademark giant naans.

The mantle was inherited by Welcom Group Corporate Chef MS Gill. Today's Exec Chef is J.P. Singh. After studying Hotel Management at Dadar, Mumbai he started out as Demi Chef at the Sea Rock Sheraton in Mumbai before working his way up to taking the reigns at Bukhara in 1991. Since then, he has travelled the world promoting Bukhara cuisine as far as South America, Europe, the USA and New Zealand.

For several years the Bukhara has been being voted as one of the 50 World's Best Restaurants and Asia's Best Indian Restaurant by Britain's Restaurant Magazine, and the world's best Tandoori Restaurant by this Cobra Good Curry Guide, with judges from around the world, including India's pioneering food journalist Rashmi Uday Singh. The likes of Presidents Bill Clinton and Putin, Prime Minister Tony Blair, and their likes of Mick Jagger, Bill Gates, Bryan Adams, Tom Cruise and just about everyone on the A-list, make a bee-line to the Bukhara.

Your editors have been there some 20 times since 1983. Indeed we have taken some of our Gourmet Tour Groups there *(see page 62)*. Most love it; some do not; after one fabulous meal I made the mistake of asking one of our Group (a Mr Stuart Hughes from Rosendale,Lancs) how he had enjoyed it. He replied *'Do you want the honest truth.'* At that point I knew I did not. But I said *'Yes'*. He said *'It was uncomfortable, I did not get enough to eat, the food was bland and I can get better in Rusholme!'* Oh dear! ... it was the first day of a 16 day tour!

Quote from an anonymous American! *'Never have I been so disappointed. Kebobs (sic) were dry, grossly over spiced, and just not good. The dahl (sic) was, however, fabulous. The tree stumps you sit on (it is decorated as if it were a campsite) made it the most uncomfortable eating hour of my life. It was also far and away the most expensive place I ate in India -- fully New York or London prices. Avoid the hype, and avoid the restaurant. If you are staying at the Sheraton the daily buffet in the "coffee shop" was fabulous'.* How we laughed!

Never mind Lancs and Yanks; the ITC directorate got it wrong too. But not anymore ... they reckon to have served 3 million diners since they opened. They book months in advance, and even come to Delhi's Sheraton for the Bukhara.

They cannot all be wrong.

List of Contributors

This Guide is possible thanks to the many Curry Club members, and others, who have sent in reports on restaurants. Especial thanks to the following regular, prolific and reliable reporters (apologies for any errors, duplications, omissions, and for the tiny print necessitated by space considerations).

A: Martin Abbott, Gloucs; Colin Adam, Kilwinning; Ray Adams, Kimberley; Meena Ahamed, London; F. Ahmed, Salisbury; Diane Aldsworth, email; Alex, email; Paul Allen, Chatham; Maria Allen, Milton Keynes; Tony and Lesley Allen, Rugby; MF Alsan, Rugby; G Amos, Wirral; Capt R Ancliffe, BFPO 12; Apryl Anderson, Ponteland; Bill Anderson, Berwick Upon Tweed; Karen Andras, Nottingham; Lisa Appadurai, Benfleet; Robin Arnott, Stafford; Mrs M Asher, Woodford Green; Dave Ashton, Warrington; Jo Ashton, Elland; Allan Ashworth, York; Berry Ashworth, Compton Bassett; Michelle Aspinal, Chester; Darius Astell, Southampton; Rachael Atkinson, Cheshire; Simon Atkinson, N5; Y Atkinson, IOM; Claire Austin, Stoke; Arman Aziz, N4.

B: Tom Bailey, Alresford; John Baker, Loughton; Raji Balasubramaniam, Bangalore; Mridula Baljekar, Camberley, Kim Baker, Hatfield; Mr & Mrs ML Banks, Enfield; Keith Bardwell, Hertford; Ian Barlex, Ilford; Trevor Barnard, Gravesend; Christopher Barnes, Ashton; Derek Barnett, Colchester; Tony Barrel, Hounslow; R.Barry-Champion, Market Harborough; Joanne Bastock, Saltash; Mike Bates, Radcliffe; Shirley Bayley, Worthing; Karin and Angela, Rugby; Mr MJ Beard, Stafford; Joyce Bearpark, Murcia Spain; Dave Beazer, Cornwall; DJ Beer, Ross-on-Wye; Derick Behrens, Bucks; Ian Bell, Cheshire, Matt Bell, Derbys; P Bell, Carlisle; Sam Bell, Coventry; TW Bennett, Sherborne; Becky Benson, Worcs; John Bentley, Northampton; Ron Bergin, Gerrards Cross; Ian Berry, Goole; Ian and Jan Berry, Sheffield; Martyn Berry, SE3; Michael Berry, email; Shirley and Nick Bertram, Surrey; Kenneth Beswick, Lincoln; DJ Betts, Bexhill; Jonathan Bick, Cardiff; Brian and Anne Biffin, Fleet; Colin Bird, Welwyn Garden City; BH Birch, Hyde; Jim Birkumshaw, Derbys; James Birtles, Manchester; Chris Blackmore, Bristol; David Bolton, Lichfield; Mrs C Bone, Norfolk; A Boughton, SE27; L Le Bouochon, Jersey; J Bowden, email; Mrs I Bowman, Rochester; Julie Bowman, email; Robert Box, Knottingley; Alan Boxall, Burwash; Sean Boxall, Andover; F Boyd, Stranraer; Iain Boyd, Wealdstone; Roderick Braggins, Peebles; Amanda Bramwell, Sheffield; Susan Brann, Worthing; Susan Brann, Worthing; Dave Bridge, Wallasey; Michael E Bridgstock, Northants; Sandra Brighton, Nelson; Steve Broadfoot, Anfield; Susan Brann, Worthing; John and Susan Brockington, Sutton Coldfield; Paul Bromley, SE13; Robert Brook, London; Nigel John Brooks, Stoke on Trent; David Brown, Leeds; IA Brown, Fernhurst; Janet Brown, email; Mark Brown, Scunthorpe; Steve Brown, Twickenham; DA Bryan, York; Rachel Bryden, email; RC Bryant, Witney; Robert Bruce, Thornaby; Heather Buchanan, Inverness; Dr TM Buckenham, SW11; Mrs J Buffey, Sutton Coldfield; LG Burgess, Berkhamsted; DABurke, London, A Burton, Weston-super-Mare; Bob Butler & family, email; Sanah Butt, Middlesex.

C: A C, email; D Cadby, Swindon; Barry Caldwell, Chesterfield; David Caldwell, Brownhills; Stan Calland, Kingsley; Hugh Callaway, Cleethorpes; Duncan Cameron, Fordoun; Frank Cameron, Dundee; HS Cameron, Wirral; Alex Campbell, Ramsey Campbell, Wallasey; Hartley Wintney; Mrs E Campbell, Harrogate; N Campbell, Edinburgh; Josephine Capps, Romford; L Carroll, Huddersfield; James Casey, Wiltshire; Peter Cash, Liverpool; Mark Caunter, Guildford; TM Chandler, Farnborough; Desmond Carr, N8; J Carr, Birkenhead; TO Carr, Warrington; BR Carrick, Wakefield; DL Carter, Huntingdon; Mrs M Carter, Colchester; Madeline Castro, Bury St Edmunds; Dr WF Cavenagh, Norfolk; Neil Chantrell, Warrington; Hilary J Chapchal, Leatherhead; Mr & Mrs DR Chapchal, Leatherhead; John Chapman, Leics; od Chapman, e-mail; Paul Chapman, Leighton Buzzard; Mr & Mrs Chatfield, Wimborne; Rajender Chatwal, Bicester; Dr GT Cheney, Salhouse; Paul Chester, Cuffley; Kathryn Chitty, Merseyside, Quest PR Ltd; Dave Christian, email; Sqn Ldr PF Christopher, Ferndown; Alexis Ciusczak, Capistrano Beach, CA; Imogen Clist, Les Routiers in Britain, email; Peter Clyne, SW11; VA Coak, Penzance; Alan Coates, Sheffield; Louise Coben-Sutherland, Enfield; CH Coleman, Sussex; Robin Collier, Mid Calder; Chris Coles, Biggin Hill, Billy Collins, Wirral; Mrs J Collins, Portsmouth; CJ Comer, Basingstoke; Rhys Compton, Cheltenham; A Conroy, Durham; Joseph Coohil, Oxford; Neil Cook, Royston; Peter Cookson, Notts; Mr LW Coombes, Devon; Alan & Margaret Cooper, Llansteffan; Kim Cooper, Basildon; DW Cope, Whitchurch; Dr JC Coppola, Woodstock; Will Coppola, Oxford; Nigel Cornwell, Orpington; John Costa, Tunbridge Wells; MJ Cotterill, Bristol; Ron A Couch, email; Stephen Cowie, SW16; Steve Cowling, Shropshire; Julie Cozens, Oxon; Dr AM Croft, Cornwall; Roderick Cromar, Buckie; C Cross, Poole; Yasmin Cross, Huddersfield; Major & Mrs FJB Crosse, Salisbury; Robert Crossley, Huddersfield; F Croxford, Edinburgh; Frank and Elizabeth Crozier, Redruth; Gordon Cruickshank, Banffshire; R Cuthbertson, Southampton.

D: S Daglish, Scarborough; P Dalton, Wirral; Jan Daniel, Felpham; Mr & Mrs PE Dannat, Eastleigh; Martin Daubney, Hitchin; Gary Davey, W4; Alasdair Davidson, Heswall; Adrian Davies, NW3; Gwyn Davies, Wirral; Mrs JC Davies, Leeds; Josephine Davies, Swansea; Lucy Davies, Essex; Paul Davies, Chiddingfold; Mrs G Davies-Goff, Marlow; Colin Davis, Tatsfield; Ian Dawson, Mirfield; DM Day, Preston; Michael Day, West Bromwich; Angela Dean, Solihull; Peter Deane, Bath; Gary & Katy Debono, High Wycombe; David Dee, Ruislip; Elizabeth Defty, Co. Durham; Neil Denham, The Netherlands; R Dent, Bishop Auckland; Les Denton, Barnsley; Richard Develyn, St Leonards; Nigel Deville, Uttoxeter; Ken Dewsbury, Somerset; Richard Diamond, Romsey; RC Dilnot, Broadstairs; Graham Divers, Glasgow; James Dobson, Burscough; S Dolden, Rochester; R Dolley, W11; Donna, Worthing; Clive Doody, Surrey; Keith Dorey, Barnet; Neil Downey, Worthing; Sarah Dowsett, Swindon; Anna Driscoll, Cape Province; Mrs J Driscoll, BFPO; Hazel Drury, Bromborough; Diane Duame, Wicklow; Eric Duhig, Hornchurch; Sheila Dunbar, Pinner; James Duncan, West Kilbride; Jon Dunham, Northants; Mark Dunn, E18; Rachael Dunn, Hemel, Robin Durant, Brighton; Martin Durrant, Chester; Avishek Dutt, London, Mr & Mrs JA Dywer, Birmingham.

E: A Edden-Jones, Bristol; Bruce Edwards, Norwich; Dave Edwards, Rugeley; Fred and Hilary Edwards, Surrey; CM Eeley, Witney; Rod Eglin, Whitehaven; Wendy Elkington; Ray Elliott, Worcester; Chris Ellis, email; H Ellis, Worthing; Peter Ellis, London, PT Ellis, W'rtn; Stuart and Christine Ellis, email; Mrs G Elston, Woodley; Tony Emmerton, Chorley; Mark Evans, SW5; Mr & Mrs A Evans, Manchester; Brian Exford, Derbys.

F: Colin Fairall, Hants; Gary Fairbrother, Crosby; J.M.Fairhurst, Baldock; Hazel Fairley, Guildford; Chris Farrington, Cherry Hinton; Graham Faulkner, Dorking; Joy Fawcett, Sheffield; John Fearson, Bucks; Denis Feeney, Glasgow; Kevin Fenner, Rothley; Bill and Laraine Field, Newcastle-upon-Lyme; Stephen Field, Norton; Mick Fielden, Glossop; AJ Finch, Enfield Wash; Duncan Finley, Glasgow; Maureen Fisher, Woodford Green; Bernard Fison, Holmrook; John Fitzgerald, Great Missenden; David Flanagan, Orkney; Gerry Flanagan PepsiCo Germany; Merly Flashman, TN12; Colin & Toni Fleet, Dorset; Dr Cornel Fleming, N6; KD Flint, Kempsey; Fiona Floyd, Truro; Stephen & Elizabeth Foden, Lynton; Chris Fogarty, Enfield; Gareth Foley, Porthcawl; Neil Foley, Essex; IE Folkard-Evans, Manchester; SR Tracy Forster, Beds; Rod Fouracres, Glos.; Rosemary Fowler, Midhurst; John W Fox, Doncaster; Linda Foye, Barry; Theresa Frey, Fareham; Chris Frid, North Shields; Steve Frost, Kingston; Ben Fryer, Worthing; Alan Furniss, Wraysbury; June Fyall, Bronwydd; Mrs MAJ Fyall, Dyfed.

G: Gail & Brendan, Orme; Stephen Gaines, Middlesex; MJ Gainsford, Burbage; Leo Gajsler, Geneva; Harry E Garner, London; Mrs FE Gaunt, Stonehouse; Phillip Gentry, Bexleyheath; Brian George, Wolverton; Nick & Julie Gerrard, Gwynedd; CM Gerry, Cyprus; G Gibb, SE21; Robert (Bob) Giddings, Poole; Michael Gill, Leeds; Emma Gillingham, Huddersfield; Andrew Gillies, Edinburgh; AV Glanville, Windsor; Ms D Glass, Liverpool; A Glenford, Lincoln; Nick Goddard, Stevenage; Andrew Godfrey, Seer Green; Matthew Goldsmith, Burgess Hill; Mr & Mrs A. Goldthorp, Halstead; John Goleczka, Pensford; Michael Goodband, Perhore; Mrs A Gooding, Aylesbury, email; Bryn Gooding, Corfu; Dr G Gordon, Kidlington; Mrs J Gorman, Strood; Ian Gosden, Woking; Bill Gosland, Camberley; Mr and Mrs J Gough, Brough; David Gramagan, Formby; DC Grant, Enfield; Kathryn Grass, Wigan; Alan Gray, Erskine; DR Gray, SW11; A Greaves, Chesterfield; Andrew Greaves, Derbyshire; Rachel Greaves, Tavistock; Denise Gregory, Nottinghamshire; Jonathan Green, Cathays, Michael Green, Leicester; Nigel Green, Orpington; Richard Green, Gerrards Cross; Sheila Green, Barrow; A Gregor, Boston; Frank Gregori, NW10; Andrew Grendale, Ingatestone; A Griffiths, Milton Keynes; JK Greye, Bath; M Griffiths, Northampton; Dave Groves, Walsall; Lynda Gudgeon, Roopa Gulati, London; Willenhall, Louis Gunn, Chelmsford.

H: Karen Haley, Telford; John Hall, Cullercoats; Andrew Halling, Leigh; Stephen Hames, Bewdley; Alan Hamilton, Wakefield; Tina Hammond, Ipswich; Geoff & Janet Hampshire-Thomas, Kirkland; Neil Hancock, Derby; Ray

Hancock, Chester; David T. Hanlin, email; Dorothy Hankin, Fordingbridge; Sharon Hanson, Derby; Glynn Harby, Knaresborough; Martyn Harding, Powys; Roger Hargreaves, Stoke; J Harman, Brentwood; Gerald Harnden, Westcliff-on-Sea; Justin Harper, Hemel,; Dawn Harris, Dubley; Paul Harris, BFPO; David Harrison, Dursley; Mr and Mrs I Harrison, Warwickshire; Mark Harrison, Oxon; Patrick Harrison, Cambridge; Louise Hartley, Edinburgh; David Harvey, SE24; S Harwood, Lewes; John K Hattam, York; Sally Haseman, Surbiton; Christopher & Linda Haw, Dewsbury; Ann & David Haynes, Bournemouth; John Haynes, Saffron Walden; DI Hazelgrove, West Byfleet; M Hearle, Tunbridge Wells; Kevin Hearn, Newcastle; Bernice Heath, Nottingham; Andy Hemingway, Leeds; Terry Herbat, Barnsley; Georgina Herridge, W9; T & M Hetherington, Preston; Victoria Heywood, Burton; Roger Hickman, N1; Stuart Hicks email; Pat & Paul Hickson, Chorley; Janet Higgins, Blackburn; Mrs S Higgins, Blackburn; Mrs B Higgs, Cotty; Dave Hignett, Newcastle-upon-Tyne; Alec Hill, Wigan; Carolyn Hill, Nottingham; Stephen Hill, Chesterfield; Barry Hills, Surrey; David Hindle, W5; Bharti Hindocha, Richmond; Daniel Hinge, Bishop Auckland; Mrs MJ Hirst, Kent; SC Hodgon; Daniel Hodson, Abingdon; Peter Hoes, Bingley; Bernard Hofmiester, Berlin; P Hogkinson, Sheffield; Duncan Holloway, Windsor; Kevin Hooper, St Austell; Linda Horan, Wirral; Will H Horley, Barnsley; Peter Hornfleck, Farnborough; Jerry Horwood, Guildford; Dr MP Houghton, Rugby; Neil Houldsworth, Keighley; JK Howard, Enfield Wash; P Howard, Hornchurch; David & Val Howarth, Derbs; Mrs J Howarth, Oldham; Kathy Howe, Carlisle; Simon Howell, Gillingham; Bruce Howerd, Tongham; Lynn Howie, Sanderstead; Deh-Ta Hsiung, London; Jan Hudson, Hemel Hempstead; Tom Hudson, Jarrow; Chris Hughes, Wraysbury; Paul Hulley, Stockport; SP Hulley, Reddish; HL & S Humphreys, Stoke-on-Trent; AG Hunt, Southend-on-Sea; John & Frances Hunt, Langport; Paul Hunt, Essex; Roger Hunt, Sidmouth; Vince Hunt, Manchester; Penny Hunter, Brighton; Sheila Hunter, Dundee; Humayan Hussain, Journalist; Dr M Hutchinson, Gwynedd; Mike Hutchinson, Stafford; Mrs V Hyland, Manchester; Jeffrey Hyman, email.

I: DM Ibbotson, Sheffield; Nick & Mandy Idle, Ossett; Ken Ingram, Leeds; G Innocent, Dawlish; Mrs G Irving, Redditch; Robert Izzo, Horsham.

J: Dr AG James, Wigan; O Jarrett, Norwich; Sue Jayasekara, Essex; Sally Jeffries, Heathfield; L Jiggins, Dagenham; Bal Johal, email; G John, Wirral; Maxine & Andrew Johnson, Leiden; Colin Johnson, Southall; Peter Johnson, Droitwich; Paul Jolliffe, Exeter; CML Jones, St Albans; Clive Jones, NW; Gareth Jones, Tonypandy; Kate Jones, Leiden; Mark Jones Newport, Gwent; RW Jones, N9; Shirley Jones, SE13; WA Jones, Flints; Wendy Jones, Clwyd; Michael Lloyd Jones, Cardiff; Esther Juby, Norwich; Surjit Singh Jutla, Reading.

K: Tessa Kamara, W13; Sarah Kaikini, Surrey; AD Kantes, Northants; Chris Keardey, Southampton; Anthony Kearns, Stafford; David R Keedy, T & W; Russ Kelly, Seaforth; Prof. and Mrs Kemp, Royston; D Kennedy, Edinburgh; Mr & Mrs MJB Kendall, Hook; David Kerray, Akrotiri; John Kettle, Dover; JS Kettle, Banbury; Saul Keyworth, Essex; M. Arif Khan, London; Stephen Kiely, N16; John Kilbride, Glasgow; David King, Biggleswade; Mike King, Sussex; John & Jane Kingdom, Plymouth; Alyson Kingham, Oldham; Frances Kitchen, Langport; Peter Kitney, Banbury; J & P Klusiatis, Reading; Drs Heather & Mark Knight, Oxford; Ana Knowles, Walton on Thames; Drs MJ & A Krimholtz, SW14.

L: Caz Lack, Kent; Martin Lally, Chester; Colin Lambert, Bucks; Mrs Langley, email; Alan Lathan, Chorley; Clive Lawrence, email; Cass Lawson, Swindon; Ronnie Laxton, London; Jonathan Lazenby, Mamhilad, Gwent; Gary Leatt, St. Brelade, Jersey; Andrew Lecomber, Durham; DH Lee, Waltham Abbey; Jackie Leek, Dartford; Simon Leng, Wakefield; David Leslie, Aberdeen; Russell D Lewin, NW2; A Lewis, Sherborne; CK Lewis, Maidenhead; Margaret Ann Lewis, Ashford; R Lewis, Rayleigh; Pat Lindsay, Hampshire; David Lloyd, Northampton; David Lloyd, Oswestry; Eleanor & Owen Lock, Geneva; Peter Long, Cheltenham; J Longman, Bodmin; John Loosemore, Orpington; DA Lord, Hove; Julia & Philip Lovell, Brighton; AP Lowe, Tolworth; Peter Lowe, Lewes; Mr & Mrs DN Luckman, Horley; Jeremy Ludlow, Dorset; Mrs H Lundy, Wallasey; Graeme Lutman, Herts; Tim Lynch, Romford; Jamie Lyon, Burscough.

Mac/Mc: M Mcbryde, Watford; David Mackay, Twickenham; Darren McKenzie, T&W; David Mackenzie, Darlington; Lin Macmillan, Lincoln; Deb McCarthy, E6; Patrick McCloy, N8; Vanessa McCrow, Teddington; David McCulloch, NW11; Michael McDonald, Ellesmere Port; David McDowell, Telford; BJ McKeown, Seaford; Ian McLean, Brighton; Dr and Mrs J McLelland, Mid Calder; Alan & Jean McLucas, Solihull; Dr FB McManus, Lincolnshire; Alan McWilliam, Inverurie.

M: Chris Mabey, Swindon; Rakesh Makhecha, Harrow; Chloe Malik, email; Richard Manley, Wirral; Cherry Manners, Hatfield; Emma and Peta Manningham, email; E Mansfield, Camberley; Clive Mantle; JF Marshall, Bedford; Geraldine Marson, Winsford; Colin Martin, Nuneaton; Derek Martin, Marlow; Jane Martin, SW19; PR Martin, Southend; DH Marston, Southport; DJ Mason, Cleveland; LJ Mason, Leeds; John Maundrell, Tunbridge Wells; Gilian May, Hayes; Peter F May, St Albans; Simon Mayo, Farnborough; Simon Meaton, Andover; John Medd, Nottingham; Tim Mee, Harrow; Sue & Alf Melor, Hanworth; Nigel Meredith, Huddersfield; Sujata Mia, Middlesex; Andy Middleton, Rotherham; H Middleton, Coventry; Simon Mighall, St Neots; PJL Mighell, Canterbury; Robert Miles, Hertfordshire; Catherine Millar, BFPO; DR Millichap, Horsham; BW Milligan; AJ Millington, Woodford; Sally Millington, N10; Mr & Mrs P Mills, Mold; Mary Mirfin, Leeds; Al Mitchell, Belfast; Jonathon Mitchell, Alton; F Moan, Cuddington; Sarah Moles, Buxton; Jon Molyneaux, Peterborough; Mrs SE Monk, Gisburn; AV Moody, Portsmouth; Christy Moore, Dublin; Christy Moore, London; DM Moreland, Willington; S Morgan, Feltham; Tim & Katherine Morgan, Scotland; Ian Morris, Gwynedd; Miranda Mortlock, Suffolk; Peter Morwood, Wicklow; A Moss, Colchester; Caroline Moss, Solihull; K Mosley, email; Paul Motley , email; Mrs L Muirhead, Glasgow; David Muncaster, Stoke; Andy Munro, Birmingham; Joan Munro, Leyburn; Annette Murray, Thornton Cleveleys; JL Murray, Enfield; RG Murray, Carlisle; Drs Heather & Harry Mycook.

N: Simon Nash, Cheshire; Mrs PG Naylor, Salisbury; Hugh Neal, Kent; Jeff Neal, Bolton; Marcus Neal, Liss; Rob Neil, Ashford; A Nelson-Smith, Swansea; Liam Nevens, Stockton; Tony Newbold, email; Rebecca Newman, Hayes; Tony Newman, Margate; J Newsom, Lancing; Clive Newton, Northwich; John Nicholson, Bromborough; Nick, e-mail; P & D Nixon, Basildon; Mrs DA Nowakowa, Tiverton; Robert Nugent, SE31; Canon Peter Nunn, Glocs; Jody Lynn Nye, Illinois.

O: Beverley Oakes, Essex; AM O'Brien, Worthing; Eamon O'Brien, Holland; Pauline O'Brien, London; DC O'Donnell, Wetherby; Elise O'Donnell, Wolverhampton; Mary O'Hanlon, Dr M. Ogden, Barnsley; Ann Oliver nee Cridland, email; N Oliver, London; Helensburgh; Sheila Openshaw, Hampshire; David O'Regan, Leeds; Joanne Osborne, Bromborough; Steve Osborne, Bucks; Chris Osler, email; Jan Ostron, Felpham; Judith Owen, SW6; William & Sue Oxley, Southampton.

P: Trevor Pack, Rushden; RH Paczec, Newcastle; M Padina, Mattingley; Mr & Mrs GG Paine, Coventry; Keith Paine, Tilbury; GJ Palmer, Gainsborough; RS Palmer, Norfolk; Mrs A Parker, Birmingham; Mr GM Parker, Birmingham; John MF Parker, North Yorks; Philip Parker, Matlock; Bill Parkes-Davies, Tunbridge Wells; Angela Parkinson, Clitheroe; Nick Parrish; Brian Parsons, email; M Parsons, Fareham; Roy Parsons, Richmond; Donald Paterson, East Grinstead; GM Patrick, London; Paul, email; Mrs PA Pearson, Bristol; Mrs G Pedlow, Hitchin; David and Dandra Peet, Surrey; Mrs Barrie Penfold, Bourne End; J Penn, Southampton; Elaine & Martin Perrett, Dorchester; AJW Perry, Bristol; Graham Perry, Truro; Ian Perry, Essex; MJ Perry, E17; Ian Pettigrew, Edinburgh; Christopher Phelps, Gloucester; Adrian & Angela Phillips, Ammanford; Diane Phillips, Hyde; John Phillips, Wrexham; Jonathan Phillips, Saffron Walden; Steve Phillips, Wokingham; Colin Phipps, Scarborough; Sara Pickering, Northolt; Dave and Sandra Peet, email; Jack Pievsky, Pinner; Dirk Pilat, e-mail; Mike Plant, Essex; Susan Platt, Bury; D Pool, SE2; K Pool, Leyland; SR Poole, Runcorn; Tony Pope, Derbyshire; Steve Porter, Walsall; Julia Pounds, Brighton; RL Power, Sutton Coldfield; Dave Prentice, Dartmouth; Steve Prentice, Devon; Tim Preston, Barrow; Alison Preuss, Glencarse; Jeff Price, Bristol; Mr J Priest, Sawbridgeworth; Dr John Priestman, Huddersfield; D Pulsford, Marford; Janet Purchon, Bradford; John Purkiss, Stourbridge; Steve Puttock, Chatham; Julie Pyne, County Down.

Q: Sheila Quince, E11.

R: Diane Radigan, Welling; Harish B Raichura, Reading; Rohit Rajput, email; Kevin Ramage, Berwick; Clive Ramsey, Edinburgh; Alison Ratcliff, Halstead; KJ Rayment, Hertford; RC Raynham, Chelmsford; CR Read, Epsom; Mark Read, Romford; Guy Reavely, Surrey; Kim Reeder, South Shields; Debbie Reddy, W12; Francis Redgate, Nottingham; Steven Redknap, Ashford; I Reid, Fife; Lorraine Reid, Edinburgh; Duncan Renn, Dursley; Richard, email; Derek Richards, Bewdley; Sean Richards, Dover; Michael & June Richardson, Hull; Simon Richardson, Gainsborough; Steve Ridley, email; Mike Ridgway, Buxton; Mathew Riley, SE3; Lindsay Roberts, Lancaster; Margaret Roberts, Rubery; Peter Roberts, Shipston; Stewart & Anne Robertson, Leamington; Simon Roccason, Willenhall; Pat Roche, Chislehurst; J & P Rockery, Leicester; KG Rodwell, Harston; R Ronan, IOW; John Roscoe, Stalybridge; Brian Roston, Pontefract; John Rose, Hull; WJ Rowe; Steve Rowland, Matlock; Gareth Rowlands, email; Mrs EM Ruck, Darlington; DC Ruggins, Chalfont; JA Rumble, Rochford; Paul Rushton, Nottingham; K Ruth, W1; Bob Rutter, Blackpool; EJ Ryan, Effingham; N Ryer, Mansfield.

S: George and Mrs J Sadler, Thetford; MB Samson, Hertfordshire; Pauline Sapsford, Milton Keynes; MR Sargeant, Cornwall; Mark Sarjant, Guildford; GM Saville, Egremont; Mike Scotlock, Rayleigh; Mike Scott, Holmer Green; MJ Scott, SE26; Nicky & Don Scowen, Romford; Tim Sebensfield, Beeston; L Segalove, N2; M Seefeld, W5; Patrick Sellar, Maidstone; Richard Sellers, East Yorks; Philip Senior, Liverpool; N Sennett, Hull; David Sewell, Aldershot; Mrs DA Seymour, Burnham-on-Sea; Richard Shackleton,

Wakefield; Brian Shallon, Camberley; Sarah Shannon, B'hm; Jeane Sharp, St Albans; Mark Shaw, Swindon; Michelle Shaw, Ilford; Mrs Loraine Shaw, West Yorks; Deborah Shent, Nottingham; Barrie Shepherd, Bishopston; Howard & Mary Sherman, Upton-by-Chester; Theresa Shilcock, Derbyshire; Ewan Sim, Leeds; Carolyn Simpson, SE13; P Simpson, Livingstone; Jennifer Singh, Enfield; Jeff Slater, E6; John G Slater, Hants; Joy Slater, Northum; William P Sloan, Camberley; Else & Harald Smaage, Sauvegny; David Smith, Norwich; David Smith, Swindon; Denis Smith, Swindon; EK Smith, Edinburgh; Gillian Smith, St Andrews; Hazel Smith, Llandrinio; Howard Smith, Cardiff; Jim Smith, Cork; LP & A Smith, Gibraltar; Mark Smith, Lancashire; Nora Smith, Cardiff; RB Smith, BFPO; Sue Smith, Northampton; Susan Smith, Devon; Sylvia Smith, Northum; Colin Snowball, Cheltenham; Tim Softly, Leigh; Robert Solbe, Surrey; Peter Soloman, Middlesbrough; M Somerton- Rayner, Cranwell; Maurice Southwell, Aylesbury; Gill Sparks, Halifax; Andrew Speller, Harlow; GD Spencer, Stonehaven; Mrs P Spencer, Norwich; Andy Spiers, Brighton; R Spiers, Wolverhampton; CP Spinks, Church Langley; Chris Spinks, Ilford; John Spinks, Hainault; Martin Spooner, Wallsend; DJ Stacey, Cambridge; Mrs WL Stanley-Smith, Belper; Mr & Mrs M Stanworth, Haywards Heath; John Starley, Birdingbury; Nigel Steel, Carlisle; Avril Steele, Crossgar; Bob Stencill, Sheffield; John Stent, Liss; Ian Stewart, Potters Bar; Tim Stewart, Norfolk; Roger Stimson, email; Tina Stone, Illford; Barry Strange, Kent; Rob Struthers, Brighton; Mrs MB Such; Steve Sumner, W.Yorks; FD Sunderland, Plympton; FC Sutton, Poole; Andrew Swain, Sudbury; Carolyn Swain, Leeds; Gary Swain, Coventry; DL Swann, Parbold; Frank Sweeney, Middlesbrough; Gill & Graham Swift, Beeston; MS Sykes, Dorrington; Dr John Szewczyk, Lincs.

T: Richard Tamlyn, Bovey Tracey; Nigel & Gill Tancock, Newbury; Steve Tandy, Cleveleys; Bernard Tarpey, Failsworth; Bob Tarzey, email; Andrew Tattersall, North Yorks; CB Taylor, Wolverhampton; Colin Taylor, Preston; Jeremy Taylor, Newport, Gwent; Kevin Taylor, Sevenoaks; Ken Taylor, Sevenoaks; Mick and Penny Taylor, email; Peter Taylor, Kingston-upon-Hull; Philip & Vivien Taylor, Cromer; Roger Taylor, Hamela; Len Teff, Whaddon; Mrs PF Terrazzano, Leigh-on-Sea; RL Terry, Kent; Michael Third, Nothum; André Thomas, Stoke; Christopher & Niamh Thomas, Barnet; DG Thomas, Gloucestershire; DL Thomas, Peterborough; Mrs J Thomas, Cumbria; Mark Thomas, Exeter; Nigel Thomas, Lincoln; Dr DA & AHE Thombs, Slimbridge; Alan Thompson, Clwyd; David & Lisa Thompson, SE10; Richard Thompson, Rainham; Bill Thomson, Ramsgate; Paul Thomson, Salford; J Thorne, South Benfleet; Richard Tilbe, Wokingham; Mrs BM Clifton Timms, Chorley; Joan & Ken Timms, West Sussex; Mrs M Tindale, Beverley; Alan Tingle, Hayling Island; Graham Todd, Crawley; Tom and Charlotte, Leeds; Joan Tongue, Huddersfield; Tom and Charlotte, Leeds; Alex & Sarah Torrence, Cleveland; SR Tracey-Forster, Bronham; Bernard Train, Barton; Leigh Trevitt, Bishops Stortford; R Trinkwon, Ferring; Kevin & Sarah Troubridge, Chelmsford; Dr JG Tucker, SW17; Paul Tunnicliffe, Cleveland; Martin Turley, Belgium; Don Turnball, Geneva; Mrs SM Turner, Stroud; R Twiddy, Boston; S Twiggs, Lower Kingswood; Jeremey Twomey, Leamington; John Tyler, Romford.

V: David Valentine, Forfar; Alan & Lesley Vaughan, Paington; Dorothy (Dot) Vaughan-Williams, Penyffordd; Puja Vedi, London; Mrs B Venton, Chipstead; Richard Vinnicombe, Camberley; Mr & Mrs T Vlismas, Crymyoh; Sarah Vokes, Dorking; Gordon Volke, Worthing.

W: Phil Wain, Merseyside; PM Waine, Manchester; R Waldron, Oxon; Alison Walker, Droitwich; Andrew Walker, Aklington; Katherine Walker, London; Dr JB Walker, Burnham; John Walker, Chorley; Dr PAW Walker, Wirral; William Wallace, West Kilbride; Alison Walton, North Shields; Brian and Maureen Walsh, Market Harborough; Jennie Want, SW20; Mrs J Ward, Wakefield; Cathy Ward, Slough; Pamela Ward, Birmingham; Simon Ward, Croydon; John Warren, Lancs; Mrs G. Warrington, Hyde; Nicholas Watt, Houghton; RG Watt, Bromyard; Duncan Weaver, Bury St Edmunds; Stephanie Weaver, Northants; Andy Webb, Aberdeen; Peter Webb, West Byfleet; TG Webb, Peterborough; Nick Webley, Llandeilo; Dave Webster, Gateshead; Harry and Marina Webster, Nottingham; Andrew Wegg, SW16; Michael Welch, Reading; J Weld, Eastleigh; Dave Weldon, Hale; Mr and Mrs Wellington, Market Harborough; John Wellings, Edinburgh; AD West, Leicestershire; Laurence West, Torquay; Dr PJ West, Warrington; Joyce Westrip, Perth, Australia; Sarah Wheatley, Leavesden; James and Bethan Whitelaw, Market Harborough; George Whilton, Huddersfield; Andy Whitehead, Swindon; Mr & Mrs DW Whitehouse, Redditch; George Whitton, Huddersfield; Peter Wickendon, East Tilbury; Jennette Wickes, Fleet; PM Wilce, Abingdon; Malcolm Wilkins, Gravesend; Chris Wilkinson, Cumbria; Geoffrey Wilkinson, Orpington; Babs Williams, Bristol; Mark P Williams, Bromley; P Williams, St Austell; Raoul Williams, Cambridge; Ted Williams, Norwich; David Williamson, NW3; David Williamson, Stamford; BP and J Willoughby, Devizes; Bob & Eve Wilson, NW2; Garry Wilson, e-mail; Dr Michael Wilson, Crewe; Major Mike Wilson, BFPO 140; John Wirring, Swindon; Mrs AC Withrington, Hindhead; David Wolfe, SW1, Hugh Wood, Brough; W Wood, Hornsea; John Woolsgrove, Enfield; JL Wormald, Leeds; Geof Worthington, Handforth; Howard Worton, email ; Mrs C Wright, Glasgow; Mrs CF Wright, Stockport; Clive Wright, Halesowen; D Wright, Rotherham; John D Wright, St Ives; Georgina Wright, Nottingham; Lynn Wright, Newark; Mick Wright, Beds.

Y: Tracy Yam, USA; Stephen Yarrow, NW11; EJ Yea, Cambridgeshire; Rev. Can. David Yerburgh, Stroud; Andrew Young, Cumbria; Andy Young, Penrith; Mrs B Young, Basildon; Carl Young, Nottingham; Mrs E Young, Ilmington.

What We Need to Know

We need to know everything there is to know about all curry restaurants in the UK. And there is no one better able to tell us than those who use them. We do not mind how many times we receive a report about a particular place, so please don't feel inhibited or that someone else would be better qualified. They aren't. Your opinion is every bit as important as the next person's. Ideally, we'd like a report from you every time you dine out – even on a humble takeaway. We realize this is hard work so we don't mind if your report is very short, and you are welcome to send in more than one report on the same place telling of different occasions. Please cut out the forms on the last page. Or you can even use the back of an envelope or a postcard, or we can supply you with more forms if you write in (with an S.A.E., please). If you can get hold of a menu (they usually have takeaway menus to give away) or visiting cards, they are useful to us too, as are newspaper cuttings, good and bad, and advertisements. So, please send anything along with your report. Most reports received will appear, in abbreviated form, in the Curry Magazine (the Curry Club members' regular publication). They are also used when preparing the next edition of this Guide. We do not pay for reports but our ever-increasing corps of regular correspondents receive the occasional perk from us. Why not join them? Please send us your report after your next restaurant curry.

Thank you.

Pat Chapman
Founder, The Curry Club
PO Box 7
Haslemere
Surrey
GU27 IEP

E-mail it to pat.curry@virgin.net

RESTAURANT REPORT FORM

Photocopy or scan this form. Mail it or e-mail it to the address below.

Whenever you have an 'Indian' meal or takeaway, The Curry Club would like to have your opinion.
Your Name and address ....

....

....

Your phone number .... Your e-mail address ....

Restaurant name: ....

Street no and Streetname: ....

....

Town: .... County: ....

Postcode: .... Telephone: .... e.mail: ....

Website: .... Date Visited ....

REPORT
Please tell us everything... your first impressions, the welcome, cleanliness, your table – was it appealing? Nice things waiting for you on it? the menu, quantities, quality, service, background music, comfort, decor. The food? How were the toilets? First visit? Been before? Would you go back/ recommend to friends? Overall was the restaurant good, bad or indifferent?

Please continue on separate sheets of paper if required
Please return your info to: The Curry Club, PO Box 7, Haslemere, Surrey. GU27 1EP. <www.patchapman.co.uk>

RESTAURANT UPDATE INFORMATION

Photocopy or scan this form. Mail it or e-mail it to the address below.

Your Name and address ....

....

Your phone number .... Your e-mail address ....

Even if you do not fill in a report overleaf, you may be able to give us vital information, such as that below. DO YOU KNOW OF ANY:

NEW CURRY RESTAURANT OPENINGS:

Restaurant name:

Street no and name:

Town: County:

Postcode: Telephone:

CURRY RESTAURANT CLOSURES OVER THE LAST FEW MONTHS,

Including any listed in this Guide

Restaurant name:

Street no and name:

Town: County:

Postcode: Telephone:

HYGIENE OR OTHER OFFENCES

Please back up with a local press cutting if possible

Restaurant name:

Street no and name:

Town: County:

Postcode: Telephone:

YOUR FAVOURITE RESTAURANT(S)

If possible, in descending order, best first

Restaurant name:

Street no and name:

Town: County:

Postcode: Telephone:

ANY OTHER CURRY RESTAURANT INFORMATION?

Please continue on separate sheets of paper if required

Please return your info to: The Curry Club, PO Box 7, Haslemere, Surrey. GU27 1EP

The 2008 Cobra Good Guide Curry Quiz

This *Guide* is all about facts, features and fun., and for the first time, in the *Guide* we bring you something we used to entertain our Curry Club members with in the iconic *Curry Magazine* . We used to get dozens of replies, and I know we will this time, by throwing it open to all, including restaaaurant personnel.. It will make you work hard, because, guess what, it is not in county order ... We have jumbled it up! You will have to read the *Guide* from cover to cover, and you may like to know that there are 250,000 words to read!!! We know because we wrote them all! But it really is worth it. Your answers must state which restaurant is involved and quote the *Guide* page number. We would prefer your answers by e-mail if you can please. The most articulate, amusing and detailed response will get first prize. Judges include Cobra Beer's Lord Billimoria of Chelsea and Dominique and Pat Chapman, the *Guide* proprietors and editors. The good news: is that first prize is a year's worth of Cobra Premium Indian Beer. If we get more than one set of correct answers do have a tie breaker(s). The Runners-up will also get prizes. Competition cut-off date: 31 October 2008. Winner runners up and answers will be announced after that date in Tandoorti Magazine and on my website. <www.patchapman.co.uk> Judges decision is final. We regret we will not enter any correspondence re this quiz nor any entries.

1. Where did the mayor's speech remind the ed of comedian Frank Carson saying, *'Thank you, Mr Mayor for shortening the winter!'*?

2. Who claims he was was also the personal valet to President Bill Clinton?

3. Where was Rob the accountant's stag night?

4. Who is a nice man, dreadful wig?

5. Which restaurants have railway connections?

6. Who has branches in Multan, Pakistan Germany and Australia?

7. Which restaurant sells the cheapest popadom?

8. Where can you find vegetarian Punjabi cooking?

9. Who sells a whole jar or pickle or chutney at £2.70 each?

10. Who is the chef at the venue where the Curry Club hold its Saturday Morning Cookery Courses?

11. Where did Pat get a chilli heat warning in 1961?

12. What is the name of the pregnant woman who correctly believed a curry fix would start her labour and at which restaurant?

13. Which restaurants serve curry breakfasts?

14. Which restaurant is in a garden centre?

15. At which restaurant was Steve Osborne glad not find Batwing Bhaji following a bat-walk evening at the local castle?

16. Whose *Guide* gets read a couple of times daily because it lives in the 'smallest room? And what is his job?

17. Who celebrated his rise to the **TOP 100** by marking the occasion with a glittering social evening?

18. Who serves chicken and egg pullao rice?

19. Who went "round the world in 74 days" and their full names please?

20. Where did British soldiers go 'doolally' and what does it mean?

21. What are Lampries and where can you get them?

22. Whose website tells us about the 'Tandoori Murder? and who was accused of it?

23. Where is the Argee Bargee (curryhouse)?

24. Where can you find Surti cooking?

25. Who promises aphrodisiacs?

26. What are Nippies?

27. Where did the ed first encounter Vark? And what is it?

28. Who makes 'hook kebab', a leaf-wrapped meat attached by hooks linked to one another and cooked in the tandoor.?

29. Whose logo beats cars for speedy home del?

30. Where is the civil war re-enacted and by whom?

31. Who has used several of Pat's copyright Balti

Cookbook photos on their menu without permission?

32. About which restaurant does Pat have a pop at their silly rules(there are at least two, but one will do)

33. Where is there a mural which is typically Rajasthani, ie a cross between Guernica and Muffin the Mule?

34. At which restaurant do the directors believe that the food served at most UK establishments has been "Anglo-sized"?

35. Where can you find Udipi vegetarian cuisine?

36. What has 'Heart in Hand' to do with Tandoori?

37. Where can you get Indian Kosher food?

38. Which restaurant has seven different cooking units used in India for thousands of years?

39. Why was Rod's mum Mrs Pat Chapman embarrassed?

40. Where can you find Surti cooking and what is it?

41. Where did a green lizard live and what crawled up the wall?

42. What did the 'clean-up' authorities banish and where? Clue: wheeled stalls selling the world's most exquisite Bhel Puri.

43. Who is Imtiaz Qureshi?

44. Where is Flamingo served, and what is it? (don't panic – it isn't what you think!)

45. Where is a bottle of wine £399.95? and just to make it easy it was the restaurant where Wills eat before passing-out

46. Which restaurants has the earliest opening hour?

47. And which opens the latest?

48. Which prolific reporter questions why he bothers to put his stomach at the disposal of research rather than enjoy his curry at somewhere he knows is good?

49. What is Cobra's Elephant beer?

50. Who are the three people on the picture below and what are their roles?

Town Index

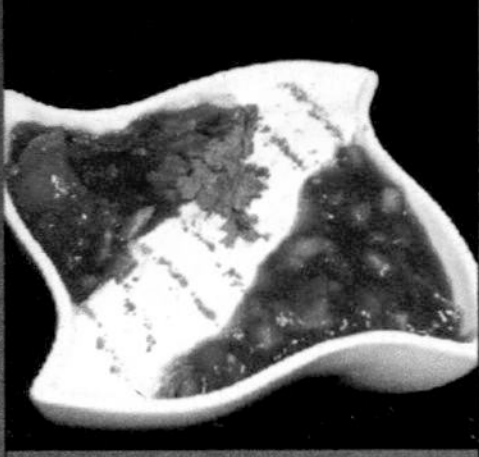

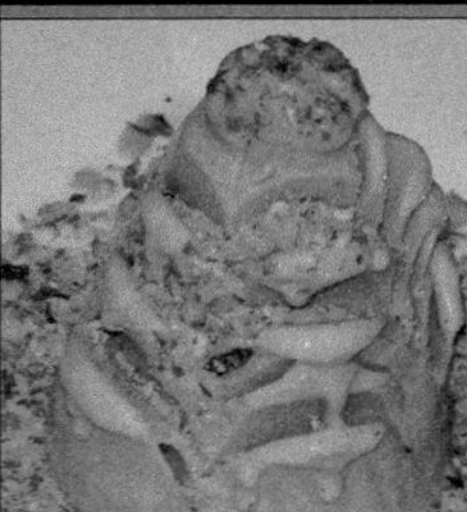

Awarded
Cobra Good
Curry Guide
Best Punjabi
Award UK
from
1999

Welcome to Brilliant Restaurant

At the heart of our business is devotion to authentic, fresh and superbly prepared food. We do everything we can to ensure that those who choose to dine with us have a 'Brilliant' time.

We look forward to welcoming you.

Gulu